Diploma in Child Care and Education

Penny Tassoni · Kate Beith
with
Harriet Eldridge · Alan Gough

Heinemann
Child Care

Heinemann Educational Publishers,
Halley Court, Jordan Hill, Oxford OX2 8EJ
A division of Reed Educational & Professional Publishing Ltd

Heinemann is a registered trademark of Reed Educational & Professional Publishing Limited

OXFORD   MELBOURNE   AUCKLAND
JOHANNESBURG   BLANTYRE   GABORONE
IBADAN   PORTSMOUTH NH (USA)   CHICAGO

© Penny Tassoni, Kate Beith, Harriet Eldridge and Alan Gough 2000

First published 2000
02 01 00
10 9 8 7 6 5 4 3 2 1

A catalogue record for this book is available from the British Library on request.

ISBN 0 435 40164 5

Pages designed by Wendi Watson

Typeset and illustrated by ⋀ Tek-Art, Croydon, Surrey

Printed and bound in Great Britain by The Bath Press, Bath

Acknowledgements

Penny Tassoni would like to thank her family for their continued support during the process of producing this new edition. Particular thanks to to Maplehurst and Beaky's nursery in Hastings which has allowed materials to be used once again. She is also grateful to those students and lecturers who have commented on the previous edition and, in doing so, have influenced this new edition.

Harriet Eldridge would like to acknowledge the following people for their help and guidance with chapters 10 and 15: Lizzie Buckley, Health Visitor, Hastings and Rother Trust; Isobel Meikle, Tutor in Health and Social Care, Worcester; Dr Lucy Haswell; Sue Walters, sick children's nurse, Hastings and Rother Trust; Judith Perkins, psychiatric nurse, Hastings and Rother Trust; and Anna Woodhouse, Occupational Therapist, Liverpool. Brenda Lewis, Clive Vale Nursery, provided information for Chapter 4 and Louise Burnham gave guidance about the format of the National Curriculum. A big thank you also to the second-year NNEB students at Bexhill College who have kindly allowed examples of their work to be included, and to Mary James and Penny Tassoni for their time and support.

Alan Gough would like to thank Sandra Gough for her invaluable help in providing ideas when his mind went blank!

Kate Beith would like to thank all her colleagues and the children at The Chiltern College for their invaluable support, and her dad for all his love.

The authors and publishers would like to thank the staff, pupils and parents of The Chiltern College, Reading and Cuttleslowe Nursery, Oxford. Our thanks also to the following for permission to reproduce photographs and other copyright material:

Gareth Boden
CACHE
Child Accident Prevention Trust
Collections/Lesley Howling
Collections/Sandra Lousada
Collections/Fiona Pragoff
Collections/Anthea Sieveking
Collections/Paul Watts
Jennifer Enderby
Sally and Richard Greenhill
Kidscape
Her Majesty's Stationery Office
The Makataon Vocabulary Development Project
Science Photo Library/Mark Clarke
Science Photo Library/Garry Watson

Contents

Contents

Contents

Introduction

CHAPTER 1

Introduction

Starting on any new course is a time of mixed emotions – excitement, interest and maybe some nervousness. This book is designed to give you both the information that you will need to complete your course as well as some practical help in undertaking some of the coursework. This introduction is divided into two sections:

1 Starting your course

2 Principles of child development

Starting your course

The aim of this first section is to look at ways in which you can prepare yourself for the demands of your course.

Most child care courses combine:

- practical work with children, that is, work experience in a placement
- knowledge gained through lectures and private study
- assignments or tests.

Practical work with children

Wanting to work with children will be the main reason why you have joined your course. Work experience or placements with children will form a large part of your course and will provide you with hands-on experience and training. It is important that by the end of the course you are not only competent to work with children but also confident. Your course tutor will probably organise a range of placements and experiences for you. You will need to learn how to fit in and how to gain knowledge from different placements.

Placements

During the course, you should be given a range of placements which may include nurseries, schools and families. Some colleges also manage to arrange placements in special schools and also in hospitals. Placements do not receive payment for taking students, and course tutors check that the placements are able to provide plenty of training opportunities.

The importance of placements

Placements give students the opportunity to practise their skills and also to carry out coursework – for example, planning activities with children, observing children. They also help you decide what area of early years and education you may want to work in after finishing the course. At the end of each placement, your placement supervisor will fill in a report about your progress. This report is important, as you must show, by the end of the course, that you are practically competent to work with children.

Placement supervisors

In each placement, you will have a supervisor who will show you around and tell you what is expected of you. Placement supervisors are often experienced members of staff and are used to working with students.

The role of the placement supervisor includes:

- liaising with the college and course tutors
- organising shift or work patterns
- supporting students by helping them with activities, signing observations and giving advice

■ filling in a report about students' progress at the end of their placement.

If you have any difficulties during your placement, you should try to talk to either your course tutor or your placement supervisor.

Visiting a placement for the first time

Most students feel quite nervous when they go into a placement for the first time. This is normal. Remember, the placement has offered to have you and your supervisors and fellow workers will not expect you to be able to do everything perfectly the minute you start.

Before your visit

■ Find out the name of your supervisor, the address of the placement and the telephone number.

■ Ask what time you should arrive on the first day.

■ Make sure that you know exactly where you are going and how you are going to get there.

■ Ignore any stories from other students about the placement, particularly if they are gloomy. Be ready to make up your own mind.

Good practice on your first day

✔ Smile!

✔ Arrive on time, looking like an early years worker, not a fashion model.

✔ Make sure that you have paper and pen.

✔ Introduce yourself clearly – one student was mistaken for the new cook and put in the kitchen!

✔ Look positive and enthusiastic and make sure that you write down any information that you may forget – e.g. daily routine; the names of the people you will be working with.

✔ Learn as many of the children's names as possible.

✔ Try to help where you can – e.g. undoing aprons, sharpening pencils.

✔ Look carefully to see where things go and try to remember.

✔ At the end of the session, help with the clearing up and setting up for the next day.

✔ At the end of the day, make sure that you have said goodbye before leaving.

✔ If you have enjoyed your day – tell your supervisor.

Common problems

What should I do at lunch time?
On the first day you should always take your own lunch. You will find out later if there is a canteen or if you are expected to eat with the children.

Lunchtimes are often the best time to get to know the other staff. It may be tempting to pop home or into town, but this will mean you do not get to know people well.

Lunchtimes are also used to prepare for the afternoon session. If you go out every time, it may look like you are trying to get out of working.

What should I wear?
Every setting has its own, often unwritten, dress code. This means that in some settings staff wear jeans, but in others they are smartly dressed. On your

first visit, it is probably best to look for something smart but casual. You will know that you have understood the dress code if you blend in – if you stick out, then you will need to rethink your clothes.

Footwear can be a problem for some students. High heels will probably be uncomfortable and in some cases dangerous to children – for example, if you accidentally step on their feet. Trainers or soft shoes are often more comfortable and kinder on the feet.

Note: Do not embarrass your supervisor by asking for permission to wear certain items of clothing – such as jeans – in a placement where no one else is wearing them. Most supervisors do not like being put on the spot – and will tend to say yes rather than tell you what they really think.

Am I allowed jewellery?
It is a good idea to keep jewellery to a minimum. Necklaces and dangly earrings can be pulled by children and rings get clogged with dough and paint. The test is to look at other staff members and be guided by what they are wearing.

I need a cigarette, what should I do?
Smoking and caring for children do not go well together. Many employers ask specifically for non-smokers,

especially if they are looking for nannies. Consider giving up, if you can, during the course.

If you do need a cigarette, you will have to wait until a break or lunchtime. You must never smoke in view of children and you must ask your supervisor where you can go. Sneaking off for a cigarette in the toilets with a window open is not the answer!

What happens if I am ill and cannot go in to the placement?
Do not panic! Telephone the placement as soon as you can and explain why you cannot come in. Remember to apologise for any trouble this may cause them. You should also telephone your course tutor or college to let them know.

What happens if I hate the placement?
Many students, especially if they have been in another placement before, find the new setting hard to like at first. It is important that you give yourself and the setting a chance. One day is not sufficient to judge a placement. If, after a few days, you are still not sure, you should talk to your course tutor. Try to work out exactly what it is that is making you feel unsettled.

I feel really uncomfortable in the staffroom.
This is a common feeling among students. First of all, make sure that you are not sitting in anyone's place or that you have not taken someone's cup. Always offer to pay for coffee or tea and ask where you should sit before taking your place.

Remember that you will gradually need to establish yourself – if you avoid going into the staffroom you will never get to know the team. It is often a good idea to take something to do with you, so that if everyone is talking to each other, you do not sit feeling uncomfortable.

A good starting point in building up a relationship with a staff member is to ask them for some advice or help – for example, 'I noticed that Sam seems very aggressive, how do you think I should handle him?' or 'Would you have time to look at my observation to see if I am on the right lines?'

It is also worth remembering that staff have developed friendships with each other and that

It is common to feel uncomfortable in the staffroom at first – this will improve

breaks are their only time for catching up – especially after a weekend!

How long should I stay after a session has ended?
Working with children is only one part of being an early years worker. Clearing up, cleaning and setting up is an important part of the job. Supervisors quickly lose patience with students who arrive, carry out the 'fun part' and then go home. You should really stay until all the tasks are finished or until your supervisor says 'Look, we've nearly finished, why don't you go?'

Asking if you can go will give the impression that you are in a rush to leave. Some supervisors will say you can go, while actually feeling irritated. If you need to go because you have another job or appointment, make sure that you tell your supervisor.

Study skills

During your course, you will be asked to take notes but you will also need to conduct research using books. These are study skills and like most skills they will improve with practice.

Organising yourself

In order to succeed on any course, you will need to be organised. This means having folders and files and

keeping your work and notes in some order. It also means making sure that you take good care of your assignments, evidence and other coursework. Lost work is not an excuse that course moderators can accept.

Time management

Every year in every college, there are students who fail their courses simply because they have not used their time properly. No qualification can be gained without effort and this means that you will have to spend some time working at home instead of socialising or watching television.

The common reason people give for not completing tasks is that they cannot get started on some work unless they have a full hour or day set aside. But it is not always possible to set aside large blocks of time. You will need to use the odd fifteen minutes to start something or read part of a book. If you have six fifteen-minute slots during a week you have gained an hour and a half. You might consider using some of your lunchtimes on placement to write up observations while they are still fresh in your mind.

Working on assignments – another way of thinking

A student close to finishing her course was moaning that she did not have time to do her 2000-word assignment. The tutor said 'Would you get it in on time if I said it was worth £8000?' The student looked puzzled and the tutor explained 'That's the minimum amount of money you'll be earning if you get this qualification so if you don't do this work you'll be losing out on £8000 a year!'

The student smiled and said 'When you put it like that, it makes me think differently about doing it!'

If you do get behind with your work – do not give up! Focus on a small task that you know you can do easily and get it out of the way. Try not to start any

Timetable

Make a timetable of your normal week – i.e. when you are in the workplace, when you are in classes, when you have social commitments. You could colour code it if you like.

Then mark out times when you are free and can study.

Remember, you must leave yourself enough time to sleep and to relax. If you do not get enough rest, your work will suffer.

Prioritise

At the beginning of the week, sort your tasks into:

urgent – tasks you have to do at the beginning of the week

important – tasks that have to be done by the end of the week

other – tasks that can be fitted in around the rest

Depending on your workload and how often you are given new tasks, you may need to prioritise daily as well.

TIME MANAGEMENT

Make lists

Some people find it useful to make a list of what they have to do, and even to assign certain times during the week/day when they will complete these tasks. It can be very satisfying to put a tick by a task when you have finished it!

Remember, if you are using lists, you must be careful not to set yourself unrealistic tasks. Try to keep track of how long it takes you to do a certain type of task – e.g. writing up an observation, making notes on a chapter in a book – and then assign a little bit more time, just to be sure.

new projects and make sure that you talk to your tutor who will be able to give you some support.

Taking notes in class

Every teacher or lecturer has his/her own style of delivering material. Some use overheads, others may expect you to jot down points as you go. The aim of taking notes in class is to have something to refer back to. This means you do not have to record every word that is being said, but write down either the points that you are likely to forget or those that are very new to you. For notes to be useful, you will need to be able to understand them afterwards. This means that if you have not had time to write in complete sentences, you should try to complete your notes as soon as possible afterwards. It is also a good idea to put the date on your notes and the name of the person who has been talking to you. This means that if, afterwards, you need the notes to work on an assignment and find you do not completely understand them, you can refer back to that person.

Handouts

Handouts may seem like a wonderful alternative to taking notes, but to benefit from them, you will need to read them! It is a good idea to underline parts that are interesting or have been specifically covered in the lesson. Handouts can be used to support your ideas in your assignments, but to use them you will need to know where they came from so make sure you note down the date and the author.

Researching and taking notes from books

This is a skill that most students need some practice in. The idea of taking notes from books is to write down only the key points that you need. Try not to copy from books as this is time consuming and there is always the danger of committing **plagiarism**. Plagiarism means using other people's words in text without their permission. If you see something in a book that you wish to use in your work you must use a **reference**.

Using references to support your work

Using a reference will show that your ideas are based on current thinking found in books or magazines. For example – 'I think that James is showing normal behaviour for a three-year-old. According to Penny Tassoni, three year olds "show social skills – e.g. turn taking, sharing and concern for others" (Tassoni 1998, p.193).'

Most child care courses expect students to demonstrate their knowledge by referring to a selection of books. There are different ways of referencing quotes from books, though most courses ask students to use the Harvard system of referencing.

The Harvard system of referencing is reasonably simple. The main points are that the author's name and the date of publication are put alongside the reference, but details of the title of the book, the publisher and where it was published are listed at the end of your observation or essay.

Look at the example below.

> I saw that James used his left hand to write with. I think that this means he has a hand preference, which would be normal for his age. Tassoni states that at two years, a child 'begins to use a preferred hand'. (Tassoni 1998, p.79)

At the end of the piece of work a list of all the books that have been used for references would appear. The list must be in alphabetical order by author. The title of the book should be in italics or underlined.

Tassoni, P. 1998 *Child Care and Education,* Oxford, Heinemann

Taking notes

Most students eventually develop their own methods of using books without copying from them, but if you are not sure, you might like to try the method below:

1   Read part of the text – e.g. a paragraph.
2   Shut the book.
3   Ask yourself if there was anything in that section that was useful or interesting.
4   If so, write down what was said in note form.
5   Open the book and check your notes.

Knowledge into action

Read the article below and see if you can work out what the main points are.

30 December 1998

Hodge Announces Funds For 50,000 Nursery Places For 3-Year-Olds

Margaret Hodge Minister for Employment and Equal Opportunities today announced £41.5 million to provide 50,000 new and free nursery places for three-year-olds.

The money which will be available in 1999-2000 is the first stage towards meeting the Government's commitment to double nursery places for three-year-olds. The free places will be provided by a range of providers – including local education authorities, playgroups and private nurseries.

190,000 extra places will be available by 2001-2, taking the proportion of three-year-olds in free places to 66%.

Mrs Hodge said:

"This is a very exciting new development. We have delivered free education for all four-year-olds whose parents wish it, and can now begin to expand free nursery education for three-year-olds. Over the next three years, we will double the number of places available for three-year-olds – offering much greater opportunities and diversity of provision to parents.

"Nursery education brings the greatest benefits to disadvantaged children, so we are giving preference in the first year to helping 50 authorities in areas of greatest social need. The money will be available from September 1999 in order to allow the authorities time to plan their expanded provision.

"The new places will be delivered through existing Early Years Partnerships. We expect that the places will be of high quality. We have made clear that the places should not be in reception classes and that they must be appropriate for children of this age. Providers of Government-funded places for three-year-olds will have to work towards the Desirable Learning Outcomes and be inspected by OFSTED.

"It is absolutely essential that the quality of staff working with three-year-olds is maintained which is why a new Standards Fund for the training and development of early years staff working with three-year-olds has been established."

The Minister for Women, The Rt Hon The Baroness Jay welcomed the injection of new money into early education. She said:

"Children benefit from interacting with other children of their own age, and this measure will help them to do so. But there are benefits for parents as well. The parents of young children who are already in paid work may find that the availability of good quality care for their children helps them to balance more effectively their working and family lives. Those parents who do not work but wish to do so may find that access to an early education scheme helps them to overcome one of the biggest barriers to employment."

DfEE press release from December 1998
You might like to do this exercise in pairs.

Choosing the right book

There is little point in using books that you do not understand, because you are more likely to make mistakes or find yourself copying out text. Sometimes it is useful to start with a very basic book and then use more specialist books as your understanding increases. Most students find they need to use a range of books and magazines in order to show that they have researched the subject adequately.

Where to look for information

There are several places where you can look for books, magazines and other information for your assignments and coursework (see the diagram below).

Coursework or assignments

During the course, you will be given coursework and assignments to complete. Assignments are used to test your understanding and knowledge of a module and unit. For the Diploma in Child Care and Education you will also need to show that you are able to plan and prepare activities for children and also carry out observations. This is done by compiling two separate portfolios which are graded at the end of the course.

European Office

For information about European countries, you can write or phone the European Office. If you want to find out information about a particular country, then you can telephone their embassy or consulate in London.

Public library

Most large libraries have reference sections with up-to-date books. Librarians are able to look up subject areas. Reference sections also keep back-copies of newspapers and some magazines.

Government departments

All government departments have information departments and publish leaflets.

College library

Your college library should have a range of books on your subject area. It is also worth looking in other sections such as history, sociology and psychology for more specialist information needed for some assignments.

Placements

Many placements will have books that could be useful for your course. Most supervisors will be happy to let you use them while you are at the placement and may even point you in the right direction if you are stuck on finding out information.

SOURCES OF INFORMATION

Voluntary sector organisations

For some assignments you may find it useful to contact voluntary organisations – e.g. NSPCC for child protection leaflets. Most voluntary organisations do not charge for leaflets, but will want you to send a stamped addressed envelope. Do not use their helplines when asking for information. Useful organisations are listed at the end of each chapter.

Town or county hall

Your local town or county hall will have some local and regional information which may be helpful to you.

Internet

The Internet can be a good source of information as many government departments, local authorities and voluntary organisations have websites. Some public libraries have Internet facilities and your college should also have Internet access. (Useful websites can be found at the end of each chapter.)

Coursework will be set by your course tutor who will give you guidance as to how to set out your folders.

The principles of child development

As part of your course, you will study aspects of child development. You will need to show that your knowledge of children is used when planning activities or managing children's behaviour. A large section of this book looks at the five key areas of a child's development:

- physical development (Chapter 5)
- cognitive development (Chapter 6)
- language development (Chapter 7)
- emotional and social development (Chapter 8).

As a student starting a new course, it will help you to understand the following underlying principles of child development. See also pages 101–103.

All aspects of child development are integrated. The five key areas of child development are so closely linked that a difficulty in one area tends to affect the others. For example – a child who has difficulty in communicating may find it difficult to socialise with other children.

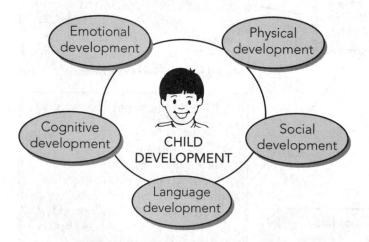

There are several theories about how children learn and develop. It is important to look at all of the theories outlined in each chapter. Research into how children learn and think is ongoing which means that new research and tests may alter and shape current theories.

Every child is an individual. This means that although we can look at general patterns of development, there will always be variations. For example, most babies are sitting up by nine months, but some will be sitting unaided at seven months. In this book, there are several charts that show the general pattern of development. These can be used only as a guide because of the differences between individual children. An important skill in working with children is to focus on their individual pattern of development and to look at ways of helping them progress at their own pace.

There are many factors that can influence children's development. Although we can look at the general patterns of child development, we must recognise that there are several factors that can affect children's overall development. These are recognised as being social, environmental and genetic. For example, children who are discriminated against tend to have low self-esteem which in turn affects their cognitive and social development.

Psychologists studying children's development are divided as to how much of a child's development results from genetics and human instinct and how much results from environmental and social factors, such as where they are living and what early experiences and opportunities are available. This is often referred to as the nature versus nurture debate.

Think about it

The nature versus nurture debate is an interesting one. Would you be a different person if you were born in another country with a different set of parents?

A final word

You may still feel nervous and wonder if you will manage the course, but remember that every year thousands of students receive qualifications in early years work. If they can do it, so can you!

Check your knowledge

- Give three aspects of the role of your placement supervisor.

- What are the main things you need to do in preparation for starting a placement?

- What is plagiarism?

- List four places where you could get information when writing up an assignment.

- What are the five key areas of child development?

Anti-discriminatory practice

CHAPTER

2

Anti-discriminatory practice

What is equality of opportunity?

In many ways equality of opportunity is about fairness in our society. It means that everyone has the same rights regardless of things such as family background, appearance, lifestyle or medical history.

Understanding equality of opportunity is important for everyone who works with young children. Equality of opportunity in early years settings means making sure that every child will be able to take advantage of the opportunities that the setting provides. It also means that, as early years workers, we are able to help children learn about being fair to others.

The rights of children and their families

A good starting point when looking at anti-discriminatory/anti-bias practice is to look at the rights of children and their families. Rights are important as they set down some benchmarks and this helps people know what treatment they are entitled to. Rights work only if people understand and know about them. This section looks at the rights of children and their families.

The rights of children

In recent years, there has been an understanding that not only do children need protection, but they should also have their own rights. The 1989 Children Act was a landmark as, for the first time, legislation about children was pulled together and their needs and welfare put first. It clearly set out that children

have the right to a basic standard of care, nurture and upbringing. Two years later, in 1991, the United Kingdom signed the United Nations Convention on the rights of the child.

The convention, which has to date been signed by 191 countries around the world, does five main things; it:

- reinforces fundamental human dignity

- highlights and defends the family's role in children's lives

- seeks respect for children – but not at the expense of the human rights or responsibilities of others

- endorses the principle of non-discrimination

- establishes clear obligations for member countries to make sure that their legal framework is in line with the provisions of the Convention.

(See the end of the chapter for details of how to gain further information about the Convention.)

In addition to children having rights, there is also a move among policy makers to consult with children more widely. This has meant the introduction of children's forums and even school councils.

The Universal Declaration of Human Rights

After the Second World War, leaders of countries worked together to try to create peace. An organisation was formed called the United Nations which aims to promote peace and harmony in the world. The Universal Declaration of Human Rights was established in 1948 and, although not legally binding on countries, has been a considerable influence on the way we think about people's rights. Article 1 of the Declaration is quite well known and really sums up what equal opportunities should be about:

'All human beings are born free and equal in dignity and rights. They are endowed with reason and conscience and should act towards one another in a spirit of brotherhood.' Article 1

Citizen's rights

This country at present does not have civil liberties laws, although it has signed up to certain European treaties on human rights and is a member of the United Nations. It is increasingly recognised that having rights that are legally enforceable can give citizens some power. This can help prevent discrimination as a person can then appeal to a court if he or she feels his or her rights have been infringed.

As well as legally enforceable rights, successive governments have also been keen to develop charters for public services such as the health service. The patients' charter, for example, states the level of service that a patient has the right to expect. There are charters for most areas of public service including a taxpayers' charter, a patients' charter and a rail users' charter.

Balance of rights and responsibilities

While it is important that individuals within a society have some rights, it is important that they also take on board some responsibilities. A good example of recent legislation is the 1989 Children Act. This Act gave parents rights, such as the right to choose a child's name, but it gave parents responsibilities as well. As early years workers we must make sure that we put children's welfare and rights first at all times – even if this may cause discomfort. This is one of our responsibilities towards children.

Attitudes and values

This is often the starting point when looking at equal opportunities. When people's attitudes and values differ it can affect their treatment of each other. Your values and attitudes may influence your behaviour

and the way in which you relate to others including children and their families.

All of us learn at a very early age how to relate to other people and how others may relate to us. We learn to put a high value on certain characteristics, such as good looks, while perhaps learning to be uncomfortable with those who wear different clothes or have a different lifestyle from us.

Although our attitudes and values form part of our identity, it is important that they do not stop us from accepting and valuing others.

Think about it

We often tend to work, learn and socialise with people who hold similar views and attitudes to ourselves. In pairs, look at the statements below and consider how strongly you agree or disagree with them.

1 Convicted murderers should be executed.
2 Cannabis should be legalised.
3 Divorce is far too easy.
4 Babies should be cared for by their mothers.
5 Abortions should be banned.

How do children learn values and attitudes?

Young children develop their own attitudes and values by watching and learning from the behaviour and reactions of those around them. When presented with a new object or situation they are unsure of, babies will often look at the parent as a guide. This is often called **social referencing**. Children learn values and attitudes in this way from several sources including:

■ family

■ early years workers and teachers

■ friends

■ peers.

The family is probably the most powerful influence on children's attitudes and values. In their home, children learn about their own family's feelings about other people.

Stereotypes

Sometimes our attitudes and values have not been formed from our experiences, but are based on stereotypes. Most of us hold stereotypes of one form or another and some of these will have been learnt in our early years while others will have come from books, magazines and television. Collins dictionary defines a stereotype as a 'standardised image or conception of a type of person' – a fixed image of a group of people. For example, a stereotype of an obese person might be that they are lazy or greedy.

Think about it

Look at the list below and consider what the stereotype image for each group is.

What do they wear, how do they act?

- Football supporters
- Train spotters
- Second-hand car dealers
- Scientists
- Nurses

What stereotype is shown in this picture?

Can you think of any other stereotypes?

Stereotypes can make us think that we know what a group of people is like and this may change our attitude towards someone who belongs to a stereotyped group. Once we meet people from these groups, we often realise that our thoughts about them were not accurate. This is why it is important for early years workers to introduce activities and visits from many different people to show children the falsehood behind stereotypes.

Prejudice and discrimination

Using stereotypes, we can find ourselves judging people without knowing anything about them. This is called **prejudice** – literally pre-judging. In some situations we may pre-judge someone favourably – for example, we might expect a minister of religion to be kind – but in other situations our thoughts about a person might be negative. People have all sorts of prejudices, but prejudice becomes more serious when people's actions are affected by their prejudice. There are different levels of action based on prejudice and in the news we often see examples of extreme behaviour caused by prejudice.

Allport (1954) who studied prejudice and discrimination defined five stages of behaviour that could be shown by groups or people acting from prejudice.

1	Verbal	Hostile talk, insults and jokes
2	Avoidance	Keeping a distance, avoiding, crossing the road
3	Discrimination	Exclusion from housing, rights, employment, etc.
4	Physical attack	Violence against an individual from a group or against their property
5	Extermination	Violence against whole groups – e.g. massacres

Discrimination in our society

At present in our society, groups of people are being unfairly treated because of prejudice. In extreme cases, individuals are physically attacked on the basis of their skin colour or lifestyle, but more often groups of people are discriminated against and receive less favourable treatment than others.

There are many terms to express discrimination and the following is a list of terms which you may come across when reading about discrimination:

Types of discrimination

Racism	Discrimination based on the belief that some races are superior to others
Sexism	Discrimination based on the belief that one gender (usually male) is superior to the other
Ageism	Discrimination because of the age of someone – e.g. too young for a job or too old for life-saving treatment
Disablism	Discrimination because of a disability or medical condition
Sizeism	Discrimination because of someone's physical size

In addition, people can be discriminated against because of their family background, social class, income or because they are homosexual or lesbian.

Institutional discrimination

Although discrimination often arises from individuals' stereotyped or prejudiced attitudes, sometimes it can result from a group or organisation treating certain people differently from others. This type of discrimination is often known as **institutional discrimination** and is likely to occur as a result of a company's policies or practices. In the workplace, an example of institutional discrimination would be a company which advertises for staff who are 'fit and active' when the job is, for example, desk based. This would discriminate against people with certain disabilities who might be quite able to do the job.

General effects of discrimination

Discrimination not only affects individuals in our society, who are not given the same life chances as others, but it affects society itself.

- The best people may not always be given jobs or positions of power.

- Views and attitudes of groups of people may not be represented – e.g. there are not many black women judges, or Asians in the police force.

- Groups of people may turn against society because they feel that they have nothing to lose and are not part of any system.

Think about it

Discrimination is often subtle and difficult to prove. This type of discrimination is often called indirect. The examples below show how indirect discrimination can affect individuals' lives.

Inderjeet has left school and is finding it difficult to get work. His friends with the same qualifications have had no problems. He is sure that his name and racial origin are stopping employers from interviewing him.

Katherine works for a large company. She has had some promotion, but has noticed that some of the men who started at the same time as her have had more promotions, even though she is well qualified and her work is of the same standard.

Simon has a birthmark on his face, which is very visible. He wanted to work in sales and has had many interviews. He is sure that he hasn't been offered the posts because of his appearance.

Zainab has a slight learning difficulty which means that she cannot always remember everything that she is told. She is fine if instructions are written down or if she is given them one at a time. In every other way, she is perfectly capable and has learnt to overcome this minor difficulty. She was offered a promotion to another department and felt that she should mention this to her boss. A week later, she was told that, unfortunately, the company had over-estimated its staffing requirements.

1 Why would it be difficult for the people involved to prove that they have been discriminated against?
2 Why might this type of discrimination affect these people's lives?

Children and discrimination

During their early years children are developing their sense of identity, self-worth and self-esteem. They are learning how others see them and treat them. They react to what they experience and see around them. By the age of three or four, children have started to understand racial and gender differences.

Being a victim of discrimination can affect children's life chances in many ways.

- It can damage their developing sense of self-worth and self-esteem.

- They may grow up with a view of themselves as inferior.

- They may not try out new activities for fear of failing.

- They may achieve less at school.

- They may develop serious emotional and social problems later in life – e.g. finding it hard to form relationships.

The diagram on page 16 shows why children may be discriminated against.

Early years workers have a strong role in promoting equal opportunities within their settings – they need to make sure that every child feels valued and also that children learn to value and respect others.

Laws to support equal opportunities

To try to fight discrimination there are several laws: The diagram on page 17 shows the available legislation.

What is equality of opportunity in child care?

Equality of opportunity means treating all children with the same fairness but this does not mean treating all children in exactly the same way. Children are individuals and to treat them all in the same way will mean that most will not have their individual needs met – a child who is shy will need

---

ISSUES Positive action

It is recognised that some groups of people who have been traditionally discriminated against are under-represented in society. This means, for example, that there are very few black women Members of Parliament or disabled magistrates. Interviewers often select the interviewee who shares their attitudes and values.

To try to balance this situation, some organisations have a policy of **positive action**. This means that they may guarantee interviews for certain groups of people, or ensure a quota of interview candidates from a certain group. Critics of positive action say it is very unfair, while others say that this is the best way of breaking the cycle of discrimination.

Look at the advert opposite which shows that the organisation is taking positive action in favour of disabled people.

In pairs, consider what your views are on positive action.

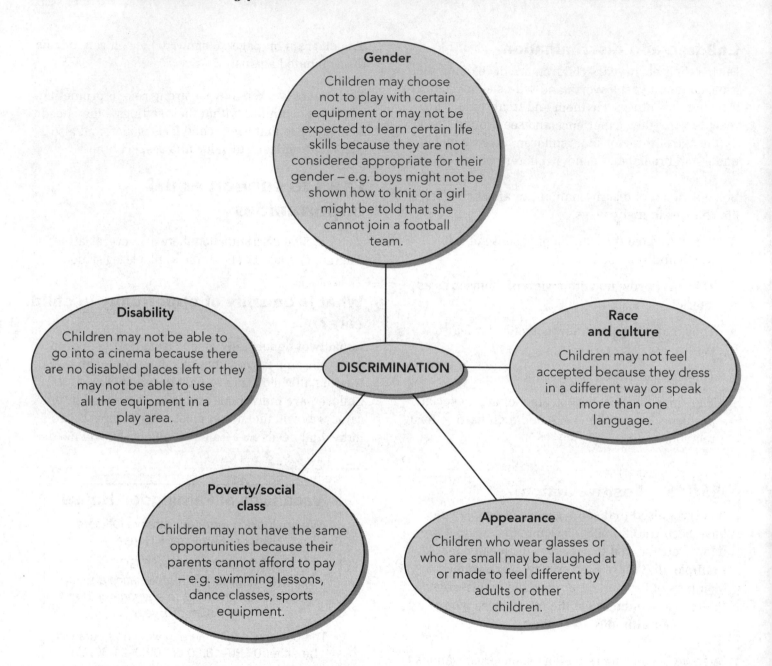

Gender

Children may choose not to play with certain equipment or may not be expected to learn certain life skills because they are not considered appropriate for their gender – e.g. boys might not be shown how to knit or a girl might be told that she cannot join a football team.

Disability

Children may not be able to go into a cinema because there are no disabled places left or they may not be able to use all the equipment in a play area.

DISCRIMINATION

Race and culture

Children may not feel accepted because they dress in a different way or speak more than one language.

Poverty/social class

Children may not have the same opportunities because their parents cannot afford to pay – e.g. swimming lessons, dance classes, sports equipment.

Appearance

Children who wear glasses or who are small may be laughed at or made to feel different by adults or other children.

more reassurance and adult support than a child who is comfortable with other children. Children who have experienced discrimination will need sensitive encouragement to overcome the hurt and rejection they feel. All children need to learn to respect and value each other.

Codes of practice and procedures

The Children Act 1989 requires early years settings to have an equal opportunities policy which is looked at during the setting's registration. Policies usually refer to the aims and values of the organisation and

the procedures cover what actions are taken in particular situations – for example, what to do if a child makes a racist comment. Of course it is very easy to have a policy, but more difficult to make sure that the policy is put into practice. For this reason, many settings develop codes of practice which set out how to make the policy work. Many employers ask employees to sign a code of practice so that everyone in a workplace understands the values of the setting.

When drawing up a policy it is always best to involve parents and staff as this will ensure their support and in the long term make the policy more effective.

Race Relations Act 1976

Protects individuals against discrimination when:

- applying for a job
- at work
- joining a club
- renting a home
- buying or selling a house
- in education and training.

The Commission for Racial Equality (CRE) was set up to enforce the Act and to give advice on improving equality of opportunity in the area of race and ethnicity.

Sex Discrimination Act 1975

Protects individuals from sex discrimination when:

- applying for a job
- at work
- renting a home
- buying or selling a house
- in education
- buying goods and services.

Men and women are entitled to fair and equal treatment. The Equal Pay Act 1972 stated that wages should be the same for a particular job regardless of whether the worker is male or female.

The Equal Opportunities Commission was set up to support the laws affecting sexual discrimination.

Disability Discrimination Act 1995

Covers those who have or who have had a disability.

Protects individuals against discrimination on the grounds of disability when:

- applying for a job
- at work
- buying goods and services
- buying or renting property.

No commission was set up to enforce the Act.

EQUALITY OF OPPORTUNITY LEGISLATION

Children Act 1989

Far-reaching legislation that affects children and their rights.

The main points of the Act are:

- The well-being of the child is paramount.
- Parental responsibility is stressed.
- Statutory services for children 'in need' were introduced.
- Partnership with parents is important.
- Individual children's race, culture, language and religion must be respected.
- Co-ordinated services.
- Services must be designed to meet the needs of individual families.
- Children must be protected.
- Children are best cared for in their own families.
- Children's own feelings and wishes should be taken into account.
- Parents and extended families continue to play a role in a child's life even when that child lives away from home.

Early years providers must be registered and inspected regularly.

Good equal opportunities policies will affect all aspects in a setting including:

- recruitment and selection of staff
- admissions procedures
- curriculum offered to children
- activities and equipment
- relationships with parents
- food and drink.

Reviewing and evaluating policies

Organisations and settings have to constantly evaluate the success of their policies in achieving their aims. It is important that policies are reviewed regularly because otherwise the issues may be forgotten. Staff may need to look hard at what is happening in their settings and decide if the policies are really working.

- Is there an effective complaints procedure open to all parents?
- Is there any evidence of name-calling or bullying among the children?

Knowledge into action

Tinnie Tots nursery has an excellent reputation for providing good-quality care. The local social services department has asked them to take a three-year-old boy from a family of refugees. The boy speaks no English and will need a considerable amount of support.

One of the parents tells the nursery assistant that it is not fair on the other children to give so much attention to this one child, especially as he is not even British. She says that surely there must be a policy to make sure that all children are treated the same.

Why is it important for parents to understand a setting's equal opportunities policy?

In pairs, role-play the nursery assistant's answer to the parent.

- Do all children have access to equipment?
- Are there any groups of children that seem to dominate play areas?
- Do staff ever humiliate or embarrass children?
- How are individual children's needs met?
- Are books and other images showing positive images of groups that are traditionally discriminated against?

Putting good practice into effect

To be able to challenge any form of discrimination, early years workers must be able to recognise that it is happening. Sometimes discrimination can be hidden and harder to detect – for example, an early years setting that does not have any images of ethnic minorities on posters or in books – even though there are no negative images, it is still discrimination.

Direct discrimination – challenging remarks

Occasionally you will have to deal with children who behave inappropriately or make discriminatory remarks. For example, in a home corner, a group of girls saying to a boy who wants to join them 'We don't want you in here, because boys can't play properly,' or a child saying 'I don't like Charlene's hair.'

It is important that we do not ignore offensive remarks, even if children are just echoing what they may have heard elsewhere. Depending on how old the child is, we can do any of the following.

- Ask the children what they meant and where they heard it.
- Tell the children that what they have said is not appropriate.
- Tell the children why their remarks are hurtful.
- Correct any information that is untrue – e.g. 'Chinese people have slitty eyes.'

Knowledge into action

In pairs, choose one of these scenarios and work out a role-play to show other members of your group how you would handle the situation.

1 *A parent comes to see you to say that her boy had been called stupid and fat by one of the other children.*
2 *You overhear a member of staff asking a child what her favourite food is. The child says that she likes chapattis and dahl. The member of staff says to the girl 'I don't know how you eat that kind of funny food.'*
3 *A father asks if you can stop his three-year-old son from playing with dolls and prams.*

- Support the other child or children and make sure that they know we care about them.
- Mention the incident to the supervisor.
- Consider whether the setting needs to look again at its policy on equal opportunities.

Direct discrimination – bullying

Children need to be encouraged from an early age to deal with bullying and discriminatory attitudes although adults must always support and protect them. Bullying is never harmless fun and you must always act if you suspect that a child is being bullied – for example, by talking to your supervisor about your concerns. Children can be taught techniques that empower them. Kidscape is a charity that produces several activity packs that teach children what to do if they are being bullied (see below).

Confronting and combating discrimination and discriminatory practices in settings

There may be times when early years workers recognise that discrimination is taking place in their early years setting. This may be intentional or unintentional – for example, a setting may forget that some parents cannot afford to pay for their children to go on an outing. It is important for early years workers to be ready to challenge any discriminatory practice that they see. This does not necessarily have

Bullying

SIGNS AND SYMPTOMS:
(from Stop Bullying! KIDSCAPE)

A child may indicate by signs or behaviour that he or she is being bullied. Adults should be aware that these are possible signs and that they should investigate if a child:

- is frightened of walking to or from school
- is unwilling to go to school
- begins to do poorly in school work
- becomes withdrawn, starts stammering
- regularly has books or clothes destroyed
- becomes distressed, stops eating
- cries easily

- becomes disruptive or aggressive
- has possessions go 'missing'
- has dinner or other monies continually 'lost'
- starts stealing money (to pay bully)
- is frightened to say what's wrong
- attempts suicide or runs away
- has nightmares.

These signs and behaviours could indicate other problems, but bullying should be considered a possibility and should be investigated.

to be done in a confrontational way, but it is essential that something is done or said. In some cases, a simple reminder or comment may work well, but where discrimination appears to be more deep seated, it may need reporting to the supervisor or manager in a more formal way. All settings should have an equal opportunities code or policy and this should include procedures for combating discrimination.

Why promoting a positive environment is important for all children

The UK today is a diverse multicultural society. In schools and nurseries there are children from many different races and cultures speaking many different languages. This is a rich cultural mix which has many positive effects for children.

- Children learn that everyone is different and special.

- Children are exposed to the wider world. They learn that there are different languages, different ways to pray and different ways to prepare food.

- Children gain learning opportunities by tasting a range of foods, listening to a range of music, hearing and seeing different art forms. This can help children to be more creative.

- Children learn how to value each other through being in a positive environment.

Creating a positive environment – valuing children and parents

A positive environment is a caring and loving one. It accepts that all children are special and provides for children with special needs as well as being multicultural. To create a positive environment involves five main things:

1 valuing children

2 valuing parents

3 showing positive images of children

4 being a good role model

5 planning an anti-bias curriculum.

Valuing children

We know that children's self-esteem and confidence will affect their behaviour, emotional well-being and in the long term their ability to fulfil their potential. This means that early years workers must be able to praise children and make them feel confident about their own identity.

Occasionally some early years workers find it difficult to praise children freely because something in their own childhood is holding them back – for example, they might not have been given much praise as children. This means that as early years workers we must examine our own attitudes and experiences to make sure that they are not stopping us from valuing children.

Positive attitudes towards families

Children will pick up very quickly on the attitudes of staff. They will see whether a staff member seems to be interested and friendly with their parents. This means that early years workers need to understand that there are a variety of child-rearing practices which are equally valuable. There is no such thing as a 'standard' household and children come to settings with a wide range of experiences. Where parents have lifestyles that are different from yours, you will need to be sure that you do not make judgements based on your particular views of parenting – which may be very different.

Think about it

Michael is four years old and goes to nursery. One day Michael's mother says to the nursery nurse that it will be her partner who will be picking up Michael at the end of the session. At the end of the session, a woman comes and says that she is collecting Michael. At first the nursery nurse says that there is some mistake, before realising that this is the partner of Michael's mother. The nursery nurse is embarrassed.

1 Why might the nursery nurse's reaction make Michael feel different from the others?

2 Why is it important for early years workers to remember that children come from a variety of households?

We can also show we value parents by involving them. They may wish to help in the setting or be able to provide information, resources or books – for example, families that have more than one language might be able to lend books and music tapes.

Promoting positive images

Early years workers need to make sure that they are showing children positive images of others. In a setting, all equipment, pictures, books, activities and the way the nursery is organised should reflect all children in a positive light – for example, books that show strong and capable characters who also happen to be black, disabled or female. This is particularly important when children are in settings or areas that are not multicultural or have no children with special needs. Positive images also help children who may in some way be in a minority in their setting, as all children need to feel proud of who they are. For example, children who wear glasses need to see images of other children wearing glasses.

Knowledge into action

Find out which are the four most popular children's books in your placement.

Why do they appeal to children?

Do they provide positive images?

Select the book that best encourages equality of opportunity – for example, showing positive images of age, race, culture, gender, etc.

Good role models

We know that children gain some of their attitudes and values from watching others. This means that early years workers need to be good role models.

- Language must not be prejudiced – 'I thought you were a big, strong boy'

- We must make sure that we are not dismissive of things that we are not familiar with – 'This

strange-looking fruit is called a plantain,' or 'I wouldn't like to wear one of those!'

- We must make sure that children see us co-operating and respecting everyone who comes into the setting, so that they learn that everyone must be treated well.

- Children will also need to see us being open-minded and genuinely interested in other people and their beliefs. We can do this by showing children objects from different countries – e.g. clothes, musical instruments and paintings.

Planning an anti-bias curriculum

Louise Derman-Sparks (1989) talks about implementing an anti-bias curriculum. Anti-bias should permeate every aspect of a setting and is more than just celebrating the occasional festival. All nursery equipment should reflect the anti-bias and ensure that all children feel valued and at home in the setting regardless of their background.

- To ensure co-operation and respect, discussions with children should stress similarities between people and races rather than emphasising the differences.

■ Children should be encouraged to look at others' points of view – e.g. 'If someone said that unkind thing to you, how would you feel?'

■ Children need to be able to feel good and confident about themselves and be able to say 'That's not fair,' or 'I don't like that.'

■ Children should feel that they can stand up for themselves and for others in unfair situations.

Good anti-bias practice

✔ Have a comprehensive equal opportunities policy.

✔ Check and review the success of the policy.

✔ Plan the curriculum to ensure an anti-bias approach.

✔ Check the books and equipment for negative images.

✔ Encourage positive interactions.

✔ Allow children to talk about their feelings.

✔ Value the community and home language used in the nursery.

✔ Encourage partnerships with parents.

✔ Tackle name-calling, bullying and discrimination.

Anti-bias practice empowers children.

Social and legal factors in caring for disabled children and those with special needs

What does the term 'special needs' mean?

Although the term is widely used, there is no absolute definition of special needs. When the term is used by professionals it usually refers to children who have specific difficulties, particularly in the area of their growth and development.

The idea of children with particular needs has been strengthened in law by two pieces of legislation: the Children Act 1989 and the Education Act 1980/1993.

The Children Act 1989 used the term children 'in need' to define a child who is 'unlikely to achieve or maintain, or to have the opportunity of achieving or maintaining, a reasonable standard of health or development without provision for him or her of service by a Local Authority.'

The Education Act 1993 states that a child has 'special educational needs' if he or she has a greater difficulty in learning than most children of the same age and requires special educational provision.

What does the term 'disability' mean?

There are many forms of physical and mental disability which may have come about through illness or accidents, developmental problems before birth, birth injuries or congenital (inherited) conditions. Disabilities vary widely – from severe disabling conditions such as cystic fibrosis to minor disabilities that hardly affect people's lives. Some may be immediately obvious – for example, mobility or sensory impairment – others may be less obvious – for example, mild learning difficulties, dyslexia, or long-term conditions such as asthma or diabetes.

Disabilities fall into the broad categories on page 23.

The language to describe disability varies. Some groups prefer to be called 'disabled people' which they feel is a straightforward description of the situation. Others prefer the term 'people with disabilities' which they say concentrates on the person not the disability. The term 'handicapped' is not often used today. However, terms such as 'dummy', 'mental' or 'spastic' are still used in ways which can damage children and families.

Think about it

Why should the terms 'dummy', 'mental' or 'spastic' never be used to describe children or their disabilities?

Disability discrimination

Ways in which children and their parents are discriminated against

Disabled children and their families often find that they are discriminated against in several ways.

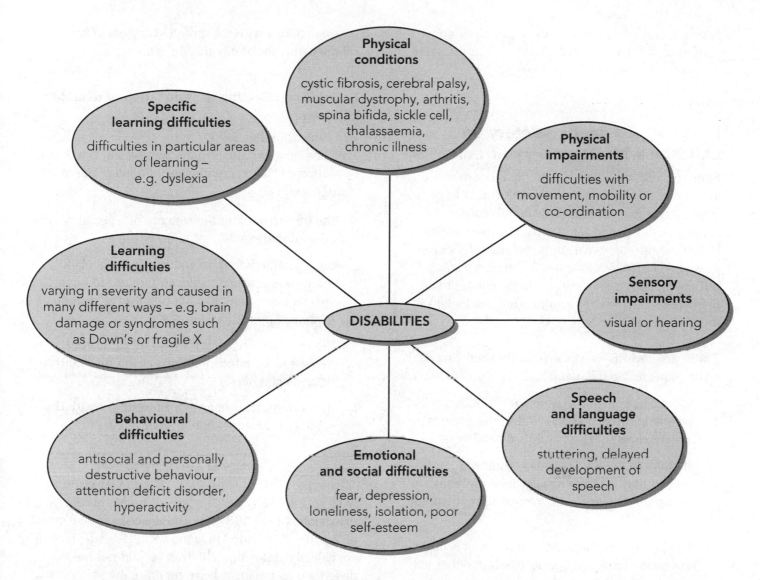

- Parents are often not given adequate support to care for their children and often have to stop work to look after them, which, in turn, may mean they have to rely on state benefits.

- Many schools lack the resources and staff to help disabled children, which often means that the children are not able to achieve their potential.

- Services to disabled children and their families may be cut when local authorities need to save money.

- Parents often have to fight to get the best treatment or resources for their children, and some are unable to cope with this constant battle, which, in turn, can affect the care and support they are able to give their children.

- Disabled children are often treated differently in public places. Access to shops may be a problem and members of the public may stare at them. In the past, some restaurants have refused to serve disabled children because they were afraid that the children might upset the other customers.

- Other children in the family may not receive as much attention because their parents need to care for the disabled child. This can affect development.

The effects of discrimination have been discussed earlier in this chapter and apply equally to the disabled. Children who are disabled or who have other special needs have the same rights and should receive the same opportunities as other children. They should be treated as unique individuals and should not be labelled or stereotyped as this is discrimination.

It is important that discriminatory practices and attitudes to the disabled are challenged in the same way as other forms of discrimination.

ISSUES   Cosmetic surgery on children with Down's syndrome

Some parents of children who have Down's syndrome are opting for their children to have cosmetic surgery so that their facial features are more like those of other children. Children with Down's syndrome have some learning difficulties. The surgery itself does not affect their learning difficulties, but it does reduce tongue length and bring together the eyes and make them look like most other children.

There are several viewpoints on this controversial issue. Look at the following.

■ Changing a child's appearance in this way is wrong because it suggests that the parents are ashamed of their child's disability.

■ If children have this surgery they will not be judged only on their appearance and may, therefore, find it easier to cope in mainstream schools.

■ If children have this surgery other people might not realise they have special needs and they may not, therefore, receive the support they need.

■ It is up to each family to decide what is best for their children.

■ Children should not have operations that might be painful unless they really need them.

In pairs, consider what you think about this issue.

Disability legislation

There are several laws in place to protect people from discrimination if they are disabled. In addition to an individual country's own laws, the United Nations Convention on the Rights of the Child states in Article 23 that a disabled child has the right to special care, education and training to enable

him/her to live with the 'greatest degree of self-reliance and social integration' as possible.

Legislation affecting the education of disabled children

The Education Act 1981
This law brought about major changes in the education of children with special needs. The main changes were:

■ the introduction of the concept of 'special educational needs'

■ the introduction of procedures for schools to monitor and assess children thought to have special needs which could result in a 'statement of special educational needs'.

■ the requirement by law for local authorities to make special educational provision for children with special needs

■ the recognition of parents as partners with the school in the education of their children.

The Education Act 1993
This is the current legislation affecting children with special educational needs. It builds on the provisions of the 1981 Act and describes the concept of 'learning difficulty' in some detail. This legislation specifically states that children should not be described as having a learning difficulty solely because their home language is not the language in which they will be taught.

Code of Practice for Special Educational Needs (1994)
This code provides guidance on putting the Education Act 1993 into practice – it is not a law in itself. Local education authorities and school governors must use the Code of Practice when assessing and planning for children with special educational needs in schools.

The Code of Practice covers:

■ partnerships with parents

■ considering parents' wishes about the school they would like their child to attend

- special needs policies

- appointing a special needs co-ordinator (SENCO)

- keeping a register of children with special educational needs

- using a five-stage method of identifying and assessing a child's needs

- working co-operatively with other services – e.g. health

- parental right of appeal.

It is important that children with special educational needs are identified as early as possible so that they can get the support they need.

The final stage of assessment is the issuing of a 'statement of special educational needs' – you may hear the phrase 'a statemented child' – that will identify what the child requires in terms of extra support. This means that the school and LEA will have to provide additional resources for that child.

Children with special needs are entitled to study the full National Curriculum and should be given every support to do so. However, many schools and LEAs are reluctant to statement children under five because it can lead to 'labelling' a child at a very early age.

Knowledge into action

*Ask your tutor or placement supervisor where you can find a copy of the **Code of Practice for Special Educational Needs (1994)**. Look carefully at its contents. Make notes on any parts of the code that you have seen working in practice in your placements.*

Integration into mainstream (inclusive education)

A major outcome of the legislation and Code of Practice described above has been the integration of children with special needs into mainstream schools. Many local authorities now have 'integration policies' which set out their plans to bring this about. Some authorities aim to get rid of all their special schools

where disabled children used to be cared for all together in one place. However, many keep a small number of special schools – for example, schools for the deaf.

Integration is thought to ensure that children with special needs do not feel different, that they receive less discrimination and that other children learn to accept disability as a normal part of everyday life.

ISSUES   Mainstream or special schools

There are many viewpoints on whether children should be integrated into mainstream schools or not. Look at the viewpoints below.

- Mainstream schools can help everyone learn how to respect and value one another. Special schools make disability seem like something to be hidden away.

- Money spent on providing transport to special schools is wasted and could be used to provide better staffing and facilities for special needs children in their local area.

- Children with special needs should have the same educational opportunities as other children.

- Special schools focus attention on the disability rather than on the parts of the curriculum that children can achieve.

- Children can be protected from bullying or from being different by attending special schools.

- Mainstream schools cannot cope with children who have profound special needs. Equipment and facilities are better in special schools.

- Parents can feel more supported by each other and by staff.

In pairs, discuss how you feel about this issue.

In your work placement, are there any children with special needs?

individual needs. This Act is described in more detail earlier in this chapter (page 17).

Knowledge into action

1 *Li-Ann is four and lived in China until a year ago. She had polio as a baby and now uses a wheelchair.*
2 *Amy is three and a half and has cerebral palsy. She has some difficulty with motor skills and her speech is indistinct, but she wants to join in with all the nursery activities.*
3 *Darren is three and has behavioural difficulties. He kicks and bites the other children in nursery and fights his carers. He refuses to use a potty and still wears nappies.*

In pairs, discuss these scenarios and create a list of the ways in which you could promote the children's self-esteem.

However, not everyone agrees that integration is the best provision for all children.

Where children have complex and profound special needs they sometimes wish to remain in special schools where they can receive high levels of care and learning support. Here they are in a protected environment where specialist teachers and nursery nurses can work with them to ensure that all their needs are met.

Legislation affecting the care of disabled children

The Children Act 1989

This is a very important piece of legislation that affects many aspects of the way in which children are cared for. The Act covers children who are disabled and is described in more detail earlier in this chapter (page 17). It states that health, education and social services for children should be co-ordinated so that a seamless service may be offered.

The Disability Discrimination Act 1995

This Act provides employment rights for the disabled and states that children with special educational needs should have school places appropriate to their

Self-confidence and self-esteem

Like all other children, children with special needs need to feel good about themselves. Some children with special needs have physical problems that may make them appear unattractive and open to destructive comments, bullying or teasing. It is important that you are aware that all children need to be protected from hurtful and stereotyped attitudes as these damage the child's confidence and well-being. Teaching assertiveness techniques to disabled children can empower them and help them to stand up for themselves – this, in turn, raises their self-esteem.

Children need clear information about disability – whether they are disabled or not – at a level they can understand. They need to have their questions answered honestly and know the correct language to use to describe disability without embarrassment.

Empowerment and advocacy

Disability legislation and practice today stress the need to encourage children to make their own decisions and gain some control over their lives. This is known as **empowerment** and is a right for every child. Sometimes children with special needs find it difficult to communicate their needs and desires and require an independent adult (an advocate) to speak for them. Parents can be their child's advocate, or a child's health visitor or social worker – some local authorities employ children's rights officers.

Case study

A family has just entered the UK as refugees from persecution in their own land. The family speak limited English and the children are deeply affected by their experiences in their home land. One child has moderate learning difficulties and needs to be assessed in order to receive a statement of special educational needs.

The family cannot speak for their children and have no knowledge of the education system or of any rights they may have. A family case conference decides that an advocate and language worker are needed for this family.

Medical and social models of disability

Disability is often still viewed as a tragedy for children and families in much the same way as illness or disease. This is the 'medical model' which focuses on the disability not the child and, in particular, on the medical aspects of the disability. Within the medical model the disabled are viewed as helpless and are given little or no control over their lives. Decisions are taken for them by medical professionals who, it is suggested, know what is best for them. Some disability groups view the medical model as patronising and discriminatory.

The social model of disability, while understanding that there may be a need for medical care, puts forward the view that the disabled are able to take control of their own lives and make their own decisions. Disability groups campaigned for equal rights for the disabled and put forward the view that it was in society itself that the problems lay. The social model of disability views society as creating barriers through discrimination and prejudice which prevent the full participation of the disabled. For example, if a person in a wheelchair cannot get into a library because there is no ramp, it is society which is disabling that person, not the fact the person is in a wheelchair. There is now a legal obligation to provide facilities for the disabled in most public places.

Early years workers should promote a social model of disability and encourage disabled children to become as independent as possible – without pressure or unrealistic expectations. Children should be encouraged to make their own decisions and be supported as necessary and early years settings should ensure there are no barriers to their full participation.

Supporting families

Positive partnerships should be made and maintained with parents or primary carers of disabled children. Like all parents, they will be the most important source of information on the particular needs, abilities and preferences of the child. In the case of children with disabilities or special needs, this information will help staff to give the appropriate support, rather than offering support based on the 'category' of disability.

Families with a child who has special needs have particular needs of their own that arise from a demanding caring role. Most families have help in caring for their child at home through community services but these vary from place to place. Local authorities have a duty to provide a range of support services to promote and safeguard children's welfare, minimise the effect of the special need and help the child to stay within the family. Services have to be culturally appropriate and offer flexibility and choice.

Types of services include:

- day nurseries/family centres
- sponsored childminders or playgroup places
- respite care
- carers' groups
- breakfast and bedtime support
- holiday play schemes
- after-school clubs
- full-time residential care and education
- key workers
- foster carers.

National voluntary organisations

The voluntary sector may provide toy libraries, pre-schools, adventure playgrounds – via the Handicapped Adventure Playground Association (HAPA) – home visiting and other services. Many voluntary associations, such as MENCAP or SCOPE, are set up to support particular groups and have achieved a great deal for the groups they represent.

Knowledge into action

Investigate the work of a national voluntary sector group that exists to support children with special needs and their families – for example, RNIB. Find out why the organisation was set up, what their aims and goals are and the range of services they offer. Give a short talk to other students on your findings.

Portage

This is a home-teaching service – usually for pre-school children – that is used to support children with a variety of conditions – for example, learning difficulties, Down's syndrome or language delay. The programme concentrates on developing fine and gross motor skills; self-help and independence; stimulation; and learning and social skills. Sometimes portage workers also teach Makaton signs, which assist in developing language. Makaton is usually used alongside speech, facial expression and body language.

Residential and non-residential settings

When disabled children are placed in residential settings particular issues emerge. Children need a key worker with whom they can identify and bond. Usually children can bond to a small number of key people. It is important that children see their families regularly and go home from time to time if possible and that their sense of identity within their community is not lost. Residential homes need to have an ethos of independence and empowerment for the children, and the children need to be able to feel 'at home'. In the past, abuse of children in residential homes has taken place and safeguards are now being put into place to prevent this happening as far as is possible.

Developmental factors in the care and education of disabled children

Impairments and disabilities affect children's growth and development according to their type and severity. This chapter cannot cover the range of conditions and strategies used to assist in promoting development. Strategies to minimise the effects of disability and realise the child's potential are usually developed both for individuals and groups of children with similar needs – for example, the development of British Sign Language as an alternative first language. The social model of disability which is now widely accepted means that services to children with special needs must be designed to ensure that there is no

Knowledge into action

Laura is three years old. Her parents and the portage worker have identified independent feeding as the next step for Laura, as at present she is still being spoon-fed. The portage worker breaks down the steps of helping Laura to feed herself and draws out a programme. The first three steps are:

Step 1   Laura's hand is to be put around a spoon with a parent's hand on top.

Step 2   Laura's hand is to be put around a full spoon and guided into her mouth with a parent's hand on top.

Step 3   Laura is to be given a full spoon and be guided from the wrist.

Matthew is four years old and his parents have identified putting on a coat as his next task.

In pairs, can you work out the small steps that Matthew will need to learn before being able to put his coat on by himself?

barrier to the child achieving its full potential and this means provision of a 'disability-friendly' nursery with a range of modified and additional equipment.

Generally, play activities are graded in difficulty and the children are encouraged to move on at their own pace. All children need to succeed and should not be put into situations where they will fail. Activities with no right or wrong way of performing can build self-esteem. Small steps are best, with praise and encouragement for success.

Specialist therapies such as Bobath – specialist physiotherapy for cerebral palsy – or conductive education – from the PETO Institute in Hungary – may be part of the treatment the child receives to promote development. Sometimes you will be involved in working with children and families to support these therapies and with other children with conditions like cystic fibrosis who require intensive physiotherapy.

Difficulties with mobility

Children may require:

- ramps
- lifts
- grab rails
- wide entrances
- wheelchair space
- large toilets with washing and changing facilities
- facilities for nappy and catheter care

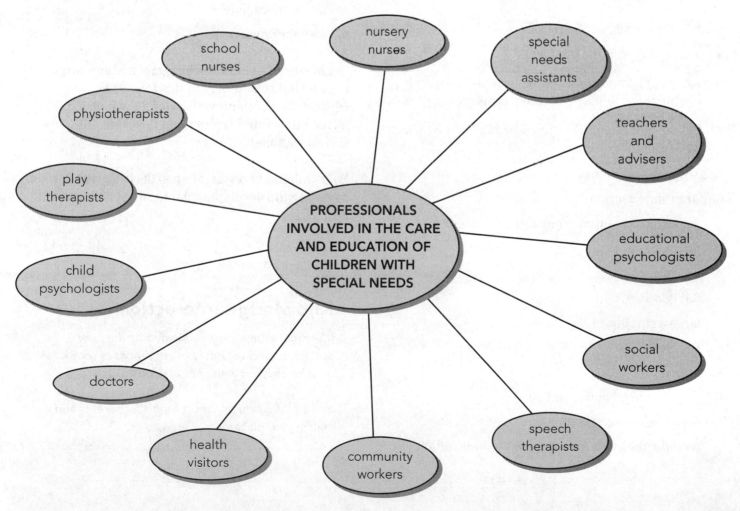

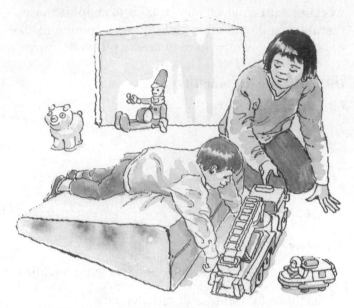

A wedge can help children play

- suitable seating

- soft play areas

- adapted toys and equipment

- wedges or foam slopes to support children and enable them to play with their arms free

- lightweight equipment for some children who lack co-ordination or muscle control.

Sensory impairments

Children may require:

- consistent layout of room and equipment

- plenty of light

- no clutter

- day-glo strips

- large-print books

- Braille books

- tapes

- use of recognisable symbols

- plenty of sensory equipment

- raised edges to tables to prevent items falling off.

Role of the nursery nurse and other professionals

There are many professionals involved in the care and education of children with special needs. These include:

- nursery nurses

- special needs assistants

- teachers and advisers

- educational psychologists

- social workers

- speech therapists

- community workers

- health visitors

- doctors

- child psychologists

- school nurses

- physiotherapists

- play therapists.

Qualified early years workers and nursery nurses have a vital role to play in this team. They can support the care and welfare of the whole child including health; learning and development; play; and educational activities.

Your training in observation skills is a great asset in assessing the developmental needs of children with disabilities.

Knowledge into action

Investigate the services provided by the local authorities and voluntary organisations in your local area for children with special needs.

You could produce a short report for parents and the staff in your placement.

Check your knowledge

- What is the difference between prejudice and discrimination?
- List the main groups of people within society who face discrimination.
- Why is it important for equal opportunity policies to be reviewed?
- What does the term 'institutional racism' mean?
- Outline the main pieces of legislation that deal with discrimination.
- What is meant by the expression 'medical view' of disability?
- Outline the advantages of mainstream schooling for children with 'special needs'.
- What is 'portage'?
- What is a 'statement of needs'?

Resources

Further reading

Commission for Racial Equality – 1989, *From Cradle to School*, CRE, London

Council for the Disabled – 1995, *Help Starts Here*, NCB, London

Dare, A and O'Donovan, M – 1997, *Good Practice in Caring for Young Children with Special Needs*, Stanley Thornes, Cheltenham

Department of Health – 1989, *Children Act*, HMSO, London

Derman-Sparks, L – 1989, *Anti-Bias Curriculum*, National Association for the Education of Young Children, Washington DC

DfEE – 1994, *Code of Practice on the identification and assessment of special educational needs*, HMSO, London

Equal Opportunities Commission – *An Equal Start*, EOC, Manchester

HMSO – 1991, *The Children Act Guidance and Regulations Vol. 6 Children with Disabilities*, HMSO, London

Issues series *Bullying*, Independence Publishers, Cambridge

Issues series *Disabilities*, Independence Publishers, Cambridge

Issues series *Equal Opportunities*, Independence Publishers, Cambridge

Milner, D – 1983, *Children and Race: 10 years on*, Ward Lock Educational

Siraj Blatchford, I – 1994, *The Early Years – Laying the Foundation for Racial Equality*, Trentham Books, Staffordshire

Woolfson, R – 1991, *Children with Special Needs*, Faber and Faber, London

Working Group against Racism in Children's Resources – 1990, *Guidelines for the evaluation and selection of toys and other resources for children*, WCARCR, London

Useful contacts

Disability Alliance Educational and Research Association
Universal House
88–94 Wentworth Street
London E1 7SA
020 7247 8763

CHAPTER 3

Foundations to caring

Parents trust early years workers to provide a safe and pleasant environment for their children. Parents who leave young children to return to work often worry about the effects that this will have on their children. A number of studies in America have compared groups of children – those with working parents and those with a parent or parents who have stayed at home. One of the largest studies (Kagan et al, 1980) would suggest that children receiving high-quality daycare fare no differently from children whose parents stay at home. The emphasis is on the setting's ability to provide high-quality care and attention. This section looks at ways in which we can create a positive environment and those ingredients that produce quality.

The jigsaw below shows the pieces that all need to be put together in order that children can thrive and develop in our care.

This chapter is divided into five sections:

- The characteristics of a positive environment
- Professional practice
- Physical care
- Health and safety requirements
- Diet, nutrition and food.

The characteristics of a positive environment

This section looks at the ingredients that make up a positive environment and the ways in which we can help provide them.

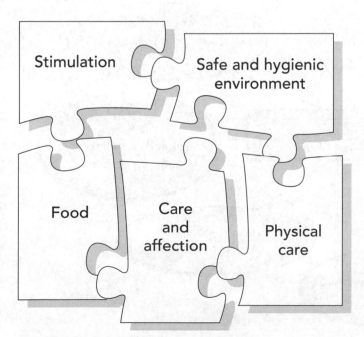

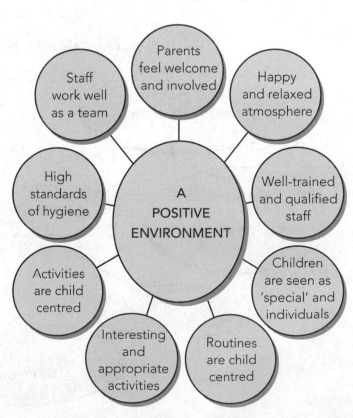

Understanding the term 'environment'

The term 'environment' is an all-encompassing one. It covers not only what we can see, hear, touch and smell, but also the atmosphere that prevails within a setting. This means that as well as ensuring the physical environment is a safe and pleasant one, we also need to make sure that children and their families feel welcome and wanted when they enter. A positive early years environment is therefore one in which all aspects of a child's experience are thought about and where staff are continually looking for ways to make sure that every child is benefiting from being in the environment.

Providing a hygienic environment

Good standards of hygiene in all areas of early years settings are vital to avoid infections. Infections are caused by bacteria or viruses which, given the right conditions, can multiply rapidly – for example, in theory a single bacterium can produce a colony of 250,000 in six hours! Babies and young children are particularly at risk of infections because their immune systems are not as developed and they therefore find it harder to fight off the invading viruses and bacteria once inside the body. The fact that some bacteria are now resistant to antibiotics means that high standards of hygiene are more important than ever as a way of preventing infection.

How bacteria and viruses enter the body

There are three main ways in which bacteria and viruses enter the body:

1 Ingestion – swallowing of bacteria and viruses
Ingestion will take place when babies and young children put toys or their fingers into their mouths. It is also the key way in which food poisoning takes place as infected food and drinks are swallowed.

2 Inhalation – breathing in droplets in the air
Many infections are caused by airborne viruses which are breathed in – a good example of this is influenza and the common cold.

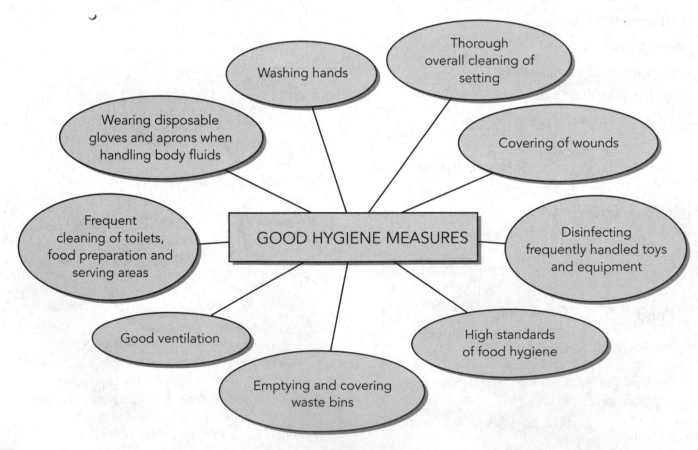

3 Inoculation – bacteria and viruses entering through punctures in the skin – e.g. cuts and grazes
Cuts, grazes and any openings on the skin provide a direct entry for bacteria and viruses to enter.

The term 'cross-infection' is used when viruses or bacteria from one person spread to another.

Preventing infection

Although it is not possible, or even desirable, to remove all viruses and bacteria, a good standard of overall hygiene can prevent viruses and bacteria from either multiplying to dangerous levels, spreading or entering the body.

Using disposable gloves

Most early years workers will find that they come into daily contact with body fluids – blood, vomit, faeces, urine or mucus. They may wipe noses, change nappies or clean up accidents and spills. It is good practice, and in most settings a requirement, that disposable latex gloves are used when staff are likely to be in direct or indirect contact with body fluids. They should be thrown away immediately after the task has been completed.

Disposable gloves are vital for two main reasons:

- They protect the wearer by preventing the viruses and bacteria from entering any skin abrasions or cuts.

- They prevent the spread of bacteria and viruses which might otherwise be carried on the hands of the person.

Using disposable aprons

As well as disposable gloves, disposable aprons should also be worn when handling body fluids. This prevents bacteria from contaminating clothes which might then cause cross-infection.

Handwashing

Handwashing can prevent the spread of bacteria and viruses from one person to another and also prevent the bacteria and viruses from being ingested or swallowed. This means that handwashing should always take place before food is handled or eaten and that staff should make sure that they not only

encourage children to wash their hands frequently, but that they themselves also do so frequently.

Thorough and frequent cleaning

Thorough and frequent cleaning using products containing disinfectants is essential, particularly in washing, toileting and food preparation areas. The standard of cleaning needs to be higher than in households as there are more opportunities for bacteria and viruses to be present when there are more people in an enclosed space. Most settings use a solution of sodium hypochlorite (bleach) and water, in the proportion of 240 millilitres to 5 litres, as an overall disinfectant. It is also important to take care and follow manufacturers' instructions when using cleaning products, as they are hazardous substances.

Providing good ventilation

Airborne bacteria and viruses build up in enclosed spaces. By providing good ventilation, we can 'dilute' the build-up of bacteria and viruses. Viruses and bacteria flourish in warm, humid conditions and so washing areas and steamy kitchens can provide the perfect environment unless they are well ventilated. Perfect conditions also exist in winter when most buildings are centrally heated and the weather outside is damp. This means that even when it is cold outside, some form of ventilation must be provided – for example, a window left slightly ajar.

Taking responsibility for hygiene

Although many settings employ cleaners and caretakers, it is everyone's responsibility to maintain a hygienic environment. This means that staff should have a high level of personal hygiene – which includes short nails, frequent handwashing and tied back hair. Staff should also carry out frequent checks on all areas of the early years setting and in addition make sure that toilet areas are actively cleaned throughout the day. Areas often 'look' clean when in reality they may be harbouring bacteria and viruses. Staff should also make sure that they keep the setting tidy as it is hard to clean thoroughly when it is untidy. Finally, hygiene, particularly in food areas, is taken so seriously by environmental health teams that they have the power to close down settings without warning if levels of hygiene are considered unsafe!

Routine cleaning

Area/item	Method
Hard floors	Wash with disinfectant every day and during the day if there are spills. Floors in wash areas and kitchens need particular attention.
Carpeted areas	These should be thoroughly vacuumed and arrangements made for them to be shampooed regularly.
Toilets, hand basins, sinks	Bacteria favour damp conditions to multiply and so these areas need to be cleaned at least once a day to prevent the spread of infections. Attention should be paid to handles on toilets and doors in these areas.
Door handles	Frequently used door handles should be wiped each day with disinfectant.
Tables	Tables should be wiped over at the end of each activity with disinfectant. If they are used to serve food, they should be cleaned at the beginning and the end of the meal. The legs of the table should also be given attention.
Chairs	The backs and sides of chairs are often handled and if they are used at food tables can become dirty. Chairs should therefore be wiped over frequently.
Bins	Bins should be emptied regularly and covered over. Separate bins are needed for waste paper and for soiled waste materials. Waste materials such as nappies should be put in a bag and then put into a covered bin. This bin should be out of reach of children.
Feeding equipment	Beakers, plates, cutlery – anything used to serve food – must be cleaned thoroughly. Staff should wash their mugs properly as dirty mugs are a common cause of infections in staff rooms.
Toys and frequently handled equipment	Wipe down with disinfectant, rinse if necessary. Pay particular attention to objects such as pencils if children suck the ends and toys that babies put in their mouths.
Cuddly toys, bedding and soft furnishings such as cushions	Surprisingly high levels of bacteria can build up on fabrics. This means that cuddly toys, bedding and cushion covers, etc. need to be washed regularly – at least weekly. Toys that are not easy to clean should be discarded.

Providing a safe environment

Young children do not have a sense of danger and so are very vulnerable to accidents. Accidents often happen very quickly, but a good understanding of their causes and ways in which they can be prevented can dramatically reduce the risk of accidents in settings. It is essential that early years workers are active in preventing accidents and do not fall into the trap of believing that accidents are inevitable.

Did you know?

Child Accident Prevention Trust (CAPT) report that unintentional injury is the leading cause of death and disability to children aged 1–15 years. They report that in 1998, a staggering 2.25 million children visited Accident and Emergency Departments following accidents. An estimated 10,000 children a year will be permanently disabled as a result of accidents.

Potential hazards

Cause of injury or death	Examples of potential hazards	
Falls	Unlocked windows Baby walkers Pushchairs Highchairs Climbing frames	Slides Stairs Steps Climbing on to furniture Baby being left on raised surfaces
Cuts	Knives Sharp edges on furniture or equipment Corners on furniture at eye level	Glass doors Broken equipment such as bikes
Choking and suffocation	Pillows for babies under one year Cords and ribbons on garments Games with skipping ropes Plastic bags Small parts from badly manufactured toys	Tops and lids Peanuts Toys unsuitable for age of children – e.g. small toys such as Lego
Poisoning	Cleaning fluids Medicines Plants	
Scalds and burns	Hot liquids and drinks left unattended Matches and lighters Unguarded radiators and gas fires Kettles	Baths Cookers Irons
Electric shocks	Electric plugs that are uncovered Electrical equipment unsupervised	
Drowning	Baths Paddling pools Buckets of water Fishponds	

Think about it

You have started work as a nanny for two young children aged 2 and 3 years. You notice that one of the children's teddy bears looks as if it needs a wash. When you mention this to the parent, she replies that she doesn't normally wash the children's toys as a little bit of dirt is probably good for them. She also says that when she last tried to wash the youngest child's teddy bear, he cried for the whole morning.

Working in pairs:

- Consider how you would continue this conversation.
- Consider strategies to prevent the children from becoming upset when their toys are washed.

Understanding the causes of accidents

It is helpful for early years workers to be aware of the key causes of accidents to young children. Based on statistics provided by the government, CAPT's data suggests that one of the major causes of accidents to young children is falls. It is also interesting to note that boys are statistically more at risk of accidents than girls from around the age of nine months. According to CAPT, the main causes of accidents are:

- falls
- striking a person or object
- cutting, piercing or crushing injuries
- suffocation and choking
- poisoning
- scalds and burns.

Identifying risks

Every setting and environment will have its own risks. This means that early years workers need to be able to identify the risks and take measures to prevent them. See the safety spider diagram on page 289. There is a good range of safety equipment available and this, combined with good supervision and commonsense, can prevent many injuries to children.

Safety equipment

Equipment	Purpose
Reins and harnesses	To prevent children from falling out of highchairs and from running into the road
Safety gates	To stop children from climbing stairs and from going into certain rooms, such as toilets and kitchens
Play pen	To have a safe area for children in, for example, a kitchen
Smoke alarm	To detect smoke and to raise the alarm
Fire blanket	These smother flames – kept in kitchens to throw over a pan that has caught fire
Catches for windows and cupboards	To prevent children from opening windows and cupboards
Catches for doors	To prevent doors from slamming on to children's fingers
Rubber mat	To prevent children from slipping in a bath
Saucepan guard	To prevent children from tipping pans on cookers on to themselves
Electric plug sockets	To prevent children from putting their fingers into sockets
Plastic film	To cover glass and make it safer – e.g. a glass window in a home setting
Plastic corner covers	To put on furniture with sharp edges
Fire guards	To put around heaters and radiators to prevent children from being burnt
Car seat/booster cushion	To protect children and babies if a car suddenly brakes or is involved in an accident. Car seats need to be fitted correctly and must be correct size for the age and weight of the child. To avoid the risk of injury from airbags, it is considered safer for babies and children to travel in the rear of the car.

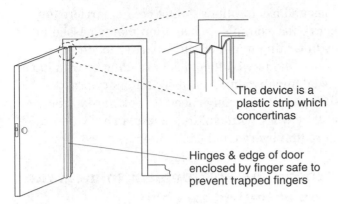

An example of safety equipment

The device is a plastic strip which concertinas

Hinges & edge of door enclosed by finger safe to prevent trapped fingers

The importance of supervision

It is important for early years workers to take active responsibility for safety in their settings. Most accidents are preventable and children and their parents rely on us to keep them safe. One of the major ways in which we can do this is by actively supervising children. This means watching them carefully and thinking about what is happening. A child who is playing with a cord or ribbon might put it around another's neck or might start chewing it. The level of supervision needs to be increased when working with younger children and babies as they have little sense of danger and are therefore extremely vulnerable to accidents. Toddlers, for example, become interested in climbing and may also be less steady in their movements than older children.

How accidents can be avoided

As well as understanding and checking for hazards, accidents can also be prevented by using safety equipment correctly. It is sadly not unusual for safety equipment to be available and then not used. Early years workers have a duty to use safety equipment at all times and to report hazards that are not being managed in the environment (see also page 57). Safety equipment also needs to be checked regularly to make sure that it remains effective.

Good practice – remember

The keys to preventing accidents are:

✔ good and active supervision at all times

✔ an awareness of hazards in the environment

✔ correct use of safety equipment at all times.

Providing a stimulating environment

As well as being in a safe and hygienic environment, children also need stimulation. Lack of stimulation in children's early lives can affect their later overall development. This has been seen in cases where children have been extremely deprived – such as in Romanian orphanages in the 1990s where children had basic care but little attention and stimulation. This resulted in stunted growth as well as poor language and cognitive development. Stimulation is therefore a key feature of high-quality early years settings.

The spider diagram below shows some of the factors that contribute to a stimulating environment.

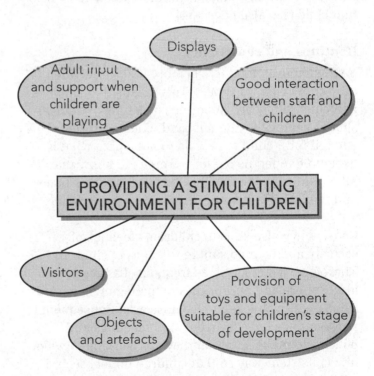

Displays

Adult input and support when children are playing

Good interaction between staff and children

PROVIDING A STIMULATING ENVIRONMENT FOR CHILDREN

Visitors

Objects and artefacts

Provision of toys and equipment suitable for children's stage of development

Although there are many ways of stimulating children, one of the most important factors is the quality of adult input. Adults can interact with children, plan activities for them and help them play by providing appropriate toys and equipment. In order to be able to provide the stimulation that children need, adults need to be skilled at choosing equipment and play opportunities, which means having a good understanding of child development and how to plan activities.

Providing a reassuring and secure environment

Children need to feel that they are in a safe, caring and loving environment if they are going to be able to settle and separate from their parents. There are many ways of providing this reassuring environment, but a key factor for most young children is whether they can build a relationship with, or attachment to, the people who are caring for them. As it is hard for children to come into a new setting and make several attachments at the same time, most settings help children separate from their parents by providing a key worker system. The key worker system is now considered to be good practice. The idea is that one adult in the setting takes responsibility for a particular child and that they build a special relationship with that child (see also page 184).

Routines and consistency

Young children tend to feel more reassured when they know what to expect. This means that routines and consistency are important in settings. Routines should be flexible and not rigid, but structured enough for a child to be able to anticipate what is likely to happen next – for example, to know that after going outside they will be washing their hands and that after story time, they will be going home.

Consistency also adds to children's feelings of security and is important for all ages of children. Therefore, factors such as frequent changes of staff, atmosphere and approaches to managing behaviour can all cause children to feel insecure. Consequently, most settings have frequent staff meetings and policies to make sure that they are working together in a consistent way so that children do feel secure.

Supporting and promoting anti-discriminatory practice and equality of opportunity

High-quality early years settings recognise the importance of children both learning to value each other and also feeling that they belong. Anti-discriminatory practice means that all children and their families, and indeed everyone who comes into the setting, should feel welcome and that they belong. For staff working to provide this atmosphere, this means being very careful to make sure that their

values and assumptions do not create barriers for others – for example, information that is passed on only in writing might create a barrier for those parents who have difficulties in reading or who have a visual impairment. Anti-discriminatory practice also means that settings need to look hard at the way that they work with children and plan activities to ensure that every child can benefit.

Adapting the environment to meet the needs of individual children

Many settings work with children who have special or particular needs. This means that in some cases the physical environment needs to be changed to meet these needs. There are no blanket solutions to how the environment should be adapted when working with individual children: each setting will need to work with the child's parents or other professionals to find the best solutions. The following case study shows how one setting was able to adapt the environment to suit an individual child's needs.

Case study

Poppy is three years old and has a visual impairment. The setting was advised to place reflective strips on the floor which would allow Poppy to find her way between different areas of the nursery. Staff were also asked to keep any changes to the nursery's layout to a minimum so that Poppy could create a conceptual map in her head to help her find her way around. Staff were also vigilant about keeping the floor between areas tidy and free of obstacles to prevent Poppy from falling over. Large pieces of equipment such as jigsaw puzzles and construction kits were also bought so that Poppy could develop her fine motor skills. Staff also found that, as they worked with Poppy, they found new ways of helping her. One member of staff brought in a brightly coloured tray which meant that smaller objects showed up on it, another member of staff sewed a bell into a beanbag so that Poppy could join in with throwing and catching activities more easily.

Ventilation, heating and lighting

The ventilation, heating and lighting in a setting contribute to the overall atmosphere because they affect our comfort. We have looked at how good ventilation can help prevent the build-up of viruses and bacteria in the air. Good ventilation is also important in buildings to prevent the build-up of the poisonous gas carbon monoxide from gas boilers and central heating systems, which means that air vents should never be blocked. Good ventilation can be provided by opening windows slightly.

The temperature of the setting is also important to overall comfort and health. Settings that are too hot encourage the growth of bacteria and viruses and also make children feel tired and irritated. A good working temperature is considered to be between 18 and 21°C.

It is also important to consider the lighting arrangements in settings. Natural light and sunlight are important to the body, with hormones being released in response to light. Where natural light is not sufficient, the lights should be bright enough for children to be able to play in without incurring eye strain. Poor light can result in headaches, while flickering fluorescent lights can trigger migraines and epileptic attacks.

Layout

The layout of a setting can affect the atmosphere that is created as well as having a practical impact on the way children and staff interact and behave. Layouts vary enormously from setting to setting because each will have its own restrictions as well as aims. A sleep room for toddlers might be decorated in peaceful and restful colours, such as pastels, to encourage children to rest, while elsewhere in the same setting a very 'busy' atmosphere might be created to encourage children to explore and be active.

As every setting is different, there are no perfect solutions, but many practical issues such as storage, tidiness, children's behaviour and even the amount of parental involvement can be affected by the layout. A well-designed reception area, for example, can encourage parents to feel welcome, while creating small focused play areas can help children to concentrate on particular activities. It is therefore a good idea for all settings to examine their layout closely from time to time and consider if it is using the available space effectively.

Observation

Choose one area of your placement setting. Ask your supervisor if you can carry out an observation of this area. Using an event sample as a method, note down who uses this area. You might like to do this for an hour.

1 How is this area being used?

2 Is the current layout an effective one?

3 Can you see any difficulties that are occurring?

Principles of good layout

When planning a layout, there are some general principles that apply to most settings:

Health and safety

■ Fire exits and other access points should be free from obstructions.

■ Good use should be made of natural light.

■ There should be enough space for children and staff to move safely from one area or activity to another.

■ Free-standing furniture, such as cupboards, should be stable.

■ Good visibility is needed to allow staff to supervise children easily.

■ Radiators and lights should be kept clear to prevent fire hazards.

■ Sufficient storage is needed to prevent accidents being caused by objects left around.

■ The layout needs to allow for thorough cleaning.

Encouraging children's independence

■ Equipment and toys need to be accessible for children.

■ Areas need to be created to encourage children to focus on tasks.

Areas in a setting

Area	Reason	Requirements
Sleep room or rest area	To allow younger children to rest or sleep away from the noise and activity of the setting	Mattresses; large cushions; blankets; story tapes; books; children's own comfort objects
Messy play or 'art and craft' area	To allow children to use materials such as dough, water, sand and paint	Flooring that is easy to clean; access to wash facilities; tables; chairs; water and sand containers; painting equipment; aprons
Role-play area	To allow children to use role play without feeling that they are being observed by adults	An area which gives children some privacy; dressing-up clothes; props
Story area	To encourage children to look at books and also to have an area for groups to work in – e.g. at story time	Carpeted area; cushions; comfortable chairs; books
Physical play area	A place where children can move and run around freely using equipment such as tricycles, climbing frames, etc. Some settings have space outdoors, while others have to create this space inside.	Sufficient space for children to be able to run and move around equipment without injury; a selection of large equipment if possible, such as climbing frames, slides; small equipment such as hoops, balls and cones

- Aprons, washing areas should be easily accessible for children.

- Storage should encourage children to help with tidying away.

Stimulation
- The layout should help the environment look interesting.

- Areas need to be created that allow objects and artefacts to be displayed.

- Space should be allowed for child-height displays.

Other factors
- Space needs to be used effectively.

- Enough space needs to be allowed for the specific type of activity – e.g. physical play often requires a large area of space.

Creating specific areas

Many settings also try to create specific areas for certain types of activity or play – for example, an area for 'messy play' or an area where children can lie down and perhaps look at books or listen to story tapes.

Children also benefit from having an area where they can 'hide' away and play – this is why children love Wendy houses, playing in tents or building their own tents. The type of play in these areas tends to be imaginative play (sometimes called pretend or role play – see also page 278).

Displaying children's work

Displays create a good atmosphere in settings. They help raise children's self-esteem as they can see that their work is being valued. Displays also help parents and others become more aware of what is happening in settings and allow parents to talk to their children about what they have been doing. For displays to continue to be eye catching they need to be changed regularly.

Types of display
There are many ways in which children's work might be displayed as the spider diagram opposite shows.

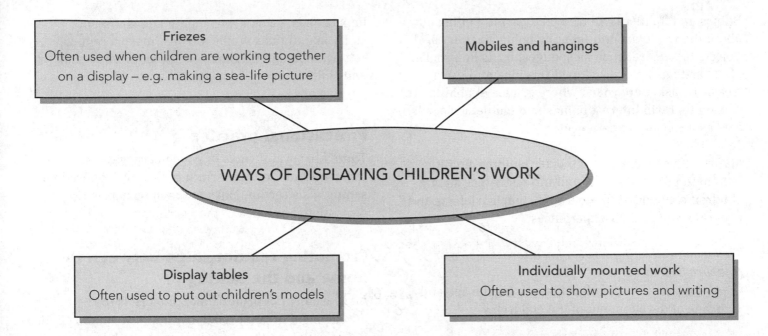

Friezes
Often used when children are working together on a display – e.g. making a sea-life picture

Mobiles and hangings

WAYS OF DISPLAYING CHILDREN'S WORK

Display tables
Often used to put out children's models

Individually mounted work
Often used to show pictures and writing

Tips for creating interesting displays

- Remember that displays should merely enhance children's work not change it.

- Use varied backgrounds – e.g. fabric, corrugated cardboard.

- Label each child's work with his/her name.

- Take photographs of the children as they are painting or modelling and display these alongside their work to show the process.

- Add notes to explain to parents and others what the child has done – e.g. 'Josh enjoyed painting a picture of his favourite animal – his pet dog'.

- Make sure that any labels are neatly presented and correctly spelt. Use a computer if necessary.

- Use a heading.

- Good displays can take time. Make sure that you have allowed yourself enough time.

Maintaining displays
Displays at child height often need some maintenance. Children often want to touch their work and so paper can become ripped or labels can fall off. This means that displays should be checked regularly and little repairs carried out.

Think about it

Look at this photograph of a display:

What makes this display eye catching?

Encouraging children to relate to the world around them

Children need to explore and respect the world around them. This means helping children to find out about plants, wildlife and insects, as well as other features of the outdoors such as weather and buildings. Most settings try to do this by either taking children outdoors or bringing objects inside for children to observe more closely. Some settings are able to encourage children to do some planting and gardening while others have to grow things inside.

Babies and toddlers can also take part in finding out about the world around them by being given natural objects to explore, such as sponges, fruits and shells. Many settings have developed this idea and use a treasure basket approach where groups of objects are chosen that will interest babies and toddlers. This acts as a sensory experience.

Many settings working with older children find it helpful to put up displays and interest tables so that children can look at photographs, touch artefacts and generally widen their experiences.

Tips when collecting objects for interest tables or treasure baskets
- Make sure that the object is safe for the age and stage of development of the children.
- Make sure that objects are clean.
- Do not put anything out that is so precious that you will be upset if it is damaged.
- Provide magnifying glasses for older children to look through.
- Encourage children to hold and touch objects.
- Encourage older children to draw objects that they are interested in.
- Consider labelling objects.
- Encourage children to talk about what they are feeling.
- Consider using feely bags.

Think about it

Every setting and place has its own atmosphere.

Think about a place that you enjoy being in.

Try to analyse what the atmosphere is like and why you like it.

Professional practice in support of creating a positive environment

As well as the physical environment, the adults working in the environment will have an enormous impact on creating a welcoming atmosphere for children and their families. The atmosphere in a setting, although invisible, is extremely important and children are quickly able to sense whether it is a positive one.

Professional practice

There are several ways in which early years workers can contribute to the warmth of the atmosphere in a setting. This section looks at the importance of professional practice in the workplace.

Promoting relationships between the home and the setting

A key element of professional practice is the development of good relationships between the child, their family and the staff. This enables children to feel comfortable and relaxed as the care is more likely to meet their needs and feel less disjointed and separate. Establishing a good working relationship with parents requires good interpersonal skills and an understanding of, and respect for, the role that parents play in children's lives. Although, the ways in which settings work with parents and the skills required is covered in chapter 18, the spider diagram opposite shows some of the key ways in which most settings try to build relationships between the setting and home.

Teamwork

Most settings will have several members of staff working in them. Good teamwork helps create a pleasant atmosphere not only for children and families, but also to work in. Teamwork requires patience, tact and the ability to think about and support others. A team is made up of individuals, so people in a team tend to have different values, preferences and skills. This can create tensions but, when everyone is pulling together, can create a dynamic and effective team that is able to respond to the needs of all the children and families in a setting. There is more information about effective teamwork in chapter 19. You might, however, like to look at the following checklist and consider your strengths and weaknesses and then ask others who know you if they would agree with you!

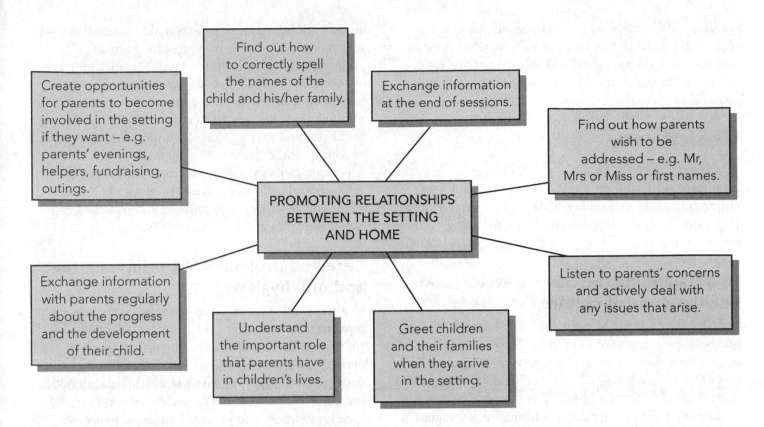

Create opportunities for parents to become involved in the setting if they want – e.g. parents' evenings, helpers, fundraising, outings.

Find out how to correctly spell the names of the child and his/her family.

Exchange information at the end of sessions.

Find out how parents wish to be addressed – e.g. Mr, Mrs or Miss or first names.

PROMOTING RELATIONSHIPS BETWEEN THE SETTING AND HOME

Exchange information with parents regularly about the progress and the development of their child.

Understand the important role that parents have in children's lives.

Greet children and their families when they arrive in the setting.

Listen to parents' concerns and actively deal with any issues that arise.

Teamwork checklist

Statement	Yes, no or sometimes
I enjoy working with others.	
I am good at taking the initiative.	
I am able to help others without being asked.	
I am ready to listen to what others say.	
I can follow instructions carefully	
I am not moody.	
I am willing to put forward my own ideas.	
My work is of a high standard.	
I am ready to seek help if I am unsure.	

Lines of management and reporting

It is important for students, employees and helpers in a setting to understand the level of responsibility that they have and who they should report to. This avoids confusion and inappropriate information being passed on. Most settings have clear lines of management and reporting that mean that staff and others understand their duties but also their level of responsibility.

Most settings will allocate a placement supervisor to students so that if the student needs guidance he/she knows who to ask. Most settings also explain to students that they should not pass on any information to parents without checking with their supervisors as they may unknowingly breach confidentiality.

Confidentiality

Understanding what is and isn't confidential can be hard for new students. The main rule is to consider anything that you have learnt during the course of your work or placement in a setting to be confidential. This means that you should not pass on any information that you have learnt about staff, children or their families to anyone outside of the setting. If you have any concerns about what you can and cannot pass on, you should always talk to your placement supervisor or tutor. (See also page 1 and page 93.)

Physical care

The physical care of babies and children is important. It is another part of the jigsaw that helps children to grow and thrive. This section looks at how to provide physical care for children, including washing, toileting and helping them to rest and sleep.

Understanding the basic physical and health needs of children

In order for children to grow and develop, certain needs of the body have to be met. These are very basic needs, but are essential nonetheless. Failure to meet them can have a dramatic effect on children's overall development, and yet in this country we tend to take them for granted. It is sobering to remember that, in some countries of the world, these needs are not always met and hence the mortality rate of children is much higher as they can easily succumb to infection and illness.

Providing basic care for children

We have seen that there are some basic care needs that are important for children's overall well-being and for their day-to-day comfort. The early years

worker therefore has a role in making sure that these are met. The first step in being able to meet children's needs is to find out exactly what they are. To do this effectively, early years workers need to liaise with parents as care needs such as washing and toileting can vary from child to child and from family to family. It will also be important to encourage children to take responsibility for some aspects of their care needs as this encourages self-reliance and self-esteem (see also pages 167 and 173). The chart opposite outlines some of the basic care needs that children have.

Care and protection of skin, hair, feet and oral hygiene

Meeting children's personal hygiene needs helps to prevent skin and other infections but also helps children to feel comfortable. The extent to which early years workers become involved with meeting children's personal hygiene needs will depend on the setting in which they work. Early years workers who care for toddlers and young children in their own homes are likely to be more involved in this aspect of children's care.

Factors that might influence how children's care needs are met

It is essential that we find out from parents how we should care for children's hair, skin and teeth. Every family has its own personal hygiene routines and preferred products. These are sometimes influenced by religious practices and medical needs as well as social morals and cultural traditions. One family might, for example, boycott certain skincare products because they are unhappy with the manufacturer's policies, while another family might be trying to avoid certain products because they irritate a child's skin.

Caring for children's skin

Our skin is actually considered to be an organ – the largest one in the body. Skin has an important function since it acts as a barrier protecting our internal organs and preventing infection from entering, as well as protecting us from the harmful rays of the sun. Skin also helps to regulate our internal temperature by producing sweat. Sweat needs to be washed off our

Basic care needs of children

Need	Reason	What early years workers should do
Changing nappies	Helps prevent soreness and infection.	Nappies should be changed at regular intervals and early years worker should always change a nappy when it is dirty or wet (see also page 379).
Helping with toileting	Helps prevent children from having accidents and losing confidence. Wiping children's bottoms properly can prevent infection.	As children get older, they should be encouraged to take increased responsibility, with adults being on hand simply to offer support.
Hand washing	This is a major way of preventing the spread of bacteria and viruses.	Younger children will need to be shown how to wash their hands, while older children will need to be reminded and praised when they wash their hands thoroughly.
Keeping noses clean	This prevents children from developing ear infections and also prevents the spread of infection to others. This is one care need that is often overlooked although it can prevent the spread of colds.	Young children cannot blow their noses and so, when they have a cold, their noses need to be wiped frequently. Older children may need to be reminded to wipe their noses and be praised for doing so.
Feeding (see also page 61)	Children need regular intake of fluids and food in order to remain healthy.	Early years workers may help children by cutting up food, helping them to feed themselves and also by being observant and checking that children are not hungry or thirsty.
Washing and care of skin	Helps prevent spread of infection and of diseases of the skin.	Early years workers may wash children's faces and, depending on where they work, may help children to take baths or showers.
Care of hair and teeth	Helps prevent spread of infection and tooth decay and helps detect headlice in hair.	Early years workers in home settings often have a particular responsibility for the care of children's hair and teeth.

bodies regularly as otherwise it combines with dead skin cells and bacteria to cause sore areas and skin inflammations. Washing skin and, where necessary, moisturising it, is therefore the main way in which we care for children's skin.

Washing skin
There are two main methods that are used to wash skin all over – bathing and showering. Many families prefer to shower because they believe that it is more hygienic and, increasingly, showers are becoming a standard fitting in new homes. Some families will want their child to shower because this is a practice

in their religion. It is therefore important to ask parents if they have any particular preferences. (See page 377 for how to bathe a baby.)

Good practice – Washing children

✔ Make sure that the water is not too hot – 63°C is a recommended temperature.

✔ Have everything to hand.

✔ Make sure that all the skin is washed and rubbed down.

✔ Encourage older children to wash themselves.

✔ Use soap products sparingly.

✔ Never leave a child unattended near water.

Skincare in the sun

It is now understood that exposure to the sun can cause skin cancer (melanoma) and also premature ageing of the skin. Skin cancer is currently responsible for 1000 deaths a year in people who, over a period of time, have been exposed to the sun. Children have delicate skin that burns easily and so particular care must be taken in the summer months when the sun is at its strongest. The following advice from health professionals should be followed when there is strong sunlight:

▪ Keep babies under 6 months out of direct sun.

▪ Keep children out of the direct sun between 11 a.m. and 3 p.m.

▪ Keep children covered up – using T-shirts, sunhats, etc.

▪ Use a high-factor sun cream – not less than 15 SPF.

Looking after children's hair

The way in which children's hair needs to be cared for will depend on their hair type and also the parents' wishes. This means researching how best to care for the child you are looking after. It is, for example, common for black children to have oil rubbed into their hair which nourishes it rather than washing it with shampoo and also for it to be braided.

Looking out for headlice

Headlice have made a dramatic reappearance in many settings. Headlice are parasites that live on the human scalp. This means that hair should be checked for headlice and advice should be sought as to the best treatment. This may include special chemical lotions, electric combs or regular combing with a fine-toothed comb.

Signs that a child has headlice might include:

▪ itchy heads

▪ small scabs caused by the bites on the scalp

▪ tiny white or yellow eggs attached to the hair (nits)

▪ small, brown, quickly moving creatures.

Choice of skin and hair care products

The choice of skincare product may be influenced by any of the following:

▪ Type of skin – some children may have dry skin that requires regular moisturisers or oils, such as cocoa butter.

▪ Allergies or skin conditions – children with eczema, other skin conditions or allergies may use specific products that are particularly gentle on the skin.

▪ Manufacturer – some parents may have a preference as to the manufacturer.

▪ Type of hair – some children's hair does not benefit from being shampooed as this makes it dry and brittle or dull and lifeless. Hair oils might be used instead.

Caring for children's feet

Feet support our weight when we stand and walk, while also bending to help us move forwards. Babies and children's feet grow rapidly and it is important that any socks, shoes or other footwear do not restrict this growth. Blisters and corns can also be caused by footwear that is too small or badly fitting. It is suggested that, whenever possible, children should be allowed to go barefoot and that babies are not put into shoes until they are walking steadily.

Oral hygiene

Care of the teeth and mouth is important to prevent bacterial build-up. Some bacteria in the mouth is 'friendly' while other bacteria causes teeth decay. The most important way to prevent the build-up of bacteria is by regular brushing of the teeth which literally removes the bacteria. This is best done after meals and before going to bed. Dentists also advise that sugary drinks and products containing sugar or acid, such as juice, are avoided between meals.

Children's needs for rest and sleep

Sleep and rest are important for all animals, and humans are no exception! Scientists do not completely understand the body's need for sleep but studies have shown that, without sleep, humans cannot not function properly. Without enough sleep, concentration, mood and memory are all affected, and where sleep deprivation is severe the brain can suffer long-term damage. One theory about sleep is that the body needs time to rest and recover while the brain needs time to gather and sort information.

What happens while we are asleep?

When we are asleep, the body's functions slow down. This means that our breathing, heart rate and other body systems slow down. During the time that we are asleep, the brain is active. There appear to be two types of sleep phase, with both being required in order for us to wake feeling refreshed. Having enough sleep is particularly important for children because, during sleep, growth hormones are released from the pituitary gland.

> ## Did you know?
>
> You will spend a third of your life asleep!
>
> Drivers falling asleep are the major cause of deaths on the road.

Understanding children's sleep requirements

The amount of sleep that children and adults need is different. As we get older, we tend to need less sleep, with most adults requiring between seven and eight hours of sleep, while most children under five years will need at least twelve hours a day, although this can vary from child to child. This does not necessarily mean that children will sleep for twelve hours at a stretch, as young children often have naps in the daytime as well as sleeping at night. It is important to find out from parents the sleep patterns of children and, wherever possible, make sure that a child's sleep routine is catered for. Keeping to a sleep routine helps children, as their body will be ready to sleep at certain times. It also helps avoid the problem of parents being unable to get their children off to sleep because they are not tired in the evenings.

Helping children to sleep

Most young children under four years will need an opportunity to have a nap, or at least a rest, during the day. There are many ways of helping children to settle to sleep and individual children may have specific requirements such as having their comforters with them or being gently rocked. Children will also benefit from being with familiar adults when it is sleep time. Most 'sleep clinics' that help parents and carers with children with difficulties in sleeping suggest that a 'wind down' period is planned before children are expected to sleep. This may mean reading a story or doing something that is calming for the children. A routine also helps children and this is why it is important to talk to parents about their child's sleep patterns and routines.

Checklist for helping children to sleep

- Check that the room is well ventilated and not too hot or cold.
- Make sure that the mattress and bedding is dry, clean and comfortable.
- In group care settings, check that there is enough room between mattresses.
- Darken the room as this signals to the brain that it should be sleeping.
- Allow some time for the children to relax and rest before going to sleep.
- Create a calm and peaceful atmosphere around the children.
- Make sure that the children are not hungry or thirsty.
- Check that children wearing nappies are clean and dry and that children out of nappies do not need the toilet.
- Make sure that children have their comforters if needed.
- Follow the sleep routine of the children – this may mean staying next to them until they have fallen asleep.

Waking children

Many children may feel groggy and disorientated when they first wake up. This means that plenty of reassurance must be given to children, especially if they are being woken up. Many key workers of younger children find it helpful to wake them by simply stroking the backs of their hands and quietly talking to them. After waking, children should be offered a drink, as the body loses water during sleep. Most children will also need the toilet or to have their nappies changed. Many children will still need some time before they are ready to run around and may wish to rest for longer with their comforters.

Helping children to rest

Some children find it difficult to take a nap during a session. It is important not to force children to sleep and so when they are not sleepy, we should encourage them to rest and have a 'quiet time'. This could mean reading a story to them, allowing them to watch television or putting on a story tape. The key to any rest activity is that it encourages children to be passive rather than active. A passive activity means that the brain and the body can slow down and so help the body to rest.

Building periods of rest into daily routines

As well as having opportunities for rest periods and naps, children will need time to relax and rest at different points in the day. This means that when planning a daily routine for young children we should make sure that there are opportunities for children to be able to play in a relaxed and restful way. We might, for example, have a story time shortly after a time spent running and playing outdoors in order for children to calm down and rest. Other activities that are restful include drawing; playing with small world toys such as farm animals and play people; as well as watching television.

Signs and symptoms of potential concern when meeting children's basic needs

Early years workers need to be observant when caring for children. It is important to look for any early signs of infection, skin abrasions or injuries.

In some cases we may suspect that a child is becoming unwell (see also page 222) or, sadly, that they are being abused (see also page 416). The chart below shows some of the common skin and other conditions that we should be looking out for. If you notice that a child has a skin or other condition, you should make a note of it and talk either to your supervisor or to the parents.

Signs to look out for when meeting children's basic needs

Concern	Signs and symptoms
Athlete's foot	Skin between toes is itchy and flaky – caused by a fungal infection.
Warts	These are caused by viruses and can be present on hands, knees and also on the feet (verrucas).
Corns	These are hard areas of skin that are caused by the pressure of shoes or footwear. They are often a sign of ill-fitting shoes.
Eczema	Itchy skin and red prickly-looking rash.
Headlice	A small parasite living on the human scalp (see also page 234).
Nappy rash	A sore red rash around the genital area. It is often caused by ammonia in the urine coming into contact with the skin (see also page 381).
Chapped skin	Sore, cracked skin caused by inadequate drying of the area.

Bladder and bowel control

Leaving nappies is a significant step for children and also their parents. It signals the first steps towards independence and so is an important milestone in children's lives. The term 'toilet training' is often used to describe the process of moving out of nappies, although this suggests that children can somehow be taught to do this. This is not the case, as gaining bladder and bowel control is largely dependent on the maturity of the child's nervous system.

Recognising when children are ready to move out of nappies

Although there are different approaches to toilet training, it is generally considered advisable to wait until children are showing physical and other signs that their bodies are ready. It is, however, important to work with parents and respect their wishes if they have other ideas or approaches that they wish to take.

Signs that children may be ready include:

- they realise when their nappy needs changing

- their nappy is dry for long periods – this indicates that they are gaining some bladder control (from eighteen months to three years)

- an interest in potties and toilets

- enough language or communication skills to indicate that they need to go to the toilet.

It is also a good idea to start by leaving a nappy off a child and showing them a potty when you know that their bladder is likely to be full. If a child seems fretful or resists sitting on a potty, it is important not to become irritated and cross. This may indicate that the child is not fully ready to start the process and it is often best to simply put a nappy back on and try again after a few days or even weeks. Keeping calm is essential as children must not feel under pressure to 'perform' – this tends to cause them to become overanxious and will result in their feeling too tense to allow the bladder to release the urine. The speed in which children master the process tends to vary, with most children having a few accidents at first.

Handling accidents

Accidents are inevitable, especially in the first few weeks of being out of nappies – children do not often understand the signals that their bodies are sending them until it is virtually too late. If they are engrossed in an interesting activity, they will often not notice that they need to go. It can therefore be helpful to watch carefully and remind children from time to time. If accidents occur, it is important to be as matter of fact about them as possible so that the child does not become worried. This means that it is a good idea to take the child to a quiet place, help them to get washed and changed into fresh underwear and clothes. Wherever possible, it is a good idea to let the child take as much control of this process as possible so that they can remain feeling self-reliant. The wet or soiled clothes should then be rinsed out and placed in a plastic bag, ready for laundering. It is important to remember to wear disposable gloves at all times during this process. Parents should be kept informed of any accidents, but this should be done away from the child so that they do not lose confidence or, in the case of older children, become embarrassed.

Equipment for toilet training

There is equipment available that can make toilet training a little easier and attractive for children:

- Clothes that unfasten easily

- Inner toilet ring

- Small step to help them reach the toilet if necessary

- Attractive potties

- Clean towels and interesting shaped or perfumed soap

- Soft toilet paper.

It is also possible to read stories about toilet training, although it is important to make sure that they do not put pressure on the child.

Encouraging handwashing

As part of the toilet training process, we need to get children into the habit of washing their hands afterwards. This is essential in preventing infections from spreading, as bacteria is present in bowel motions. Children need to learn to wash their hands using hot water (63°C) and soap and to dry them thoroughly afterwards. It is now suggested that paper towels are the most hygienic way of drying hands in group care settings.

Signs and symptoms that might be a cause for concern

When helping children to use the potty or toilet, you should look for any signs of illness or abnormality – for example, you might notice that children are in pain as they produce bowel motions: this could be a sign of constipation. It is also important to remember that problems in going to the toilet can sometimes be a sign of sexual abuse (see also page 416).

Infections of the bowel and bladder can be painful for children and so it is important to pass on promptly any concerns that you have to your supervisor or the parents.

Signs and symptoms of bowel and bladder infections

Symptom	Could indicate
Difficulty in passing bowel motion	This is often a symptom of constipation in children. It can cause the children pain which in turn puts them off from passing a motion – this becomes a vicious circle as the stools become harder and less easy to pass.
Itchiness, white discharge	This can be a symptom of thrush – medical attention will be required.
Itchiness around the anal area	This can be caused by a threadworm infection (see page 231).
Diarrhoea	This will need urgent attention (see page 230).
Pain when passing urine/blood in the urine	Seek medical attention.
Strong-smelling urine	This can be caused by an infection or could be a sign of dehydration. Seek medical attention.

Health and safety requirements

On pages 36–39 we looked at the importance of providing a safe environment for children. This section looks at the legal framework designed to protect children and adults in the workplace as well as aspects of good practice in relation to maintaining a healthy and safe environment.

Think about it

Simon has just had his second birthday. His father has come into the nursery to say that over the holiday he has begun to take Simon out of nappies at home. He has designed a star chart so that Simon will get a sticker and a lollipop every time he 'performs'. Simon is also being forced to sit on a potty for 10 minutes during mealtimes before getting his pudding. He wants the nursery to carry on with this regime when Simon is with them. When asked by the key worker how Simon is reacting, the father concedes that Simon has been tearful and that success has been limited. The father blames this on Simon not concentrating hard enough. In pairs discuss the following points:

- Why might Simon find it difficult to control his bladder and bowel movements?

- Should the nursery follow the parent's wishes?

- How should the key worker handle this situation?

Health and Safety at Work Act 1974

The Health and Safety at Work Act is the major piece of legislation that all employers need to be familiar with. The aim of the Act is to protect employees and it imposes major responsibilities on employers who can be heavily fined if they breach the Act. Since the introduction of the Act, additional regulations have also been written which employers also have to comply with.

Main features of the Health and Safety Act 1974

The Act imposed duties not only on employers, but also on employees.

Duty of employers
Employers must ensure the health and safety of their employees – they must show that they have taken all

possible steps to do so. In practice most employers do this by providing training, safety equipment, carrying out regular checks and also by writing and implementing a health and safety policy.

Employers with more than five employees also have to carry out a risk assessment which identifies the potential hazards to employees and shows how the risks are to be managed or eliminated. In early years settings, for example, changing a nappy is a potential risk as an early years worker may contract an illness such as polio or *E. coli*. This risk cannot be eliminated completely as nappies need to be changed but can be 'managed' by providing, and insisting that employees wear, disposable gloves.

Employers also have to display information about the Health and Safety at Work Act for employees – look out for a large poster in staff or rest rooms.

Duty of employees
Although the main responsibilities for Health and Safety fall on the employers, under the Act employees also have legally binding responsibilities.

These are:

■ to comply with their employer's safety procedures

■ to use the safety equipment that is provided

■ to report hazards

■ to act with regard for their own and others' safety.

Think about it

An early years worker is changing a child's nappy without wearing disposable gloves. The supervisor asks why this is happening. The early years worker replies that she hates wearing them, and in any case there are not any gloves left in the box and she has not had time to tell anyone yet.

1 How is this employee breaching the Health and Safety Act 1974?

2 If you have been employed, have you ever been tempted not to use safety equipment?

Health and Safety regulations

There are a number of health and safety regulations that have been introduced since the original act. These look at specific areas of health and safety – for example, first aid and fire precautions. Outlined below are the regulations that early years settings are likely to have to comply with, although some settings might have to comply with others. This means that it is important for employers and people in settings who have responsibility for health and safety to find out what regulations they need to comply with. Information can be gained from the government agency responsible – the Health and Safety Executive (see address and website at the end of this chapter).

Health and Safety (First Aid) Regulations 1981

The regulations that relate to first aid lay down a minimum standard. In reality, early years settings will need to exceed this standard by having at least

An example of part of a risk assessment

Potential hazard or procedure	Dangers posed by the hazard	Ways of minimising the risk
Bleach	Accidental poisoning Fire risk Skin irritant	Lock bleach away in kitchen cupboard Follow manufacturer's instructions when using Use protective clothing
Changing nappies	Infection	Use disposable gloves and aprons Put soiled nappies into bags provided Clean changing areas after use Wash hands before and after nappy change

one qualified first aider on site at all times. It is also important to remember that first aid qualifications need to be updated. To comply with the regulations, employers have to appoint one person to be responsible in the event of an accident and to keep a first aid box. There are no legal requirements as to what a first aid box should contain as this will depend on the individual needs of settings. Below is a content list for a first aid box suggested by the Health and Safety Executive:

Suggested contents of a First Aid box
- A leaflet giving general guidance on first aid
- 20 individually wrapped sterile adhesive dressings (assorted sizes)
- 2 sterile eye pads
- 4 individually wrapped triangular bandages (preferably sterile)
- 6 safety pins
- 6 medium-sized (approximately 12 cm x 12 cm) individually wrapped sterile, unmedicated wound dressings
- 2 large (approximately 18 cm x 18 cm) sterile individually wrapped unmedicated wound dressings
- 1 pair of disposable gloves.

In addition, most first aid boxes also contain scissors.

Control of Substances Hazardous to Health Regulations 1994 (COSHH)

These regulations – often known as COSHH – will affect early years settings, as most settings use cleaning products or have other materials that could potentially be hazardous. As a result of the COSHH regulations most settings make a list of materials that they have which could potentially be dangerous and show how they intend to make sure that any risks are minimised.

Reporting of Injuries, Diseases and Dangerous Occurrences Regulations 1995 (RIDDOR)

In order to monitor and, if necessary, investigate accidents and diseases these regulations insist that workplaces keep a note of any injuries, diseases and dangerous occurrences. This means that settings must have an accident reporting system and that any incident that has resulted in an employee needing three or more days off work is reported to the Health and Safety executive. Most early years settings keep two accident books, one for staff and another for children. It is important that they are kept in central places and are filled in promptly.

Fire Precautions (Workplace) Regulations 1997

It is important that early years settings have a system for quickly evacuating children and staff in the event of a fire. Settings should keep records of fire drills and make sure that fire equipment, such as extinguishers and alarm systems, are functioning properly. Fire exit signs need to be clearly displayed as well as instructions to be followed in the event of a fire.

Most settings ask their local fire prevention officer to give them up-to-date advice and to help them look out for potential hazards.

Good practice – Fire precautions
✔ Fire exits must be kept unlocked and unobstructed at all times.
✔ Fire exits must be clearly signed.
✔ Regular checks on fire equipment should be carried out.
✔ Drills should be carried out regularly.
✔ Instructions for use in the event of a fire should be clearly displayed.

DATE AND TIME	EMPLOYEE	NATURE AND CAUSE OF INJURY	TREATMENT	SIGNATURE
22/10/99	Louise Cullington	Cut to right thumb in kitchen caused by knife slipping	Washed and cold water compress Plaster	L Cullington
5/12/99	Nadyia Rayan	Small cut above eye caused by a toy thrown in the toddler room	Ice compress and washed with water	N. Rayan

Employee accident record

✔ Registers should be kept up to date during the day.

✔ Car parking arrangements should ensure access for emergency service vehicles.

Additional regulations

In addition to the Health and Safety at Work Act 1974, early years settings will also be affected by other pieces of legislation including the Children Act 1989 and the Food Handling Regulations 1995.

Children Act 1989

Within this act there are several requirements that are directly related to health and safety. Checking that these requirements are fulfilled is currently met by the local authority, although this is likely to change and become the responsibility of OFSTED following the introduction of the Care Standards Bill.

Annual registration and adult:child ratios
Under the Children Act, settings that provide care for more than two hours for children under the age of eight years must be registered. Settings are inspected and given a certificate which has to be renewed each year. The qualifications and background of staff has to be appropriate. Currently each local authority can impose its own adult:child ratios, providing that these meet the guidance of the Children Act. The new Care Standards Bill is likely to introduce universal ratios and standards across the country. This will prevent situations where neighbouring authorities have different expectations of settings. It is recognised that younger children and babies need more adult input and supervision and so currently the adult:child ratios for babies and toddlers is higher than for older children.

The chart below outlines commonly found minimum adult:child ratios, although it will be important to find out what these are in your area.

Examples of adult:child ratios

Age of children	Number of staff or adult helpers to children
0–2	1:3
2–3	1:4
3–5	1:8

Food Handling Regulations 1995

These regulations cover anyone who is selling or providing food whether or not this is for profit. Many settings prepare and serve food for children and so they must comply with these regulations. The food safety laws are enforced by Environmental Health Officers who are employed by local authorities. Early years settings that prepare food should be aware that environmental health officers have wide-ranging powers which include being able to close down a setting if necessary!

Understanding how the regulations affect settings
There are three main ways in which the regulations affect settings.

1 Settings should be registered with the environmental health team in the local authority. This means that environmental health officers are aware of places in their area which are serving and preparing food. Most environmental health officers make a visit each year to inspect the premises and also to offer advice.

2 Settings must also make sure that their premises are suitable for the preparation and serving of food. Food premises should:

■ be clean and maintained in good repair

■ be designed and constructed to permit good hygiene practices

■ have an adequate supply of drinking water

■ have suitable controls in place to protect against pests

■ have adequate natural or artificial light

■ have sufficient natural or mechanical ventilation

■ provide clean lavatories which do not lead directly on to food rooms

■ have adequate handwashing facilities

■ be provided with adequate drainage.

3 Settings must also make sure that the people handling food have sufficient training or supervision to ensure that basic food hygiene is sufficient. In practice, most settings send staff on courses such as the Basic Food Hygiene certificate.

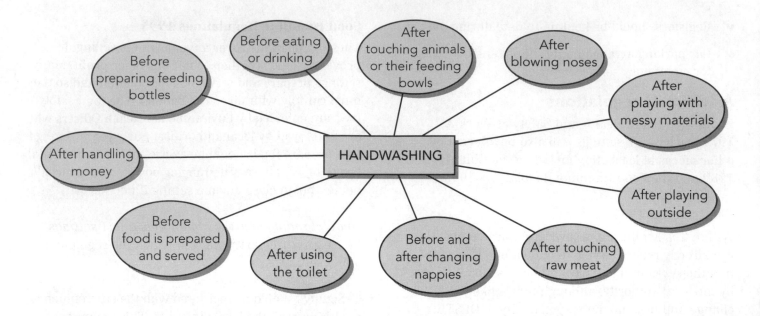

Handwashing in settings

As part of making sure that the environment is a healthy and safe one, settings must develop good handwashing and personal hygiene routines for staff and for children.

The spider diagram above shows examples of when hands must be washed to avoid infections and cross-infection.

Using equipment and materials to maintain health and safety

We have seen that employees have a duty to use the safety equipment provided by their employers and also to make sure that their actions do not create accidents. This means that the safety equipment that is provided to protect children has to be used correctly by staff and failure to do so could lead to disciplinary measures in some settings. On page 38 is a chart showing the types of safety equipment that might be used with children. In addition, most settings will also provide protective items to keep staff safe. Most settings understand that the cost of providing safety equipment is clearly outweighed by the benefits or the financial risk of being fined or sued if preventable accidents take place in their setting. A serious accident to a child could damage the reputation of a setting and potentially lead to its being closed down.

Caring for animals in a safe and hygienic way

Some settings have pet animals, visit farms or occasionally bring in animals for children to observe and touch. Learning how to respect and care for animals can be beneficial for young children, but the potential health and safety hazard created must be managed properly.

The spider diagram opposite shows some of the hazards that might be associated with bringing pets into early years settings.

In order to maintain children's health and safety when caring for or visiting animals, early years workers must be careful about the type of animal that they bring into contact with children and if necessary seek guidance about any potential risks. Local veterinary practices are usually helpful as well as the RSPCA (see address and websites at the end of this chapter).

Good supervision remains the key to making sure that children remain safe and also that they wash their hands thoroughly after touching any animals.

Children also need to understand that animals are not toys and need to be treated with respect. They must also learn to watch and not interfere with wildlife.

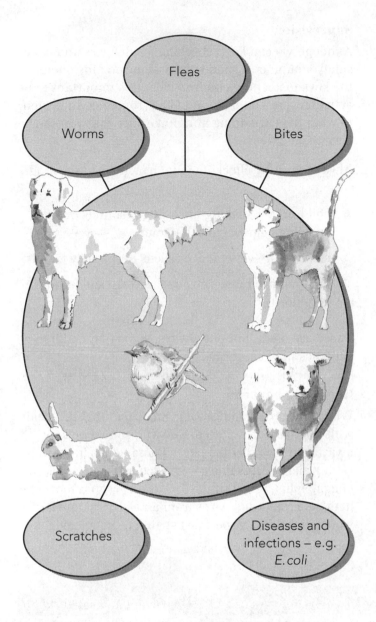

Good practice – Contact with animals

✔ Ensure children wash their hands thoroughly after touching animals.

✔ Do not allow children to touch animals when they are feeding – some animals may bite.

✔ Keep a distance when observing wildlife.

✔ Ensure good supervision.

✔ Do not encourage children to touch dogs that they do not know.

Identifying and reporting potential hazards

It is important for early years workers to be able to spot hazards and also to report potential dangers. Every setting should have a policy which allows adults to report any hazards. There are many reasons why hazards may appear in the environment but these include:

◼ wear and tear – frayed carpets, cracks in equipment, screws coming loose, etc.

◼ human error – leaving out bleach, forgetting to close safety gates

◼ vandalism or thoughtlessness – broken glass, dog mess, used syringes

◼ accidental damage – broken windows, glass breaking on a floor, temperature control on water system being faulty

◼ weather conditions – ice on pathways.

Equipment and signs of wear and tear

Type of material	Examples of equipment	Signs of wear and tear
Plastic	Chairs, sit-and-ride tricycles, plastic see-saws, cups and plates	Cracks, fading colours, sharp edges, chips
Metal	Outdoor climbing frames, safety gates, pushchairs, highchairs	Signs of rust, flaking paint, bent parts
Wood	Blocks, jigsaw puzzles, chairs	Splinters, cracks, rough edges, flaking paint
Fabric	Reins, harnesses, baby bouncers	Threadbare, fraying, seams coming undone

Although it is a good idea to carry out daily checks, an environment that appeared to be safe for children in the morning may not necessarily remain so in the afternoon. This means that early years workers need to be vigilant at all times.

Indoor safety – wear and tear

Most settings carry out daily routine checks indoors at the start of the session. Unfortunately, it can be easy to overlook hazards that are created by wear and tear as this is gradual and may not always be obvious. It can therefore be helpful to have regular inspections of equipment in settings in order to look out for wear and tear. Equipment that is identified as being dangerous should be removed or repaired immediately.

Knowledge into action

Design an indoor safety checklist based on your current work placement.

Outdoor safety

It is always a good idea to check an outdoor area before allowing children to go outside as animals and strangers may have access to it and so have created a hazard.

Supervision

Although we can keep checking for dangers and using safety equipment, good supervision remains one of the keys to keeping children safe. It is important to be active in your supervision of children, look and listen to what they are doing and make sure that you can clearly see them.

Always react by checking what exactly is happening when:

- children are making loud, angry sounds or showing aggressive behaviour
- children are very quiet or silent – especially toddlers
- children are boisterous or there are squeals of laughter.

These are often, but not always, signs that children's activities may be unsafe.

Reporting hazards

When a hazard is noticed it is important that it is dealt with promptly or reported. Children should be kept away from the potential hazard, and adults in the setting alerted. In some cases, such as a broken piece of equipment, it will simply be necessary to remove the item, while exposed wires from an electrical appliance would mean that a specialist should be contacted.

Things to check in outdoor areas

Area/equipment	What to check
Fences and access points	Gates should be securely fastened and fences checked to prevent children from 'disappearing' and to prevent strangers or animals from gaining access to children.
Plants and animals	Check for dog, cat or bird mess. Clean and disinfect if necessary. Make sure that plants are not poisonous and that children are not allergic to them. Look out for swarms of wasps in summer.
Outdoor equipment	Check for wear and tear, cleanliness and even vandalism.
Water	Make sure that children do not have any unsupervised access to ponds, swimming pools or other water.
Other hazards	Check that litter bins are covered and that tools and gardening equipment have not been left out. Remove clothes lines.

Being a positive role model

The social learning theory suggests that children imitate the behaviour of others, particularly adults. This means that, through our actions, we can help children to pick up good health and safety habits such as blowing noses, drying hands thoroughly. We can also help children to understand why these things are necessary by explaining our actions to them – for example, 'I'll come and join you once I have washed my hands because I've just finished helping Nadia with her nose.' It is also useful to talk to children about hazards in their environment so as to encourage older children to report any potential difficulties.

Drying hands thoroughly

Using knives and forks correctly

Closing safety gates

Reacting calmly during fire drills

Washing hands using soap

Keeping hair tied back

Wearing aprons during messy activities

Tidying away objects to avoid accidents

Safe management of daily routines

There are many everyday routines that take place in early years settings which have health and safety implications, these include:

- home times
- meal times
- nap times.

Home times

Home times need to be carefully managed. It is important that children are handed over to the person who is supposed to be collecting them to avoid potential confusion and also in some cases to comply with contact or custody arrangements. This means that early years workers must not let children go home with someone else unless they have been asked by parents to do so. It is usual for settings to ask parents to write in a note if they wish their child to be taken by someone else or there is to be a change in the usual arrangements. Early years workers also need to check that older children who may be waiting independently (for example, in school settings) do not simply wander off or out of sight. Home times can be busy periods in early years settings, as it is often a time when parents wish to exchange information with staff, people are coming and going, and there is a generally a lot of bustle! Settings therefore need to be alert to the dangers of children getting out of main doors. Settings often develop a range of strategies to cope with these potential difficulties.

Different ways of managing home time include:

- preparing the children and their belongings before parents arrive
- taking the children out to the cloakroom area to meet parents in small groups
- encouraging parents to come into the setting and prepare the children themselves
- increasing the supervision at home times.

Knowledge into action

1 How does your setting manage home times?
2 What are the advantages of this system?

Health and safety at meal and snack times

Meal times are important points in the day, but they too have health and safety implications.

- Make sure that children have washed and dried their hands before eating.
- Never leave children unattended with drinks or food in case they choke.

- Before giving children food, check that they have no allergies – e.g. peanuts or milk.
- Make sure that babies and toddlers are strapped into their highchairs.
- Make sure that food is not too hot or too cold (frozen foods such as lollipops can cause burns).
- Supervise children carefully – look for allergic reactions or choking.
- Wipe spills up straight away.

Health and safety at sleep and nap times

Sleep and rest are essential for young children as we have seen on page 49. It is also important that health and safety procedures are still observed.

- Make sure that babies and toddlers are not overdressed.
- Ensure that the temperature of the room is suitable.
- Make sure that there are no potentially dangerous toys or objects lying around.
- Regularly check on sleeping children.
- Make sure that bedding is clean and dry.
- Do not give pillows to babies and toddlers as there is a danger of suffocation.
- Place babies on their backs to sleep.
- Ensure that toddlers or babies cannot fall out of their cots or beds.
- Remove any ribbons or garments with them; necklaces; or other items that might choke children.
- Make sure that any cuddly toys are clean and safe.

Managing emergency procedures

All settings should have emergency evacuation procedures in the event of a fire or other emergency such as a gas leak. Most settings carry out drills every three months so that children and staff become familiar with them. Drills also allow the member of staff responsible for health and safety to assess the speed and efficiency of the procedures. Adults should also comment if they can see any difficulties with the procedure. The way that procedures are carried out will vary from setting to setting, but the following

should always happen:

- Early years workers should respond quickly, but calmly.
- Children should be given clear instructions about what to do in a reassuring way.
- A register should always be taken outside and checked.

It is extremely important that, during the drill or real emergency, early years workers talk to the children and reassure them. Some children are frightened by the sound of the alarm, while other children may become overexcited. After a drill is over, it is a good idea to praise children for being sensible and allow them some time to settle back down again.

Knowledge into action

1 Who is responsible for the emergency procedures in your setting?
2 How often are drills held?
3 Where are the emergency procedures displayed?

Health and safety on outings and trips

Most early years settings plan outings and trips as these provide good learning opportunities for children. Outings can be as simple as taking children for a walk or to a park. Whatever the scale of the outing or trip, early years workers need to look at the health and safety aspects and prepare accordingly. Parents must give their consent before children go on outings and adult:child ratios must conform with the guidelines currently given by the inspection unit of the local authority. This is often a ratio of one adult to every two children under the age of five. As well as obtaining parents' consent, it is also important, when preparing for trips to public places such as theme parks or sea-life centres, for a member of staff to visit before the trip. This means that any potential hazards or difficulties can be considered – e.g. toilet arrangements, prices, size of crowds.

During the outing or trip, it is essential that good supervision is maintained at all times to prevent children from becoming lost or being involved in accidents.

Wherever possible, a first aider should accompany the children and it is generally advisable for adults to take charge of small groups and ensure that they are safe and together. On large-scale outings involving many children, registers should be taken several times and the leader of the trip should always have emergency contact details with them. When packed lunches are being taken, it is important that they are stored somewhere cool to avoid the danger of food poisoning. It is also important during hot weather that children are offered plenty to drink and are kept out of the sun.

Health and safety on trips

Potential hazards and difficulties on outings	Children becoming separated from group Children being involved in accidents Food poisoning Stranger danger Dehydration Sunstroke Children becoming tired and irritable Motion sickness
Items to take	First aid kit Emergency contact numbers List of children's names Sun cream and sunhats Drinks Food Nappies Spare clothing Sick bucket Reins and harnesses where necessary Medication such as inhalers Comforters Pushchairs

Think about it

Choose one place in your area, where you could take 15 children aged 2-4 years on an outing.

1 Describe what children might gain from their trip.

2 Explain the steps you would take to ensure that the children remained safe while on the outing.

3 Consider the cost of the outing.

4 Draft a letter explaining to parents the purpose of the outing and asking for their consent.

Collections/Lesley Howling

Providing food and drinks for children

As part of children's day-to-day care, early years workers are likely to be involved in preparing and giving children food and drinks. This section looks at some of the main principles of diet and nutrition.

Food is life

Food is so much a part of everyday life, that we tend to take it for granted, yet without food we cannot live. The food that children eat is especially important as it helps them to grow and gives them energy so that they can develop. Some scientists have also found that the food we eat in our childhood may affect our health in later life. A healthy diet in childhood is one indicator of high life expectancy.

Food is also fun and pleasurable and mealtimes bring opportunities for children to socialise.

Nutrients

In order for the body to be able to function well, it needs **nutrients**. The body needs five types of nutrients. These are:

■ fats
■ carbohydrates
■ proteins
■ mineral elements
■ vitamins.

In addition, the body also needs water, which is not strictly classed as a nutrient. To gain all the nutrients the body needs, we have to take in a range of foods – this is what is meant by a **balanced diet** as, although one food – for example, milk – may contain several nutrients, no single food can, over time, give the body everything it needs.

At different time in our lives, our bodies may need different amounts of nutrients – for example, children when they are growing, adolescents during growth spurts, and women when they are breastfeeding.

The role of nutrients

There are two main functions of nutrients which are:

- to provide the body with material for growth and repair
- to provide the body with energy.

The chart below shows how nutrients help the body. It also shows where these are found in common foods. Some foods appear in more than one group, because they contain more than one nutrient.

Nutrients work with each other

Without realising it, when we eat we are creating a chemical mixture, as all food can be reduced down to chemical formulae. There are some nutrients that, because of their chemistry, work only if they are combined with another.

Calcium and vitamin D	Calcium is absorbed by the body only if it is taken with vitamin D. If children do not have enough calcium and vitamin D in their diets there is a risk of a disease called **rickets** which affects the bones.

Nutrient	Benefits to the body	Examples of foods
Fats	Energy Also needed for the body to absorb vitamins A and D	Butter, olive oil, margarine, vegetable oils, as well as present in meat and fish and dairy products
Carbohydrates	Energy	Bread, pasta, flour, potatoes, sweet potatoes, plantains and bananas, vegetables
Proteins	Energy Growth and repair	There are two types of proteins. Proteins that are found in meat, fish, soya and dairy products can be absorbed by themselves by the body, while proteins found in vegetable products such as peas, beans, lentils, need to be eaten in combination with other food so that the body can take in the protein – e.g beans on toast, lentil and barley soup.
Mineral elements	There are many minerals needed in a balanced diet. The role of some has not yet been fully identified	Traces of mineral elements are found in many vegetables, particularly if eaten with skins.
Iron	Helps blood to carry oxygen	Red meat, broccoli, spinach, plain chocolate, egg yolk
Calcium and phosphorus	Used for maintaining and repairing bones and teeth	Milk, cheese, yoghurt, and other dairy products. They are also added to white flour.
Fluoride	Used for maintaining and forming teeth and bones	Sea fish, added into some water, also often taken in by the body through toothpaste.

Nutrient	Benefits to the body	Examples of foods
Vitamins	Many diseases are caused by lack of vitamins, even though the amounts needed by the body are very small	
Vitamin A	Healthy skin, growth and development. Needed for maintaining good vision	Fat-soluble – found in fats – dairy products, cheese, margarine, apricots, fatty fish
Vitamin B group	Growth and development, appetite, helps release energy from other foods, good for the nervous system	Bread, flour, meat, yeast, pasta, rice, noodles – added to some breakfast cereals
Vitamin C (fragile – easily destroyed by cooking processes)	Needed for forming bones, teeth and blood vessels, needed for skin	Fresh fruits and greens – e.g. oranges, kiwis, potatoes, blackcurrants, cabbage
Vitamin D	Needed for bones and teeth	Dairy products – e.g. milk, cheese, yoghurts, and fish, added into margarine
Vitamin E	Not completely understood, but links to fertility, protection from cancers and heart disease	Vegetable oils, green leafy vegetables, milk, nuts
Vitamin K	Helps blood to clot	Green vegetables – e.g. spinach, broccoli, peas

Iron and vitamin C	Iron, which is important for the blood, is more easily absorbed in the body when vitamin C is also taken. Lack of iron causes a condition called anaemia – common symptoms include extreme tiredness.
Vegetable proteins	Vegetable proteins found in foods such as pulses, lentils, corn and barley can be absorbed by the body only if more than one of them is eaten. This means that vegetarians need to combine vegetables at meals – e.g. beans on toast, pulse and bean stew.

Diets that lack nutrients

The table above clearly shows that every nutrient is important in keeping the body healthy. The term **malnutrition** is used when one or more nutrients are lacking from a diet. Although in theory someone may be taking in enough food (in quantity), they may not be getting the right nutrients – for example, before it was known that vitamin C was needed, sailors on long journeys suffered from a disease called scurvy, even when they had plenty of food.

The term **undernutrition** is used when people are not getting enough quantities of food.

Symptoms of malnutrition/undernutrition in children may include:

- tiredness, lack of energy, mental alertness
- failure to gain in height and weight
- lowered resistance to infection – e.g. colds, sore throats
- bleeding gums
- poor skin and hair condition.

Regular health checks on babies and young children mean that severe malnutrition is usually spotted by health professionals.

Undernutrition and severe malnutrition are extremely rare in Western countries, although our diets and lifestyle can cause us other problems such as obesity and heart disease.

Nutritional values of food

The energy that food gives us is measured in kilo calories or in kilo joules. In order for the body to have enough energy, it must take in enough food. The amount of food or energy that the body needs varies according to our age and our lifestyle. This means that a man who works as a builder will probably need more calories than a man of the same age working in an office.

As children are growing, their requirements for energy are quite high and the table below shows that boys need more energy than girls.

Meeting children's energy requirements
If you take into consideration the size of children's stomachs, you will see that they have high energy requirements – for example, the table below shows that a boy aged seven will need as much energy as an adult woman.

To meet these high energy requirements, children's fat intake is often higher than adults' – for example, it is recommended that all children under the age of five should be given full-fat milk.

Meeting children's energy requirements does not mean giving lots of sweets and sugar. Although these foods are high in energy, they do not provide the other nutrients that children also need, such as vitamins and protein.

Finding out about nutrients in foods

Most food products list their ingredients and also a breakdown of the main nutrients.

The effects of different food preparation methods on nutrients

The way food is cooked and prepared can alter the nutrient content. For example, boiling fresh vegetables means vitamin C is lost into the water. (Using the water to make a sauce can save them. Alternatively, you can steam the vegetables which helps them retain more of the vitamin C.)

Recommended calorie intake

Boys	kilo calories	Girls	kilo calories
4–6 months	690	4–6 months	645
7–9 months	825	7–9 months	765
10–12 months	920	10–12 months	865
1–3 years	1230	1–3 years	1165
4–6 years	1715	4–6 years	1545
7–10 years	1970	7–10 years	1740
Men		Women	
19–50 years	2550	19–50 years	1940

Think about it

TYPICAL NUTRITIONAL INFORMATION				
	Per 100g		Per 50g pack	
Energy	2257	kj	1129	kj
	540	kcal	270	kcal
Protein	6	g	3	g
Carbohydrate	48	g	24	g
Fat	36	g	18	g
INGREDIENTS				
potatoes, vegetable oil, salt.				

Label from crisps

ADDED INGREDIENTS		
(greatest first): peach, sugar, water, glucose syrup, modified starch, milk protein, stabiliser (pectin), flavouring, citric acid, colour (lutein). Minimum 7% fruit.		
CAUTION		
ALLERGY ADVICE: MAY CONTAIN MINUTE TRACES OF NUTS		
NUTRITION		
TYPICAL VALUES	PER 100g	
Energy value (calories)	341 kj (81 kcal)	
Protein	3.7 g	MEDIUM
Carbohydrate (of which Sugars)	14.6 g (10.5 g)	HIGH MEDIUM
Fibre	0.4 g	MEDIUM
Sodium	0.1 g	MEDIUM
PER POT (150 g)		
Energy value (calories)	512 kJ (122 kcal)	

Label from yoghurt

1 Which product is the higher in protein?
2 Which product is the higher in calories?
3 Overall, decide which of these products would be the better for children.

Planning a balanced diet

To plan a balanced diet, it is important to consider what children will be eating over a number of days. A balanced diet needs to be varied to ensure that the body gets all the nutrients it needs. It is also important that children develop a range of tastes, otherwise they will find it difficult to like new foods.

Some groups of food are particularly good for children and can be used regularly when planning a menu for them. These include the foods in the diagram opposite.

The key to planning a balanced diet is to make sure that children eat a variety of foods and that, whenever possible, these are freshly prepared rather than manufactured – for example, fresh fruit salad rather than tinned fruit; fresh grilled meat rather than burgers. It is also important for early years workers to check whether children have any dietary needs or requirements – for example, allergies to food or religious preferences (see page 73).

The chart on page 66 shows a weekly menu for a day nursery.

The menu includes ice cream and chips. Although these foods are not thought of as 'healthy', they can still be included as part of a diet, providing that they are offered only from time to time.

Providing drinks for children

Water, although not strictly a nutrient is needed by the body. The body's weight is two-thirds water. It

ISSUES Salt in food

Some food manufacturers put salt into their foods to add taste and also as a preservative. It is known that too much salt is not good for the body, especially for children. Salt is not allowed to be added to products for babies, but there is no protection for children. There are many food products aimed at children, such as crisps, tinned pasta and beans, that exceed recommended salt levels for children. Some manufacturers say that there is little demand for low-salt products and that if they were to change the salt levels, consumers would not buy their products.

At present, few food products list the amount of salt on their food labels, although they show the amount of sodium in a product. If you multiply this by 2.5 you will find out the amount of salt. The recommended amount for adults is 6 grams a day.

1 Work out how much salt is in a can of beans.
2 Do you think that consumers are aware of salt as an issue?
3 Whose responsibility is it to make sure that food products are healthy?
4 Do you think that manufacturers should target children in their advertising?

Weekly menu for a day nursery

	Day 1	Day 2	Day 3	Day 4	Day 5
Breakfast	Milk Cereal Chopped apple	Flavoured milk Toast Banana	Milk Yoghurt Cereal	Orange juice Cereal Toast	Milk Pancakes Chopped apple
Mid-morning	Diluted orange juice Banana	Water Grapes	Milk Cheese straws	Milk Raisins	Water Satsuma
Lunch	Pitta filled with tuna and sweetcorn Fresh lychees Water	Turkey curry with rice Yoghurt Water	Macaroni cheese Broccoli Ice cream and fresh fruit Water	Shepherd's pie Carrots and peas Blackcurrant fool Water	Trinidad fruit stew (made with plantains) Banana and custard Water
Mid-afternoon	Cheese and biscuits Milk Water	Dried fruits – apricots, raisins Milk	Mango Milkshake	Rice crackers Hot chocolate	Carrot, celery and dips Water
Tea	Chicken and rice Salad Strawberry mousse	Jacket potatoes with a choice of fillings Fresh fruit salad and ice cream	Sausage and lentil stew Bread rolls Fromage frais	Home-made pizza Rice pudding	Fish fingers, peas and chips Crème caramel

helps the body to control its temperature and is involved in some way in most of the body's functions – e.g digestion, blood circulation.

Knowledge into action

You have been asked to plan the meals for a day for two children aged three and five years.

1   *Write down a plan of the meals and snacks that you would offer.*
2   *Explain how these meals would cover the nutrient requirements of these children.*

The term **dehydration** is used to describe a lack of water in the body. Dehydration is dangerous, particularly in children. This means that children should be offered drinks frequently, especially in the summer or after vigorous physical activity, when the body may lose water through sweating.

The best drinks for children are water and milk. Water is good to quench children's thirst and milk is good as it contains many nutrients. Sugary and sweet drinks are not advised as they can spoil children's appetites and may also cause dental decay.

Foods to avoid giving to children

Some foods should not be given to children, either because they could damage their health or because they may encourage poor eating habits.

Salt	By law, salt cannot be added into baby foods. Too much salt can affect the water balance in children's bodies. This means that foods such as crisps and salty snacks should not be offered regularly. Salt should not be added to foods as they are being cooked as children may develop a taste for it and it is thought to cause high blood pressure in adulthood.
Nuts	Young children should not be given nuts as, although nutritious, there is a danger of children choking on them. Products such as peanut butter have also been linked to increasing nut intolerance among children.
High-fibre foods	In adult diets, high-fibre products such as bran are desirable. Fibre helps digestion, but is not nutritious. However, if children are given too much bulky food, their stomachs have less space to take in the more nutrient-rich foods.
Undiluted fruit juices	Fruit juices might seem like a good alternative to sugary drinks, but they do contain natural sugars and acids that can cause dental decay. This means that all fruit juices given to young children should be diluted.
Uncooked eggs	The current advice is that babies and young children should not be given uncooked eggs due to a risk of contracting **salmonella**. Salmonella is a type of food poisoning. This means, for example, that soft-boiled eggs should not be given as the yolk is not completely cooked and also home-made mayonnaise should not be given as it contains uncooked eggs.

Helping children eat a balanced diet

We have looked at the importance of eating well and why food is important in helping children's growth and development. Early years workers have a strong role to play in making sure that children enjoy food and that they eat a range of different foods.

Being a good role model

A good starting point, when helping children to eat well, is to look at our own attitudes towards food. Children will need to see the adults around them eating a sensible and varied diet. If we tend to eat our own food in a rush or eat unhealthy snacks in front of children, they will learn that meals are not important. If adults are on diets they should avoid making this obvious to children because it will not encourage children to eat well.

Making mealtimes fun

Eating and enjoying food is an opportunity for children to socialise and develop social skills. It is often a chance for families and groups in settings to sit down together and share news. Mealtimes should be relaxed, as this allows children to eat more. Early years workers can also present the food in interesting ways, for example:

- Picnics – Children love the idea of choosing their own food and eating outdoors. Indoor picnics with cuddly toys can also brighten up rainy afternoons.

- Buffets – Allowing children to choose their own foods from a variety.

- Making pictures from food – e.g. faces and shapes.

- Taste testing – asking children to taste different variations – e.g. spoonfuls of different yoghurts.

- Cut food into interesting shapes – e.g. sandwiches into stars and circles.

- Give food fun names – e.g. 'Mickey mouse's cheese' or 'Dinosaur's dinner'.

- Finger foods – Even older children enjoy eating with their fingers – e.g. chicken legs and dips.

How much should children be expected to eat?

It can be difficult for adults to know how much children should be given at each meal. The best guide is often the children themselves and early years workers should try to follow a child's appetite. The amount of food a child will eat at each meal often varies from day to day, although children tend to become very hungry just before a growth spurt. It is important that children who are still hungry after finishing their meal are offered more food, providing it is nutritious and healthy.

It is a good idea when serving food to try putting small quantities on the plate and offering a second helping, rather than put so much on a plate that the child feels overwhelmed. Older children can be asked if they would like to serve themselves.

Sometimes a lack of appetite means that children are off-colour and may be incubating a cold or other infection. Forcing children to eat may result in their vomiting later on.

If children have not eaten much at a meal, they may become hungry later. It is not a good idea to give them large snacks in between meals, as they may not be ready for their next meal.

Sally & Richard Greenhill

Children love eating outdoors

ISSUES No pudding unless you finish!

In some families, there are strict rules about children not having a pudding if they have not finished their main meal. It is important for early years workers to respect the views of parents, although you may have different ones. Look at the following arguments and, in pairs, discuss this issue.

The arguments for:

■ Letting them have a pudding means they will never learn to eat up the main meal.

■ If they are not hungry enough for the main meal, they can't be hungry enough for pudding

■ It is more important that they eat their main meal than the pudding.

■ They are more likely to eat up foods they don't like if they know they can have a pudding.

The arguments against:

■ The danger is that you are teaching that pudding is a reward and that sweet things are nicer.

■ Children may not ask for a large helping of main meal in case they are too full for their pudding.

■ Insisting that children have an empty plate teaches them to eat more than they really want.

■ The pudding should be seen as part of the meal, not as a reward. The pudding should be just as healthy as the main meal.

■ Making a child finish his/her main meal can spoil the atmosphere at the table.

Changing tastes

Children's tastes and preferences for foods often develop and change. This means that a child who used to eat mushrooms, may start rejecting them, while a food he/she used to dislike may be eaten with relish. This can be quite frustrating for adults preparing meals.

Children should never be forced to eat, as there is a danger that food can become a battle-ground. Parents have different views about how to handle situations when whole meals are rejected rather than an individual item of food. Some parents are happy to provide an alternative meal, while others refuse to do so. If you are working in a family, it is important that you work with parents to agree a strategy. This could be encouraging children to help in the preparation of the meal or making meals that have a do-it-yourself feel such as a barbecue or jacket potatoes with a choice of fillings. Some very young children respond well to a little 'marketing' – for example, 'These carrots are special, because they are called Peter Rabbit carrots!'

Think about it

You are working as a nanny to Jo who is three years old. Jo's mother has left a meat and vegetable stew for you both (which is very good). Jo refuses to eat any of it saying that he hates it. He pushes away his plate. He drinks all his milk and asks to leave the table.

In pairs, consider what you would do.

Snacks

Most adults can manage on three meals a day, but children's stomachs are smaller and their nutritional requirements are large. This means they will often become hungry between meals. Snacks can be offered to children, providing that they are nutritious and not too filling. It is a good idea to plan times for snacks, so that they are not too close to mealtimes.

Good snacks are nutritious and encourage good eating habits – e.g. slices of fruit, milk, dried raisins and apricots, savoury biscuits, cheese and yoghurts.

Unhealthy snacks give children poor eating habits and a taste for high-fat or sugary products. They fill children up without giving them nutrients such as vitamins. Examples of poor snacks include crisps, chips, ice cream, chocolate bars, sugary drinks and sweets.

Introducing new tastes

It is reasonably easy to introduce new tastes into the diets of children under two years, as their preferences are not too strong. It is often harder with older children as they may have strong food preferences. In some meals, new tastes can be added gradually without children necessarily realising. Broccoli and spinach, for example, can be added into some dishes, so that children acquire a taste before having it as a separate portion.

It is important that new foods are introduced in a positive way. Children can be told that they can taste a small amount before deciding whether or not to have some. This encourages them to taste without putting pressure on them. Children should be praised for trying out new foods, even if they do not like them. Allowing children to add sauces to new foods is also acceptable to most parents as a way of encouraging them to try.

New tastes can also be used as learning activities in settings – for example, fruit tastings or tasting food from other cultures.

Poverty and children's diets

Poverty is a major issue affecting children's welfare and development. In Chapter 16, Provision of services in the UK, we look at the general effects of poverty on families, but poverty can also affect children's diets.

There is a strong link between a family's income and its diet. Children whose families are on high incomes tend to have a healthier diet than those living on state benefits. There are many reason why families find it difficult to give children the right types of foods if they are on a limited income:

- Cooking facilities may not be adequate in some types of accommodation – e.g. a family might not have access to a proper cooker or cooking equipment.

- They may not have enough money to buy all the ingredients needed to make a tasty meal. Some foods, such as milk and cheese, are reasonably priced, but to make a whole meal often means using small amounts of ingredients, such as stock cubes, eggs and flour, and families may not have enough money to buy all of these at once.

- Families living on low incomes tend not to have store cupboards, buying in only what they need at the time. This means that meals can be repetitive.

- Families may not be able to take advantage of lower prices in superstores because of a lack of transport. Food may have to be bought locally and at a higher price.

- Some local foodstores might not have the turnover to ensure the freshness of fruit and vegetables.

- Families might not be able to take up offers, such as 'Buy two get one free', or buying in bulk, because they can afford only small amounts at once.

- Cooking often involves using gas or electricity. When money is short it may seem cheaper to reheat food or buy take-aways.

- Most families living on low incomes find they tend to cut back on food, as this is a cost they can more easily control. Rent and other costs, such as electricity or water, are less flexible.

- Some parents, when faced with long periods of living in poverty, find it hard to be motivated to cook. Depression is often linked to anxiety and poverty.

- Some parents may not have the skills or knowledge to prepare healthy food.

- Parents may prefer to give their children processed foods because they know they will eat them. Buying fruit or healthy foods might waste money if children are not going to eat them.

Parents such as Shirin are more likely to buy processed foods such as tinned soup, pies and crisps because they are filling and cheap. They are often tasty and little preparation is involved. Families on low incomes cannot afford to waste food and therefore tend to stick with the same foods. This means the children's diets tend to be less varied.

Case study

Shirin is twenty years old and has two children. She lives by herself in a small flat. She works part-time as a cleaner and finds it difficult living and coping by herself. Her low income means that she often tries to save money on food so that she can buy nappies and clothes for the children. She knows that fresh fruit is good for children, but still prefers to buy them sweets and other foods such as ice cream. She does this because she wants to give them treats and these types of food treats are cheaper than buying them toys. The children enjoy chips and burgers and Shirin finds this type of fast food useful, especially when she is working, as it saves her time and they eat everything up.

She has tried to cook some 'proper' food, but the children didn't really like it and she had to throw some of it away. She buys quite a lot of tinned food because it keeps for a long time and is easy to prepare.

Processed foods

Processed foods are often cheap, but do not always contain enough nutrients for a healthy diet. The manufacturing process often destroys vitamins. Vitamin C, for example, is destroyed by cooking at high temperatures and is very fragile. (In home cooking, the water can be saved to make sauces or gravy.) Food products such as pies and pizzas often do not contain much protein or meat as it is cheaper for the manufacturer to add in other things such as starch and fat.

Processed foods can also give children poor eating habits as they become used to the taste of sugar, fat and salt.

Meeting and understanding the dietary needs of children

It is important that early years workers talk to parents about the dietary requirements of children. Some children may have medical conditions which affect their diets, others may not be able to eat some foods because of religious or cultural beliefs.

Diabetes

This is a medical condition which means that the pancreas is unable to regulate the sugar levels in the body. Most diabetics avoid sugar in their diets, but need to have regular balanced meals and snacks. If you are caring for children with diabetes, it is essential that their dietary requirements are strictly followed. Early years workers may also need to record accurately the amount of food that children have had during the day.

Coeliac disease

This disease means that the body is unable to absorb food properly. The cause is unknown, but it generally develops shortly after weaning. Children with this condition must avoid gluten, which is found in cereal products such as wheat flour and oats.

Food allergies and intolerance

Some children may not be able to eat certain foods as their bodies react to them. Intolerance can cause children to develop skin conditions or may aggravate asthma. Occasionally, a food intolerance can be potentially fatal as the body goes into **anaphylactic** shock. This means that the airways swell and sufferers find it difficult to breathe. Nuts and shellfish are two common triggers for anaphylactic shock. The potential danger of nuts in products means that most food manufacturers now label products that contain even small traces of nuts. Early years workers caring for children with nut allergies must be very careful about the food they offer as nuts may be hidden ingredients – for example, many chocolate bars contain small traces of nuts.

Other common food intolerances include:

- lactose – found in milk and some dairy products
- histamine – present in strawberries and ripe tomatoes
- tartrazine – a yellow food colouring found in some soft drinks and sweets.

It is very important to check food labels carefully for potentially allergenic substances, particularly if you are working with a child with known allergies.

Dietary customs

Food is an important part of life, and for centuries it has also been linked to religious beliefs. Food is used in all cultures and religions to celebrate life events such as birth, festivals, weddings and even death. As Britain is a multicultural society, it is important for early years workers to understand the significance of food and how it is eaten so that we can respect and meet all children's needs.

Think about it

How is food used in your family to celebrate events such as marriage, birth and religious festivals?

Respecting ways of eating food

Every culture and country has slightly different 'table manners' which often depend on the types of food being eaten. Knives and forks are not the only way of eating food. Some children in settings may be used to eating food from small bowls with spoons or using their fingers. This means that early years workers need to be careful not to criticise children who seem to lack table manners – for example, having elbows on the table. Most children who are exposed to more than one culture learn to adapt their eating habits just by watching other children and adults.

Respecting diets

There are some foods which we may not personally wish to eat, but are considered delicacies in other cultures – for example, horse meat or raw fish. In the same way, some people with strong beliefs might not wish, or be permitted, to eat foods that we eat – for example, bacon, beef and prawns. It is important for early years workers to respect these differences and make sure that, if parents have asked us not to offer certain foods to their children, that we do not do so.

Opposite is a chart that shows the main dietary customs of the major religions where certain foods are restricted or forbidden.

The word 'some' means that some members of these groups may eat these products.

Some religions also have strict rules about how foods should be prepared.

Halal and Kosher meat
■ Halal meat is meat that has been slaughtered and prepared in accordance with the Muslim faith.

■ Kosher meat has been slaughtered and prepared in accordance with the Jewish faith. Meat that has been killed in this way is available from specialist butchers.

Both faiths believe that eating meat that has not been slaughtered properly is wrong.

Vegetarians and vegans
Some parents may have strong feelings about eating meat or animal products.

■ Vegetarians eat no meat or fish, but will eat products that come from animals, such as milk, cheese and eggs.

■ Vegans eat no meat, fish or any food product derived from animals.

If children are vegetarian or vegan, it is important to find out how best they should be provided for. It is also important to remember that items such as stock cubes or gelatine are made from animal products.

Celebrating with food

It is important that children grow up understanding that there are different foods in the world. We can teach children about cultures and religions by planning food festivals. We can ask parents if they have any recipes or equipment that would be useful and even ask visitors in to settings to show us how to prepare food. For example, in one setting, a nursery assistant approached her local Chinese take-away and the owner came into the nursery with Chinese food for the children to taste!

Where possible, food should be as genuine as possible, to prevent stereotyping – the French do not live on a diet of frog's legs and snails!

Dietary customs of major religions

Food	Muslim	Jew	Sikh	Hindu (mainly vegetarian)	Rastafarian (mainly vegetarian although take milk products)
Lamb	Halal	Kosher	Yes	Some	Some
Pork	No	No	Rarely	Rarely	No
Beef	Halal	Kosher	No	No	Some
Chicken	Halal	Kosher	Some	Some	Some
Cheese	Some	Not with meat	Some	Some	Yes
Milk/yoghurt	Not with rennet	Not with meat	Yes	Not with rennet	Yes
Eggs	Yes	No blood spots	Yes	Some	Yes
Fish	Halal	With fins, scales and backbones	Some	With fins and scales	Yes
Shellfish	Halal	No	Some	Some	No
Cocoa/tea/coffee	Yes	Yes	Yes	Yes	Yes
Fast periods	Ramadan	Yom Kippur			

Think about it

Jacob's parents are Jewish. They have asked the nursery to make sure that Jacob is not given any food that contains pork or pork products and have also provided the nursery with a simple guide to make sure that Jacob is not inadvertently given any foods that are not permitted. The cook has made a quiche that has some ham in it. One of the nursery assistants picks out the ham pieces and tells you that providing no one says anything, Jacob or his family will never know. You know that, although the ham has been removed, the food would still be considered unclean in Jacob's faith.

1. In pairs, consider what you would do in this situation.
2. Why is the other assistant wrong to imagine that it does not really matter?

Observation

Ask permission to observe a group of children as they are eating their packed lunches. Record in list form what each child has in his/her lunch box. Write down the order in which children eat their food – for example, Anne starts with sandwiches and then has a chocolate roll. Record what food children leave.

Note down if children look at each other's lunches and whether any comments about food are made. What do the children talk about?

Ask the children after lunch what they enjoyed most about their lunch. If they have left any food, you might ask them what they left.

Ask the children who chooses what is put in their lunch box.

Interpreting this observation
Look at each child's lunch and consider its nutrient value.

Would the meal have provided enough energy (calories)? – look on page 64 for the recommended daily amount of calories for different age groups and assume that lunch needs to provide between a third and a quarter of these calories.

What did children say about any food they had left?

Were there any common foods in lunch boxes – for example, crisps?

What social benefits did children gain from sharing lunch together?

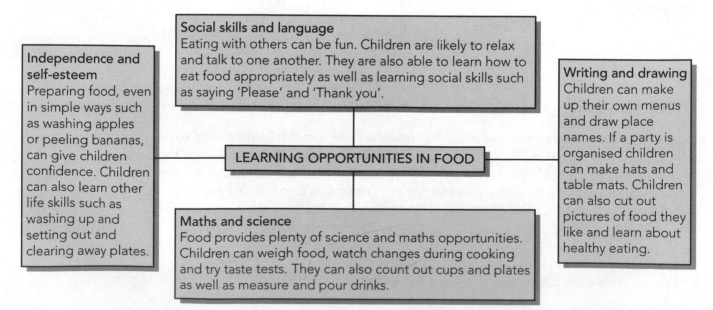

Independence and self-esteem
Preparing food, even in simple ways such as washing apples or peeling bananas, can give children confidence. Children can also learn other life skills such as washing up and setting out and clearing away plates.

Social skills and language
Eating with others can be fun. Children are likely to relax and talk to one another. They are also able to learn how to eat food appropriately as well as learning social skills such as saying 'Please' and 'Thank you'.

LEARNING OPPORTUNITIES IN FOOD

Writing and drawing
Children can make up their own menus and draw place names. If a party is organised children can make hats and table mats. Children can also cut out pictures of food they like and learn about healthy eating.

Maths and science
Food provides plenty of science and maths opportunities. Children can weigh food, watch changes during cooking and try taste tests. They can also count out cups and plates as well as measure and pour drinks.

Learning opportunities

Food and mealtimes can provide children with many learning opportunities, particularly if they are encouraged to take an active part in preparing food.

Check your knowledge

- List five places in a nursery where good hygiene practices should be observed.

- Describe the ways in which an early years worker might recognise that a child is tired.

- When should children be given their first pair of shoes?

- How might an early years worker know that a child is ready to be toilet trained?

- Explain the reasons why most settings display children's work.

- Make a list of safety equipment that should be provided when working with children under two years.

- What are the five main nutrients needed by the body?

- In what types of food can carbohydrates be found?

- What is the difference between malnutrition and undernutrition?

- Why should children not be given uncooked eggs?

- What is meant by the term environment?

- Explain the three ways in which bacteria and viruses enter the body.

- Explain the reasons why settings should keep a supply of disposable gloves.

- What is meant by the term 'risk assessment'?

- Consider ways in which we can help children in a setting to feel secure.

Resources

Further reading

HMSO 1998 *Manual of Nutrition* London, HMSO

A useful reference book to find out more about food and nutrition. It gives detailed information about nutrient content in foods.

Issues series *Vegetarianism*, Cambridge, Independence Publishers

Issues series *Food for Thought*, Cambridge, Independence Publishers

Useful contacts

British Nutrition Foundation (BNF)
High Holborn House
52–54 High Holborn
London
WC1V 6RQ
020 7404 6504

Ministry of Agriculture, Fisheries and Food (MAFF)
Publications Department
London
SE99 7TP
0645 556000

The Food Commission
94 White Lion Street
London
N1 9PF
020 7837 1141

British Red Cross Society (BRCS)
9 Grosvenor Crescent
London
020 7235 5454

Child Accident Prevention Trust (CAPT)
18–20 Farringdon Lane
London
EC1R 3AU
020 7608 3828

Useful websites

Centre for Advanced Food Research
http://hotel/uws.edu.au/~geoffs/

Mayo Foundation for Medical Education and Research
http://www.mayohealth.org/mayo/9511/htm/ecoli.htm

Think Fast
http://www.thinkfast.co.uk

World Health Organisation (WHO)
http://www.who.ch/programmes/emc/bsefacts.htm

CHAPTER 4

Observation and assessment

The ability to observe and record children's development and behaviour is a major part of many child care courses. This chapter is designed to give you an understanding of how such records are used in settings as well as giving you some guidelines so that you can succeed in your own observation and assessment.

Why do we observe and assess children?

Recording children's development and behaviour is an important part of an early years worker's role.

- Observation is when you watch a child do a task.

- Assessment is when you ask a child to carry out a specific task or group of tasks.

There are several reasons why early years workers and other professionals keep records and assessments on babies and children.

To check a child's overall development

Health visitors and doctors regularly check children to see if there are any developmental difficulties. These routine checks are considered important for detecting and diagnosing any problems early on. Early years workers may assess a child on entry to a

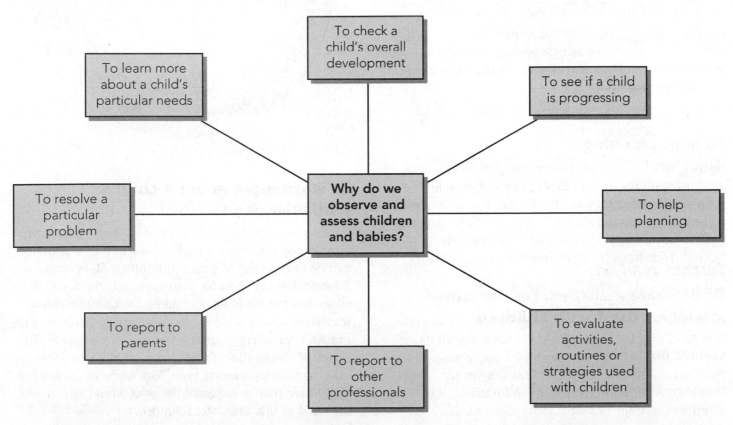

To check a child's overall development

To learn more about a child's particular needs

To see if a child is progressing

To resolve a particular problem

Why do we observe and assess children and babies?

To help planning

To report to parents

To report to other professionals

To evaluate activities, routines or strategies used with children setting, so that they will know if the child has any particular needs and also in order to track the child's progress later.

To see if a child is progressing

Regular assessments are also made on children to ensure that they are making progress – both in their overall development and in specific areas.

A class teacher might carry out an assessment to see if a child's skill in reading was progressing, whereas an early years worker might look at how well a particular child was using scissors

To help planning

Early years workers should be using observations and assessments to help them plan activities for individuals or for groups of children. For example, as a result of observing a child's physical skills, an early years worker might decide that that child would benefit from some throwing and catching activities.

To evaluate activities, routines or strategies used with children

It is good practice to carry out observations in order to check that activities or strategies being used with children are having an effect. This may in turn show that a different approach needs to be taken. For example, in order to help a child learn to share, an

early years worker could plan a series of activities where the child has to work co-operatively with other children. An observation at the end of the programme would help the worker to consider whether he/she had been successful.

In early years settings, staff may also need to consider changing the overall routine – for example, if it is noticed that children become very noisy after outdoor play. An observation would be carried out to find out why this happens.

The diagram below show how observations and assessments can help early years workers plan more effectively.

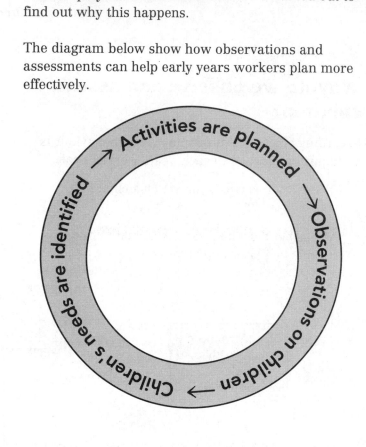

Activities are planned → Observations on children ← Children's needs are identified →

To learn more about a child's particular needs

If it has been recognised that a child has a particular strength or weakness, observations and assessments can be carried out to gain more information. The information can then be used to plan activities and strategies for the child. Occasionally, assessments may show that a child needs more specialist help. For example, an early years worker may, as a result of a series of observations, find that a child's language skills are not developing well. The early years worker could then plan some activities that would encourage the child to talk and interact more.

Think about it

A nursery manager looks through the accident book and notices that several accidents are happening in one part of the outdoor play area. She and her staff have already looked to see if there are any obvious reasons for an increase in accidents there. However, no particular reason has been found. The manager asks one of her assistants to carry out some observations to see if they can discover a reason for the accidents.

The nursery assistant quickly discovers that this is a very popular area with the children which means there are more squabbles and also more chances of children running into one another. After a team meeting, it is decided to stagger the outdoor play times so that fewer children are in this area at any one time.

To resolve a particular problem

Sometimes observations are carried out on children to find out more about a particular problem that has arisen. For example, if a parent mentions that her child has said he has no friends, the early years worker could carry out a series of observations concentrating on the child's social interaction with other children. These observations might show that the child has no difficulty, or they might pinpoint a particular problem.

To report accurately to parents

Keeping records and carrying out observations on children allow early years workers to pass accurate information on to parents. It means that parents can be kept informed of a child's progress which shows them that their child is being seen as an individual and that the staff really know and understand their child.

To report to other professionals

Records based on observations and assessments are often used in reporting to other professionals. An example of this is when children move setting or school. Passing on accurate information can help the

Brightlands Day Nursery
107 St. Georges Road
Cheltenham
Gloucestershire
GL50 3ED

Tel : 01242 230938

Progress Reports to the Parents

Child's name: Alexander   Date: 7th December

On behalf of all the staff at Brightlands Day Nursery

Areas of learning

Personal, social and emotional development	Knowledge and understanding of the world
Experiences: ie. Toileting, Personal Hygiene, Putting on coats. Alexander is a popular child at nursery. He is able to mix with children of all ages. Alexander is able to go to the toilet on his own, and understands that he has to wash his hands after going to the toilet. Alexander is also beginning to put his coat on by himself without any help.	Experiences: i.e. Sand, Water, Trips out Alexander likes going for walks. He is aware of the environment surrounding him and is very well behaved. He also loves playing in the sand and water. He gets very involved in both of these activities. He enjoys socialising with his friends during this time.
Communication, language and literacy	**Physical development**
Experiences: i.e. Books, Stories, Singing. Alexander enjoys looking at books and listening to stories. He has now begun to sing on his own but prefers to do this in a small group. Alexander is very good at his letterland. When Alexander is looking at books he like to tell his own story from looking at the pictures, he has a good imagination.	Experiences: i.e. Outside Toys. Alexander is an energetic child who loves to play outside, he likes to run around a lot letting off some energy in a fun way. He really enjoys playing football with the other children and enjoys playing on the toys provided.
Mathematics	**Creative development**
Experiences: i.e. Construction Toys, Games, Threading. Alexander is good with his numbers but prefers to play number games with blocks or Duplo. He does, however, love to build new models with these materials. Alexander also enjoys threading, modelling, making new creations with the beads. He sometimes loses concentration easily and can be distracted if something else is going on in the room.	Experiences: i.e. Painting, Colouring, Collage, Playdough. Alexander loves doing creative play, especially painting or junk modelling. He likes to take great care over his painting and colouring and is always pleased with his achievements. When Alexander is colouring he shows good imaginative skills, and he holds a pencil well.

Schools have to produce a written report for parents at least once a year

new setting prepare for the child and may, in turn, help the child to settle in more quickly. Observations and assessments are often needed when children are seeing other professionals because they have a developmental delay or impairment. For example, a speech therapist might wish to know if the child's speech impairment was causing him/her difficulty in relating to the other children.

Understanding the limits and scope of observations

While observations can identify that a child's development and behaviour is of concern, it is important that early years workers do not attempt to 'diagnose' the underlying reasons as we are not doctors or psychologists. Finding out the underlying cause can be extremely important and should therefore be left to other professionals, such as speech therapists, paediatricians, educational psychologists, who are specialists in their area. This means that if early years workers have concerns about a child's behaviour or development they should pass these on to their supervisor so that the parents can be informed.

The role of other professionals in observing and assessing children

Although early years workers have a role in observing and assessing children, other professionals may also keep records on children. Some professionals, such as health visitors and doctors, routinely carry out checks on all children. Other professionals carry out observations and tests specifically to diagnose and treat a child who has been referred to them. Sometimes, early years workers will be asked to carry out specific observations for these professionals. This means that it is important for you to have an understanding of their roles.

Health visitors

Health visitors advise on and monitor all aspects of a child's development. They carry out routine assessments on babies and children. These include measuring a child's growth, hearing and vision as well as other areas of development – for example, language, cognitive and emotional development.

Family doctors

A family doctor – general practitioner (GP) – also carries out some routine tests, but often concentrates on the overall health and well-being of a child. Doctors have an important role as they are often responsible for referring children on to specialists if they need specific assessment or treatment.

Speech therapists

A speech therapist works with children and adults who have a speech impairment. A speech therapist works regularly with a child and devises a programme to help improve the child's speech. It is also common for parents or early years workers within settings to carry out certain parts of a

	5. MOTOR SKILL – FINE MOVEMENT		COMMENT
a	Can build a tower with 9 cubes		
b	Can build 3 steps from 6 cubes from a model		
c	Can build 4 steps from 10 cubes from a model		
d	Thread large beads on to a lace		
e	Left-handed		
f	Right-handed		
g	Works well with either hand		
h	Uses scissors – with difficulty adequately skilfully		
i	Can copy a circle triangle cross square		

Health visitors check children's physical development as well as other areas of development

programme. Speech therapists carry out an initial assessment of a child's language and also make assessments during the programme to see how the child is progressing. Speech therapists may also ask for feedback from parents and early years workers.

Educational psychologists

A child is referred to an educational psychologist if there are concerns about the child's cognitive or behavioural development. The psychologist makes an initial assessment of the child, talking to parents and early years workers before diagnosing the difficulty. Specific tests often form the basis of the assessment – for example, asking the child to solve problems or put pictures in a sequence. Educational psychologists are also responsible for drawing up a 'statement of special needs' which is reviewed annually. The statement is important as it requires the local authority to meet the child's needs (see also Chapter 2).

Child psychiatrists

Children are referred to a child psychiatrist if there are concerns about their emotional development. A child psychiatrist carries out an initial assessment which involves talking to parents, the child and other people responsible for the child. Strategies for helping the child may be suggested and his/her progress is regularly monitored.

Play therapists

Children who have difficulty in expressing their feelings and are showing signs of disturbance may be referred to a play therapist. They are often referred by a child psychiatrist as part of a strategy for helping the child. A play therapist concentrates on working with the child through play and often records after each session the types of play that the child is attracted to. By analysing what has happened in each session, the therapist can consider what progress the child has made and also develop a strategy for future sessions.

Working with other professionals

If a child is being monitored or helped by other professionals, early years workers may be asked to keep records or to carry out observations. It is essential that these records are accurate and that the information that the professional needs is being recorded. Sometimes, a professional may give a pre-printed sheet on which the information can be recorded – for example, a checklist.

You should remember to:

- make sure that the observation or assessment is carried out in the way that has been asked
- date and sign the sheet
- store the records carefully
- remember that the information gained when working with another professional is always confidential.

ISSUES in record keeping

There are many issues involved in record keeping.

- Who should have access to the records?
- Where should records be stored?
- How can records be checked for accuracy?
- Who should be allowed to carry out observations and assessments?
- Who can give permission for observations and assessments to take place?

Until quite recently, it was commonplace for educational settings, healthcare institutions and others, such as banks, to keep records without letting the public see them. Nowadays, however, it is considered good practice for any records kept by professionals to be 'open'. This means that parents can ask to see their child's medical and educational records. This allows them to check that the records are accurate and, if necessary, ask for them to be changed. The law has also strengthened the right of members of the public to see information stored about them.

1998 Data Protection Act

The Data Protection Act came into force in March 2000 and replaced the previous act. It asks anyone processing personal information, such as financial records or details to register with the Data Protection

Commission. The previous act covered only the processing of information stored on computer, whereas the current act applies to paper records as well. Anyone processing personal data must comply with the eight enforceable principles of good practice below.

Information must be:

- fairly and lawfully processed
- processed for limited purposes
- adequate, relevant and not excessive
- accurate
- not kept longer than necessary
- processed in accordance with data subjects' rights
- secure
- not transferable to countries without adequate protection.

Think about it

Below are two organisations that may hold information about you. In small groups, think of some other organisations that may store information about you.

1   Previous schools
2   Fan clubs, magazines and book clubs

What sort of information are you often asked for? Have you ever asked to see your school records? Why do you think that some people may be afraid of asking to see their records?

Policies in settings relating to observations and assessment

Every setting should have a policy that addresses the questions outlined on page 81. It is important that all early years workers understand what their setting's policy says. This means that students must ensure that they are allowed to carry out observations and also that they know whom to ask for permission to perform observations. It is usual for early years settings to tell parents that their child's progress will be monitored and then gain permission from them to keep records about the child.

Application form

Please use Capitals

Child's	Age Now	D.O.B.	Admission Date Desired
Nationality	Religion		First Language

Please tick boxes for sessions, remember to include lunch session if required.
For Full day tick all 3 boxes.

	8.30–12.00 ☐	12.00–1.00 ☐	1.00–4.30/5.00 ☐	FEES ☐
Monday				
Tuesday				
Wednesday				
Thursday				
Friday				

Do you wish to pay weekly, half term or by term ....
Parents or Guardians
Name in full .... Address ....
.... Tel No Home ....
Tel Work Mother .... Tel Work Father ....
Emergency contact i.e., Grandparents, friends ....
Doctor's Name .... Doctor's Tel No ....

In Confidence
Any other information you feel we ought to know so that your child's sessions at Nursery can be happy, secure and trouble free, i.e., allergies, physical problems

....

Outings & Emergency Hospital treatment
I give my consent for .... to be taken out of Nursery on occasional outings.
I give my consent for .... hospital treatment if needed in my absence.
Signed ....

Policy Document
I have read the document and agree with the school's policy.
I understand and give permission for routine observations and assessments to be carried out by staff members and supervised students. I understand that I have full access to these if I require.
Signed ....

Confidentiality

Confidentiality is an extremely important issue when keeping records on children. The records can be used only in the child's best interest and any information gained by early years workers is confidential. It is essential that children's records are stored safely and that only parents, appropriate staff members and other professionals have access to them. This means that other parents should never be given information about other people's children.

The role of parents in making sure records are accurate

Parents often have an extensive knowledge of their children. They have been with them and seen them develop over a long period of time and in a variety of different situations. It is, therefore, important that settings and professionals ask parents for information about their children. For example, health visitors often ask parents to tell them what their child can do, because, on a short visit, children are likely to be wary of a stranger and may not complete tasks that they would otherwise complete, such as building a tower of bricks. Parents are also able to give us a rounder picture of the child, as a child may play differently at home with older brothers and sisters. It is quite common for children who are quiet in early years settings to be extremely noisy at home!

Remembering the rights of children and primary carers

It is important for anyone carrying out observations to remember that observations should be carried out only in the child's best interest. This means that it is unethical to set up situations that might cause the child or his/her parents distress and that all information gained during the observation and subsequent evaluation should be treated in confidence.

Entry assessments

Many early years settings and schools will assess children when they first come into the setting. This helps them to find out about the child's strengths and any areas of weakness which may make it hard for the child to participate in activities. Entry assessment also allows settings to monitor a child's progress and later assessments are then matched against the initial ones to determine progress in different areas.

Baseline assessments

Baselines assessment is the name of the entry assessment that is currently carried out when children start their first year in state schools. Baseline assessment tasks and scoring systems vary between different education authorities, although the purpose of them is to measure children's performance at the end of Key Stage 1 against their initial entry scores. They also help to identify any children who may need further support. The reception teacher or classroom assistant carries out a series of tasks with individual children and notes their performance. At the time of writing, these assessments take place within the first weeks of the autumn term, although with the introduction of the Foundation Stage, this timing is under review.

Factors for consideration when carrying out observations and assessment

In some ways carrying out observations on children is a little like being a scientist. We collect information, process it and then reach conclusions. The only problem is that children are not objects or chemicals and their behaviour and reactions can trigger feelings and thoughts in us. Most early years workers know, or have already met, the children on whom they are carrying out the observations and assessments. This can mean that they may already have formed an opinion about the child. This is likely to cloud their judgement and may mean they are not objective in their recording.

Making sure an observation or assessment is objective

In order to assess children in an objective way, we need to consider our own attitudes and values towards children. If we have preconceived ideas about what a child is like, we are more likely to look and record the type of behaviour that we expect rather than the actual behaviour. To make an observation or assessment as accurate as possible, we must be careful that any prejudices and stereotyped ideas we have about the child are stripped away (see also Chapter 2 on the dangers of stereotypes).

Observations and assessments need to be part of an ongoing process

Imagine that someone looked at what you are doing now and based all their conclusions on what they saw. They might come to decide that you work and study hard. This may well be the case – on the other hand, perhaps you do not look at books very often! It is important to remember that we should not read everything into one single assessment.

Think about it

Lisa has been working with Sam – a three-year-old boy – on his speech. She thinks that he has made a lot of progress and now she has been asked by the speech therapist to complete a checklist. All she needs to do is put a tick if he can do a task and a cross if he can't.

On one particular task, he came very close to achieving it, so Lisa decided to put a tick instead of a cross because he had tried so hard. This was not an accurate recording.

1 Why do you think Lisa did not record accurately?
2 Was she right to put a tick instead of a cross?
3 Why do you think that some tests on children are carried out by strangers?

In order for records of children to be accurate, several observations should be made – preferably using different recording techniques. This allows early years workers to gain an overview of a child's learning and development. This should make observations more objective.

The advantages of being a non-participant observer

One of the difficulties in observing and assessing children is not knowing if your presence is affecting their usual behaviour. This is why many early years workers prefer not to observe while they are involved in the child's game or activity. The phrase **non-participant** observer is used to describe situations where observers have distanced themselves from the child.

In a non-participatory observation:

- the child may show more spontaneous behaviour

- the observer will be able to concentrate more effectively on aspects he/she wants to record

- the observer may find it easier to be objective about the child

- the observer will also be able to see what is happening around the child – e.g. if there are other children playing alongside.

Is this child happy, sad or just concentrating?

The main disadvantage of being a non-participant observer is that, if you are trying to assess one particular area of a child's development, you may not actually get to see it.

The advantages of being a participant observer

Sometimes, to correctly assess a child, it may be necessary to ask him/her to carry out a task – for example, 'Can you tell me what the colour of this car is?' In such cases the observer is involved with the child and is therefore a participant observer.

In a participatory observation:

- the observer can record specific types of behaviour that the child might not demonstrate otherwise

- the child may be more responsive because a familiar adult is present.

There are two distinct disadvantages to being a participant observer and in general, unless you need to see specific areas of competence, you should try to record the child's behaviour without becoming involved.

- The child's normal behaviour is likely to be changed by being with an adult.

- The observer may find it difficult to record information while interacting with the child.

Methods of observing and assessing children

There are many methods of observing and assessing children. Most child care courses ask students to show that they can use a range of methods.

Open and closed data

When we carry out an observation or assessment we are collecting information or data. Different recording methods collect data in different ways. It is important to understand that some data is thought of as 'open' whereas other data is thought of as 'closed'.

- Open data gives information that can have different meanings.

  For example, you record in note form that a child hesitates before correctly naming a toy's colour.

  From this one piece of information, there are several possible conclusions, for example:

  - he could not remember the colour

  - he was thinking more about the toy

  - he was nervous that he might give the wrong answer.

- Closed data gives information that has only one conclusion because it has been recorded in a way that does not allow for different meanings.

  For example, a child hesitates before correctly naming a toy's colour.

  The observer simply ticks that the child knows his colours.

During your course of study you will be collecting both types of data because you will use a range of methods. However, you should note that it is difficult to show a good depth of knowledge about a child's development if you concentrate on using closed data.

Structured and naturalistic observations

We can observe children either doing a task or activity that we have prepared for them or doing something of their own choice.

- In a structured observation we know the type of behaviour or learning that we are likely to see – e.g. observing the way a child plays with dough.

- In a naturalistic observation we record behaviour or learning that occurs spontaneously – e.g. a child falling over and another child offering comfort.

Cultural bias in accepted measurements

Most observations and assessments are measured against 'normative' development and behaviour. This means that we might look at a three-year-old's physical development and consider whether it is within an accepted range by referring to charts of normative development or milestones. It is now accepted that in some cases the accepted milestones or measurements may be flawed because in general they were based on a cross-section of Caucasian (white) children. This means that accepted measurements may not always be relevant to certain groups of children – for example, babies whose families have Chinese origins tend to be lighter in weight and smaller than babies of Anglo-Saxon origins. As well as physical variations between cultures there are also different parenting styles that in turn can affect children's behaviour. An example of this is attachment and bonding. In some cultures, babies and toddlers spend more time with their mothers and so react differently (and more strongly) to being separated from them.

The potential for cultural bias in accepted measurements means that it is important to see 'milestones' simply as guides to behaviour and development.

Different methods of recording children

There are many methods of recording and assessing children. It is important that early years workers are familiar with all of them. Most methods need some practice and each method will have its advantages and disadvantages.

Written records

Written records are a way of collecting open data. They are used for recording a child's development or behaviour over a short period of time. They provide a snapshot of what a child was doing.

Written records

Advantages	Disadvantages
Only a paper and pen is needed.	It can be used to record only for a very short period – e.g. 3–5 minutes.
Allows spontaneous observations to take place – e.g. you may be able to record something at short notice.	It can be difficult to record everything that is happening.
Provides open data that can be interpreted later.	Notes need to be written up quickly afterwards, otherwise details may be forgotten.
Both structured or naturalistic observations can be carried out using this method.	

Equipment required:

Paper and pen.

Carrying out a written record

The idea of a written record is to write down as much as you can see and hear in the period in which you are observing. This means that you need to write quickly and also you decide what to focus on. You might plan to record a certain activity – for example, watching a child paint (structured observation) or you might decide to record some event that interests you (naturalistic observation).

It is common practice for written records to be in the present tense – 'He is looking at the book,' and not 'He looked at the book.' This means that when it is read, it will sound like a running commentary.

Checklists and tickcharts

Checklists and tickcharts are structured assessments of children. The information gained is closed data. They are often used in settings to assess children in particular areas of their development. There are many standard checklists and tickcharts that are used by early years workers or other professionals. Checklists and tickcharts are quick and simple to use and can be referred to later to check the progress of children.

Child's name .... Date ....

Date of birth .... Observer ....

Developmental checklist

By 12 months	Yes	No	Sometimes
Walk with some help?			
Pick objects with finger and thumb?			
Transfer items from one hand to the other?			
Look for an object hidden under a beaker?			
Look at a person who is speaking to him or her?			
Make tuneful babbling sounds such as Da-da			
Respond to different sounds e.g. drum, bell			
Imitate gestures such as pat a cake and bye bye			
Hold beaker using two hands?			
Use fingers to eat finger foods such as squares of bread?			
Pick up dropped toys?			
React to the word 'No'?			
Reacts to own name?			

Equipment required:

Pen, checklist or tickchart.

Using a checklist or tickchart

You can use standard tickcharts or checklists or you can draw up your own. If you draw up your own it is important to make sure that it is detailed enough, otherwise you might find it difficult to draw any conclusions. Tickcharts and checklists are a good way of recording the development and behaviour of several children and this means that you can see how children of the same age can vary in their behaviour.

Tickcharts and checklists can be used while children are engaged in normal activities or an activity can be structured allowing a particular behaviour to be recorded – for example an observer might set up an activity where children have to cut out a picture.

It is important to remember that if an observer specifically asks a child to carry out a task, the way in which the child carries it out will be influenced by the observer's presence.

Checklist or tickchart

Advantages	Disadvantages
Simple and quick to use.	Closed data means that there is no record of how easily a child achieved a task.
Can be repeated with children at a later date to check their progress.	It does not give a rounded picture of the child – only of their performance at the time the assessment was carried out.
Can be used with several children to give a broader picture of an age range.	Only the skills that are being assessed are recorded. A child may be able to do more than the assessment suggests.

Event samples

Event samples are used to record the pattern or frequency of a particular behaviour. They are often used where there are some concerns about a child – for example, if parents feel that their baby cries all the time. An event sample could be used to provide information about when, why and how long the baby actually cries.

Event samples are useful because they focus on one type of behaviour and may give early years workers not only an idea of how often it is occurring but also background as to why it may be occurring.

Recording takes place only when the behaviour occurs, which means that event samples can be carried out over longer periods of time if necessary – for example, a child who is thought to be aggressive might have his/her behaviour tracked over a week or more.

The way an event sample is laid out will depend on the type of information that is required.

The example below was used to record the amount of speech a child was using during a session at nursery.

Event	Time	Situation	Social group	Dialogue
1	9.16 am	Curren is hovering near the painting	Susan + 2 children table	A–C 'Do you want to come and paint a picture too?' C–A nods head
2	9.27 am	Curren is finishing painting	Susan + 2 children	A–C 'Have you finished?' C smiles 'It's a lovely picture. Tell me a little bit about it.' C–A 'It's my mum. Can't take my apron off.' A–C 'Wait still, I'll do it.' Curren hands apron to Susan and runs over to sand area
3	10.12 am	Curren is waiting for his drink at snack time	Curren is sitting next to Ahmed. Jo is handing out drinks	A–C 'Milk or squash, Curren?' C–A 'Milk.' A–C 'Can you remember the magic word?' C–A 'Thank you.' A–C 'Good boy.'
4	10.19 am	Curren is putting on his coat in the cloakroom area	Jo + 5 children	C–A 'Can't put coat on.' A–C 'Keep still. There you are. You can go out now.'
5	10.36 am	Curren is waiting for his turn by the slide	Jo + 2 children	A–C 'Good boy. It's your go now.' C smiles C–A 'I go fast down now.'

Equipment required:

Pen and prepared chart.

Carrying out an event sample

Event samples can be very interesting and versatile. You could look at how much food a child eats during the day, the number of times a child sucks his/her thumb or even how often a child speaks to an adult.

The most important part of carrying out an event sample is the preparation. You will need to design a chart that records the information that is needed. This means that a chart that looks at the frequency of a child biting will not be of any use when recording the number of times a child sucks his/her thumb. The best way of designing a chart is to consider what information would be useful in order to explore the behaviour.

A chart to look at the frequency of a child's speech would probably include:

- how long the speech lasts
- who the child speaks to
- what the child says
- what the child is doing.

Once you have drawn up a chart, you will need to fill it in whenever you see the behaviour. You may need to ask other adults to help you, as you may be working with another child when the behaviour occurs.

Event samples

Advantages	Disadvantages
Provides open data.	Needs to be carefully prepared.
Is quick and easy to use.	Other adults may have to be asked to help.
Builds up a picture of a specific behaviour.	

Time samples

Time samples are a useful way of carrying out an observation over a period of time because recording is not continuous. The idea of a time sample is that at regular periods of time a child's activity is recorded. Time samples can be used to look at children's specific behaviour or more generally at their activity during a session.

Time	Activity	Social group	Comments
11.00	Snack time	Whole group	Anna is sitting with her legs swinging on a chair. She is eating an apple. She is holding it in her left hand and she is smiling. She puts up her hand when a staff member asks who wants a biscuit.
11.15	Outdoor play Climbing frame	Anna and Ben	Anna is on the top bar of the climbing frame. She is smiling at Ben. She is calling 'Come on up here!'
11.30	Taking coats off	Anna, Ben and Manjit	Anna unzips the coat and pulls out one arm. She swings around and the coat moves around. She laughs and looks at Manjit.

This time sample is recording a child's general activity every 15 minutes during a morning.

Equipment required:

Pen, prepared sheet and watch.

Carrying out a time sample

You will need to decide the length of the time sample and then consider how many samples you will need. For example, if you wish to find out what a child does during a morning's session, you may decide to observe the child all morning at 15-minute intervals. A time sheet is then prepared. Some timesheets have separate columns so that types of activity or behaviour can be noted.

Time	Interaction	Social group	Activity	Comments
10.00 am	None	Amy, Jo and Sam	Dough table	Pippa is rolling out dough and smiling
10.10 am	Talking to self	Alone	Dough table	Pippa is making pretend cakes
10.20 am	'I want it, it's mine.'	Chris	Painting easel	Chris has snatched the paintbrush. Pippa tugs it back and shouts at Chris.

This is an example of a time sample where the observer is particularly interested in the language that the child uses.

It is not a good idea to space out the intervals between recordings too much, otherwise you may miss a lot of the child's activity.

To carry out the observation, you need a watch and to jot down what the child is doing at the times marked on the sheet. Each 'sample' should be a snapshot of what the child is doing, although if the child is engaged in an interesting activity, you may decide to record for longer.

Time samples

Advantages	Disadvantages
Children's activity can be recorded for longer periods.	Good timekeeping is needed. It is easy for the observer to forget to record.
Open data is being collected.	The child may show some interesting activity outside of the time sample.
This is a simple method to use.	Other adults may be needed if observations extend over a day.
Specific behaviour as well as children's general activities can be observed.	

Target child observations

The aim of a target child observation is to look at the activity of one or more children and record what they

are doing over a session. This method relies on using codes because it would be impossible to write for long periods. Target child observations are also known as pre-coded observations. The main difficulty with a coded observation is that the observer must be skilled at using the codes. Of all the methods, this requires the most practice.

Many early years settings use this as their main method of carrying out observations, which means that students benefit from learning how to carry out this method competently. Target child observations can be used either to track a specific type of behaviour or to see generally what children are doing.

Target child

Child's name	Annie	Sex	Female
Age	3 yrs 4 months	Date	22/3/99

Time	Activity	Language	Task	Social group
1 minute	T.C scooping sand with hands	T.C directing himself	Sand	Sol
2 minute	T.C scooping with beaker		Sand	Sol
3 minute	T.C patting down sand in beaker	A–T.CV 'Are you going to make a sandcastle?'	Sand	A
4 minute	T.C turning beaker over	T.C–A 'It won't come out'	Sand	A + 1 C
5 minute	T.C Protects sandcastle	T.C–C 'Don't it's mine'	Sand	A + 1 C

Code

T.C = Target child	A = Adult	
Sol = solitary	C = Child	

Equipment required:

Pen, chart and copy of codes.

Carrying out a target child observation

It is important to choose codes that you will remember, although there are some standard codes that you can use. It is a good idea to start with a short observation so that you can get used to using the codes. Eventually, you will be able to record for longer and longer periods. Skilled early years workers are able to use this system to track more than one child at a time. The data provided is open, but quite limited in detail. Concentration is important and this observation cannot be done while the observer is engaged in any other activity.

Target child observations

Advantages	Disadvantages
The only written method that allows children's activity to be tracked over a continuous period.	The observer needs to be able to use the codes.
Several children can be observed at once.	Data is limited, although not closed.
Specific activities can be observed.	The observer has to concentrate hard.

Sociograms

A sociogram is not an observation as such, because behaviour or activity is not recorded. The idea of a sociogram is to track children's friendship groups. This is an interesting exercise, although it is not suitable to carry out with children below school age.

The children are asked to give the names of the three children that they most enjoy playing with.

In the sociogram (next column), you may notice that although Daniel has named three friends, he has not been named. This may mean that he is not played with or it may be that the other children forgot to name him! It is important that you do not read too much into the data.

A sociogram

Name	Friend	Friend	Friend
Sarah	Inger	Elizabeth	Jenny
Daniel	Jo	Tom	Michael
Tom	Inger	Michael	Jo
Michael	Stephen	Jo	Tom
Elizabeth	Inger	Jenny	
Jenny	Sarah	Inger	Anne
Inger	Elizabeth	Jenny	Sarah
Stephen	Jo	Michael	
Anne	Elizabeth	Jenny	Inger
Jo	Tom	Michael	Stephen

Equipment required:

A chart showing the children's names and spaces to write in the names they give, pen.

Carrying out a sociogram

To carry out a sociogram, you will need to prepare a chart similar to the one above that lists the children's names. It is a good idea to ask each child individually who they like playing with, otherwise they may be influenced by the others around them. Once you have completed this, you need to look closely at who has named whom. It is a good idea to use sociograms as a starting point for other observations. For example, you may be interested in observing children who

Sociograms

Advantages	Disadvantages
Reasonably simple method.	Data is closed.
It is a way of looking at groups of children.	Some preparation is needed. Asking children can be time consuming.
	Relies on what children choose to say.

seem to be frequently named in play situations. It is essential not to assume that the sociogram represents an accurate picture of children's friendships as some children name only those with whom they last played. Class teachers are often interested in the results of sociograms to see if children are beginning to form settled relationships. It is useful to repeat a sociogram again after a few weeks to see how stable the friendships are.

Why are students asked to carry out observations and assessments?

Most child care courses require students to put together a portfolio of observations. Although students will need to be able to carry out observations and assessments when they are employed, it is also an excellent way for students to show that they have understood how the theories of child development relate to practice. It also shows that students are able to assess and identify children's needs at different ages and stages of their development.

Unfortunately, carrying out observations and assessments is a skill that requires practice. This means that most students need to produce many observations before they are truly competent.

To help you learn the skill of observing children, we have included in this book 15 observations using different methods that link to different areas of study.

Observations

Area of study	Method of observation	Chapter	Page
Attachment theory	Written record	4	99
Nutrition	Chart	3	74
Behaviourist theory	Written record	6	127
Cognitive stages of learning	Written record	6	130
Pre-operational stage	Written record	6	131
Language development	Event sample	7	142
Moral development	Written record	8	160
Social interaction	Sociogram	8	170
Gender concept	Written record	8	173
Behaviour	Event sample	9	207
Symbol use	Written record	11	260
Exploratory play	Written record	11	261
Object permanence	Written record	15	366
Object permanence	Written record	15	367
Nappy changing	Written record	15	382

Presentation of work

There is a difference in the way settings and students lay out observations. Students are using observations and assessments as a way of demonstrating their knowledge and so are required to write up and make comments about what they have seen. Most child care courses ask that the students present their work using the following sections.

Details of the observation, signature of workplace supervisor

Students are asked to provide information about the observation they are submitting. Details help the tutors to look particularly at the interpretation and consider whether the student is coming to appropriate conclusions. Some courses provide front sheets to make sure that students remember to include all the details.

Aim and rationale

A statement about why the observation or assessment is being carried out and what the student is hoping to observe.

Observation/Assessment

The record of the observation and assessment, using one of the above methods.

Interpretation

(The heading 'evaluation' can also be used.) In this section students come to some conclusions about what they have observed. They should also look at the child's age and consider if the learning or development is typical for the age range. Where possible, students should also write about how the actions of the child link to child development theories. Students should also consider whether the observation method that they used was effective.

Recommendations

This section identifies the child's immediate needs and considers ways of meeting them – for example, a child who can steer a tricycle might now be ready to use a tricycle with pedals.

Personal learning

Students write about what they have learnt from carrying out the observation, either in terms of knowledge gained about the children, the setting or about the method of recording they used. For example, 'From carrying out this observation, I have found out that Samantha can read some words. This has taught me that some four-year-olds perhaps pick up words if they are familiar with a book.'

References and bibliography

At the end of the piece of work, books used for research are listed in alphabetical order by author.

Confidentiality and students' observations and records

Observations and assessments on children are confidential. Normally observations and assessments carried out by early years workers would be shown only to supervisors and parents. They would also be stored in a safe place.

Think about it

Sharon is studying on a child care course. She has carried out several observations and assessments. One day she tells her supervisor that she has left her file on the bus. The supervisor asks if she had anything in the file that would identify a particular child. Sharon nods her head and says that she has written up an observation, but hasn't had time to change the child's name.

The supervisor is cross and explains that this child's family is living in a refuge because the father has assaulted the mother and one of the other children. The supervisor feels that if the father finds out where the child is during the day, he would be able to work out where the whole family was staying.

Afterwards Sharon complains bitterly to her friends, saying that it wasn't her fault, because nobody had told her about this child before and there was little chance that the father would get hold of the file anyway.

1   Why is Sharon wrong to believe that she should have been told about this child before?
2   Can you think of any other circumstances where a child's identity or location may need to be kept confidential?

This is not the case with the observations that students carry out. This means that we have to protect the identity of children in the following ways.

- Use only children's first names.

- Change children's names if they are unusual or could lead to the child being identified.

- Give the type of setting, not the actual name – e.g. write nursery not 'Tiny Tots'.

- Write children's ages as years and months – e.g. 3 years, 4 months. Do not write down their date of birth.

- Photographic records should not be used unless permission is gained from the parents and from the setting.

- Make sure that your files contain either the college telephone number or your own, so that if necessary it can be returned safely.

The test of a confidential observation should be that if anyone else read it, would they be able to identify the setting or the child?

The role of your workplace supervisor

Your supervisor will expect you to carry out observations and also conduct activities with children, as your tutor will have explained that this is a requirement on the child care course. Most supervisors are very keen to help you and should be able to give you time and advice. To help them, you need to be organised and sensitive to the demands on their time. Very few supervisors will be in the position where they can drop everything to read through your observations. This means that you need to find out when it is a convenient time for you to carry out observations and also make sure that, when they offer help, you are appreciative. Some supervisors will be able to talk you through what you have recorded only 'after hours' or during your lunch break.

Once you have written up your observation, you will need to ask for a signature. Most supervisors are interested in seeing what you have written, either in order to help you further or because they would like to find out more about the children you have been

studying. In any case, supervisors have the right to look at students' work because they are signing to say that it is a fair record of what took place.

Preparing to carry out an observation

Asking permission

This is the first thing you must do before even beginning to plan an observation. It is a good idea to ask your supervisor well in advance, usually the day before. This allows the setting to make sure that you are not included in any of their activity plans for the session when you hope to carry out the observation. On the day of the observation, it is a good idea to check again that it is convenient for you to carry out the observation, because sometimes circumstances may have arisen which mean it is no longer convenient – for example, a parent is coming to look around the setting.

Making sure that you are properly equipped

You should know beforehand which method you intend using. Some methods require preparation or equipment and it is important that you do not forget anything.

Most recording requires a pencil, plenty of paper and something to lean on.

Finding a good location for observing children

It is not always easy to be a non-participant observer as children are often keen to find out what you are doing. You may decide to look for somewhere in the room where you are partially out of sight or allow some time before you start writing so that the children can become used to your presence and lose interest in what you are doing.

Checklist for carrying out observations and assessments

✔ Ask permission from your supervisor.

✔ Make sure that you have everything that you will need to hand.

✔ If you are carrying out a non-participant observation find somewhere to sit and observe.

✔ Make sure that you record the date and time on your notes.

✔ Write up what you have recorded in full as soon as possible – lunch breaks are ideal times!

Evaluating your observations and assessments

There is little point in carrying out an observation or assessment unless you process the information in some way and draw conclusions. This next step is often called interpretation or evaluation. The aim is to look at the information, compare it to information you already have from other sources, such as books, and then draw some conclusions.

Linking your observations to normative development

You will need to show that you can compare children's behaviour and development to the normative development or milestones. 'Normative development' means development that is expected of children at certain ages.

This means that if you have observed a three-year-old girl turn-taking, you should look to see if this is considered to be normal development. (It is!) This in turn allows you to come to a conclusion that the child you have observed is showing social skills that most children of her age group are demonstrating.

In this book, there are several charts that should help you to do this.

- Physical development – pages 109–112
- Cognitive development – page 135
- Language development – pages 143–144
- Social and emotional development – pages 161–163
- Behaviour and goals for behaviour – pages 196–199
- Milestones for babies – pages 362–365.

Think about it

In pairs, look at the following snippets of information.

- A two-year-old hugs her parent's legs when she sees a stranger.
- A four-year-old pushes another child down the slide.
- A child of fifteen months has a vocabulary of twenty words.
- A three-year-old finds it difficult to use a pair of scissors.
- A baby of six months is trying to feed itself.

Now find out whether these children are showing learning and behaviour that is typical for their age.

Linking theories of child development to your observations

To show that you have understood the theories of child development, you should be able to link them to some aspects of children's behaviour. For example, you might see a baby of nine months cry when his mother leaves the room. This is typical behaviour for this age of child, but it also shows that the child knows who their primary carer is. This behaviour fits in with Bowlby's theory on attachment.

In this book, we have outlined many theories of behaviour and development.

It is important to include references to theorists in your work. A correct link to theories of child development shows that you can link theory to practice.

Theorist	Areas of development	Page
Bowlby	Attachment to primary carers and effects of separation	177
Erikson	Personality and emotional development	157
Freud	Personality and emotional development	155
Bandura	How children learn and behave	126
Skinner	How children learn and behave	126
Piaget	How children learn concepts and stages of play and moral development	127
Vygotsky	How children learn concepts and play	131
Bruner	How children learn concepts and language	132

Whilst carrying out this observation I noticed that the boys were quite imaginative in their play as they used a few pieces of Lego which was joined together as a gun. According to Davenport, Piaget's theory says that both boys should be in the pre-operations stage where symbolism is used.

"By about two years of age a child can let one object stand for (or symbolise) something else." (1994)

During this observation I noticed that both Sam and Jake were quite aggressive in their play, ie, they spoke about making guns and shooting someone, according to Davenport the TV may have an effect on a child's level of aggression. Davenport outlines an experiment done by Stein and Friedrich in 1972 about children and TV violence.

The example in the previous column shows how a student has linked normative behaviour and also a theory of development in her interpretation.

Using references to support your work

In order to support your ideas, you will need to use references. For example, you might think that the behaviour you have seen is normal for a three-year-old, but how can you prove this?

Using a reference will show that your ideas are based on current thinking found in books or magazines. For example – 'I think that James is showing normal behaviour for a three-year-old. According to Penny Tassoni, three-year-olds "show social skills – e.g. turn-taking, sharing and concern for others".' (Tassoni 1998)

Most child care courses expect that students will demonstrate their knowledge by referring to a selection of books. There are different ways of referencing quotes from books, most courses ask students to use the Harvard system of referencing (see Chapter 1 for more information)

Using observations and assessments for planning purposes

One of the key ways in which early years workers use observations and assessments is for planning. If you understand the stage of development of a child and can work out any particular needs that they have, you should be able to plan more effectively for them. For example, a child who can steer and pedal a tricycle might be ready to transfer to using a bicycle with stabilisers, or a child who enjoys writing might be asked if he would like to write and post a letter to a relative.

Students can show that they can consider the 'next steps' for children by using a 'recommendations' section in their evaluations. A recommendation section should consider what the next steps might be for the child and the role of the early years worker in helping the child.

A step-by-step guide to writing up interpretations

Many students find it difficult to know where to start, so below is a step-by-step guide to writing an interpretation or evaluation that you may find useful.

1 Carefully read through what you have written or recorded.

It is important that any conclusions you draw are based on what you have recorded, not on what you think about the child from other days.

2 Underline, in pencil, parts of the observation

that you think may be significant to the child's learning or development – for example, a child was smiling or talked a lot during an activity. Consider asking your supervisor or tutor what they think is worth highlighting.

3 What conclusions can be drawn from what has been underlined

(even if they seem obvious to you)? For example, 'I think that the child was smiling because he was enjoying the story,' or 'The child said "thank you." This shows that the child has some social skills.'

4 Find some evidence that supports your conclusions.

How does what you have seen fit in with any theory of child development that you have learnt about? Is the child showing normal behaviour or learning for his age? For example, a child who watches another child and then copies what she is doing is showing that children learn from others (Social learning theory, page 126).

To do this you will need to refer to a selection of books and find some quotes that support your ideas (see also Using references to support your work, page 6).

On page 95, you saw an example of a student's observation. Look at this again to see how he has interpreted some of what he saw.

Knowledge into action

Read through this observation made by a student on a child in a nursery setting.

In pairs, underline the parts of this observation that you think might be significant.

> Zoe is coming over to the home corner. She is taking a wooden tomato and is placing it on a toy chopping board. She is taking a wooden knife and is sawing at the wooden tomato with the knife. She is now opening the toy oven. She is running over to the post office corner. She is taking a clip file from the post office counter. She is running back to the oven and is placing the clip file into the oven. Charlie is running towards her. He is reaching out a hand to help Zoe to put the clip file into the oven. Zoe is pushing Charlie away. She is saying to Charlie: "No don't touch — it too hot for you!" Zoe is putting an arm around Charlie's shoulders. She is speaking to me. She is saying: "Charlie is my friend." She is now speaking to Charlie whilst sawing against the table with a wooden knife. She is saying: "Go and get my shopping."
>
> Jack is rummaging through the dressing-up clothes. He is putting a postman's cap on to his head and a postbag over his shoulder. He is reaching into the postbag and is pulling out a brown paper parcel. He is handing the parcel to me. I am saying: "Is this for me Jack?" Jack is nodding his head.
>
> Zoe is pretending to pour out a cup of tea from a small teapot into a plastic cup and saucer. She is bringing over the cup and saucer to me. I am taking the cup and saucer and pretend to drink from it. I am saying: "That is a lovely cup of tea. Thank you Zoe."

Recommendations and personal learning

Once you have come to some conclusions about the child's behaviour and development, you will need to show that you would be able to act on what you have seen.

Recommendations

Under the heading 'recommendations' you can write about:

- activities or strategies that might help the child

- whether it might be advisable to carry out a further observation and why.

Think about it

In pairs, look at the following snippets of observations.

1   … picks up a red crayon and says 'This is like my red shoes.'

2   … leans over and watches the boy next to him draw.

3   … holds the hand of a child who is crying and shows her a toy.

4   … takes hold of the teddy and says 'Go to bed now.'

Can you match them up to the following conclusions?

a   This shows that the child is aware of other children's needs.

b   The child is playing imaginatively and may be repeating phrases that he has heard.

c   This shows that the child knows the names of her colours and can match colours.

d   This shows that the child is aware of the actions of other children and is interested in what they are doing.

Personal learning

Under the heading 'personal learning', you should show what you have learnt by carrying out the observation or assessment. You could write about:

- the advantages or disadvantages of the recording method you used

- what you have found out about the particular child or group of children that you studied

- what you have learnt by studying this area of development and behaviour

- what you have learnt by watching other early years workers

- how what you have found out will help you work with children in the future.

Common mistakes

Observing and assessing children does take some practice and it is normal to make some mistakes along the way. As you learn more about children's development, you will find it easier to make comments in your interpretation.

Below is a list of common mistakes that are made by students, often in the first year of their course.

Aims

The aims are too vague, which means the observations are not detailed or focused enough.

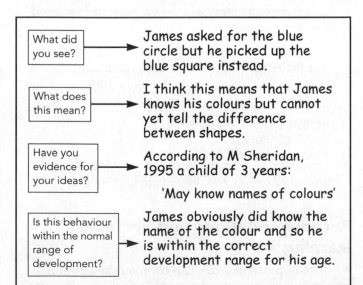

What did you see?	James asked for the blue circle but he picked up the blue square instead.
What does this mean?	I think this means that James knows his colours but cannot yet tell the difference between shapes.
Have you evidence for your ideas?	According to M Sheridan, 1995 a child of 3 years: 'May know names of colours'
Is this behaviour within the normal range of development?	James obviously did know the name of the colour and so he is within the correct development range for his age.

Personal Learning
    I feel that by observing the children at play and by relating this to the theories in the books I used, I came to really understand the importance of role play to children of this age group — that it is essential to their development as people. It seemed to me to be a way of a child rehearsing roles in later life. I feel therefore that it is very important to ensure that children have the means to play in this way — dressing-up clothes, a home corner, police station, etc., so that they are helped to grow and develop to the greatest extent possible.

Recommendations:
    I felt overall that the children concerned needed to be encouraged to continue with as much role play as possible. Zoe seemed very unselfconscious about this form of play, but I felt that some of the other children needed encouragement to relax and to enjoy it more. I felt that it would be my role as nursery nurse to encourage them and to help them to relax in this form of play. Also perhaps it would be my role to help them to expand on the play by making suggestions in an unobtrusive way and to help some of the shyer children to join in.

REFERENCES

Bee 1977   *The Developing Child*
Longman

Bruce and Meggitt 1977 *Child Care and Education*
Hodder and Stoughton

Davenport 1994   *An Introduction to Child Development*
Collins

Avoid aims such as 'to watch a child playing'. Make aims detailed – for example, 'to look at how a child interacts with others as they are playing'.

Observations and assessments

- Observations and assessments are not detailed enough – e.g. checklists are too vague or written records do not show enough information.

- The wrong recording method has been used to meet the aim.

- Students record things that have not happened – e.g. 'He didn't say thank you.' Make sure that you only record what you see and hear!

- Commenting on children's behaviour and development in the observation section – e.g. 'Mary smiles because she is enjoying being with Simone'. Remember that, in the observation section, you should record only what children are actually doing. Do not try and explain their behaviour in this section.

Interpretation

- Information that has not been obtained during the observation or assessment is used in the interpretation – e.g. 'Mark was not concentrating, which is his normal behaviour.'

- References are used inappropriately. It is important that, if you use references, they support your ideas – e.g. to show they have seen conservation, students should use a reference about Piaget's work *not* Freud's!

- Comments are made without showing where the evidence is in the observation. 'He seems to enjoy painting,' rather than 'During the observation, I saw that Michael was smiling. This may indicate that he enjoys painting.'

- Many students miss opportunities by not looking carefully enough through the observation sections or by not considering how what they have seen relates to the theories of child development.

Think about it

This interpretation by a student contains some good points, but also has some mistakes.

There are three good points, two glaring errors and one missed opportunity. See if you can find them!

> During this observation I noticed that Sam and Jake played co-operatively together. According to Sheridan by the age of three a child
>
> 'Joins in active make believe play with other children' (1997)
>
> As Sam is three and Jake is four years old, both children are within the normal development for their age range.
>
> Whilst they were playing, I saw that Sam picked up a stick and pretended that this was a gun. I think that this shows that Sam is able to use symbols in his play. This fits in with Piaget's stages of play and development. 'Children are learning to use symbols in their play. This means that a child might use a stick to stand for a magic wand . . .' Tassoni (1998)
>
> I also noticed that Sam and Jake were quite aggressive in their play i.e. they spoke about making guns and shooting someone. I think that this means that they may have been influenced by something that they have seen. This may fit in with the Social Learning Theory which Bowlby developed.
>
> I saw that as they were playing Sam and Jake were able to share equipment. I think that this means that they are developing some social skills. According to Tassoni (1998) children at 3–4 years are showing social skills 'They show social skills – e.g. turn taking, sharing and concern for others'
>
> This shows that Sam and Jake are showing behaviour appropriate for their ages.

- Not focusing on the areas of development stated in the aims – e.g. a student writes in the aim that he is looking at physical development, but the interpretation mentions only the child's social development!

- Language used is not professional – e.g. 'Sadie almost *blew her top* when Pete snatched her car!'

Recommendations and personal learning

- A good piece of work can be spoilt by appalling recommendations. 'I recommend that as Sarah cannot sit still, she should be kept in to teach her how to behave.'

■ Remember that recommendations need to show an understanding of the needs of children and how an early years workers can help to meet these.

■ Criticising settings – e.g. 'I think that Sarah is really bored and should be given more exciting activities by the staff.' This type of comment is not acceptable, as students are not in the position to judge the competence of the settings. Most supervisors will find any criticism of the setting to be a serious matter.

References

■ Incorrect referencing – e.g. not putting the author, date and page in brackets after the quote.

■ Forgetting to list books in alphabetical order by author at the end of the piece of work.

An idea for observation that you could carry out

Written record

Aim: To observe how easily a child separates from the carer at the beginning of a session.

Observation

This observation can be carried out on children of many ages. You will need to position yourself where you can clearly see the child arriving in the setting. Look out for the following details:

■ Does the child hold on to the parent's hand or walk ahead of the parent?

■ What is the facial expression of the child on entering the setting?

■ Does the child take off his own coat or is he helped?

■ Does the child leave the parent immediately?

■ Is there some ritual to saying good-bye?

■ How quickly does the child settle down?

■ What activity does the child go to?

Interpretation

Look at Chapter 8, Emotional and social development, and read the following:

■ Bowlby's theory of attachment

■ Helping children to separate from their parents.

Recommendations and personal learning

■ Would it be an idea to repeat this observation again on the same child or another child of the same age?

■ Are there any activities that could help the child feel more comfortable when separating from the carer?

■ Have you learnt anything from this observation about settling children in?

■ Was the written record a good observation method?

There will be further suggestions for observations throughout the book.

Check your knowledge

- Give three reasons why observations and assessments are used in professional child care settings.

- Name three professionals who also carry out observations and assessments on children as part of their role.

- How can students learn about child development from carrying out observations?

- Why should children's identities be protected?

- What steps should students take before carrying out an observation on a child?

- What are the main disadvantages to carrying out a checklist or tickchart?

- What is meant by the term 'open data'?

- Why can open data sometimes be more useful than closed data?

- What is the difference between an event sample and a time sample?

- Why can sociograms be used only as indicators to children's friendship patterns?

Resources

Further reading

Bartholomew, L. & Bruce, T. 1993 *Getting to Know You: A guide to record-keeping in early childhood education and care*, London, Hodder and Stoughton

Bentzen, W. 1993 *A guide to observing and recording behaviour*, New York, Delmar Publishers Inc.

The developing child

UNIT
Introduction

Learning about child development is important for early years workers. If we know when and how children gain skills, we will then be able to meet their needs more effectively. Child development is also of interest to psychologists who study the way we learn and think. This means that much of our knowledge about child development has been based on research carried out by psychologists. There are different branches of psychology, but developmental psychology looks at the way we grow and develop and includes areas such as how we learn language and personality development.

Who's who in psychology?

While it is not essential for early years workers to study psychology in depth, it is important to have an understanding of some of the main theories of development as these have, over the years, shaped the practice of early years workers. A good example of this is the way that we now recognise the importance of comfort objects for young children, while previously, many early years settings took them away from children.

There have been many studies carried out by psychologists over the years and some pieces of work have been particularly influential. The chart on page 102 shows the key figures in developmental psychology and where you will find them in the next few chapters.

The nature versus nurture debate

At the heart of the nature versus nurture debate are two questions:

■ Are our personalities, behaviour patterns, thoughts, etc. a result of our genes ? – *or*

■ Are our personalities, behaviour patterns, thoughts, etc. a result of environmental influences such as the way we were brought up or where we live?

Psychology (and thus child development) is a relatively new area of study. Many of the first

psychologists were trained as biologists. This means that many of the early theories were influenced by the idea that we inherited skills, abilities and behaviour. Work by psychologists such as Skinner have since shown that our behaviour can also be shaped and so have come to the conclusion that our personalities, behaviour and skills are a result of the environment that we are brought up in.

Think about it

In pairs, think about characteristics that you share – e.g. you might both have a good sense of humour. Now consider some of the differences – e.g. does one of you worry a lot about your coursework?

Now think about the following question:

Do you think that people's personalities, skills and abilities are inherited or that we are the result of our upbringing?

The way in which development is measured

Children's development is measured in order that health and education professionals can identify any problems and, where possible, take steps to intervene. While everyone working with children recognises that children develop at slightly different rates, the pattern and sequence of development is the same for all children. Over the years, by studying

Developmental psychology – theorists and theories

Name	Area	Key theory	Comments	Chapter
Bandura, Albert	Behaviour/learning	Social learning theory	Bandura showed that children can learn through imitating others.	6
Bowlby, John	Attachment	Maternal deprivation	Bowlby showed that, for healthy development, babies and young children need to form a bond with their parents or key carers.	8
Erikson, Erik	Personality and emotional development	Psychosocial stages of development	Erikson based his theory on Freud's work. He considered that our personalities carry on developing into adulthood.	8
Freud, Sigmund	Personality and emotional development	Psychosexual stages of development	Freud made a distinction between our conscious and unconscious minds.	8
Pavlov, Ivan	Behaviour/learning	Classic conditioning	Through his works with dogs, Pavlov showed that humans can learn through association.	6
Piaget, Jean	Learning/cognitive development	Stages of cognitive development	Piaget suggested that children's thinking passes through stages.	6
Skinner, Burrhus Frank	Behaviour/learning	Operant conditioning	Skinner suggested that behaviour can be manipulated through the use of reinforcements.	6
Vygotsky, Lev	Language/cognitive development	Zone of Proximal Development	Vygotsky placed emphasis on the importance of adults in helping children understand concepts.	6

thousands of children, an expected pattern and range of development has emerged. This means that children's progress can be checked against this range.

The measurement of development begins at birth, when babies' first reflexes are checked, and carries on through their childhood. (See page 218 for more information on health checks.)

Although all areas of development link together, they are often looked at separately in order to measure them. The spider diagram opposite shows the areas of development that are commonly studied:

Emotional and social development are often looked at together because, as they are so interrelated, it can be hard to assess them separately.

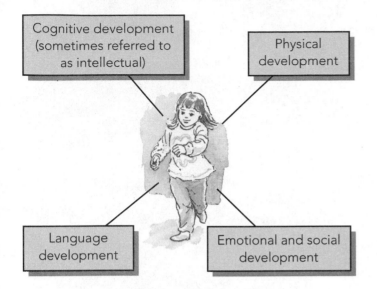

In order to assess children's development, observations, measurements and tests are carried out. The results of these are then compared to developmental charts that show the range of development that children of the same age might be expected to show. Developmental charts are often referred to as 'normative measurements' (the word 'norm' means 'average').

In some areas of development such as cognitive development, health and educational professionals look out for specific things or 'milestones', such as a child knowing his primary colours or being able to build a tower of three bricks.

Factors affecting development

Sometimes children do not show the expected development for their ages and stages. This can happen for a variety of reasons – for example, babies who are not responded to or spoken to may have delayed language while some babies might be born with conditions that will affect their ability to communicate. In the following chapters we look at each area of development and the common factors that might result in developmental delay.

Helping children who do not show 'normative development'

The early detection of children who are not showing the expected patterns of behaviour is now considered extremely important. This is why assessment and health checks on children are conducted regularly. There are many reasons why children might not show expected development and finding the cause of the developmental delay is the first step towards helping the child. Once the cause of the developmental delay is found there is a range of services that may be offered to the child and her family. These include portage, speech therapy and physiotherapy. (See also pages 27–30 for information about children with special needs.)

Is development continuous or does it occur in stages?

Another aspect of development that is looked at by psychologists is whether development happens as a continuous process or whether it occurs in stages. You will see that some of the theories in the following chapters are 'stage' theories – for example, Freud's psychosexual stages of personality and Piaget's stages of cognitive development. Such theories are based on the idea that development passes through defined and separate stages and that each stage will have recognisable features – for example, in language development children babble before they speak words, and so babbling is seen as a stage in itself. Other psychologists feel that development is more gradual and that it is a continuous process. This means that stage versus continuous development is another area of debate for psychologists.

Think about it

Many early years workers feel that children don't jump from stage to stage, but that development is often so gradual that it would be hard to see sudden jumps on a day-to-day basis, although over a few weeks they can see that children's development has progressed.

1 In your work setting, ask the staff what they think.
2 Do they think that children's progress fits into stages or do they see that the development is continual?
3 You might like to ask if there are any areas of development which seem particularly stage like.

CHAPTER 5
Physical development

This section looks at children's physical development and growth. Although closely linked, there is a difference between growth and development. Growth is the process by which cells divide to increase the size of the body, whereas development is the process by which children master the control of their body. For information about the growth and development of babies aged 0–1 years see Chapter 15.

This chapter is split into seven sections:

- Growth and measuring growth
- What is physical development?
- Principles of physical development
- How physical development is measured
- Factors affecting growth and measurement
- The implications of delayed or impaired physical development
- The role of the adult in promoting physical development

Growth and measuring growth

Growth

Growth and physical development are closely linked. Physical development in areas such as walking cannot be achieved until the bones in a baby have grown long and strong enough to support the body's weight. The process of growth begins from the moment a baby is conceived. The mother's fertilised ovum or egg divides and then divides again. The process of growth ends around eighteen years later when the body is mature.

During the period of growth, there are times when some parts of the body grow more quickly than others – for example, many parents are amazed to see how their older children's legs suddenly grow more rapidly than other parts from around the age of nine or ten.

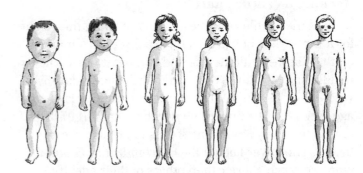

Changes in body proportions between birth and adolescence

The process of growth results in changes to children's body shape. At birth, a baby's head makes up about a quarter of overall height but, by the time the body reaches maturity, the head accounts for only just over an eighth.

Measuring growth

Even before babies are born, health professionals are keeping an eye on their growth. This is done by using ultrasound scans, weighing the mother and also by feeling the abdomen (see also page 357). Measuring growth is important for many reasons. It acts as an early warning system and may indicate an underlying difficulty with the health or development of a child (see page 113–116 for information about factors affecting growth and development).

After birth, the growth of babies and children is carefully monitored by weighing and measuring them. Health professionals such as midwives and health visitors do this routinely either in a child's own home, a doctor's surgery or a family health clinic.

Three measurements are taken:

- Head circumference
- Height
- Weight

The results of the measurements are usually plotted on to graphs. These graphs are called percentile charts – often known as centile charts. Over a period of time the growth rate can be tracked. Growth is also compared with the average ranges of growth for children of the same age. There are separate centile charts for boys and girls, as boys are generally heavier and taller than girls.

Reading a centile chart

Look at the centile chart below. It is showing the height for a three-year-old girl. There are three lines marked on the chart – a middle one and two outer ones. The middle line plots the average height for girls. Our three-year-old girl is much taller than most other girls of her age. She is on the upper line which is marked 97. This means that only 3 per cent of girls of her age are this height. The lower line on the chart indicates children who are much shorter than others of their age. If a child's height was plotted on this line, it would mean that only 3 per cent of children are this short.

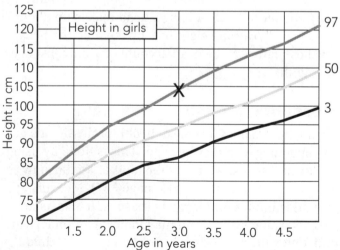

The expected pattern of height gain in girls of 1–5 years

Think about it

Can you think of any reasons why the expected weight patterns of girls might be slightly different from those of boys?

What happens if children are above or below the outer lines?

If children are above or below the outer lines, health professionals are likely to check that there are no abnormalities, such as a child not producing sufficient growth hormones. Health professionals also look at the overall picture and compare the height, weight and head circumference measurements together. Most children's measurements correlate – that is, if a child is tall, he or she is also likely to be heavier than the average. (See pages 113–116 for information about factors affecting children's growth and development.)

Did you know?

As babies and children inherit some of their physical characteristics, including height, from their parents, there are differences in height, weight and head circumference between babies from different cultures and race. For example, French children are, on average, slightly shorter and lighter than babies born to parents of Anglo-Saxon heritage.

What is physical development?

Physical development is the process by which children gain control of their movements. Most children have learnt all the basic skills that they require by the age of six or seven. Afterwards, children just become more skilled at using these movements – for example, they tend to be able to run faster or use two or more skills at once.

Physical development is important for children's overall development for three key reasons:

- *It allows new learning to take place* – a baby who learns to crawl can then start to move and explore his environment, touching items that interest him.

- *It allows further development to take place* – once a child has learnt one skill, she can then build on this skill.

- *It affects children's confidence and self-esteem* – children who have learnt to ride a tricycle feel good about themselves, while older children who feel that they are no good at skipping may lack confidence.

The physical development of children is often grouped into the following areas:

Fine motor

This broad term covers the smaller movements. It can be broken down into the following categories:

Fine manipulative skills
These are small movements that are needed when children write, draw or put together a jigsaw puzzle. You should note that although many fine manipulative activities often involve a degree of hand-eye co-ordination, hand-eye co-ordination is actually a separate skill. A feely bag, for example, requires fine manipulative skills, but no hand-eye co-ordination.

Fine motor skills
These are small movements using the whole hand and wrist, such as twisting a door knob or opening a jar

Gross motor

This broad term covers the large movements. It can be broken down into the following categories:

Gross motor skills
These are whole limb movements used when, for example, a child kicks a ball.

Locomotive skills
These are the movements that children use in order to walk, run and jump.

Co-ordination

Sometimes children will need to be able to co-ordinate more than one type of movement or skill at once. For example in order to skip with a rope, children need to be able to move their arms while jumping. This is what is meant by co-ordination. There are some specific types of co-ordination that most children need to develop, these include:

Hand-eye co-ordination
Some activities such as throwing and catching or writing can be done more easily when the eyes guide the hands. Most children therefore learn to co-ordinate the information received by their eyes and use it to guide their hands. (For children with visual impairment they may learn to co-ordinate sounds, such as instructions or a bell in a ball, with control of their hands.)

Running is a gross motor skill

Turning the pages of a book is a fine motor skill

Throwing a Frisbee is a gross manipulative skill

Drawing is a fine manipulative skill

Foot-eye co-ordination
There are some activities that involve the eyes guiding the feet. Although there are more examples of hand-eye co-ordination, children also need some foot-eye co-ordination in order to do the following: climb stairs; run; kick a ball; avoid obstacles.

Balance
The ability to balance comes with age as the body learns to co-ordinate its movements with the information being received by the central nervous system.

Think about it

Look at the list of actions that you may have done today. Consider what types of physical movement were involved – e.g. fine manipulative, gross motor.

- Eating breakfast
- Getting dressed
- Closing the door
- Turning pages of a book
- Running for a bus

Principles of physical development

The growth and development of children is an incredible process. Babies are born with instinctive reflexes and little control over their movements and responses, yet, within a few years, most babies are able to run, talk, draw and socialise. Studies over time have shown us that development is a process and certain principles seem to govern this process:

■ Physical development is continuous.

■ Physical development is sequential.

■ Physical development is closely linked to the nervous system.

Physical development is continuous

In some ways physical development is like a flowing river. Children do not suddenly jump from being able to crawl to being able to walk. The process by which the development takes place is continuous and goes on being so until we reach maturity. The process flows because different skills are brought in and combined together, thus children trying to walk must learn to balance as well as have the muscle development and bone development to take their weight.

Physical development is sequential

As we watch children growing and developing, we see that a pattern emerges and that, like driving a car, development has to go in a certain order. A baby cannot run without first learning to walk, in the same way that you cannot accelerate if the motor is not switched on.

The speed at which children work their way through the pattern of development varies, which is why some babies crawl at seven months while others crawl at ten months. Health professionals track babies' development carefully and can see if babies are 'stuck' at any stage or if their pattern of development is unusually slow (see also page 218).

Although the speed at which babies and children work their way through the pattern of development does vary, most children acquire certain skills by predictable ages. These skills are often referred to as milestones, and health professionals and others use milestones as a way of checking children's progress. The term 'normative measurement' or development is also used instead of milestones and on pages 109–112 there is a chart showing normative development for children aged 1–8 years.

Some key aspects of sequential development

There are two key aspects to the sequence or pattern of development that we can observe in children.

Losing involuntary reflexes

Babies are born with certain involuntary reflexes which are controlled by the central nervous system. These reflexes are present at birth and enable babies to survive. As part of the sequence of development, we will see that these disappear and are replaced by voluntary control – for example, when the baby wants to move its arm or clasp an object.

Direction of development

There is also a sequence to the way in which voluntary control is gained. In simple terms this can be remembered as downwards and outwards.

Some key stages in gaining voluntary gross motor control

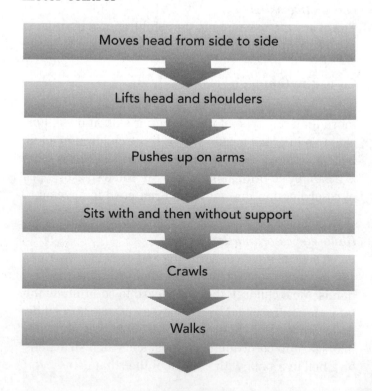

Moves head from side to side

Lifts head and shoulders

Pushes up on arms

Sits with and then without support

Crawls

Walks

Downwards

Gross motor (whole body) movements begin with gaining control over the head, then the neck and back and finally the legs.

Outwards

Fine motor (control of the hands, wrists and lower arm) movements begin with jerky movements of the whole arms, whole hands and then eventually fingers. This means that children will not be able to control their individual finger movements until they are able to control their whole hand action.

Physical development is closely linked to the nervous system

The nervous system is the body's information-gathering, storage and control system. Its 'headquarters' is the central nervous system (CNS) which is made up of the brain and the spinal cord. Information is sent to the CNS from the sense organs via nerves that fan out through the entire body. As a result of the information, the CNS sends out instructions to muscles (including muscles controlling speech), glands and internal organs.

In some cases we are conscious and in control of these instructions – for example, you are hungry and so you decide to unwrap a chocolate bar – while other instructions are made involuntarily – for example, flinching when you are hurt. When babies are first born, they show a number of involuntary movements and reflexes but, as the central nervous system matures, it is able to interpret information and remember responses. This means that more voluntary control is gained.

The maturation of the central nervous system takes time, and so some functions such as gaining control of the bowel and bladder cannot take place until there is some maturity (see pages 50–51 for more information about bladder and bowel control). This effectively means that while we can encourage children's physical development by praising them and stimulating them, thus helping the central nervous system to remember movements, we cannot 'fast track' children.

How physical development is measured

In order to be able to assess children's development, most health professionals and early years workers refer to 'normative development' charts or milestones. These give an indication of whether a child's skills and rate of development are similar to other children's. It is important to understand that normative charts or milestones are only guides as children develop at different rates.

In addition to looking at milestones, the rate at which children are mastering skills can be looked at by using checklists and noting down the date when a skill is first seen.

Age	Fine manipulative skills	Gross manipulative skills	The carer's role	Toys and equipment
12 months	■ Picks up objects with thumb and forefinger ■ Picks up and holds toys such as rattles ■ Points to objects ■ Holds cup with help ■ Puts small objects in a container	■ Mobile – either crawling, rolling or shuffling ■ (Some children may be walking) ■ Sits up unsupported for long periods ■ Walks with assistance ■ Tries to crawl up stairs	To support this stage of development, carers need to supervise carefully and give plenty of praise and encouragement. We need to spend time playing alongside the child – e.g. making a tower of bricks for them to knock down or putting a cuddly toy in their truck to push along.	■ stacking beakers ■ large balls ■ push-and-pull toys ■ bricks

Age	Fine manipulative skills	Gross manipulative skills	The carer's role	Toys and equipment
15 months	<ul><li>Holds and drinks from cup using two hands</li><li>Builds tower of two blocks</li><li>Makes marks with crayons</li><li>Tries to turn pages in books</li></ul>	<ul><li>Crawls down stairs feet first</li><li>Walks independently</li><li>Seats self in small chair</li></ul>	Carers need to supervise children of this age very carefully, as they are keen to explore and may start to climb. Children enjoy discovering new toys especially if they make sounds. We can help children by showing them how to use toys and by playing alongside them. Children of this age can often follow simple instructions – e.g. they may collect their hat and put it on. These early self-help skills need to be encouraged and praised so that children gain in confidence.	<ul><li>picture books</li><li>bricks</li><li>shape sorters</li><li>toys that make music</li><li>large crayons</li></ul>
18 months	<ul><li>Strings four large beads</li><li>Turns door knobs and handles</li><li>Pulls off shoes</li></ul>	<ul><li>Bends down from waist to pick up toys</li><li>Squats down to look at toys</li><li>Rolls and throws a ball</li><li>Walks down stairs with adult help</li><li>Pushes and pulls toys whilst walking</li></ul>	The main role of the adult is to allow children the time and space to play. Children are likely to spend more time playing alone and may play quite repetitively – e.g. putting objects into and taking them out of boxes. As children gain in self-help skills – e.g. taking off shoes and coats – they need to be praised and allowed time to complete the task.	<ul><li>prams</li><li>rocking horses or chairs</li><li>threading toys</li><li>bricks</li><li>toys to ride on</li></ul>
2 years	<ul><li>Uses a spoon to feed him or herself</li><li>Zips and unzips large zippers</li><li>Places five rings on a stick</li><li>Puts on shoes</li><li>Draws circles and dots</li><li>Builds a tower of five to six bricks</li><li>Begins to use a preferred hand</li></ul>	<ul><li>Kicks a ball that is not moving</li><li>Climbs on furniture</li><li>Puts together and pulls apart snap-together toys</li><li>Walks up and down stairs confidently</li></ul>	Children of this age are enjoying exploring their environment and are beginning to have favourite toys and activities. Going to play parks and using swings and rocking equipment are a particular treat. Children's self-help skills are developing although there may be times when children become frustrated – e.g. an arm of a coat may be twisted and they cannot get their hand through. Praise and encouragement need to be offered and we need to look at ways of making children feel independent.	<ul><li>ride and sit on toys</li><li>push-and-pull toys</li><li>shape sorters</li><li>bricks</li><li>crayons</li><li>dough</li><li>picture books</li></ul>

Age	Fine manipulative skills	Gross manipulative skills	The carer's role	Toys and equipment
3 years	■ Turns pages in a book one by one ■ Holds crayon and can draw a face ■ Uses a spoon without spilling ■ Washes and dries hands with help ■ Puts on and takes off coat	■ Walks and runs forwards ■ Walks on tiptoes ■ Throws large ball ■ Kicks ball forward ■ Jumps from low steps ■ Pedals and steers a tricycle	Children of this age are starting to enjoy playing together and enjoy new challenges. Adults need to provide stimulating activities that allow children to develop fine movements – e.g. painting, cooking – as well as opportunities to engage in pretend play.	■ large outdoor apparatus ■ puzzles ■ paints and crayons ■ dough ■ sand and water ■ tricycles ■ prams ■ dressing-up clothes
4 years	■ Buttons and unbuttons own clothing ■ Cuts out simple shapes ■ Draws a person with head, trunk and legs ■ Puts together 12-piece puzzle	■ Walks on a line ■ Aims and throws ball ■ Bounces and catches large ball ■ Runs, changing direction ■ Hops on one foot ■ Pedals and steers a tricycle confidently	Children at this age are gaining in confidence and are able to become more independent. We can encourage them to wipe up spills, pour drinks and tidy away. This will help prepare them for school. Most children of this age enjoy being busy and playing co-operatively	■ balls ■ climbing frames ■ slides ■ materials for creative activities ■ crayons ■ glue ■ scissors ■ puzzles ■ construction toys ■ books
5 years	■ Forms letters, writes own name ■ Draws recognisable pictures of trees, houses, people and animals ■ Colours in pictures neatly ■ Dresses and undresses easily ■ Completes 20-piece jigsaw puzzles ■ Cuts out shapes using scissors quite accurately ■ Draws around a template	■ Skips with a rope ■ Runs quickly and is able to avoid obstacles ■ Is able to use a variety of large equipment – e.g. swings, slides ■ Throws large ball to partner and catches it ■ Hits ball with bat or stick	Children are starting to enjoy playing games with rules – e.g. snakes and ladders, chase etc. Adults can help by introducing new games into their play – e.g. hide-and-seek – as well as encouraging children to make up their own games. Adult support and encouragement is needed as there may be times when arguments break out! We should also be encouraging children to be as independent as possible – e.g. folding their clothes when changing, hanging up their coats.	■ hoops ■ balls ■ roller-skates ■ bicycles with stabilisers ■ large equipment ■ creative materials – e.g. paints, crayons, card and paper ■ construction toys ■ board games

Age	Fine manipulative skills	Gross manipulative skills	The carer's role	Toys and equipment
6–7 years	■ Is able to sew simple stitches ■ Cuts out shapes accurately and neatly ■ Handwriting is evenly spaced and may be joined ■ Drawings are detailed and representative ■ Makes a simple sandwich ■ Ties and unties laces	■ Rides a bicycle without stabilisers ■ Runs ■ Chases and dodges others ■ Hops, skips and jumps confidently ■ Kicks a ball with direction ■ Balances on a beam or wall	Children of this age are independent and able to do many day-to-day tasks – e.g. tidying away, laying the table. They are gaining in confidence and enjoy trying out new activities – e.g. making models, origami, cooking. They are starting to have preferences and their own hobbies – e.g. some children will be learning to swim whilst others may go to karate or dance lessons. By eight years some children may need to be encouraged to join in some types of physical activities. This is often due to self-consciousness – e.g. they feel that they are not as good as other children.	■ bicycles ■ skateboards ■ roller-skates ■ balls ■ bats and rackets ■ kits – e.g. modelling kits, origami ■ jigsaw puzzles ■ board games

Physical checklist

Skill	Date observed	Comments
Turns door knob and can use handles		
Jumps on the spot with both feet		
Can walk backwards		
Walks downstairs with aid		
Can build a tower of 5 – 6 bricks		
Can turn the pages in a book one at a time		
Can fold a piece of paper in half		
Kicks large ball		

Observation

Using written record as a technique, watch a child doing one of these tasks.

■ Putting on or taking off a coat

■ Doing a jigsaw puzzle

■ Playing with construction bricks

■ Drawing or painting

During the observation

■ Observe whether the child is right- or left-handed.

■ See how easy the child finds the task.

■ Does the child look for support or help?

■ Is the child carrying out the activity confidently – e.g. smiling?

Interpreting the observation

■ Look at the physical development charts and consider how the child is developing compared to other children of their age.

■ What have you learnt about this child's physical skills?

■ What activities could you plan to help the child develop or to reinforce the child's skills?

Factors affecting physical development and growth

There are many factors that can affect children's growth and development as the spider diagram below shows:

These can be grouped into three categories:

- Antenatal
- Perinatal
- Postnatal

Antenatal factors

The term 'antenatal' is used to mean the time from conception up until birth. There are many influences during this period that might later affect children's growth and development. During the first twelve weeks of life the foetus is particularly vulnerable as this is the period when all the major organ structures are developing. It is now recognised that good antenatal care is important and can reduce the levels of infant mortality. (See page 357 for more information about antenatal care.)

Heredity

Most people resemble their natural parents, grandparents or cousins in some way. This is because our cells inherit genetic information from both of our parents. This information will shape the way we look, grow and even our susceptibility to certain diseases.

Understanding how the information is stored
Every cell in our body (with the exception of sperm and ovum) contains 46 chromosomes which are grouped in pairs, thus making 23 pairs. The chromosomes act like a library of information. The chromosomes are in turn made up of long strings of a chemical that has become known as DNA (deoxyribonucleic acid) with each string being divided further into sections called genes. Genes control specific characteristics such as the colour of your eyes or whether your hair is curly. Everyone, with the exception of identical twins, has a different DNA makeup.

Understanding how the genetic information is passed on
At conception the sperm and the ovum combine. These are the only two cells not to have 46 chromosomes arranged in pairs. They have 23 chromosomes which means that when conception takes place, 23 chromosomes from the ovum combine with 23 chromosomes from the sperm which then gives the cell the usual number of 46. The 46 chromosomes combine into pairs.

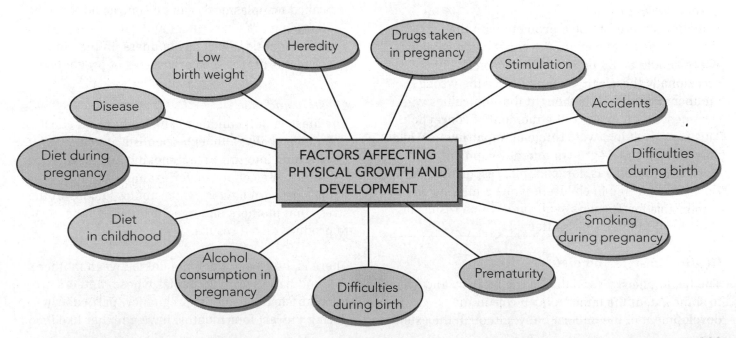

How genetic information might affect physical development and growth

A person's height is a good example of how inherited information might affect our growth. People who have parents and grandparents who were tall for their generation are more likely to be tall.

At the time of writing, scientists are making significant breakthroughs in understanding the genetic makeup or 'blueprint' of the human body. This work is beginning to throw more light on why people may be more susceptible than others to certain diseases.

There are many medical conditions and diseases that children might inherit from their parents which can affect their growth and/or physical development. A good example of this is sickle cell anaemia which is an inherited blood disease that limits the oxygen-carrying capacity of the blood.

Did you know?

A lovely example of how genes might affect our development is tongue rolling! Try rolling your tongue by bringing the sides of your tongue in (a little like making a straw). The ability to do this is an inherited one!

Chromosomal disorder

Sometimes there can be a problem with the chromosomes that contain the genetic information. There should be 23 pairs of chromosomes but occasionally these can be damaged or the wrong number produced. It is thought that difficulties with chromosomes happen at the moment of conception. This can result in a wide range of impairments which may affect a child's growth and development. An extra chromosome is, for example, responsible for Down's syndrome in children, while a missing one is responsible for Turner's syndrome which results in short height in those girls affected.

Health, lifestyle and diet

The health, lifestyle and diet of the mother, and even to some extent the father, play a role in the development of the unborn baby, although the extent of this is only just beginning to emerge. An example of this is the discovery of the importance of the health of both parents before conception. Prospective mothers are being encouraged to increase their intake of folic acid as this has been shown to help prevent the condition of spina bifida.

Health

During pregnancy, the embryo or foetus shares its life-support systems with its mother. This means that any drugs that the mother takes will also be passed on to the embryo. Similarly, if the mother contracts a disease this too can be transmitted to the baby. This means that pregnant mothers are advised not to take any medication during pregnancy that is not prescribed for them by their doctor and also to avoid the following:

- Contact with people who have German measles. German measles or rubella, if contracted by the mother in the early stages of pregnancy, can cause severe abnormalities in the baby, such as deafness or congenital heart disease.

- Eating foods that contain unpasteurised milk. A bacterial infection called listeriosis can be contracted from eating foods such as unpasteurised cheeses. This can cause miscarriage or stillbirth.

- Contact with cat's excrement. A rare infection called toxoplasmosis can be contracted through handling cat's excrement and can cause abnormalities, such as blindness, in the embryo or foetus during the early stages of pregnancy.

Lifestyle and diet

The lifestyle of the mother can also have an effect on the unborn baby, although scientists are still researching into this area. Smoking and large quantities of alcohol can, for example, mean that babies are born lighter, while studies looking at the stress that mothers undergo during pregnancy seem to produce mixed results.

There is, however, a definite link between mother's diet and baby's growth. Babies whose mothers are malnourished during the pregnancy, particularly during the last four months, have a higher likelihood of being born lighter and even of dying during the first year. Bee (1998) suggests that they also seem, at birth, to be less responsive and so less likely to learn from their early experiences. It is important to note that being malnourished does not mean not having enough to eat but means not eating enough of all the nutrients required by the body. (See pages 61–62 for more information about diet.)

Difficulties during the pregnancy

Difficulties in the pregnancy can also affect a baby's physical development and growth. Antenatal screening helps identify potentially fatal conditions such as pre-eclampsia and rhesus incompatibility (see also page 357).

Perinatal factors

Perinatal factors are difficulties that occur during the birthing process. The birthing process is not without risk for the baby or the mother. This is why in earlier times many religions had ceremonies to give thanks for the safe arrival of babies.

Anoxia – lack of oxygen

This can happen for several reasons – for example, the baby being slow to breathe or the umbilical cord that supplies the baby with oxygen being squeezed during the birth. Lack of oxygen at birth can cause a range of problems including cerebal palsy or learning difficulties.

Low birth weight

The weight of a baby at birth can influence its future development. There are many reasons why a baby might be born with low birth weight. Common ones include:

- prematurity (babies born early)
- failing placenta
- poor maternal nutrition
- multiple births.

In some cases, babies who have a low birth weight may show signs of developmental delay. This is particularly the case with premature babies as they are not fully developed when they are born.

Postnatal factors

Postnatal factors are influences that might affect children from birth onwards. These factors can be considered to be environmental ones such as where children grow up, their diet and the way they are cared for. In some cases, we might find that children's environment and their genetic disposition come together to shape their development – for example, a child who grows up in a home with pets and who has a genetic pre-disposition to allergies might develop asthma in response to the animal hairs present. There are many postnatal factors that can affect children's physical development and growth, these include:

- diet
- quality of care
- accidents
- infections
- poverty
- abuse and neglect.

Diet

The food that children eat is extremely important to growth and development. Children who do not have enough food (undernourished) or a balanced diet (malnourished) are likely to show signs of developmental delay. A study where school children were given vitamin drops showed a clear improvement in cognitive development. (See pages 61–62 for more information about diet.)

Quality of care

The quality of care that babies and children receive can affect their growth and development. As mentioned in Chapter 8, children need love, care and stimulation in order to grow and develop. Sometimes children who are not thriving are not receiving the quality of care that they need. Unhappy children may not feel like playing or eating and thus do not grow and develop.

Providing a good environment for children must therefore be a priority for early years workers, especially when they are looking after children for considerable periods of time.

Accidents

According to Child Accident Prevention Trust (CAPT), an estimated 10,000 children a year are left disabled as a result of accidents. This means that early years workers need to be extremely vigilant when caring for children and checking that their environment is a safe one. (See pages 36–39 for more information about preventing accidents.)

Infections

Infections such as measles or whooping cough can affect children's physical development. This is why the government is keen to vaccinate young children. (See page 215 for more information about immunisation programmes.) Children can also be affected in the short term by having repeated colds and ear infections as this may affect their hearing. Children who are poorly also feel tired and may not be able to concentrate and benefit from learning opportunities.

Poverty

Poverty plays an extraordinary part in the growth and development of children in many ways. Statistically, children from low-income households have a higher incidence of ill health and accidents while having lower life expectancy and educational achievements. The link between poverty, health and education has prompted the government to put funds into projects such as Surestart (see page 406).

Abuse and neglect

Children who are being abused in some way, or who are being neglected, are likely to show developmental delay in terms of their growth and development. Children who are under strain often 'regress', meaning that they go back to an earlier stage of development. (See page 416 for more information about abuse and neglect.)

The implications of delayed or impaired physical development

Although most children follow a similar pattern in their physical development, some may have delayed or impaired physical development. In some cases, a physical impairment or delay can affect other areas of a child's development. Common reasons why this may happen include:

Lack of self-esteem

Some children may lack confidence if they can see they are not developing in the same way as other children – for example, children who have not gained bladder control may feel they are 'babies'. This means that adults working with children need to look for plenty of other opportunities to help children feel good about themselves.

Lack of independence

Children who lack physical skills may need more adult assistance and so not learn to be independent. It is important, therefore, when working with children with special needs, to try to look for ways of encouraging them to take control, make choices and do as much as they can for themselves.

Difficulty in building friendships

Children might miss out on opportunities to make friends if they cannot play alongside other children. A child who is visually impaired may have difficulty in joining in an activity where throwing and catching is taking place. This means that adults working with children need to look for ways of involving them in activities with other children and looking for ways of adapting materials and activities so that they can join in.

Lack of stimulation

Once children gain some physical skills such as the ability to be mobile or to hold objects, they can explore objects and enjoy different play activities. Children who have developmental delay or impairment may not be able to move physically to get toys, nor have the strength/co-ordination to play with them. This can result in a lack of stimulation and delay in their cognitive development since young children learn and develop their concepts by being active. This means that adults working with children must make sure that they are giving them plenty of stimulation and providing a variety of toys and equipment to help them.

The role of the adult in promoting physical development

There are several ways in which adults can help promote children's physical development, many of which are also important in relation to other aspects of children's development. The spider diagram below looks at the many aspects of promoting physical development, although this section looks particularly at ways of providing physical activities for children.

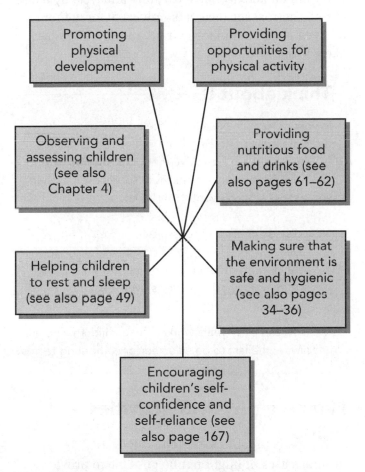

Providing opportunities for physical activity

Physical activity is very important for everyone, both young and old! Physical activity helps the body in many ways by, for example:

- stimulating the brain
- helping the digestive system
- releasing hormones
- maintaining and developing bone density

- strengthening muscles, including the heart
- maintaining and developing lung capacity.

Providing for physical activity

There are two main types of physical activity that early years workers should plan for:

- physical activity which allows children to exercise their whole bodies
- activities for children to develop their fine motor movements.

Vigorous physical activity – outdoors

Ideally children should be encouraged to have some time outdoors each day so that they can play. Many settings have planned times where children can go outside to play – for example, in a garden or a playground. Being outside is good for children's spatial awareness as they are moving in a larger space and so, wherever possible, early years workers should try to make sure that children have been outside. Settings with no outdoor area may try taking children out for walks or going to an area such as a park.

Making sure that children are safe

Children playing outside need careful supervision. The freedom that being outdoors gives children can sometimes mean they become very excited. This is wonderful for the children but it means that early years workers need to be extremely vigilant and ready to intervene if the play looks as if it might become dangerous. Early years workers also need to check that the outdoor environment is safe and that any equipment that is going to be used is also safe (see also page 57).

Promoting outdoor play for children

Many young children will benefit greatly from being able to choose their own play outside. In this way they are more likely to concentrate for longer periods and persevere. Many children under the age of five tend to combine outdoor play with imaginative play – for example, pretending that their tricycles are cars or that the climbing frame is a house. This means that it can be a good idea to put out a range of props, such as dressing-up clothes, bags and household objects, to support this type of play (see also page 278 for information about role play).

Developing specific skills

As well as encouraging children to play outdoors, adults may also need to provide activities and equipment that will develop specific skills in children – for example, throwing and catching, skipping, or kicking a ball. These skills are important as they help children's overall co-ordination although, as with planning any activity, it is important to consider each child's individual stage of development – for example, a child will not be able to hit a ball until he is able to judge its speed, which means that learning to catch usually comes before learning to hit.

Activities for developing physical skills

Skill	Type of equipment and games
Running	Tag, paper chases, running in and out of cones, running to find hoops, What's the time Mr Wolf?, obstacle courses, catching bubbles
Steering and pedalling	Prams, pushchairs, tricycles, sit-on toys, bicycles, scooters, obstacle courses
Throwing and catching	Bean bags, balloons, different types of balls, quoits
Batting and hitting	Mini-golf, mini-hockey, racquets, cricket bats, wooden and plastic bats
Climbing	Climbing frames, walls, trees
Balancing	Stilts, chalk lines for children to follow
Skipping	Skipping to music, skipping with ropes, traditional skipping games, French skipping
Kicking	Kicking large foam balls, footballs
Jumping	Jumping off walls, jumping into hoops, hopscotch, pogo sticks

Encouraging but not pressurising children

It is important for children to enjoy physical activity if they are to develop positive attitudes towards sport and exercise later on. This means that it must be a pleasant experience for them. Many early years settings do not encourage competitive games for this reason, as children may lose confidence if they are not 'winning'.

In the same way, while we might encourage children to try out an activity such as riding a bicycle by using praise and reassurance, it is unwise to force them as this will make them more afraid and therefore less likely to succeed.

Think about it

In your groups, make a list of the advantages and disadvantages of holding competitive sports events for children. When you have done this, discuss with your group how you felt at school sports events when you did not win an event.

Now discuss the following issues.

- What long-term effects might constantly coming last in races at school sports events have on children?

- How can early years workers help children who are always the last to be selected for competing teams?

Planning physical activities – indoors

In some cases, it might not be possible to provide gross motor activities outside – because of the weather or because a setting has no outdoor area. This means that early years workers need to look at ways of providing activities indoors. This may mean moving equipment and furniture in order to create a space. There are many games that can be played inside that will help children develop their gross motor movements – these are often linked to music and dance. Party games are often a good source of indoor physical activity and can easily be adapted to different ages.

Activities to promote children's fine movements

One of the major tasks for early years settings that are working with Foundation stage children is to prepare their hands ready for writing. In order to be able to write, children have to have complete control of their arms, wrists and hands. The muscles and the bones in their arms and hands have to be developed enough before they will be ready to write. In the past, children had plenty of opportunities for developing the control in their hands because they were often involved in household activities such as laying fires, dusting, polishing shoes and even washing up. Lifestyles have now changed, so many of these household chores are no longer been carried out by children. This means that early years settings need to make sure that children have plenty of opportunities to practise and develop a range of hand movements before they begin to write.

Providing opportunities for large arm and hand movements

We know from looking at the principles of children's development that the direction of development is outwards. This means it is a good idea to provide some activities that will help children to control their large arm and hand movements. This might be encouraging children to paint very large pictures, drawing on the ground with chalks, or activities such as helping to wash cars. In many European countries specific pieces of equipment help children develop their arm movements such as the piece of equipment shown on page 120.

Indoor physical activities

Name of activity	Activity
Follow my leader	The children follow the actions or movements of another child or adult. Traditionally, this game was played with children in a line, but can be adapted so that children can follow the actions while standing or sitting in a circle.
Mr Bear's honey	There are several versions of this game. Mr Bear is in the middle of the circle pretending to be asleep while another child from the circle takes the bear's honey. Mr Bear has to give chase and catch the thief before he reaches his place in the circle.
Parachute games	It is possible to buy small parachutes that have only eight handles. These can be easier to use with smaller groups or in restricted spaces. Young children enjoy the feeling of lifting the parachute up and down. This encourages their co-ordination. There are many parachute games. A popular one is called Fruit Salad. All the children are given the names of the following fruits: pineapple, pear, apple or orange. When the adult calls out the name of the fruit, the children must go underneath the parachute and find a new place to stand. This game can be adapted to introduce specific topic words – e.g. names of flowers or types of animals.
Roll a ball	Children sit in a group and roll a ball or throw a beanbag to each other when a name is called.
Musical statues	This classic party game can be adapted in many ways in early years settings. Children move to the music and then have to stand still when they can no longer hear it. Variations can be to ask children to do certain things when they can no longer hear the music such as crouch down or wave their hands in the air.

Activities to encourage fine manipulative skills

Fine manipulative movements are important as they give children strength and co-ordination. As well as activities such as threading, dough and painting, adults can help promote this area of development by using everyday opportunities such as dressing, pouring out drinks and tidying away. By encouraging children to use their fine manipulative skills in this way, we can also help then to become more independent, which in turn can make them feel confident.

Ensuring equality of opportunity

As we have seen, physical development is important, as it affects other areas of development. This means that early years workers need to make sure that all children are given enough support and encouragement to help them meet their potential. There are many ways in which early years workers might do this, including the following:

- Planning activities for individual children to promote specific areas of their development – e.g. a child who has had an accident which means that his right side is not as strong as that of another child, might benefit from throwing beanbags with his right hand.

- Adapting equipment to help children with impairments to join in – e.g. bells could be sewn into a beanbag to help a visually impaired child to hear the bag.

- Challenging the behaviour of children who are undermining others – as children get older, they tend to make comparisons and remarks about others' abilities.

- Being a good role model – some activities are seen as gender specific, such as football, skipping or dancing. Being a good role model or finding good role models is important to encourage all children to feel that they can take part.

Knowledge into action

In pairs, choose one activity that will promote fine manipulative skills for *each* of the following age ranges.

0–1 years   1–3 years 3–5 years 5–8 years

For each of your chosen activities:
- Explain why it is suitable for the age range.
- Consider the learning potential for other areas of development.
- Discuss the role of the adult during the activity.

Check your knowledge

- What is the difference between 'growth' and 'development'?

- Explain what a centile chart is used for.

- What is meant by the term 'fine manipulative skills'?

- Name one professional involved in measuring children's physical development.

- Give two reasons why checks are regularly carried out on children.

- Describe the physical skills that most three-year-olds have developed.

- Outline two factors that might affect a child's physical development.

- Write down four pieces of equipment that might encourage a child's gross motor skills.

- Outline how an early years worker might ensure that an outdoor play area was safe.

- Name three pieces of equipment that can help develop a child's fine manipulative skills.

- What is the role of the central nervous system?

- How is physical development linked to other areas of a child's overall development?

- List three factors that might affect a child's physical growth and development.

- What does the term 'normative' development mean?

Resources

Further reading

Health Education Authority 1998 *Birth to Five*, London, Health Education Authority

Oates, J. (ed.) 1994 *The Foundations of Child Development*, Oxford, Blackwell/Open University

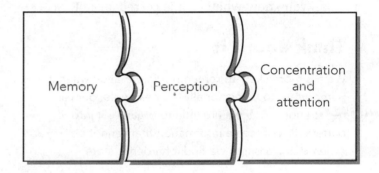

CHAPTER 6
Cognitive development

What is cognitive development?

Cognitive development is about the way our thought processes develop. It is about the ways in which we organise our thinking and come to an understanding of our environment.

Understanding how our minds and thoughts work is complex and psychologists are still trying to learn more about our brain functions. It is understood, however, that elements of brain function are inter-related.

To understand how these components are interlinked consider the following case:

Did you try to read what this message said? In order to do so, you would have needed to:

- use your memory of symbols to look for familiar signs
- concentrate on the task
- look for visual clues.

Memory

Our ability to store information enables us to build on our experiences and learn from them. Memory is,

therefore, a key component in the way we develop thoughts. Psychologists have become interested in the way we use our memories and why we remember some pieces of information, but forget others.

Studies on memory are ongoing and there are several different theories. However, many psychologists believe that we have a long-term and a short-term memory. They have also concluded that we develop different strategies to help us store information and to retrieve information that has been stored.

Short-term memory

Our short-term memories are like notepads, allowing us to work from them and then discard them when they are no longer of use to us. This may mean, for example, that while you need a telephone number you can remember it, but once you no longer need it, it is lost.

Psychologists believe that we can store information in our short-term memories for between 15 and 30 seconds, although we can increase the length of this time by using a strategy known as **rehearsal**. Rehearsal is repeating something – for example, a telephone number, over and over in order to remember it. Young children do not have this strategy which means they often forget simple instructions.

Long-term memory

Our long-term memories allow us to store information that is not necessarily needed immediately, but can be retrieved when required. It is thought that there is unlimited capacity in our long-term memories. However, this does not always mean that all the information stored can be retrieved in the same way – for example, sometimes you may not be able to remember someone's name, but if someone suggests a name, you know whether it is correct or not.

Think about it

We are more likely to remember information when it is important to us personally – for example, our car registration – or if we are able to organise it into a pattern. If we receive information that cannot be ordered or classified we find it harder to store.

Try this experiment in pairs.

Partner A calls out fifteen random numbers between zero and ten – e.g. 6, 3, 8, 9...

Partner B, after a short pause, must now try to write these down in the correct order.

How many numbers can partner B write down? Research suggests that most people can remember between five and nine numbers correctly in order, with most people managing seven.

Perception

Vision and perception are slightly different things. Our brain receives a flat, upside-down image from our eyes, yet what we perceive a full three-dimensional picture. To do this, our brain extracts as much information as it can from other senses, as well as drawing on previous experience, to convert the flat image into a fuller picture for us.

Psychologists are interested in how our brains manage to do this quickly and you may have seen

examples of perception tests that psychologists use on children and adults.

Here is the rabbit/duck test.

You should be able to see a duck or a rabbit, but you will not be able to see both at the same time!

Several studies have been carried out on animals and humans to find out more about perception. One experiment by a psychologist called Kohler involved volunteers wearing headgear that inverted the image received by the brain – everything appeared upside down.

Most volunteers found that after a short period of time their vision of the world appeared the correct way around as the brain had adjusted the information, although those volunteers who did not physically move around had much greater difficulties. This shows that in order for perception to develop, babies need to have sensory experiences and to explore their worlds.

Psychologists studying the perceptual skills of babies have found that their brains quickly learn to interpret the different forms of information around them by using their senses.

Think about it

Research shows that in order to develop their perception, babies need some stimulation of their senses.

In pairs, make a list of toys and activities that are often offered to babies and discuss how each may stimulate a baby's senses.

Attention

Attention and concentration are skills that the brain uses to focus in on some particular pieces of information. This is important because, without our realising it, the brain is busy filtering out sounds, colours, smells, thoughts and so on, which would otherwise distract us.

This does not mean that all of our attention is directed at one single activity – for example, at a party, while talking to one person, you can still hear your name being mentioned in another conversation.

Attention and concentration are important components in the learning process because, without them, children would not be able to concentrate long enough to store essential information.

Psychologists are keen to understand how we decide what to concentrate on and what to disregard.

Knowledge into action

Listen to the noises in the room you are in.

Write down the noises that you can hear.

When someone talks to you, are the noises as loud?

Why do some children find it easier to work and play in quieter environments?

> ## ISSUES   Attention deficit hyperactivity disorder (ADHD)
>
> This disorder has been treated with some scepticism by the medical profession, although it seems to be generally recognised now.
>
> Children with this disorder find it hard to concentrate and attend even for short periods. They lack concentration. ADHD is often identified through children's impulsive actions and motor activity. It is thought that this is due to the brain being either under-stimulated or over-aroused. Some families and dietitians have blamed the use of chemicals in foods which act as stimulants. This has led to some children being put on special diets. The diagnosis of ADHD has often been controversial, with many experts believing that some children's problems are the result of poor behavioural management. They point out that many children who are put onto behavioural modification programmes improve (see page 207). A drug called Ritalin – now widely used in America – acts as a depressive. In this country, many families with children who have ADHD tend to feel they are unsupported by the medical profession.
>
> Have you worked with children with this condition?
>
> Why do you think that the medical profession is reluctant to give children Ritalin?

How children learn

There are many theories about how children learn, but they follow three essential strands:

- behaviourist theories
- social learning theories
- constructivist theories.

Many psychologists believe that these theories are not necessarily competing theories but may complement each other.

It is useful and necessary for early years workers to understand how children learn, so that they can use different strategies when working with children.

Behaviourist theories

Pavlov (1849–1936) – Classical conditioning

Ivan Pavlov was a physiologist who was working on dogs' digestive systems when he noticed that he could influence their behaviour. He noticed that when they saw the feeding bucket, they would start to salivate, even though they were not eating. As a result of his observation, he started to do some more work which resulted in a theory called classical conditioning.

Pavlov started to ring bells just before feeding the dogs. After a short period, the dogs would start to salivate just on hearing the bells, even when there was no food given. The dogs had learnt to do something that they would not otherwise have done.

It is suggested that humans also learn some things in this way. For example, a child who had been sick on the day she wore a blue jumper might associate the jumper with being sick and not want to wear it again, even though she knew it was not the jumper that made her sick.

Think about it

Have you ever had an experience that gave an object or place a strong association?

Thorndike and Skinner – Operant conditioning

It is generally accepted that the theory of operant conditioning started with Edward Thorndike (1874–1949) although B F Skinner (1904–1990) developed and refined it.

Thorndike devised a puzzle box from which a cat could escape by learning to operate a catch and a lever. If it escaped it was rewarded with food. He noticed that cats learnt to escape by a process of trial and error and that, over time, they remembered how to free themselves and get the food.

Thorndike is famous for his Law of Effect, which says that:

> If a response is followed by a satisfying state of affairs it tends to be repeated. Other responses fade away.

Skinner developed the theory further. He called pleasant experiences positive reinforcement and bad experiences negative reinforcement. He also showed that by ignoring behaviour, the behaviour might disappear (see page 193).

Operant conditioning is very powerful. It means that if you have a pleasant experience, you are more likely to repeat your behaviour. For example,

This child has learnt that by pressing a button, she can make a chicken pop up

a baby shakes a rattle, likes the sound and shakes it again. In this way the baby learns what to do with a rattle.

Bandura (1925–) – Social learning theory (see also page 159)

Social learning theorists agree that we learn much of our behaviour through conditioning – positive and negative reinforcement – but they add to the work of conditioning by suggesting that we also learn by observing others' behaviour, which they call observational learning.

Albert Bandura was able to show that children learn from watching others.

In a famous experiment in 1965, he looked into the effects that seeing aggressive adults had on children. He showed three groups of children a film in which they saw an adult hit an inflatable doll. There were three endings to the film.

1 Group A saw only the beating.

2 Group B saw the adult being praised and rewarded for beating the doll.

3 Group C saw the adult being punished for beating the doll.

Afterwards, the children were given the same doll and their behaviour was observed. Groups A and B imitated the aggressive behaviour that they saw, while children in group C were less aggressive.

Think about it

Can you think of any skills that you learnt by watching other people?

Why is it important that early years workers are aware that children are watching and learning from them?

Observation

You may be able to record a child learning and copying from an adult in this way. There are many situations in settings where children copy the movements or skills of an adult. Always remember to ask the adult who is working with the children if you can observe him or her (not everyone likes to be observed!).

Using written record, look out for these types of situation:

An adult playing alongside children

- at the dough table – e.g. the adult starts making cakes

- in the sand tray – e.g. the adult makes sandcastles

- in the water tray – e.g. the adult tries to make objects sink.

Also, see if children copy adult actions such as crossing legs, yawning or tidying up.

As you observe, notice whether or not children keep checking to see if their actions are similar to the adult's.

What have the children learnt by copying the adult?

Constructivist theories

Constructivist psychologists suggest that rather than the children learning because of things happening to them – for example, being given praise – they learn from action and from exploring their own environment.

Piaget (1896–1980)

Jean Piaget was a Swiss zoologist who is widely recognised as having influenced the way young children are taught. He became interested in the way children's thought processes developed while working on intelligence tests. He noticed that children were routinely giving the same 'wrong' answers and became interested in why this happened. Over a period of years he studied children, including keeping a diary on his own children. He discovered that children's answers were not random, but followed a logical pattern based on conclusions drawn from their own experiences. Piaget called their conclusions *schemas*. An example of a schema that is common among young children, is to believe that everyone lives with a parent figure. For example, a young child might watch an adult break something and comment 'His mummy will be cross with him!'

How children develop and adapt schemas
Piaget believed that children are able to adapt their schemas when they have new experiences. This process is often called **assimilation** and **accommodation**.

- **Assimilation** occurs when children find that an existing schema fits another situation. For example, a child might find that putting on a cardigan is similar to putting on a coat.

- **Accommodation** happens when children realise that their schema does not 'fit' what is happening. This forces the child to develop a new schema based on the latest experience.

Look at this example of how a child 'accommodates' a new concept.

1 Rosie drinks orange juice out of a red beaker.

2 She develops a schema that all red beakers have orange juice in them.

3   She is given another drink of orange juice out of the red beaker and this confirms her schema.

4   Rosie is then given a red beaker that has milk in it.

5   She now has new information that shows her that her schema does not fit.

6   Rosie then develops a schema that all red beakers have orange juice or milk in them.

Eventually, Rosie will come to understand that beakers are used for many drinks and that beakers come in many colours.

Stages of conceptual development
Piaget also felt that as well as learning about their world by developing and adapting schemas, children also seemed to pass through four stages of conceptual development which linked to their biological development. He used several tests to show the different stages in the cognitive process.

Object permanence At first babies do not have a mental picture of the world. They learn through their senses. This means that if they cannot see an object, they believe that it no longer exists. At around eight months, babies seem to develop the concept of object permanence. If they are shown an object and it is then hidden, they look for it or cry.

Egocentrism Children under the age of six or seven tend to be 'self-centred' in the way they view the world. This does not mean they are selfish, but that they do not have the concept to understand that – for example, what you can see depends on where you are sitting. Piaget showed this in a test where children were shown three model mountains. A doll was placed in different positions and children were asked what they thought the doll could see. Their answers reflected what they were able to see.

Piaget called the concept of being able to see things from someone else's view 'decentring'.

Animism Children under the age of six or seven tend to imagine that objects and animals have the same thoughts and feelings as they have. For example, if a child bumped himself on a table he might say 'Naughty table.'

Children's drawings often show animism – for example, a cat with a smile:

Conservation Piaget had several tests to see if children could understand that, even if a material changed shape or form, its other properties would remain the same.

Piaget suggested that most children under six would not be able to conserve, but many psychologists have found that younger children are able to conserve.

Piaget's test to demonstrate conservation

Volume

1 Children are shown two identical beakers with the same amount of drink in them.

2 One of the drinks is poured into a taller, thinner beaker in front of the child.

3 Children are asked if there is any difference in the amount of drink.

Children who can **conserve** know that there is still the same amount of drink.

Mass

1 Children are shown two identical balls of dough.

2 One piece of dough is flattened or rolled into a sausage shape in front of the child.

3 Children are asked if they are the same or different.

A child who can **conserve** understands that the amount of dough is still the same, but the shape has changed.

Number

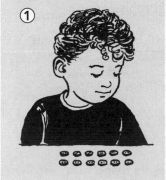 

1 Children are shown two lines of buttons or counters.

2 One line is spaced out in front of the child.

3 Children are asked if there are still the same number of buttons.

Children who can **conserve** know that as nothing has been taken away, the same amount is still there.

Observation

Try out one of the conservation tests with three or four children of different ages between three and seven years.

■ Make sure that the children see you change the objects – for example, pouring the drink into another container.

■ Ask the children if there is any difference in the amounts.

■ Ask the children why they have come to their conclusions.

Interpretation
■ Were children under six years able to conserve?

■ Did the children hesitate in their answers?

■ Look at the table below and consider which stage these children are in.

Piaget's four cognitive stages of learning

Stage	Age	Title	Stage of learning
1	0–18 months/ 2 years	Sensory motor	■ Babies learn about their environment from their senses. ■ They are **egocentric** – they see the world from their viewpoint only. ■ At around eight months they start to develop the idea that a person or object they cannot see still exists – **object permanence**. ■ They learn mainly from trial and error methods.
2	2–6/7 years	Pre-operational	■ Children are using language to express their thoughts. ■ They are starting to use symbols in play – e.g. a stick becomes a wand. ■ They are **egocentric** – seeing things from their viewpoint only. ■ They tend to think that non-living things and animals have the same feelings as them – **animism.** For example, a child might draw a picture of a worm with a smile. ■ They tend to be taken in by how things look and appear.
3	7–11	Concrete operations	■ Children can see things from another's point of view – **decentring**. ■ Children can reason more easily and are less fooled by appearances. They are able to **conserve**. ■ Children can use abstract symbols – e.g. mathematical signs and writing – and are developing complex reasoning skills. They still need physical objects to solve some problems – e.g. counters. ■ They understand that non-living objects do not have feelings.
4	11–18+	Formal operations	■ Children are able to think in the abstract. This means that they can manipulate ideas in their head – e.g. solve sums in their head. ■ Children are more logical and methodical when trying to solve a problem – e.g. not using a trial and error approach. ■ Piaget suggested that not everyone would move on to this stage.

Piaget's ideas that children go through stages of development have been influential, although there are three main criticisms of his work.

1 His suggested ages of the stages underestimate children's abilities. In subsequent testing, children have often been able to conserve and decentre at much younger ages than he suggested. In part, this may be due to the way that he tested children.

2 Some psychologists feel that the idea of stages is not accurate and that children learn as more of an ongoing process.

3 Piaget's work has also been criticised as being culturally biased as he used white European children for his studies, including his own daughter.

Nevertheless most psychologists accept Piaget's starting point that children are active in their own development and use their experiences to develop their understanding of the world.

Vygotsky's theory of cognitive development

Vygotsky (1896–1934) and Piaget were working on similar lines, but Vygotsky's work was unknown in the West until it was translated from Russian in 1962. Vygotsky – like Piaget – suggested that children were active in their learning, although he placed much more emphasis on the role language played in the cognitive process. The social development of the child is also an important part of cognitive development as the child is seen as an apprentice, learning with the help of sensitive adults through language.

Observation

There are many observations that can be carried out with children aged two to seven who are in the pre-operational stage.

Animism

Ask some children aged between three and five to draw you some pictures of animals.

▩ Do the children represent these animals with smiles or expressions?

▩ Ask the children why they have given them these expressions.

▩ To make your observation fuller, you should also be looking to see what fine manipulative skills the children are using.

Decentring

Psychologists carry out a test called the Sally-Anne test, which you can do with individual children. It is a good idea to do this separately with a number of children of different ages.

Show the child two dolls.

Tell the child that one doll is called Sally and the other is called Anne.

Give both dolls a box or a basket. Put a counter in Sally's basket.

Tell the child that Sally is going for a walk and remove her from sight.

Tell the child that while Sally is not there, Anne sneaks up and takes away Sally's counter and puts it in her own box. Show this to the child.

Ask the child where Sally will look for her counter when she comes back

Children who can decentre will know that Sally will look in her own box. Children who cannot decentre will say that Sally will go and look in Anne's box.

Vygotsky is particularly noted for his idea that children had unlocked potential that adults had to discover. This is referred to as the Zone of Proximal Development (ZPD). The ZPD is the gap between what the child is currently able to do and what he has the potential to do. In some ways, the ZPD is like a bud waiting to flower and providing the adults tend to the plant, the bud will open. Vygotsky's work influenced other psychologists such as Jerome Bruner.

Bruner's theory of cognitive development

Jerome Bruner (1915–) agreed with many areas of Piaget's work, but built on the ideas of Vygotsky. He too felt that children organised according to their experiences and that they are active in their learning. He did not agree that children passed through stages, but rather that they developed different ways of thinking. He called these modes of representation. There are three modes; children start with one mode and gradually develop the other two. We can use all three modes as adults.

A major difference between Piaget and Bruner was the link between language and thought. Bruner thought that the appearance of language allowed children to think in a symbolic mode because language allows us to categorise things. He also felt that adults have an important role to play in this process. Children can be helped to learn how to use symbols and thus speed up the cognitive process. For Piaget, the adult's intervention would make no difference because children would not be able to use symbols until they were biologically ready.

The role of the adult
Bruner felt that adults need to be active in helping and encouraging children in their learning. He talked about **scaffolding** – the idea of helping children to find their way to the top of a problem. Adults make the scaffold by providing elements of a problem, maintaining children's interest and pointing out information or giving support that will allow them to increase their knowledge and reasoning.

An example of this would be if an adult provided a child with some materials and asked the child to make a bed for a cat. Rather than leaving the child with the problem, the adult could guide the child.

- What sort of bed do you think cats like?
- How big do you think the bed needs to be?
- Shall I show you how to use these scissors?

The aim of the adult is not to teach children, but to allow them to reach their own solutions.

Bruner also felt that older children, or children who had gained a concept, could 'tutor' other children.

Bruner's three modes of representation

Mode	Approximate ages (although adults might use all three modes)	Description and use
Enactive	0–1	Information is stored according to physical movements. When something has to be remembered, the movement is recreated. Adults may still use the enactive mode to learn physical skills such as icing a cake and wall papering.
Iconic	1–7	Information is stored using images which may be based on smell, hearing or touch. A smell may trigger a memory.
Symbolic	7 onwards	As not everything can be pictured, we use symbols such as language, music and numbers to store information.

Cognitive development and concepts

Many people confuse cognitive development and intelligence. Cognitive development is about the process of thinking, organising information and learning abstract concepts. There is a link between cognitive development and intelligence, although defining what we mean by intelligence is quite difficult.

What do we mean by an abstract concept?

Part of the process of cognitive development involves being able to understand abstract ideas or concepts.

An example of an abstract concept is blue.

> Look at three blue things in the room you are in. They are likely to be different shades.
>
> How did you know they were blue?
>
> If you had to explain what makes something blue, you would find it difficult. You simply know that blue is blue!

Colours are examples of concepts. Your brain has learnt to categorise and store information which means that you are able to look at a colour and name it.

Concepts that children need to learn

Children need to learn many concepts. Some concepts they will learn just through seeing and experiencing. Other concepts will be learnt through

---

ISSUES   Measuring intelligence

From the beginning of the 20th century, it was thought that intelligence in children could be measured. This was a very attractive idea, because, if it was possible to know how intelligent a child was, schools could group children according to their potential. The first intelligence tests were developed by two French men in 1905 called Binet and Simon with the aim of looking to see which children would have difficulty in school. The test concentrated on measuring vocabulary, and mathematical and verbal reasoning.

The Binet-Simon test was revised by an American team of psychologists in the 1930s and became known as the Stanford-Binet test. In the 1950s, Britain's secondary education system was based on the principle of intelligence-testing at the age of eleven. Following an examination – commonly called the Eleven Plus – children were put into either grammar schools – which followed an academic curriculum – or secondary modern schools – which were supposed to be more practical.

Unfortunately, these tests were found to be measuring not intelligence but children's knowledge and language skills. This disadvantaged children who had potential but whose language skills were underdeveloped. Children who did not pass the test often felt that they had failed in some way and in the 1970s testing in this way was phased out.

Nowadays, intelligence-testing is treated with much caution and the latest theories of intelligence suggest that there may be different types of intelligence. This would explain why some people are talented in one area but may have difficulties in other cognitive areas – for example, talented artists might find it difficult to organise and understand their business affairs because they had poor mathematical reasoning.

To find out more about this theory of intelligence, you could read about Sternberg's triarchic theory of intelligence – for example, in *The Developing Child* by Helen Bee (Addison-Wesley, 1996).

1   If there were a perfect test, do you think that children should be tested?
2   Are there any dangers in testing for intelligence?

being supported by the adults around them. Adults have a key role in doing this. In many ways, adults should see themselves as supporters rather than as teachers. The idea of supporting children is sometimes called **facilitating**. The idea behind facilitating is that the adult should be there to provide activities, equipment and encouragement which, in turn, allows children to explore their world. It is generally accepted that young children need to be active in their learning. They need to do, rather than watch! (See also page 136 for activities and methods of working with children.)

The spider diagram below shows some of the key concepts that children learn during their early years.

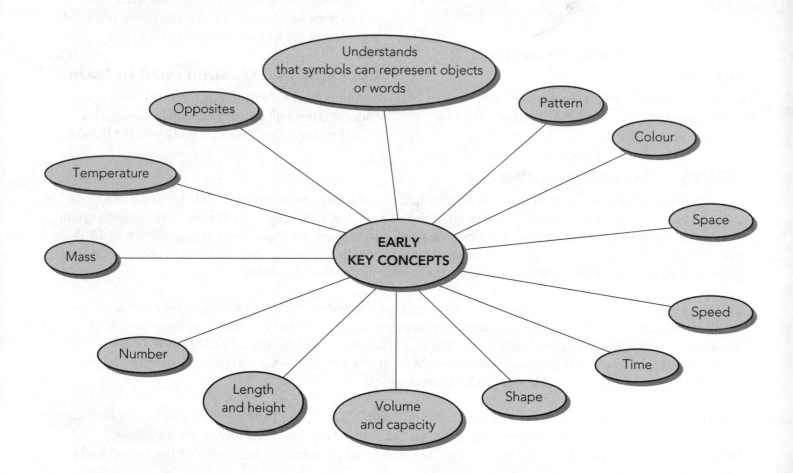

Stages and sequences of cognitive development

It is very difficult to give milestones for cognitive development as children's acquisition of concepts depends on their play experiences and their own individual pattern of development. The chart opposite attempts to look at some of the stages and ages of learning concepts. It is based on some of the work done by NFER/Nelson which is often used in devising portage programmes (see page 28).

Activities and equipment to help cognitive development

There are some activities and pieces of equipment that can help children's cognitive development. A major part in the thinking process is the ability to classify, store and retrieve information. This means that activities that encourage children to have any of these skills are particularly valuable.

Probable sequence of tasks in children aged 0–6 years

Age	Probable sequence of tasks
0–1 years	■ Looks for an object that has been removed ■ Places an object in a container when asked ■ Finds an object that has been seen and then hidden
1–2 years	■ Takes out objects one by one from container ■ Points to parts of the body ■ Scribbles ■ Points to a named picture
2–3 years	■ Completes a three-piece puzzle ■ Copies a circle ■ Matches textures ■ Is able to point to little and big – e.g. 'Which is the big teddy?' ■ Matches three colours ■ Stacks beakers in order
3–4 years	■ Tells if an object is light or heavy ■ Is able to repeat a simple story ■ Matches one to one – e.g. putting a cup with each saucer ■ Points to long and short objects ■ Is able to sort out simple objects ■ Knows primary colours ■ Names three shapes ■ Counts ten objects with support
4–5 years	■ Picks up a number of objects – e.g. 'Find me four cubes.' ■ Names five textures ■ Names times of day associated with activities e.g. bedtime, dinner time ■ Names eight colours ■ Matches symbols (letters and numbers) ■ Is able to decide which object is the heavier ■ Places objects beside, behind and next to ■ Counts by rote up to twenty
5–6 years	■ Counts accurately up to 20 items ■ Prints own name ■ Arranges objects in order of size ■ Names days of week in order ■ Tells month and day of birthday ■ Sight reads ten or more words ■ Predicts what happens next ■ Points to half and whole objects e.g. half a cake ■ Counts up to a hundred by rote

Activities and equipment to help promote cognitive development

Construction toys	Concepts	Cognitive skills
Puzzles Shape sorters Tray puzzles 3-piece puzzles 12-piece puzzles 3-D puzzles	Children learn about shape and space. They also learn to sort and match. As they become older, trial and error learning will decrease as they start to use reasoning skills to work out the position of pieces.	■ Classifying ■ Attention and concentration
Sorting objects Buttons Plastic shapes	Children are able to sort, order and classify objects according to colour, shape or size. Children can be asked to find all the blue cars or all the yellow buttons.	■ Classifying ■ Attention and concentration
Sewing cards **Threading beads**	Children learn about patterns and also colours.	■ Classifying ■ Attention and concentration
Kim's game	This is the game where objects are put on a tray and then one is removed. The children have to work out which one is missing.	■ Memory ■ Attention and concentration
Construction toys Duplo Lego Wooden bricks Popoids	Children learn about space, shape and structures. They can also experience matching and sorting as well as being encouraged to think about size.	■ Classifying ■ Attention and concentration
Matching games Lotto Pairs Pelmanism Snap	These types of game help children sort and match. Pelmanism can help children's memories as they work out where they have seen a matching card – cards are put face down; children choose a card and then work out where its partner is.	■ Classifying ■ Memory ■ Attention and concentration
Feely bags	These encourage children to use their senses to work out what object is in a bag.	■ Classifying ■ Memory ■ Attention and concentration

Factors affecting cognitive development

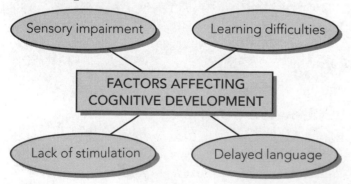

Not all children will show the expected sequence of cognitive development. There are many reasons why this may happen

Learning difficulties

Some children do not show the expected cognitive development because they have learning difficulties. There are many causes of learning difficulties, including: inherited conditions such as Fragile X syndrome; brain damage as a result of an accident; oxygen deprivation at birth.

Sensory impairment

Children with a sensory impairment may show some delay in cognitive development because, in the early years of a child's life, the central nervous system that processes information relies heavily on the senses to bring in information. Children who have severe sensory impairments, such as complete hearing loss, are usually identified quickly by routine surveillance tests. It is common for very slight impairments to be missed, so it is essential that early years workers look for any signs that a child may have a sensory impairment. A child, for example, who appears to be clumsy might actually have a visual impairment which means he is not able to see things clearly.

Delayed language

In children's early years, language and thought are closely linked. Very young children cannot, for example, keep their 'thoughts' inside themselves until they are around five years old. They express their thoughts in words, sometimes quite embarrassingly! It is therefore common to find that children with language delay may also show some signs of delay in their conceptual development.

Good practice when working with children who are showing developmental delay

✔ Choose activities that are practical.

✔ Check that activities are suitable for the child's current level of understanding.

✔ Repeat activities frequently.

✔ Break down concepts and activities into smaller steps.

✔ Look for plenty of different ways of presenting the same concept.

✔ Avoid children becoming frustrated and tired by an activity.

✔ Praise children for their efforts.

Why is stimulation essential?

We have seen that children need to be active in their learning and that adults need to provide activities and opportunities that will help them to learn some key concepts. The early years worker has an important role in this as long-term damage can occur when children are not given such stimulation. Children who are not given challenging learning and play opportunities will find it difficult to achieve their full potential and may develop worrying behavioural patterns.

Disruptive/attention-seeking behaviour

Some behavioural difficulties are caused by lack of stimulation. This is particularly well documented in older children who can become disruptive and attention-seeking in their behaviour. They may not settle down to work and so falsely lead adults into believing they are not capable of doing the work. Their challenging behaviour may also lead to adults disciplining them, which in turn may lead to their developing a low self-esteem.

Case study

Jack was a classic case of poor behaviour resulting from a lack of stimulation. He was five years old and particularly disruptive in the classroom. He would not settle down to a task and stopped other children from working. Staff working at the school began to believe that Jack must have some major learning difficulty. His teacher and mother met to talk about Jack's behaviour. During the conversation, his mother revealed that, from the age of two, Jack had been able to do complex jigsaw puzzles. He even did them face down, without a picture, to make them harder. Although the mother did not see the significance of her remark, this information made the teacher realise that she was probably working with a child who was particularly able and that the tasks in class had been too easy for Jack, thus contributing to his behaviour. Jack's behaviour improved dramatically once he was given more demanding activities.
(The story of Jack is a true case history.)

Withdrawn behaviour

Most people daydream because their attention has wandered, but sometimes under-stimulation can cause children to withdraw more permanently.

They seem to retreat to their own worlds and gradually become less and less communicative and sociable. The effects of this withdrawn behaviour can be long-term as, during this time, children are missing out on opportunities of learning to socialise and use language.

Regression and reliance on comfort habits

In extreme cases, such as those seen in orphanages in Romania in the early 1990s, children whose cognitive development is not being stimulated may repeatedly show comfort behaviour – for example, rocking, head banging and masturbation. In these cases, children are gaining stimulation from sensory experiences in the absence of cognitive ones being provided for them.

Knowledge into action

It is important to provide practical activities that will help children understand concepts such as colour.

Choose one of the following concepts.

- *colour*
- *size*
- *shape.*

Plan two practical activities to develop this concept for each of the following age groups.

- *2–3 years*
- *3–5 years*
- *5–7 years.*

Check your knowledge

- Explain the links between attention and concentration, and cognitive development.

- Why are Pavlov's dogs famous?

- Outline the way in which Bandura was able to show that children learn from watching others.

- What are Piaget's four stages of cognitive development?

- Describe one test that is used to see whether children can conserve.

- What are the main criticisms of Piaget's work?

- What is meant by the expression 'Zone of Proximal Development'?

- Name four concepts that children need to learn about.

- Why do young children need to learn by doing, rather than by being taught?

- Choose four pieces of equipment and explain why they might encourage children's cognitive development.

- Describe three factors that might affect children's cognitive development.

- Is it possible to measure children's intelligence?

- Why is memory so important to children's cognitive development?

Resources

Further reading

Bee, Helen *The Developing Child*, London, Harper Collins
(At the time of writing, this book was out of print, but you should be able to get hold of a copy from a library.)

Flanagan, Cara 1996 *Applying Psychology to Early Child Development*, London, Hodder and Stoughton

Gross, Richard 1996 *Psychology – The Science of Mind and Behaviour*, London, Hodder and Stoughton

Mc Iven, Rob & Richard Gross 1997 *Developmental Psychology*, London, Hodder and Stoughton

The developing child

Language development

As a professional working with children you need to understand how children learn to communicate and also the ways in which adults can promote children's language development.

What is meant by language?

One might think that language is about being able to talk. This is not the case: language is about being able to communicate. Although at first most children will use speech to communicate, it is important not to forget that reading, writing and signing are all ways of communicating with others. Deaf children may use a sign language such as British Sign Language (BSL) to express themselves and to understand others, while children with multiple disabilities may use a computer to write and receive messages.

These are the common features of any language:

◾ It is a way of communicating.

◾ It has rules that are understood by those using it.

◾ It is made up of sounds, gestures and symbols that have meaning for those using it.

◾ It allows the user to be creative and expressive – i.e. a user can make up and use his/her own sentences, provided that they fit the overall 'rules' so that others can understand.

For children to learn a language, they need to learn the rules – or grammar – of a language as well as the meanings of words. This is a gradual process for children and one in which adults have an important role.

The uses of language

We use language in many ways. It helps us to socialise, express our needs and recount events to others. Psychologists, such as L S Vygotsky (1896–1934) and J S Bruner (1915–) have suggested that there is a further link between language and cognitive development. Vygotsky thought that by the age of two or three years, children use language to help them control their behaviour and thoughts. This would explain why children of this age often direct themselves by talking out loud.

Children often talk to their toys – this can be an important part of the learning experience

Stages and sequences of language

Humans are not unique in being able to communicate with each other. Animals, such as whales and even

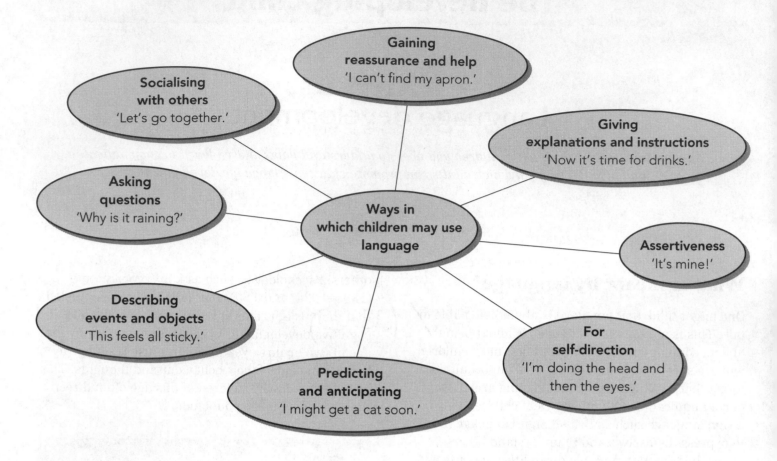

bees, are able to pass information to each other. This has made some psychologists, such as A N Chomsky (1928–), wonder whether we are born with an instinct to learn language. He called this instinct a **language acquisition device**.

Observation

Carry out an event sample on a three- or four-year-old for at least an hour. Note down each time the child uses language. Analyse in your interpretation the ways in which she used language. Look at the stages and sequences of language development in the chart on page 143 and consider where this child's development fits.

(For information about how to carry out event samples see page 92.)

Other psychologists, such as B F Skinner (1904–1990), have suggested that children learn language in the same way that they learn other skills – by reinforcement. For example, a baby gurgles, and the parent smiles at the baby; the baby is pleased to gain the attention and repeats these sounds; the baby's behaviour has been reinforced.

Although the way in which children learn language is not fully understood, they seem to pass through stages and sequences of development.

Stages of language development

The chart below shows the sequence in which children learn to communicate with others. As with other areas of development, it is important to remember that children vary in the speed with which they reach these milestones. This means that some children of eighteen months may have twenty or more words, whereas other children of the same age may be using ten.

Pre-linguistic stage	
0–3 months	■ Cries to show hunger, tiredness and distress. ■ Recognises different tones of voices. ■ Coos and gurgles when content. ■ By three months can recognise carer's voice and is soothed by it. ■ Smiles in response to others' faces.
3–6 months	■ Still cries to show distress, but is more easily soothed. ■ Babbles and coos. ■ Babbles consist of short sounds – e.g. 'ma ma da da'. ■ Laughs, chuckles and even squeals.
6–12 months	■ Babbling makes up half of a baby's non-crying sounds. ■ Strings vowels and consonants together to make repetitive sounds – e.g. 'mememememe, dadadadadada'. ■ Babbling becomes more tuneful and inventive and by nine months most of the sounds used are the ones needed for the language being learnt. ■ At ten months understands about seventeen words – e.g. 'Bye bye.' ■ Uses gestures to ask for things – e.g. points hand and whines to show adult what he wants. ■ Enjoys games – e.g. Pat-a-cake.
Linguistic stage	
First words **12–18 months**	■ First words appear at around twelve months, although will only be recognisable as a word to carer – e.g. 'dede' to mean drink. ■ Words are used to mean more than one thing depending on the intonation the baby uses – e.g. 'dede' is used to mean 'I want a drink,' 'My drink is finished' or 'I want more drink.' (Linguists call these one-word expressions *holophrases*.) ■ By fifteen months children will have about ten words that their carers can understand.
18–24 months	■ Two words are put together – e.g. 'Bye bye dog.' ■ Telegraphic speech appears, with children using key words in a grammatical way – e.g. 'Dada come.' ■ Children's vocabulary increases with children learning 10–30 words in a month. ■ By two years, most children have 200 words.
2–3 years	■ Quickly learns new words. ■ Uses plurals – e.g. 'dogs'. ■ Makes errors – e.g. 'sheeps', 'drawed'. ■ Starts to use negatives – e.g. 'There no cats.' ■ Starts to use questions – e.g. 'Where cats?'
3–4 years	■ Imitates adult speech patterns accurately – e.g. 'We liked that, didn't we?' ■ Speech is understood by strangers. ■ Sentences contain four or more words and are grammatical. ■ Vocabulary is large, with children knowing parts of their bodies, names of household objects, animals. ■ Errors are still made especially when using past tenses – e.g. 'I taked it.' ■ Knows and understands nursery rhymes. ■ Enjoys asking questions.

Linguistic stage *(continued)*	
4–8 years	■ From four years on, children develop and refine language. Mistakes become fewer and children start to enjoy using language as a means of socialising with others, expressing their needs and recounting what they have done. ■ By five years, vocabulary is about 5000 words. ■ Uses complex sentences correctly. ■ Enjoys telling and hearing jokes. ■ Understands that language can be written with symbols. ■ By eight years, most children are fluent speakers, readers and developing writers of their language.

Pre-linguistic stage

The first stage in the process of children learning to use a language is often referred to as the pre-linguistic stage. This is an important stage, because, although babies are not able to use the rules and words of the language, they seem to use this stage to learn about *how* to communicate. Psychologists have noticed that this pre-linguistic stage is common to all languages and that the early babbles of babies all over the world are similar. This supports the idea that we are born with some instinct to communicate with others.

During the first year of life, babies rapidly learn how to communicate with their carers, so that by the age of twelve months, most babies understand what is being said to them and are starting to communicate their needs by pointing or by showing their carer objects.

Linguistic stage

At around twelve months, children start to use words. They develop their own word for an object or person and use it consistently. Often it is only the carers who can understand what is meant by this word. Children then go on to use **holophrases** – using a single word to express several meanings by changing the sound and using gestures. Gradually children put two words together to form a mini-sentence – for example, 'Drink no.' Linguists call these two-word sentences **telegraphic speech**. Telegraphic speech allows children to be more expressive and gradually verbs

This baby is in the pre-linguistic stage of development and learning how to communicate with his carer

appear in speech as well as nouns – for example, 'Dada gone.' or 'See cat.'

Learning the rules

The rules of a language – the grammar – are learnt gradually. Children imitate the word order that they hear, but often cut down the length of the phrase. An adult may say 'Look at that poor cat,' but the child will say 'Poor cat.' While learning the rules of a language, children often make mistakes. Roger Brown (1925–), who looked closely at children's speech, called these mistakes **virtuous errors**. He suggested children made these errors because they were trying to apply what they knew to all situations. For example, a child might use and hear the word 'played'. The child then adds -ed to all verbs when trying to express something that has happened – you may have heard children say 'I swimmed a long way,' or 'I maked it.' These are examples of virtuous errors and as children gain more experience in using language, they will disappear.

Components of language development

Although we have looked at the stages of language development in children, it is important to understand that in many ways language development is like a jigsaw puzzle and there are many parts to it.

Listening

Listening is an important skill for children to master. To listen means to take notice of another person's communication. For children with sensory impairment, 'listening' may mean following another's signs or lip-reading. Relationship counsellors suggest that people do not spend enough time listening to others and this often means that relationships fail. Active listening means showing someone that you understand what they are saying by nodding your head, smiling and repeating or 'reflecting' back phrases that they have said:

But really the other person should be listening!

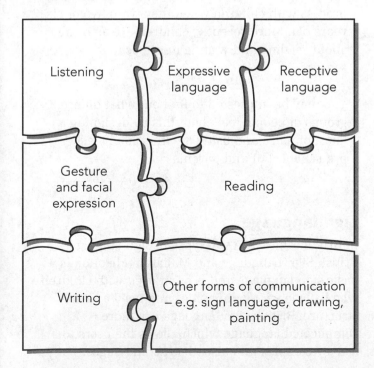

Receptive and expressive language

Receptive language is the phrases and vocabulary that we understand, whereas expressive language is what we actually use. This means that you may not use a phrase such as 'Thanking you kindly,' but you are able to understand it.

When children are acquiring new language, first it becomes part of their receptive language and then, when they know how and when to use it, it becomes part of their expressive or active language. If you have learnt another language, you may remember being able to understand some of it, although you could not speak it.

Knowledge into action

Listening is a skill that tends to be underdeveloped in adults as well as in children!

Try out your active listening skills with a partner for three minutes. See if you can listen to them talk about one of these subjects:

Family
College
The last good film they saw.

To check that you have listened actively repeat back the gist of what you have heard.

Facial expression and gesture

Children need to learn to read others' facial expressions and gestures in order to communicate effectively. Babies are quick to learn this skill and will smile in response to seeing an adult smile. Imaginative play, using equipment such as a home corner or small world toys, helps children to explore gesture and facial expressions.

Collections/Sandra Lousada   *Collections/Fiona Pragoff*   *Collections/Lesley Howling*

Can you read these people's expressions?

Children who are exposed to more than one culture need to learn that facial expressions and gestures are not universal – for example, in some cultures, eye contact when talking to an adult is considered to show lack of respect.

Some children with communication difficulties – for example, autistic children – can find it difficult to correctly read the faces and expressions of others.

Reading and writing

Our society today is a literate one. Being able to read and write is considered an essential skill. Think of the number of signs, labels, books and instructions that you have read in the past week. Most children learn to read and write once they have mastered the spoken word. Studies have repeatedly shown that children who start school with good language skills learn to read and write more quickly. To read and write a child needs to understand that symbols can have meaning, and so need to have reached this stage in their cognitive development. Jean Piaget (1896–1980) and J S Bruner (1915–) suggested that most children are ready to do this when they are seven years old. In contrast to Britain, most other European countries do not attempt to teach reading until children are six years old.

ISSUES in child care and education

There has been fierce debate around the age at which children in this country should be taught to read and write. Traditionally, schools began this process with children when they were five or six years old. More recently, children are learning about reading and writing in pre-school settings.

You may be interested to find out what different groups of people feel about this by designing a questionnaire and using it with school teachers, pre-school staff and parents.

Sign language

In Britain, there are two types of sign language – British Sign Language and Makaton. Makaton is a basic sign language and is often used with children who have learning difficulties and need a simple structure. British sign language is a more complicated language which allows the users to convey complex and also abstract messages.

Signing is used with children who have difficulty in using the spoken word. As a language, signing is not as versatile as other languages because there is a limited vocabulary. This means that facial expression and gesture play an important part in the communication process.

It is a good idea to learn some signs so that you can greet parents or children who sign.

Other forms of communication – drawing and painting

Cave drawings and scrolls show us that drawing and painting have been used as a method of communication for thousands of years. Children often use drawing and painting as a way of expression and communication. In the same way that children develop languages in stages, children also seem to pass through drawing stages.

Scribble stage

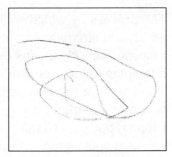

Circular shapes emerge within the scribbling

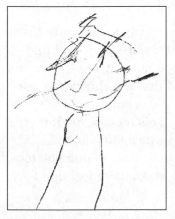

Circular shapes become more regular and lines are added that eventually represent features and limbs

Trunk and more features are added

Children start to draw more items such as houses, trees and birds

Stages of drawing

Most children start by drawing themselves or their carers.

From six years onwards, some children become reluctant to continue drawing. One suggestion is that the decline in children's motivation to draw may partly be a result of mastering reading and writing.

Multilingual children

Some children speak more than one language. They may use one language at home, another at school and a third as part of their religion. Children who are able to use two languages are known as bilingual, whereas children who are able to use three or more languages are considered to be multilingual. Although cognitive development is closely linked to language, psychologists are unsure whether the ability to use more than one language makes any difference to a child's achievement. Studies have shown that some bilingual and multilingual children may be more creative in their thinking, although if the children's home languages are not valued, they may actually underachieve. (See section on racism and multilingualism, page 149.)

Contexts in which children are multilingual

There are many bilingual and multilingual children in Britain: some children will be part of larger cultural communities such as Bangladeshi, whereas other children will have learnt another language from one of their parents. It is important to understand the different contexts in which multilingual children live, as children will have different needs depending on their circumstances. There are three broad contexts in which children use other languages.

Large cultural communities

In some towns and cities, there are large cultural groups living together that speak languages other than English. Children from these communities often have a rich home language and may come into settings with some English, but needing support as they have grown up mostly hearing the home language used by the community.

Dispersed cultural communities

Case study

Dora lives with her parents and grandmother who own a restaurant. At home, she speaks Greek, but in the restaurant she hears her parents speak English. She goes to a school where there are no other Greek-speaking children, although on Sundays and at other times she meets other Greek families in the area as there is a small but thriving community of Greeks.

There are many small cultural communities living in towns and cities, who do not necessarily live near each other, but spend time together – examples of these communities include Greek, Turkish and Chinese. Children from these families will be exposed to both English and the parents' home language. This may mean that they come into settings with a good knowledge of both languages, although the home language will be dominant.

Isolated speakers

Case study

Marie-Lise speaks French to her mother and English to her father. Most of the time she hears English as her mother and father communicate in English and her mother has little social contact with other French people in the area.

There are many children who have one parent whose first language is not English. These children are spoken to in another language. Children growing up in such families will probably have considerable understanding of English as they will hear it alongside the other language and quite often English will become the dominant language as they will not hear enough of the other language.

Understanding the language development of multilingual children

Children who are learning more than one language at a time tend to be slightly slower in learning to talk and communicate. It is thought that this is because the child is having to absorb more than one language system. This early delay in speaking does not affect children's overall language development, provided they are given adequate support.

The process by which young children learn additional languages is through absorption and association. This means that they gradually associate a language with a person or a situation and are able to respond in the language they hear. In the same way that you might use the word 'Ta' with your friends, but use 'Thank you' with your lecturers, children learn which phrases to use with non-English speakers and which phrases to use with English speakers.

Although some young children may speak more than one language, it is not until they are older that they start to understand that they are using more than one language. Most children find that it is difficult to use their home language in situations where they are used to speaking in English. This means that if they are asked what the word for saucepan is in their home language, they may not be able to immediately think of the word. This may make them feel that they are failing in some way.

By the age of eight, children will understand that they are using more than one language and start to be aware of equivalent words and phrases – for example that saying 'Merci' to their father, is the same as saying 'Thank you' to an English speaker.

Children need to master their home language

It is now widely recognised that in order for most multilingual children to achieve, their home language also needs to be supported. Studies have shown that unless a child has mastered one language he will find it difficult to make progress in others. This is why in some settings where there are children who have little English, teachers are employed who can carry on supporting the child's home language. Some communities organise after-school activities in order that the child can learn to read and write in her home language.

Racism and multilingual children

It is sad that, instead of valuing all children who can speak more than one language, the approach often taken in our society is to value some languages and not others. Society often sees the ability to speak a European language, such as French or German, as an advantage, whereas speaking Punjabi or Urdu may not be valued in the same way.

Speaking another language is actually part of a child's self-identity so, when a child's home language is not recognised or valued, the child is being sent the message: 'We don't care about your family or your culture.'

Emotional and social needs of children

It is important to recognise that children who are multilingual will have emotional and social needs as well as needs connected with their language development.

Common feelings amongst children who speak more than one language include:

Embarrassment

Children may feel embarrassed and different from other children. They may pretend that they do not speak another language.

Rejection

Children may feel that their home language, and consequently their home life, is not important and valued. This is particularly true of children who speak non-European languages. Staff may stop children from speaking together in their home language.

Helping children who are multilingual

Not mixing languages

To help very young children learn which language they should be using, it is important that the people around them stay in one language – for example, an English speaker should not start speaking to them in their home language. This prevents children from mixing up their languages.

Gaps in vocabulary

As children are learning languages by association and absorption, they may find themselves in some situations where they have a word in only one language. A child may know the word for bed in his home language as this word is used at home, but not know the word in English. Similarly, children may wish to tell their parents that they have been playing with Playdough but know this word only in English.

> ## Think about it
>
> With a partner, continue this list of words or phrases that are mostly used in school settings.
>
> - Book corner
> - Assembly
> - Lining up time.
>
> Now continue this list of words and phrases that are mostly used at home.
>
> - Pillowcase
> - Settee
> - Doorbell.

If children are unable to find the words and phrases they need to express themselves, there is a danger that they will stop talking about what they are doing. This means they may not tell their parents what they have been doing, or that they may never talk about their home life in settings. Many settings used to working with multilingual children aim to involve parents in the setting in order to solve this problem. Parents may be asked if they would like to spend some time in the setting or early years workers may work with parents to make sure that children learn the English words that are used at home.

The importance of having a multicultural ethos

In many ways, helping children who are multilingual is about creating an atmosphere in which they feel comfortable. Settings that have a good understanding of equal opportunities will be able to do this easily, as they will already have activities and materials that promote an understanding of different cultures and languages. (See Chapter 2 on promoting multicultural awareness.)

Being sensitive to children's needs

An early years worker needs to be sensitive to the needs of individual multilingual children in the same way as to those of any other child. It is important that the child does not feel like a 'party turn' because he can speak another language. There may be some children who are keen to stand up and sing a song in their home language, whereas for another child this would be embarrassing.

The most useful way of helping children feel comfortable in a setting is to build a good relationship with them. This may mean spending some time playing or talking to the children by themselves and encouraging them to talk about their family. Children can sense when someone really cares for them and this 'caring' is, in the end, the best way to help children value themselves and their culture.

Involving and valuing parents

All children need to see that their parents are liked and valued. If the setting is able to build a relationship with parents, multilingual children will be more likely to value their language.

There are many ways in which this relationship can be established – for example, parents could come in to help or early years workers could ask the parents if they would like to see some of the activities that the child has been carrying out.

Language delay in children

There are many reasons why children's language may be delayed, including:

- physical conditions – e.g. a cleft palate or enlarged tongue
- learning difficulties – e.g. autism
- hearing impairments, either temporary – e.g. glue ear – or permanent
- stutters or stammers
- shyness
- lack of stimulation and language input
- more than one language being learnt.

Hearing impairments

Hearing difficulties are a common reason for children's language being delayed. Not all hearing difficulties are permanent, as children who have had repeated colds can build up fluid in their ears, which can cause a slight hearing loss.

It is important for early years workers to be aware of some of the indicators of a child not hearing well. Sometimes parents may not have spotted that their child has a hearing loss, believing that the child's lack of response is due to naughtiness or deep concentration.

Possible signs that children are not hearing well include:

- lack of response when name is called
- looking at speaker's mouth intently
- appearing to be in own world
- lack of interest in formal group activities – e.g. story time
- appearing to be forgetful when given instructions
- mispronouncing names and words.

If a child seems to have some of these signs, you should mention your concerns to your supervisor or to the parent, if this is appropriate.

Overall development and language delay

There is a strong link between language and children's overall development. Children need language in order to socialise with each other, express their needs and develop their thought processes.

If language is delayed, children are more likely to have some behavioural difficulties stemming from frustration.

Common behavioural difficulties linked to language delay include:

- clinging
- tearfulness
- aggressiveness – biting, hitting, throwing objects
- difficulties in socialising with peers.

Difficulties in communication

If children have language difficulties, it is important for early years workers to be sensitive to their needs. Parents and other professionals are often able to give advice about how to help a child communicate. Strategies will vary from child to child. Some children may take you to the objects that they want, whereas others may show you what they need by looking or pointing to it. Working with children with language difficulties requires a flexible, calm and patient

Makaton can help children overcome communication difficulties

approach. Early years workers may need to spend some time playing and working with individual children or staying alongside them as they join in a group. Children will often become frustrated when they cannot make themselves understood and will need reassurance and understanding rather than being disciplined.

For children who have communication and learning difficulties, programmes such as Makaton can help. Makaton was designed to develop communication, language and literacy and today is a popular and widely used total communication programme, which uses speech, signs and written symbols and can help children to develop and overcome their communication difficulties.

Stutters or stammers

It is common for young children to stutter or stammer. This often happens because their minds are working more quickly than their tongues or they are afraid that another child will interrupt them. Most children grow out of this, but for some children, stuttering and stammering becomes a habit.

Early years workers can help children by showing them that they are listening to them. This can be done by making good eye contact, sitting down with the child and smiling. The aim is to relax the child and therefore calm their speech. It is not considered good practice to finish off children's sentences – this is likely to make them more worried about being interrupted.

Children who have persistent difficulties are likely to be referred to a speech therapist.

Specialist help

Children with delayed language are often referred to a speech therapist. A speech therapist will devise an individual programme for a child. For example, a child who has difficulty in pronouncing some sounds would be given exercises to correct this.

In some cases early years workers will be asked to carry out the child's programme or will be given advice about how to support the child.

Promoting children's language

Adults have a strong role in helping children's language to develop. This role begins at birth, when parents and carers talk to babies in a special way. This is called Motherese or Baby Talk Register. This way of communicating with babies and young children helps them to learn words and phrases, because sentences are simplified, short and repetitive – for example, 'Look at the duck. It's a big duck, isn't it? Look, the duck is coming here. Say hello to the duck.'

Age	Role of adult
0–6 months	■ Good eye contact, running commentary and repetition of phrases – e.g. 'I think you're feeling hungry now, aren't you? Are you hungry?' ■ As babies begin to babble they need praise and recognition that they are trying to communicate.
6–12 months	■ Getting down to the level of the child and making eye contact is important. ■ Children need to feel they are being understood and listened to. ■ Sometimes children will point to objects and want the adult to follow them or pick up the object. Helping the child to communicate in this way will give the child confidence. ■ Rhymes, songs and books can be introduced. ■ Children still need plenty of adult input and running commentary – e.g. 'It's time for a bath now. You like your bath, don't you?'
12–24 months	■ Children start to use their first words. Sometimes adults will need to guess what the child means and must expect the child sometimes to be frustrated when they are not understood. ■ To help children learn new words, adults must continue to use running commentary and encourage the child to talk back. ■ Most children are becoming interested in books and enjoy nursery and finger rhymes.
2–4 years	■ Children at this stage are keen to talk and communicate, although they may start to stutter or stammer. Adults need to allow children enough time to think and answer. They must be patient, as children often enjoy repeating questions and asking for stories and rhymes over and over again. ■ We can help children with their pronunciation and grammar by using the same words but correctly – e.g. 'I felled down.' – 'You fell down did you? Shall I look at your knee?' ■ Children will often practise their language skills by playing in an imaginative way. Adults can encourage this by providing dressing-up equipment, home corners and small world toys – e.g. Playmobil, train sets.
4–8 years	■ Children are becoming quite fluent in their speech. ■ Adults need to extend children's vocabulary and help them to use language as a way of thinking. Open questions can be used when working with children. This means asking questions where children have to give more than a one-word answer – e.g. ' Why do you think the ice melted?' ■ Children also need to learn the skills of listening and this means that we must be good role models for them by listening to them. ■ We could also plan activities that will encourage listening skills – e.g. musical games, activities that need children to follow instructions. ■ It is common for children to use words they have heard without understanding their meaning – e.g. swear words – and we may need to explain that some words are not nice. ■ From about the age of six, children will start to read for themselves, although they will still need stories and poems read to them. Studies have shown that if children see adults reading, they are more likely to develop the reading habit.

Babies and young children need this type of running commentary so that they can learn the rules of communication and start building some receptive language.

Think about it

Michael has a slight hearing loss which has affected his ability to pronounce words.

Although he is understood by his family, others find it difficult to understand him. He is four years old and attends nursery. When he cannot make himself understood, he tends to lash out and become aggressive. He finds it difficult to play with other children as they do not always understand what he is saying. Michael is having some speech therapy and it has been decided that one member of staff in the setting will work with him every day.

Why might Michael need this extra support from one particular member of staff?

What type of games might encourage Michael to talk?

Communicating with children

✔ Make eye contact.

✔ Smile and look patient.

✔ Allow children time to think about what they want to say.

✔ Do not finish sentences for them.

✔ Do not interrupt to hurry them along.

✔ Listen to what children are saying!

✔ Correct grammar by echoing back their sentence correctly 'He took your ball, did he?'

✔ Ask open questions – e.g. 'What are you doing?' rather than closed questions, which can be answered with only one word – e.g. 'Are you enjoying that?'

✔ Make sure that you are speaking clearly and correctly.

✔ If you really do not have time to listen properly, explain this to the child and suggest a time when will be able to listen – and make sure that you do!

✔ Be sensitive to the needs of bilingual and multilingual children.

Think about it

Look at this conversation between an adult and a child who is drawing.

Adult   Are you enjoying that?
Child   *(Nods head)*
Adult   What's it meant to be?
Child   It's my mum and my house and my sister and… (adult looks away)
Adult   Oh that's very nice. When you've finished remember to hang up your apron.

■ What mistakes has the adult made in this conversation?

■ In pairs, write your own conversation between an adult and a child who is drawing.

■ In what ways would your conversation help to develop a child's language?

Check your knowledge

- Outline the link between cognitive development and language.

- Name four ways in which children might use language.

- What is a Language Acquisition Device (LAD)?

- Give an example of and explain what is meant by the term 'virtuous error'.

- What is the difference between receptive language and expressive language?

- What type of language skills would you expect most three-year-olds to show?

- Explain why different groups of multilingual children might not have the same language needs.

- Explain why multilingual children might have gaps in the development of their vocabulary.

- Give two reasons why children's language might be delayed or impaired.

- Explain two ways in which an adult can encourage a two-year-old's language development.

- Explain two theoretical approaches to language development.

- Describe two methods of communicating that do not rely on the spoken word.

Resources

Further reading

Lee, V. & Das Gupta, P. 1995 *Children's Cognitive and Language Development*, Oxford, Blackwell/Open University

Petrie, Pat 1989 *Communicating with Children and Adults*, Edward Arnold

The developing child

Emotional and social development

Being with other people and learning to build relationships is an important social skill that children need to develop. Helping children to develop these skills is, therefore, a crucial part of working in early years.

This chapter looks at the theories of emotional and social development, of self-image and self-esteem. It also examines loss and separation and looks at how early years workers can help children to manage their strong emotions.

Theories of social and emotional development

An interesting question that has not yet been fully answered is 'What makes me the way I am?' We are all different – some of us are outgoing and talkative, some of us are quiet and reflective. It is generally accepted that our childhood experiences will affect our personalities. This means that, as early years workers, we need to be aware of some of the main theories of emotional and social development.

Psychoanalytical theories

The Greek word 'psyche' means spirit or mind and psychoanalytical theories use the exploration of the mind as the starting point for explaining our behaviour and personality.

Two famous psychoanalytical theorists are Sigmund Freud (1856–1939) and Erik Erikson (1902–1994). Both their theories are based on the idea that:

- our behaviour is guided both consciously and unconsciously by our minds

- our personality is formed during our childhood

- children pass through stages at certain points in their childhood

- our personality is affected by how well we cope with each of these stages.

There are many similarities between Freud and Erikson's theories, but the main differences are that:

- Freud's stages are called **psychosexual stages** because he put emphasis on the physical pleasures that were associated with each stage

- Erikson's stages are called **psychosocial stages** because his emphasis was on the child's exploring relationships.

Sigmund Freud (1856–1939)

Freud is well known because he was the first theorist to consider that we have an **unconscious** mind. Freud was interested in the way people say and do things without always realising them – for example, sucking the tops of pens.

The unconscious mind and moral development
Freud suggested that we have an unconscious mind that is split into three parts:

1 id
2 ego
3 superego.

The **id** is that part of our mind that represents our desires and needs. Freud thought that babies were all id – as they are unable to consider other people's needs.

The **ego** emerges later as children begin to consider the consequences of their actions and also start being able to plan the best way of meeting the powerful id's demands – for example, the id wants a sweet, the ego considers that the best way of getting the sweet is by behaving well.

The third part of the unconscious mind is the **superego**. This part of the unconscious is the moral part. The superego is that part of us that knows right from wrong – in other words, our conscience.

Freud suggested that in our subconscious minds there is often conflict between the id and the superego – that is, what we really want to do versus what is the right thing to do. For example, if you were hungry and saw a bar of chocolate belonging to someone else on the table – your id would be urging your ego to plan how to take it, your ego would be considering the consequences of taking it, while your superego would be telling your ego that the chocolate belongs to someone else and that you would be punished if you took it.

It is surprising how many people feel that this type of dialogue often happens inwardly when they are faced with temptation.

Freud suggested that gradually children develop all three parts of the unconscious, which would mean they could gradually make moral decisions.

Stages of emotional development

Freud felt that we are all driven by the need to satisfy some basic needs and pleasures. He called this drive or energy the **libido**.

He suggested that there were five stages through which we pass in childhood and on which our drive – or libido – concentrated. The stages link to the physical development of the body. Freud felt that if we did not pass through these stages satisfactorily, part of our energy or libido would be stuck – or **fixated** – there. This would affect our behaviour and personality.

The table opposite looks at these five stages.

Oedipus complex

Freud is famous for talking about the Oedipus complex. Freud suggested that boys in the phallic stage are in love with and desire their mothers, but unconsciously realise they cannot marry their mothers because of their father's presence. He suggested that boys are not only jealous of their fathers, they are also afraid of them. (Freud felt that they were afraid of being castrated.) This causes them a dilemma – Should they love their mother and risk their father's anger? Freud felt that most boys resolve this dilemma by deciding to make friends of their fathers by copying their actions and interests.

Although many people laugh at this idea, it is noticeable that boys of this age do tend to hold on to their genitals when they are worried and that, at this age, they start to model themselves on their fathers!

Freud suggested that a similar complex existed for girls – the Electra complex, where girls desire their fathers.

Criticisms of Freud's work

There have been many criticisms of Freud's work, although his thinking changed the way that people with emotional problems are treated. He concentrated more on the development of men rather than women, and he is seen as putting too much emphasis on the physical and sexual drives that people have as a way of explaining behaviour. He will always be famous because he was the first theorist to make people aware that some of our actions and reactions are unconscious. For example, the expression 'Freudian slip' is used when someone says something that she did not mean to, such as saying your ex-boyfriend's name to your current boyfriend.

Understanding how theory may link to practice

Working with children Freud felt that children need enough time to explore different parts of their bodies. For example, in the oral stage, a baby may wish to suck, even though it has finished its feed. Freud felt that stopping children from exploring during the different stages might prevent them from successfully completing that stage.

In the anal stage, when most children are being toilet trained, Freud's theory suggest that children should not be put under too much pressure and that they should not be trained too early.

Freud's five stages of emotional development

Age	Stage	Area of pleasure	Features of stage	Effects on personality and behaviour if *fixation* occurs
0–1	Oral	Mouth	Babies are gaining pleasure from feeding and sucking. They will also be weaned during this stage.	Behaviour linking to pleasures gained in the mouth – e.g. overeating, smoking, thumb sucking. Also naivety: 'Swallows anything they are told'!
2–3	Anal	Anus	Children are learning to control their bowel movements. They learn that adults praise them when they master toilet training or can be angry with them if they do not.	Freud argued that if children were toilet trained too early and were too controlled, they would develop 'controlling' habits – e.g. extreme tidiness, meanness, stubbornness – while if children did not have enough encouragement to become toilet trained, they would become overgenerous, gushing in personality.
4–5	Phallic	Genitals	Children are exploring their bodies and are noticing their genitals. They are also learning about their gender. Freud felt that girls needed to adopt the gender role of their mothers, while boys had to separate from their mothers and follow the gender role of their fathers (see also Oedipus complex).	Vanity, recklessness
6–12	Latent	None	Freud felt that this was a resting period for children in terms of their emotional development.	None
13–18	Genital	Genitals	Children are developing into mature adults. If they have passed successfully through the other stages they will be able to make strong relationships with the other sex.	

Observations You might be able to refer to some of Freud's theories in your observations.

- Children sucking their thumbs – oral stage
- Small boys clutching their penises – phallic stage
- A child pushing his father away or stopping his parents from cuddling – phallic stage
- Children exploring their bodies – e.g. playing doctors – phallic stage

Erik Erikson (1902–1994)

Erikson was a student of Freud and there are a lot of similarities between their theories. Erikson accepted Freud's stages of psychosexual development and built on them. One of the main differences is that Erikson felt that the stages of development were linked to cognitive and social development rather than led by physical needs. It is interesting to see that Erikson also believed that our personality kept on developing into adulthood.

Erikson's stages of personality development

Age	Dilemma	Stage	Effect on personality
0–1	Basic trust versus mistrust	Babies have to decide whether the world and the people around them are safe and friendly or hostile.	If babies do not have their needs met, they may decide their world is a hostile one. This can mean they find it harder to form relationships later.
2–3	Autonomy versus shame and doubt	Children are learning to explore their environment and develop some control over their bodies and bowel movements. They may try to do things for the first time – e.g. dressing.	If children are not given encouragement to explore or are made to feel guilty about toilet accidents, they may feel doubt about themselves. This can mean they will be less independent when older.
4–5	Initiative versus guilt	Children are increasingly able to plan and carry out activities. They also need to learn about their gender role – similar to Freud's phallic stage.	Children need to feel they are independent, although they also need to learn what the boundaries on their behaviour are. Too much control of the child may result in a fearful, dependent child, whereas a very permissive attitude may leave the child without any guilt or conscience.
6–12	Industry versus inferiority	In these years, children are comparing themselves to other children.	Children who experience failure and notice that they are not as competent in some areas as their peers, may lose confidence and feel inferior. Children in this stage who meet only with success may become over-confident and lack humility and empathy.
13–18	Identity versus confusion	Adolescents need to consider their identity – sexual identity and also what they wish to become in the future.	Ideally, at the end of this stage, adolescents have a firm idea of who they are and what they want to go on and do. If they have not worked through this stage, they may 'drift'.
19–25	Intimacy versus isolation	This age group may be considering whether to live alone or find a partner to settle down with.	Adults must decide whether to form a couple or stay single. If this conflict is not resolved, they may find themselves unable to commit to a relationship.
26–40	Generativity versus stagnation	Adults in this stage are often having their own children or are making progress in their careers.	In this stage, adults are trying to make an impact on the future. Most people have children or try hard in their careers. If adults feel they have not left their mark on life, they may feel bitter and resentful.
41 plus	Ego integrity versus despair	Adults in this stage are thinking more about their mortality.	In this stage, adults are trying to come to terms with themselves and the way they have lived their lives. They may feel satisfied and accepting of themselves or they may feel depressed and bitter.

Erikson considered that there were twelve stages in the development of our personalities. He saw each stage as a dilemma and believed that how we coped with the dilemma would affect our personality.

> ***Understanding how theory may link with practice***
> **Working with children** A large part of Erikson's theory suggests that, in order for children to go successfully through each stage, they must gain enough confidence. This means that adults working with children need to make sure that they give them enough time to explore and take the initiative as well as giving them plenty of praise.

Observations You might be able to refer to Erikson's theory in your observations by considering what stage the child is in. You may also be able to show that you are aware of how important it is for children to gain confidence.

- A child looking at another child in a way that suggests comparison – Industry versus inferiority

- Babies having their needs met quickly – Basic trust versus mistrust

- Toddlers having a go at dressing themselves – Autonomy versus shame

- Adults praising children – building confidence which is important in all stages.

Albert Bandura's social learning theory

In Chapter 6, we looked at Bandura's social learning theory. Here we must consider the theory in terms of how children may develop their personalities.

Social learning theory suggests that children model their behaviour on the behaviour of the adults around them. Thus, children who have parents who are visibly generous and kind towards others are more likely to develop these characteristics.

Criticisms of the social learning theory
It is true that children often share characteristics, speech and actions with their parents, but the theory does not explain why some children in the same family develop such different personalities. Neither does it explain why children gradually develop moral codes.

Moral development of children
Jean Piaget (1896–1980)
An important part of socialisation is understanding what is right and wrong. Piaget looked at children's moral reasoning. He was particularly interested in observing children play and the rules that they developed while playing. He also told children stories to examine their reasoning of right and wrong. For example, a tale of one child who broke several plates while helping a parent and another who threw one plate down in a temper. He noticed that young children tended to concentrate on the damage caused when deciding what was naughty rather than whether the act was an accident, saying that the child who had dropped several plates was the naughtier.

Piaget therefore concluded that moral reasoning changed according to their cognitive development – a child in the pre-operational stage would be able to think only in terms of behaviour being either right or wrong – whether behaviour would be punished or not – whereas a child in the formal operational stage starts to be able to consider other elements – for example, whether an act was deliberate.

Kohlberg (1927–1987)
Lawrence Kohlberg's work also looked at how children think about right and wrong. Kohlberg devised a series of tests to find out what children and adults thought about different dilemmas. From these tests he concluded that there were three main stages in children's and adults' moral development, although each stage is divided into two.

Kohlberg concluded that not everyone would reach the final stage or even the final level. Research done since in different countries seems to support Kohlberg's view of a stage-like development of morality.

Criticism of Kohlberg
There has been some criticism of Kohlberg's work because he mainly used boys in his first studies. Since that time, his work has been used with children in several countries and this has shown that the stages do occur in the order that Kohlberg suggested with relatively few differences between cultures.

Kohlberg's stages of moral development

Level	Age	Stages	
Pre-conventional	6–13	1	Obeys rules to avoid punishment.
		2	Behaves well to avoid punishment and to gain reward.
Conventional	13–16	3	Conforms to behaviour in order to win approval and acceptance of others – 'good girl/boy'.
		4	Being good means doing one's duty and conforming to authority – laws are there and need to be obeyed.
Post-conventional	16 plus	5	Laws need to be obeyed, but only if they are fair and the majority of people accept them – some questioning of authority.
		6	We must act according to our own conscience and this should be our guide as to whether to obey authority or not.

Linking theory to practice

Working with children The work of Piaget and Kohlberg shows us that children are not able, at a young age, to tell the difference between right and wrong and are often showing good behaviour to avoid punishment or to gain reward. This means that concepts such as ownership of objects will not be automatic for children and they will need explanation as to why they cannot have everything that they see. It also means that children will be prone to temptation as they are still developing a sense of conscience – for example, they may take another child's biscuit.

Knowledge into action

Many people find Freud's ideas interesting and he is easy to find in most psychology books.

Find out about Freud's ideas on dreams.

Why did Freud place so much importance on dreams?

What is meant by a Freudian slip?

Why has Freud been so influential in counselling and psychotherapy?

Observation (structured observation)

It might be interesting to test Piaget's and Kohlberg's theories with children. You might consider using a test like the one below to see a child's reasoning.

- There was a boy who didn't like his dinner. He threw his dinner on the floor and the plate broke.

- There was a boy who was helping his father to wash up. He knocked over a tray of cups. Fifteen of the cups fell to the floor and broke.

- Was one of the children naughtier than the other?

It is important to tell the tales carefully and not to indicate, through facial expression, what you are feeling. After a child has given his answer, carefully record his reasons for this answer. It is always interesting to repeat these types of dilemma with children of different ages – to observe how children of different ages are developing.

Stages and sequences of emotional and social development

Learning to build relationships with others is an important skill that children develop over time. It is a gradual process, but by the age of eight, most children socialise well and are able to understand the needs of others and act in an acceptable way.

The following chart outlines the stages and sequences of emotional and social development of children, but as with any area of development, children will reach different stages at different times. We should always concentrate on building up a 'picture' of a child rather than thinking about what is 'normal'.

From birth to one year

Important social skills are learnt in the baby's first year. Babies learn some of the skills of socialisation. They learn that making eye contact, smiling and laughing can keep their carer's attention.

This first year is also critical in terms of emotional development. Babies need to develop a strong bond – or attachment – with their carers. In some ways, developing this bond may be instinctive as, at birth, babies are able to recognise the smell of their mother and are quickly soothed when they hear her voice. Babies who have a strong bond or attachment with their primary carer at the end of their first year will be more comfortable when they socialise with others.

Age	Development
1 month	Watches primary carer's face
3 months	Smiles and coos.
	Enjoys being handled and cuddled.
6 months	Laughs and enjoys being played with.
8 months	Fears strangers.
9 months	Plays peek a boo.
	Discriminates between strangers and familiar adults.
12 months	Is affectionate towards family and primary carers.
	Plays simple games such as Pat-a-cake.

1–2 years

During this year, children learn more social skills. They are able to play with their primary carers and are comfortable with other familiar adults. They start to explore their environment but need the reassurance that their primary carer is nearby. At the end of this year, children often start to notice other children and become able to play alongside them.

In terms of emotional development, children are very dependent on their primary carer. They will protest and cry if their primary carer leaves them and it is important that they are left with someone who is familiar to them. Although they are still dependent on their primary carer, they are starting to realise that they are individuals. They recognise and begin to use their own names.

The end of this year also marks a change in many children as they become increasingly aware of what they want. They begin to show anger and frustration if they cannot have their needs met immediately.

1–2 years *(continued)*	
15 months	Begins to explore environment if familiar adult is close by.
	Begins to use words to communicate with.
	Has a stronger feeling of being an individual.
18 months	Language is increasing.
	Points to objects to show familiar adults.
	Explores environment and shows some independence but still needs familiar adults.
	Strong emotions – e.g. anger, fear and joy – are shown.
2 years	Plays near other children – parallel play.
	Begins to talk when playing – pretend play.
	Imitates adults' actions.
	Strong emotions – e.g. anger, fear and joy – are shown.

2–3 years

This is an important year in a child's life although it is often not an easy one for carers – hence the expression 'the terrible twos'!

Children in the first part of this stage are keenly aware of what they want to do, although they become easily frustrated, because their own physical and language skills are not developed enough to meet these desires. They also find it difficult to understand why they cannot have what they see, because they lack the concept of ownership or objects being unsafe. Frustration is often vented through temper tantrums or inconsolable crying. These tantrums and strong feelings lessen as children gradually develop more language and physical skills.

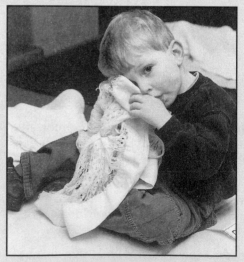

Carers working with this age group need to be very sensitive and organised so that children are not often in a position where they can become frustrated.

Children often need their comforters with them during this year to help them feel more secure, especially as many children will also be having their first experience of being separated from their primary carers on entering pre-school settings. This is an important step as children learn to socialise without the backup of their primary carers. The first experiences of separation need to be carefully handled and children entering pre-school settings will need a lot of reassurance from early years workers. (See pages 176–82 for more on separation.)

There is also a wide variation in the way children progress over the year so it is hard to put times to these steps.

A child with a comforter

2–3 years (continued)

During this year most children will:

- move out of nappies
- have a strong sense of their identity, including their gender and age
- be happy to leave their primary carer for short periods
- start taking an interest in other children and playing with them
- show concern for other children – e.g. telling primary carer if baby is crying
- start to wait for their needs to be met.

3–4 years

This is a more settled year for children. Most of them are happy to leave their primary carers and socialise with other adults and children. The first real friendships start to develop, with children seeking out particular friends. Social skills – e.g. turn-taking, sharing and concern for others – are shown. Emotionally, children still need reassurance from their immediate carers, but are more independent and may play by themselves for longer periods. They still feel strong emotions, and quarrels and temper tantrums are still apparent at times.

Many children will still be reliant on their comforters, especially when they are unwell or unsure of a situation.

- affectionate towards family, friends and carers
- wants to help and please primary carers and other familiar adults
- imitates – in play – actions seen – e.g. putting teddy to bed, feeding dolls
- shares playthings
- plays with other children – mostly pretend play
- shows concern for other people – e.g. rubs back of crying baby.

4–6 years

In some ways the expression 'I can do' sums up this period of a child's life. Emotionally, most children are feeling confident and express themselves in terms of their achievements – e.g. 'I got a sticker today,' or 'Look at me, I can climb this now.'

They may start to use words and actions in imitation of other people.

Playing with other children is increasingly important and some children start to make close friendships. At this time, children start to play with children of their own gender which may link to their understanding of gender roles.

6–8 years

By the end of this period, most children are skilled communicators and their social skills are well developed. This means that they often have stable friendships and are able to share, play and understand others' viewpoints. They become more aware of their abilities and may start comparing themselves to their peers. Some may start losing confidence in certain areas – e.g. drawing or reading – and it is important for adults to support them during this time.

The importance of a positive environment

In Chapter 2, we looked at how to create a positive environment for children. In terms of emotional and social development, a positive environment is crucial if children are to grow in confidence and security. The main needs of children are:

- love and affection
- security and stability
- opportunities to socialise.

Love and affection

Children need unconditional love. This means learning they are loved and valued for who they are, not what they do. Knowing that they are loved and will always be loved gives children lifelong security. Bowlby's and other subsequent research shows that if children have been deprived of this type of love, they have severe problems in forming relationships in later life (see also page 177).

It is mostly parents and close family members who can give children this unconditional love, but early years workers should be doing something similar – valuing and caring for them unconditionally. A positive environment which offers this unconditional caring is welcoming of all children and in such an environment children are not worried about failure or doing something wrong.

Security and stability

A positive environment for children is also a predictable one where children feel they are being protected and cared for. Children come to understand that there is always an adult there for them to turn to if they need reassurance. It is interesting that when children feel secure in this way, they are more likely to be independent and self-reliant, whereas children who are not settled often demand more attention.

Routines

Most children gain stability by having some kind of routine. A routine allows them to understand that there is a pattern and order to events. Once children have understood the pattern, they can anticipate what is going to happen next. For example, children may know that, after story time, it will be home time. Early years workers can help young children to see the pattern by explaining to them what they will be doing – for example, 'It's Tuesday, so after lunch we'll be going out for our walk.'

Setting boundaries and providing consistency

In the same way that children need some sort of routine to help them feel secure, they also need to learn that adults' expectations of behaviour are constant. This means that children know what they can and cannot do and that these limits do not change day by day – for example, knowing they must put an apron on before painting or that they must wait their turn at the slide. Children become confused when rules seem to change – for example, being told one day that they are not to throw stones and another day nobody seeming to care. This often results in children showing challenging behaviour – almost as if they are trying to work out who is in charge.

Opportunities for children to socialise

Children need some opportunities to socialise and play with other children. This is important, because they will develop their social skills through being with other children. There are now plenty of opportunities for children of all ages to socialise – for example,

parent-and-toddler groups, playgrounds and activity clubs, such as Rainbows, Beavers and Woodcraft.

Early years workers have an important role in providing activities that help children socialise together and learn the skills of co-operation and negotiation.

Factors affecting social and emotional development

There are many factors that can affect children's emotional and social development. Delay in another area of development may mean children lack opportunities to socialise or that they are suffering from lower self-esteem as a result of this delay.

The diagram below gives some examples of how children's development in other areas may affect their social and emotional development.

There are also other factors that can affect children's emotional and social development.

Genetic disorders and learning difficulties

Some children have genetic disorders or learning difficulties which limit their ability to develop emotionally and socially. This may be because they have communication difficulties or because the part of the brain that is responsible for understanding others' responses is not functioning.

Language development

Children who cannot express themselves may find it harder to develop relationships with other children. They may not be able to engage in role play which children aged between two and six use as a way of exploring relationships.

Cognitive development

Children who have learning difficulties may not be able to play at the same level as other children or they may not understand that other children have needs and feelings. As children get older, they often play games that have set rules. To be able to play in this way, children need to have reached a certain cognitive understanding.

SOCIAL AND EMOTIONAL DEVELOPMENT

Physical development

Most children use physical skills in their play – e.g. they may use fine manipulative skills to do puzzles or to explore materials. Children who have difficulties with their physical development may find it harder to join in with other children. As children become older – particularly boys – they begin to value physical skills and this can mean some boys feel inferior.

Poor attachment

We have looked at the need for children to receive unconditional love in order to feel secure. Sometimes parents/primary carers are not able to form a bond that is strong enough to allow this unconditional love. This attachment or bond needs to be established in the first few months of a baby's life. There are many reasons why the bond is not always formed – for example, postnatal depression, premature birth, illness of either the baby or the primary carer. Sometimes primary carers are unable to form the bond because they are under emotional strain – for example, their partner has left them. Health visitors, midwives and other professionals routinely look out for such difficulties after the birth of a baby and offer support to families who are finding it hard to care for and love their child.

Delayed or impaired language development

Children who have delayed or impaired language development can find it harder to form relationships with people other than family members. This is often because other people find it hard to understand and communicate with the child. It is not uncommon for children with language delay or impairment to show signs of frustration and aggression. This means other children are less likely to choose to play with them. When this is the case, early years workers need to actively support the child. This may mean playing alongside the child and the other children or acting as go-between to explain to the other children what the child is trying to express.

Poverty

Children living in poverty may lack opportunities to socialise and develop their communication skills. Extra activities such as swimming or gym clubs where children meet others may be too expensive or difficult to get to. As children become older, they may start to feel different from other children – for example, they may wear clothes that have been passed down or may not have pocket money to spend at the school fair. As most children like to feel the same as their peers, these differences can cause children to lose confidence.

Cultural differences

Where children's family backgrounds are different from those of their peers, they may lack confidence. This is particularly common with older children who may be afraid their friends will reject them. They may hide differences in culture rather than be proud of them – for example, not telling anyone when they are fasting. For children to fulfil their potential, they need to be confident about their cultural identity.

Sometimes, young children may not have had the opportunity to socialise because of their parents' culture – for example, children from a travelling family may not have been to a nursery or playgroup.

Environmental factors

It is a common mistake to think that children from rural areas have wealthy parents. This is not the case and many families in rural areas are living in poverty. It can be hard for the parents to use facilities, such as libraries and parent-and-toddler groups, because public transport is scarce. This means many children living in these areas lack opportunities to socialise. The same difficulties can apply to families living in some housing developments on the outskirts of towns and cities.

Social skills

Social skills help us to be accepted by others and are so much a part of our everyday life that we often use them without thinking. Children need to learn social skills in order to be accepted by their peers, which means learning the code of behaviour used by others. Codes of behaviour can vary from culture to culture, so children with a different cultural background may need more support from the adults around them.

Think about it

What social skills have you used in the last 24 hours?

Can you remember how and when you learnt them?

Why are these skills important for children to learn?

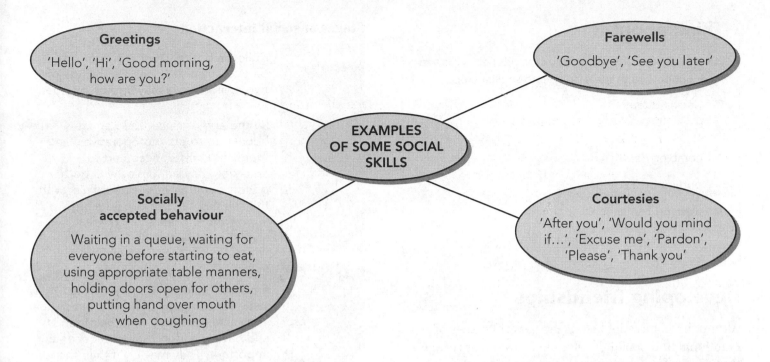

Helping children gain social skills

It is thought that most children learn the social skills they need by copying the adults around them. This means that early years workers need to be good role models so that children learn appropriate phrases and actions. Children need to see and hear early years workers saying 'Please' and 'Thank you' and being thoughtful in their actions.

Learning social skills is a gradual process as, at first, children do not have the cognitive skills necessary to consider others. Children under three will need to be reminded to say 'Please' and 'Thank you' and will to be encouraged to share with others. It is important that children are praised for showing appropriate social skills, as this will make them more likely to repeat them.

Self-help skills

Self-help skills – for example, being able to put on a coat, use the toilet and wipe up a spill – are extremely important for children. By mastering such tasks, children gain confidence, as they are taking control of a small area in their lives. Many self-help skills require physical co-ordination and some practice, so children need to be praised for their efforts.

When helping children to carry out self-help skills, adults need to ensure that they do not expect more than the child can manage. Early years workers can avoid this by observing children and considering what might be the next step for them. Sometimes play opportunities will be the starting point for children to learn a self-help skill.

The flow chart below shows how an early years worker planned a series of opportunities so that children learnt how to pour out drinks.

1 Sessions of water play using pouring equipment – e.g. jugs, cups, bottles, etc.

2 Children encouraged to water plants outside with watering cans and bottles.

3 Children practise pouring out using toy tea sets. They also practise wiping up spills!

4 Children take turns pouring out drinks at snack time.

Think about it

In pairs, choose one of the following self-help skills and work out how to break it down into smaller steps:

- brushing teeth
- tying laces
- combing hair
- putting on a coat
- washing hands
- getting out toys and equipment.

Developing friendships

Although we have looked at the general stages of emotional and social development, we must recognise that friendships are often the source of much happiness and sadness in children's lives. The nature of friendships changes as children grow and become more emotionally dependent on their friends. The chart opposite outlines the ways in which children develop friendships.

Helping children relate to each other

Adults have a strong role in helping children relate to each other. The diagram below shows the key ways in which this can be done:

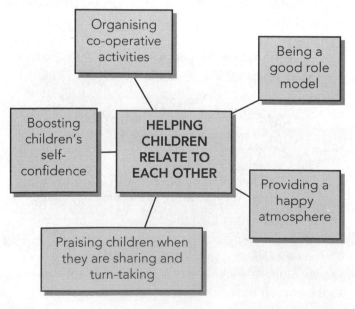

Stages of social interaction

0–2 years	Children notice other children, particularly older ones. By the age of two, children are playing side by side.
2–4 years	By the age of three, children are beginning to play co-operatively and friendship preferences start to emerge. They often play with both genders and friendships are fluid, with the choice of activity being more important to children than who else is involved in the activity.
4–7 years	The first stable friendships begin to emerge. Children actively start to seek the company of their friends. They share willingly with their friends and having a friend starts to become important. They may cry if their friend has not come to school that day. They are starting to choose same-sex friends.
8–11 years	Friendships are based more on compatibility, with children sharing common interests. They have strong same-sex friendships and there are some gender differences between the sexes. Boys tend to gather in larger groups and are more likely to be involved in activities such as sport, while girls often meet in pairs and spend more time sharing confidences.

Being a good role model

Children often model themselves on adults they admire. This means they need to see the adults around them co-operating with each other and working as a team.

Praising children

Young children need praise and perhaps a reward when they are co-operating with each other. This may mean, when a group of children are playing well together, that we tell them how well they are doing or, when children have worked well on an activity, we give them a star or other reward for their co-operation.

Providing activities

Some activities are particularly good for making children feel part of a group or for helping them to co-operate – for example, sand, dough and home corner as well as adult-led activities such as playing Lotto or cooking. Some activities may be part of the everyday routine – for example, passing around snacks or joining in with a rhyme at story time. When planning activities, adults need to be sure that the children will be able to manage the level of co-operation needed so that they do not fail. For example, children under two will be unable to share, although games such as Peek-a-boo will teach them how to play.

Boosting children's self-confidence

Children who are relaxed and confident are able to socialise more easily. They send out positive signals to other children and so make friends quickly. Boosting children's self-esteem and confidence over a long period will help them become more relaxed. To do this, early years workers need to make each child feel special and valued. (See page 173 for more about the importance of children's self-confidence.)

Providing a happy atmosphere

Children are more likely to share and make friendships if they are part of a happy environment. This means there should be a commitment to equal opportunities, so that children learn to be understanding and accepting of others. It also means that children should be given plenty of individual time and attention so that they, in turn, are able to be generous with other children.

Why are some children more popular than others?

You may already have noticed that some children seem to be more successful in their friendships than others. This is an area that is beginning to be researched more, because it seems that children who find it difficult to play with others are more likely to have problems with their relationships in adulthood. For example, a study by S W Duck (1991) suggested that children who were rejected by their peers were more likely to display signs of alcoholism,

schizophrenia and delinquent behaviour in later life. It seems likely that if we can detect the 'loners' early on and help them play with others, bullying and later social isolation can be avoided.

Characteristics of popular and unpopular children

There have been many studies (many by Kenneth Dodge) that have looked at why some children seem to be more popular than others. Below is a list of some of the characteristics that seem to be noticeable in popular and unpopular children.

- Popular children have good social skills – e.g. being able to join a game gradually rather than demand to take it over.
- Popular children may be physically more attractive (Langlois et al, 1994).
- Unpopular children are more likely to be aggressive towards their peers.
- Unpopular children tend to be disruptive in play situations – e.g. knocking over another's work.
- Unpopular children are more likely to wrongly interpret situations, believing that others are hostile towards them.

Helping children who have difficulties relating to others

Some children find it hard to form relationships with other children. There are many reasons for this, including children who have been bullied or have not had opportunities to mix with other children. It is vital that adults around them try to help them learn the skills they need, as children who find it difficult to socialise with others can become victims of bullying or potential bullies.

If a child seems to find it difficult to socialise with others, it may be a good idea to carry out a series of observations on the child, to discover the areas in which he is having difficulties. You could carry out a time sample over a session to see what areas they seem confident in – for example, a child might be able to play alongside children, while finding it difficult to share equipment or co-operate with others.

Observation

A sociogram is an interesting way of finding out about children's friendships. It works well with school-age children as younger ones tend to have less stable relationships.

You simply ask each child in a class to name three of his or her friends, preferably when the friends are not present! You can then see who has named whom.

In your evaluation, consider the following points:

■ Are there any children who were not named?

■ If so, had they had any absences recently?

■ Which children were the most frequently named?

■ Do these children have any siblings in the school?

■ Were these children the oldest ones in the class?

■ Did children show any gender preference? – e.g. boys naming only boys?

It is important to realise that a sociogram gives a good indication of friendship patterns, although it is important to follow up any findings with a recorded observation – for example, a time sample at playtime on a child who has not been named. It is also interesting to repeat the sociogram after a few weeks to see which friendships are stable.

Name	Friend 1	Friend 2	Friend 3
Jo	Simon	Ian	Darren
Darren	Peter	Jo	Simon
George	Owen	Curren	Jo
Owen	George	Peter	Ahmed
Ahmed	Owen	Simon	Peter
Peter	Ian	Jo	Darren
Jose	Simon	Ahmed	Ravi
Simon	Darren	Curren	Ravi
Curren	Simon	Jo	George
Ian	Jo	Peter	George
Ravi	Becky	Sedgee	Simon
Sarah	Becky	Anne	Kirsty
Kirsty	Anne	Becky	George
Becky	Sedgee	Sarah	Ravi

Strategies for helping children

Children who have difficulties in playing with other children can lack confidence. A good starting point is to make them feel good about themselves. You can achieve this by playing with them and praising them when they show social skills that will be attractive to other children – for example, waiting for their turn when playing a game or passing you a piece of equipment.

Once the child appears more confident, you can introduce activities with other children – for example, a board game for three or four players: you remain a participant in the game, but gradually take a less active role. As the child gradually shows the social

skills needed to play with peers, you can plan less structured activities until the child is able to join in with the others. In addition, you could teach the child to follow the lead of other children in order to join in their game. Rather than ask children if it is alright to join in, the child could instead imitate what the others are doing.

Seeking further help

It is also important for early years workers to refer children on to other services if they feel a child has serious difficulties in co-operating and playing with others. Such difficulties may be signs of a deeper psychiatric or medical problem that may need further investigation.

Self-concept and self-esteem

We often hear the words self-image and self-esteem, but it is important to understand what they mean.

Self-concept We know that we are all different, but what are we really like? The way we view ourselves is called our self-concept. Sometimes the words self-identity or self-image are used as well.

Self-esteem Once we have developed a self-concept, we then judge ourselves – do we like who we are? Our self-esteem is based on our judgement of ourselves. If we are reasonably comfortable with ourselves, we will have a high self-esteem or, in other words, be confident. If people do not like themselves they have a low self-esteem.

Self-concept
What am I like?

Self-esteem
Do I like who I am?

Developing a self-concept

Babies and children gradually develop a self-concept. This is a process that carries on throughout our lives as our circumstances change – for example, when a woman has a baby, she will probably start to see herself as a mother: this is a new role.

The chart below looks at ways in which children start to realise they have their own identity.

Stages of self-concept development

2–3 months	Babies begin to realise that they are separate beings from their parents. They learn this by realising they can make things happen around themselves – e.g. if a child pushes a rattle, it moves.
9–12 months **Object permanence**	Babies start to realise objects are still there even if they cannot see them. Piaget referred to this as 'object permanence'. Once babies have an understanding of object permanence, they gradually understand that objects and people continue to exist even when they are out of sight.
Self-awareness	The next stage for children is to work out what they are like. In the same way that a wooden cube is hard and firm, the child needs to ask what her own properties are.
21 months **Self-recognition**	At around 21 months, most children recognise themselves in a mirror. To test this, experimenters put a spot on a child's nose and then show the child a mirror. Do children touch the reflection or their nose? Children who have self-recognition touch their nose.
2 years	Most children know their names, their gender and whether they are little or large. By the age of two, most children have a feeling of identity and it is interesting that this coincides with their becoming more assertive and wanting to do things for themselves.
2½ onwards	Children use imaginative or role play – e.g. home corner and dressing up. They play helpers, babies, mothers and 'baddies'. It is thought that this type of play helps children explore different roles.
5–7 years	Children are able to give a full description of themselves – e.g. 'My name is...', 'I have a brother.'

Knowledge into action

Kylie is four years old and has not had many opportunities to play with other children. She finds it hard to share and play with other children in the setting and often seems happier playing alone in the sand. Her father is concerned that she is not mixing with other children.

Why might you decide to carry out an observation on this child?

What method would you use and when would be the best time to carry it out?

How could you encourage Kylie to play with other children?

Gender concept

Understanding that you are a boy or a girl plays a major part in developing a self-identity. Babies are not born knowing they are female or male and it is interesting to see how children gradually understand what their gender is. More important is the way children also start to learn about the gender roles in their culture – how men and women behave. Research carried out across several countries and cultures suggests that all societies have stereotyped gender roles that children learn from an early age, although the stereotypes vary from culture to culture.

Apparently, along with other stereotyped characteristics, German women are considered to be jolly and Pakistani men emotional.

How do children learn gender stereotypes?

There are several theories as to how children learn about the stereotypes attached to gender in their culture.

Social learning theory Some psychologists feel that children learn about gender roles through observing the behaviour of the men and women around them as well as through their own treatment by adults around them. A study by Smith and Lloyd (1968) in which adults played with identically dressed children showed that they played differently with babies depending on their name – the adults played more gently with the babies who had feminine names.

If children do learn about gender roles in this way, early years workers should consider whether their attitudes and behaviour are shaping the way children see gender. For example, if you are a woman, are you showing children that women can use a drill and a screw-driver or, if you are a man, are you showing that you can cook and clean?

The chart below looks at how children learn about gender roles.

Cognitive theory Some psychologists feel that children work out a **schema** to make sense of what it

Stages of gender concept

9–12 months	Babies react to male and female faces differently.
18–24 months	Young children start to choose gender-stereotyped toys.
By 2 years	Children can point to a picture of a child of their gender.
2½–3 years	Children can identify the gender of other children through properties such as girls having longer hair or through clothes.
3–4 years	Children start to associate tasks and possessions with gender – e.g. drills are used by men, irons are used by women.
5–6 years	Children have understood gender stability. They know that if you dress a boy in a pink dress, he is still a boy.

means to be a boy or a girl. A schema is like a set of rules that children work out for themselves based on their experiences. Their experience may suggest that girls wear dresses or have longer hair. They may also decide that boys play with some toys and not others. As with Piaget's stages of development, it is interesting that, by the age of seven, children seem to have definite views of what boys and girls should be doing, although, as they become older, they tend to become more flexible. This would fit in with Piaget's view that between the ages of seven and eleven, children like to use and apply rules, but once they are older, they can be more abstract in their thinking and this allows them to be more flexible.

Freud felt that, at around three years, children tried to be like their mothers or fathers and thus copied their behaviour. He felt that boys were secretly afraid and jealous of their fathers and that, unconsciously, they copied their father's behaviour hoping to make a friend of him. Freud called this the Oedipus complex (see also page 156).

The difficulty with this theory is that many boys who do not have a father figure in their lives, still manage to develop a masculine sex role.

Self-esteem

Self-esteem is sometimes called confidence. How confident you feel about yourself depends on how much you like yourself. Nobody completely likes themselves, although the wider the gap between being the person you would like to be and the person you think you are, the lower your self-esteem.

Why is having high self-esteem so important?

Having high self-esteem allows us to fulfil our potential. If we are not confident, we may not think we can do a job or study for a course. Low self-esteem affects the choices that we make – for example, a woman with low self-esteem might stay in a relationship where she was being abused because she felt she deserved to be treated badly.

Children who feel positive about themselves have high self-esteem. This means that they are more

---

Observation

There are some interesting observations that can be carried out on children to find out about their attitudes towards gender.

You can ask school-age children what they would like to be when they grow up and why they would like to do this.

■ Are the occupations gender specific?

■ Do they want to be like one of their parents?

You can also tell this story to school-age children and ask them the following questions.

Robbie is a six-year-old boy who likes to play with Barbie dolls. His father tells him that he shouldn't do this and buys him toy cars instead.

1 Why does Robbie's father get cross with him?
2 Should Robbie stop playing with Barbies?
3 Is there a rule that boys should not play with Barbies?

You can ask children the following question to find out if they have gender stability.

When you were born, were you a boy baby or a girl baby?

Children under four years old may say that they were just a baby, but now they are a boy/girl.

likely to try out new things, be ready to seek help and make friends more easily. Children with low self-esteem are less confident and can be easily put off if they think they may fail. Sometimes children with low self-esteem deliberately misbehave because they are afraid of trying hard and then failing.

Think about it

Harriet is six years old. She tries to hit a ball with a bat. She misses. She tries again and then misses. She looks around and sees that her friends can all hit the ball. After a few minutes, she gives up and snatches the bat away from one of her friends. She is told to behave. Two minutes later she snatches and throws away her friend's ball.

Why is Harriet no longer trying?

Why does she deliberately misbehave?

How could an early years worker help her?

How do children decide whether they value themselves?

There seem to be several sources of information that we use when evaluating ourselves.

1 Our direct experiences;

2 The importance of the skill or attribute;

I see that I am the slowest runner in the class.

Being a fast runner is very important to my friends.

My friends say I run like a tortoise.

3 Judgements and labels from others.

Direct experiences

Children's self-esteem can be affected by their experiences. If they experience repeated failure at an activity, they may draw the conclusion that they are not very good at it. At around six years old, children also become more aware of how others around them are performing. Comparing ourselves with others and deciding that we are not as good is damaging to our confidence.

The value attached to the skill or attribute

Some skills or attributes are valued more than others. For example, in our society, being slim is valued and this means that children who are not slim can have a lower self-esteem. Sometimes a child may be good at something, but if they do not consider it valuable, they will not gain self-esteem – for example, a boy who is a good reader might not consider this important if the rest of his friends value being a good footballer.

Judgement and labelling by others

The way we think about ourselves is often linked to the way others value us. Children are quick to pick up messages that others around them send out. Comments are sometimes made in front of children such as 'He's quieter than his brother,' or 'Can you work with Jo because he is slower than the others?' These types of comment are potentially damaging, as the children use them to judge themselves. Children who hear positive comments about themselves will gain confidence. However, it is important to remember that self-esteem is not fixed, because we consider regularly how we feel about ourselves. This means children need to hear praise and positive comments consistently.

Specific factors that can affect children's self-esteem include:

- ethnicity and multilingualism
- gender
- special needs
- abuse and neglect
- poverty.

Children who have different needs or backgrounds from other children can sometimes develop low self-esteem. They are often unsure about their differences and can easily come to the conclusion that they are not as valued as others. For example, we have seen on page 150 that children who speak more than one language can sometimes feel embarrassed, while children who have learning difficulties can feel they are not as good as other children. Children who are in some way different from their peers need particular support so that they can come to see themselves as valued. Early years workers need to be particularly supportive so that children vulnerable to lower self-esteem can develop a positive image of themselves.

Think about it

In pairs, think about the following questions:

- Can you remember what your worst subject at school was?

- What made you feel that you were not very good at it?

- Did you carry on trying hard in this subject?

- Did you ever feel that you were labelled as not being good at it?

- How would you feel now if you had to study this subject again?

Helping children's self-esteem

It is clear from research – for example, Weinberg 1978 – that children who have high self-esteem are more likely to fulfil their potential. This means that early years workers must help children to develop high self-esteem. This is not as easy as it sounds as, once a child has low self-esteem, it will take some time and a lot of effort for them to feel more confident about themselves. Remembering to praise a child from time to time is not enough!

Providing a positive atmosphere
One of the best ways to help children's self-esteem is to provide them with a positive atmosphere. Children need to feel they can experiment, fail and not be criticised. Children who are often criticised or reprimanded gradually develop a feeling that they

are not as good as others. Reprimanding children needs to be done carefully so they know that, although their behaviour is inappropriate, they themselves are still wanted.

In a positive atmosphere, children feel that they are special, noticed and valued. This means that a young child can come for a cuddle or an older child can chat to an adult about what they are doing. Settings that only value achievement can make some children feel inferior and, although we must praise children when they are doing well, it is important to consider other children's feelings. Children who are finding it difficult to read may come to the conclusion that they are less important if they constantly hear other children being praised for reading. Ideally, an atmosphere should be created where all children feel included when work or behaviour is being celebrated.

Praise
Children need to be encouraged and praised. It is important that not all praise is directed at achievement. Children can be praised because they are looking happy or have played well with another child. Children from a different cultural background can be praised for sharing their home news with you or a child living in poverty can be praised for helping a younger child. There is a danger that when children are praised only for work or for doing something well, they become afraid of failing or not performing well. This is important because, at some time or another, children will not succeed at a task – such is life – and it is essential that, when this happens, children do not lose their confidence.

Realistic expectations
What adults expect of children can influence not only the way they behave and achieve, but also how they come to see themselves. This means that we must make sure that tasks we give children are within their capability. Older children often give up if their first experience of something is failure – especially if they see another child succeed.

We must also be careful about the comments we make. Children need to hear adults saying positive things about them so they come to understand that the adults around them really believe in them.

Think about it

Look at these common phrases:

'Never mind, you've done your best.' 'Don't worry, I was no good at … … when I was your age.' 'Never mind, you can't be good at everything.'

These phrases are often used to reassure children when they are disappointed. Unfortunately these phrases can also be interpreted by children as meaning that 'Never mind, you can't do any better.' This means that some children stop trying because they feel that the adults around them do not expect them to do any better.

Look at the example below:

Yasmin is five years old. She is tired at the end of the day and is now in tears because her picture of a dog looks more like a horse.

What can you say to make Yasmin feel better?

What can you do to make sure that Yasmin does not come to the conclusion that she is no good at drawing?

Being vigilant

It is important that adults working with children look closely for early signs of children losing confidence – a child not being as keen to do something as before or a child avoiding a task or situation. If we are able to spot that a child is starting to lose confidence, it is easier to support or talk to the child. The task may need to be made easier or the child may need more adult support. Look at Tom's story opposite.

Providing play materials

It is important to provide children with plenty of opportunities and materials for exploring different roles and learning that people come in all shapes, colours and sizes. Seeing images, books and having stories about children from different backgrounds is important. Some children may not have both parents living together, other children may be using wheelchairs or wear glasses. If we introduce an understanding that everyone is different, but still special, children will be more likely to feel supportive

rather than hostile to children whose background or needs are different from their own.

Think about it

Tom is four years old. He used to be keen to go outside and play with the tricycles. Lately, he often hangs back and watches the others rather than taking a turn. The early years worker mentions this to his father and finds out that he had a fall from a tricycle the week before.

How can the early years worker encourage Tom to play with the tricycles?

Why is it important that the early years worker spends some time with him?

Most pre-school settings use home corners and dressing-up areas to help children explore their identity and the role of others. It is considered good practice to stock these areas with a variety of materials, including items from a range of cultures – for example, cooking utensils, saris, tunics, etc.

Displaying children's work

Displaying children's work can give them a big boost. Paintings, models or anything that a child is proud of can be displayed. Children can bring in objects that they like from home. Displaying work and objects shows children that you value them. It is good practice to avoid displaying only the 'best' work as this can make some children feel their work is not good enough.

Separation

There are times in all children's lives when they have to leave their primary carers. For some children this happens very early in their lives – for example, some parents return to work when their child is three months old. For other children, their first real experience of leaving their primary carers may be when they start playgroup or nursery. It is important that early years workers understand children's fears and reactions about this separation and also have a knowledge of the research that has been done into children's attachment to primary carers.

Attachment theory

Attachment theory suggests that children need strong relationships with their primary carers and that this bond or relationship begins in the first few months of a baby's life. For most babies and children, the primary carer will be their mother or father. It is generally accepted that when children do not have a strong bond with a primary carer, they find it difficult to socialise and develop relationships with others. Where a child cannot be with their primary carer, it is important that he receives a good quality of consistent loving care.

John Bowlby (1907–1990)

John Bowlby was one of the first people to recognise the need of babies and young children for a strong, stable relationship with their primary carers. In the 1950s, Bowlby was asked to study the effect on children of being in orphanages or other institutions. His findings suggested that children who were, at an early age, deprived of a relationship with their primary carer were more likely to have behavioural problems in later life.

Bowlby's report 'Child Care and the Growth of Love' (1953) changed many of the child care practices of the time.

There were three aspects to his theory of attachment that have since been developed by other researchers such as Mary Ainsworth (1913–).

- Children who have been separated from their parents are more likely to suffer from psychological problems in later life.

- Attachment is an instinct in babies. They must form an attachment by the time they are twelve months old.

- Babies' and young children's fear of strangers is instinctive. Babies start to fear strangers from the age of seven to eight months. Bowlby wondered if this was a primitive reaction which, in nature, would prevent babies from coming to harm.

Criticisms of Bowlby's work

There are many criticisms of Bowlby's work and it has been superseded by other pieces of research.

When looking at the criticisms of his work it is, however, important to remember the political, economic and social climate of the time.

The role of the mother was overemphasised
This has been a major criticism of Bowlby's early work. At the time of writing, women were the traditional caregivers and, after the war, the government was keen (for economic reasons) for women to return to their traditional roles within the home. Bowlby's later work did emphasis that babies could form an attachment with someone other than the mother.

Attachments to more than one person were not explored
Bowlby placed a lot of emphasis on the importance of one single attachment. Subsequent research (Schaffer and Emerson, 1964) has shown that as children get older, they can develop equally strong attachments to other figures such as their fathers and siblings (see page 181 for information about multiple attachments).

Quality of the substitute care was not taken into consideration
Bowlby did not take into consideration the effect of being in poor-quality care. This means that it is hard to be absolutely sure that the psychological damage done to the children was the result only of 'maternal deprivation'. Later studies have suggested that good-quality care can help children to adjust to separation as children are able to transfer the main attachment to another person (Hodges and Tizard, 1989).

Who will babies and children attach to?

Up until the 1950s, it was generally thought that babies and children automatically formed the strongest relationships with the people who fed them and met their physical needs. This is sometimes referred to as 'cupboard love'!

Several pieces of research have shown that this is not necessarily true (see Harlow's monkeys on page 178). One strong piece of research by Schaffer and Emerson (1964) showed that babies and children can form equally strong attachments to their fathers, even when the father is not the main giver. Over a period of eighteen months they visited babies at four-weekly intervals and found that most children, by eighteen months protested equally when separated from either the mother or the father. This piece of research showed that care-giving alone did not automatically mean that a child would form a main attachment.

Linking theory to practice

One of the major concerns most parents have when leaving babies with nannies or childminders is that the child will attach itself to the caregiver and not know who the parent is. Although in theory this is possible, it is unlikely, providing that the parents spend time responding to and interacting with the baby. This is the idea behind 'quality time' where the quality of the interaction and responsiveness of the parents is more important than the actual time spent with children.

Looking at the quality of attachments

There has been some research looking at the quality of babies' early attachments (see below). It would seem that, when babies and children are 'securely' attached, they are able to explore and develop their independence. Children who are attached to their parents, or another figure in their lives such as their key worker, may show the following signs:

- Actively seeking to be near the other person

- Crying or showing visible distress when that person leaves or, for babies, is no longer visible

- Showing joy or relief when that person appears

- Acute awareness of that person's presence – for example, looking up at them from time to time, responding to their voices, following their movements.

Babies and children whose attachment is less secure seem to show either indifference or clingy types of behaviour.

Harlow's monkeys

Harlow and Zimmerman (1959) raised rhesus monkeys from birth. The monkeys were put in a cage with two man-made substitute mothers. One mother was a wire mother and the other was covered in terry towelling. Half of the monkeys were fed by the wire mother and half by the cloth mother. They found

that regardless of which mother was feeding them, the monkeys 'attached' themselves to the cloth monkey. They clung on to her when they were frightened and turned to her for comfort. This study showed that providing food alone does not mean that attachments will be formed.

In a development from this study, Harlow and Rosenblum (1963) looked at what would happen if the cloth mothers 'rejected' the monkeys. One group of monkeys was randomly blasted with compressed air by their cloth mothers. These monkeys tended to spend more time clinging to their 'cloth' mothers than those in the other group. This seems to show that rejection or abuse made the monkeys insecure and made them try more often to gain some comfort even though there was a chance that they would be 'rejected' again.

Strange situation

The quality of attachments was also looked at by Ainsworth who is considered, alongside Bowlby, to be a key figure in this area of psychology.

Ainsworth and her colleagues (1978) created a scenario where babies' reactions to being left with a stranger and then reunited with their mothers (and or fathers) were measured. This scenario is now widely used to study attachment behaviour.

The scenario is known as the 'strange situation' and is divided into eight parts with each part lasting about three minutes. During the experiment, the baby (one-year-old) has some time by itself as well as with a stranger.

- Parent and baby enter room

- Parent remains inactive, baby is free to explore room

- Stranger joins parent and infant

- Parent leaves room

- Parent returns, settles baby and stranger leaves

- Baby is alone in the room

- Stranger returns and interacts with baby

- Parent returns again and stranger leaves

Ainsworth and her colleagues were particularly interested in the reactions of the baby to the parent when she left or returned and the way in which the parent interacted with the baby.

They categorised the behaviour into three types.

Type A – Anxious-avoidant
Baby largely ignores parent and shows little sign of distress when parent leaves, continuing to play. Baby ignores or avoids parent on her return. Baby dislikes being alone, but can be comforted by stranger.

Type B – Securely attached
Baby plays while parent is present, but shows visible distress when parent leaves and play is reduced. Baby is easily comforted on return of parent and carries on playing. Cries when alone because parent is not there, but can be partly comforted by stranger. Reactions towards stranger and parent are markedly different.

Type C – Anxious-resistant
Baby is wary and explores less than other types. Very distressed when parent leaves and actively resists stranger's attempts to comfort. Wants immediate contact with parent on return but is ambivalent, showing frustration and anger alongside clinginess – e.g. wanting to be held but then immediately struggling to get down.

Why are some children more securely attached than others?
Ainsworth came to the conclusion that the quality of attachment depended on the parenting that the baby received. Where parents were able to sense and predict their babies' needs and frustrations, the babies showed Type B behaviour (securely attached). This meant that they were able to explore and play, knowing that their parent was a safe base.

What happens when babies and children are separated from their main attachments?

Most early years workers will notice that as children become older, they find it easier to separate from their parents. This is because they have formed other attachments to staff and, as they get older, to other children. They have also learnt that although their

parent is absent, he or she will return later. Babies and toddlers, however, find it difficult to cope with the absence of their main attachments and will show distress.

Bowlby saw that there seemed to be a pattern to the way children reacted if they were separated from their main attachments. This pattern is often referred to as separation anxiety.

There seem to be three distinct stages of separation anxiety.

Stages of separation anxiety

Stage	Features
Protest	Children may cry, struggle to escape, kick and show anger.
Despair	Children show calmer behaviour almost as though they have accepted the separation. They may be withdrawn and sad. Comfort behaviour, such as thumb-sucking or rocking, may be shown.
Detachment	Children may appear to be 'over' the separation and start to join in activities. The child is actually coping by trying to 'forget' the relationship – hence the title detachment. The effects of detachment may be longer lasting as the children may have learnt not to trust people they care for.

Separation anxiety is clearly seen in babies from around seven months and seems to reach a peak at around twelve to fifteen months. Older children will show separation anxiety if they are separated for long periods – for example, if a parent dies or goes away for a period of time.

Separating from carers

For most children, changing settings is a daunting experience and they have many fears. It is important for early years workers to understand these fears so that they can reassure the child. Young children often have very specific fears – for example, whether they will know where the toilet is or whether their parent will know where to find them. Older children are often concerned about whether they will make friends easily and whether the staff will be nice to them.

Age and separation

The age of children will play a crucial part in their reaction to being separated from their carers.

- Babies under six months are unlikely to show any signs of distress, as they will not have formed a strong attachment with their primary carer.

- Children between the ages of one and three years are likely to show the most reaction to being separated. This means early years workers caring for children in this age range need to be particularly sensitive to children's needs.

- As children get older, they are able to understand that being separated from their carer does not mean losing them.

- Children over four are less likely to react to short periods of separation, although this will depend on their previous experiences of separation. Most children settle well, providing they know what the child care arrangements are and that they like the setting they are in.

Experiences

Children's reactions will be partly affected by their previous experiences. Children who, from an early age, have been cared for by someone other than their primary carer may be happier than those who have never been left before. Children whose previous experiences of being left were unhappy ones are likely to cling to their primary carer. This shows how important it is for the child's first experiences of separation to be good.

Children with older siblings may find it easier to separate from their primary carer as, quite often, they are already familiar with the setting and know some of the carers – for example, a child starting the same school as her brother.

Case study

Ruth has three children. Two are teenagers and the third child, Tom, is two years old. Ruth left her job when Tom was born, but two months ago, she and her husband separated. Ruth has decided to return to work and has arranged for a nanny to care for Tom. She is not very happy about this situation as she stayed at home with the other children. She feels that Tom will miss out by not having her there. Her nanny is fully qualified and experienced, but when Ruth comes home, she always questions her or finds fault with what she has done with Tom. The nanny is beginning to consider finding another job, because she feels that Ruth is 'nit-picking'.

- Why might Ruth be reacting to the nanny in this way?
- How can the nanny make Ruth feel more confident that Tom is fine?

Parents and separation

Not all parents find it easy to leave their children. There are many reasons why parents find it hard to separate from their children.

Guilt Our society still promotes images of mothers being at home with their young children. This can mean that, if parents need to leave their pre-school children due to financial pressures, they feel guilty.

Concern There have been some cases in the media where early years workers have mistreated children. Some parents are concerned about the quality of the care provided. It has been known for parents to install 'spy cameras' to check on their nannies!

Attachment In the same way that babies and children are attached to their parents, parents also have strong feelings about their children. Some parents are afraid their children will become attached to the new carers and will no longer respond to them.

Parents also need to come to terms with their children growing up and becoming more independent. Some parents find it hard when their youngest child starts school because this marks the end of a phase in their own lives.

Helping parents separate from their children
Babies and young children notice when parents are anxious or upset about leaving them. They may start crying, which in turn will make it harder for the parent to separate from them. Most parents find it very upsetting to leave a crying child and may go on to work not knowing that their child has now settled down. This can mean that a cycle develops where parents become tense before leaving the child and the child then starts to cry. Settings can help parents separate in the following ways.

- Make sure parents feel they can come in and see what is going on.

- If a parent leaves a crying child, ask if he or she would like to phone in later or peep through a window or door after a few minutes.

- Agree with the parents what should happen if the child is not settling in well.

- Make sure parents do not feel rushed by you when leaving their children.

- Listen to and note down any concerns parents have about their children – e.g. 'He didn't sleep very well.'

Think about it

Alex is three years old. His mother has been called into work suddenly and she has asked if he can attend the nursery for an extra morning. She arrives at the nursery in a rush and Alex who normally leaves her easily, clings to her. On this occasion, she cannot stay with him and she gives him a quick kiss. You spot that she seems quite upset on her way out.

1 Why might Alex be clingy on this morning?
2 How can the early years worker help Alex to settle down?
3 How might the parent be reassured?

- Give parents detailed feedback about the child at the end of the session.

- Help parents feel that they are still important to the child – e.g. 'He told me all about his trip to the park with you. It sounded like a lot of fun.'

The effects of multiple transitions

The phrase 'multiple transitions' is used when children have many carers or have to move setting many times. Children can find repeated change of carer and setting unsettling, as most prefer to have an established pattern or routine. There are many reasons why children may find themselves being cared for by a series of different people, including:

- being taken into care by social services

- their parents moving areas due to their employment

- child care arrangements breaking down – e.g. a child having a series of nannies or au pairs

- illness or bereavement in the family

- children moving around because their parents are travellers.

The effects on children of changing carer and setting can often be damaging. Children who have experienced multiple transitions may find it harder to trust their new carer as they have learnt from previous experience that the people they like and get to know seem to disappear from their lives. Early years workers caring for children who have had many transitions need to be particularly patient – children who are feeling unsettled often show unacceptable behaviour which can range from extreme attention-seeking to withdrawal and apparent disinterest. (See page 201 for strategies for dealing with inappropriate behaviour.)

Older children can find moving from school to school unsettling as it is harder for them to break into established friendship groups in the new school. They may also have a different regional accent from the children in the new setting and this may lead to them feeling less confident.

Although multiple transitions can be damaging for some children, others may be less affected, providing their primary carers are a constant presence in their lives.

Helping children to adapt to change

Where possible, children need to be prepared for any change in their care arrangements – for example, spending a day in hospital or starting at a playgroup. There are many ways of doing this, depending on the age of the children, although it is often a good idea for all children to spend a short time visiting or getting used to their new setting or carer. Early years workers need to work closely with parents to reinforce things the parent has said and they also need to understand the children's concerns. If early years workers are preparing children to move on to school, it is important they give out positive messages, as children need to be reassured that they will enjoy their new school.

Think about it

Fayed is four years old and will be starting school in the following term. His behaviour is sometimes inappropriate and he has just pushed another child down the slide. An adult says to him, 'You won't be doing that in your new school because they make boys like you stand outside the hall.'

Why is this remark inappropriate?

How might it affect Fayed's ability to settle in the new school?

Babies and young children

Children will need to build up a relationship with the person who is going to care for them. The separation process needs to be a gradual one with the time spent away from their parents building up. For example, a two-year-old might be left for just ten minutes and then on another day for half an hour. This gradual separation helps the child to see that their parent will return.

Older children

Older children who are used to separating from their parents need to visit the new setting and spend some time before actually starting. Schools often arrange for children to visit them for a morning before the start of a term. Most children are happy if the routine of the day is explained to them and they know what will be expected of them. It can be difficult to know when to tell older children about changes, as some are inclined to worry – a month is a long time for a child, although it is important for children to have enough time to understand what will be happening.

Common ways of helping children prepare for a change include:

- reading a story or watching a programme – e.g. going to hospital, starting school, starting playgroup

- arranging visits to the new carer or setting

- having people from the setting in to talk to the children – e.g. teachers visiting playgroups and nurseries

1 Initial visit to setting.

2 Information exchanged between parents and workers.

3 Parent and child spend a session in the setting.

4 Parent takes a less active role during the next visit to the setting and early years worker plays with the child.

5 Parent tells the child they are popping out for a few minutes. The early years worker reassures and plays with the child. Parent returns after a few minutes. Child is praised.

6 Parent stays with the child at the beginning of the session and gradually leaves the child for longer periods. Child builds up a relationship with the early years worker.

- involving children in any preparations – e.g. packing a suitcase for the hospital, buying items of clothing

- encouraging children to ask questions and answering these seriously

- encouraging children to act out their fears by using dressing-up clothes – e.g. making a hospital corner.

Settling-in policies

It is not long ago that children were taken sobbing from their parents' arms. There is now a greater understanding of the importance of allowing children time to adjust to settings, so most settings have a settling-in policy. Parents are encouraged to visit settings with their children and time is set aside for parents and workers to talk about the needs of the children.

Think about it

Harry's mum is very keen for him to start nursery. She does not really want to settle him in because she sees this as a waste of money – 'After all, I'm paying you to look after him. If I'm sitting there with him, I might as well be at home with him!'

In pairs, work out a role play that will convince Harry's mum about the benefits of settling him in gradually.

Parents who sneak off

Some parents prefer not to say goodbye to their children, believing that if they sneak off while the child is playing, they will not be missed. Unfortunately, this is not so. When this happens to children they become more clingy in new situations as their past experience tells them their parent may

---

Name _Curren Snell_   Date _21/4/99_

Activities

My favourite things to do today were:...

Singing five fat sausages Playing with the dough and rolling it out.

(Curren has slept longer today, he seemed very tired this morning.)

Sarah McDonnell.

Lunch

Today I ate...
- ☐ Everything
- ☑ Most of my lunch
- ☐ I wasn't very hungry

Rest

I slept for...
- ☐ ½ hour
- ☐ 1 hour
- ☑ 1½ hours
- ☐ I wasn't sleepy

suddenly disappear. It is always better that children know when their parents are leaving, even if this means a few tears at first. This way, children will learn that their parents do return and it allows parents to build up a routine around saying goodbye.

Key-worker systems

Research carried out (Robertson & Robertson, 1971) has shown that when children are separated from their primary carers, they need to build an attachment to someone else. As a result, many early years settings have introduced a key-worker system. The idea of a key-worker system is that a young child is able to form a strong relationship with one particular member of staff. The key worker will spend more time with 'their' children and really get to understand them, although other staff members will still work with these children. This helps babies and young children gain a sense of stability in the absence of their primary carer.

Key workers are also the main contact with parents. This allows parents to build a relationship with the person who is mainly responsible for their child. Most settings that operate a key-worker system have also developed ways of reporting to parents.

Ways of helping children express themselves

Young children can have very strong feelings that are difficult for them to express. Sometimes they may not have the language skills to explain what is wrong, whereas some children do not know themselves the cause of their feelings. Helping children to express

and control their feelings is an important part of being an early years worker.

The diagram opposite shows the types of feeling and emotion that children show.

Happiness and joy

It is important that children are encouraged to enjoy being happy! It is often easy to focus on children who are showing negative feelings and thoughts and forget to praise children who are showing happiness and joy. Being able to stay positive and have a sense of humour are important life skills and they can affect our ability to make friends and be employable.

Ways of encouraging children to be positive

- Organise parties in settings.
- Share jokes with children.
- Ask children at the end of the day to talk about things they have enjoyed doing.
- Encourage children to share their happy news.
- Focus on positive things – e.g. sunshine, food children are enjoying.
- Celebrate festivals with children.
- Be a good role model by being positive and happy.

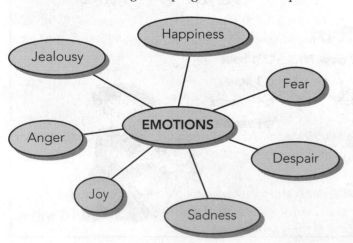

Anger

Anger is a strong emotion that many children feel. Biting, temper tantrums, kicking and shouting are common ways in which children express their anger. Sometimes they act in these ways because they want to protest, while at other times, the anger can be so strong that the child is not in control of itself. In these situations it is important for adults to stay calm and protect the child from harming either itself or other children.

- Move the child away from any equipment that might either be harmful or be damaged.
- Speak slowly and quietly to the child.
- Vocalise what he or she is feeling – e.g. 'You are feeling upset because it's not your turn yet.'

Dough	Children can twist, pound and squeeze dough, allowing them to vent their aggressive feelings. They can also choose to make something from dough which can be a positive experience.
Hammer and pegs	Children can use equipment that encourages them to bang and hit.
Musical instruments	Children can use drums, triangles and cymbals to make loud angry sounds with. This helps them to channel their energy.
Outdoor play	Vigorous outdoor play can help children vent their anger, although it is important that activities and equipment are provided so that children do not vent their anger on each other. Tricycles, climbing frames and obstacle courses can focus children's aggression.
Sand	Sand can be calming, but also good for children who need to build and then destroy. They can make mounds or sandcastles and then destroy them. Other activities – e.g. digging – can help, although a close eye must be kept on children in case, in their anger, they start throwing sand.

- Try distracting younger children with an interesting object.
- Consider giving older children the opportunity to go somewhere to cool off – e.g. 'Why don't you come with me to the library for a few minutes?'
- Praise children once they are showing more acceptable behaviour.
- Reassure the child that you still care for him.

Activities that help children express negative feelings

Sometimes children show anger because they are not feeling in control. It is a good idea to look for activities where children can be destructive or in control to vent their negative feelings.

Jealousy

Being jealous shows a deeper unhappiness and lack of confidence. Jealousy is an emotion that most adults can identify with, although often children will not know that their behaviour or sadness stems from this emotion. Most children's jealousy is shown through uncooperativeness and anger. A common reason for children to feel jealousy is because of a sibling. It is interesting that some children will say that their sibling is their best friend, yet also be jealous of them. Most children first feel this jealousy when they have to share the attention of their parent or carer with other children. Jealousy can start when a new baby is born, but it is common for children to be jealous at other times – for example, on birthdays, when a sibling is ill, or when a sibling has been somewhere interesting. Jealousy is a lonely feeling and children need to be given some extra attention when they are showing this. Becoming angry with a young child, just confirms to them that they are not loved.

Helping children overcome jealousy

In order to overcome their jealousy, children need to feel they are involved and appreciated. They may also need some extra attention.

Birthdays or celebrations for other children
- Involve children in surprises – e.g. making a cake for the other child.

- Ask children for advice – e.g. 'Do you think he'll like this?'

- Ask older children if they feel a little left out.

- Have a small present for younger children.

- Praise children for their help in making a day or celebration special.

New baby

- Involve the child in activities – e.g. nappy changing and feeding.

- Praise the child for helping you.

- Allow the child to 'borrow' toys from the baby.

- Allow the child to taste baby food, etc., if they want to.

- Have periods when the child is alone and away from the baby.

Think about it

Izzy is eight years old and has a brother Patrick who is six years old. Most of the time they get on quite well, although they sometimes squabble about toys!

Izzy is going to have a minor operation at the hospital which will mean an overnight stay. Their mother has decided to stay the night at the hospital while Patrick stays at his friend's house. On the morning of the operation, both children are sulking. Patrick is sulking because he wants to go to the hospital and knows that Izzy has been promised a special surprise after the operation and Izzy is crying because she has always wanted to stay at a friend's house.

There are 'hidden' reasons why these children are upset.

In pairs, work out what each child may really be feeling.

How would you handle this situation?

Fears

Many children over the age of two develop fears. Common fears include the dark and dogs. It is important to take children's feelings seriously and make sure you reassure them. This may mean teaching them strategies – for example, with a fear of dogs, children can be encouraged to focus on what type of breed it is, or guess what its name might be. Early years workers must also be aware that materials they read or show to children might give them fears. Stories about ghosts or scary monsters are not usually read to children under four years and young children should be protected from watching the news on TV.

Effects of loss and grief on children

It would be lovely to imagine that all the children we work with have a carefree childhood. Unfortunately, there are many painful circumstances which children are faced with, including:

- parental separation – e.g. divorce or separation

- bereavement of a close family member

- loss of a pet.

Divorce and separation of parents

The divorce and separation rate in this country has increased gradually over a number of years. The number of divorces is beginning to level off at around 40% and around 160,000 children a year are affected by divorce. The effects of divorce and separation on children have been shown to be quite considerable. A significant number of children from divorced or separated families have lower self-esteem and confidence and are less likely to achieve later on in their school life.

There are several reasons why children may be affected by family breakdown, but some children are able to adapt well, so it is important not to assume all children will have difficulties.

Reasons why children may be affected include:

- missing and grieving for the absent parent

- continuing conflict between parents

- difficulties for the remaining parent in coping alone

- effects of living in poverty – many families become reliant on state benefits after divorce or separation.

Bereavement

Some children may have to face a bereavement of a close family member or friend. This can be a difficult time for children and parents. Children may not always feel they can grieve because they do not want to upset others or they may feel they need to be 'good' and be supportive.

Understanding the grieving process

We must always remember that grief is a natural way of adapting to a loss. Children can grieve over missing a friend who has moved away, over the death of a pet or even because a favourite toy has been broken or lost.

There seem to be three stages in the grieving process and Engel (1962) suggests that they are all vital if we are truly to come to terms with a loss.

Stages	Signs
Disbelief and shock Numbness/denial	Children may behave as if nothing has happened. Children may seem dazed or withdrawn.
Developing awareness Understanding what has happened and that this is irreversible	Children may show a wide range of strong emotions, including anger, inconsolable sobbing and despair.
Resolution Coming to terms with what has happened and adapting	Children gradually talk more easily about what has happened and their feelings. Children start to join in again and seem more settled.

Supporting children who are grieving

Working with parents
Early years workers need to be sensitive to the needs of children who are grieving and should try to work with the parents. This is particularly important when children are coming to terms with bereavement, because a child may ask many people the same question to seek reassurance – e.g. 'Will I see my Mum again?' Some families may believe in a heaven, others in reincarnation or spirits. Working closely with families should help us to support the child, although we need to be sensitive as the parents may also be feeling under stress.

Activities
As well as listening to children and giving them extra attention, there are some activities that can help children come to terms with a loss or bereavement.

- Allow children to act out what they have experienced – e.g. teddy is sick and dies.

- Encourage children to draw and paint.

- Use stories and poems as a way of helping children to talk about their feelings.

- Plant and grow things so that children learn about natural cycles.

Knowledge into action

George is four years old. His baby brother died suddenly of Sudden Infant Death Syndrome (cot death) six months ago. George's family were devastated and George has shown some signs of regression. George's mother is concerned about him as he is bedwetting, and clingy when she brings him into school. She looks tired and strained and often asks a friend to collect George because she finds it hard to wait for him because of the other mothers with babies. She is finding it hard to keep going and often asks friends to take George off her so she can have a break.

Why might George also feel insecure?

How might the key-worker system help George and his mother?

What types of activity might help George to work through his grief?

What specialist help might George need if he is still unsettled?

What organisations might be able to help George's mother?

Changes in children's behaviour

Major changes in children's lives can cause them to show a range of behaviour. It is important to understand that this is often part of the grieving process. We can help them by being sympathetic, and also by providing consistent care. Many children who are under stress need more one-to-one attention from the early years worker. It is not uncommon for younger children to regress, which means they revert to an earlier stage – for example, they may start to wet themselves or wanting to be fed.

Examples of behaviour that children under stress may show include:

- attention-seeking and clinging
- being withdrawn
- inability to concentrate
- aggressive behaviour
- temper tantrums
- refusal of food
- regression.

Specialist help

Some children can be so affected by a bereavement or loss that they need specialist help. They may be referred to a play therapist or a psychologist for help. Play therapists encourage children to use play to express themselves and to come to terms with what has happened.

Check your knowledge

- Name Freud's psychosexual stages of emotional development.

- What are the three main elements of a caring environment?

- Explain two factors that might affect a child's social and emotional development.

- Outline why self-help skills are important for children.

- How can an early years worker help a child who has difficulties in playing with others?

- What is the difference between self-esteem and self-concept?

- What is the link between self-esteem and children achieving their potential?

- Outline Bowlby's attachment theory.

- What is the role of a key worker?

- Name three activities that can be used to help children with aggressive feelings.

- Outline the main criticisms of Bowlby's work.

- Describe the three stages of separation anxiety.

- Why are Harlow's monkeys famous?

Resources

Further reading

Issues series *Bereavement*, Cambridge, Independence Publishers

Schaffer, Rudolph 1995 *Early Socialisation*, Leicester, BPS Books

Turner, Patricia 1995 *Sex, Gender and Identity*, Leicester, BPS Books

Useful contacts

CRUISE
Bereavement Care
126 Sheen Road
Richmond
Surrey TW9 1UR
020 8940 4818

Compassionate Friends
53 North Street
Bristol BS3 1EN
0117 966 5202

Stillbirth and Neonatal Death Society (SANDS)
28 Portland Place
London W1N 4DE
020 7436 5881

Parentline
Endway House
The Endway
Hadleigh
Essex SS7 2AN

Parents Advice Centre
Franklin House
12 Brunswick Street
Belfast BT2 7GE
01232 238800

Twins and Multiple Births Association – Bereavement Support Group
PO Box 30
Little Sutton
South Wirral L66 1TH
0151 348 0020

Useful websites

Family Mediators Association (FMA)
www.familymediators.co.uk

Relate
www.relate.org.uk/bookshop

London Bereavement Network (LBN)
www.bereavement.demon.co.uk/

CHAPTER 9
Understanding the behaviour of children

Children are not born with an understanding of the rules of acceptable behaviour in their society: they have to learn them and adults need to help them do this. This chapter looks at how we can help children learn about appropriate behaviour and also at identifying factors that may mean children have difficulty in showing desirable behaviour. (Note that the effects of loss and grief on behaviour and strategies to help children express their strong emotions have already been covered in Chapter 8.)

What is good behaviour?

Unfortunately, there is no rule book to give children when they are born and to which early years workers, parents and other adults can refer. This means that each society, each setting and each family tends to have its own rules and boundaries – for example, in some families, children are allowed to watch TV at the same time as eating, whereas in others, this behaviour would be punished!

Our own views of what is and is not acceptable will have been formed from our upbringing and our culture. You may like to try out the exercise below.

As you may have found out, people have different views on what is acceptable or not. This means you must never assume that your expectations of appropriate behaviour will be the same as those in your setting. It is essential to find out what the behaviour policy of a setting is and to observe how staff help children to learn what is expected of them.

Expectations of appropriate behaviour also vary from culture to culture. The way in which food is eaten and

Think about it

Look at the following statements.

- Children should be taught to hold doors open for adults.

- Children should give up their seats on public transport.

- Children should not chew gum or eat sweets in the street.

- Young children should wait for a meal to end before getting down from the table.

- Children should be taught not to interrupt conversations.

- Young children should be able to choose what they wear.

- Young children should be taught to say 'Please' and 'Thank you'.

How strongly do you agree or disagree with these statements?

Give each statement a mark out of 10.

10 = complete agreement, 0 = complete disagreement

Are your marks the same as those of other people in the group?

191

general table manners are often very different – for example, in many cultures, people eat food with their fingers and lift bowls off the table to eat from.

It is essential, therefore, that, when children show behaviour which is inappropriate in our own culture, we handle them sensitively.

Knowledge into action

Every placement will have slightly different expectations of children. For example, in some placements during story time children may be asked to sit cross-legged, while in others children may not have to sit down at all.

What are the expectations of children in your placement during the following time of the day?

- *playtime or outdoor play*
- *dinnertime*
- *story time*
- *home time.*

Children need to show acceptable behaviour

Children need to learn what behaviour is appropriate in their culture, for otherwise they will not be accepted by other people. In our society, this means children who do not learn to think of others' needs and feelings will find it harder to make friends. This is why, from an early age, most parents and adults encourage children to learn to share and say 'Please' and 'Thank you'.

Promoting good behaviour

Early years workers can help children show good behaviour. There are three strands to managing behaviour:

1 understanding how children learn behaviour
2 having realistic expectations of children
3 providing consistency and a framework.

How children learn acceptable behaviour

In Chapter 6 we looked at how children learn. Most of the theories we explored are also used to explain how children learn certain behaviours. (*Remember*: children can also learn undesirable behaviour!)

Most professionals working with children use a combination of strategies based on the following theories.

Social learning theory

Social learning theory suggests that children learn from watching those around them, particularly their parents, carers and, later in life, their peers. They are likely to behave similarly to the people around them.

This theory is widely accepted and may explain why children often adapt their behaviour according to the setting – for example, at school children learn to put their hands up when they want something because that is what everyone else is doing.

Using the theory with children

The importance of good role models If you accept this theory, children need to see people showing desirable behaviour – for example, saying 'Please' and 'Thank you'. The people around them act as role models and children gradually learn to copy desirable behaviour – for example, helping others, waiting for turns. As an early years worker you need to act as a good role model at all times, so that children learn caring, thoughtful behaviour from you.

Mixed messages
If children are getting very different messages about how to behave from different people, they will be confused about how to act. This is why most parents and early years workers try to work in partnership when looking at how to manage a child's behaviour.

Poor role models
Some children may not see good role models. For example, if children experience an aggressive

parenting style, they are more likely to be aggressive themselves. (This is why early years workers should not shout or be aggressive in their actions towards children.)

As children get older, they also start to copy other children and sometimes school-age children may start to spit or swear.

Think about it

Jo is three years old and is attending a playgroup. One of the early years workers hears Jo swearing as the tower he has been building falls over. There are no other children around and Jo seems to be quite absorbed in his game. The early years worker decides not to interrupt Jo in his game, but listens to him carefully. A few minutes later, he swears quietly as a piece of brick does not fit in. Again, Jo does not seem to be swearing to gain attention.

At the end of the session, the supervisor has a quiet word with his mother, explaining that Jo has been overheard swearing. His mother explains that his grandfather has been staying with them and that he often swears. They agree that nothing will be said to Jo as he is too young to understand that some words shouldn't be used and that talking about it may make him use the word more often. Jo's mother says that next time his grandfather stays, she will keep an eye on the situation and if necessary she will talk to his grandfather.

1 Why did the supervisor talk to Jo's mother?
2 How did Jo learn the swearword?
3 Why is it important that early years workers and parents talk about behaviour together?

Behaviourist theory

The behaviourist theory can be used effectively to manage children's behaviour and to help them learn appropriate behaviour. The essence of the theory is that behaviour will be repeated when the child gains something positive and that behaviour may disappear if it is not rewarded or the outcome was particularly negative – for example, a child who is given a sticker

because they have helped tidy up is likely to want to tidy up again.

Rewards for behaviour are called **positive reinforcers** by psychologists. The most common reward given to children is praise and attention, although some settings also encourage behaviour by giving stickers, badges and treats.

Using the theory with children

The behaviourist theory is used by most settings and early years professionals to manage children's behaviour.

Timing is important

Skinner suggests that the timing of the reward or positive reinforcement is crucial. Behaviour that has been rewarded straight away is likely to be learnt and repeated, so children should be 'rewarded' as soon as possible following the wanted behaviour. For example, praise while a child is helping is more powerful than praise at the end of the day.

What happens if an action is not always positively reinforced?

It may not be always possible to 'reward' children every time they show desirable behaviour. This does not mean they will stop showing the behaviour. In fact, if behaviour is positively reinforced from time to time, it is likely to be more strongly learnt than if it is positively reinforced every time. (Think of scratch cards and lotteries. People do not win every time, but if they have won once, they believe that they will win again.) Children who are praised frequently but not all the time, will still keep showing the behaviour.

Think about it

Techniques based on behaviourist theories are often used to make us buy or consume products.

Scratch cards are apparently more addictive than playing the lottery. If someone wins on a scratch card, he is 'rewarded' instantly. The immediate reinforcement means that he is more likely to keep on playing.

1   Find out who in your group has had a scratch card win.
2   Did they buy another ticket shortly afterwards?
3   Are they still tempted to buy tickets?
4   Are their buying habits the same as someone who has never had a win?

Unfortunately this is also why some children learn bad habits that are hard to break. Look at the example below:

Day 1   A child whines for some sweets and is given some. (The child has learnt that whining for sweets is effective.)

Day 2   The child whines for some sweets and is refused them.

Day 3   The child whines for some sweets and eventually gets them. (Child has learnt that it is always worth whining because sometimes you get a reward.)

Days 4, 5, 6   The child continues to whine for sweets and, though refused, the behaviour has been established and the child continues to whine.

Day 7   If the child gets sweets today, the behaviour will be hard to break!

What happens if there is no reinforcement?
You may have been told to 'ignore' the behaviour of a child. This at first seems to be strange advice – after all, how will the child learn to behave properly? In fact, this is often a sound technique, providing the child is not harming himself or others. Skinner and other behaviourists have found that behaviour that is not 'reinforced' will often disappear. This means that if a young child is doing something to gain attention such as squealing or banging a toy on the floor, he will stop his behaviour if no attention is given. With babies and young children, it is also possible to distract them by showing them another activity or toy so that they forget what they were doing.

Think about it

You are working as a nanny. Jenny is two years old. She is constantly exploring her environment. Today, she has found that she can make a noise by hitting the stair gate with a wooden brick. The noise is very loud and irritating but she is in no danger.

Why might it be useful to ignore this behaviour?

Is Jenny being 'naughty'?

If the noise becomes unbearable, what could you do to distract Jenny?

Attention as a positive reinforcer
All children enjoy having adults' attention and it is a powerful positive reinforcer. If we praise children and give them attention when they are doing something positive – for example, playing well together – they are more likely to carry on playing in this way. It is not necessary to always give children stickers, food and other rewards, although they are useful at times. Praise and attention are just as effective.

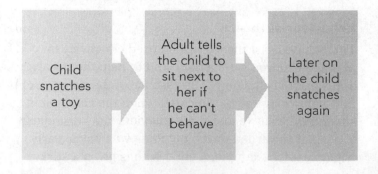

Why some children don't mind getting into trouble
For some children having an adult's attention is very important to them, even if they are getting it through being told off. Some children, therefore, will repeat undesirable behaviour to gain attention.

Self-fulfilling prophecy
This theory suggests that children are likely to behave according to the expectations of the adults around them: if an adult expects a child to be difficult, the child may well show inappropriate behaviour. However, if adults think that children are 'good', the children are more likely to show appropriate behaviour.

Adult's expectations of child	
'He's always a nuisance.'	'He's such a good boy.'
Child behaves badly.	Child behaves well.

This theory was demonstrated in a study (Rosenthal and Jacobson, 1968) where class teachers were told that certain children (who were actually chosen at random) were going to make a lot of progress. At the end of the experiment, researchers found that there was a staggering improvement in the performance of those particular children!

Why labelling children can be damaging
The self-fulfilling prophecy shows that negative labelling of a child can be extremely damaging. However, it is still common to hear negative comments in settings – for example, 'Oh, you've got James in your group – you'll have to watch him.'

Labelling children in this way increases the likelihood of them showing unwanted behaviour.

Understanding that children's needs, feelings and behaviour are linked

It is important for early years workers to understand the link between children's needs and feelings and their behaviour. Learning to control strong impulses and desires is hard for young children as they are egocentric. We can help children to some extent by giving them opportunities to express themselves (see also page 185) but we should always remember that the ability to wait for their needs to be met is dependent on children's stage of development.

The links between age, stage of development and behaviour

We have now looked at the theories of how children learn behaviour. Early years workers also need to understand that learning appropriate behaviour is a

Using the self-fulfilling prophecy with children
It is important to be very positive with children and to believe in them. We need to smile, praise them and show them through body language that we enjoy being with them.
The expectations we have of children must be realistic: if we expect too much of children they will fail. However, at the same time, it is important to expect enough of them – see chart on page 196.
If children need to be reprimanded, make sure they understand you are unhappy with what they are doing, not with them. Avoid using words such as 'naughty', as some children end up believing they were born naughty and that there is no hope of them being good.
Be positive when children have shown inappropriate behaviour – e.g. 'You're normally so good at sharing,' is better than 'I wish you would learn to stop snatching.'
Do not remind children of past failures – e.g. 'I hope you'll behave more sensibly than you did yesterday.' This contains a hidden message – 'You're likely to be naughty.'

gradual process which is linked to children's overall development, although particularly to their language and cognitive development. For example, a two-year-old will not have the concept of ownership and therefore may often snatch toys.

It is important that early years workers have realistic expectations of children's behaviour. We know that if the expectations of behaviour are too high, children can feel that they are failing, and if the expectations are too low, children may not learn appropriate behaviour for their age.

The chart on the following pages looks at children's behaviour in relation to their age and also at the role of the adult. It shows the goals for behaviour. The goals are the types of behaviour that early years workers should be encouraging, while remembering that the children will not automatically be able to show this type of behaviour.

As with any developmental chart, it must be seen as a guide since children vary greatly in their development. For example, a six-year-old child with learning difficulties may show behaviour that is normally associated with a two-year-old.

Goals for behaviour at different ages

Age	Stage of development	Goals for behaviour
1–2 years	■ actively explores environment ■ is learning from adults and will copy simple actions ■ repeats actions that gain attention ■ alternates between clinging and independence ■ has no concept of sharing or ownership, will want what is seen.	■ to play alongside other children (parallel play) ■ to carry out simple instructions – e.g. 'Can you find your coat?'

Role of adult
- **Good supervision**: children of this age do not understand the dangers around them.
- **Distraction**: to stop unwanted behaviour; children often forget what they were doing – e.g. if a child wants another child's toy, offer him another instead.
- **Praise**: to help children understand how to get adults' attention in positive ways and to help them develop good self-esteem.
- **Being a good role model**: children learn behaviour through imitating those around them.

Age	Stage of development	Goals for behaviour
2–3 years	■ easily frustrated and may have tantrums ■ less easily distracted ■ copies actions of others ■ dislikes attention being shown to other children by carers ■ cannot wait for things ■ finds sharing difficult ■ active and restless.	■ to wait for needs to be met, for example, at mealtimes ■ to share toy or food with one other child with adult help ■ to play alongside other children ■ to sit and share a story for five minutes ■ to say 'Please' and 'Thank you' if reminded ■ to follow simple instructions with help – e.g. 'Wash your hands.'

Role of adult

■ **Good supervision and anticipation**: children are trying to be independent, but lack some of the physical and cognitive skills necessary, which makes them frustrated and angry. Adults need to anticipate possible sources of frustration and support children either by offering help or by distracting them – e.g. if they do not want to go out give them a book to look at while getting them dressed.

■ **Praise and encouragement**: to help children learn what behaviour adults expect from them. Some unwanted behaviour that is not dangerous should be ignored so children do not repeat it, hoping for adult attention.

■ **Consistency**: children are trying to work out what the limits are on their behaviour. Children of this age start to form patterns of behaviour – e.g. tantrums or whining.

■ **Being a good role model**: children model their behaviour on others around them. This is especially important at this age as they act out their experiences through play.

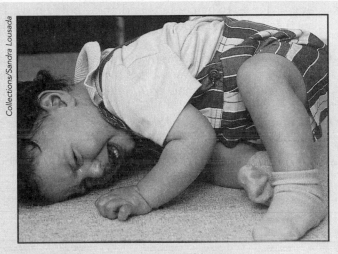
Collections/Sandra Lousada

Tantrums are often a result of frustration

Age	Stage of development	Goals for behaviour
3–4	■ follows simple rules by imitating other children – e.g. collects aprons before painting ■ able to wait for a short while ■ enjoys activities – e.g. painting ■ enjoys being with other children ■ able to play co-operatively ■ enjoys helping adults ■ occasional tantrums – often when tired and frustrated.	■ to follow rules in games when helped by adult – e.g. playing Lotto ■ to say 'Please' and 'Thank you' often without reminder ■ to take turns and share equipment ■ to follow instructions of adults most of the time – e.g. 'Shall we put the red bricks away?' ■ to help tidy up.

Role of adult

■ **Praise and encouragement**: to build confidence – makes children more likely to show desirable behaviour.

■ **Explanation of rules**: children are more likely to remember and understand rules that are explained.

■ **Good supervision**: although children are able to do many things for themselves, they are still unaware of the dangers around them. Most of the time children will be able to play well together, but squabbles will still break out.

■ **Being a good role model**: to help children learn the social skills they will need to resolve arguments and express their feelings.

■ **Supporting children**: to try to resolve their own conflicts – e.g. 'What do you think we can do to make sure you all have a turn on the slide?'

Age	Stage of development	Goals for behaviour
4–5	■ plays with other children without help from adults ■ able to communicate feelings and wishes ■ understands the needs for rules.	■ to ask permission to use other children's toys ■ to comfort playmates in distress ■ to say 'Please' and 'Thank you' without a reminder ■ to tidy up after activities.

Role of adult
- **Providing activities and tasks**: that are stimulating and allow children to develop confidence. Children of this age are keen to help adults and enjoy being busy. Tasks such as laying the table or getting objects allow children to feel independent.
- **Praise and encouragement**: to make children feel good about themselves. This is important because children often start school at this time. They need to feel they are able to be 'good'.
- **Explanation**: to help children remember and understand the need for rules or decisions.
- **Being a good role model**: to help children learn social skills, as they are copying what they see.
- **Supporting children**: and giving them opportunities to resolve potential problems themselves – e.g. 'I have some drinks here, how do you think that we can share them?'

Age	Stage of development	Goals for behaviour
5–8	■ has strong friendships ■ able to argue back ■ copies behaviour of other children – e.g. swearing or spitting ■ understands the need for rules and plays games that have rules ■ understands the difference between right and wrong ■ has many self-help skills – e.g. getting dressed, wiping up spills.	■ to follow instructions from adults ■ to apologise to others ■ to listen to others **From six years onwards** ■ to work independently and quietly in school settings ■ to be helpful and thoughtful.

Role of adult
- **Praise and encouragement**: so children do not look for other ways of gaining attention. Praise is needed as children become more aware of others and compare themselves critically.
- **Explanation**: so that children can understand the reasons for rules and decisions. Children should also be made to consider the effect of their actions on others.
- As children become older they are likely to argue back and so clear boundaries are needed and have to be enforced.
- **Being a good role model**: children are trying to understand more about the adults they are with. Speech and actions are modelled increasingly on adults they admire.
- **Providing activities and responsibilities**: to help children 'mature' as they learn more about their capabilities. Small responsibilities help children to become independent as well as giving them confidence – e.g. asking them to tidy areas of a setting or pour out drinks for other children.

Think about it

Look at these examples and consider whether these types of behaviour are usual for these ages of children.

A four-year-old snatches a ball from a two-year-old.

Two six-year-olds share out some biscuits.

A two-year-old has a tantrum when the telephone is moved out of the way.

A seven-year-old argues back to an adult.

A five-year-old cries because he has to wait for his turn.

Other areas of development affect behaviour

There is a strong link between the overall development of children and their ability to demonstrate acceptable behaviour. For example, many social skills such as sharing or turn-taking require children to think of others. Where children are delayed in some aspect of their development, they are likely to show behaviour that is not normally associated with their age. Even a slight delay can affect a child's behaviour.

Early years workers often find that many children who have a developmental delay are aggressive or have tantrums. This behaviour is often a result of children's general frustration. For example, they might see what they want, but not have the language to express their needs or the physical strength or mobility to get it. Early years workers who work with such children

need to be patient and get to know the children well, so that they can understand their needs and, therefore, prevent incidents from occurring.

Ways to help children show appropriate behaviour

Early years workers have an important role in helping children learn and show desirable behaviour. By carefully working with children we can often create a positive atmosphere in which unwanted behaviour is rare.

We have already looked at the theories of how children learn behaviour and established that adults can help by:

- acting as good role models for children (social learning theory)

- rewarding children for wanted behaviour; ignoring some inappropriate behaviour (behaviourist theory)

- having positive expectations of children's behaviour (self-fulfilling prophecy).

In addition, we can also help children show appropriate behaviour by giving them clear guidelines on what is and is not acceptable. This is often called setting boundaries and goals.

Setting boundaries and goals

Imagine playing a game where nobody tells you the rules. You might decide to work out the rules by testing what happens if you do something. Children do this when there are no clear directions and boundaries – for example, they might push another child down the slide or tip out toys to see what reaction they get from the adults.

Setting clear goals and boundaries helps children know what is expected. A goal is a target for behaviour – for example, an early years worker might remind a child that she should say 'Please' if she wants something.

A boundary sets the limit on behaviour. They are often simple rules that children learn must not be broken – for example, 'You mustn't throw sand.' Most boundaries concentrate on keeping children safe – for example, 'We never slam doors.'

Using goals and boundaries with children

✔ Use simple clear language when directing children – e.g. 'It's time to tidy up now.'

✔ Help children by reminding them of the rules – e.g. 'Yes, you can play, but remember we always wait for our turn.'

✔ Explain the rules – children are more likely to remember the rules if they understand them – e.g. 'We mustn't push each other, because someone might fall and get hurt.'

✔ Praise children when they are showing appropriate behaviour.

✔ Some rules can be written down to remind children – e.g. 'Four children can play in the sand pit.'

✔ Explain clearly what will happen if the boundaries are broken – e.g. 'I may have to take this toy away.'

Consistency

Children need to know that the rules do not keep changing. Sometimes children with behavioural difficulties have not been handled consistently by their carers. Knowing that the boundaries and goals are set helps children feel secure. This is why it is important for early years workers to work closely with parents and to have an agreed policy in a setting.

Think about it

Tara has just started as a nanny to two boys aged two and four years old. They often jump over the furniture and throw cushions on the floor. When Tara stops them from doing this, the oldest child says 'Mummy says it doesn't matter and we don't have to listen to you!'

Tara is finding it increasingly difficult to work with the children as it seems they can do whatever they want.

In pairs:

■ Work out a role play where Tara talks to the parents about the difficulties she is having.

■ What do you think might happen if Tara does not talk over the situation with her employers?

Think about it

Sally is a nanny and she looks after Freya who is three years old. Most of the time Freya is easy to work with and Sally enjoys looking after her. Recently Freya's grandmother has come to stay. She has not seen her grandchild for a few months and feels that she has a right to spoil her!

This means that when Sally reminds Freya of the rules, the grandmother steps in and tells Freya not to worry. Sally is starting to find the presence of the grandmother a strain, as Freya has learnt that if she whines enough her grandmother will give in.

1 Why is it important that Sally talks to her employer about how she is feeling?
2 Why would Freya's grandmother wish to 'spoil' her grandchild?
3 How can Sally help to work with the grandmother?

Policies in the work setting

To make sure that all staff members are working together and managing children's behaviour in the same way, settings have behaviour policies. When settings are inspected, these policies are also checked by the registration unit to see that early years workers do not humiliate or use corporal punishment on children.

Most settings also make sure that parents are aware of the behaviour policy so that, where possible, parents and carers can use similar methods.

If you are working with a child as a nanny or childminder, it is important to find out from the parents what they view as acceptable and unacceptable behaviour. An agreed approach will help everyone, including the child, work together.

Good supervision is often the key to managing behaviour

Most incidents involving inappropriate behaviour happen when there are no adults in sight or when children have become bored with an activity. Early years workers need to keep an eye on all the children they are working with and make sure that everyone has an activity that is suitable for them.

Warning signs that children are becoming bored or have found something inappropriate to do include:

- short squabbles
- equipment being thrown around or being used inappropriately
- raised angry or excited voices
- silence.

Always investigate if children are very quiet. Often with young children it means they have found something exciting – and probably dangerous – to do!

Think about it

In pairs, think back to your own childhood. What was the 'naughtiest' thing that you did?

1 What did you do?
2 How old were you?
3 Was an adult present?

Intervening when children show unwanted behaviour

We have looked at ways to promote children's behaviour, but early years workers also need to know how to react when children are showing unwanted behaviour. This will vary with the age of the children and also the behaviour they are showing. Common techniques that are used include:

No!	This single word can often stop inappropriate behaviour, especially if you make eye contact with child. It is important not to overuse this word, otherwise it will lose its impact. Also you should make sure that when it is said children are not allowed to carry on with their behaviour.
Distraction	This technique is particularly effective with younger children. The aim is to take their attention away from whatever is causing the difficulty – e.g. if a child wants another child's toy, he could be offered another toy instead. Older children may need to be distracted if the reason they are showing inappropriate behaviour is because they are bored – e.g. a group of children waiting for a story or activity might need distracting by singing some rhymes or asking them to play a simple game such as I Spy.
Explanation	Older children can often be stopped from misbehaving simply by explaining why their behaviour is not

Explanation *(continued)*	appropriate – e.g. 'If you carry on doing that, you could break a window or hurt someone.' You could also explain the possible consequences if they do not stop their actions – e.g. 'I'll have to take the ball away.'
Sanctions	Sometimes older children need to learn that there will be some sanctions if they carry on – e.g. 'If you don't sit down, you'll miss the story.' Sanctions are quite negative and it is always better to try more positive approaches first. Always think carefully before threatening a sanction as you may have to follow it through. If sanctions are threatened and then not used children will learn that you do not mean what you say.
Facial expression and body language	Many experienced early years workers are able to control children's behaviour merely by giving them a 'look'. This is an effective way of managing children's behaviour as it shows that you are calm and in control. Once children have understood that you are unhappy and they start to behave more appropriately, you can praise them.
Removal of equipment	Removing equipment should be a final measure to be used if children are damaging equipment or are likely to hurt themselves. It is important to explain to children why the equipment is being removed.
Time out	Some older children respond well to being removed from the situation that is causing them difficulty. Time out should not be used as a punishment, otherwise children are likely to feel excluded and this will increase the likelihood of further problems in the future. Never leave children on their own but, if necessary, sit away from them so they have their own 'space'.

Specific types of unwanted behaviour

There are some specific types of unwanted behaviour that early years workers may have to deal with. Often such behaviour shows that children are being affected by other factors – for example, a delay in their development – or that they are emotionally disturbed. If you are concerned about a child's behaviour, you should always mention it to your supervisor – or the parents if you are working in the home environment (see also page 204).

The chart opposite looks at some specific types of unwanted behaviour.

Think about it

Mark is three years old. He is playing with his friend Simon at the sand tray. He flicks some sand up into the air. He smiles and does it again. The supervisor walks over and says 'We don't throw sand because it can hurt your eyes.'

Mark looks her directly in the eye and smiles. He picks up a little sand and throws it into the sandpit slowly. The supervisor is sure that he has understood the boundaries, but is just trying to see what her reaction is going to be.

1 What should the supervisor say or do next?
2 Why is it important that she should intervene?
3 Why should she praise Mark once he is showing appropriate behaviour?

Factors affecting children's behaviour

Quite often the way that children behave reflects how they feel about themselves or what is happening in their lives. Most early years workers will notice children becoming more boisterous around certain times of the year!

A change in a child's behaviour can indicate a change in their circumstances and this is why it is important to exchange information with parents. Occasionally, a

Factors affecting children's behaviour

Type of behaviour	Common causes	Role of adult
Comfort behaviour ■ thumb sucking ■ masturbation ■ rocking	■ tiredness or boredom ■ fear or anxiety ■ regression ■ serious emotional disturbance. Many children show this behaviour when they are tired or under temporary stress. Occasionally, comfort behaviour may be a sign of some emotional disturbance and the child may need specialist help. Masturbation is common in very young children, especially boys, but it is rarer in children over five years old.	Consider if the child might be unwell or particularly tired. Distract the child with another activity. If such comfort behaviour is frequent and excessive, it should be reported to the supervisor or parents.
Destructive behaviour ■ throwing objects ■ head banging ■ temper tantrums ■ biting and kicking	■ frustration ■ serious emotional disturbance. This behaviour shows that the child is temporarily out of control. Sometimes the anger is caused by a deeper frustration – e.g. being bullied – or the child may have some developmental difficulties – e.g. poor speech.	Remain calm and speak quietly to the child. If necessary, remove the child from the situation – although if the child is likely to fight back, remove other children and equipment. (You may decide to seek help from another member of staff.) Once the child has calmed down, it is important to work out what caused the upset and also to make sure that the child knows that this behaviour is unacceptable.
Attention-seeking behaviour ■ clinging ■ interrupting activities ■ answering back ■ challenging instructions	■ insecurity ■ difficulties in socialising with peers ■ habit. Attention-seeking behaviour is often a sign of insecurity and sometimes low self-esteem. Older children may have learnt that this is a good way of getting an adult's attention. It can make children unpopular with other children, especially if they disrupt activities – e.g. story time.	It is often best to ignore attention-seekers, but to give them plenty of praise when they are showing more appropriate behaviour. Eventually, if they are given plenty of attention in other ways, they will lose the habit. Sometimes, long-term attention-seeking can be a sign that a child needs specialist help and you should mention your concerns to the supervisor.
Inappropriate verbal remarks ■ swearing, ■ racist comments ■ other offensive remarks	■ insecurity ■ overhearing but not understanding remarks. Most young children repeat words and phrases that they do not necessarily understand themselves, but that they have heard. Some older children may make comments to deliberately hurt and thus gain power over other children. This behaviour may mean that their own self-esteem is poor.	Manage inappropriate comments sensitively. When a young child has made a remark, ask him where he heard it and what he thinks it means. Explain that this language is not used in your setting, because other people do not like it. Where older children deliberately upset other children, it is important that they understand that this behaviour is wrong and unacceptable. Ask them why they are using it and why they wish to hurt other children.

change in a child's behaviour may indicate child abuse, in which case, you should pass your concerns on to your supervisor (see also below).

How changes in children's lives can affect their behaviour

The way children react to a change in their lives depends very much on individual circumstances as well as the age of the child and the child's understanding of the situation. Early years workers need to provide a lot of reassurance and security when children are reacting to a change in their lives. This is not always easy, because some children test the boundaries to see how secure they really are. For example, with a new nanny, children might show some quite appalling behaviour to test out what will happen and also to see if the nanny really does care for them!

Most children quickly settle down after a change in their lives, providing they feel secure and loved, although some children may continue to show some of the specific behaviours that are mentioned in the chart above – for example, attention-seeking.

Think about it

Harry is five years old and is starting school in September. His mother has noticed that at times he is quite clingy, whereas at other times he is aggressive towards his baby sister.

His mother mentions this to the supervisor at the play scheme who says that this behaviour is quite normal as he is likely to be worrying about starting school. The mother asks how she should tackle Harry's behaviour when he is aggressive as she finds herself shouting at him.

- In pairs, work out the answer that the play scheme worker should give.

- How can the play scheme worker help Harry to feel more secure?

Common changes that affect children include:

- divorce and separation of parents

- re-marriage of one parent

- moving house

- new baby in the family

- death or illness in the family

- change of class or school

- having a new carer – e.g. nanny.

Reporting and recording children's behaviour

Part of the role of an early years worker is to keep records. If a child shows a change in behaviour or a serious incident occurs – for example, one child biting another – this needs to be recorded. Records of behaviour should include the date, time and type of incident, along with how it was handled. If there were any injuries as a result of the behaviour, the accident book should be used (see page 255).

Any written records are always confidential and should be stored safely. Parents should always be informed if a child's behaviour is giving concern, although it may be the role of the supervisor or key worker to talk to the parents. Involving parents is important, as they may be having difficulties at home or they may have an idea why there has been a change in behaviour. Quite often, parents and early years workers will agree to monitor any further behaviour and then meet again if necessary. The staff will probably suggest that both the parents and the setting keep a record of the child's behaviour.

Assessing children's behaviour

If a child's behaviour is giving some concern it is important to look more closely at the child before deciding on any strategies to deal with the behaviour. There may be some triggers in the setting that are causing the behaviour or, after studying the child, it may be decided that the behaviour is not particularly abnormal. In some cases, specialists, such as educational psychologists or psychiatrists, may be involved.

Most information used to assess children's behaviour is taken from observations carried out by early years workers and other professionals and from information provided by parents.

Once enough information has been gathered, strategies can be considered to help the child.

Ways of recording children's behaviour

The main aim of recording children's behaviour is to provide an accurate picture of what is happening. Sometimes, a child may seem to be disruptive, but after looking more closely at the child and behaviour, staff may realise that the behaviour is a result of boredom. In order to build up an accurate picture, it is essential to look at the child for a period of time and to use a range of recording methods.

Early years workers may use the methods shown in the table below to record behaviour (see also pages 91–96 in Chapter 4).

Working with parents and other professionals

If children's behaviour is of serious concern, they may be referred for some specialist help. Children are often referred to these professionals by their family doctor or by their parents after concerns have been raised.

Early years workers will often be asked to a team meeting if specialists feel they need a wider assessment of the child's behaviour. Team meetings allow an exchange of information and ideas so that a picture of the child's behaviour can be built up. All information exchanged during these meetings is confidential and this trust must never be broken. Following a meeting, parents and early years workers may be given some strategies to use with the child. It is essential that any programme is followed carefully otherwise it will not be successful. It is common for early years workers to be asked to keep some further records while the child's behaviour is being changed.

Specialists involved in advising on children's behaviour include:

Play therapist   Works with children using play as a medium to allow children to express their feelings and fears.

Event sample	This method is used every time the behaviour occurs. The record should show what has happened, who the child was with and how the incident was handled.
Diary	This method is used to provide an overall picture of the child's behaviour and mood. It is a non-structured method and it is important that the person recording is able to remain as objective as she can. Diaries can build up a picture of the child's overall behaviour and participation in activities.
Sociogram	Where it is thought that an older child's behaviour is linked to his social development, a sociogram may be carried out. A sociogram is a structured observation in which children are asked to name three or so of their friends. Staff may find that a child is not being named by other children (see also page 170 in Chapter 8 and page 95 in Chapter 4).
Video recording 	Some settings may be able to video activities. Video recordings are useful because they can provide a reasonably accurate picture of a child's behaviour, providing they do not know they are being filmed.

Think about it

Look at the following event sample that was used to observe Dean's behaviour over a day. Concerns had been expressed because Dean, aged five years, had been in trouble several times in the playground.

Event	Time	Children and adults present	Incident	Action taken
1	8.55 am	Sam, Michael	Dean kicks Sam when Sam will not allow him into the line.	Dean is taken into the classroom by Mrs James.
2	10.32	Michael, Joshua and Simon	Dean walks up to the group and asks to join in the game of marbles. Michael says 'Go away.' Dean kicks the marbles.	Dean is warned by Mr Brown.
3	10.39	Kerry, Jenny and Holly	Jenny catches hold of Dean's coat during a game of chase. Dean pushes her away roughly. Jenny falls down.	Mr Brown tells Dean not to be so rough.
4	10.45	Michael, and others lining up	Dean tries to find a place in the line. Michael stops Dean from getting in. Dean kicks Michael twice in the shins.	Mr Brown tells Dean to say sorry and to find another place in the line.
5	12.17	Midday supervisor	Dean sticks his tongue out at the midday supervisor when she asks him to move away from the school gate.	Dean is sent inside to see his teacher, Mrs James.
6	12.45	Michael, Simon and Harry	Dean is playing chase with Simon and Harry. Michael calls him a 'fat idiot'. Dean pushes him over.	Dean is told by the midday supervisor to line up early.

■ Can you see any pattern to Dean's behaviour?

■ Why might it be helpful to carry out a sociogram to find out if Dean has any friends?

■ How might an adult be able to support Dean at playtimes?

■ How might providing play equipment be useful for children of Dean's age?

Observation – event sample

With your placement supervisor, choose one child whose behaviour might be interesting to observe. Carry out an event sample on this child, noting down the number of times a particular behaviour occurs, who else is involved and how the behaviour is dealt with (see also pages 87–88).

Interpretation – consider what is contributing to the behaviour.

- Is this type of behaviour unusual for this age range?

- Why might the child be showing this type of behaviour?

- Is the child trying to gain attention?

- Is there any pattern to the behaviour?

- Are there any triggers to the behaviour?

- How does the child react after the incident?

Recommendations consider how this child might be helped to control his behaviour.

- What activities might be provided?

- How could adults support the child?

- Are you able to work more closely with this child?

- Would it be useful to carry out further observations?

Personal learning

- What have you learnt about children in this age range?

- What have you learnt about this particular child?

- What have you found out about ways of managing behaviour?

- What have you found out about this observation method?

Educational psychologist	Specialises in the way children learn and behave. Carries out diagnostic tests on children's language and cognitive development.
Child psychiatrist	Works with children and family to find out what the child is thinking and feeling.
Health visitor	Advises and monitors all aspects of children's development under the age of five. Has completed training about managing children's behaviour.

Behavioural modification strategies

We know that once behaviour has been learnt, it can be difficult for children to correct it. Psychologists have developed several techniques based on the behaviourist theory to change children's behaviour. They are often known as behaviour modification techniques.

Star charts

The idea of a star chart is to reward a child for wanted behaviour in a positive and tangible way. Children are told that every time they show a certain type of behaviour – for example, they help tidy up – they will get a sticker. The sticker is put on to a chart and the

child is told that when he has a certain number of stickers he will be given another reward.

Stickers or stars are most commonly used because children can actually hold and see them. The star chart method is often used with children over four years as it not very effective with younger children.

Using star charts with children

- Make sure that children know what they have to do to get a star.

- Set achievable targets for them – if it is too hard, they will fail and come to believe they are not able to be good.

- Give the star or sticker soon after the behaviour has been shown.

- Do not use the stickers as a threat – e.g. 'If you don't behave you won't get a sticker' – the whole experience should be positive.

Changing children's behaviour gradually

Sometimes we can change children's behaviour simply by boosting their confidence and self-esteem. We can set small goals for children to work towards and make sure they achieve them. This allows them to gain praise and attention and, over a few days, they will start to show more appropriate behaviour. It is important to realise that changing behaviour is not like doing magic – patience and preparation are needed, as a real change in behaviour may take several weeks and, in between, the child will often try to revert to the previous behaviour. The message must be 'Do not give up!'

Good Dragon Star Chart

1. When you do a good thing, your teacher or parent will let you colour in a spot on the dragon.

2. When you have coloured in all his spots, you will be given a present.

Think about it

Marie has started a job as a nanny to twin boys aged three years. Their mother finds it hard at weekends to manage their behaviour as they want her attention. She often finds it easier to 'bribe' them with sweets and toys or becomes cross with them and smacks them. This Monday, Marie finds that Joshua and Stefan's behaviour is particularly challenging. They start off by clinging to their mother and then, once she has left, start throwing toys and books on to the floor. Joshua then goes into the fridge and pours milk on to the floor while Stefan starts scribbling on the walls.

Why are Joshua and Stefan showing such difficult behaviour?

What could Marie do to manage their behaviour?

Why is it important that early years workers plan activities for young children?

ISSUES   Physical punishment

Fortunately for early years workers, there is no question, as it is illegal for us to smack or be aggressive towards a child, although the law does allow parents to 'reasonably chastise'.

Many parents feel that smacking is a good way of disciplining children, although research (Rohner et al, 1991) shows that it can cause emotional tensions in the family and teach children to be aggressive. There have also been cases where children have been injured as parents can easily misjudge the strength of their actions.

It is incredible to think that in a supermarket someone can strike a child and no one will do anything, but were they to strike another adult, the police would be called!

Why smacking does not work

- It does not teach children how to resolve conflicts peacefully.

- Young children do not always understand why they have been smacked.

- The fear of a smack can lead children to lie about their actions.

- Children learn that being violent can be acceptable.

- Smacking does not show children how to control their anger.

- Children who have been smacked are more likely to smack when they are parents.

- Most parents are not very consistent about when they smack. This means that children learn that sometimes a behaviour is accepted, whereas at other times it is not.

- Parents who find that they are smacking a lot may benefit from attending a parent group such as parent link which runs classes on how to manage children's behaviour.

Check your knowledge

- Why is it important for early years workers to read and use the behaviour policy of the setting?

- How is social learning theory used when encouraging acceptable behaviour?

- What types of reinforcers can be used with children to encourage them to repeat desirable behaviour?

- Why do some children appear not to mind being 'in trouble'?

- Name three goals for behaviour that an early years worker might encourage a two-year-old to show.

- What is meant by the expression 'boundary setting'?

- Outline two factors that might affect children's behaviour?

- Name three strategies that early years workers might use to manage children's behaviour and explain how they might be used.

- What recording methods might be used to monitor and assess children's behaviour?

- What is behaviour modification and when might it be used?

- Which other professionals might also be involved with managing children's behaviour?

- Why is it important to keep records of children's behaviour?

- What is the link between children's stage of development and their behaviour?

- Explain why it is important to avoid 'labelling' a child.

Resources

Further reading

Warden, David & Christie, Donald 1997 *Teaching Social Behaviour,* London, David Fulton Publishers

CHAPTER

Health and community care

As an early years worker, you will come into contact with sick children. This chapter looks at children's health and at the needs of sick children. It is divided into six main sections:

- *health promotion and surveillance*
- *identifying common illnesses in children*
- *caring for sick children*

- *giving medicines and keeping records*
- *the effects of illness on children and families*
- *emergencies and first aid treatment.*

What is health?

The World Health Organisation defines health as 'a state of complete physical, mental and social well being and not merely the absence of disease or infirmity'. Everyone has a different concept about what health means to them and the definition of health can also include spiritual, emotional, environmental, the health of the community and societal health.

Think about it

What does health mean to you?
Do you think that everyone, including children, has 'a right to health?'

The promotion and maintenance of health

Health promotion in children and adults

The World Health Organisation defines health promotion as: 'the process of enabling people to increase their control over, and improve, their health'. This means that everyone, including children, needs the right information about their health and health issues so they can make informed choices about their lifestyle. This not only involves health education for individuals, but wider community issues, such as anti-smoking campaigns and healthy working conditions.

The health promoters

Everyone can be involved in promoting health. Early years workers and parents do this constantly through day-to-day routines, such as hand washing, and by being good role models.

On page 212 is a chart of the main people and organisations involved in promoting health.

Others with a role in health and safety include the police, who teach children to protect themselves, and provide road safety training, and the fire brigade, who teach fire awareness.

Health education

Health education aims at preventing illness. It emphasises being healthy and improving health and includes wider issues in society, such as anti-smoking campaigns.

There are different types of health education programmes: primary, secondary and tertiary health education.

Different approaches to health education
Health educators will try to get their message across in a variety of ways in order to make an impact on the targeted group.

Aims of health education programmes

Type of health education	Aims of the health education
Primary health education	This aims to improve health by giving information and advice on staying healthy. Primary health education for children includes healthy eating, care of the teeth, hygiene and road safety.
Secondary health education	This aims at educating people to change their behaviour in order to restore good health – e.g. giving up smoking.
Tertiary health education	This aims to limit the impact of a chronic illness or disability by teaching children how to reach their potential. This could involve, for example, specially adapted wheel chairs.

These approaches include:

- the medical approach, which aims to prevent illness through a series of public health measures – e.g. health screening of all children

- the educational approach, which provides information and/or the necessary skills to enable the child or parent to make an informed choice

- the behavioural change approach, which aims to encourage people to change their behaviour – e.g. giving up smoking

- the empowerment approach, which aims to help people develop the skills, confidence and self-esteem to make changes – this can be used on an individual basis or within the community and can include building up children's self-esteem through personal safety role plays

- the fear creation approach, where the health educator may try to change behaviour using frightening tactics – e.g. drink-drive campaigns which replay accidents or talk to victims of accidents.

Health educators will usually use a variety of approaches to educate. For example, when doing a topic on teeth, the children might be seen by the dentist to have their teeth checked (medical), have a talk by a dental nurse and do some worksheets (educational), be shown how to use a toothbrush and have a go at brushing some giant plastic teeth (behavioural change) – these will all help to empower the children to take some responsibility for the care of their own teeth. They could also be shown some photographs of bad teeth which might frighten children into brushing their teeth.

The role of the early years worker

Early years workers must:

- know and understand how to maintain their own personal health and that of the children in their care

- teach children about health issues, as part of the pre-school and school curriculum.

On page 213 is a table of some health promotion topics and how they can be taught to children.

Other topics could include: personal safety, road, water, rail and electrical safety.

Health education within the family
Most first-time parents have little knowledge of parenting or caring for children. They need information on pregnancy, diet, breast- and bottle-feeding, immunisations, weaning, and many other less pleasant things, like headlice! The health visitor is a useful source of this information. Early years workers may also be responsible for passing on information to parents.

Think about it

In pairs, think of an activity for five-year-olds about healthy eating.

Write out a curriculum plan. Decide what materials and resources you will need and how long it will take.

The health promoters	How health is promoted
World Health Organisation	Sets global health targets – e.g. to reduce the incidence of skin cancer and to increase the uptake of immunisations.
Government	Creates health policies and Acts – e.g. the 1990 NHS and Community Care Act.
National voluntary organisations and pressure groups	These either put pressure on the government to change policies – e.g. The Society for the Protection of Unborn Children – or give information about certain issues – e.g. The National Childbirth Trust.
The media	Provide programmes on television and radio and articles in newspapers about health issues.
Primary health care team (see page 220)	Runs clinics in surgeries and health centres. Many offer classes – e.g. asthma clinics and antenatal classes.
School nurse	Provides health screening, information and some teaching of health matters to children at school and to parents.
Dentist	Provides teaching on dental hygiene and the prevention of tooth decay.
Teacher	Teaching on health issues is part of the PSE (Personal and Social Education) programme in schools.
Health promotion unit	This unit provides training, courses, exhibitions, advice and support on any health initiative. It also offers a free loan service of health education videos, displays, books, project packs, CD-ROMS and provides leaflets and posters.

Unfortunately, those in most need of health education, are often the least likely to use the services provided or to attend clinics. This is sometimes due to fear or distrust of the services, lack of understanding about the importance of health issues, or ignorance of the available services.

Those who may be the most in need of health education and child surveillance include:

- single-parent families – if they lack support

- those living in poor housing, or in overcrowded conditions

- parents who have experienced neonatal death or Sudden Infant Death Syndrome in a child

- people who are socially isolated, including those for whom English is their second language

- people with a history of postnatal depression or mental health problems

- people with a history of congenital defects in the family.

Influences on health

There are many factors that influence the health of the children within your care; these include the following:

- Lifestyle – whether the parents smoke (increased risk of chest infections, Sudden Infant Death Syndrome and asthma), the child's diet (a good diet is necessary for normal growth and development) and amount of exercise (exercise helps to develop motor skills and increases muscle strength, joint mobility, and co-ordination). These will all affect the child's health.

- Genetic factors – children will inherit factors from both parents that may affect their health. Some conditions, such as haemophilia and cystic fibrosis (see page 227) are passed on through the genes from one or both parents to the child. There can also be an abnormality of one of the chromosomes (genetic factors), as in Down's Syndrome.

■ Poverty – the poorer the family, the greater are the health risks and the more likely the children are to suffer from chronic sickness and tooth decay. These children are less likely to attend screening and developmental checks as well as immunisations.

■ The environment – poor housing conditions (can cause an increase in respiratory infections); air pollutants (can increase the risk of respiratory problems); poor water supply (can cause water-borne diseases).

■ Response to allergens – allergens are the cause of an allergic response in some children. Some children can have an allergic reaction to anything, including some food substances, grass, animal hair or saliva and house dust mites. Children react to these allergens in a variety of ways including hay fever, asthma, diarrhoea, skin rashes, colic or headaches.

The causes of infections
Germs (called micro-organisms) which enter the body and cause illness are divided into three groups: bacteria, viruses and fungi.

■ Bacteria need warmth, moisture, darkness and food to survive and include whooping cough, impetigo, some ear infections and tuberculosis.

Health promotion topics

Subject	Aim	Activities
Teeth	To help children understand: ■ the importance of brushing teeth ■ when and how to brush teeth.	■ games involving food that is good and bad for the teeth ■ demonstration of correct tooth brushing with a large set of teeth and brush – available from the health promotion unit (HPU) ■ drawing pictures of their own teeth ■ visitor: dentist or dental nurse.
Personal hygiene	To help children understand: ■ the reasons for, and importance of, washing ■ how to wash hands correctly ■ hair care.	■ handwashing games – e.g. painting the early years worker's hands and asking the children to guess how long it would take to get the hands clean ■ videos – from the HPU ■ visitor: school nurse or health visitor.
Diet	To teach children about: ■ healthy foods ■ the importance of healthy eating.	■ drawing healthy and unhealthy lunch boxes for fictional characters ■ making posters of the different food groups ■ visitor: dietitian, health visitor or school nurse.
Fire safety	To ensure children become more aware of: ■ how fires can be caused ■ the dangers of playing with matches ■ what to do, and what not to do, in the event of a fire ■ how to make an emergency phone call.	■ booklets – from the HPU ■ books aimed at children ■ fire practice – e.g. Fireman Sam ■ role play with telephones ■ visitor: fire officer.

ISSUES in health care

Some religions, such as Jehovah's Witnesses, discourage their members from having some forms of medical treatment, such as blood transfusions. There have been cases where the courts have overruled the parents' wishes so that children might be given life-saving treatment. How far do you think that the religious wishes of parents should be taken into consideration?

Look at these points of view.

- Interfering with other people's religion is wrong.

- Children have a right to medical treatment.

- It's not fair for children to be denied life-saving treatment because of their parents' views.

- Children have a right to have their views taken into account.

- Viruses invade the cells in the body where they reproduce and are not affected by antibiotics. Examples of these are colds, flu, chickenpox, measles, mumps, rubella and AIDS (acquired immunodeficiency syndrome) caused by the HIV virus.

- Fungi – some fungi are not harmful to humans – e.g. yeast – but others can cause ringworm and thrush.

Parasites
There are some parasites which can affect humans, such as headlice, scabies and threadworms.

Some germs aren't harmful to humans – for example, there are organisms that live in the bowel and manufacture vitamin K, which is essential in the blood-clotting process.

Illness prevention

Prevention and early detection is very important and saves many lives. Many children in the UK used to die from infectious diseases, such as cholera and measles – as they still do in the Third World. The main reasons for the improvement in child health are:

- good sanitation

- clean water supply

- healthier diet

- better housing

- free health care and prescriptions

- antibiotics

- improved antenatal care

- child health screening and immunisation.

Immunisation

Immunisation against nine serious diseases is available to all babies and children at different ages. It is done at either the child health clinic or the doctor's surgery, and is often combined with developmental checks.

Immunisation is not compulsory in the UK so parents must be given information on the implications and possible side-effects of the immunisation and they may need to sign a consent form. Some parents choose not to have their child immunised for religious or medical reasons or because of previous side-effects. The doctor must be informed if the child is taking any medicines or has had a previous bad reaction to an immunisation. If the child is unwell, it is usually considered best to wait until he or she is better.

Care of a child following immunisation
Although serious side-effects are rare, some babies will have a mild reaction, often within the first 48 hours. These include irritability, a mild fever and

soreness and redness around the injection site. If any of these symptoms appear, infant paracetamol is often prescribed. A small lump may appear at the site but should disappear over the next few weeks.

MMR can produce mild symptoms of the illnesses it is aimed at preventing:

- signs of measles after seven to ten days
- signs of mumps after three weeks
- a rash like rubella after two weeks.

Very occasionally, children can develop a severe reaction to the MMR, with a high fever and convulsions.

The polio virus will be excreted in the baby's faeces for up to six weeks, so hand washing is particularly important when changing nappies.

Child health surveillance

All children need to be checked at regular intervals to ensure they are developing normally and that any condition they might have picked up is treated early and appropriate care given. For example, a child who has glue ear (see page 225) may have delayed language skills if it is not picked up and treated early.

At birth, parents are given a Personal Child Health Record Book in which health care professionals will record the results of all developmental checks, weight checks and any advice given by the health visitor.

Development charts

Every area has its own charts to record development. The Personal Child Health Record Book contains charts on which the child's weight, height and head circumference are plotted (see Chapter 5, page 106).

The immunisation schedule		
Birth	BCG	given if there is a risk of contact with tuberculosis
8 weeks	diphtheria, whooping cough, and tetanus	sometimes called the 'triple vaccine', these are given in one injection
	polio	taken by mouth
	Hib	an injection against one type of meningitis
12 weeks	as for 8 weeks	as for 8 weeks
16 weeks	as for 8 weeks	as for 8 weeks
12–18 months	measles, mumps and rubella (MMR)	given in one injection
3–5 years (pre-school)	diphtheria and tetanus	booster injection
	polio	booster by mouth
	MMR	booster injection
10–14 years	BCG	given by injection
13–18 years	diphtheria and tetanus	booster injection
	polio	booster by mouth

Health and developmental checks

There are four main ways to check a child's development:

1 by asking questions of, and listening to, parents and/or carers
2 by measuring height, weight and head circumference
3 by physical examination
4 by observation of the child during structured or unstructured activities (see Chapter 4).

After the neonatal (at birth) checks, all subsequent checks are carried out by either the health visitor or the doctor. Each developmental area is checked to ensure the child is developing at the appropriate rate. Specific areas, such as hearing are also tested.

The sooner a condition is detected, the sooner the appropriate treatment can be started, or the appropriate care organised.

If any problems are picked up on these tests, the child will be seen more regularly by the doctor or health visitor, or may be referred to a specialist.

Checks at school entry
In many areas routine physical checks are no longer done at five years, although a developmental

Health and development checks

Check	Main reasons for the check	Description of the condition
Weight Height	To ensure growth follows the norm for the child and to detect 'failure to thrive' (FTT).	FTT is when a child is not growing at the expected rate – e.g. through under feeding, neglect or a serious physical disorder.
Head circumference	To detect: ■ hydrocephalus ■ microcephaly.	Hydrocephalus (water on the brain) is associated with many congenital conditions. Microcephaly – an abnormally small head – is usually associated with mental retardation.
Heart	To detect congenital heart defect (common in Down's syndrome).	Any type of heart defect will usually need surgery. If undetected, it could cause poor growth and chest infections.
Hips	To detect congenital dislocation of the hips – 'clicky hips'.	The hip joint is dislocated; this often corrects itself, but sometimes requires splints. If not detected early, traction or surgery may be required.
Testes (in boys)	To ensure that both of the testes have descended into the scrotal sac.	The testes usually descend on their own, but may require surgery. There is an increased risk of infertility.
Spine	To detect: ■ spina bifida ■ curvature of the spine.	Spina bifida is one or more bones in the back not fusing properly. This causes a bit of the spinal cord to be exposed. It can range from mild to very serious.
Reflexes	To ensure the reflexes are normal.	Abnormal reflexes can indicate a problem with the nervous system.
Feet	To detect talipes.	Talipes (club foot) is when the foot is twisted out of shape. It may be helped through physiotherapy, or may require splinting or an operation.
Hearing	To ensure the hearing is normal.	There are many different types of hearing loss, the most common of which is 'glue ear' (see page 225). The child may be referred to an audiologist.
Sight	To detect: ■ squint ■ cataract. To ensure the child sees normally.	A squint, where one eye is not aligned to the other, is initially treated with a patch over the affected eye, and later with glasses or surgery.

assessment and height and weight checks may be carried out by the school nurse. Questionnaires are sometimes sent to the parents on health issues so that any problems can be discussed.

The role of the early years worker

Early years workers are not expected to carry out developmental checks, but you will need to know the results, especially if problems or abnormalities have been detected.

Knowledge into action

Melissa is three-and-a-half years old and has just had a developmental check. She is very small for her age and reluctant to eat.

As her early years worker, what might you be asked to do for Melissa?

What actions would the other professionals take?

Pre-school health and development checks

6–8 week check	
This is usually done by the GP at the same time as the mother's postnatal check, although the health visitor may also be involved. The baby's first immunisation will also be done.	
Parental concerns may include	feeding; sleeping.
Parents will be asked about	the baby's sight; hearing; and whether the baby smiles or coos.
Developmental checks	height; weight; head circumference.
Physical examination	hips; heart; testes; reflexes and muscle tone.
Observation	reactions of baby to mother; smiles or coos; vision – turns to the light and follows a face; hearing – startles to loud noise.
Parents will be told about	feeding; immunisations; recognition of illness; advice on Sudden Infant Death Syndrome (SIDS).
6–9 month check	
There is a long time between these two checks, but the parent or carer can visit the health visitor at the Child Health Clinic for advice and to have the baby weighed. The health visitor also does home visits. This check is usually done at around 8 months because the hearing distraction test and the second immunisation is also due. The hearing test is done by the health visitor, but the check might be done by the GP.	
Parental concerns may include	weaning, sleeping.
Parents will be asked if the baby	sits unsupported; rolls; bears own weight when held standing.
Developmental checks	height; weight; head circumference.
Physical examination	hips; testes; hearing – hearing distraction test (see opposite).

6–9 month check *(continued)*

Observation:	vision – squint; picks up hundreds and thousands using a pincer grasp; watches a falling toy; puts everything in mouth.
Parents will be told about	diet; accident prevention; care of the teeth.

Hearing distraction test
The hearing distraction test is to ensure babies can hear sounds of varying pitches. It is done in a quiet room while the baby sits on the parent's lap. One health visitor sits in front of the baby and distracts him with a toy; the toy is then hidden and someone else makes a noise behind the baby. If the baby fails the test he is referred to the audiologist, a specialist in measuring hearing problems.

18–24 month check

This is often carried out by the health visitor and may sometimes be done as a home visit. Iron deficiency, which can cause anaemia, is fairly common at this age. It may cause paleness, tiredness and headaches.

Parental concerns may include	diet; toilet training; behaviour.
Parents will be asked if the baby	pushes and pulls large toys; climbs stairs and on to furniture; uses six or more words; imitates everyday activities; obeys simple commands.
Developmental checks:	height; weight.
Physical examination:	not usually done unless there are any concerns.
Observation:	gait – how child walks; builds tower of three bricks; holds crayon and scribbles; turns pages of a book – several at a time; vision – squint
Parents will be told about	dental care; toilet training; diet; accident prevention; social contacts for the baby.

3–3½ year check
This is a pre-school check and is done by either the doctor or the health visitor.

The parents will be asked if the child	can kick and throw a ball; is toilet trained in the day; takes turns in play; separates from parent; dresses with supervision.
Developmental checks:	weight; height.
Physical examination:	heart and lungs (for wheezing), and the testes.
Observation:	builds a tower of 9–10 bricks; copies O; imitates +; gives name, age, sex or address; language – clear sentences.
Parents will be told about	accident prevention; diet; dental care; toilet training; preparation for school.

Health professionals

The chart below shows the health professionals you may come into contact with if you are caring for a child at home or in hospital.

The primary health care team
This team consists of the GP, practice nurse, health visitor, community midwife, district nurse and community psychiatric nurse, but could also contain other professionals – for example, a social worker. The team is based at the doctor's surgery or health centre and provides most health care. When a child becomes unwell it will usually be one of these professionals who sees the child first. The team meets regularly in order to provide a service to the local community which includes health education, health promotion and detection and treatment of illnesses.

Hospital-based care
Hospital care is usually centred around a children's ward with a nursing team headed by a sister. Many other health professionals are also involved, including the doctors and those listed in the table opposite.

Care in the community

Children are less stressed if they are at home, so when a child is in need of health care, this is provided whenever possible, in the community. Parents will need a lot of support if they are caring for ill children at home. This may be provided by the primary health care team and others – for example, the community paediatric nurse, an audiologist or a Macmillan nurse.

Confidentiality

Confidentiality is covered in full in Chapter 3. It is very important that all information about a child's illness or condition is kept confidential. This means you will not always know the child's medical history as this is given on a 'need-to-know' basis only. It also means you should never discuss a child with your friends or with other parents. Each work setting will have a policy on confidentiality, which you need to be familiar with.

Health professionals

Professional	Role
General practitioner (GP)	Probably the first person you will see if a child is ill; usually treat children themselves, but may also refer them on to someone else.
Practice nurse	Attached to the GP's surgery – duties include immunisations; taking stitches out and dealing with dressings.
Health visitor	Conducts child health surveillance and developmental checks on children up to school age – or older in some areas.
Community midwife	Cares for the mother and baby throughout pregnancy, labour and until 10–28 days after delivery.
School nurse	Monitors health problems in school-age children; may do surveillance checks too.
Paediatrician	Based in local hospital; a doctor who specialises in treating sick children.
Sick children's nurse	Based in hospital; specially trained to care for sick children.
Play worker	A nursery nurse who may have taken a specialist hospital play course; helps children to come to terms with being in hospital, with their condition and with any procedures – e.g. surgery – that they might be there for.
Community paediatric nurse	Hospital based; sees children at home who have been discharged from hospital and who still need specialist care; this allows children home earlier than would normally be possible – very few areas have a community paediatric nurse.
Physiotherapist	Treats disorders using physical methods – e.g. exercise, massage, heat treatment, cold water (hydrotherapy), electrical currents (TENS).
Radiographer	Takes X-rays in hospital; gives radiotherapy treatment – e.g. for cancers.
Anaesthetist	Specialises in giving anaesthetics.
Audiologist	Specialises in measuring hearing problems.
Speech therapist	Works in the hospital and community; helps children with communication problems.
Occupational therapist	Helps children who have been disabled to relearn muscular control in order to do everyday tasks.
Dietitian	Helps develop appropriate diets – e.g. for diabetic children.
Dentist	Specialises in prevention and treatment of tooth decay and gum disease.
Orthodontist	Specialises in straightening teeth and ensuring they fit together properly.

Identifying common illnesses in children

General signs of illness

Most childhood illnesses have a number of common signs and symptoms. You will need to make the initial assessment of the significance of any signs of illness, so you need to know when it is necessary to summon medical help.

There are usually some signs that a child is becoming unwell before the specific signs or symptoms develop.

Identifying symptoms in children with different skin tones

If you know a child well, you should have no difficulty in detecting illness because the child's behaviour and demeanour will change as well as the skin colour.

Darker-skinned children look greyer and may have dark rings under their eyes when not well. Check the inside of the child's bottom eyelid – this is usually pale when the child is unwell or anaemic.

Rashes, which look pink on pale-skinned children, are sometimes more difficult to see on darker-skinned

children. Some rashes may appear as raised lumps. If you press the skin near a rash or spot, you can see if it disappears or not (see meningitis, page 239).

Jaundice can be detected by pressing the nose with your finger and letting go quickly. You will see a yellowish tinge before the skin colour returns. Jaundice can also be seen in the white of the eye.

Knowledge into action

Survey five parents or carers of children from a class or nursery group and ask:

1   *How can you tell when the child is coming down with something?*
2   *Does the child usually have a temperature when sick?*
3   *Does the child's behaviour change when unwell?*
4   *Are there any games/activities that the child likes to do when off school or nursery?*

If darker-skinned children scratch spots, or have a burn, they can lose some of the skin pigmentation and end up with a pale patch. Extra care should therefore

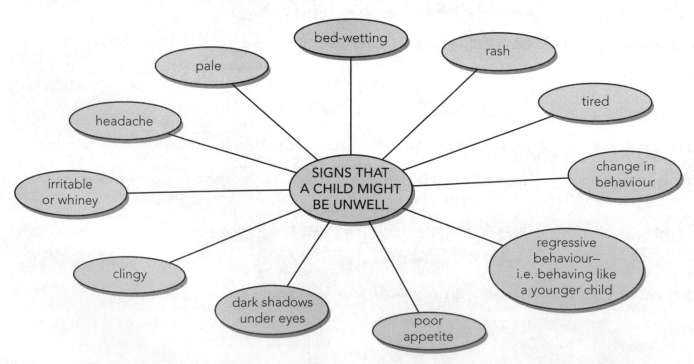

be taken to prevent children from scratching spots. Occasionally this loss of pigmentation may also happen with the use of steroid creams on eczema.

If a child is having breathing difficulties or an asthma attack, check her colour by looking for a blueish tinge on the fingertips and lips.

Childhood illnesses

This section deals with the childhood illnesses which you will come across most frequently. If you are working in a home, you will probably have to look after children who become sick. It is therefore important to know the signs of some of the commonest infections. In other settings, it is important to recognise when a child is becoming unwell and to know when to call the parent to collect the child.

Definitions of terms used

Here are some specific terms associated with illnesses:

- symptoms – what the child might be complaining of – e.g. feeling sick or having a headache
- signs – what you will notice about the child – e.g. a rash or a change in behaviour
- acute illness – generally comes on suddenly, is short lived and may well have a rapid onset of symptoms from one day to the next – it may be severe
- chronic illness – a prolonged illness with little change in symptoms from day to day; there is often, but not necessarily, a slow progressive deterioration; some chronic illnesses have acute episodes.

Colds

Children will, on average, have six to eight colds a year. They are caused by viruses and are spread by coughing, sneezing or by contact with secretions on toys and other surfaces. Colds often last five to nine days, but children can have a runny nose for one to two weeks after this.

Signs and symptoms	Treatment and care	Refer to a doctor if:
■ runny nose ■ sore throat ■ sneezing ■ cough ■ slight temperature.	There is no specific treatment available: ■ plenty of fluids to drink. To reduce cross-infection: ■ teach child to blow nose and ensure regular hand washing ■ use tissues rather than hankies and throw them away straight after use ■ put cream on nose if sore ■ use a decongestant at night if the child is having difficulty in sleeping – a chemist can advise which is most suitable.	■ child complains of earache ■ child becomes worse after two or three days ■ baby is unable to breathe properly or drink due to being congested ■ the nasal discharge remains thick and yellow after the cold has finished.

Sore throat and tonsillitis

The tonsils form one of the barriers for germs between the air we breathe and our lungs. They are composed of lymphoid tissue which contains lymphocytes – the body's soldiers in the defence system. Their role is to engulf and destroy all germs that enter the body. If there is a large invasion of germs, the tissues swell, which usually causes pain. This is what happens in tonsillitis: the throat initially becomes sore, the infection then spreads to the tonsils, which become enlarged.

Many childhood illnesses have a sore throat as one of the symptoms. It can be caused by a virus or bacterial infection, the most common being a streptococcal infection, which can cause the child to be acutely ill. The doctor may take a throat swab if he suspects a streptococcal infection. Complications which might occur are: nephritis – inflammation of the kidney – or rheumatic fever – widespread inflammation throughout the body, including the joints and the heart.

Signs and symptoms	Treatment and care	Refer to a doctor if:
■ sore throat ■ swollen glands ■ difficulty in eating ■ refusing to eat ■ snoring ■ stomach ache ■ able to see sore throat/enlarged tonsils when mouth is opened.	■ plenty of fluids ■ children's paracetamol if needed ■ soft food ■ antibiotics might be prescribed ■ if a child has repeated attacks a tonsillectomy (removal of the tonsils) may be carried out.	■ there is pus in the throat ■ there are white spots on the tonsils ■ the baby is refusing feeds ■ the child appears ill.

Coughs

Coughing is one of the body's defence mechanisms to rid itself of irritants, chemicals or germs.

Coughs can be caused by: viruses; dust; smoke; inflammation of the upper respiratory tract (colds, laryngitis); inflammation of the bronchi of the lungs (bronchitis); inflammation of the bronchioles, the small air passages of the lungs (bronchiolitis); inflammation of the lung (pneumonia); tuberculosis; asthma – a dry cough at night can sometimes be an early sign of asthma.

Signs and symptoms	Treatment and care	Refer to the doctor if:
■ cough ■ raised temperature ■ rapid breathing ■ looks and feels unwell ■ dry mouth.	■ plenty of fluids ■ avoid smoky atmosphere ■ breathing may be easier if top of bed is raised slightly ■ seek advice from doctor or chemist if parents feel a cough syrup might help ■ a cough suppressant should not be used if the child is coughing up mucus, because this will actually be clearing the lungs.	■ the cough lasts more than one to two days in an infant ■ coughing prevents feeding in babies ■ child is constantly gagging ■ child has high temperature ■ ribs sink in when child is breathing in ■ a whooping sound is made ■ child looks very unwell.

Croup

Croup is caused by a swelling in the child's trachea (windpipe) and is very common in children under four years old. In older children the air passages are wider and the cartilage surrounding them is harder, which prevents this from happening.

It usually follows a cold, but can be due to an allergy or inhaling a small object. It often starts in the middle of the night and is more common in winter. Croup is very frightening for both child and carer, so it is very important to stay calm and reassure the child.

Signs and symptoms	Treatment and care	Take straight to hospital if:
■ barking, seal-like cough ■ high-pitched crowing sound when child breathes in ■ raised temperature ■ hoarseness.	■ stay calm and call a doctor ■ steam the bathroom by running hot water into the bath; close door and windows; stay for at least 20 minutes ■ reassure child by holding and talking ■ if the child improves, take back to bed; place a humidifier in the room – or put wet towels on the radiator ■ stay with child in same room to monitor breathing.	■ child cannot talk ■ child has poor colour (blue lips) ■ child cannot be calmed ■ breathing is taking a lot of effort.

Middle ear infection (otitis media)

Infection in the middle ear is very common and often follows other respiratory infections. Infections from the upper respiratory tract can spread to the middle ear by travelling up the Eustachian tube. This tube runs from the middle ear to the back of the nose and drains fluid from the middle ear. It also helps equalise pressure. Ear infection is caused either by a virus or bacteria and some children have frequent attacks. Children who are bottle fed, live in a smoky house and have frequent colds are the most prone.

Glue ear

Glue ear is caused by a build-up of fluid in the middle ear, which, because the Eustachian tube is blocked, cannot drain. It is usually associated with upper respiratory infections, such as colds, and ear infections. It usually occurs in both ears. Glue ear affects young children; they will usually 'grow out of it' by the age of eight, by which time the air passages and Eustachian tube have grown longer and wider.

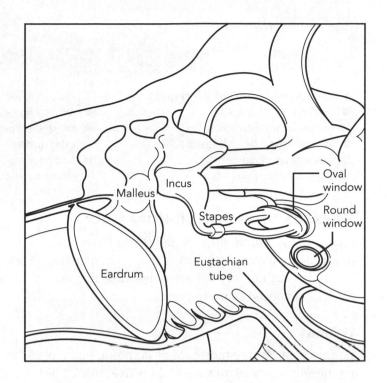

Middle ear infection (otitis media) *(continued)*

Signs and symptoms	Treatment and care	Contact doctor *immediately* if:
■ painful ears ■ child clutches ear ■ vomiting ■ ears 'crackle' and 'pop', feel 'tight' or 'full' ■ ringing or buzzing in ears ■ raised temperature ■ difficulty in hearing.	■ child needs to see a doctor ■ children's paracetamol to relieve the pain and reduce fever ■ getting child to yawn or swallow may help to relieve feeling of tightness ■ warmth against the ear, but do not allow child to sleep with a heating pad or hot water bottle – it may cause burns ■ if warmth doesn't help, try wrapping an ice pack – or pack of frozen peas – in a towel and apply for 20 minutes every hour ■ plenty to drink ■ antibiotics may be prescribed ■ do *not* pack the ear with cotton wool if the ear discharges.	■ child has a stiff neck ■ child is unsteady on feet ■ child had a head injury before the earache ■ child has a high fever and appears very unwell ■ the ear discharges pus, the pain may fade, this is caused by the eardrum perforating.

Complications

If a middle ear infection is not properly treated, the following complications may occur:
■ inflammation of the outer ear (otitis externa)
■ glue ear (chronic otitis media)
■ brain abscesses (*very* rare).

Glue ear *(continued)*

Signs and symptoms	Treatment and care
■ partial and intermittent deafness ■ behaviour changes ■ lack of concentration ■ speech may be affected ■ poor school performance.	■ a doctor will monitor the child ■ a hearing test will ascertain the degree of deafness ■ be understanding – it can be very confusing for a child to suffer intermittent hearing loss ■ occasionally grommets (small tubes) may be inserted into the ear drum to allow the fluid, which is trapped in the ear, to escape.

Illnesses of the respiratory tract

These are the commonest of childhood illnesses. Children are particularly prone to infections when they first start nursery or school because they are suddenly exposed to more germs.

Asthma

Asthma is becoming increasingly common in children. It generally starts before the child is five, but 50 per cent of children grow out of it by adulthood, especially if they were breastfed. There is often a family history of asthma, eczema or hay fever. It is potentially fatal and should always be taken seriously.

Causes
Asthma is caused by a narrowing and swelling of the airway and increased mucous production. This is due to the body's allergic response to an allergen or virus – these are sometimes called 'triggers'.

Signs and symptoms
The first signs of asthma are:

■ coughing at night

■ recurrent cough in the cold or after exercise

■ breathlessness and wheezing when the child **breathes out** (exhales).

During an attack there may also be:

■ difficulty in speaking

■ fear

■ a dry tickly cough

■ grey-blue colour to the skin especially around the lips.

Management of asthma
Once asthma has been diagnosed, the child will usually be prescribed a 'bronchodilator' drug, which will relax the muscles in the airway helping the child to breath more easily. These are often called 'relievers' and the most common is Ventolin (salbutamol). This

can be given as tablets, in syrup form or in an inhaler – which will always be blue.

If a child has regular attacks the doctor may also prescribe a 'preventer', such as 'Intal', or a steroid, such as 'Becotide', which need to taken regularly to prevent attacks. These are in a brown or an orange inhaler.

Children under five and those who have difficulty in using an inhaler might use a spacer device – such as a Volumatic or Nebuhaler – or a nebuliser, where the child inhales drug as a mist. A nurse or first aider will usually be in charge of this, but if you are caring for a child at home, you should be given detailed instructions on its use.

Volumatic

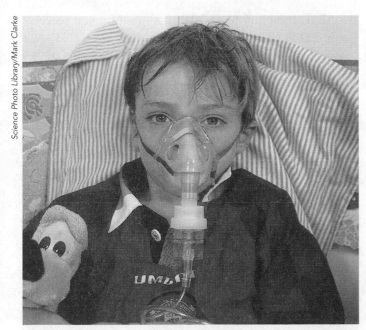

Nebuliser

Children over six might also use a peak flow meter, through which the child blows regularly – and records the results on a chart – to help detect early signs of the asthma worsening or of an impending attack.

Avoid any known triggers. The house-dust mite is a particular problem – mattresses and pillows should have a protective cover (or be vacuumed daily), bed linen should be washed at 60°C and soft toys should regularly be put in the freezer for six hours and then washed at 60°C.

Children should live normally. Exercise is very beneficial to asthmatics, although some children may be advised by their doctor to use their 'reliever' inhaler prior to exercise.

Care of a child with an asthma attack
- Keep calm and reassure the child.

- Help the child find a comfortable position – often leaning forwards.

- Give the child the **reliever** inhaler – usually blue – and allow the child to use it himself.

- If the inhaler has no effect after five to ten minutes, call 999.

- Check and record the child's breathing and pulse every ten minutes.

Cystic fibrosis

Both the respiratory and digestive systems are affected by the inherited condition cystic fibrosis (CF). The airways become infected or blocked by thick and sticky mucus, thus causing difficulty in breathing. Mucus also clogs the ducts in the pancreas, thus preventing the digestive enzymes in the pancreas from digesting fats in the digestive tract. This results in poor weight gain. Children should be watched carefully for signs of chest infections, which can cause damage to the lungs.

CF is the most common life-threatening inherited disease. Over the last thirty years the life expectancy has risen from 5 years to 31 years. In many areas babies are routinely screened for CF as part of the neonatal screening programme.

Signs and symptoms of cystic fibrosis

Signs and Symptoms	Care and Treatment
■ One in ten babies with CF is born with a blocked bowel	■ Regular chest physiotherapy, breathing exercises and exercise to keep the lungs as free as possible from mucus
■ Failure to grow normally and poor weight gain	
■ Repeated chest infections	■ A diet high in protein, energy and vitamins
■ Salty sweat	■ Medicines to enable the child to digest food properly
■ Stools are loose, oily and have a 'cheesy' smell	

Infections of the eye

Conjunctivitis

Conjunctivitis is an inflammation caused by bacteria or a virus and is infectious, so the child needs to be kept away from other children.

Care of a sticky eye
If it is sticky, the eye will need cleaning:

■ Boil a small piece of cotton wool in a saucepan and allow to cool.

■ Wash your hands.

■ Using the cotton wool, wipe the eye from the bridge of the nose outwards.

■ Discard the cotton wool and repeat the process if necessary.

■ If only one eye is infected, the child should be encouraged to sleep on the infected side to reduce the risk of spreading.

■ The child should be discouraged from touching or rubbing the eyes.

■ Eye care should be done before eye drops or ointment are given, if these have been prescribed.

Disorders and infections of the digestive system

Vomiting

Vomiting is not actually an illness but a symptom that is very common in children and often associated with infections. Some children will be sick every time they have a slight fever. However, there are many causes, as can be seen from the diagram opposite.

Food intolerance

It is not known why certain foods upset some children, but diarrhoea and vomiting in children can be due to this. The most common foods which cause an intolerance are milk, eggs, fish, nuts and artificial food colourings and preservatives.

If a food intolerance is suspected, then the child should be seen by a doctor.

Care of a child who is being sick

■ Ensure there is a bowl nearby.

■ Support the child's head when vomiting.

■ Wash the child's hands and face, and ask her to rinse her mouth out with water.

■ Reassure the child.

■ Allow the child to rest/lay his head on soft towels in case of accidents.

■ Change clothes when necessary.

■ Stay near the child.

■ Prevent dehydration (see below).

■ Wash and disinfect the bowl.

■ Once the sickness has stopped, small portions of dry food – e.g. toast – should be started gradually.

Prevention of dehydration

Children should be drinking 1–1.5 litres of fluid a day. If a child has diarrhoea and/or vomiting, fluid can be lost very quickly. Regular sips of clear water, therefore, or an oral rehydration solution, such as Diarolyte, should be given.

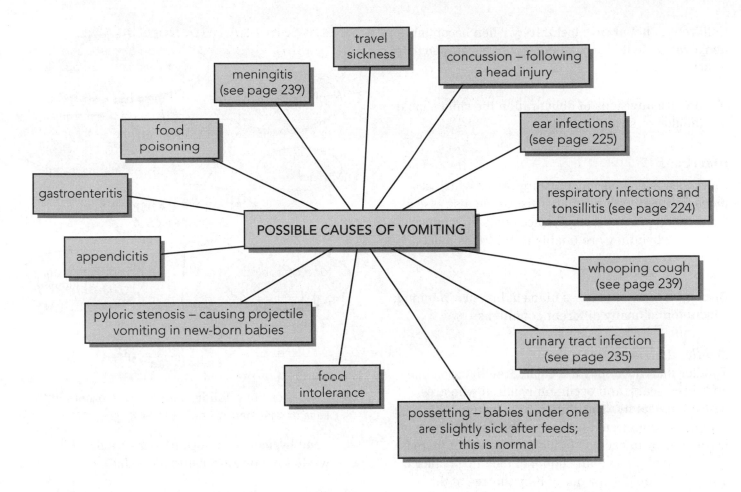

POSSIBLE CAUSES OF VOMITING

- travel sickness
- meningitis (see page 239)
- concussion – following a head injury
- food poisoning
- ear infections (see page 225)
- gastroenteritis
- respiratory infections and tonsillitis (see page 224)
- appendicitis
- whooping cough (see page 239)
- pyloric stenosis – causing projectile vomiting in new-born babies
- urinary tract infection (see page 235)
- food intolerance
- possetting – babies under one are slightly sick after feeds; this is normal

Knowledge into action

In a reception class, a child is suddenly sick all over the floor. He feels hot to touch.

What would you do to help this child?

How could the rest of the class be handled?

You manage to contact the father, who will take an hour to arrive. How can the child be cared for during the wait?

Signs and symptoms of dehydration include:

- sunken eyes
- dry mouth/cracked lips
- pasty colour and dry skin
- dark urine
- sunken fontanelle (in a baby)
- increased pulse and breathing rates
- headache
- passing no urine for six hours in the day.

Think about it

Look up one of the following in a medical dictionary or encyclopaedia:

- possetting
- intestinal obstruction
- pyloric stenosis.

Find out:

- the cause
- the signs and symptoms
- if it can be prevented.

Share your information with others in the group.

Children do not always feel thirsty when becoming dehydrated, so it is very important to encourage them to drink.

If there are any signs of dehydration the child should see the doctor straight away.

Diarrhoea

Diarrhoea is the passing of runny stools which are more frequent than normal. This can be distressing for a child, and there may be accidents in younger children when they are unable to get to the toilet in time.

Diarrhoea is not an illness in itself, but, like vomiting, a symptom of many different conditions.

Toddler diarrhoea

Toddler diarrhoea may affect children between one and three years, and occurs in children who are otherwise healthy. The child passes watery diarrhoea containing undigested food. The child should be seen by the doctor to exclude other disorders, but there is no treatment other than chopping food up smaller. The child should grow out of it by the age of three.

Care of a child with diarrhoea

- Reassure the child – it can be very distressing.

- Give regular drinks of clear fluid.

- Keep a potty nearby, if possible, for a younger child.

- Keep spare underwear handy.

- Avoid going out – except in the case of toddler diarrhoea.

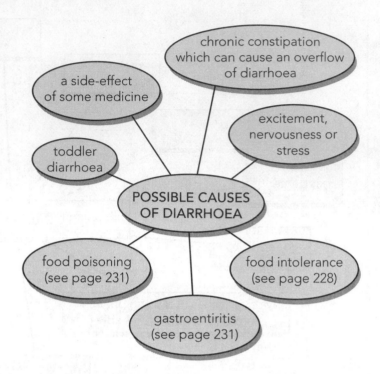

- Keep infectious children away from others in the case of gastroenteritis.

- Good hygiene is important – ensure the child washes hands after using the toilet.

- Soak soiled underwear in Napisan solution before washing.

Appendicitis

Appendicitis is an infection of the appendix – a small section of the large gut in the bottom right corner of the abdomen.

It is unusual in children under two, but is a common cause of abdominal pain in children under sixteen. It is treated by an abdominal operation in which the appendix is surgically removed.

Appendicitis

Signs and symptoms	Treatment and care
■ pain in the centre of the abdomen which moves to the right groin ■ pain is worse if the child moves ■ nausea or vomiting and diarrhoea ■ fever.	■ Take the child to hospital immediately. ■ Do not allow the child to eat or drink – because he/she will need an operation. ■ Do not give paracetamol. ■ A warmed hot water bottle may help the pain.

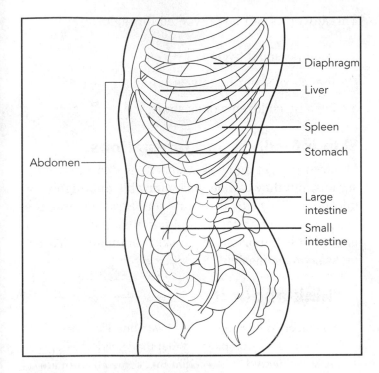

Diaphragm

Liver

Spleen

Stomach

Abdomen

Large intestine

Small intestine

Gastroenteritis

Gastroenteritis is an inflammation of the stomach and intestines. It is fairly common in children and can easily be spread from child to child by unwashed hands touching food or equipment. It can also be caused by poor sterilisation of bottles or teats. Breast milk contains an antibody against one of the viruses which cause gastroenteritis.

Food poisoning

Food poisoning is a form of gastroenteritis which is caused by contaminated food or water. The symptoms, which are similar to gastroenteritis, start 2–6 hours after eating. The doctor will need to be informed and the treatment is the same as for gastroenteritis.

Gastroenteritis and food poisoning can be prevented by:

- ensuring bottles, dummies and feeding equipment are properly sterilised
- good personal hygiene
- storing food at correct temperature
- ensuring chicken and eggs are always cooked thoroughly.

Threadworms

Threadworms are tiny worms in the digestive tract which look like threads of white cotton when excreted. Children catch them by getting eggs on their hands from food, the sandpit, playdough, clothing and other equipment.

Symptoms include:

- itching around the anus, especially at night
- sore anus due to the scratching
- occasionally white worms can be seen in the faeces.

The whole family will need to take the medication from the doctor.

Gastroenteritis

Signs and symptoms	Treatment and care	Call a doctor *immediately* if
<ul><li>vomiting</li><li>diarrhoea (6-10 times a day)</li><li>loss of appetite</li><li>general abdominal pain</li><li>fever.</li></ul>	<ul><li>Give clear fluids every 30 minutes.</li><li>Give regular sips of a rehydrating solution – e.g. Diarolyte.</li><li>Stop food and milk (except breast milk) for 24 hours.</li><li>Avoid all food initially.</li><li>When diarrhoea and vomiting have stopped, reintroduce half-strength milk, then gradually introduce food.</li></ul>	<ul><li>child is under two months</li><li>a baby has missed two feeds</li><li>there are signs of dehydration (see page 229)</li><li>child cannot keep any drinks down</li><li>there is no improvement after 24 hours.</li></ul>

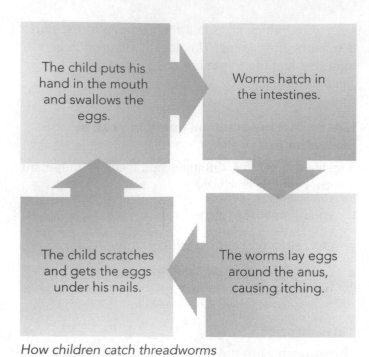

How children catch threadworms

The child puts his hand in the mouth and swallows the eggs.

Worms hatch in the intestines.

The child scratches and gets the eggs under his nails.

The worms lay eggs around the anus, causing itching.

Knowledge into action

There are several children in the nursery who have had, or have, threadworms.

Produce a fact sheet to inform parents about threadworms – the causes, prevention and treatment.

What hygiene procedures should be in place at a nursery to prevent the spread of threadworms?

Threadworms can be prevented through:

- good personal hygiene
- the use of separate towels
- keeping children's nails short.

Skin infections and infestations

Children can get many skin infections. Most are not serious, but they can be uncomfortable and highly infectious. They can also cause embarrassment to the child, and other children (and parents) may be unkind. It is important to get skin complaints cleared up as soon as possible.

Think about it

The nursery is having problems with headlice and a few parents are complaining that their children keep being re-infected. It is thought that some children are not being regularly checked, and others are being inadequately treated.

The nursery has tried sending letters home, with no effect.

What else could be done to increase awareness about headlice?

Produce a colourful leaflet giving advice to parents on how to recognise, prevent and deal with headlice.

(see page 234 for information on headlice)

Infection/infestation and *cause*	Spread	Signs and symptoms	Treatment and complications	General care
Impetigo *bacteria*	■ contact with other children ■ cut in skin, or chapped lips	■ small blisters on face – often around mouth – which ooze and form a crust.	■ antibiotic cream or medicine ■ child should not be in contact with others until it dries. If untreated it: ■ spreads rapidly ■ can cause generalised infection and septicaemia – blood poisoning.	■ separate towels and flannels ■ child should not touch the area ■ personal hygiene is important ■ bedding and flannels should be washed on a high heat.

Infection/infestation and *cause*	Spread	Signs and symptoms	Treatment and complications	General care
Wart or **verruca** *virus*	■ direct contact ■ from showers or swimming pools	■ wart – raised lump on surface of skin ■ verruca – on foot; lump is pushed in and can be painful.	■ cream from chemist ■ freezing with liquid nitrogen by doctor. If untreated it: ■ can spread to other areas.	**Verruca:** ■ use rubber socks when swimming ■ during PE, feet should be covered.
Ringworm *fungus*	■ direct contact ■ from animals, showers or soil	■ ring-shaped scaly patch on skin – usually the trunk, nails, feet, scalp or groin ■ on scalp it may cause bald patches.	■ see a doctor who will prescribe a cream – this cream *must* be used for the prescribed length of time otherwise re-infection will occur.	■ good personal hygiene ■ separate flannels and towels.
Athlete's foot *fungus*	■ bathroom floor, showers and swimming pools	■ itchy feet especially between toes ■ infected area is pale and flaky.	■ cream, powder or foot spray from doctor or chemist.	■ wash and dry carefully between child's toes ■ cotton socks ■ shoes made of natural materials ■ keep feet covered ■ separate towels.
Scabies *insect*	■ direct contact (the insect burrows under the skin and lays eggs)	■ tiny grey swellings appear especially between fingers or on wrist, armpits or sides of feet. ■ intense itching especially at night ■ frequent waking at night.	■ see a doctor ■ all the family will need treatment with an insecticide lotion (scratching can also cause impetigo).	■ isolate child ■ keep child cool to reduce itching ■ personal hygiene very important.
Cold sore *herpes simplex virus*	■ direct contact	■ tingling around mouth initially ■ small blisters which crust after one to two days – smaller and more regular than impetigo ■ itching, irritation.	■ often disappears on its own ■ anti-viral cream may be used early on ■ after infection, virus lays dormant until a 'trigger' restarts infection.	■ discover and avoid (if possible) the trigger – e.g. heat, cold, wind ■ use lip salve in winter and sun screen in summer.

Infection/infestation and *cause*	Spread	Signs and symptoms	Treatment and complications	General care
Urticaria (nettle rash or hives) *allergy*	■ contact with allergen – whatever is causing the reaction	■ smooth, raised pale lumps surrounded by a pink area ■ intense itching.	■ none – calamine lotion may reduce itching.	■ if the child suffers often, try to determine the cause – e.g. peanuts, eggs, milk, chocolate, strawberries, artificial colours and additives, fish, fruit and tomatoes.
Headlice *louse*	■ direct contact from head to head – they cannot jump	■ itching of the scalp ■ lice in the hair ■ nits – the eggs – can be seen as small white specks near root of hair, which cannot easily be removed. They are most commonly seen behind ears and nape of neck.	This changes frequently: ■ see the health visitor or school nurse for current recommendations ■ if lice are found, hair should be conditioned and combed through with a nit comb twice daily initially, and then daily for two to three weeks. If lice have laid eggs, this will ensure you rid the hair of baby lice before they too lay eggs ■ many different products on market to get rid of headlice, including one which electrocutes the lice ■ check all of the family.	**Prevention:** ■ short hair or wear long hair up ■ check hair frequently with a nit comb.

Eczema

Eczema affects about one in every ten children and is more common in children who have been bottle fed. It can start as early as two months and most children grow out of it by adulthood. There is often a family history of eczema, asthma or hay fever. The condition is usually mild, but some children are affected badly.

Think about it

The nursery has decided to let the children have their faces painted as part of their imaginative play. Two of the children have eczema and cannot do this.

What can you do to make sure they do not feel left out?

Eczema

Signs and symptoms	Treatment	Care
■ Dry, itchy rash which becomes red and starts to weep. ■ In very young children it affects the face, scalp, trunk and the outside of the arms and legs. ■ In older children it affects the bends of the elbows and knees, the feet and the hands. ■ Itchiness, especially at night.	■ Use an aqueous cream instead of soap or emollients in the bath which makes the water oily. ■ Moisturising creams should be used twice daily. ■ Creams may be prescribed by the doctor. Some of these contain steroids, so should be used sparingly. Ensure hands are washed carefully afterwards.	■ Avoid known irritants – wool; some man-made materials; biological washing powders; jewellery containing nickel; grass. ■ Watch for anything which worsens the condition. ■ Cotton gloves at night can sometimes prevent scratching. ■ Elimination diets are sometimes tried to exclude dietary causes – e.g. dairy products. This must be done with guidance from a dietitian.

Caring for the child with eczema in the nursery setting

Because eczema can be made worse through contact with many substances; it is important to find out from parents what the child is unable to touch or use. The child may not be able to play with paint, salt dough, clay, sand or water. This can obviously restrict the opportunities available for the child, and it will be up to the early years worker to find alternative activities. It might be possible for the child to play with dry sand and playdough if wearing cotton gloves.

Infections of the urinary tract

These are fairly common in children and particularly affect girls; in babies, however, it is more common in boys.

Prevention	Signs and symptoms	Treatment and care	Complications
A child who is prone to infections should: ■ drink regularly ■ pass urine at least every four hours in the daytime ■ have a daily bath or shower ■ avoid scented soaps and bubble bath. Girls should wipe themselves from front to back after going to the toilet.	**Children under two** ■ fever ■ diarrhoea ■ vomiting ■ irritability. **Children over two** ■ passing urine frequently ■ burning pain when passing urine ■ stomach and back ache ■ urine may smell and be pale or cloudy ■ bed wetting.	■ See a doctor, taking a sample of the child's urine in a small clean pot – e.g. camera film case ■ Antibiotics ■ Drink plenty of fluids.	Recurrent infections can cause scarring of the kidneys, leading to kidney failure.

Hormonal disorders

Diabetes mellitus

There are two types of diabetes mellitus: childhood diabetes and age-onset diabetes. In childhood diabetes, the body stops making insulin – a hormone which allows the body to use and store glucose properly. Without insulin, the glucose cannot be used and passes out of the body. In the past, before synthetic insulin was produced, many children died from diabetes. All children with diabetes will have to have insulin injections for the rest of their lives.

The first signs are generally:

- frequency in passing urine
- excessive thirst
- tiredness and lack of energy
- poor appetite
- weight loss.

Management of diabetes

Once the family doctor suspects diabetes in a child, a blood and urine test will be done and the child will be admitted to hospital for a short time while insulin is started. The parents and child – depending on the child's age – will be taught how to test the blood for glucose and how to give the injections.

The role of the early years worker

If you are working in a home setting you may need to do the following with the child:

- test for glucose in child's blood (a pinprick)
- record the results
- give injections
- store and dispose of syringes
- manage the child's diet: a regular, balanced diet – the dietitian will give the parents information on this.

Although it seems fairly daunting at first, the child will soon get used to it.

Hypoglycaemia

If, for any reason, the child does not eat the correct amount, takes extra exercise, or is unwell, there may be danger of a hypoglycaemic attack. This occurs if the blood sugar level drops suddenly. It is essential that everyone involved in caring for the child – for example, teachers and early years workers – knows that the child is diabetic, and what to do if the child has a hypoglycaemic attack.

Hypoglycaemia

Signs and symptoms of hypoglycaemia	What to do:
<ul><li>feeling dizzy or faint</li><li>pale, clammy skin and sweating</li><li>strong, 'bounding' pulse</li><li>shallow breathing</li><li>may become aggressive</li><li>may become unconscious.</li></ul>	If conscious<ul><li>call for help</li><li>give the child sugar, chocolate or a sugary drink</li><li>if he/she improves give him/her a little more to eat and drink and allow him/her to rest until recovered</li><li>inform the parents.</li></ul>If unconscious<ul><li>place in the recovery position (see page 255)</li><li>call an ambulance</li><li>check the child's breathing and pulse every ten minutes until the ambulance arrives.</li></ul>

Infectious diseases

The table below lists some of the infectious diseases you may encounter in your work with young children.

Illness, incubation, immunisation and severity	Signs and symptoms	Treatment and care	Call doctor immediately if:	Complications
Hand, foot and mouth disease 3–5 days *not usually serious*	■ blisters in mouth leading to ulcers ■ blisters on hands and soles of feet ■ reluctance to eat ■ mild fever.	■ plenty to drink (non-acidic).		■ none ■ mouth ulcers may last for 3–4 weeks.
Roseola infantum (very common in under-twos) 5–15 days *uncomfortable but not usually serious*	■ erratic temperature of 39–40°C ■ mild diarrhoea ■ cough ■ enlarged glands in neck ■ earache. **After 4 days:** ■ normal temperature ■ rash of tiny distinct pink spots over head and abdomen.	■ paracetamol to reduce temperature.	■ febrile convulsions ■ drowsy or irritable ■ rash appears with fever.	■ rare
Mumps 14–24 days Children can be immunised against mumps at 12–15 months as part of the MMR. *not usually serious except in adolescent boys*	■ fever. **After 1–2 days:** ■ swelling and pain on one or both sides of face under jawline.	■ paracetamol to reduce temperature ■ plenty of fluids.	■ severe headaches ■ abdominal pain.	■ orchitis – inflammation of testes – in adolescent boys, which very rarely can cause infertility. **Rarely:** ■ meningitis ■ encephalitis (inflammation of the brain).
Chickenpox (varicella) (common in children under 10 years) 2–3 weeks *can be serious in older children and adults, especially pregnant women*	■ rash starts on head and behind ears ■ pink spots turn to blisters which dry and form scabs ■ spots often come in crops ■ slight fever and headache ■ child may *feel* well.	■ nails should be kept short ■ calamine lotion to relieve itchiness ■ keep child out of sun – this makes spots and itching worse ■ soft food if mouth is affected.	■ coughing ■ seizures ■ abnormal drowsiness ■ unsteady when walking.	■ secondary infection from scratching ■ scarring ■ pneumonia ■ chest infection ■ encephalitis (inflammation of the brain).

Illness, incubation, immunisation and severity	Signs and symptoms	Treatment and care	Call doctor immediately if:	Complications
Measles 10–14 days Immunisation is available for children at 12–15 months. *can be serious*	■ generally unwell initially ■ Koplik's spots (bluish white spots) appear on inside of cheeks ■ temperature, runny nose, red eyes and cough ■ flat, blotchy red rash starts behind ears and on face, and spreads to rest of body ■ photophobia (dislike of bright light).	■ paracetamol to reduce fever ■ plenty of fluids ■ nurse in a slightly darkened room.	■ earache ■ rapid breathing ■ drowsiness ■ fits ■ severe headache ■ vomiting.	■ otitis media (see page 225) ■ pneumonia ■ encephalitis.
Erythema infectiosum (5th disease or slap face) (very common in under-twos) 4–14 days *not usually serious*	■ bright red cheeks (as if they had been slapped) and pale area around mouth ■ temperature. **After 1–4 days:** ■ blotchy lace-like rash may appear on arms and legs and occasionally on trunk lasting 7–10 days ■ rash may get worse when warm ■ child may feel well.	■ paracetamol to reduce temperature.		■ can be serious if child has sickle cell disease or thalassaemia – hereditary blood disorders.
Rubella (German measles) 14–21 days *usually mild and not serious, except to pregnant women – it can cause serious effects on unborn child*	■ slight fever ■ swollen glands behind ears and at back of neck ■ rash of tiny flat pink spots which are not itchy and start on face and spread to body and limbs – these last only a few days.	■ keep children away from pregnant women ■ give paracetamol to reduce temperature.	■ joint pain ■ any signs of meningitis.	■ encephalitis ■ can cause serious defects to the foetus if a woman contracts rubella in first 12–16 weeks of pregnancy ■ child is infectious for four days before rash develops, therefore inform pregnant women who have had contact with child.

Illness, incubation, immunisation and *severity*	Signs and symptoms	Treatment and care	Call doctor immediately if:	Complications
Pertussis (whooping cough) 7–10 days Immunisation can be given to children at 8, 12 and 16 weeks. *can be a very serious infection*	■ starts like a cold ■ bouts of short dry coughing ■ long attacks of coughing followed by a whoop (deep intake of breath) ■ vomiting ■ a cough may last for months.	■ consult a doctor as soon as whooping cough is suspected ■ antibiotics – need to be given early ■ soft non-crumbly food ■ plenty of fluids ■ sit child up during an attack ■ it is very frightening, so reassure child and stay close by especially at night.	■ if child has poor colour – grey/ bluish/pale ■ difficulty in breathing ■ baby not feeding.	■ weight loss ■ dehydration ■ pneumonia ■ bronchitis ■ encephalitis.
Meningitis (infection of the lining of the brain and spinal cord) 2–14 days There are 3 types: **Viral** **Bacterial** Hib vaccination can prevent one type of bacterial meningitis in children under four (see page 216) **Meningococcal** *always very serious*	■ signs of cold/flu to start with ■ drowsiness ■ temperature ■ nausea or vomiting ■ severe headache ■ photophobia (dislike of bright light) ■ stiff neck ■ joint pains ■ rash: flat purple spots which do not fade if pressed. **Babies may also:** ■ arch their backs ■ have a shrill cry ■ have a bulging fontanelle	**Depending on the cause** ■ antibiotics in bacterial meningitis ■ will be nursed in hospital and given intravenous fluids ■ darkened room.	■ immediately meningitis is suspected.	■ brain damage ■ deafness ■ epilepsy ■ death.

The rash in meningitis is very distinctive and can be recognised by doing the glass test: press a glass over the spots. If the rash is due to meningitis the rash will not fade when pressed whereas other rashes will.

Caring for sick children

When children are unwell, they may regress to an earlier developmental stage. They often become clingy and have a short attention span. Most children will also sleep and rest more when they are ill.

If you are caring for children at home they will probably be happier having a bed made up on the sofa during the day, because it can be isolating being in their bedroom.

In a nursery setting, the child should be kept away from other children and have a bed made up in a separate area, if possible, until the parents can pick the child up.

Routine

Children need the security of a routine to continue when they are unwell. Drinks, meals and rest times should, where possible, continue at the usual times. If the child cannot be cared for by the parent, then a familiar adult needs to be around, as well as any comfort objects.

Case study

When Rohini arrives at nursery in the morning, she is more clingy than usual and when her mother leaves she hangs around you and is not really interested in playing.

At break time you notice she is very hot, and while helping her to remove her jumper, you notice that she is covered in small spots that look like bites.

What could be wrong with Rohini?
What would you say to her mother on the phone?
How do you think the mother might feel?
What advice could you give to Rohini's mother?
How could you care for Rohini until her mother comes to collect her?

Food and drink

Do not worry if children 'go off' food when they are unwell, as long as they are drinking well. In order to help the child fight infection, try to give drinks which are high in vitamin C – for example, blackcurrant,

orange, lemon or cranberry juices mixed with water. Offer a drink hourly to reduce the risk of dehydration (see page 228).

Food should be presented in small appetising portions.

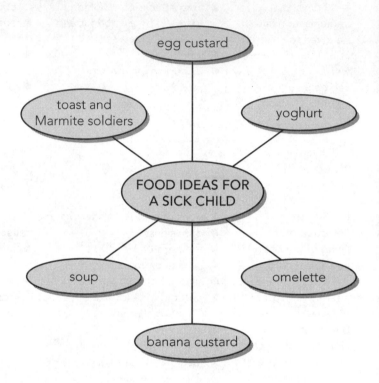

FOOD IDEAS FOR A SICK CHILD: egg custard, toast and Marmite soldiers, yoghurt, soup, omelette, banana custard

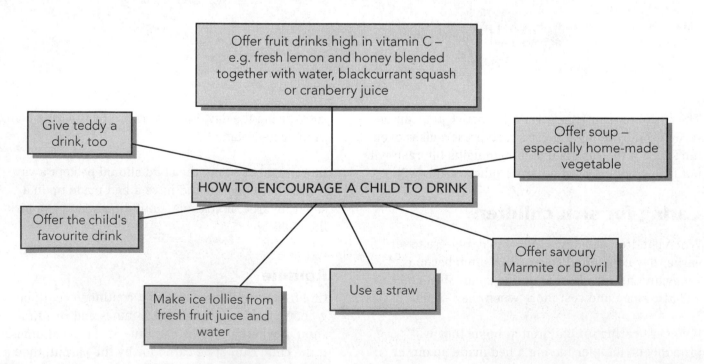

HOW TO ENCOURAGE A CHILD TO DRINK: Offer fruit drinks high in vitamin C – e.g. fresh lemon and honey blended together with water, blackcurrant squash or cranberry juice; Give teddy a drink, too; Offer soup – especially home-made vegetable; Offer the child's favourite drink; Offer savoury Marmite or Bovril; Make ice lollies from fresh fruit juice and water; Use a straw

Play activities for sick children

When children are first ill, they often need to sleep for longer periods of time and are not often interested in doing much, except perhaps having a simple book read to them. When they start to recover, they still need plenty of rest, but will tend to become bored and frustrated. They therefore need activities which are short and simple and do not require too much concentration.

Activities for children who are unwell

Books	Young children often have favourite stories which they like to have read to them over and over again. The local library or the child's school may be able to provide school-age children with further reading.
Story tapes	These can be obtained from the local children's library and enable the child to listen to the best bits over and over again!
Treasure box	This is a collection of toys, books and games which is kept aside and used only occasionally to provide something different for the child to play with.
Puzzles	These can be done on a tray and need to be fairly simple to prevent the child from getting frustrated.
Games	Board games and simple card games can provide good quality time that an early years worker, sibling or family member can spend with the child. These can be borrowed from the local toy library, if you have one near you.
Family photographs	If a child has a very poor concentration span, then photos of familiar people, pets or places can relieve boredom and provide a good talking point.
Plasticine or playdough	These activities can help a child to express some of their feelings and frustrations and need not be too messy if done on a tray.
Drawing, colouring or sticking	This is a good activity for all ages. Older children can also do simple word puzzles and word searches.
School work	The school can provide school-age children with some appropriate work to help prevent them from getting too far behind if they are to be away for a period of time.
Friends and family	Providing the child is not infectious, a visit from friends and family can prevent him from becoming isolated. It will also help to maintain friendships.
Video	There are some very good short videos that can be used occasionally when a child is unwell and that can help stimulate the imagination. They should not, however, be relied on too heavily, especially in chronic illnesses, because children can become too dependent on the television to provide them with entertainment.
Role play	Playing with a medical kit with a teddy or doll can help the child express feelings about the illness.
Fuzzy felt	Stories can be 'acted out' on felt boards, including hospital scenes.

Knowledge into action

Devise a routine for a four-year-old girl who has tonsillitis. Include periods of rest, food, drinks and activities.

Hygiene

It is important to continue with children's normal washing routine when they are unwell, but it can sometimes be better to give them an overall wash instead of a bath. Hair brushing and teeth cleaning should continue as normal.

It is also important to ensure that the carers reduce the risk of cross-infection. The following precautions should be taken:

- Use tissues instead of hankies and dispose of these correctly.
- Wash hands after being in contact with the children's tissues, clothes and bedding.
- Use gloves if in contact with body fluids.
- Ensure the room is adequately ventilated.
- Wash children's clothes and bed-clothes frequently on a high heat.

Knowledge into action

You are working as a nanny for Michael, who is three years old, and Laura who is three months old. Michael has a terrible cold and you are concerned that Laura might catch it too.

What can you do to help prevent Laura from catching the cold?

Handling and disposing of body fluids

Because many infections, including HIV and hepatitis, can be passed on by contact with body fluids, the early years worker must always follow the workplace's health and safety regulations.

You will rarely know if a child is HIV positive and must therefore be vigilant in all hygiene matters.

The health and safety policy will include the following:

- Disposable gloves should be worn when in contact with blood, urine, vomit and faeces.
- Cuts and grazes should be covered by waterproof plasters.
- Hands should be washed after contact with spillages (even when gloves are worn).
- In the work setting spillages of blood should be:
  - covered by 1 per cent hypochlorite solution (bleach)
  - wiped over using disposable cloths which should be placed in the appropriate bag (yellow) for incineration
  - then the area should be washed with warm soapy water.

Knowledge into action

Find out from your placement:

Who is in charge of health and safety?

What is their policy for handling and disposing of body fluids?

Taking a child's temperature

The normal body temperature of a child is 36.5–37°C. It will vary throughout the day, being higher in the evening, after exercise and in hot weather. Babies, who have a very immature temperature-regulating mechanism, can show a big fluctuation in temperature.

In young children the temperature is usually taken under the armpit or by using a fever strip on the forehead. The temperature will be 0.5°C lower than if taken by mouth.

Thermometers

The four different types of thermometer are:

- Digital thermometer, which is easy to read, unbreakable and fairly quick to use.

- Mercury thermometer, which is difficult to read and can be hazardous because it is made of glass and contains mercury, which is poisonous.

- Fever strip, which is easy to use by placing the strip on to the child's forehead. The strip changes colour and shows the temperature of the child. It is not as accurate as the other methods.

- Infra-red thermal scanning thermometer, which is very expensive but very accurate. It is placed in the ear and takes only a few seconds to give a reading. It is usually used only in hospitals and doctors' surgeries because of the expense.

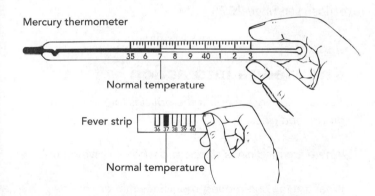

Mercury thermometer

Normal temperature

Fever strip

Normal temperature

Care of a child with a temperature

A raised temperature is an indicator that the body is fighting an infection. High temperatures can cause febrile convulsions (see below) and it is therefore recommended that the child should be cooled.

Ways to reduce a child's temperature

- Remove clothing down to the underwear.

- Maintain room temperature at 15°C (60°F).

- Paracetamol syrup can be given to children over three months with parental consent.

- Offer cool drinks regularly.

- If the temperature is over 38.5°C, use tepid sponging – dip a sponge into warm water which is a few degrees lower than the child's temperature, and

Taking a child's temperature – the steps

Collect the thermometer and a book or toy to distract the child.

⬇

Show the child the thermometer and tell her what you are going to do.

⬇

If using a mercury thermometer, shake it until the mercury is at its lowest point.

⬇

Sit the child on your knee.

⬇

Place the thermometer under the child's arm, ensuring the bulb is directly in the armpit.

⬇

Wait until the readings have stopped changing or until the digital thermometer bleeps.

⬇

Record the temperature and clean the thermometer.

⬇

Ensure the thermometer is put of children's reach.

sponge over the child's skin. Do not dry the skin. Repeat until the temperature falls below 38.5°C. The temperature should not fall too quickly.

Febrile convulsions

One in twenty children has a febrile convulsion due to a high temperature. It occurs in children of six months to five years and children who have had a convulsion have an increased risk of further convulsions. (For action in case of febrile convulsion or fit, see page 256.)

Checklist for caring for an unwell child

✔ Make the child's bed up on the sofa in the sitting room.

✔ Ensure the child drinks every hour when awake.

✔ Keep a covered jug of drink in the room.

✔ Ensure the room is warm and well ventilated.

✔ Sit with the child as much as possible.

✔ Draw the curtains slightly if the light is distressing the child.

✔ Keep a box of tissues and a sick bowl handy.

✔ Ensure the bedclothes are washed frequently.

✔ Have plenty of books, puzzles and simple activities to do with the child.

Giving medicines and keeping records

Medicines

It may be necessary for children to be given medicine while in your care. Each setting will have a policy on this, and will have a form for the parent to fill in. This is completed before medicine can be given.

In most settings medicine is given by the first aider. If you are caring for a child at home you need to get permission from the parents before giving any medicine. You also need to have the following information about the medicine:

■ the reason it is being given

■ whether it should be given before or after food

■ storage (some medication needs to be stored in the fridge)

■ expiry date

■ side-effects.

You will then need to record all medicine given, the time and the dosage.

Storage of medicines

All work settings have to abide by the Control of Substances Hazardous to Health Regulations (1994) (COSHH) when storing medicines. All medicines should be kept locked away and out of reach. The only exception is inhalers – which need to be accessible to the appropriate child – and medicines that need to be kept in a locked fridge. Children are very curious and also surprisingly quick at opening bottles and packets, so real care must always be taken. In the home setting, medication should never be kept in a handbag – young children love to search through any bags that are left lying around.

Medicines supplied to children should always have a child-proof lid on – be warned though – these delay a child only slightly in getting the container open.

(For the action to take in accidental poisoning or overdose see page 257.)

Knowledge into action

Ask your supervisor about the policies for storing and giving medicines.

Where are medicines stored and who can give them?

What are the commonest medicines that are needed by the children in the setting?

Where are children's inhalers kept?

Ask if you can see the forms that the parents need to fill in.

Date	Name of child	Medicine	Dose	Time or circumstance for taking the medicine	Signature of parent	Time given and by whom
16/7/99	Hazel Jackson	amoxycillin	5 ml	1 pm	M Jackson	1 pm HE
16/7/99	Hazel Jackson	ventolin inhaler	2 puffs	If Hazel becomes wheezy during PE, games or playtime.	M Jackson	

Knowledge into action

In pairs, discuss what you could do in the following situations.

While working as a nanny, you notice that the children's mother always leaves her contraceptive pills out by the kettle. You ask her about it and she says that she has to keep them out , or she will forget to take them, and that the children cannot reach them.

In the home setting, the child's grandmother comes to visit the children once a week. You notice that she always puts her handbag, containing her blood pressure tablets on the floor. When you mention it to her she says that she gets the child-proof tops put on, and therefore there is no problem.

In the nursery setting, a father leaves some medicine for his daughter and fills in the appropriate form. He states on the form that it is very important that it be given at the correct time. When the first aider comes to give the medicine, she notices that the medicine is past the expiry date. When you try to telephone him, he is out of the office.

Giving medicine

It is very important to approach a child with a positive attitude when giving medicine. Medicines are generally supplied in syrup form for children under twelve, and are flavoured and usually sugar-free. They are supplied with a 5 ml spoon or a syringe. Syringes are often used with babies and young children. They are easy to use because they ensure you are accurate with the dose and there is less likelihood of any being spilt. Most children take their medicine readily, but some are reluctant and need persuasion – try making it into a game, offering their favourite drink afterwards, or if the taste is really unpleasant to the child, the child's parent could talk to the doctor about changing the flavour. Some medicines, such as iron, have a very strong taste which is difficult to disguise.

Checklist for giving medicines

✔ Read the label on the medicine to ensure it is the right one and to check the dose and time the medicine should be given.

✔ If you are giving a non-prescription medicine – e.g. paracetamol – check that the dose you have been asked to give matches the instructions provided.

✔ Check the expiry date.

✔ Shake the bottle if necessary.

✔ Always use the measure that is provided with the medicine – teaspoons are *not* equivalent to a 5 ml measure.

✔ Pour medicines from the bottle with the label facing upwards, to prevent drips ruining the label.

✔ Ensure that the child takes the full dose – medicine should not be added to drinks because the full dose might not be given.

✔ Ensure that the medicine is stored correctly.

✔ Record the date and time you gave the medicine.

✔ For a baby, sterilise the syringe.

✔ Never pour medicines from one container to another.

The commonest types of medicine that need to be given to a child are antibiotics and paracetamol:

Antibiotics are prescribed for a bacterial infection normally for five, seven or ten days. It is very important that, even if the child becomes better after two or three days, the prescribed course is completed, otherwise the infection may re-occur. If a child develops a rash or diarrhoea, or any other side-effects from the medicine, the doctor should be contacted before the next dose is given.

Case study

You are looking after a two-year-old girl called Sophie, who has an ear infection. Her mother has asked you to give her the next dose of her antibiotic after lunch at 1 pm.

What do you need to find out from the mother?

When you try to give the medicine, Sophie is very reluctant to take it. What could you do to encourage the child to take it?

How would you record what has been given?

Paracetamol syrup (such as Calpol) is commonly given for teething, aches and pains, and for reducing a temperature. It is important that the dose is correct for the age of the child, that it is given no more frequently than every four to six hours and that a child is not given more than four doses in 24 hours.

Keeping records of children's health

As part of the admissions procedure in an early years setting, the parent will be asked to complete a health form. Staff will then know about the child's needs and what to do if a problem occurs. For example, if a child has a severe allergy to peanuts, staff need to ensure that cooking ingredients do not contain nuts.

Records need to contain the following information:

- name and address of child
- next of kin's contact number
- two further contact names and their telephone numbers
- GP's name, address and telephone number
- long-term illnesses
- allergies
- medication
- special diet
- difficulties with hearing, speech or vision.

It is important to have three contact numbers so that if the child is unwell during the day and the parent is out, someone else can be contacted. It is obviously better for the child to be at home when not feeling well.

All records of a child's health are confidential, and should be known only by those that really need to know. Parents might not want other people to know that their child has a particular health problem because he might be treated differently. This means you will probably not be aware if a child has a potentially infectious condition, such as hepatitis or HIV, which is why it is so important to ensure hygiene precautions are always taken (see page 242).

Records will always be kept locked away and be updated regularly, usually annually. If they are kept on computer, they will be subject to the Data Protection Act (see pages 81–82).

If you are looking after a child at home, you will need to make records of the child's illness, in order to show the parents, or doctor, if necessary. You will need to record the child's temperature, medication given, and any changes in the child's condition. If you are concerned that a child's condition is deteriorating you should always contact the child's parents and seek medical assistance.

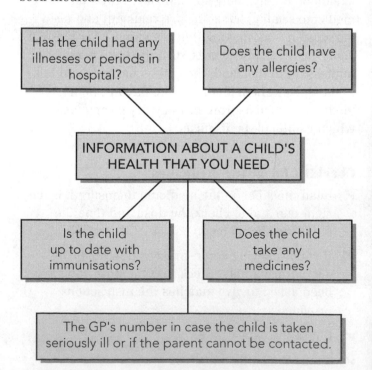

Knowledge into action

From your placement try to find out:

What information is requested on the child health form?

Where are these stored?

How often are they updated?

Who has access to them?

Reporting illnesses

When you are looking after children it is important to find out the parent's contact number and to know the child's medical history.

Whom to contact when a child is unwell

The parent
If children are unwell or their condition changes then the parent should always be informed. It is also important that the parent is made aware of any falls or accidents, especially head injuries, which have occurred during the day.

The GP
If for any reason you are unable to contact the parent, you may need to contact the family doctor (the GP) if the child is unwell.

Calling a doctor out
If it is necessary to call a doctor out to the child, they will need to know:

- the child's name, age and address
- all of the child's symptoms
- when the illness started
- the child's temperature (see pages 242–243)
- any long-term health problems and medication.

If you are unsure what to do, it is always safest to seek medical help. Children, especially babies, can deteriorate very quickly.

Emergency services

In an emergency, it will be necessary to dial 999 (or 112) and request an ambulance. You will be asked for:

- your name, telephone number and address
- the name, age and sex of the child
- the signs and symptoms of the child.

While waiting for the ambulance, continue to reassure the child and note down any changes that occur. Ensure that the child's parents are called and arrangements are made to care for any other children you are looking after at the time.

Someone will need to accompany the child to hospital – usually the first aider – but it could be the child's key worker.

The other children in the setting will need reassurance and, if necessary, a brief, simple

Knowledge into action

In pairs, role-play the telephone call you would make in one of the following situations.

You are looking after a baby of six months who has been mildly unwell. His temperature suddenly shoots up to 39°C, he is sick and very fretful.

A three-year-old boy called Paul who has had a bad cold for two days complains of a headache and stiff neck. He is very sleepy and is sick. His temperature is 38.6°C.

Laura is two and is feeling unwell and a little hot. Later on, when you take her temperature, it is 38.8°C. Just as you are about to start cooling her down, she starts having a convulsion.

Emergencies

When to seek medical assistance	What is an emergency? You must dial 999 immediately in any of the following cases
■ any pain which is causing obvious distress to the child ■ rash with any other symptoms ■ severe earache ■ jaundice (except babies under six weeks) ■ headache – in conjunction with other symptoms in a child under six, or following a head injury ■ urine dark, smelly or abnormal colour ■ stiff neck with other symptoms ■ abdomen hard, tender and bloated ■ signs of dehydration (see page 229) ■ breathing difficulties ■ very drowsy. **Further reasons to see a doctor with a baby:** ■ baby is 'not himself' – not interested in surroundings, or sleeping more than normal ■ fontanelle – either swollen or sunken ■ vomiting or diarrhoea for longer than six hours ■ refusing a bottle ■ dislikes being handled ■ dry nappies.	■ breathing stops ■ difficulty in breathing and/or blue lips ■ unconsciousness ■ signs of meningitis (see page 239) ■ severe abdominal pain ■ heavy bleeding ■ chemical in the eye ■ swallowing of poisons ■ severe burns ■ fits or convulsions ■ asthma attack not getting better after ten minutes or getting worse ■ breathing difficulties.

explanation of what is happening. It is important that everyone remains calm and the routine is maintained in order to disturb the child and the other children as little as possible.

The effects of illness on children and their families

All illness is stressful for the child and the family, but the effect of the illness on the child will depend on:

■ the illness itself, and the treatment

■ how the family copes with the illness and the support they receive

■ how often the child is away from nursery or school and how often she is in hospital – the longer the child is ill or in hospital, the greater the effect on her development.

An acute illness of short duration which doesn't require hospitalisation should not effect the child's development at all. A chronic illness can place

restrictions on a child and limit his opportunities. Epilepsy, for example, can mean a child is not allowed to play on or use some equipment. The drugs used to treat epilepsy can cause a child to be drowsy, lethargic and clumsy, and can also dampen his curiosity, which will hinder development.

Many children suffer from 'glue ear' (see page 225), and suffer intermittent hearing loss. This can affect their language development, and might mean they miss some of what is said to them.

Absence from school or nursery

A chronic illness which necessitates absences from nursery or school, can affect the child's social, emotional and cognitive development. The child will lack the stimulation offered by a learning environment and will also be restricted from learning through observation and imitation of others. The child will also be away from friends for long periods, which can affect his ability to make and sustain friendships.

Minimising the effects of illness on a child's development

Unless children are very unwell, they need to be provided with activities to stimulate them and to promote normal development. Because they may have a shorter attention span, activities need to be changed frequently. Children who are chronically sick need to be given a sense of control over their condition and should be allowed to be involved in any decisions about their care – this should help them develop some independence and increase their self-esteem. There are some ideas for things to do with a sick child on page 241.

In hospitals there are specially trained play workers (see page 205) who give children appropriate activities to aid their recovery, but children will still depend on their family and carer to provide care and stimulation.

If children are worried about their illness they will show signs of stress, and therefore need reassurance and plenty of opportunity to talk and ask questions.

Knowledge into action

In pairs, think how you might provide play activities in the following situations.

A child who is being kept isolated in a room.

A three-year-old girl who has extremely itchy eczema (see pages 234–235), and needs to be distracted to prevent her from scratching.

A five-year-old boy who has to have his tonsils out the following day, but is very anxious.

The effects of a child's illness on the family

Even if a child has a short illness this can cause a disruption to the normal routine of a household and be a worrying time for the parents. If a child has a chronic condition or has repeated visits to hospital, this can totally disrupt the whole of the family's life,

including that of the other children in the family. Parents may need to go through a grieving process before they can accept the implications of the illness. Due to the restrictions the illness may place on the child, it is easy to be over-protective and not encourage independence; this can hinder the child's emotional development. For example, if a child is epileptic and has frequent fits, the parents will naturally be anxious about her being on a climbing frame.

How a parent may feel

Guilty
This may be due to:

- having to leave the child (or other children) with someone else

- not having enough time to spend with the sick child

- feelings that the illness might in some way be their fault.

Parents need constant reassurance and help with household tasks so they can spend more time seeing to the needs of the children. The health visitor may be able to arrange for some help at home.

Anxious
This may be due to:

- the nature of the child's illness

- how other family members are coping

- financial matters – if a child is in hospital it can cause extra expense.

Parents need information about the illness and the treatment, which the GP or hospital staff can provide. They also need someone to listen to their concerns. If they have a spiritual adviser, this can provide tremendous support. A social worker may be able to help with any financial problems.

Exhausted
Exhaustion can be caused by:

- lack of sleep

- anxiety

■ the extra work involved in caring for the child and the rest of the family.

Other family members could help by sitting and playing with the child to give the parent a break.

The worries and needs of the carer will reflect those of the parent, if all the main day-to-day care of the child is her responsibility.

Siblings

Other children in the family will also be affected by the child's illness. They may feel jealous of all the attention the ill child is getting and may want to be ill themselves. They may also feel guilty for thinking unkind thoughts about a brother or sister.

These children might become attention-seeking or develop behaviour problems. They therefore need someone to spend time with them away from the unwell child, and to reassure them that they are still loved. Older children will understand if they are told what is wrong with their sibling and can be involved in playing games and reading to him.

Case study

You've been asked to baby-sit for two children of three and five years for an afternoon. The five-year-old is recovering from a week's stay in hospital, having had a minor operation. The mother is on her own with the two children, with no family support, and wishes to go back to her part-time college course, which is one afternoon a week.

How do you think the mother might be feeling and why could it be beneficial for her to have a break?

What do you need to find out from her about the children?

What activities/games could you prepare to amuse both children, bearing in mind that the five-year-old might be tired and will need some rest?

Admission to hospital

When a child is admitted to hospital it is an extremely stressful time for everyone. This is especially true if it is in an emergency, because the child cannot be prepared beforehand. If it is known that a child is to be admitted to hospital, the child and family can be prepared appropriately.

Think about it

Read about Bowlby's research on attachment (pages 177–179). How should this be reflected in our practice, particularly when helping children face hospitalisation?

The way a child copes with the admission will depend on a variety of factors, including:

■ age and stage of development

■ personality

■ type of illness

■ length of stay in hospital

■ parent's anxiety

■ atmosphere of the hospital and the support given by the hospital staff.

It has been recommended that a child should start to be prepared for admission about a week beforehand, but can be exposed to appropriate books and games before this. Each hospital will have their own procedures and booklets for a child's admission but the preparation will usually include some of the examples included in the following chart.

If a child is well prepared and the family is not unduly anxious, the child is more likely to co-operate with medical procedures and less likely to have behaviour problems afterwards, or be stressed – which would delay recovery.

Before admission, allow the child to help pack her bag. Make sure you pack the child's comforter and any favourite toys and books. The hospital booklet will advise you on what else to bring.

Procedures and strategies for helping a child who is being admitted to hospital

Books	The local children's library will have a variety of books about hospitals.
Booklets	A booklet for children should be available from the hospital explaining in simple terms what will happen in the hospital. Parents should be given a booklet informing them of all hospital procedures and about the specific illness or condition their child has. It has been shown in studies that children will imitate their parents' (or carers') fears, so it is important that these are dealt with by being as informed as possible.
Videos	Some hospitals have a video about their hospital or about specific procedures, such as having an operation.
Play sessions	If children are given the opportunity to play with pretend hospital equipment and are able to act out what is likely to happen to them with dolls or teddies, they will cope much better with the hospital stay. This can be started at home with the early years worker and continued in hospital with the play worker.
Verbal information from the hospital	There will be an opportunity for parents and carers to be fully informed by the hospital staff. Children can then be told in a simple way what is likely to happen. It is always important to be totally truthful in answering children's questions. Ensure that children know if someone is going to stay with them for the whole time.
A hospital visit	If this can be arranged, it can certainly help both parents and children feel more comfortable about the admission. Let children see the playroom and point out all the different toys.

The hospital will allow a parent or carer to stay with the child all the time, and if she is having an operation, to accompany her to theatre. If it is not possible to stay all the time, there is always an open visiting policy.

Play will continue to be important in hospital because it can:

- help communication between child and staff
- help prepare a child for theatre or other procedures
- allow the child to act out any fears
- provide some sort of normality for the child
- provide a distraction.

The early years worker's role when a child is in hospital is to support the child, the parents and any other children. It is obviously a time of great stress for the whole family but will be much less stressful if the family feel well supported. The parents may want to talk, have time alone or have a few extra chores done around the house.

If a child is admitted as an emergency there can be no preparation and therefore the child and family will be much more frightened. It is important to be as calm as possible – even if you don't feel it – and explain everything to the child step by step.

Children in isolation

It is occasionally necessary for a child to be placed in a side ward and to be kept isolated from everyone else. There are two reasons for this:

- If the child is infectious and it is necessary to protect others from getting the infection.

- If the child has a vulnerable immune system and is very prone to catching infections from other people. This could occur with leukaemia. Visitors will be restricted and everyone who visits the child will have to wear a mask and gown. Toys may have to be sterilised before being taken to the child, which will limit the number of toys the child can have.

The needs of the child and parents

The main problem is boredom for both child and carer, because of the restrictions of being stuck in one room. It is really important that, if possible, someone stays with the child at all times. This can cause extreme pressures on the family, especially if there are other children to consider.

The child will need to be able to express his fears and anxieties and have all his questions answered. He will need the comfort of a routine, and have meals and drinks which he enjoys. The child will also need stimulation and the play worker will be able to help in providing ideas and activities for the child to do, such as those on page 241.

The parents need as much support as possible from family and friends and from the hospital staff in order to support the child. Other children still need to be cared for and household chores and bills, etc. still need to be dealt with.

Children with life-threatening terminal illness

Cancer is the most common life-threatening disease in children, but there is a 70 per cent rate of overall cure. The most common type of cancer is leukaemia, in which there is an overproduction of immature white blood cells (which help fight infection) in the bone marrow; this means that there are fewer red blood cells (which carry oxygen around the body), and platelets (which help in the blood-clotting process). This can cause the child to be anaemic and tired, to have swollen glands and joint pains and to bruise easily.

Problems and needs of the child

Am I going to die?	Children need to be told the truth so that they are able to come to terms with what is happening to them. This is probably best done by the parent but can be supported by the hospital staff. A spiritual adviser can be invaluable in helping the child.
Coping with the side-effects of the treatment	These can be very distressing for children, especially older children, who are very conscious of the hair loss. Wigs or baseball caps can be worn to reduce the embarrassment.
Support	Other than the family, carers and hospital staff, the child's friends can be encouraged to visit. If there are other children on the ward who have a similar illness, the children will be able to support each other too.
Play	Play is very important for the child. It can allow him to act out any fears and help him come to terms with his condition.
Routine	Routine should continue as much as possible. This includes continuing to discipline the child if necessary because he needs the security of knowing that some things remain the same as always.
Decision-making and independence	A child who is in hospital can become very dependent on other people for making decisions and providing care. If the child is given choices about day-to-day issues, it can help him to cope emotionally.

Treatment of cancers may include:

- surgery, which will aim to remove the cancer and prevent it spreading, this will often be followed by chemotherapy and/or radiotherapy

- chemotherapy, which is used especially on cancers that are widespread, such as leukaemia, and which destroys fast-growing cells – side-effects include sickness and diarrhoea, anaemia and hair loss

- radiotherapy, which is a deep X-ray therapy that shrinks the cancer or slows down the growth – side-effects include nausea and hair loss

- bone marrow transplant, which can be used to treat leukaemia if other methods have failed: a compatible donor needs to be found, which may be a member of the family; the child will then have radiotherapy or chemotherapy to destroy his own bone marrow, which contains the cancer cells; this is then replaced by some of the donor's bone marrow.

The needs of the family

Once a child has been diagnosed as having a life-threatening illness, the consultant will inform the parents about the condition, the treatment and prognosis and will also put them in contact with someone they can call at any time to ask questions. They will initially be in shock and will not really take in what they have been told, so they need an opportunity to talk this over again during the following few days. The early years worker will need to be a good listener over this period and also have to deal with her own shock, and the child's illness.

The family as a whole will continue to need support, which can be provided by the hospital staff, specialist counsellors, spiritual advisers, or other parents who are going through, or have been through, similar experiences. Support can also be obtained from one of the voluntary organisations such as Action for the Sick Child.

The child may have periods of remission when he goes home. This can be a stressful time initially, especially if some treatment needs to be continued at home. The family will, however, be supported by either Macmillan Nurses, a health visitor or, in some areas, a community paediatric nurse.

Knowledge into action

Find out what statutory and voluntary bodies there are locally that are able to provide support to the family of a child who has a life-threatening illness.

Case study

Mohammed is six years old and has been diagnosed as having leukaemia. He has had a course of chemotherapy, which made him feel very ill, and it has caused some hair loss. He has now been sent home for a while before further tests are done and another course of treatment starts.

There are three other children in the family who are seven years, four years and eighteen months.

1 What are Mohammed's needs and how can the early years worker help meet these needs?
2 How can the early years worker support the parents?
3 How might the other children be feeling about their brother's illness, and how could the early years worker support them?
4 Mohammed wants to see some of his school friends, but is worried about how they may react to his hair loss. What could the early years worker do to help in this situation?
5 Plan out one day's routine for the child while the other three children are at their grandparents.

Emergencies and first aid treatment

Because babies and children are prone to accidents, it is recommended that all early years workers complete a first aid course and keep up to date with first aid procedures. This section will give a summary of some first aid procedures, but it is meant for revision only, and not as a substitute for a course.

In a work setting, always call the first aider for any accident or incident. In a home setting, you will need to be able to deal with any incident until an ambulance arrives (see page 247 for calling emergency aid).

Emergencies

The priorities for dealing with any situation are known as the 4 Bs:

- breathing – this has to be the first priority, to ensure that the child is breathing
- bleeding
- breaks
- burns.

Breathing

Resuscitation

> **Important note**
>
> Do not attempt resuscitation unless you have been specifically trained in it. Call for a first aider or an ambulance.

The flow chart opposite shows the sequence for resuscitation of a child.

The order in which this sequence occurs is easily remembered by the letters: DR ABC:

D anger
R esponse

A irway
B reathing
C irculation

A child who has been unconscious, even for a short time, must be seen by a doctor or go to hospital.

What to do in an emergency situation

- Stay calm
- Assess the situation – are the casualty, yourself or any other children in any danger?

Resuscitation

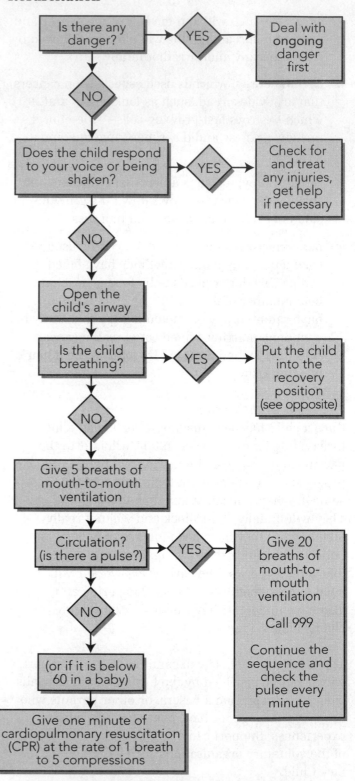

- What's wrong? – make a quick assessment of what is wrong with the child and call for help if necessary.

Recovery position

Put 2 fingers under the child's chin and 1 hand on the forehead.

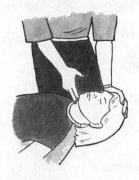

Gently tilt the head well back. Straighten limbs. Bend the arm nearest you so that it is at right angles to the child's body.

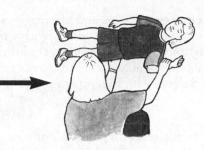

Bring the other arm across the child's chest. Place the hand against the child's cheek – with palm outwards.
Pull up the child's far leg, just above the knee – using your other hand.

Pull on the far leg and roll the child towards you, still pressing the hand against the cheek – until the child is lying on his side.

To stop the child rolling too far, use your knees as support. Bend the upper leg so that it is at a right angle from the body.

Make sure the child's head is well back – to keep airway open and stop him from breathing in vomit or choking on his tongue.

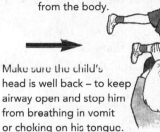

Make sure the upper arm is supporting the head.

- Deal with the emergency and reassure the child until help arrives.

It is far more common to deal with minor injuries, such as cuts and bruises, than life-threatening situations.

The table opposite shows common minor injuries and their treatment.

Informing parents

Parents obviously need informing about *all* accidents that occur. When there has been a serious injury, the parents need informing immediately. Many settings will inform parents of minor injuries when the child is collected, either by a written note or verbally.

Recording accidents

By law, *all* accidents to children, staff and visitors need to be recorded in an accident book. The following information needs to be included:

Injury	First aid treatment
graze	■ Rinse with clean water.
nose bleed	■ Tip head forward and pinch nose just below bridge. ■ Seek medical advice if it continues for 30 minutes.
foreign object in the ear or nose	■ Do not try to remove it. ■ Take the child to hospital.
bruises and sprains	■ Apply cotton wool dipped in cold water. ■ For a sprain, rest the limb, apply an ice pack and apply a bandage. Raise the limb.

- the name of the injured person and the first aider
- what happened and where
- the date and time of the accident
- the treatment given.

255

Treatment of injuries

Injury/incident; *symptoms*	Treatment
Bleeding	■ Check for objects in the wound but do not remove them. ■ Apply direct pressure to the wound with a pad. ■ Raise the injured limb above the level of the heart. ■ Apply extra pads if necessary, but do not remove the old pad. ■ Lie the child down with the legs raised to prevent shock. ■ Call for help.
Breaks (fractures); *pain, loss of movement, swelling and bruising, possible deformity of limb*	■ Do not move the child unless in danger – e.g. from falling equipment. ■ Help the child to support the injured limb above and below the injury and support with pads. ■ Call an ambulance.
Burns	■ Run under a cold tap or dip into bowl of water (or any cold liquid) for ten minutes. ■ Remove watches and rings from the site. ■ Cover with a clean, non-fluffy cloth. ■ Chemical burns need 20 minutes of cold water. ■ Call 999 for a severe or chemical burn. ■ **Do not** apply cream or butter.
Choking; *difficulty in breathing and speaking, flushed face, may clutch throat or chest*	■ Encourage child to cough. ■ Ask to lean forward and give five slaps between shoulder blades. ■ If this fails, give up to five chest thrusts. ■ Then up to five abdominal thrusts (but not in babies under one). ■ Call an ambulance. ■ Repeat the cycle. ■ If the child stops breathing, start resuscitation.
Fit; *sudden rigidity of the body, twitching and jerking of the limbs, the back may arch, eyes may roll upwards, breath-holding, possible incontinence, loss of or altered consciousness*	■ If possible, remove anything which could cause injury and protect the head by putting something underneath it. ■ **Do not** restrain the child. ■ When the fit finishes, place the child in the recovery position (see page 255) and reassure the child on regaining consciousness. ■ Call for an ambulance unless the first aider knows that the child has occasional fits. ■ If the fit is due to a febrile convulsion, the child will need to be cooled. ■ The child should never be left alone.
Head injury	■ Apply a cold compress to the head. ■ Sit down and rest. ■ Watch for signs of concussion – e.g. headaches, vomiting, dizziness, unusual drowsiness. ■ Go to hospital if the child was unconscious, even if only for a short time.

Injury/incident; symptoms *(continued)*	Treatment *(continued)*
Swallowed poisons	■ Dial 999 for an ambulance. ■ Ensure you have the bottle of tablets or medicine to take to hospital – it is essential you record how much you think has been taken. ■ Do not make the child sick – but if he is, check the vomit for tablets, and take a sample with you. ■ Reassure the child. ■ If the child is unconscious, place him in the recovery position (see page 255). ■ Record any changes in the child.
Severe allergic reactions; *anxiety, difficulty breathing, swelling and puffiness of face, neck and eyes, red, blotchy skin*	■ Call for an ambulance. ■ Reassure the child. ■ Help the child into a comfortable position. ■ Record the pulse and breathing. ■ If the child becomes unconscious, follow the DR ABC of resuscitation.

Think about it

Jessie came home from school saying she fell over in the playground and hurt her knee. That evening she went to bed early with a headache and during the night she was sick twice. The following morning she was still feeling unwell. Her brother mentioned that she had hit her head when she fell.

In pairs, answer the following.

Why might Jessie be feeling unwell?

Might her mother have treated her symptoms any differently if she had been told about the head injury earlier?

What should have happened to prevent this from happening?

Suggest ways in which the school might have passed on details of the injury to the mother.

What should have been written in the accident book?

Check your knowledge

- List three groups – either professionals or organisations – who might be involved in health promotion.

- What types of checks are routinely carried out on children?

- Name three diseases that children are vaccinated against.

- What are the common signs of an asthma attack?

- Give three causes of vomiting in children.

- What are the signs of chickenpox?

- What steps should be taken if a child has a raised temperature?

- What steps can be taken to limit cross-infection?

- Describe three circumstances when medical assistance should always be sought.

- What should a carer do if he suspects that a child has taken a poisonous substance?

Resources

Further reading

British Medical Association 1995, *Complete Family Health*, London, Dorling Kindersley

Health Education Authority 1998 *Birth to Five*, London, Health Education Authority

Middlemiss, Priscilla 1998 *Child Health*, London, Hamlyn Publishers

Red Cross 1997, *First Aid Manual*, London, Dorling Kindersley

Valman, Dr. B. 1997 *Children's Medical Guide*, London, Dorling Kindersley

Useful contacts

Health Information Wales
Ffynnon-Ias
Ty Glas Avenue
Llanishen
Cardiff CF4 5DZ
0800 665544

National Eczema Society (NES)
163 Eversholt Street
London NW1 1BU
020 7388 4097

National Meningitis Trust
Fern House
Bath Road
Stroud GL5 3TJ
01453 751738

National Asthma Campaign
Providence House
Providence Place
London N1 0NT
020 7226 2260

Useful websites

Health Education Authority (UK)
http://www.hea.org.uk

CHAPTER
What is play?

'In play, a child always behaves beyond his average age, above his daily behaviour, in play it is as though he were a head taller than his normal self.'
(Lev Vygotsky 1978)

Play is a very important aspect of a child's life. Children determine their own play and the adult's role is to give opportunity and guidance where necessary. A child's period of play can be as demanding as an adult's time at work. As with adults, children spend far more time on and give far more effort to an activity that they have chosen for themselves.

Watch a child building a model from Lego and you will note the concentration, enthusiasm and determination shown by a child who is 'only playing'. Materials such

as Lego allow children to experiment with ideas without any fear of failure. They can transfer what they have learnt about the world around them into tangible objects which can then be used for play. A child who is given a worksheet has only to make one mistake to feel a sense of failure, which will then lead to a reluctance to attempt that activity in the future. A 'mistake' with Lego (or sand/water) is easily rectified and developed as a challenge.

Children of all ages need to have the opportunity to learn from experimentation and exploration. In settings for 0- to 5-year-olds, these opportunities are structured by the adults to form the framework of an early years curriculum. The foundation stage of the curriculum is based on the early learning goals and ends at the *end* of the reception year. This stage should underpin all future learning. In primary schools, children aged 4 to 7 years 11 months will experience a more structured curriculum, which should include learning through play, working towards Key Stage 1 of the National Curriculum.

The following flow chart illustrates the ways that the curriculum from 0 to 7 years 11 months can be delivered through learning-based play.

The aim of this chapter is to promote an understanding of the play and learning opportunities offered to children in a variety of group care and educational settings. The chapter will lead to a better understanding of:

■ the purpose and potential of play activities

■ an effective play environment and materials

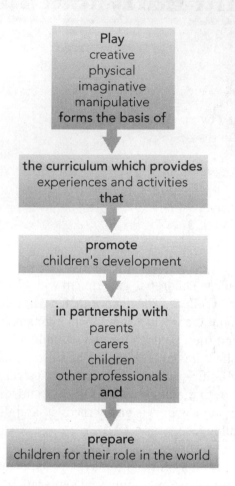

Play
creative
physical
imaginative
manipulative
forms the basis of

the curriculum which provides
experiences and activities
that

promote
children's development

in partnership with
parents
carers
children
other professionals
and

prepare
children for their role in the world

- the value of different types of play:
  - creative
  - social
  - physical
  - imaginative
  - manipulative.

Theories that influence play and education provision

Nowadays, play is generally accepted as an essential part of an early years curriculum. There are a variety of approaches to play and the provision will vary according to the needs and developmental stages of children. The following theorists have had an enormous effect on learning through play and are seen as pioneers in the early years education world.

Friedrich Froebel (1782–1852)

Froebel founded his first kindergarten in 1840. He believed in outdoor and indoor play and invented

finger play, songs and rhymes. He valued **symbolic behaviour** through play: this is where children understand that they can make one thing stand for – or symbolise – something else – for example, a yoghurt pot can symbolise a cup of tea. He felt that children were able to learn at their highest level through imaginative play. He was also well known for encouraging **block play** which he called *gifts* – encouraging children to understand a variety of mathematical concepts and relationships through play with various wooden blocks. After his death the idea of his child-centred kindergarten became popular in both Germany and the rest of Europe.

Observation

Plan a block play activity, with a set of wooden blocks, to encourage a child to be a symbol user.

Observe the response of the child to the activity and evaluate your observation.

Maria Montessori (1870–1952)

Maria Montessori was a doctor in poor areas of Rome in the early twentieth century. During this time she observed children's development and saw them as **active learners**. She did not believe in imaginative play as Froebel did and felt that children needed to experience concepts such as shape, size and order through **structured play**.

She also felt that, at different stages of their development, children are particularly receptive to certain areas of learning and that the adult must guide them through these. Montessori believed that children would become independent learners if they worked on their own. She did not encourage play and encouraged freer creative work only after they had studied a sequence of exercises often using specifically designed **didactic** (instructional) materials. Her methods are still popular in Montessori schools around the world.

Rudolph Steiner (1861–1925)

Steiner believed in community education and the importance of maintaining relationships between child and teacher. He placed great importance on a vegetarian diet and proper rest. Adults were encouraged to observe children's temperament as a way of planning their work with them. Children with special needs were encouraged to be part of the community and to be considered by other children. He believed in three phases of childhood that were:

1   **The will** – fusing of the body and the spirit (0–7 years).
2   **The heart** – the rhythm of the heartbeat meaning feelings are important at this stage of development (7–14 years).
3   **The head** – a period of thinking (14 years onwards).

A number of schools in Europe are Steiner communities and follow his original methods.

Margaret McMillan (1860–1931)

During her professional life Margaret McMillan became a member of the Froebel Society, believing first-hand experience and active learning to be important. She felt that children could develop into the whole person through play. McMillan, along with her sister, Rachel McMillan, pioneered nursery schools as an extension of home, working in partnership with parents. She also believed in access to a wide variety of materials through **free play** and emphasised that children could not learn if undernourished or deprived in any other way. She encouraged school meals and medical services. She also placed a great importance on high-quality early years training and encouraged imagination and inventiveness.

Susan Isaacs (1885–1948)

Susan Isaacs was also influenced by Froebel. She placed a high value on play and felt that through it children would have a balanced view of life. Movement in learning was important and desk-based learning discouraged. Parents were seen as the main educators of children. Isaacs advised that play should encourage children to explore their innermost feelings.

Spontaneous and structured play

There are two types of play that will be supported by early years workers.

Spontaneous play is when children play in their own way and, making their own choices, build their self-esteem and confidence. The role of the adult is to provide as much variety of equipment and materials as possible, allowing the children time to play.

Structured play is when the play is planned by adults who may work alongside the child developing a particular skill.

The diagram on page 262 shows what children aged 0 to 5 years learn through play.

As they grow from 5 years to 7 years 11 months, play becomes structured and more social skills are developed, adding the following to the list overleaf.

■   value of working as a team
■   developing leadership skills
■   awareness of the needs of others
■   winning and losing appropriately
■   playing by rules.

Observation

Observe a group of children in an exploratory play activity in an area such as the home corner.

In your evaluation, consider how the children related to each other and what the children were gaining from the play.

ISSUES in child care and education

It is an interesting fact that Isaacs felt that children should have a nursery-based education until the age of seven, a feeling echoed by many early years professionals today who are against the current trend of four-year-olds being offered places in schools.

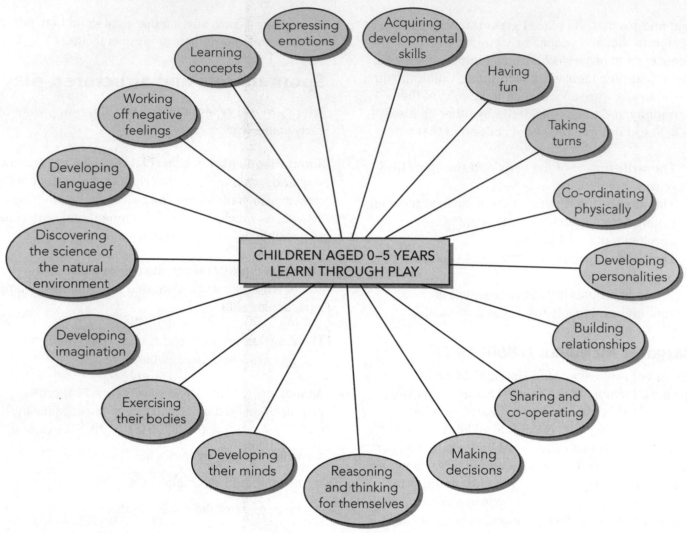

CHILDREN AGED 0–5 YEARS LEARN THROUGH PLAY

- Expressing emotions
- Acquiring developmental skills
- Learning concepts
- Having fun
- Working off negative feelings
- Taking turns
- Developing language
- Co-ordinating physically
- Discovering the science of the natural environment
- Developing personalities
- Developing imagination
- Building relationships
- Exercising their bodies
- Sharing and co-operating
- Developing their minds
- Making decisions
- Reasoning and thinking for themselves

In order to help early years workers appreciate the great potential of play, Janet Moyles defines it as a *spiral of learning*:

'Rather like a pebble on a pond, the ripples from the exploratory free play through directed play and back to enhanced and enriched free play, allowed a spiral of learning spreading ever outwards into wider experiences for the children and upwards into the accretion of knowledge and skills.'

Her approach to play is one adopted by many early years practitioners – acknowledging it as a necessary part of our lives and structured by the environment, materials or contexts in which it takes place. This approach defines play as a learning medium that has excellent potential.

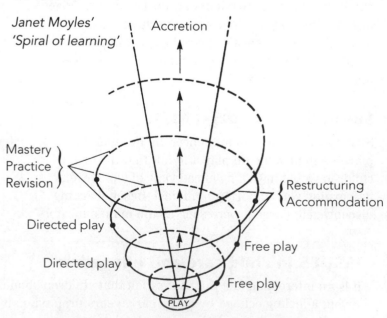

Janet Moyles' *'Spiral of learning'*

Accretion

Mastery
Practice
Revision

Restructuring
Accommodation

Directed play

Free play

Directed play

Free play

PLAY

Source: Janet Moyles 'Just Playing', The Role and Status of Play in Early Childhood Education, Open University, 1989

Stages of social play

There are four stages of social play, which need to be developed in a natural process.

The chart below shows the four stages of social play:

The four stages of play

0–2 Solitary play	2–3 Parallel play
Children play alone, with the reassurance of an adult being close by. They explore the world around them and enjoy adult-directed games such as peek-a-boo.	From two years of age, children are more aware of each other. They may play alongside each other without playing together.
3+ Associative play	**3+ Co-operative play**
From three years children watch and copy each other.	By three years children play together, talk and decide what they want to play.

Choosing play materials and equipment

The equipment that early years workers provide for children must be suitable for developing the appropriate skills and providing for different types of play. Carefully study the chart on pages 264–265, which shows the play equipment most likely to be suitable for children of different ages.

Buying play equipment and materials

There is a wide variety of toys and equipment available. As they will have a great deal of use it is worth using the following checklist when buying new items.

■ Does it have a recognised safety mark?

■ What age is it suitable for?

■ Can it be stored appropriately?

■ Is it versatile?

■ Is it hygienic?

■ How many children will benefit from playing with it?

■ Are spare parts easily available?

It is also important to remember that items in the home can provide a variety of play opportunities – for example, yoghurt pots for pouring and pegs for sorting.

Children with special needs

Children with special needs must always be carefully considered when planning activities. Equipment may need to be adjusted, the layout of an activity considered and extra time may be needed.

Case study

Parveen has a hearing impairment and has to wear a special radio aid, as does any adult communicating with her. She is playing at the construction table when she asks Jo, an early years worker, to help her. He too wears an radio box and makes sure that he gives Parveen space and sits opposite her so that they can have eye contact and communicate using the radio boxes.

You will notice that Jo adapted this activity to accommodate Parveen and allow her to play to her full extent.

Play in the curriculum

The National Curriculum is discussed in more detail in Chapter 13. In schools, learning and play experiences are linked to the National Curriculum and in pre-school settings to the early years curriculum using the six areas of learning called the early learning goals.

In Year 1 of school, learning and play experiences are linked to the National Curriculum and in pre-school

Choosing play materials and equipment

Age	Play needs of the child	Indoor equipment	Outdoor equipment
1–2	The child is mobile and gaining gross motor and fine manipulative skills. The child needs plenty of opportunities to strengthen her muscles and develop co-ordination.	Push-and-pull toys Toys that make music Dolls Trolleys Building bricks Posting toys	Paddling pool Baby swing Small slide
2–3	Children are starting to notice and play with other children. Their language is increasing and much of their play is pretend play. Children are gaining confidence in physical movements and enjoy playing outside. Children of this age can be easily frustrated and have a short concentration span – less than 10 minutes – so they need opportunities to be independent in their play and a range of activities. There should be plenty of equipment as children find it difficult to share with each other.	Dressing-up clothes Home corner equipment – e.g. tea sets, prams, cooking utensils, pretend telephones Building blocks Toy cars and garages Dolls and cuddly toys Dough Paint Jigsaw puzzles Musical instruments	Paddling pool Sand and water tray Slide Climbing frame Swings Sit-and-ride toys Tricycles
3–4	Children are starting to co-operate with each other and enjoy playing together. Most of their play is pretend play. Pieces of dough become cakes; tricycles become cars! Children enjoy physical activity, gaining confidence in being able to use large equipment – e.g. climbing frames. They are also developing fine manipulative skills and beginning to represent their world in picture form.	'Small world' play – e.g. playmobil, Duplo figures Dressing-up clothes Home corner and equipment Dough and other malleable materials Water and sand Construction toys such as train tracks, building bricks Jigsaw puzzles	Climbing frame Slide Paddling pool Tricycles Bicycles with stabilisers Balls and beanbags
4–6	Children are more interested in creating things – e.g. making a cake, drawing cards and planting seeds. They enjoy being with other children although they may play in pairs. Children are beginning to express themselves through painting and drawing as well as through play. They are enjoying using their physical skills in games and are confident when running and climbing.	Materials for recycled modelling Cooking activities Dough and other malleable materials Jigsaws Home corner Construction toys Small world play – e.g. Duplo people Simple board games Toy animals	Mini-gardening tools Skipping ropes Hoops Climbing frame Slide Tricycles Different-sized balls

Age	Play needs of the child	Indoor equipment	Outdoor equipment
6–8 contd.	Children are confident and can play well with other children. They are starting to have particular play friends and are able to share ideas about their play. Games that involve rules are played and rules are added and changed as necessary! Most children enjoy physical activity and play organised games. Sometimes this age can be very competitive. Children are also keen on making things – either of their own design or by following instructions.	Creative materials – e.g. recycled modelling, crayons, pieces of card and paper Board games Jigsaw puzzles Complex construction toys Books Collections – e.g. stamps, stickers	Balls Hoops Bicycles Roller-skates Skipping ropes Climbing frames Slides Swings

settings and reception classes the six areas of learning called the early learning goals are used. This is known as the foundation stage which finishes at the end of the reception year.

A sound understanding of the early learning goals will enable early years workers to plan an appropriate curriculum through play and to focus on the sequence and pace of learning that will help children to achieve those goals. The early learning goals are organised into six areas of learning:

- Personal, social and emotional development
- Communication, language and literacy
- Mathematical development
- Knowledge and understanding of the world
- Physical development
- Creative development.

The early years curricula in the UK vary, but there are many similarities between the frameworks, which are based on learning through play. While Wales works towards the desirable outcomes it is the early learning goals that are referred to. If you are working in countries that are not working towards the early learning goals you will need to consider this when planning activities and experiences for children.

In Chapter 14, Work with young children, you will have the opportunity to study the development of the curriculum and its activities.

Different types of play

Play can be planned for children in a number of ways allowing them to develop a variety of skills. Play is often categorised in four groups:

- creative
- physical
- imaginative
- manipulative.

Creative play

Creative play is an important means of encouraging children to *experiment* and *explore* the world around them. It helps them discover, through their senses, the properties of different materials. If provided with a wide range of activities they can develop physical, social, emotional and intellectual skills. When activities are led in a positive way, children can gain a great deal of satisfaction from creative play and so increase both their confidence and self-esteem.

You should always remember that the end product should never be stressed in creative play: there should be no competition. Children often enjoy the process more than the end product. However, all children should be praised for their efforts so that they feel pride and satisfaction rather than disappointment and frustration.

As an early years worker you need to understand the difference between the creativity of adults and that of children.

Adults will often have a very definite end result in mind when they start a piece of creative work. This sometimes results in frustration and dissatisfaction. Adults usually have a more developed sense of physical co-ordination.

Children, unlike adults, will not always have visualised a definite end product. They are more likely to explore and enjoy the creative material that they are using.

Materials for use in creative play

Sand and alternative materials

If you are in a nursery or school setting you will probably have a sand tray. However, sand can also be provided in a baby's bath, a washing bowl or a sandpit in the garden. Special play (silver) sand is available, which is soft and does not stain hands. Sand can be used in a wet or dry form. Children can use it to create an imaginary environment for diggers, animals and other toys. With simple containers, sand can be dug, raked, scooped, patted and moulded. A sand tray is also an area where children can learn to play creatively together, sharing their imaginative experience.

Sand can also be used as part of a collage picture or to provide an interesting sound in a shaker made from a clear plastic bottle. Sawdust, beans or peat can also be used in collage activities but take note of the health and safety issues on page 269.

Water

From an early age, water plays an important part in creative play – starting in the bath! It is inexpensive and can encourage creativity in endless ways. Children will play at a water tray, washing bowl, paddling pool or bath for a long time. In creative play, water can be transformed by adding ice, colouring, bubbles and even a variety of smells such

Water plays an important part in creative play

as lavender or lemon. You can give children a variety of equipment to stimulate their imaginations – from buckets and bottles to sophisticated water wheels, or, if your funds are limited, children will gain as much creativity from different-sized yoghurt pots and an empty washing-up liquid bottle.

Creative play does not have to have an end product. Sand and water play are excellent examples of this. The children can simply enjoy using their imaginations to play creatively.

Painting and drawing

There is a wide variety of drawing materials on the market – for example:

- pencils

- coloured crayons

- felt-tipped pens

- wax crayons

- chalks.

Children can use these as a medium on their own or mixed together. Drawing can be 'free' or topic related. Children can use drawing materials, such as wax crayons, to explore and rub a variety of textures – for example, bark and walls. The medium provided to 'draw' on will encourage children to explore their imagination. Papers can range from thin tissue to thick paper that children can make themselves.

Children can use a variety of brushes, depending upon their **manipulative stage**. Do not discount household brushes that can be used on large areas. There are many other things that can be used to apply paint. Here are a number of ideas but there are many more:

- potato printing

- scrubbing pads and nailbrush painting

- blowing paint with straws

- painting with rags or scrunched up newspaper

- printing with a roller – a bought one or one made from a kitchen roll

- sponge painting

- drawing with wax and painting over with coloured paint

- roller painting using an old deodorant bottle

- finger painting.

Knowledge into action

Look at the resources in your work setting and choose one that would encourage a creative play activity.

How do you think the children will benefit from this activity in relation to the early learning goals?

Paint can be bought ready-mixed or in powder form. The type of paint you provide for a creative activity will depend upon the consistency required. You can create your own inexpensive thick paint from powdered glue and powdered paint. Other materials such as glitter and sand can be mixed with paint to give them a different texture. Glues, such as PVA, will give a shiny finish.

With a variety of textures to paint on and a variety of techniques children will have a real chance to express their creativity through imaginative experience.

Malleable materials
Malleable materials can be bought in forms such as clay or Plasticine, whereas materials such as playdough can be made at home or in the work setting. Dough or clay can be used in a raw form or cooked to make it more permanent – it may then be glazed or painted and varnished. Dough used for cooking is also creative: children can create their own shapes or use commercial cutters.

Children will enjoy rolling, shaping, moulding and cutting dough or clay.

Papier-mâché can also be provided – either as strips of paper dipped in glue or soaked pulp that can be moulded and dried out ready for painting.

Wonderful cornflour and 'gloop' (soap flakes and water) activities can be provided in shallow trays. Very young children enjoy pushing this medium, holding their hands in the air and watching it fall slowly from their fingers.

Collage
Collage can be an imaginative and creative experience for children from a very young age. As an early years worker, your role is to provide the children with a variety of materials – for example:

- different textured and patterned papers and cards

- a variety of fabrics

- ribbons, wool and textured thread

- pasta and beans – there is some controversy about using food for creative activities: some people are concerned that it is a waste to use food in this way.

Always make sure that a strong glue is provided as it is very frustrating for a child to watch all the pieces fall off a collage picture on the way home.

Constructions

This is often referred to as recycled modelling and can be an excellent form of creative play if a variety of materials are provided. Your modelling collection could include:

- kitchen rolls (avoid toilet rolls as they can harbour bacteria)

- cereal and food boxes (avoid egg boxes: possible salmonella infection and allergic reaction)

- cheese boxes (good for wheels)

- large and small cardboard boxes

- a variety of packaging waste – e.g. Cellophane, tissue etc.

- provide a variety of adhesive media (Sellotape/ PVA/scola cell) and scissors to cut pieces to the required size and shape (remember to think about the health and safety issues – see page 269).

Many manufacturers will provide off-cuts of materials to schools, nurseries and playgroups at no charge.

Your role is to encourage the children to make effective choices and to enjoy creating their construction.

The role that creative play has in a child's development

The diagram opposite shows ways in which creative play can help development in children of different ages.

Children with special needs

Children with special needs will need to be considered individually according to their stage of development. A child with visual impairment will benefit from tactile creative activities such as clay work, whereas a child with limited manipulative control may need thicker pencils or brushes. Creative play can help children with low self-esteem if they are sensibly led.

Creative play and the early years curriculum

Creativity can be found in all areas of the curriculum. *Imagination* is the tool children use to play creatively. If you observe children during their play you will see them using their imagination – whether it is in the home corner, during a cooking activity or playing outside in the sandpit. Creative activities may well be part of an overall theme or project and the children can be stimulated through:

- discussion and conversation

- visits

- photographs and pictures

- books.

Good practice – setting out and presenting materials

✔ Set out creative materials in an attractive and safe way that enables all the children in the setting to have access to the activity.

✔ Choose the activities according to the development level of the children.

✔ Remember that the environment will influence the activity. For example, on a rainy day when you had planned to foot paint on a long piece of paper outside you may well need to abandon the idea owing to lack of space inside.

✔ Make sure that the activity is suitable for the number of children involved. For example, a clay

How creative play helps children develop

> **0–3-year-olds**
>
> Learn through senses and movement and can enjoy:
> - finger paint
> - crayons and non-toxic felt pens
> - playdough
> - water play – carefully supervised
> - sand.
>
> Children will become easily frustrated if task is too difficult.
> Manipulative skills are still developing.

> **3–5-year-olds**
>
> - wet and dry sand
> - water – to encourage investigation
> - variety of pens, paints, painting activities, cutting and sticking
> - construction
> - clay and dough.
>
> Will enjoy exploring different materials.
> Manipulative skills are developing.

> **5–8-year-olds**
>
> As for 3–5 years, but creative activities will be influenced by Key Stage 1 requirements.
> Will use creativity to learn about other topics.
> Able to learn some specific creative skills and follow instructions.
> Develop concentration span and manipulative skills.

activity should involve only a small number of children so that you can carefully supervise them.

✔ Consider the sensory development that is to be encouraged and how best to do this.

✔ Always allow for investigation and experimentation.

✔ Be aware of any child who has special needs – you may need to provide adapted space, equipment and materials.

Health and safety requirements of a creative play activity

For children to experience and enjoy an activity, having the freedom to use their imaginations in a variety of ways, the activity provided must be safe and the health of the children protected. You will play a very important part in taking the necessary actions and raising the children's awareness of health and safety issues.

When choosing creative materials you should ask yourself the following questions.

▪ Can the item be swallowed?

▪ Is the item poisonous in any way? – e.g. uncooked kidney beans

▪ Could it irritate the skin or cause damage to eyes?

▪ Is the item too sharp or pointed?

▪ Can any other damage be caused?

Materials should be non-toxic and have the appropriate safety marks. Small parts should not be used for children under three years in case they swallow them. Seeds, beans and pulses can be dangerous or sometimes poisonous. Surfaces and floors should be wipeable and stable. Protective coverings must be used when necessary. Children should be provided with overalls to cover their arms and bodies. However, they will inevitably get paint and glue on their clothes. You can help by providing washable materials and asking the parents not to dress children in their 'best clothes'.

Access and supervision

There must be plenty of space around the activity to allow for freedom of movement by all children, including those with special needs, such as cerebral palsy, or children in wheelchairs. If the materials are laid out to indicate how many children can take part, this will help prevent too many children joining in at any one time. Numbers should be limited if close supervision is required. If there is a choice of activities available, then children may be able to take a turn later in the session.

When the activity is closely supervised you will be able to:

- help children use materials and equipment appropriately

- make sure they are safe

- support their creativity

- encourage them to share experiences.

Some activities and materials can be dangerous if they are not *very* closely supervised – for example:

- bubble blowing can cause the swallowing of paint

- water play can prove fatal

- pen tops can cause choking

- ice can burn

- scissors can hurt children if they are not correctly used but children need access to scissors that can cut the materials being used.

When encouraging children to develop their creative play, always remember that each child is an individual and that all children will respond to encouragement and praise.

Physical play

The term 'physical play' is a term that can be used to describe the type of play in which children use their large muscles and exercise their whole body. They learn to control large and small muscles and develop co-ordination, and surplus energy is expended.

When children are older, physical play may lead to the enjoyment of more competitive sporting and athletic activities. This is sometimes called 'athletic play', 'outdoor play' or 'play involving large muscle movements'. This type of play often involves the use of large apparatus or equipment. The following chart shows the type of equipment that can be used for physical play at different ages and stages of development.

Physical play equipment can be situated indoors or outdoors and can provide opportunities for:

climbing	walking	jumping
rolling	running	sitting down
balancing	hanging	sitting up
pushing	sliding	hopping
skipping	bending	pulling
swinging	kicking	crawling.

There are ten components of co-ordinated movement that are required for the body to move efficiently.

The ten components of co-ordinated movement

Apparatus must allow children to develop these different areas and also take into account children with special needs. Equipment should be challenging for those children who are ready, and secure for those who need to consolidate and practise their skills.

When providing large apparatus equipment, make sure:

- it is situated away from fences or other obstructions, which could cause accidents

- adequate space is allowed

- there are clear guidelines for adults and children on the use of apparatus

- all equipment is placed on safety surfaces

- it is within sight of supervisors

Physical play equipment

Type of equipment	Play and developmental potential	Age range
Trampolines	Children enjoy bouncing and this allows them to develop their sense of balance while giving them a sense of achievement. Jumping and bouncing strengthens leg muscles and builds stamina.	3–8 years Some trampolines have handles, which means that children from three years can use them safely under close adult supervision.
See-saws and rockers	Children enjoy working in pairs and can enjoy the sensation of moving from side to side and up and down. Balance and co-ordination skills are improved.	Rockers can be suitable for children of eighteen months. See-saws are generally for children aged between three and eight years.
Play tunnels	Play tunnels can be used in many ways. Children can use them as places to hide as part of a game. They can also be used as part of an obstacle course and can often link into other pieces of equipment such as tents. Play tunnels can develop co-ordination between the arms and legs and general agility.	2–6 years Younger children may become frightened in a tunnel and older children may get stuck.
Slides	Slides help children learn to climb and build up confidence in balancing. Children enjoy the sense of achievement from completing the movement. They enjoy the sense of risk-taking and challenge as they climb.	18 months–8 years+ Different heights of slide are available, ranging from two steps upwards.
Swings	Swings give children much pleasure as they enjoy the rhythmic movements. As they learn to co-ordinate their movements they build up strength in the legs and upper body as well as their ability to balance.	From 9 months–8 years+ Baby swings are available which prevent children from falling out.
Climbing frames	Co-ordination and balance are developed through climbing. Leg and arm muscles are strengthened and children enjoy the challenge and the feeling of adventure. Climbing frames can be used as part of a game – e.g. it becomes a house or ship. Co-operative play is often seen when older children are using climbing frames.	From 3–8 years+ There are a variety of styles of climbing frame available.
Ropes and rope ladders	Children enjoy learning to climb up ladders. This helps their sense of balance and co-ordination. They enjoy the challenge of this activity. Ropes can be used to swing on which strengthens arm muscles. Ropes can be used as part of children's games.	From about 4 years
Sit-and-ride toys Tricycles Bicycles Go-karts	These are versatile and popular with children. They can make moving around part of their games and can play co-operatively together. Many skills are developed, including the ability to judge speed, steer and pedal. Leg muscles are strengthened and general co-ordination is developed.	1–8 years+ The range of equipment means that very young children can enjoy feeling mobile.

- the equipment is supervised

- you are aware of any potential hazards, which will help prevent accidents

- the equipment is regularly checked for damage or rust.

1	**Space and direction**	Identifying position of body in relation to surroundings – this is constantly changing.
2	**Balance**	Controlling the movement of the body by transfer of weight, moving backwards, forwards, sideways.
3	**Rhythm**	Developing movement flows and co-ordination.
4	**Physical self-awareness (body image)**	Understanding the way the body moves and what each part of the body can do.
5	**Fine muscle development**	Physical co-ordination of toes, fingers and eyes.
6	**Large muscle development**	Particularly around the pelvic and shoulder girdles.
7	**Basic body movement**	Moving skilfully and freely without thought.
8	**Symmetrical activity**	Right and left side. To develop both sides of the body.
9	**Hand/eye co-ordination**	Ensures the working together of hands, eyes and arms.
10	**Eye/foot co-ordination**	Ensures the working together of eyes, legs and feet.

Knowledge into action

Your work setting is in need of new outdoor apparatus and you have been asked to research the market, and provide a report on what is available.

Include the following points in your report:

- *location and space for the apparatus*

- *how the equipment will be used – e.g. how often, by which age groups, level of supervision*

- *the options on the market*

- *advantages and disadvantages in terms of cost, durability, safety and appearance*

- *your recommendations.*

Manipulative play

Manipulative play involves children using their hands. 'By the end of the foundation stage most children will be able to "handle tools, objects, constructive and malleable materials safely and with increasing control."' (QCA). Children develop hand-eye co-ordination as they usually concentrate carefully on what they are doing. Sight and touch are, therefore, important parts of manipulative development. Young babies can be observed in early manipulative play: exploring their own hands. This sense of touch is one of the earliest sensory experiences and leads on to an increased control of the finer muscles and fingers, development of perception and accurate hand-eye co-ordination.

As an early years worker, you have an important role in providing appropriate and stimulating materials for **gross** and **fine** manipulative play.

Gross manipulative play encourages the use of the whole hand (and arm) or leg to grasp, push, hit, pick up or release – for example, throwing a ball.

Fine manipulative play encourages the use of the finer muscles of the fingers and thumb. In this type of play, children learn to use their fingers independently – for example, unscrewing a lid, cutting or using a pencil.

Both types of play depend upon the movement of the hands.

Providing manipulative play to promote children's development

When providing materials for manipulative play they must be appropriate for the child's stage of development. A child will easily become frustrated if unable to hold a toy or become bored with tasks that are far too easy. The chart on pages 273–275 shows how children are likely to play at different ages and what sort of toys would be suitable for them.

You will also notice from the chart that other developmental skills are used during all levels of manipulative play. For example, children may:

- develop their language and mathematical skills by describing the activity, counting items and playing with shapes

- develop their perception by observing what happens during their play

- develop their cognitive skills by sorting and matching shapes

- develop their self-esteem by making their own creatures out of items such as Duplo and building bricks

- express themselves through manipulative play activities.

Manipulative play

		Suitable manipulative toys
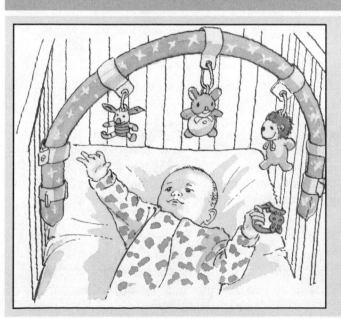	**0–3 months** Finger play; discovering hands; may hold given object for a few moments	Rattle placed in hand; objects above cot or chair that make a sound when touched

Manipulative play *(continued)*

		Suitable manipulative toys
	**3–6 months** Starting to use pincer grasp and move objects from one hand to another; watches object and follows objects and people	Soft toys; toys that rattle; things that will withstand banging and are visually stimulating and tactile
	**6–9 months** Reacts to people and objects; developing pincer grasp; points with index finger; looks for objects that have been dropped	Small objects to encourage pincer grip (supervise closely as they will taste them!); building bricks and toys that can be built and knocked down
	**9–12 months** Developed pincer grip; bangs objects and enjoys throwing toys down and pointing to them	Pull-along toys – with sound; balls to roll; containers with objects in to put in and take out; stacking toys

Manipulative play (continued)

		Suitable manipulative toys
	1–2 years	Pushing toys; building bricks; simple construction toys; large crayons and pencils; wooden lift-out puzzle with knobs to grasp
	2–3 years	Construction toys – e.g. Duplo; stickle bricks; thick puzzles in a frame of about six pieces No small parts as children will put them in their mouth
	3–5 years	Small world toys – e.g. Playmobil or train sets; construction toys; medium-sized interlocking puzzles

Case study

Daniel was sitting on the kitchen floor with a small saucepan. He kept looking in the saucepan. Tim took some wooden pegs out of a bag and placed them in the saucepan. Daniel took the pegs out of the pan using a pincer grip and threw them on the floor. Tim placed them in the saucepan again. Daniel smiled while he was taking the pegs out. He also began to bang the saucepan on the ground, enjoying the sound. Tim quickly gave Daniel a small wooden spoon which he could grasp and enjoy the noise it made when it banged against the saucepan.

The case study above shows how Tim, an early years worker in a home environment, supported Daniel, aged 11 months, in a manipulative play activity.

In the activity Tim:

- provided Daniel with the appropriate equipment for him to develop **fine manipulative play**

- did not dominate the activity but enabled Daniel to lead his own manipulative play time

- used everyday objects that are always available.

Setting out equipment for manipulative play

Whatever your work setting you will probably have a variety of equipment and materials to set out for manipulative play. For all equipment you should observe the guidelines below when setting it out.

- Always present equipment **attractively**.

- Give the children **choice**.

- Allow children to **experiment**.

- Avoid setting out too many toys as this will not enable a child to **enjoy** choosing an activity.

- Place equipment such as Lego in the **middle** of a table so **all** the children can have access.

- Make sure the surface is **clean** and **stable**.

- Make sure the surface is at the **right height** for the children.

- Make sure the equipment is **appropriate** for the ages of the children involved.

- Make sure there is **space** for the children to move easily.

- Consider **access** required for children with limited mobility or wheelchair use.

- Consider **tactile** equipment for a child with visual impairment.

- Make sure that toys such as jigsaws show **positive** images of people.

Providing the right materials for manipulative play

There are many play materials available for all stages of manipulative play. The materials listed on page 277 range from low to high cost and small to large. All are safe if used for the appropriate developmental stage and supervised appropriately. This list is just a start, you will be able to add many other items to it yourself that you have seen in shops, catalogues or your work setting.

Manipulative play and the curriculum

Manipulative play will also support the curriculum plans of a playgroup, nursery or school. Such activities will be as carefully planned as any other activities provided for the children. Remember the early learning goals and be aware that manipulative play is an important part of any curriculum and the achievement of these learning outcomes.

We have considered providing activities for children with varying needs and how important it is to adapt the equipment and space as appropriate. It is worth mentioning that left-handed children also have specific special needs. Children who are left-handed should have the same opportunities as their peers but may need extra help when learning to write; or special equipment – for example, left-handed scissors will be needed. Don't be fooled by scissors sold as ambidextrous – there is no such thing!

Knowledge into action

Different settings will vary in the way they plan their activities. Look at the curriculum plan in your work setting and note how many activities develop the manipulative play of the children in your care. If you work in a home environment and don't have such a regulated plan try to visit a setting that does.

Storing manipulative play materials

Manipulative play materials can be inexpensively and attractively stored. As children get older they may be in a position to have access to them and put them away.

- **Large plastic boxes** are useful. Do not fill them too much, otherwise children will be unable to look for what they need.

- **Drawstring bags** can hold materials such as Lego and undo to provide a play mat.

- **Small plastic boxes** such as empty ice cream cartons with lids provide adequate storage for small items such as beads.

- **Label** all containers clearly with letters and recognisable pictures – cut from catalogues or drawn – of the materials inside. Materials can then be located easily and children's reading skills are also encouraged.

It is your responsibility as an early years worker to present a variety of materials and equipment for children to encourage them to observe, investigate and meet challenges and to develop their manipulative skills.

Think about it

Plan a manipulative play activity for a group of three-year-olds. You will need to consider the:

- length of time the activity will take

- materials needed

- space and location.

Write down how the activity will develop manipulative skills.

Link the activity with as many areas in the early years curriculum as you can.

Materials for manipulative play

Small equipment	Drawing and painting equipment
<ul><li>puzzles – all varieties</li><li>construction toys – such as Duplo and Meccano, straws</li><li>pegs/peg boards</li><li>beads, cotton reels, cards for threading and stacking</li><li>sewing – cards, fabric</li><li>interlocking shapes</li><li>dolls for dressing</li><li>musical instruments</li><li>objects for sorting – buttons, shells.</li></ul>	<ul><li>crayons – thick and thin</li><li>pencils, pens – felt-tip – washable – non-toxic glue, paper, collage pieces</li><li>cotton reels – threading, stacking</li><li>recycled modelling</li><li>printing shapes</li><li>water</li><li>sand.</li></ul>
	Other
	<ul><li>materials for cooking, dough, clay</li><li>physical play – ball play – throwing, catching</li><li>home corner play.</li></ul>

Imaginative play

In imaginative play, children pretend they are other people or that they are in situations. This often happens naturally during their play as they act out situations for pure enjoyment or to make sure of their own world. You will probably have watched children instigating their own imaginative play – perhaps running around as aeroplanes or crawling along the floor as a dog. At other times imaginative play is instigated by an early years worker so that children can explore familiar or new situations and fantasy worlds. Work settings can support and provide a number of imaginative play activities to allow children to safely explore their own feelings and the world around them.

The diagram below shows the key roles of the early years worker in providing suitable equipment and materials to stimulate role play.

Using imaginative play to develop skills

Imaginative play is an excellent way of developing children in many ways. Children as young as 18 months will use role play to develop their imagination. They may also develop their:

- manipulative skills
- social skills
- emotional skills
- sharing skills
- self-confidence, feeling of security
- language and communication skills.

Before you think about planning suitable imaginative play for the children that you work with, think about how children need to be encouraged to communicate:

- listening
- looking – understanding what is being communicated through body language, such as the nod of a head or a smile
- talking – being talked to and talking with other people (a telephone is essential)
- writing and drawing – provide examples of signs, marks, etc. Provision of paper and pencils will encourage children to communicate by putting marks on paper.

Remember these three areas when planning imaginative play for the children in your care.

Children from 18 months upwards will respond to imaginative play that is set up in a suitable area of an early years environment.

Imaginative play can link in with a theme or curriculum plan in your work setting.

Case study

Chris, an early years worker with three- to four-year-olds, made a boat with the children as part of their topic relating to the theme of 'Journeys'. The materials involved were two large cardboard boxes that the children helped to paint, hats that were donated and telescopes made out of kitchen tubes! These materials were appropriate for this simple imaginative play and varied enough to encourage the involvement of the children. The children were able to get in 'the boat' and create their own world and yet be visible to their supervisors.

In this case study you will have observed how an imaginative play area can link into an overall curriculum plan.

Knowledge and understanding could be covered by:

- a discussion of how different types of boats are made

- drawing maps in the role-play area to show where they might sail the boat

- making boats from a variety of trays and testing them in the water tray.

Mathematics could be covered by:

- talking about the 3-D shapes used to make the boats – e.g. cubes, cylinders

- setting a maximum number of children in the boat and illustrating with a drawing

- making and selling tickets for the boat – use of money

- putting boats in the water tray and asking children to put a specified number of play people in each.

There are many contexts for imaginative play. Here are some of them:

- doctor's surgery/hospital
- café
- farm
- office
- hairdressers
- beach
- school
- variety of homes.

Through their imagination children will be able to understand and experience the theme that is being explored.

Child-led imaginative play

This can occur in a theme-led imaginative play area or spontaneously in everyday play. There is imaginative play that can be totally unplanned – for example, one child might be playing under a climbing frame using it as a jungle and very soon two or three other children might be joining in this imaginary play.

The home corner plays an important part in imaginative play

Remember that imaginative play does not just occur when children are dressing up. Here are other activities in which you might observe some interesting imaginative play:

- small world play, such as Lego or Playmobil
- puppets/dolls
- books and stories
- sand and water play
- painting and drawing
- playdough

Hats are one of the most important parts of imaginative play. By providing a box of different hats children are able to role play many different characters.

Creating a home corner to encourage imaginative play

It is possible to create a home corner that will encourage not only imaginative and spontaneous role play, but also an understanding of the children's own world and the wider environment.

Knowledge into action

Does the home corner in your work setting encourage children to explore their own and other cultures?
If you work in a home setting, are there ways that this is done?

279

The equipment you provide will affect the quality of children's play and learning and the way that they develop their attitudes towards other people.

Resources that should be provided to reflect other cultures include:

- a range of cooking utensils
- clothes and hats
- artefacts, such as furniture.

Consider the following points when setting up a home corner:

- Resources should reflect a multicultural society and help children to recognise, understand and value the differences between them.

- Reasons and explanations for resources supplied should always be given. Parents may be willing to visit your work setting to discuss food, festivals or clothes from their culture.

- Children do use stereotypes in their pretend play and are often only copying situations and relationships they have observed. Early years workers can channel this behaviour by providing dressing-up clothes and experiences that do not specify gender, such as a female doctor or a female police officer.

Safety of equipment

All the equipment you provide should be safe to use. Everything should be regularly checked before use and repaired or replaced when appropriate. Where possible, all equipment should comply with the required safety standards.

Remember that:

- clothes should be kept on hangers and regularly cleaned and mended
- equipment must be checked for rough or sharp edges, splinters or flaking paint
- beads and necklaces should be safely strung and not made from materials such as seeds or glass that could be swallowed easily.

Children with special needs

Always consider children with special needs when setting up an imaginative play area. A child with a wheelchair will need plenty of space, while a child with visual impairment may need textured and brightly coloured equipment.

Children with behavioural needs may benefit from adult involvement in their imaginative play as long as the adult does not dominate the situation. For example, a child who has a new baby brother or sister might be talking crossly to a doll in the home corner: this could be a chance for you to gently discuss what they are acting out.

We must remember that, whatever the age or setting:

- time must be made for imaginative play
- imaginative play can link in to the work setting's theme or curriculum plan
- plenty of space, outside and inside, must be given to imaginative play
- adults can be involved, but only when appropriate
- clothes and equipment must be safe and secure
- stereotyping must be avoided
- cultural diversity should be celebrated
- imaginative play can take place spontaneously in many activities other than the home corner
- if imaginative play is provided in an appropriate and sensitive way it will help children to develop their language and communication skills effectively.

Check your knowledge

- Outline the work of Maria Montessori.

- What is the difference between structured and unstructured play?

- What types of outdoor equipment can be used for four- to six-year-olds?

- What is meant by the term solitary play?

- Describe the play needs of three-year-olds.

- Name three materials that might be used in creative play.

- How can manipulative play help children's overall development?

- Describe four things to be considered when choosing toys for children.

- Why should the home corner reflect our multicultural society?

- Think of three pieces of equipment that might encourage physical play and explain how they might help children's development.

- Briefly explain Janet Moyles' Spiral of Play.

- What is the value of outdoor play in the early years curriculum?

- What are the principles of accident prevention when providing equipment and materials for young children?

- List six ways in which an imaginative play area might develop a child's confidence.

- Briefly describe three ways to support imaginative play.

- What are the ten components of co-ordinated movement?

- What influence has Susan Isaacs had on current early years education?

- Explain the importance of water play in the early years curriculum.

- How can you ensure an anti-bias view in physical play activities?

- What is the role that creative play has in a child's development?

Resources

Further reading

Bruce, T. *Time to Play in Early Childhood Education and Care*, London, Hodder and Stoughton

Moyles, Janet R, 'Just Playing': *The Role and Status of Play in Early Childhood Education*, Open University, 1989

Petrie, Pat 1994 *Play and Care*, London, HMSO

Useful contacts

National Association of Toy and Leisure
68 Churchway
London NW1 1LT
020 7387 9592

UNIT 6 Play, curriculum and early learning

CHAPTER 12
Learning through play

This chapter looks at the:

■ stages of development and learning

■ provision of an environment that supports and encourages learning through play

■ the role of the adult in supporting children's learning and development

■ the principles of effective communication with young children.

Teachers need to be clear not only about what they would like children to become under their guidance but about what children were actually like when the process began' (Donaldson, 1978). So Margaret Donaldson sums up part of the problem encountered in teaching children. It is essential to have as much knowledge as possible about what children already know so that one can find the correct starting point.

The chart below shows the way children play and learn at different stages

Age	Play and learning development
0–6 months	Watching adults closely Exploring by using the mouth and by touch Playing alone with toys such as rattles and baby gyms
6–12 months	Exploring by using the mouth and by touch Watching and copying adults Repeating movements such as dropping a rattle Enjoying simple games such as peek-a-boo Exploring toys alone
12–18 months	Learning through trial and error – e.g. banging two cubes and discovering the sound it makes Repeating actions that they have enjoyed Beginning to play with adults and notice other children Playing and 'talking' alone
18 months–2 years	Learning through trial and error Imitating other children and adults Exploring things with mouth Possibly carrying out repetitive actions – e.g. putting things in and out of boxes or scribbling on several pages Watching other children but not joining in Enjoying playing with adults as well as by themselves

Age	Play and learning development *(continued)*
2–3 years	Beginning to show some reasoning skills – although still learning by trial and error Imitating adults and other children Starting to use symbols in their play – e.g. a stick becoming a wand Beginning to play alongside other children Most of their play is 'pretend' play – e.g. telling off toys
3–4 years	Showing more reasoning skills and asking questions such as 'why' Starting to concentrate for longer on a play activity that interests them Recognising shapes and letters Solving jigsaw puzzles through a mixture of reasoning and trial and error Playing co-operatively together and taking turns with other children Playing imaginatively – e.g. playing in the home corner, dressing up
4–6 years	Showing more understanding and using reason based on their experiences Starting to use and understand symbols – e.g. writing and reading Starting to understand simple rules in games Playing co-operatively, taking turns and enjoying table-top games
6–8 years	Enjoying using rules and understanding the need for rules Showing reasoning skills but still using some trial-and-error learning Playing in small groups and making up their own games which tend to have rules Enjoying playing competitive games but not always coping with losing Tending to play with children of their own sex

Learning through play

There are various theories about the stages of cognitive development in children but there is one theorist who has provided the basis for most early years provision, Jean Piaget.

Jean Piaget (1896–1980)

Jean Piaget is recognised for the way he has influenced current understanding of how children learn. The research that he conducted highlighted the fact that children do not think in the same way as adults and the ways in which they gather and process information are unique to childhood. Although some of the results of his research have been disputed, the basis of it is fundamental to a curriculum with the child at the centre. There are three stages of learning that children aged 0 to 7 years 11 months may pass through:

- sensory motor stage (age 0–2)

- pre-operational stage (age 2–7)

- concrete operational stage (age 7–12).

The diagram in Chapter 6 on page 130 outlines these stages in more detail.

Assessing children's stage of development

Assessment of children's progress is vital if we are to offer them activities appropriate to their stage of development and discover any areas of concern that may need extra attention. When assessing children it is important that they are assessed in a variety of ways.

Assessment needs to take place in a variety of settings in case there are certain settings that are upsetting to the child. Differences of personality between child and adult can lead to a false impression of a child's capabilities, so ideally more than one person should assess the child.

An activity needs to be assessed in more than one way to ensure the child has understood the concept – for example, when counting objects, do not always put them in a straight line. To fully grasp the concept of counting, a child needs to be able to count in a line, in a circle and in a haphazard layout. Some children will need to remove each object, as it is counted, to ensure they do not count it twice.

Be aware that trying to assess a child's knowledge in a group situation presents problems. Many children love to come up with the correct answer and you will often receive the answer from another child, rather than the one you are trying to assess.

There are a variety of ways of assessing children in order to prepare them for their next stage of learning or to assess their curricular needs. It can be done through:

- record keeping
- observations
- baseline assessment
- Standard Assessment Tasks (SATs).

Record keeping

Record keeping on children aged 0 to 5 years is done in a variety of ways from a simple diary for a young child to a more complicated assessment of a child's areas of development before he enters school. As these records are used to assess a child they must be accurate in order to build up a picture of the child's learning needs. In Chapter 14, Work with young children, you will find practical examples of records that are kept in order to support the needs of the child and provide the appropriate curriculum. Parents should also be involved in the record keeping on their children.

Observations

Spontaneous and planned observations are an excellent way of finding out a child's developmental needs or discovering if an area of learning, such as a constructive play area, is being used appropriately or may need to be reviewed. It is important to remember that in order to be effective the curriculum must be constantly reviewed by any early years team. You will find Chapter 4 a useful guide to developing your observation skills.

Baseline assessment

A baseline assessment is an assessment of a child's capabilities on entry to an early years setting. All five-year-olds entering schools undergo a standard baseline assessment that covers reading, writing, speaking and listening, mathematics and social development.

Standard Assessment Tasks (SATs)

SATs are used to assess children at the end of each Key Stage of the National Curriculum. Children are now also assessed before Key Stage 1 in order to establish a baseline.

Without baseline assessment there is no way that the teacher marking the SAT can have a realistic idea of the starting point of each child. Baseline assessment allows teachers to assess the capabilities of each child within a short time after starting school. This period, hopefully, allows the child time to settle into a new setting before being assessed and also gives the teacher knowledge of any areas that have not been fully covered during the child's pre-school education. The SAT results will then give a truer portrayal of a child's progress during his time at school, taking into account those children who may not have received any pre-school education whatsoever.

Providing an environment that encourages and supports learning through play

All children should be given full access to the curriculum. It is therefore very important that equipment and materials used should be accessible to all of the children.

Children with English as an additional language

Some children's first language may not be English and some may not have any understanding of English at all. This does not mean that they should not be given the same opportunities as those who do. The provision of good-quality picture books will benefit all of the children in the early years setting, but images must be checked to ensure they do not give inappropriate messages. It is not safe to assume that recent publications are free from negative images. Other equipment used that may contain negative images includes posters, jigsaws, lotto games and card games. Remember that it is not necessary to speak the language in order to play in the sand or the water. Any type of tactile experience (playdough, clay, etc.) is ideal for children who do not speak English and they will soon start to absorb language from the children playing around them. In the home corner, a child from another culture can be made to feel welcome through the provision of cooking utensils, dressing-up clothes, and so on, from other cultures. Another area which will be accessible is the early years setting garden (physical play does not demand language as a prerequisite).

Promoting a world-view

It is essential to represent a balance of cultures in any early years setting and not just those represented by the children in the setting. A variety of play opportunities should be provided that take account of people's cultural and religious beliefs. As stated in the Early Learning Goals (QCA 1999), by the end of the foundation stage most children will:

- understand that people have different needs, views, cultures and beliefs, which need to be treated with respect
- understand that they can expect others to treat their needs, views, cultures and beliefs with respect.

Avoiding gender stereotypes

Roughly equal proportions of males and females populate the world. The early years setting environment should reflect this situation.

As with race and culture it is important that books, posters and other equipment are checked for negative images – for example, women always doing the housework and men always doing DIY. However, do not remove all images of these situations because that would offer a totally unrealistic view of the world.

Adult role models can be very useful. If you know a male nurse or a female fire fighter, let the children see that they exist! Do not have a fire station in the home corner because you do not think the boys will play in a baby clinic. Encourage the boys to use the baby clinic too. Find images and people to support your case.

Think about the language you use with the children. At the end of the session don't say, 'Let the mummies in.' Men will collect some of the children and many of the women collecting may not be the mothers of the children.

Many popular early years songs and rhymes were written when no thought was given to gender stereotyping. It is quite easy to change words without altering the metre or the meaning of a song – for example, 'Five little men in a flying saucer' can easily become 'Five astronauts in a flying saucer.' There is then no question of gender stereotyping. Remember, though, avoid change for change's sake – the children should still be able to enjoy songs and rhymes.

All children should help to tidy up, take turns to head the line for outside play, hand out drinks or whatever else needs to be done during the day. There are no girls' jobs and boys' jobs, there are just jobs!

Knowledge into action

In your early years setting class, there are 26 children (13 boys and 13 girls). One of your parents complains that his little girl never uses the computer because the boys always push her out of the way. She tells him that she is never first in the line for outside play and, therefore, is never able to play on the bikes. How would you deal with this parent?

Knowledge into action

Use your knowledge of the need to present a balance of cultures in the home corner to plan a suitable area which will make children from the Indian sub-continent feel welcome. Consider involving parents and other colleagues.

Special needs

Hearing impairment

If you have a listening centre it should be in a quiet area of the early years setting so that the children are able to hear clearly taped stories, etc. Children who have a hearing impairment will need extra help, which can be given through provision of headphones with adjustable volume controls.

At story time children who have a hearing problem should be placed near the person reading the story to ensure they are able to hear clearly. If a child is disruptive in story sessions it is always worth moving that child nearer to the reader. If the child is experiencing difficulty with hearing it will solve the problem. If not, you will have the child where you can more easily control him or her.

Visual impairment

A child with visual impairment will benefit from provision of books with clear bold pictures. It is essential that such a child should be seated near the front at story time.

Tactile activities and peg jigsaws are very useful for providing access for visually impaired children.

Wheelchairs

If a child is confined to a wheelchair, the early years setting should provide tables, sand trays, etc. that offer access. The provision of beanbags and cushions in the book corner will allow the child to look at books in comfort. Floor toys and jigsaws will also be accessible to the child.

Left-handed children

Children who are left-handed require some specialised equipment. It is difficult for a left-hander to cut accurately with a right-handed pair of scissors, so left-handed scissors must be provided. Left-handed children will draw and cut spirals in a different way from right-handers. If a child is practising letter formation, a left-hander will start in a different place from a right-hander. Left-handed children must position the paper differently when writing or drawing and, if a left-hander is seated next to a right-hander they may knock elbows when they are trying to write or draw, so ensure the left-hander is seated to the left side of the right-hander.

Activities, materials, equipment and resources for promoting and supporting learning

In any setting, there will be a wide range of abilities and interests and the resources provided should reflect this range. Children's chronological age does not always match their developmental stage so one cannot assume that, for example, all three-year-olds need the same provision. Some activities lend themselves to children of all ages and stages. For example, sand offers to each child whatever they choose to get from it: one child will enjoy the sensation; another will appreciate the difference between wet and dry; another will have developed the vocabulary to express these differences – all of them will have access to the activity at different levels.

Jigsaws are a different matter – the number of pieces and the style can limit access to them so it is necessary to provide a range of styles and a range of levels of difficulty.

Some children love to sit at a table and draw while others prefer to race about and roll around the floor.

During the course of the day all of these children should be catered for, and encouraged to use the appropriate area at the appropriate time. The early years setting should be separated into areas that allow for these different types of activity – a quiet area for table activities and books; an easy-to-clean area for sand, water, malleable and art activities with a tiled or linoleum floor; a role-play area; a small world imaginative area; and a floor area for large construction toys, floor puzzles and some small world play. There should be a good balance of sedentary (sitting down) and non-sedentary activities available for the children. Activities provided should allow the children to explore for themselves and to use materials provided in their own way. At the same time, opportunities should be taken by adults in the early years setting to guide the children and to extend their learning.

Outside play is very important for children

Outside play must be available to the children to provide them with fresh air and give them a chance to expend their excess energy.

When choosing resources one must take into account those children who are the same age but at different stages of development in the setting. You should not aim all activities at the average – children are individuals and should be treated as such.

Books

Picture books are suitable for those children whose first language is not English and for younger children, but will be enjoyed by many of the children in the setting. Some children will be interested in catalogues and books of a technical nature – provision should be made for them. Board books may be more suitable for those children who have not yet acquired the skills required to handle books correctly.

Jigsaw puzzles

Peg puzzles, inset puzzles and interlocking puzzles of varying degrees of difficulty should be provided.

Construction equipment

Large and small equipment should be provided to take into account the varying manipulative skills of children in the setting. Pictorial instructions should be provided to help the children to construct a wider range of models than would otherwise be possible – if the instructions are laminated, they will last much longer.

Creating a safe, stimulating, caring and carefully planned environment to enhance children's learning

Providing a stimulating environment

Within the early years setting, the environment should be bright, colourful and stimulating to children. This can be achieved in a number of ways.

Displays

These must be the **children's work**! (An exception would be an interest table set up by the adults. Children should be encouraged to contribute to this table). The role of the early years worker is to enhance the child's work by the way in which it is displayed. Children love to see their work on the wall, and so do the parents!

Displays do not have to be a major event, depicting a scene connected with the theme. While these can be wonderful, so can a display of children's artwork or drawings. There is not always time to put together

(contd. on page 290)

Use floor toys in an area that is not used as a thoroughfare.
Someone may fall over the toys and receive an injury.

Keep toys away from doors.
An opening door may hit the children.

All doors should be fitted with two handles,
one of which must be above child height.
This will ensure no child is able to open
doors without the help of an adult.

Keep toys away from fire exits.
They may cause an obstruction
in the event of a fire.

Ensure there is a gate to close
off any steps.

Remove any broken or
damaged toys immediately.

Keep all medicines and
cleaning materials out of reach
of the children.

Place sand and water trays
on a non-slip surface.
If no such surface is provided,
any spillage should be
regularly removed to avoid
the danger of anyone slipping.

Do not place kettles, saucepans,
etc. where a child may reach
them.

SAFETY

Encourage children to walk
indoors, to prevent accidents.
The bathroom/toilets is a
particular danger area.

If there is a kitchen or laundry in the
early years setting the door should
be closed at all times. No child
should be allowed access unless
under close supervision by an adult.

Cover all electric sockets with
plastic safety plugs. Children
will then be unable to put
their fingers or other objects
in them.

Cover the sandpit with a net
to avoid fouling by cats.

Do not leave appliances
plugged in with trailing wires
where children will be able to
reach them.

Check all gates to ensure no
child is able to get out
of the area.

The garden/outside area should be governed by rules that are known to all staff and visitors.
Children should be reminded of the rules, which should be justified in terms they understand.
Before the children are permitted to play in the outside area a check should be made for the
following dangers:
- broken glass
- syringes
- stones on grassy areas
- fungi
- nettles
- poisonous weeds
- broken or damaged toys.

(contd. from page 288)

the elements required for a scene and not every early years worker is good at display; it is better to do a simple display well than a complicated display badly.

Do *not* always choose the 'best' work for display. All children have the right to have their work displayed and even if you, or the parent, do not think that the picture looks like what it is meant to be, the child does and that is what counts! Displays should be interactive and contain a variety of lettering styles. Lettering should not appear only in the title of the display and should not always be the result of the use of templates.

When displaying children's work it is important that it is not always presented on a flat plane. 3-D displays, interest tables, lift-the-flap displays, hanging displays all add to stimulation of interest in the children and visitors to the early years setting (displays do not have to go on a wall).

Asking questions will add greatly to the interest engendered by a display – for example, 'Can you find three frogs hidden in this picture?' will encourage children to study the display more carefully than a display with no words or just a title.

The argument that words in displays are wasted on children who cannot read does not hold water. The children will know that those squiggles say something and will ask. This stimulates enquiry and conversation

and helps the children realise that print carries meaning, that letters are formed in a certain way.

Displays should be at child height wherever possible or they will be denied access to what is, after all, their work. They should be changed regularly so as to maintain the interest of the children.

Knowledge into action

The theme in your setting is autumn.

Think of ways to make a display that will generate the maximum possible interest from the children in your setting.

Posters and friezes

Posters can be used as a separate entity or incorporated into a display and can add a great deal to the early years environment. They should be relevant, bright, colourful and free from any inappropriate images. This is an area where it is possible to portray positive multicultural images for the benefit of both children and visitors to the early years setting.

ABC, number and nursery rhyme posters and friezes displayed around the early years setting can add to the education of the children in an implicit way. Other posters and friezes will stimulate questions from the children, and so further their education.

Book corner

Children will appreciate the joy of books far more if they are provided with a variety of stimulating, colourful ones that are in good condition and are presented by adults who display a joy of books themselves. Provision of a quiet, cosy, comfortable carpeted area with cushions and beanbags is more likely to encourage a love of books than a noisy area with linoleum on the floor. A listening centre with taped stories can add another dimension to this area.

Home corner

A home corner that is relevant to the children will help stimulate their interest and increase their knowledge of the world. Some children are very happy to play in a house situation while others prefer a hairdressers. Whichever you choose, there must be some relevance to the children's experience. Do not have a role-play area based on the Amazon rainforest unless you have talked to the children about it first.

Sand, water and malleable materials

If children are provided with a tray of water, sand or other malleable material there will always be those who choose to play with it completely unadorned. However, if care is taken to make this area of the curriculum stimulating by the addition of carefully selected items, the number of children who visit it can be greatly increased and the necessary learning outcome can be achieved.

Making an area stimulating will increase the number of children who visit it

If sieves are placed in wet sand and moulds in dry the children will gain some very important scientific concepts through discussion with an early years worker combined with exploration of the materials provided. By adding small world elements to sand, water and malleable materials, more children will be encouraged to participate in the activity. Natural materials should be used wherever possible.

Do not just have a basket of toys which all go in the sand or the water every day. These activities require as much thought as the maths table or any other area of the curriculum.

Outside area

The outside area should offer opportunities for a variety of physical activities that help the physical development of the children. There must be room for the children to run and to climb on apparatus with safety surfaces underneath. Balls, hoops, quoits and beanbags should be provided to enhance the children's throwing, kicking and catching skills. Bicycles and tricycles are another type of apparatus that is popular with the children but, if money is in short supply, this area is the one most likely to be covered at home.

Adult intervention will help the children to learn in areas where they are unable to do so on their own. Use as many natural materials as possible. Children love to climb on logs and to hide in bushes. They enjoy gardening and sweeping leaves so provide them with the tools to do so. Provide bird tables and binoculars so that the children can observe and appreciate nature. Children need to learn to care for their environment and must be encouraged to respect the birds and animals and not to pick the leaves off the trees.

Provision should be made for outside play in all weathers, therefore a covered area is invaluable.

Knowledge into action

Plan an imaginative play area to be set up in a covered area outside. Consider the importance of extending outdoor experiences in the same way as indoor opportunities.

Pets

Pets in the early years setting can be used to teach the children how to care for animals, but should be kept only if there is someone who is willing to look after them properly. A poorly kept pet will provide the children with a very poor example. *Always check the latest ruling on pets as regulations change periodically.*

Provision that builds on a child's experience and background

As with adults, children are far more interested in pursuing a course that fits in with their previous experience. They are able to relate what they know to what you are trying to tell them. For example, a topic on the seaside will mean little to a child who has never been outside the city boundaries and how many children have been in space? These topics are not completely out of the question but a lot of work must be done to ensure the children have a sound background knowledge of the topic.

Case study

Ben was a lovely little boy and sat with his dad while the teacher at the early years setting made a home visit. Dad obviously cared a great deal about Ben and spent a lot of time talking to him. They talked about what lovely toys Ben had to play with and what a lively child he was. The teacher remarked on how difficult it must be for Ben to use up his excess energy in the small flat where he and dad lived. 'Yes,' said dad, 'I wish I could take him out more but I'm a single parent and work long hours. My parents help but they don't live anywhere near a park and, quite frankly, don't see the need for him to play in the open. They think that if they let him watch a video and buy him a burger that they're providing him with good care. I am grateful to them but feel that Ben's missing out.'

When Ben started at the early years setting, he had no idea of how to cope with playing in the garden because it was outside his experience. Thanks to a home visit, the staff at the early years setting were forewarned of the problem and were able to deal with it appropriately.

The first step with children is to learn about their backgrounds. The best way to do this is with a home visit prior to the child starting at the early years setting. If this is not possible, as much information as possible must be gained from the parents. Having obtained this information, it is possible to plan according to the needs and interests of the children and be forewarned of difficulties that may arise – for example, covering a project on the circus when one of the children is frightened of clowns. Knowledge of a child's background can also prevent potential problems with Mother's Day and Father's Day card-making activities.

How to care for and maintain the equipment, rooms and materials

Equipment used by children should be regularly checked for signs of wear or damage. Any such equipment should be removed immediately and replaced or safely repaired. Children should not be presented with equipment which has been defaced or which has pieces missing. It is very frustrating for a child to almost finish a puzzle then realise that a piece is missing or to be unable to complete a lotto game because it is incomplete.

Slotted spoons and collanders provided with sand will allow children to learn the different properties of sand

Good practice – maintaining equipment, rooms and furniture

✔ Check books regularly for torn pages and any signs of scribbling. Children will think that this is acceptable if they see it in books presented to them. These books can, however, be used to show children what not to do.

✔ Check the room every day for signs of any danger to the children. Worn carpets, damaged linoleum, cracked or broken glass are all hazardous and must be dealt with. Check that fire exits are not blocked and that doors close properly. Windows should open easily and radiators should not be too hot for the children to touch (if at all possible, radiators should be caged).

✔ Check that materials to be used by children are clean and safe.

✔ Change and clean sand regularly.

✔ Change water every day.

✔ Materials used for modelling must conform to the latest safety initiatives (eggboxes, eggshells and toilet roll middles are always contentious).

The role of the adult in supporting children's learning and development

Differentiating between adult-directed and child-led activities

Adults need to introduce new concepts to children in order to expand their existing knowledge. To do so it is necessary to have some form of directed activity. For example, a child does not automatically know which side to put the paint on when engaged in a printing activity and children very often fail to identify the correct side of the paper to apply glue to when making a collage. Children can often solve these problems by a process of trial and error but adult intervention can help to prevent a child from giving up through frustration.

Working with a child on a one-to-one basis, an adult can give direction by offering strategies to help the child perform a task – for example, where to start formation of letters and ways to touch-count

accurately. One must never forget, however, to allow children the opportunity to try their own ideas. A child learns a great deal by experimentation. If we cut out activities such as emergent writing, we will create a generation of children who are so concerned about 'getting it wrong' they will not try to write anything of their own accord and we will be in danger of removing the individuality of children and replacing it with an attitude of 'everyone is the same.'

Case study

A mature student training to teach in the early 1990s carried out a study with children on emergent writing.

'To help me to obtain examples I set up a railway booking office in the home corner. Tickets were provided as examples and blank "ticket books" and writing implements were provided so that the children could write their own tickets for the customers. When I went to the booking office to ask for a ticket to London, I was given one of the real tickets by the child in charge. I told him that I had a really bad memory and would not be able to remember when the train would leave or what platform to go to. He told me the relevant details but I said that I would forget and could he write it down for me. He scribbled a variety of symbols on a piece of paper and told me that this was the information I required. I thanked him for his help and went off with my example of emergent writing. By further questions and by provision of paper for the children to write during their play, I gathered a lot of emergent writing, both directed and undirected.

Recently, I tried to get one of the children in my nursery to write a shopping list for me so that I could buy some items from our role play supermarket. He asked me how to spell the items I had asked for and would not, despite my encouragement, try to write anything for himself. Is this an indication of how we are teaching children that there is only one way to write from an early age and that they must not attempt to try for themselves? If so, it is a very sad sign of the times in which we live'.

How do you think we can encourage children to explore emergent writing?

There are times when children should be given a completely free rein to produce whatever they want from an activity or to choose to do whatever they want. It must be remembered, however, that some children find it very hard to choose and will require some guidance. At all times, the adults are responsible for ensuring that the free choice does not lead to situations which are unsafe or out of control.

There are also times when the adult is aiming for a particular end product from an activity. The children need to realise that there are times when it is necessary to produce a specified result.

Children need to have occasions when they choose the direction of an activity. Areas where this will occur frequently are: outside; in the role play area; at the imaginative table; and in the sand and water. Supervision of these activities will allow the adults to determine where intervention may be of use.

Knowledge into action

Closely watch the children in your care and, when possible, make a spontaneous observation of a child who is choosing the direction of an activity set up by adults.

You may choose the water tray, sand area, role-play area, etc.

The difference between structured and spontaneous activity

All children need some form of structure in their lives and all establishments are governed by constrictions of time and space that inevitably lead to the necessity for some structure to the day. Even so, there should be room within the structure of the curriculum for spontaneous activity. Children act upon the moment, they do not plan their day ahead as adults do. If one has planned to talk to the children about sunshine and it rains, there is nothing to be gained by ploughing on regardless with the original plan. If you do, the children may well think that you are mad and will certainly fail to maintain an appropriate level of interest. By abandoning your plans and leading the

children in activities connected with rain, you will immediately gain their interest in what you do. The plans you made to discuss sunshine can always be used at a later date. By their very nature, spontaneous activities will not wait, so make the most of them.

Think about it

Revise the section about Janet Moyles' Spiral of Play in Chapter 11 (page 262). Consider its importance when studying the difference between structured and spontaneous activity.

Learning opportunities in everyday routines

Throughout the day, there are continual opportunities for learning with children. When children first arrive at the early years setting, they learn to search for their coat peg, which will be marked by a picture or their name (early matching and reading).

Registration time or welcome group is a good time for children to practise speaking and listening skills. An opportunity exists here to use the children for some practical mathematics. Ask the children to get into groups (boys/girls; colour of hair; type of shoe fastening, etc.). You can then talk about 'more/less' and 'the same' or use the information to produce simple graphs. Using the groupings when lining up and so on can reinforce the knowledge gained by the children in forming these graphs.

Group time can be used for mathematics and language and literacy. A child can be asked to count the children and to hand out the milk. Children can learn to recognise environmental print on milk cartons and snack packaging.

Outside time offers opportunities for one-to-one correspondence of buttons to buttonholes, arms to sleeves, etc.; work on pairs (gloves, boots); counting buttons, fingers in gloves. Boots and gloves offer a good opportunity to discuss right and left. Discussion of parts of the body covers knowledge and understanding of the world. Children should be encouraged to use a degree of independence when dressing themselves for the outside area and to hang up their coats when they return to the early years setting.

When outside, there are opportunities to discuss the weather and the environment (knowledge and understanding of the world). Children on the climbing frame are higher and lower, the tricycles go faster and slower, providing work on opposites. Many social skills are learnt outside (sharing, caring for each other and the environment, negotiation, turn-taking, waiting patiently).

Tidying up time helps the children to learn about the passage of time. By using egg-timers of varying length to dictate the time available for tidying up, children can learn about relative periods of time. There is a lot of opportunity for teaching personal and social skills at this time (taking responsibility, helping others, negotiating areas of responsibility). Children need spatial awareness to put equipment into storage containers effectively. Listening skills are needed to follow instructions; self-confidence and clear articulation are needed to carry messages and to issue instructions.

Knowledge into action

Consider the following two situations and discuss in groups how and why you would develop learning opportunities from each situation.

At registration time with a group of three- to four-year-olds, a child brings in a large shell that she found on the beach during her holiday.

You are playing with a group of two- to three-year-olds in the sandpit when an aeroplane flies over.

Being sensitive about when to intervene in children's activities to support learning and development

There is no set answer to when it is right to intervene in children's activities. It depends on the activity and on the children involved. Children need to become skilled in resolving their differences and solving their own problems but there are times when negotiations break down or they become frustrated with what they are doing. At this stage, adult intervention can help save the day.

In the area of art it is important to avoid over-direction. The end result of an activity should be the child's work, not that of the adult. The adult can offer ideas and strategies but needs to take care that these ideas do not overpower those of the child. The same principle applies to music. Children need free expression to develop their skills. Avoid overuse of stencils and templates as these can give children a stereotypical view of an object and remove their ability to portray things for themselves.

Children need free expression to develop their skills

If children are asked to draw themselves they should be allowed to complete their own portrayal first before any discussion about any omissions there may be.

Children need to experiment with print and too much intervention by adults can stifle this ability. When a child is starting to learn to form letters, adult intervention is needed to indicate the correct starting point.

Encouraging and supporting children's independence, self-reliance and self-confidence

Independence

There are many occasions during the day when a child can be encouraged to act independently. Encouragement of independence does not mean leaving the child to get on with it.

Ideas for helping children become independent through play

- Encourage children to put aprons on themselves.

- Encourage children to choose and put out puzzles, games and other equipment.

- Allow children to practise dressing skills by providing interesting dressing-up clothes.

- Encourage children to help clear away – e.g. wiping tables, putting away games.

- Praise children when they are trying to be independent.

Provision of a structured free-play session that offers activities in all areas of the curriculum encourages the children to choose for themselves, but there will always be children who need encouragement to settle down to an activity. In areas such as the home corner, imaginative area and sand and water trays where children often play together in groups, it may be necessary to encourage a less confident child who finds it hard to gain entry to the existing group.

There are responsibilities which can be offered to children to help boost their self-confidence, but you must be careful that these responsibilities are not offered to a child who will find them overwhelming. Asking a child to go and find out what is on the art table may not seem a difficult task, but to a shy child who would rather remain in the background, it can be daunting. It is, therefore, vital that you know the children and their personalities. Some children will love to hand round the milk at group time, others will not.

All of the children must be given the opportunity to assume responsibility and care must be taken that

the confident children do not dominate proceedings to the extent that no other child gets a chance.

Dressing up can encourage independence

Case study

Saima is aged four years and one month, the second of five children. English is not her mother tongue. Saima has attended the nursery for a term and is a shy and solitary member of the group. She chooses to go to the home corner from the start of the session and remain there for as long as possible. When asked to move to another activity, she will always choose to visit an undirected activity. The staff would like to use the home corner as an area where they can work with children like this to deliver the curriculum. Unfortunately, with a ratio of 13:1, it is not possible to do this often.

One day, the home corner was not being used at the start of the session and the class teacher took the opportunity to direct the girl to work with the early years worker on the carpet. They engaged in block play, which resulted in good interaction between the child and the early years worker. The girl took turns to build a tower and choose blocks from a box containing mixed colours. She used far more structured English than the staff had realised she possessed. The information obtained from this activity was entered in her records to help plan for her future progress. Had this child previously taken the easy way out and stayed in a familiar setting? As she presented no behavioural problems, busy staff did not often redirect her from the home corner, thus depriving her of the opportunity to add to her experience.

Effective communication with young children

It is important to realise that all adult support for children revolves around the appropriate use of language. This applies in all settings and with all ages. All children need to talk and to be talked and listened to (unless there is a physical reason why they cannot do so). Routine activities during the day – for example, climbing the stairs, discussing things seen on a walk, washing up – should be used as opportunities to speak to a child.

It is important to be on the same level as the child when talking to him

Case study

Hannah came to nursery at the age of three possessing a very limited vocabulary. There appeared to be no reason why she should not be able to use more words. Investigation by nursery staff discovered the reason for the problem. Hannah's mother had not thought that there was any need to speak to her as she watched plenty of television and videos. She did not see the need to speak to a child who was not speaking to her. After all, what was the point? Hannah had thus been deprived of any form of conversation for the first three years of her life. She would now find it extremely difficult, if not impossible, to catch up with her peers. Hannah now attends a special school.

How to communicate with and listen to young children

When speaking to young children it is very important to be on the same physical level as the child. Failure to do so can inhibit the conversation by:

- an inability to hear clearly what the child is saying – don't forget that many children speak very quietly

- an adult towering over a child can seem very intimidating and may lead a less confident child to be reticent about communicating.

The location of the conversation can have a great bearing on the direction it takes. As previously stated, many children have very quiet voices which will be very hard to hear if you are speaking in the middle of a noisy, crowded room. If you and the child find it necessary to shout at each other it will not lead to a productive conversation. **Never** shout if it can be avoided.

When speaking to children, use language that they understand. You must remember that a young child does not have the same vocabulary as an adult.

Think about it

Curran is three years old and refuses to tidy away at the end of sessions.

Today he has been playing with bricks, but is sitting with his arms crossed rather than helping to clear away.

Should Curran be forced to tidy up?

Why is it important for children to clear away?

Can you think of three strategies to encourage him to join in?

Knowledge of the child's background, interests and abilities will help in holding a conversation on an appropriate level. Using open questions will give children a chance to state their opinions and ideas rather than the single-word or short-phrase answers indicated by closed questions. Be aware that the phrasing of a question can lead to a child providing the wrong answer – for example, 'You don't want to play do you?' commands a very different answer to 'Do you want to play?'

ISSUES Partnership with parents

It is important to remember that a partnership with parents is at the centre of positive care and education for young children. It is this partnership that will help early years workers to gain the information they need about a child to facilitate effective communication.

Give the child time to speak. If you want to hear what children have to say, time must be allowed for them to formulate and articulate an answer. If you do not allow sufficient time the conversation will become one-sided and you will have learnt nothing about the child nor understood what the child had to say.

Lack of experience

Children learn vocabulary by hearing words spoken by others. If a child has not had this experience it can lead to communication problems. Children may lack the vocabulary to articulate their thoughts or adults may be using words that children do not understand.

Talking and listening activities for young children

Speaking

Children enjoy playing lotto games and usually play by one person showing the picture and the others finding the one that matches. Extend the children's descriptive skills by getting them to describe what is on the card rather than show it to the other children.

Puppets are a good way to get children to speak. They will often assume the character of the puppet and children who normally say very little can be found chatting happily as their assumed character. More confident children will narrate plays with puppets and decide on the story line that will be followed.

Small world play is another area where children will put themselves into the shoes of the character they are playing with. If you are a dinosaur you can do and say all sorts of things that a little boy or girl cannot.

In the role-play area, careful selection of scenarios can lead to the acquisition of valuable new vocabulary. The children will put this new vocabulary to good use as they perform the roles of their adopted characters. Role-play areas should include a telephone whenever possible as this will generate wonderful conversations.

If children have a diary or similar 'News Book' they will enjoy telling an adult about what they have done outside the early years setting. The adult can perform an important function in extending the child's vocabulary and descriptive powers. For example:

Child: 'I've got a new dog.'
Adult: 'What kind of dog?'
Child: 'I don't know.'
Adult: 'Tell me what it looks like.'
Child: 'It's white with black spots.'
Adult: 'That's a Dalmatian. I know a story about 101 Dalmatians. Have you ever heard it?'

This start to the conversation can lead to a discussion about the film and others seen at the cinema. The adult can read the book and discuss it with the child, thus adding to the child's store of knowledge and vocabulary.

When reading a book discuss the contents with the child. This will help to increase the child's vocabulary and provide an opportunity to introduce words like illustrator, author and index, in addition to encouraging the child to participate in a conversation with an adult.

At storytime, ask the children questions about the book you are reading to them and get them to provide a full answer (open question), not just a yes or no (closed question). Ask the children to help you to tell a story, thinking up the plot as they go. This makes them think very hard and is a good exercise in descriptive language.

At storytime, ask the children questions about the book

Many children like to 'show and tell' items they have brought from home. This can be a useful speaking and listening exercise but it has a number of drawbacks.

■ Some children dislike talking in front of others.

■ Some children cannot sit still and concentrate while waiting for their turn.

■ Not all chilren will be able to bring an item in, and those that cannot, are likely to feel left out.

If you wish to have such a session, consider holding it at a small-group time when the wait is not so long and the number of children is easier to control. Link the show-and-tell to the theme or to a letter or colour. This will avoid a procession of cuddly toys and will give an opportunity to those children who are less well off. Limit children to one item each. Assign one day per week to this session if you are going to hold it as a whole-class activity or it will encroach upon the rest of the week.

Listening

There are many activities that can be used to develop the listening skills of the children.

■ A small story group is a good opportunity for children to listen. Tell them that you are going to read them a story that was written down by a friend of yours. Explain that this friend is not very good at writing things down and you are sure that there are some mistakes in it. Ask the children to let you know if they hear something wrong with the story, and then begin to read. (You must choose a well-known story or the children will not realise that there are errors. Even well-known stories have more than one version, so be prepared for children to miss mistakes and to call out where the story differs from the one they know. The children will be very excited by this activity and it is essential to have control strategies handy.)

■ Sound lotto games are a very useful item. The children have to listen carefully to identify the item portrayed on the card. Be aware that many shop-bought lotto games contain sounds and images with which the children may be unfamiliar. Try to produce your own game by recording sounds which occur every day in the early years environment or ensure the sounds that the children are expected to identify are very easily distinguished and familiar.

■ Questioning the children during and after a story is a good way of ensuring that they listen attentively to what is being read. Children are generally eager to please and like to answer correctly. Tell them before you start that you want them to listen very carefully as you might ask them about the story. Make sure that they can hear you and see the book or you may not get the answers you expect.

■ If the children gather together at any time during the day prior to moving on to the next stage of the session, you can use this opportunity to encourage them to listen. Send them off by name, colour of shoes, initial letter of name or any other means you can think of. Whispering the children's names is a good way of ensuring that they listen very carefully.

■ In a small group, tell the children that you are going to say some words and that some of them will rhyme. Demonstrate what a rhyme is – children do not necessarily know. Ask the children to indicate when they hear two words that rhyme.

■ Games like 'Simon Says' encourage the children to listen carefully.

■ Take the children for a listening walk. You do not have to go far, the garden will suffice. Ask them to listen carefully for a short period of time and then tell you what they have heard.

- Play music to the children and ask them to listen very carefully. When the music has finished ask them how the music made them feel.

- Play the children a small selection of musical instruments. Hide the instruments behind a screen and play them all again, except one, then ask the children to identify which one you left out.

- Clap a simple rhythm and ask the children to try to copy it.

The use of non-verbal communication

When communicating with young children it is important that they become aware of the importance of gestures and facial expressions. It is also your role to encourage eye contact where appropriate, remembering that autistic children can find it difficult to do this and some cultures consider eye contact disrespectful.

With young babies the tone of voice and touch are important ways of developing communication skills.

Participating with children in an appropriate manner

Children need clear, consistent guidelines on how to behave. These guidelines must be understood by all the children and adults in the early years setting in order to avoid confusion (see also Chapter 9).

Be fair but firm with children and you will gain their respect. This does not mean shouting or using physical punishment. If children know where they stand they will respond more appropriately. There will always be children who test the boundaries of acceptable behaviour and it is necessary to have a range of behaviour management strategies to deal with this. If you find that you are unable to deal with a child it is worth asking another member of the early years team to help. Children may have adults that they respond to better than they do to others.

Always maintain a sense of humour. This will be of great assistance to you and will be appreciated by

the children. You should not expect children to understand jokes; this is an advanced skill and is not possessed by many children of the age covered by this book.

Never get the children overexcited unless you are sure that you can calm them down again. A lot of work has to go into making the children realise that when you say stop you mean stop.

Do not try to be one of the children. It is possible to have fun with them while maintaining a degree of respect. Children will not listen to someone they do not respect.

Songs, rhymes, finger plays and musical activities

Songs and rhymes

Songs and rhymes for young children should be fun and easy to learn. Children, like adults, learn things better if they are fun. They should have a relevance to the children. It is a good idea to link songs and rhymes to the theme or to a story just read, but avoid songs or rhymes which are theme-related but uninteresting.

It is good for children to learn traditional songs and rhymes but you need to be aware that some of the vocabulary and content may be unfamiliar and will need to be explained by an adult.

Give the children some choice in what they sing, but remember that you are leading the session, and be prepared to say no to a fifth rendition of 'Baa Baa Black Sheep'. Introduce new songs and rhymes to the children but not so often that they do not have time to become familiar with them.

Involve the children in songs like 'Five currant buns' and 'Five little ducks went swimming one day.' This adds to the enjoyment and you will be surprised how well the children will behave when waiting to be chosen!

Keep a list of songs and rhymes in categories. Songs and rhymes for children cover a large part of the early years curriculum – for example, there are number songs, colour songs, songs about jobs and animals. 'Little Tommy Tadpole' deals with life cycles. 'Head, shoulders, knees and toes' deals with body parts and is also good for physical exercise.

Finger plays

Children enjoy finger plays because it is often the case that they can do them while the adult cannot. This kind of activity will develop their manual dexterity skills.

A finger play like Tommy Thumb can be used to encourage children to speak in a group. By replacing Tommy Thumb with the name of a child, you can say, for example: 'Billy Smith, where are you?' and, hopefully, get an answer from a child who does not normally speak in a group.

Knowledge into action

Look at the following themes

Birds	Ourselves	Water
Animals	Weather	Farms

In pairs, try to write down three songs, nursery rhymes or finger plays that could be used as part of the theme.

Music

Musical instruments are a wonderful way for children to demonstrate their feelings. An angry child can beat on a drum and relieve a lot of frustration, which might otherwise be aimed at another child. A shaker can be used to demonstrate a variety of moods and it is very good practice for the children to try to play them to match a given mood.

Exposure to music from different cultures can help create respect for other cultures and can also boost the self-esteem of children in the early years setting who come from that culture.

Play different styles and moods of music to the children and ask them to say or show how it makes

them feel. If you have access to a hall, use music for children to interpret through dance.

Children should be given access to live music as this adds a new dimension to musical appreciation and enables them to see how musical sounds are produced.

Devising and using home-made items

As previously stated, a home-made sound lotto can contain sounds which are far more relevant to children than any manufactured lotto. Children will love to help make home-made musical instruments, such as guitars (cereal box, cardboard tube, elastic bands) and shakers (any container you can find filled with a variety of pulses, seeds, etc.). This activity will cover technology in the making and music in the using. By choosing different fillings for the shakers and different thicknesses of elastic band, you can also cover pitch and tone.

Use photographs you have taken as a basis for discussion. Make a puppet theatre and encourage the children to make puppets to use in it. Recording a story on to a tape will increase the children's interest. They like to hear a story read by someone they know.

If you make your own dominoes, games and snap cards you can gear them to the children's interests. If you are not confident at drawing, use photographs.

Preparing for story time

Adequate preparation of a book is essential so that the reading is smooth and clear. Children look forward to a story and deserve to be given your best effort.

Always ensure that you read the book you have chosen before presenting it to the children. There are several reasons for this:

■ The book may contain negative images.

■ You may feel the need to amend the text for some reason.

■ It may be too long for the time you have available to read it.

You will need to think of ways to extend the story by asking questions in appropriate places and knowing what to do if you receive a different answer from that expected.

It is always a good idea to find rhymes or songs that link to the story in case there is time to spare. There is nothing worse than sitting with a group of children and not knowing what to do next.

Read the book in front of a mirror to check that you are holding it correctly so that the children can see the pictures. There may be times when you would rather read the words, and then show the pictures; this is perfectly acceptable but you must tell the children that this is what you are going to do.

Tape yourself reading a story so that you can get an idea of whether your inflection is correct. A story that sounds the same all the way through is very boring.

Use of puppets

Puppets can be wonderful story props. It is possible to buy puppets quite cheaply if you keep a look out for them. Choose those that can be used with a variety of stories. Make your own to suit your needs – a puppet made from an old sock can be as interesting as one which cost a lot of money. It all depends on how you use it. The children can operate the puppets for you but be careful that you are able to control both the puppeteers and the rest of the children.

snake sock puppet

felt finger puppet

string puppet

Make a puppet theatre with the children and then make puppets with them with which to tell a story. Use an overhead projector or a strong light to tell a story with shadow puppets or, on a large scale, use the children as shadow puppets.

Other props

■ Cut felt into the shape of characters in a book to portray the story on a flannel graph. Use Fimo or some other modelling material to make items

Read a story that you like – the more you enthuse, the more the children will enjoy it

featured in a story. Back them with Velcro or button magnets and use them to tell the story.

■ Make items from the story with salt dough, which can then be handled by the children.

■ Make up a prop box with real items that link to the story. The children will love to act out the story with you.

■ Use an item like a carpet, an old hat, a violin, an old book or an old trunk to make up your own story with the help of the children.

■ Get the children to act it out without the aid of props.

Start a story and ask the children what they think will happen at various stages (if possible, do some follow-up work and make a book of the end result).

Always make stories as interesting as possible. Use props only if you feel it is appropriate; it is no use using props and then losing control of the children. Read a story that you like; the more you enthuse, the more the children will love the story. Don't worry about who is watching – you cannot read children an interesting, lively story with a paper bag over your head.

Selecting and setting out a range of books to interest young children

Books that are bright and colourful with clear images attract young children. Books with dull, uninteresting pictures will not come across as something worthy of investigation. Use your knowledge of the children to provide a range of books in line with the range of interests enjoyed by them. Choose a mixture of well-known and new stories.

Check books for:

■ inappropriate images

■ scribbles or drawings

■ damaged pages

■ missing pages.

Use different types of book – for example:

■ board books

■ picture books

■ books made by the children in the setting

■ textured books

■ lift-the-flap books

■ 'through the hole'-type books

■ bath books

■ big books

■ story books

■ factual books

■ ABC books

■ colour books

■ number books

■ books like 'Ketchup on your Cornflakes' – by Nick Sharratt, published by Scholastic (hardback) and Hippo (paperback) – with sections to change into different pictures.

■ books with photographs of familiar people and places.

Knowledge into action

Visit your local library or bookshop and find three books that would be suitable for a group of three- to four-year olds. Note down the titles, authors and publishers of each book and why you chose them.

Compare your lists with the rest of the gorup and note down what they have chosen.

Check your knowledge

- Outline the ways in which 18-month- to two-year-olds play.

- How can left-handed children be helped when developing their manipulative skills?

- What safety aspects should be considered when planning a layout for children?

- Why is it sometimes important for adults to be involved in children's play activities?

- Describe three activities that will encourage children's listening skills.

- Explain how props can help storytime.

- What are the advantages and disadvantages of 'show and tell'?

- How can a variety of play opportunities promote a world-view in the early years curriculum?

- How will children be expected to respect their own and other people's beliefs by the end of the foundation stage?

- What is the difference between a structured and a spontaneous activity?

- What is the importance of non-verbal communication?

- Briefly explain how musical instruments can encourage children to express their feelings.

- Describe two activities that could encourage a three-year-old child's talking skills.

- What are the important things to remember when displaying children's work?

- List the checks that should be made before children play in an outside setting.

- How can gender stereotyping be avoided during a snack time for six-year-old children?

- Where would you place a listening centre in an early years setting? Give your reasons.

- How can you assess a child's stage of development in order to provide appropriate play activities?

- What is baseline assessment?

- Explain how Jean Piaget influenced the current understanding of how children learn.

Resources

Further reading

Bonel, Paul 1993 *Playing for Real*, National Children's Play and Recreation Unit

Moyles, Janet (ed.) 1994 *The Excellence of Play*, Oxford University Press

Useful contacts

National Centre for Play
Moray House College
Cramond Campus
Cramond Road North
Edinburgh EH4 6JD
0131 312 6001, ext. 292

National Play Information Centre
359–361 Euston Road
London NW1 3AL
020 7383 5455

Play, curriculum and early learning

The curriculum for the under 8s

At the time of writing, the United Kingdom has no single early years curriculum. Each country – England, Scotland, Wales and Northern Ireland – follows its own early years curriculum designed for that country – although the child-centred approach is similar. It is the Foundation stage for England that is referred to in this book.

There are three separate curricula (or curriculums) which apply to children under eight years old. The curriculum for 0–3s is based on activities and experiences that link to a child's overall development and children are encouraged to learn through their senses. However, this chapter is based upon the two curricula that are laid down by the QCA for children aged three years and above who are in government-funded settings.

The Early Years Curriculum *is based upon the 'early learning goals' and is designed for children from three to five or until they reach the end of the reception year. This is known as the Foundation Stage and should prepare children for Key Stage 1 of the National Curriculum.*

The National Curriculum *applies to children of compulsory school age in maintained schools, including special schools. It is organised in four Key Stages. Key Stage 1 is for pupils aged five to seven years in school years 1 and 2.*

The National Curriculum was established before the Early Years Curriculum. It first became law in the Education Reform Act of 1988.

The Early Years Curriculum

In 1990 the Rumbold Report was published, which reported on research into the most appropriate learning experiences for three- to five-year-olds. As a result of this research, the School Curriculum and Assessment Authority (SCAA) – now renamed the Qualifications and Curriculum Authority (QCA) – published the 'Desirable Outcomes for Children's Learning on Entering Compulsory Education'. The outcomes were set out under six areas of learning:

■ Knowledge and understanding of the world

■ Personal and social development

■ Language and literacy

■ Mathematics

■ Physical development

■ Creative development.

The aim was to provide a curriculum which all children could follow and which would provide a foundation for later achievement, once the children were of school age. The outcomes were derived from the nine subjects in the National Curriculum at Key Stage 1.

From September 2000 the new early learning goals were implemented by all settings that receive funding for three- to five-year-olds. It was the intention that the desirable outcomes should be reviewed alongside the National Curriculum. This new foundation stage will last until the end of the reception year and will ensure continuity for children as they move from their early years settings into primary school.

The early learning goals are:

■ Personal, social and emotional development

■ Communication, language and literacy

■ Mathematical development

- Knowledge and understanding of the world
- Physical development
- Creative development.

The Curriculum for 0–3s

The early years curriculum for three- to five-year-olds is now widely recognised and is based upon the children's previous development and an organised learning structure. However, the learning goals that provide a basis for three- to five-year-olds may not be right for babies and toddlers. Please read Chapter 14 for more information about a curriculum for babies.

Early years workers and teachers work together

> **ISSUES**
>
> Treasure baskets are an important way of developing a baby's learning through sensory experiences. Two videos about treasure baskets are available from the National Children's Bureau.

The role of the early years worker in the delivery of the early years curriculum

In a school setting

In a school, an early years worker will usually work alongside a teacher. The early years worker and the teacher should aim to work in partnership, each recognising the strengths of the other. Each will have differing skills that, when combined, will cover all aspects of working with young children. The teacher may have trained for four years to degree level in Early Years (3–8); or may have trained for three years for a Certificate in Education (Cert.Ed) or Bachelor of Education (B.Ed); or have taken a one-year Post Graduate Certificate in Education (PGCE) following a three-year degree course, which may or may not have been connected with education. The early years worker will have trained for two years or more to work with children aged 0–8 and will be able to offer particular help with children in the lower age range of the early years.

Responsibility for planning lies with everyone involved with the child. Teachers and early years workers in the setting plan the curriculum for the child at school but need to bear in mind input from parents and carers. Some children will have an individual education plan tailored to their needs, which is formulated in conjunction with professionals from agencies outside the setting – for example, speech therapists, educational psychiatrists.

Early years workers' roles are changing but it is up to them to ensure they remain up to date with the issues that affect them and the children in their care. Participation in professional development is essential if the profile of early years work is to be raised to the extent that the appropriate rewards are forthcoming – for example, job satisfaction, higher salaries and professional recognition.

The early years worker should help to plan and carry out the curriculum, assuming equal responsibility for story and group times. Children benefit from the input of more than one adult; this reduces personality clashes and means that children benefit from different teaching styles. The teacher may well take overall responsibility for the planning and record keeping, doing the bulk at home. In the case of meetings outside school – for example, Child Protection – it will often be the teacher who attends (if it is impractical for both to attend).

Home visits are invaluable and should, ideally, be carried out before the child starts at the early years setting. A very good insight into the background of a child and his or her family may be gained. The child and carer will see adults from the early years setting in the comfort and security of their home surroundings. These visits should be made in pairs for reasons of safety and security.

The early years worker in a school has a responsibility to report to the class teacher who is then responsible to the teacher in charge of the setting or, in a nursery school, to the headteacher.

In a day care setting

The role of the early years worker in a day care setting is very different from that in a school. There is often more emphasis on the care aspect than on education. Not all children attend a day care setting every day as they do in a school setting. Planning therefore becomes more complex. However, the ratios in a day care setting are usually better than the 13:1 in a nursery class and the 10:1 in a nursery school. These ratios, if used to advantage, can overcome the difficulties presented by sporadic attendance and so lead to delivery of a balanced, well-planned curriculum for the children.

Personal, social and emotional development

- Encourage sharing and taking turns – board games are good for this.
- Encourage children to impose their own limits on numbers in the home corner, water, sand, etc.
- If children cannot impose their own limits, encourage them to follow your limits.
- Give the children clear guidelines and ensure all staff interpret them the same way.
- Set a good example in the way you talk to and treat others in the setting.
- Encourage children to sort out their own problems – e.g. sharing the bicycles.
- If the children cannot sort out their own problems, offer strategies – e.g. 'Have one more turn then let someone else have a turn.'
- Stress the children's positive aspects – e.g. praise, stickers, star of the day, etc.
- Learn about other cultures, religions.
- Teach the children to respect each other.
- Use positive language – e.g. say 'Please walk' not 'Don't run'.
- Always give a child a chance to avoid confrontation.

Mathematical development

- Talk to the children about age, buttons, pairs of gloves/socks, house numbers, car registration numbers – numeracy.
- Count the children at group time.
- Cook with children – weighing, counting – 1:1 correspondence.
- Get the children to set places at the lunch table – 1:1 cutlery items.
- Offer children milk and a snack – 1:1 correspondence, e.g. child to milk
- Make graphs of eye colour, etc. with the children – data collection.
- Line up the children in height order – relative size, ordering by size.
- Group the children by various criteria – sorting.
- Discuss whether there are more boys than girls, etc.
- Observe shapes in the environment.
- Conduct weighing activities – e.g. a see-saw is a simple weighing machine.
- Talk about opposites.

Remember that mathematics is not only numeracy and can be covered in all areas of the setting, not just at the maths table – e.g counting the legs on the spiders in the sand tray, sticking shapes on a collage, painting five ducks on a pond at the art table.

Knowledge and understanding of the world

- Provide well-planned activities in sand and water.
- Provide more structured activities – e.g. magnets, magnifiers, reflection, etc.
- Talk about healthy food at mealtimes – and brushing teeth.
- Discuss personal hygiene – e.g. hand washing.
- Discuss the need for and carry out physical exercise.
- Discuss the weather and the natural environment.
- Take full advantage of spontaneous events – e.g. sight/sound of fire engines, ambulances, aircraft.
- Take walks around the area and talk about buildings, jobs and other features.
- Talk to the children about your own life and culture, providing examples of your home life and culture/language if appropriate.
- Provide technological activities – e.g. 3-D modelling, construction equipment, IT. (You must have a sound understanding of these activities in order to provide appropriate guidance.)
- Talk about the sequence of the day or the week.
- Discuss events in the lives of the children.

This area includes children's developing knowledge and understanding of the environment, other people and features of the natural and man-made world to provide a foundation for historical, geographical, scientific and technological learning. **Good planning will enable knowledge and understanding of the world to be delivered through the topic.**

Language, communication and literacy

Talking and listening

- Talk to children at a level appropriate to their understanding.
- Talk to children about their interests.
- Extend the child's vocabulary.
- Listen to children and add to the conversation.
- Provide activities to promote language – e.g. role play, small world, stories, Lotto, Guess Who? games.
- Work on phonics, letter recognition and names.
- Talk about books – e.g. left – right flow of print, print carries meaning, turn pages from front to back, title page, illustrator.
- Ask the children to carry verbal messages and follow and issue instructions.

Reading

- Read to children and stress that print carries the meaning.
- Run a finger under the words as you read so that children can see the relationship between the words and the sound.
- Look for words and letters that match.
- Observe and discuss print in the environment – e.g. crisp packets, burger boxes, road signs, etc.

Writing

- Provide children with a variety of writing media (pens, pencils, chalk, charcoal, etc.).
- Provide sand, tea, rice, etc. so that the children can experiment in it with their writing.
- Help with pencil control – e.g. correct size of pencil, correct pencil grip, provision of fingergrips if necessary.

Many children are not ready to read and/or write until they are more than 5 years of age

Physical development

- Provide activities to develop manipulative skills – e.g. threading, cutting, small construction.
- Offer help with threading, cutting, pencil grip, dressing/undressing.
- Encourage children to perform physical activities in the appropriate place. For example, by using positive language to explain, in terms the child will understand, why it is not safe to run or roll around in the setting; telling the child that running, climbing, and so on take place outside or in the hall – if the setting has such facilities.

Physical development (continued)

Inside activities could include large construction, dancing, action songs or role play – but these need to be in a safe, large area.

- Play games – e.g. football, throwing and catching, rolling hoops.
- Help children to ride bicycles and tricycles.
- In PE, teach the children how to find a space that is safe to work in – e.g. unable to touch nearest child with arms outstretched.
- Stress the importance of fitness.
- Talk about the children's interests – e.g. football, ballet, swimming.

Creative development

Imagination

- Encourage role-play in the home corner and outside.
- Provide a variety of dressing-up clothes and role-play equipment.
- Provide structured drama activities – e.g. making faces to match a mood, acting out a story.
- Provide a variety of small world activities.

Art

- Provide a variety of activities to encourage the acquisition of new ideas and new skills. For example, marble rolling using a circular tray: cut paper in a variety of colours to complement the colours of the paint and to fit into the bottom of the tray; provide shallow dishes with paint and different-sized marbles. Children learn to:
  - select colours (paint and paper)
  - handle the tray carefully to avoid the marbles falling on the floor
  - roll the marble in the required direction by tipping the tray so that the paint goes where they want it to.
- Provide a wide range of artistic media.
- Allow the children free access to a wide range of art materials for 2-D and 3-D work, including scissors, Sellotape and glue.
- Provide a balance of directed/undirected activities.
- Provide a balance of activities which do/do not involve paint.
- Display finished work attractively, using work by all the children.
- Do not take work from children if they do not want you to have it – ask them to do two, one for you and one for them.

Sound

- Observe sound in the environment.
- Provide sound tables.
- Use sound lottos.
- Play music – use instruments from a variety of cultures.
- Listen to live/recorded music in a variety of styles and from a variety of cultures.
- Study pitch/tempo.
- Compose music – young children can do so with pictograms.
- Study rhythm – e.g. clapping.
- Sing songs:
  - from different cultures
  - in different languages
  - old ones and new ones
  - chosen by staff/children
  - with/without accompaniment.

Drama and dance

Ensure there are opportunities for:
- free expression
- interpretation of moods
- interpretation of action words – e.g. bang, crackle, float
- interpretation of actions – e.g. leaves falling from a tree)
- fun dancing – e.g. musical bumps, etc.
- retelling a well-known story.

The role of the early years worker as a key worker for a group of children can be of great help in ensuring the curriculum is delivered as efficiently as possible. A key worker should be responsible for all aspects of planning, record keeping and delivery of the curriculum for all children in the setting, but with particular emphasis on their key group. Liaison with parents and other professionals is the responsibility of the person who has the greatest knowledge of the child and the situation. However, there will be times when that responsibility falls to the nursery manager or deputy manager.

Supporting delivery of the early years curriculum

The tables on pages 307–309 provide points of good practice when supporting delivery of the areas of learning experience in the early years curriculum.

Providing a curriculum designed to meet the social, cultural and linguistic needs of all

Language

Always avoid the use of language which would be unfamiliar to the socio-economic class of the children in your care. Match your language to the requirements of the audience you are addressing and make allowance for children who do not speak English; use support staff who are hearing impaired; use sign language. Make allowance for regional dialects.

Promoting cultural, religious and social equality

Ensure that images in any books or posters, etc. you use do not exclude any child on the grounds of social class or culture. Ensure that there are positive images of all social classes and cultures – this will help stress that all people are to be valued. Observe other cultures, but not in a token way. Make it fun and interesting and ensure that you research them in some detail. Observe festivals and involve any children, parents or members of the community from that particular culture.

Do not ask the children to bring in items for a topic if you feel it may be beyond the economic means of

their parents or carers or if it may cause offence. Be aware that some topics may cause offence – for example, Hallowe'en can be a problem. Be aware of the difficulties which may arise with certain religions – for example, if there is a Jehovah's Witness in the setting.

Educational ability

Always plan a broad ability range to allow all children access to the curriculum.

The National Curriculum

The National Curriculum was first introduced in 1988 to all schools in England and Wales (Scotland and Northern Ireland have their own versions) to ensure that a consistent education or core curriculum would be taught throughout the compulsory school years.

Between the ages of five and eleven years, all children study the same nine subjects – English, maths, science, history, geography, technology (design and technology; information technology), art music and physical education. Each subject is divided into **attainment targets** or levels to ensure that progress can be monitored as children progress through their schooling. At the end of a **key stage** (see below) the school will need to report the results of their assessments in the core subjects of English, maths and science to the parents and wider community. These are known as **standard assessment tasks** or **SATs**.

Key Stage	Age of pupil	Year group
1	5–7	1–2
2	7–11	3–6

At the end of Key Stage 1, the majority of pupils will have attained Level 2; at the end of Key Stage 2, they will have attained Level 4.

Individual subjects are divided into **programmes of study**, which set out the knowledge and skills which must be taught to children. In science, for example, there are four programmes of study – experimental and investigative science; life processes and living things; materials and their properties; and physical

Materials and their properties

	Pupils should be taught:
1 Grouping materials	a: to use their senses to explore and recognise the similarities and differences between materials; b: to sort materials into groups on the basis of simple properties, including texture, appearance, transparency and whether they are magnetic or non-magnetic; c: to recognise and name common types of material – e.g. metal, plastic, wood, paper, rock – and to know that some of these materials are found naturally; d: that many materials – e.g. glass, wood, wool – have a variety of uses; e: that materials have specific uses – e.g. glass for windows, wool for clothing – on the basis of their properties.
2 Changing materials	a: that objects made from some materials can be changed in shape by processes including squashing, bending, twisting and stretching b: to describe the way some everyday materials – e.g. water, chocolate, bread, clay – change when they are heated or cooled.

processes. Within each of these areas, the curriculum defines what should be taught, although how it is taught depends on individual schools and teachers.

The table above shows an extract from the Key Stage 1 in Science.

All schools, except those in the private sector, must offer the entire National Curriculum. The only exception to this is for those children who have a statement of **Special Educational Needs** and who therefore need some variation within the curriculum for teachers to provide appropriately challenging work.

The Literacy Hour

The curriculum is under constant scrutiny and modification, with two new initiatives in recent times – the **Literacy Hour** which was introduced in September 1998 and the **Numeracy Hour** which was introduced in September 1999. These are both frameworks for teaching that have been set up to improve standards in English and maths on a national level. All teachers have been trained and advised in methods of teaching and classroom organisation to help with the introduction of these initiatives.

The **National Literacy Strategy** is aimed at raising literacy standards in schools. It sets out reading objectives for reception to Year 6, when pupils should be fully literate. The work is focused on:

- *word level work* – phonics, spelling and vocabulary

- *sentence level work* – grammar and punctuation

- *text level work* – comprehension and composition.

In the Literacy Hour this framework should be taught as outlined in the diagram below:

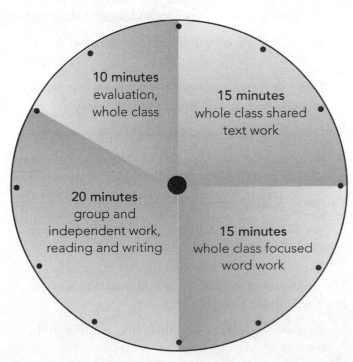

The Numeracy Hour

The **National Numeracy Strategy** was introduced as a way of promoting higher numeracy standards in schools.

It is based on four key principles. They are:

- dedicated maths lessons every day
- direct teaching and interactive oral work with whole and class groups
- an emphasis on mental calculation
- controlled differentiation, with all pupils engaged in mathematics relating to a common theme.

Children should have dedicated maths lessons every day. At the end of the foundation stage they should be able to:

- say and use the number names in order in familiar contexts
- count reliably up to 10 everyday objects
- recognise numerals 1 to 9
- use language, such as more or less, greater or smaller, heavier or lighter, to compare two numbers or quantities
- in practical activities and discussion, begin to use the vocabulary involved in adding and subtracting
- find one more or one less than a number from 1 to 10
- begin to relate addition to combining 2 groups of objects, and subtraction to 'taking away'
- talk about, recognise and recreate single patterns
- use language such as circle or bigger to describe the shape and size of solids and flat shapes
- use everyday words to describe position
- use developing mathematical ideas as methods for solving practical problems.

The following nine subjects are included in Key Stage 1 of the National Curriculum:

- **English** – speaking and listening, reading and writing

- **Mathematics**
- **Science**
- **Technology**
  - Design and technology
  - Information technology
- **History**
- **Geography**
- **Art**
- **Music**
- **Physical education**

Knowledge into action

There are many different views about the numeracy and literacy requirements. Discuss these strategies with other early years workers when on a primary school placement and find out what they think.

Special educational needs

The National Curriculum provides early years workers with much greater flexibility for response to the needs of pupils with identified special educational needs.

The role of the early years worker in the primary school setting is rapidly developing as four-year-olds are being offered places in schools. The early years workers' knowledge of the early years curriculum will make them a valuable part of the team. They will support the teacher in the care of the children and work as a part of the team to provide suitable learning activities.

Supporting delivery of the National Curriculum

The following tables provide points of good practice when supporting delivery of the National Curriculum at Key Stage 1.

English

- Give a child time to speak and an environment that offers encouragement. A shy child should not be forced to stand in front of the class and speak.
- Listen to the child and do not interrupt. Let children have their say rather than you having yours.
- Make it plain through your body language that you are listening.
- Help to extend the conversation if necessary. Give help with any words that the child may not understand.

Responding appropriately

- If a child is speaking to a large group, stress the need to speak in a clear voice so that anyone at the back will be able to hear.
- Explain to children that a clear description of an item may be necessary so that everyone will know what they are talking about.
- Provide an environment that will not make it difficult for children to be heard or their confidence may be undermined.
- Value what the child says.
- Get down to the child's level.
- Interpret if necessary. The child may want to tell you, then you can pass on the information.
- Some children may find it easier to speak through a puppet or other medium.
- Ensure the audience is quiet and listening carefully before a child starts speaking.

Develop children's awareness of standard English

- If a child says something that is incorrect, repeat it in the correct way. Do not say 'that was wrong,' or you will undermine the child's confidence.
- Read stories that contain standard English so that children are given good examples.

How to help pupils read aloud with developing fluency

To be able to read aloud fluently children need:

- time and patience on the part of the listener
- practice which is enjoyable, not a chore
- strategies which will help them to read the words – e.g. whole word, building words from individual letters.

How to help pupils recognise familiar words accurately and easily

- Point out the words when reading a story.
- Repeat words and show what they look like.
- Look for familiar patterns in words – e.g. mummy has 3 ms, daddy has 3 ds.

How to help pupils express opinions about events or ideas in stories or poems

- Give time for expression.
- Value all initial ideas and write them down – they can be filtered later.

How to help pupils communicate meaning through written words and phrases at an appropriate level

- Provide opportunities for writing in the home corner.
- Encourage the children to use symbols and letters to convey meaning – emergent writing.
- Discuss familiar letters from the child's name.
- Write down the child's thoughts – shared writing.
- Demonstrate different purposes for writing, e.g. shopping lists, labels etc. – modelled writing.
- Discuss how the print in a book conveys the meaning of the story.

Listening

- Impress upon children that we all have a right to be heard and that everyone has something of value to offer.
- Remind children that, if they are speaking, it will not be possible to hear someone else.
- Speak clearly so that children understand and do not need to ask you what you are saying.
- Use vocabulary appropriate to the children's level of understanding.
- Make sure that you are speaking in an area that is not too noisy.

Encourage children's ability to develop and expand their ideas
- Show an interest in what children are saying. Encourage them and offer your own ideas if necessary.
- Help to develop the story – e.g. if a child says a character went to the shop to buy some bread, ask what the character could buy to put in the bread for sandwiches.
- Find a story or pictures that relate to the idea and let children find further ideas within them.
- Allow time for children to develop an idea without having to rush. If there really is no time, find a later occasion when the idea can be brought to full fruition.

Developing children's ability to adapt to the needs of the listener
Explain to children:
- that the listener may not understand or share an interest and that it may be necessary to give an explanation
- the need for appropriate vocabulary
- the need for a tone of voice to suit the audience
- how visual aids can help – e.g. if talking about a particular toy it helps to show that toy to the audience
- that on a one-on-one basis eye contact is important
- the importance of proximity to the audience
- that some people have difficulty hearing or seeing
- that some people do not understand English and there may be a need for someone else to explain what is happening to them.

Mathematics

How to help pupils understand the concepts of number
Children's first experience of numbers can include:
- car registration or house/flat numbers.
- numbers as sets – e.g. 5 sweets, 4 cows.
- numbers used for counting.

Before children have the words to express number they can see that five sweets is more than two sweets and will say that is not fair. They can be given early experience of counting by the use of rhymes – e.g. One, two, three, four, five, once I caught a fish alive – and by counting as they go up and down the stairs or do up the buttons on their coat.

Numbers in the environment include car registrations, house numbers, and telephone numbers. Numbers are spoken about with reference to prices in the shop and ages of children.

Ordinal numbers – 1st, 2nd, 3rd – can be taught by talking about the order in which drinks are served or the order in which children line up, etc.

When counting sets of objects, children can become confused by the fact that, for example, they are counting a set of six objects, holding one object and saying six. They need to understand that six is the name of the set. Children can often count to quite large numbers by rote but this does not mean that they have any understanding of number.

Children can get an idea of the size of a set by showing them sets that are obviously different:
- Ten Lego bricks is obviously more than two Lego bricks.
- Give children five counters and ask them to make patterns with them to reinforce the 'five-ness' of five.
- Use pairs of socks, shoes, etc. to reinforce the 'two-ness' of two.

Mathematics *(continued)*

- Use number tables to reinforce number concepts e.g. a table for five could include a hand with five fingers, a five number rhyme, etc.

When children are counting they need to learn strategies to help them to count efficiently. For example:

- Touching each object as it is counted will reinforce the fact that it has been dealt with and does not need to be counted again.
- Moving an object away from those still to be counted will ensure it is counted only once.

How to help pupils know number bonds and relationships between numbers

Children learn best from practical activities, for example:

- Give them Unifix cubes in two colours and ask them to make towers with the bricks as many ways as they can. If there are six red bricks and six blue bricks, ask the children to make towers six bricks high. They will get the following combinations: 6 blue/0 red, 5 blue/1 red, 4 blue/ 2 red, 3 blue/3 red and vice versa.
- Curve stitching: mark a horizontal and vertical axis on a piece of card. Number each axis zero to a chosen number – e.g. six. Punch holes in the card at each number and get the children to stitch between the numbers which total six, using a different coloured thread each time. This will help them to learn the number bonds within six.
- Older children could be given squared paper – e.g. three squares by three – and two different coloured pens and asked to colour the squares in a number of ways. This will help them to recognise number bonds within nine.

Number relationships can be reinforced by practical activities. Using the children, see if there are more boys than girls, more blondes than brunettes, etc.

How to help pupils develop mathematical language

Once again this area should be approached through practical activities:

- Comparative size – e.g. stories such as Goldilocks and the Three Bears and The Three Billy Goats Gruff.
- Ordinal numbers – lining up, races in the garden.
- Shape – in the environment.
- Time – 'What time do we tidy up?' 'How long does it take to tidy up?'
- Counting: objects in the nursery or buttons on coats.
- Opposites: people and objects in the nursery – e.g. tall/short, old/young.
- Colours: eyes, clothes, Lego bricks.
- Pattern: in nature, Unifix cubes – e.g. red first, blue next, etc.

Comparing tall and short children can teach about opposites

Science

How to develop children's skills, knowledge and understanding of science through play

- Sand: children can learn about the properties of sand by playing. They learn that dry sand will not build a sandcastle and wet sand will not pass through a sieve.
- Water: putting washing-up liquid in the water will help children realise what will happen if the water is whisked. Water wheels give a good insight into the power of water and lays down the foundation for discussion of hydro-electric power in secondary school.

Science (continued)

- Malleable materials: a range of malleable materials – e.g. playdough, clay, cornflour and water, shaving foam, shredded paper, wood shavings – can help children gain valuable scientific knowledge and understanding.
- Dressing up: stimulates discussion about materials. Looking in the mirror encourages talk about reflection.
- Toys and equipment: the children can be encouraged to talk about what the toys are made from.
- Construction equipment: 'What is it made from?' 'How should it be used?' 'Will Lego be stronger if the bricks are bonded?'
- Paint: how to make it thinner/thicker; 'Why should it be different consistencies?' 'What colour will we get if we mix these two together?'
- Jigsaw puzzles: 'What are they made from?'
- Imaginative area: discussion can be generated about animals, cars, roads, railways, aircraft, etc.

How to help pupils realise the importance of science in everyday life and its relevance to personal health

- Discuss and demonstrate how appliances work – e.g. refrigerator, freezer, cooker, kettle.
- Talk about central heating and other forms of heating and what effect they have on our lives.
- Talk about the weather – e.g. 'How does it affect us and the way we live?'
- All children have minor illnesses. Talk to them about the importance of doctors and medicine.
- Talk about personal hygiene and tooth brushing.

How to help pupils use computers in their work as and when appropriate

- Before working with the children, make sure you are aware of how the computer works.
- Give the children guidelines on who is allowed to switch the computer on/off and who can touch the disks, dials, buttons and switches.
- Show the children how to use the keyboard and the mouse.
- Explain fully to children and be sure they understand what to do before leaving them to get on with it.
- Do not use the computer for the sake of it. If there is a better way of teaching available, use it.

How to help pupils ask scientific questions and know how to respond

- Set up a colour-mixing activity. This will provide ideal opportunities to ask questions such as 'What will happen if I mix yellow and red?' Some children will then ask their own questions about what will happen if they mix certain colours.
- Don't do everything for the children. Encourage them to guess what will happen and form their own hypotheses.
- When a child asks a question, give an explanation of your answer. If you do not, the child will have gained nothing from having asked the question.
- Plan activities that can be completed only by the child asking questions.

Helping children to investigate familiar everyday objects

- Set up a table with a variety of mechanical objects – e.g. clocks, cameras, etc. – and allow the children to take them apart with screwdrivers.
- Look at the bikes in the garden and discuss the workings with the children.
- Make collections of objects – e.g. keys, cameras, clocks, locks, etc. – for the children to study.

Allow children to use the computer when relevant

Science *(continued)*

- Arrange trips to 'hands-on' museums and centres.
- Investigate mechanical toys.
- Visitors to the setting can bring in equipment for the children to investigate – e.g. doctor, fire-fighter, etc.
- Introduce everyday objects to the home corner – e.g. telephones, radios, etc.
- Use nature tables and interest tables to bring everyday objects into the setting.

Remember that whatever you do, the safety of the children is paramount!

Knowledge into action

1   *Choose a creative activity that would be suitable for a small group of three- to four-year-olds. Make a plan for the activity, listing the objectives for the children with reference to all six desirable outcomes.*

2   *Make a list of at least ten speaking and listening activities that would be suitable for a group of children following the National Curriculum Key Stage 1. Note which particular skills the activity would make use of.*

Check your knowledge

- What are the titles of the current early learning goals?

- Describe ways in which the desirable outcome of mathematics can be covered with children.

- What areas of the curriculum are children tested in at Key Stage 1?

- Suggest four activities to help children's speaking and listening skills.

- On what is a curriculum for 0–3s based?

- What was implemented by the DFEE in September 2000?

- How long does the foundation stage last?

- Why is it important for a child to be involved in the planning of a curriculum?

- Briefly describe why an 'end product' is not always essential in a curriculum?

- How does the National Curriculum provide for children with special needs?

- Who designed the National Literacy Strategy?

- List the three main areas that the strategy focused upon.

- What is the Literacy Hour?

- What are the four key principles of the Numeracy Strategy?

- List at least three things a child should be able to do by the end of the foundation stage.

- Who may work alongside a teacher in an early years setting?

- Briefly describe how you could help a five-year-old to use a computer in a science activity.

- Briefly describe an activity to encourage four-year-olds to take turns.

- Why is a key worker important in the delivery of the early years curriculum?

Resources

Further reading

Pascal, C. & Bertram, T. (eds) 1997 *Effective Early Learning*, London, Hodder and Stoughton

Whalley, M. 1994 *Learning to be Strong: Integrating Education and Care in Early Childhood*, London, Hodder and Stoughton

The National Numeracy Strategy, DFEE

The National Literacy Strategy, DFEE

CHAPTER 14

Work with young children

The most important role of any early years worker is to encourage children to explore the world about them through a variety of safe and stimulating experiences. These experiences are planned in the framework of a **curriculum** which provides different learning opportunities. Although curriculum planning varies according to the setting it should always be varied, enjoyable, and allow for spontaneity to support every child's individual learning needs and stage of development.

In Chapter 11 we covered the theoretical perspective of how children learn. Such theory is important and, if you understand Jean Piaget's theory of children's stages of learning, this will lead to good practice and to recognising the responsible role that the adult has in curriculum planning, implementation and assessment.

Although Piaget's work has been criticised, as children can develop earlier than he suggested, his idea that they need to learn at their own pace has been accepted. Carefully read the table below to revise Piaget's **Stages of learning** and **Stages of play** as a way of children gaining an understanding of their world.

Piaget's stages of learning and play

Age	Title	Stage of learning	Type of play	Common play features
0–2	Sensory motor	Discovering world around them and what can happen.	Practice and mastery play	Learning to control bodies. ■ Through play they explore their bodies. ■ They explore their environment and their effect on it. ■ Play can be reflective.
2–7	Pre-operational	Development of thought process. Start to use symbols in play. See and feel to learn about things – e.g. counting up with counters.	Symbolic play	Using language to communicate. ■ See in play. ■ Learn to use symbols in play – e.g. a pot may be a cup of tea!
7–11	Concrete operational	Development of logical thought. Follow rules of games. Can use and understand symbols – e.g. numbers and letters.	Play with rules	Developing an understanding of rules. ■ Play with board games. ■ Developing logical thoughts.

Piaget's ideas are widely recognised and have acted as the foundation for many early years and school settings using play as a basis of learning.

From studying other chapters in this book you will now understand that learning is **holistic** – i.e. a child is learning all the time and most subjects or curriculum areas cover other subjects and areas – and, although early years workers have to divide a curriculum and cover all areas of development, a child should not be constrained by subject boundaries.

This chapter will enable you to discover the importance of curriculum and routine planning and lead to a better understanding of:

▪ the curriculum and planning

▪ the importance of play in the curriculum

▪ assessing children's needs

▪ the three stages of curriculum planning:

   – long-term planning

   – medium-term planning

   – short-term planning

▪ curriculum and detailed play for 0–3-year-olds

▪ curriculum and detailed play for 3–5-year-olds

▪ curriculum and detailed play for children aged 4 years to 7 years 11 months

▪ home-made resources

▪ routines for children.

Approaches to curriculum planning and delivery

There are a number of possible approaches to planning the curriculum. The main ones are detailed below.

Structured

In this approach the work is planned by adults with a learning outcome in mind. They then guide the children towards achieving this outcome – within the time limits and given the ability of the children involved. For example:

Lotto game e.g. Galt First Lotto
The learning outcome is for the children to develop their descriptive skills, abilities in speaking and listening, turn-taking and positional language.

The game is set out and each child is given a baseboard. Sit with the children and, without showing them to the children, describes the lotto cards by what is shown in the picture. Start with a fairly difficult clue and, if none of the children guess, make the clues gradually easier until someone does. (Clues can thus be geared to the ages and stages of the children involved.) After a time you should encourage the children to try.

Unstructured

An adult provides planned activity which the children use in their own way and gain from as much or as little as they choose. The outcome of this activity may well not be what the adult had anticipated. For example:

Dry or wet sand, a log, real leaves and plastic minibeasts
The children will hopefully learn about properties of natural materials (sand, wood, leaves) and, with adult help, the names and categories of minibeasts.

The children may be content to hide the minibeasts under the leaves or the log. They may choose to play with the sand and ignore everything else or take the minibeasts out of the sand and play with them because they do not like the feel of the sand.

Experiential

Children learn from life and their environment. Opportunities to learn are drawn from events happening in the environment; for example, if it is snowing, the children take 'snow' as the theme for the day.

Thematic

Thematic learning is used to deliver the curriculum to the children in a way that is relevant to their experience and understanding. For example:

A shop (any kind)
You need to provide:

- a variety of real and toy items for sale

- items should represent a variety of cultures

- a cash register with real money (foreign coins are good). Real 1p pieces are cheaper to use than plastic money and more realistic. Children at nursery age do not need to know about the different denominations. Older children do, so you will have to use plastic money. As many people use cheques and credit cards, it would be a good idea to provide something to represent these methods of payment.

- a telephone with paper pad or diary to take orders, pencils and a variety of pens to write with.

- price lists and posters (some real and some written by the children).

- shopping bags (not plastic carrier bags) – some with shop names would help to introduce environmental print.

- dressing-up clothes, e.g. coats and hats, handbags – these should contain the same as you might have in your handbag (junk mail, bus tickets, etc. to encourage literacy).

- a sign on the door, written by the children – open/closed; name of shop; hours of opening.

- a number on the door and prices on articles will encourage number recognition.

For planning purposes the curriculum is divided to represent the sum of children's experiences. This can be done in a variety of ways, but will generally support the **early learning goals for children's learning** which specify goals for children's learning on entering compulsory education.

This stage is called the foundation stage, it starts when children are three years old and finishes at the end of the reception year in primary school before they progress to Key Stage I of the National Curriculum.

The early learning goals are organised in six areas of learning and are as follows:

- Personal, social and emotional development

- Communication, language and literacy

- Mathematical development

- Knowledge and understanding of the world

- Physical development

- Creative development.

QCA's guidance on young children's learning states that 'Most children are expected to achieve the early learning goals by the end of the foundation stage. Practitioners should plan a curriculum that helps children make good progress towards, and where appropriate beyond, these goals.'

There are different approaches for curriculum planning which you will discover during your training and throughout your professional life.

By planning a curriculum, in whatever form, you can be confident that all the learning experiences, opportunities and activities that you feel children should have will be identified and organised. A planned curriculum for children aged 0–7 years 11 months may sometimes sound formidable, but, if based on play, it is the only way to ensure children are given the opportunity to develop fully.

Below are some guidelines to planning an early years curriculum.

Good practice – planning an early years curriculum

The curriculum must:
- ✔ be appropriate for the ages and stages of development of the children involved

- ✔ use the children's interests as a basis and their needs to explore and practice

- ✔ cover all aspects of a child's learning and development with reference to the six early learning goals for children aged 3–7 years 11 months

- ✔ support children's individual needs, including special educational needs and English as an additional language

✔ promote children's health and safety

✔ involve parents, visitors and other professionals

✔ encourage equality of opportunity.

Knowledge into action

Consider the curriculum at your work setting. How does it meet the seven guidelines to planning an early years curriculum.

Planning a curriculum is made up of many tasks and involves children, practitioners and parents. In order to develop practice it is important to review the curriculum as a cycle.

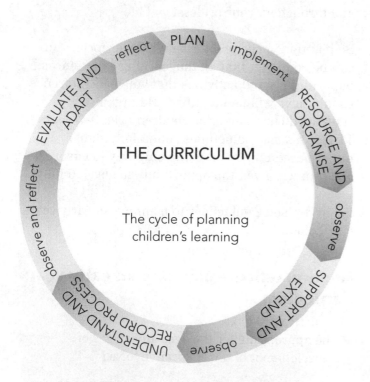

THE CURRICULUM

The cycle of planning children's learning

PLAN — implement — RESOURCE AND ORGANISE — observe — SUPPORT AND EXTEND — observe — UNDERSTAND AND RECORD PROCESS — observe and reflect — EVALUATE AND ADAPT — reflect

The importance of play in the curriculum

It is important to recognise the value of play in children's learning. Susan Isaacs (see page 261) wrote

'Play is a child's work and the means whereby he grows and develops.'

Taking into account the stages the children have reached, play activities can develop and expand each child's knowledge and understanding. In Berkshire Education's document 'A Curriculum without Bounds' a child's need to play is clearly defined in a list of objectives as portrayed in the spider diagram on page 323.

Play is often planned for in the curriculum in a variety of ways. As you will remember from Chapter 11 play is often categorised in five areas:

■ creative

■ physical

■ imaginative

■ manipulative

■ social.

Assessing children's needs

Any curriculum plan needs to take into account the particular age, stage and needs of the children it is planned for. Two important tools in assessing children's needs are **observation** and **record keeping**.

Observation

Through observation and assessment of the children in your care you will be able to plan an appropriate curriculum that allows the children to gain maximum benefit from its content. Sometimes observations are intuitive but others will have a clear aim and will identify:

■ particular needs of children

■ strengths and weaknesses of the curriculum.

The case study opposite is an example of how observations can support curriculum planning.

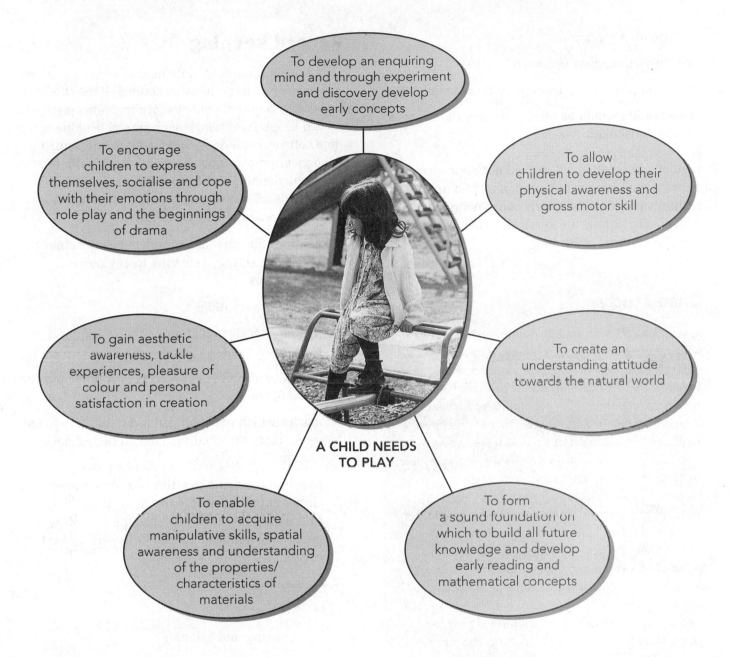

To develop an enquiring mind and through experiment and discovery develop early concepts

To encourage children to express themselves, socialise and cope with their emotions through role play and the beginnings of drama

To allow children to develop their physical awareness and gross motor skill

To gain aesthetic awareness, tackle experiences, pleasure of colour and personal satisfaction in creation

A CHILD NEEDS TO PLAY

To create an understanding attitude towards the natural world

To enable children to acquire manipulative skills, spatial awareness and understanding of the properties/ characteristics of materials

To form a sound foundation on which to build all future knowledge and develop early reading and mathematical concepts

Case study

In the Hawthorn Nursery School it was decided to observe the outside play area as the team were concerned that it was not an extension of the indoor planned nursery activities. Over a period of two weeks, two members of the team observed the area and noticed that the children were often unsettled as there was not a great enough variety of activities for them. As a result, it was decided to create a peaceful area away from the bikes, plan a variety of daily activities to develop gross manipulative play, and provide a creative table and a role-play area. When weather permitted children would be able to flow freely between indoor and outdoor activities and the team would plan them as an area. After developing this new approach to the curriculum it was decided to monitor the changes and meet as a team to evaluate the observations and review the changes.

In this use of observation:

- the curriculum was reviewed

- a new approach to outside play was formulated

- observation would be used to review the changes to the curriculum.

Individual observations, if carried out appropriately, can reveal the learning potential of a child and assess that child's progress. The early years team will then be able to assess how the curriculum is meeting the needs of individual children.

Case study

Joseph was three years five months. His key worker, Alison, noticed that he was reluctant to play with other children and that he tended to focus on activities that he could do on his own, such as drawing and puzzles. The team agreed that Alison should observe Joseph's involvement in planned activities over a period of a week. It was observed that Joseph became easily involved in activities that he could do on his own, such as free painting, making a mask, designing a car out of recycled material and completing an animal floor puzzle. He watched children play in the home corner, water tray and sandpit but did not join in. As a result of these observations, the team decided to help Joseph to develop his confidence and communication skills by encouraging him gradually to play with small groups of children in planned group activities that are part of the curriculum plan and any spontaneous opportunities that may arise.

Through observation the team were able to identify areas of the curriculum in which Joseph needed to become more involved in order to develop some of his communication and social skills. It may be that some future group activities will be planned with reference to Joseph and that Alison, as his key worker, will work alongside him to develop his confidence and encourage him to play with other children.

Record keeping

This area of recording individual children's progress has developed in early years settings since OFSTED inspectors required evidence of comprehensive record keeping. Although such record keeping can be time consuming it does help evaluate and contribute to curriculum planning. Records can sometimes show that a curriculum is not supporting children's learning as effectively as it should. There are a variety of records that may be used:

- child profiles that are completed as the child enters the setting, referring to any needs or preferences

- written observations

- mental checklists that may refer to acquired skills

- portfolios of children's work, with comments added by staff, children and parents as appropriate

- diaries which may be filled in by staff for parents, referring to the children's day in the school or nursery

- **baseline assessment** – this is an assessment of a child's capabilities on entry to an early years setting. All five-year-olds entering schools will undergo a standard baseline assessment that covers:

  - reading

  - writing

  - speaking and listening

  - mathematics

  - personal and social development.

Children with special needs will benefit from professional observation and record keeping. Other professionals may be involved in the record keeping, such as a health visitor, speech therapist, or an LSA (Learning Support Assistant) working with a statemented child. If the records are shared with parents it may help if they add to the records with their experiences outside the setting. If parents and staff can share and discuss records this can enhance a child's development.

The three stages of curriculum planning

There are three stages involved in the planning of any early years or national curriculum.

They are

- **Long-term planning** This creates a framework to give a structure and coherence to a curriculum. It is often done for a period of one year, but may be shorter in early years settings such as day care provision for children under five.

- **Medium-term planning** This looks in more detail at particular aspects of the curriculum, perhaps for one month, half a term or a full term.

- **Short-term planning** This concerns the individual needs and interests of children on a daily or weekly basis.

Long-term planning

When you are a student and spend time in a placement, it is likely that the long-term planning will have already been formulated by the permanent team. But you may be asked to form a daily or weekly plan within the overall long-term plan. If you are in this position you must always ask to see the long-term plan of the setting so that you can plan effectively within this framework.

Long-term planning will help to ensure that the aims of the setting in all six areas of learning (or areas of development for younger children) are met, enabling children to develop their full potential. It is important to remember that under-fives can attend early years settings for a variety of times, from a few hours a week to a full week. The curriculum should offer learning opportunities to cover the six areas of learning or development for all children, no matter what number of sessions they attend at the setting.

The following questions will need to be considered:

- Will the curriculum focus on a particular area of learning at certain times, for example, numeracy in the morning when the children are fresh?

- How will children with special needs, including those who have an IEP (individual education plan), be accommodated?

- Will any particular events, such as fixed religious festivals, be part of the planning?

- Are there ways of providing a variety of activities that offer a balance of learning opportunities, perhaps within a topic or a theme?

- Are there ways of maximising the potential in all activities to help the children's areas of development?

- How will the curriculum be reviewed with reference to the results of observations and record keeping?

The stages of long-term planning are as follows:

1 Discuss and agree the curriculum plan. (This will be influenced by what you want children to learn in your setting according to their developmental needs.)
2 Decide what learning experience you will need to meet these aims. (For example, role play, construction games, cooking, local visits, etc.)
3 Look at the six early learning goals or perhaps areas of development for younger children and decide whether the learning experience you have planned will help them progress towards these learning goals.
4 Review your resources for sufficiency, suitability and availability. It may be that more resources, such as costumes for the home corner, or utensils for a cooking activity, have to be purchased.

Medium-term planning

This is required to focus on one particular aspect of learning – for example, **time**: this will develop the idea of night/day, routines, sense and duration of time. Various aspects of learning may be considered in one medium-term plan.

The stages of medium-term planning are as follows:

1 Discuss **how** a particular aspect of learning can be developed – for example, using stories, role play, investigation, etc.
2 Consider the language that might be used – e.g. for time, 'early' in the morning, 'late' at night, etc.
3 Plan activities for different-sized groups of children and children with particular needs.
4 Decide on the role of the adult in working alongside the children – e.g. reading stories to a group of children, playing alongside children, investigating different time pieces.
5 Check the children's learning by observing and questioning in order to develop planning.
6 Develop planning by, for example, allowing children to practice their home language in play, providing additional learning experiences such as making clocks, drawing pictures for daily routines – e.g. cleaning teeth, breakfast time, etc.
7 Ensure that the appropriate learning goals are considered.
8 Consider how the children can be involved in the planning process.

Short-term planning

This may be carried out on a daily or weekly basis. If it is carried out weekly it must be flexible enough to allow for spontaneous learning. Some activities will be **adult-led**, such as story telling and cooking, while others will be experiences freely selected by the children where staff supervise and are aware of key questions to ask, such as 'Why are there stars in the sky?'

How to carry out curriculum planning

This section will focus on the different ways of planning, implementing and evaluating curriculum activities that will promote children's learning and development. The promotion of equality of opportunity and anti-discriminatory practice will be considered throughout. You will find it useful to refer to chapters 11, 12 and 13, which discuss in detail the range of activities and experience that you can include in your planning.

Curriculum plans will vary according to the needs of the children and the setting they are in. You will find that settings will formulate their own styles. One major influence will be the ages of the children to the considered.

Children of 0–3 years will benefit from curriculum plans relating to the five areas of development emphasising sensory experiences. The five main areas of development are:

- physical
- cognitive (intellectual)
- emotional
- social
- language.

For children of this age the **process** – for example, playing with the sand – is more important than the result – for example, the sandcastle (in fact, their enjoyment is likely to come from knocking it down).

Children of 3–6 years will need to experience their learning through play. Any curriculum planning will relate to the early learning goals. It is acknowledged that children may attend a variety of settings before they begin primary school and that the only way to value and build upon children's previous learning is for early years workers to work in partnership with parents and other adults.

The foundation stage referred to by OFSTED begins when children reach the age of three and ends at the end of the reception year. The foundation stage curriculum is organised into the six areas of learning referred to earlier in this chapter as the early learning goals.

Children of 5–7 years 11 months will require curriculum plans that mainly relate to Key Stage 1 of the National Curriculum. They will include numeracy and literacy strategies. A school curriculum plan is the responsibility of the teacher, although enlightened settings will involve all early years workers in the class in the curriculum planning.

ISSUES

It is important to remember that many five- to eight-year-olds attend out-of-school and holiday clubs. The activities in these settings will be based on play and not linked to the National Curriculum, so a plan of activities may be introduced here that promotes more freedom of choice rather than a school-based curriculum plan. For example, there may be more opportunities for outdoor play and children may well be involved in the planning of such activities.

When planning a curriculum you may be required to focus on a range of activities and experiences that concentrate on one area of play or one area of the early years curriculum. It may be your responsibility to lead one of the activities and write it up as a detailed plan. You may also be required to make a resource that supports the children's learning in the activity. (Later in this chapter you will have the opportunity to consider a curriculum plan for three- to five-year-olds based on a range of activities and experiences to meet the early learning goals. In addition you will read about a resource relating to an activity plan that is designed to support a school curriculum plan for children aged five to seven years eleven months.)

Knowledge into action

Members of your group will be able to share a variety of curriculum planning experiences in different settings. Collect as many examples of curriculum plans as you can during your course and discuss them with other members of your group.

The stages in curriculum planning

Whatever the type of curriculum plan you are involved in implementing, you will be expected to:

- identify the aims of the plan
- explore the rationale for the plan
- explore the learning which may take place for the children
- explore the learning which may take place for yourself
- create an overall plan of activities/experiences that can be included in the curriculum plan
- describe these activities/experiences in detail
- implement and evaluate activity plans when required.

You will then be expected to create resources to be used as part of an activity plan.

It is essential to remember that planning will vary according to the curriculum plan concerned. For example, a curriculum plan for young babies will focus on development but can be encouraged in routines and individual contact between baby and carer while, in a National Curriculum plan, the focus will be upon meeting the learning goals in the required areas of learning. All plans will require detailed preparation by the early years team.

Identify the aims of the plan

In order to decide on the aim of any curriculum plan, it is essential to find out about the children for whom the plan is intended and the setting that they are in. Much of this work will be carried out by observing the children and planning as a team with other years practitioners and parents. In the curriculum plan likely to meet because resea

327

'Practitioners have a crucial role in this learning and should draw on a range of teaching and care strategies and knowledge of child development. Children deepen their understanding by playing, talking, planning, questioning, experimenting, testing, repeating, reflecting and responding to adults and to each other. Practitioners need to plan learning experiences of the highest quality, considering both children's needs and achievements and the range of learning experiences that will make them progress. Well-planned play is a key way in which children learn with challenge and enjoyment during the foundation stage.'

So, before planning a curriculum or detailed activity, it is essential to gather information about the children by:

- observing the children
- talking to the children
- talking to the parents
- talking to other early years practitioners
- researching the developmental stages of the children involved
- reflecting and reviewing children's developmental records.

The information gathered will include:

- the **children's play preferences** – e.g. they might like energetic physical activity or play involving particular manipulative equipment
- the **children's routine** – e.g. is the planned activity going to take place before or after lunch when the children are fresh or tired?
- ...**ildren's developmental stages** – e.g. are ... pl... do a fine manipulative task such as
- the a... parent... skill tha... e.g. do they need to ... staff and ... icular

such as playing a musical instrument or cooking?

- **health and safety issues** – e.g. ensuring that there is enough space to play safely.

Your aim may also relate to any topic or theme that the setting is exploring.

Case study

Consider the following situation.

Sophie, a student in a nursery school, was part of a team planning a range of experiences for children aged one to two years to promote their physical development. The team planned this particular curriculum together and Sophie included this in an assignment for college. She wrote the aim as:

'To develop the physical skills of a group of one- to two-year-old children over a period of a week through a variety of indoor and outdoor play experiences.'

Think about the stages of planning that Sophie went through in order to arrive at this aim and how she will have considered the needs of the children, working in partnership with both parents and colleagues.

1. List at least three experiences Sophie was aiming to offer the children.
2. Which early learning goals were these experiences working towards?
3. How was Sophie aiming to develop the children's numeracy skills?

Explore the rationale for the plan

The rationale for any plan is the reason why the plan is to be implemented. All the work carried out when establishing a clear and appropriate aim will help to focus on the rationale. In explaining the reasoning for any plan you should consider:

- the area of development to be focused on
- any assessment to be achieved
- the link to any theme or topic
- the variety of experiences to be offered.

the National Curriculum. They will include numeracy and literacy strategies. A school curriculum plan is the responsibility of the teacher, although enlightened settings will involve all early years workers in the class in the curriculum planning.

ISSUES

It is important to remember that many five- to eight-year-olds attend out-of-school and holiday clubs. The activities in these settings will be based on play and not linked to the National Curriculum, so a plan of activities may be introduced here that promotes more freedom of choice rather than a school-based curriculum plan. For example, there may be more opportunities for outdoor play and children may well be involved in the planning of such activities.

When planning a curriculum you may be required to focus on a range of activities and experiences that concentrate on one area of play or one area of the early years curriculum. It may be your responsibility to lead one of the activities and write it up as a detailed plan. You may also be required to make a resource that supports the children's learning in the activity. (Later in this chapter you will have the opportunity to consider a curriculum plan for three- to five-year-olds based on a range of activities and experiences to meet the early learning goals. In addition you will read about a resource relating to an activity plan that is designed to support a school curriculum plan for children aged five to seven years eleven months.)

Knowledge into action

Members of your group will be able to share a variety of curriculum planning experiences in different settings. Collect as many examples of curriculum plans as you can during your course and discuss them with other members of your group.

The stages in curriculum planning

Whatever the type of curriculum plan you are involved in implementing, you will be expected to:

- identify the aims of the plan

- explore the rationale for the plan

- explore the learning which may take place for the children

- explore the learning which may take place for yourself

- create an overall plan of activities/experiences that can be included in the curriculum plan

- describe these activities/experiences in detail

- implement and evaluate activity plans when required.

You will then be expected to create resources to be used as part of an activity plan.

It is essential to remember that planning will vary according to the curriculum plan concerned. For example, a curriculum plan for young babies will focus on development but can be encouraged in routines and individual contact between baby and carer while, in a National Curriculum plan, the focus will be upon meeting the learning goals in the required areas of learning. All plans will require detailed preparation by the early years team.

Identify the aims of the plan

In order to decide on the aim of any curriculum plan, it is essential to find out about the children for whom the plan is intended and the setting that they are in. Much of this work will be carried out by observing the children and planning as a team with other early years practitioners and parents. In this way the aim of the curriculum plan or related activity will be more likely to meet the needs of the children concerned, because it will be based on actual observation and research.

As stated in *Curriculum Guidance for the Foundation Stage* (DFEE/QCA, May 2000), the success of early year learning provision is dependent on partnerships:

'Practitioners have a crucial role in this learning and should draw on a range of teaching and care strategies and knowledge of child development. Children deepen their understanding by playing, talking, planning, questioning, experimenting, testing, repeating, reflecting and responding to adults and to each other. Practitioners need to plan learning experiences of the highest quality, considering both children's needs and achievements and the range of learning experiences that will make them progress. Well-planned play is a key way in which children learn with challenge and enjoyment during the foundation stage.'

So, before planning a curriculum or detailed activity, it is essential to gather information about the children by:

- observing the children

- talking to the children

- talking to the parents

- talking to other early years practitioners

- researching the developmental stages of the children involved

- reflecting and reviewing children's developmental records.

The information gathered will include:

- the **children's play preferences** – e.g. they might like energetic physical activity or play involving particular manipulative equipment

- the **children's routine** – e.g. is the planned activity going to take place before or after lunch when the children are fresh or tired?

- the **children's developmental stages** – e.g. are they able to do a fine manipulative task such as threading beads?

- the **children's needs** – e.g. do they need to practise particular skills?

- the **available resources**, including staff and parents – e.g. do any parents have a particular skill that they could share with the children,

such as playing a musical instrument or cooking?

- **health and safety issues** – e.g. ensuring that there is enough space to play safely.

Your aim may also relate to any topic or theme that the setting is exploring.

Case study

Consider the following situation.

Sophie, a student in a nursery school, was part of a team planning a range of experiences for children aged one to two years to promote their physical development. The team planned this particular curriculum together and Sophie included this in an assignment for college. She wrote the aim as:

'To develop the physical skills of a group of one- to two-year-old children over a period of a week through a variety of indoor and outdoor play experiences.'

Think about the stages of planning that Sophie went through in order to arrive at this aim and how she will have considered the needs of the children, working in partnership with both parents and colleagues.

1 List at least three experiences Sophie was aiming to offer the children.

2 Which early learning goals were these experiences working towards?

3 How was Sophie aiming to develop the children's numeracy skills?

Explore the rationale for the plan

The rationale for any plan is the reason why the plan is to be implemented. All the work carried out when establishing a clear and appropriate aim will help to focus on the rationale. In explaining the reasoning for any plan you should consider:

- the area of development to be focused on

- any assessment to be achieved

- the link to any theme or topic

- the variety of experiences to be offered.

Case study

Chris considered the following rationale for a cooking activity she was planning for a small group of children in the day nursery where she was on student placement.

The aim of a cooking activity for three- to four-year-olds in a day nursery, relating to a curriculum plan based on the theme of 'shape' is *'to encourage children to explore the topic of shape while making biscuits during a cooking activity'*.

I have decided to make biscuits with the children using shape cutters that they will be able to manage. The recipe will be suitable for them as they will be able to look at recipe cards that have pictures and words. The children will also benefit from the process of stirring the mixture, rubbing the mixture and rolling it out. It will be an activity that has many things for them to do and, as it doesn't take long to cook, will provide quick results. The children will be able to name and choose the shape cutters for their biscuits, which will be squares, triangles, circles and rectangles. They will be able to share the biscuits with their friends, discuss the shapes and take one home in a paper bag to show their parents what they achieved in their cooking activity in the nursery.

1 On which area of development was Chris focusing in her plan?
2 Why has she chosen to make biscuits using shape cutters?
3 What are the experiences that Chris will offer to develop the children's numeracy skills?
4 Will there be an opportunity for Chris to observe and assess the children's recognition of shapes during this activity?

Explore the learning which may take place for the children

From a clearly focused rationale the learning outcomes for the children will be easy to explore. The learning outcomes should show a clear idea of the way children can learn from the curriculum or activity plan. These outcomes will be written as a result of your planning with other early years workers and parents stating what you would like the children to learn as a result of the plan. The chart below shows what you will need to do in working towards the learning outcomes for the children.

How to work towards learning outcomes

Learning Outcome	Example
Ensure you build upon what the children already know and can do.	You can find this out by talking to parents and colleagues and looking at records.
Carefully consider the needs of each child.	A child may have a learning need, physical need, or transitory need – e.g. change in their lives caused by the birth of a sibling, or moving house.
Maximise the potential of the activities, including for those who have special educational needs or an individual educational plan.	Ensure that the activities are stimulating – e.g. has a collage activity got enough textured and coloured materials for the children to use?
Identify the early learning goals, area of development or key stage you want the children to meet.	If your aim is to develop fine manipulative skills you could provide a range of interesting activities to do this, such as threading brightly coloured beads, painting with textured paints, drawing with coloured chalks in the outside play area.

Learning Outcome	Example
Ensure children are involved in the planning.	If children are involved in planning an activity, such as a hairdressers in the role play corner, they will hopefully gain more from it and take more responsibility for the area.
Identify the routines of the children, particularly those which may affect or be affected by the curriculum plan.	Children might make their own snack and have it in the garden rather than at their table in the nursery. In a case like this, ensure that the children are told in advance that their snack time will change. Remember that routines are very important for children's emotional stability.
Consider concepts to be developed and skills to be related to the learning outcomes.	If a concept such as **up and down** is to be developed. carefully think about the variety of ways it can be explored – e.g. using scales, climbing up and down steps, etc.

The spider diagram below shows where the information is gathered from.

Remember that the curriculum must have an anti-bias view and allow each child to reach his full potential in his learning. Children must feel secure and valued. Ensure that your curriculum plan allows for the involvement of every child.

'*No child should be excluded or disadvantaged* because of ethnicity, culture or religion, home language, family background, special educational needs, disability, gender or ability.' (*Curriculum Guidance for the Foundation Stage*, QCA, 2000)

Here is an example of the learning outcomes that can be written as part of the planning of the activity:

Case study

Tom planned a clay activity, making animals, for a group of three- to four-year-olds. The activity was in the context of a theme around farm animals. Tom planned the learning outcomes by considering how the children would learn and thus benefit from the activity, the needs of the children, where the activity would take place, what they had learnt about animals in the topic so far and the type of manipulative activities they had previously experienced. As Tom was a student on an eight-week placement he gained information from parents and colleagues to plan these outcomes and was given permission to read the children's records to help understand their needs. Tom understood that in planning an activity it should be possible to extract a variety of learning outcomes. As a result the potential learning outcomes were that each child would:

- develop her listening skills by listening to the instructions for the activity

- interact with adults and children by discussing thoughts and ideas during activity

- develop language to describe the touch and texture of the mixture and the end product

- develop recall of events in topic

- share materials and tools with each other and develop self-esteem through enjoyment

- develop manipulative and hand-to-eye skills by rubbing clay, rolling out and creating shapes

- use senses to explore texture and the way it changes through the process

- develop an understanding of shape, size, colour

- use mathematical language through phrases such as more than and less than

- enjoy the activity and have fun.

Questions

1 How did Tom consider the needs of each child when planning this activity?
2 Name the areas of development on which he wanted to focus.
3 How did Tom ensure the children's interest could be used during the activity?
4 Which concepts did Tom want the children to develop during this activity?

Explore for yourself the learning which may take place

When training you will be acutely aware of what you are gaining from taking an active part in curriculum planning, implementation and evaluation. However, it is important to remember that qualified early years workers should also always be aware of what they will learn when an activity takes place. The day any early years worker stops learning is most probably the day she should retire! As with the potential learning for the children, your potential learning will relate to the aims of your curriculum plan. Your learning will relate to:

- the area of learning to be developed – this may relate to the early learning goals or national curriculum

- the activity/ies to be implemented

- the way the children learn

- the way each child's needs are met

- the way the activity/ies are anti-bias

- the importance of planning effectively

- the way other early years workers participate in the activity

- the importance of working as a team

- how the health and safety policy is observed.

Case study

Emma has nearly completed her training and has been part of a team planning a short-term weekly curriculum plan based on the project 'water'. In the project the children will carry out different water-play-based activities, take a trip to the local pond, make instruments that will make water sounds, make water sounds and grow watercress. The imaginative play area will be a beach in Australia, where one of the children's parents comes from.

By taking part in this weekly plan and planning the imaginative play areas Emma hopes that she will learn:

- how a short-term curriculum plan is carried out by a team of early years workers

- how the children use their senses to investigate objects and materials in the water-play activities

- how the children are involved in the planning of the activities

- how each expectation of learning is met

- how children's needs are met

- how children are grouped

- how the resources were used

- how successful the overall organisation of the plan was

- how a broad range of learning experiences was used.

1 How long is the short-term curriculum plan Emma is involved in?
2 Which early learning goals will the children work towards during this short-term activity plan?
3 How will the children learn about water during this project?
4 How has Emma incorporated a world-view in this project?
5 What is the broad range of learning experiences that the children will have during the week?

Create an overall plan of activities/experiences

There are many ways in which activities/experiences are set out in a curriculum plan. As stated before it is essential to work with the other early years workers in your setting to make a plan that can be understood by all those adults supporting the children. It is important to remember that plans are often displayed in the settings for parents to read. Carefully re-read the section about the age range of curriculum planning in Chapter 13 (pages 306–307).

When creating an overall plan, as discussed, detailed information must be gathered to ensure that the curriculum plan is suitable for the children concerned.

The second stage is to decide how long the curriculum plan will last. It will be useful to revise the section earlier in the chapter that refers to short-, medium- and long-term planning (page 325).

Knowledge into action

When you have read the section of this chapter about curriculum planning for different ages consider how the planning of a curriculum for one- to three-year-olds might vary from one for six- to eight-year-olds.

Most curriculum plans will be created by a team of early years workers whose disciplines will vary according to the setting. Most teams will have an initial brainstorm where a variety of ideas is discussed and related to the relevant areas of learning. The activities should be varied and stimulating, allowing for individual needs and choice. Some settings may record this brainstorming session. Read the examples of brain-storming and activity plans on pages 348–351.

Once the ideas have been selected the team will decide:

- the equipment and materials needed
- where the activities will take place
- who will facilitate each activity.

The next step is to ensure that the plan:

- follows health and safety guidelines
- promotes a world-view and is anti-bias
- links to the relevant learning goals
- will be recorded appropriately
- is balanced and flexible
- can be realistically supported by staff
- is able to meet each child's needs
- is evaluated after implementation.

Plans will then be presented in a variety of ways. There are no set ways to present a plan. Whatever the style of curriculum plan, it should refer to the relevant learning outcomes and how the activities will be planned to meet them. Incorporated in or alongside a curriculum plan will be the detailed organisation of the activities showing:

- who is involved in each activity
- whether it is a small- or large-group activity
- the resources and equipment to be used
- the rationale for each activity.

Individual Learning Programmes (ILPs) are prepared when a child has specific needs and may require special support that is not allowed for in the general plan of activities and experiences. Such programmes will be planned by a variety of early years workers, specialists and parents and may be designed to meet a temporary need or may be for a child who has severe difficulties.

An ILP cannot be planned until a child has been observed, assessed and his needs clearly identified. The plan will then have to be integrated into the overall plan of the setting. A detailed plan of activities may well show how a child's individual needs will be supported. For example, a child who has severe hearing loss may require a key worker to work alongside them during a language activity.

Implement activity plans

When planning an activity or experience as part of a curriculum plan, detailed preparations must take place in order for the activity to be successful. As discussed, remember that the aim and learning outcomes for the child and yourself will be considered. The next stage is to plan in detail how you will carry out the activity. It can be written in list form starting from consulting with your supervisor to clearing away the activity – **always considering how the children can be involved in each stage**. Use the following checklist when writing a detailed plan.

- Is the activity accessible to all children?

- Will the activity promote an anti-bias and a world-view?

- Will the activity help to develop the children's social and interpersonal skills?

- How will the activity develop the children's language?

- What will the children do in the activity?

- What will the adults do to support the children?

- How many children can participate in the activity?

- Where will the activity take place?

- How long will the activity last?

- What resources and equipment will be needed?

- How will health and safety requirements be met?

- What ratio of adults/children will be needed?

- How will the activity meet the learning outcomes required?

Types of activity

The detailed planning of an activity will ensure its implementation runs smoothly. It could be based upon one of the following experiences:

- Cooking activity

- Science activity

- Technology activity

Case study

Here is an example of a detailed activity plan. Megan implemented a successful art activity with a group of five-year-olds. The activity is an observational painting session of some sunflowers in the school garden. Megan's detailed plan is as follows:

Before the activity:

- Discuss the idea with supervisor.

- Decide where and when the activity will be carried out.

- Discuss how many children can be involved and allow space for X with wheelchair.

- Find out when the activity will take place.

- Organise materials, paints, brushes, water, etc.

On the day:

- Arrive early to prepare materials.

- Prepare easels and equipment.

- Prepare area outside.

When children arrive:

- Talk about sunflowers and activity.

- Ask them to write names on paper.

- Explain how they can use colours and paint.

- Allow them to paint their own view of sunflowers.

When they have finished:

- Praise them and discuss activity if they want to.

- Ask them to place paintings on rack.

- Ask them to replace aprons.

- Encourage them to wash their hands.

- Ask them if work may be displayed.

Questions

1 How effective do you think Megan's detailed plan is?

2 Has the plan taken into account any unexpected occurrences such as rainy weather?

3 What would you add to this plan?

- Mathematics activity
- Music activity
- Storytelling activity
- Language/literacy activity
- Physical activity.

There are many more experiences that could be used. It will be useful for you to read chapters 11, 12 and 13 to review the many experiences that children aged 0–7 years 11 months can be offered.

Evaluate plans

Evaluation is an essential part of any planning process as it will consider if the children's needs were met and will affect future plans. Evaluation will include how the children were involved, comments from colleagues, children's comments and some form of record keeping and assessment.

Observation of children may be recorded formally or informally, according to the setting. This will help to evaluate the activity and focus on each child's needs.

Colleague feedback may take place in an evaluation team meeting, informally or in a formal feedback session. It is important that feedback is constructive and supportive.

Parental feedback may be spontaneous and may be positive or negative. Discussion may take place at a more formal meeting such as an open evening. Criticism may be considered and evaluated.

Children's feedback will be honest and spontaneous and should always be taken into account when evaluating an activity. Any good setting will ensure that there is time to evaluate as part of the planning process. This may take the form of a comment on a plan or a meeting of early years workers.

When writing an evaluation of an activity you have planned, carefully consider the following:

- Did the children enjoy the activity?
- Did you enjoy the activity?
- Which part of the plan was successful?

- Which part of the plan could have been improved?
- What did the children learn?
- What did you learn?
- Did you achieve your aim? Did your plan deviate from the aim?
- What would you change if the activity were to be repeated?
- How will this activity affect future planning?

How to create a resource that will be part of an activity plan

A resource is something that can be used to support an activity you have planned. Resources can be made or collected and could include a variety of items such as

- games
- books
- audio tapes
- story props
- story boards
- puppets/dolls
- sensory materials
- musical instruments.

As an example:

Consider how important puppets are and how they can be used to support a variety of activities – perhaps as a way of emphasising an area of learning or to reassure an otherwise unsure child. Why not supply a collection of puppets for free play?

Any resource that will be provided must be

- safe
- durable
- age appropriate
- anti-bias
- relevant to the activity
- well presented.

A curriculum plan for children aged 0–1 year

A curriculum for children aged 0–1 year has a very different focus from the activities and experiences that are planned for older children. The early years curriculum for 3–5-year-olds is now widely recognised and is based upon their previous development and an organised learning structure. However, the learning outcomes that provide a basis for a 3–5-year-old curriculum may not be right for babies and toddlers.

Consider the following areas that are essential when planning a curriculum of learning activities and experiences for children aged 0–1 year.

- The baby's day should be looked at as a whole and not as a series of activities, and importance should be placed on the learning opportunities that can arise from individual contact, routines and spontaneous play.

- It is important to focus on the baby's current skills, abilities and interests and to value these in their own right.

- Adults are at the centre of a baby's learning and experiences and if they have the time to communicate fully with an individual baby they will be able to develop a warm relationship which will result in the baby developing at the right level and rate appropriate for his or her age. An adult can also encourage a baby to become aware of other children. In recent years, there has been much research done into babies' ability to communicate with each other and it is considered wrong for babies to have no social contact with each other.

- The physical care and routine of a baby's day is a vital part of the 'curriculum' as it can enable the adult to give complete attention to the baby and support his or her personal development.

- Babies as individuals must lead the curriculum as they develop their own thinking and do not operate as part of a group.

- The curriculum does not have to result in end products such as painting and models that can be shared with parents at the end of the day.

Sharing what you have seen and heard is of great importance.

With these concerns in mind carefully consider the following short-term (weekly) curriculum plan for a group of 0–1-year-olds in a day care setting.

The **long-term plans** of *The Red House Nursery* are to develop the babies' five areas of development through a variety of sensory experiences based upon individual babies and the adults with whom they have close contact. Detailed record keeping is implemented to ensure that both parents and early years workers consider the curriculum together.

The **medium-term plans** are loosely based upon the nursery's theme of 'animals' but the babies' team are encouraged to consider the importance of spontaneous learning through routines and physical contact.

The **short-term curriculum plans** for the babies' aged 0–1 year in The Red House Nursery are for a period of five days.

The aim and rationale of the plans is to provide an appropriate range of activities and learning opportunities for a group of babies aged 0–1 year and promote all areas of development. The nursery theme of animals is used when appropriate but importance is placed on integrated care and stimulation.

When planning the weekly curriculum, the early years workers started by producing a spider plan of ideas referring to the five areas of development (see page 337).

They then drew up a weekly plan as shown at the bottom of page 337.

The learning outcomes for the child

Throughout the week's activities and experiences each child will have the opportunity to:

- develop physically through the use of a variety of activities – e.g. cushion mountains, the paddling pool and textured mats – and in spontaneous play and routines – e.g. feeding and nappy-changing time

- develop cognitive skills by exploring the activity basket of textured animals through sight, touch and taste and exploring the variety of filled bottles and other nursery toys

- develop language skills by listening to music such as animal song tapes, visiting the local duck pond, communicating with carers and having time to listen to sounds

- develop emotionally by enjoying the physical routines of the day such as nappy changing, feeling positive about developing self-help skills such as holding a spoon or cup and feeling secure at sleep times, etc.

- develop socially by being with carers, other children and enjoying experiences such as the visit to the duck pond.

Rationale for the above chosen activities

Activity basket – will relate to the theme of animals by being filled with a variety of toy animals of different textures, encouraging all areas of development. Physically, the children will be encouraged to explore the basket, sit unaided and develop hand-eye co-ordination by manipulating the objects. There may be some interplay of babies using the basket. Independence may be developed and it is hoped that the babies will be satisfied. They will be encouraged to explore and choose items. The adult will supervise from a distance and change or wash items as appropriate.

Visit to duck pond – will relate to the animal theme. Children will enjoy the fresh air and perhaps point to and recognise ducks in a different environment. Language may be developed through repetition of names and sounds. This will be a social event in the company of other adults and children. Children will benefit according to their needs.

Hand painting – the children will have the opportunity to explore texture, recognise colour, enjoy a varied sensory experience and enjoy the routine of hand washing afterwards. They may listen to instructions and have fun!

Baby gym – this activity will give individual babies a chance to stretch, pull, swing arms and kick legs. They may enjoy exploring the items and listening to sounds.

Textured mats in garden – in a fresh air environment, the babies will be able to explore the different textures through touch when lying, crawling, sitting, walking or shuffling.

Plastic bottles – safely filled in a variety of shapes and sizes with different fillings, such as coloured water, pasta, coloured balls, etc. Babies can roll, push, feel and bang them and listen to the sounds they make.

Animal books and pictures – sturdy books and pictures, some on walls, relating to the animal theme and ducks visited at the pond. Babies will enjoy looking at these with their key worker and perhaps pointing to animals and making noises – repeating sounds.

Music – animal songs – listening to tapes, clapping, copying movements, recognising animal sounds and enjoying rhythm. Some quiet music to lie down and listen to.

Wooden shapes and sorters – to experience natural material and practise manipulative skills when holding shapes.

Cushion mountains – to enjoy crawling and climbing through and over a variety of shaped and textured cushions with safe fillings. Baby may copy movements of adult. Peek-a-boo behind cushions?

Water play – to take place inside and outside in baby bath or paddling pool. Closely supervised. Encourage babies to experience the calming sensation of water, to kick, splash and play with a variety of objects that may float or can be used to pour.

How the activity basket activity was planned in detail

Through playing with the treasure basket children will:

- develop their large muscles by stretching for items in the basket, sit alone, manipulate and

Red House Nursery 0–1 years group spider plan

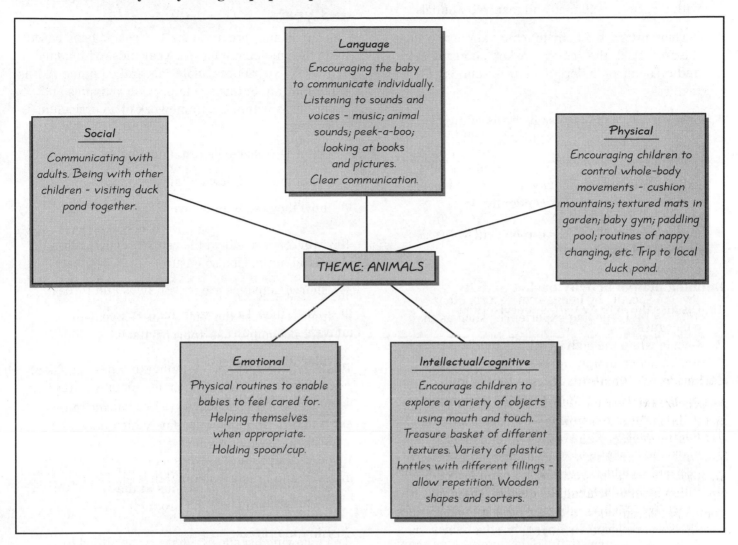

Red House Nursery 0–1 years group weekly curriculum plan

	Morning	Afternoon
Monday	Treasure basket	Visit to duck pond
Tuesday	Hand painting Baby gym	Music – animal songs
Wednesday	Textured mats in garden	Wooden shapes and sorters
Thursday	Plastic bottles – variety of fillings	Cushion mountains
Friday	Animal books and pictures	Water play

This is a plan of activities available during the week that are provided alongside a variety of other toys, equipment and experiences. Emphasis is placed upon the benefit that the babies gain through the experiences of their routines and contact with key workers.

develop hand-eye co-ordination when playing with a variety of shapes and textured animals

- develop intellectually by touching and exploring the animals in the activity basket, choosing them and recognising different shapes, sounds and textures.

- develop their language skills by listening to sounds and perhaps recognising animals.

- develop their emotional skills through feeling satisfied during the activity, perhaps releasing tension and playing independently.

- develop social skills by experiencing some interplay if appropriate.

Detailed plan of activity basket activity

1 Discuss the activity with supervisors and colleagues.
2 Decide when the activity will be available.
3 Find a safe and appropriate basket. Collect a variety of animals that fit in with the animal theme. Ensure that they are safe, and varied in texture, shape, size, colour and sound.
4 Fill the basket with animals.
5 Place the basket on the floor, giving babies a safe peaceful area to sit and explore without distractions.
6 Encourage babies to join in the activity and supervise carefully, giving them space to explore objects on their own.
7 At the end of the activity, older babies may enjoy putting objects into the basket.
8 Clear the activity away but be prepared to repeat it for other babies who may have been asleep, arrived after the activity, or who were not interested at the time.

Knowledge into action

*Re-read the **detailed plan** of the activity basket activity. Then, using the same approach, write the objectives and detailed plan for a different activity with 0–1-year-olds. You could choose either an activity from your own work setting or use one of the activities on page 337.*

A curriculum plan for children aged 1–3 years

The curriculum provision for 1–3-year-olds is based upon the curriculum for 0–1-year-olds, with added activities, experiences, materials and equipment. It is still important at this age to provide activities and experiences within the framework of a curriculum based on:

- what 1–3-year-olds can manage

- what they find fascinating

- how they relate to the world around them.

Key workers are still at the centre of curriculum provision but must also ensure:

- shared activities are only in twos and threes

- they recognise the feelings of 1–3-year-olds, offering comfort as appropriate

- they encourage children to begin to play together

- they encourage children to have a role in the domestic routine of the day, which may include clearing-away activities

- they develop practical child-centred activities and show the activity to parents at the end of the day (even if there is no end product).

The following list shows what can be added to the 0–1-year-old curriculum to make it suitable for 1–3-year-olds.

- playdough – different colours and smells (be aware of children who may be allergic to artificial food colouring).

- sand play (special play sand) – indoors and outdoors

- non-toxic chubby crayons and felt tips

- thick paint – particularly to encourage finger and hand painting or object painting

- continue to develop use of the treasure basket

- a wider variety of toys and equipment to be used to develop the senses

Spider plan of an activity basket for The Red House Nursery weekly curriculum plan

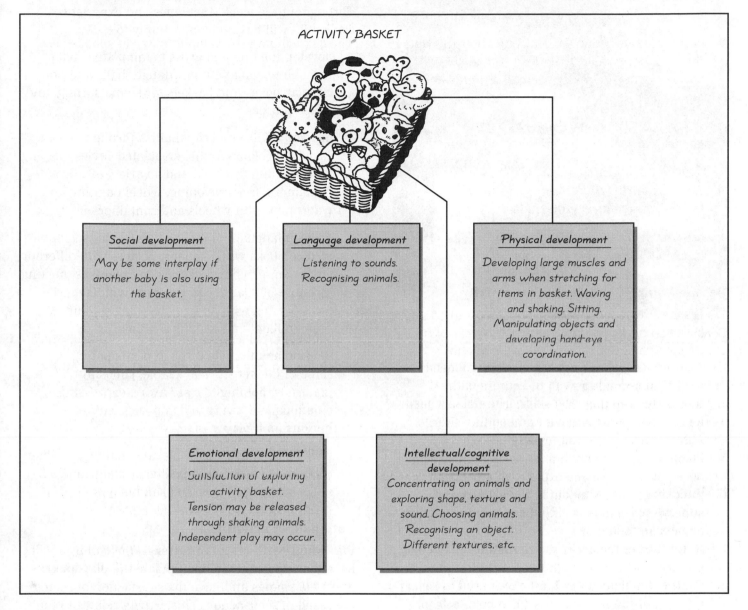

ACTIVITY BASKET

Social development

May be some interplay if another baby is also using the basket.

Language development

Listening to sounds. Recognising animals.

Physical development

Developing large muscles and arms when stretching for items in basket. Waving and shaking. Sitting. Manipulating objects and developing hand-eye co-ordination.

Emotional development

Satisfaction of exploring activity basket. Tension may be released through shaking animals. Independent play may occur.

Intellectual/cognitive development

Concentrating on animals and exploring shape, texture and sound. Choosing animals. Recognising an object. Different textures, etc.

- space – wide and free – to crawl, learn to walk, run, jump, kick, throw, etc.

- play props to develop role play such as tea sets, dolls, etc.

- construction bricks to create towers

- trucks and tricycles

- boxes and baskets to put things in

- books with pictures and simple text

- music, singing and finger-play activities

- water play – always supervised.

The **curriculum plan** is for the 1–3-year-olds at The Ark Day Nursery based on the theme of 'colours and shapes'.

The **long-term plan** of The Ark Day Nursery is to encourage the 1–3-year-olds' five areas of development through a variety of play experiences, working towards their involvement in an early years curriculum at the age of three years old. Detailed developmental records and diaries are kept to assess individual children's needs and to discuss these with colleagues and parents when planning the curriculum. For example, Sam, aged two years and

Construction bricks can be used with 0–3-year-olds

six months, has visual impairment and will need a range of textured equipment and carers with appropriate communication skills. The nursery team work closely with his parents and health visitor to adapt some of the curriculum activities when appropriate.

The **medium-term plan** of the 1–3-year-old department of The Ark Day Nursery is based on the theme of colours and shapes. Spontaneous learning through routines and individual communication with early years workers are important, whether they fit in with the theme or not.

Knowledge into action

Are there any children with special needs in your setting?

If so, how are they considered when planning activities?

The **short-term plan** of the department is based on the circle shape, although not *all* the activities will link to this. This curriculum plan is based on a five-day week.

The learning outcomes for the children

Throughout the week's activities and experiences each child will have the opportunity to:

- develop the fine and gross manipulative skills through playing with playdough, balls and hoops, circular boxes and baskets for shape sorting, and shape puzzles

- develop intellectual capabilities through using a variety of colours for finger-painted circles, playing with wet and dry sand and a variety of containers, free crayoning, wheel painting and water play with wheels and containers

- develop language skills through looking at simple picture books with captions, posters with different circles on, playing with dolls and blankets, making a picture of a large circular plate with favourite food, playing with an imaginary tea set and pretend food, and making a circular cake

- develop emotionally through participating in some of the activities available, choosing materials, helping to clear away, expressing emotions and trying to do up large circular buttons on a play mat

- develop socially by sharing cake making, making a picture of a circular plate with favourite food, some interplay, water and sand play.

Rationale of activities

Playdough with circular cutters – the children will have the opportunity to manipulate the playdough, press the shapes and have the satisfaction of seeing the result of their action. This activity relates to the circle theme and encourages the use of language – e.g. 'round', 'circular', etc.

Water play with wheels and containers – through the experience of water play, the children will be encouraged to understand what happens to the wheels when they pour water on them.

Simple picture books about wheels and shapes – children will be encouraged to be aware of the link between the printed word and speech and will enlarge and develop their concept of circles. Enjoyment of books will be encouraged.

The Ark Day Nursery – five-day curriculum plan: 1–3 years

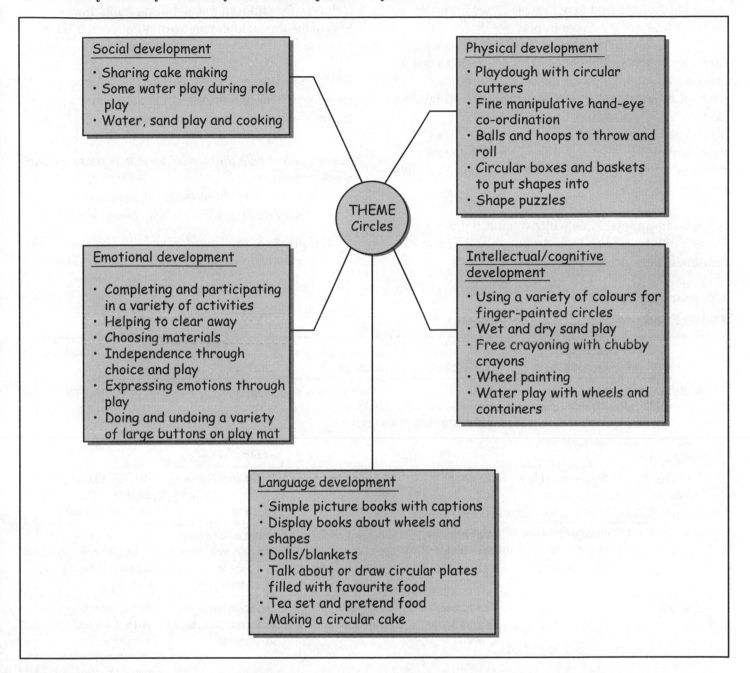

Social development
- Sharing cake making
- Some water play during role play
- Water, sand play and cooking

Physical development
- Playdough with circular cutters
- Fine manipulative hand-eye co-ordination
- Balls and hoops to throw and roll
- Circular boxes and baskets to put shapes into
- Shape puzzles

THEME Circles

Emotional development
- Completing and participating in a variety of activities
- Helping to clear away
- Choosing materials
- Independence through choice and play
- Expressing emotions through play
- Doing and undoing a variety of large buttons on play mat

Intellectual/cognitive development
- Using a variety of colours for finger-painted circles
- Wet and dry sand play
- Free crayoning with chubby crayons
- Wheel painting
- Water play with wheels and containers

Language development
- Simple picture books with captions
- Display books about wheels and shapes
- Dolls/blankets
- Talk about or draw circular plates filled with favourite food
- Tea set and pretend food
- Making a circular cake

Shape puzzles – this will develop manipulative skills, hand-eye co-ordination and also spatial awareness.

Poster with different circles – this will help children to recognise different sorts of circles – for example, wheels, boxes, etc.

Coloured finger-painted circles – this will develop creativity through using paint in an exploratory way; seeing what happens when colour is placed on circle with finger.

Balls and hoops – this will develop gross manipulative skills through throwing and rolling the balls and hoops during outside play. Children will learn to 'circle' them.

Wet and dry sand – this will enable children to experience the different properties of wet and dry sand through using different utensils.

Tea set and pretend food – this will enable children to act out feelings and experiences. They may also socialise and use language in play.

Circular boxes and baskets – this will help to teach children to shape and sort and understand the concept of matching. It will also develop manipulative skills.

Free crayoning – this will develop manipulative skills and enable children to exercise choice. It is a creative play activity.

Dolls and puppets – this will give children the opportunity to express their emotions and to play out real-life experiences with dolls and blankets.

Large buttons – this relates to the circle theme. It is a chance for children to start developing their self-help skills through playing with buttons on a large play mat.

Wheel painting – this will encourage children to consider wheels within the circle theme and will enable them to enjoy wheel painting.

Now consider how the 'circle' book was planned and made a resource:

- Collect a variety of photographs and pictures of everyday circular objects – e.g. cakes, wheels, etc.

- Cut pieces of thick card, place the pictures attractively on card, leaving a space for short text.

1–3 years group

The Ark Nursery weekly curriculum plan

	Physical	Intellectual	Language	Emotional	Social
Monday	Playdough with circular cutters	Water play with wheels and containers	Simple picture books about wheels and shapes	Help clear away playdough Choice of books Independence in water play	Some interplay during water play
Tuesday	Shape puzzles	Coloured painted circles	Discuss poster with different circles on	Independence in shape and finger painting	May discuss poster with others and share paints
Wednesday	Balls and hoops	Wet and dry sand play	Tea set and pretend food	Express emotions through role play and playing independently	Interplay may take place in all activities
Thursday	Circular boxes to sort shapes	Free crayoning using chubby crayons	Dolls and blankets	Independence in play and choice of crayons	Some interplay with dolls and blankets. Take it in turns to use crayons
Friday	Do up variety of large buttons on a play mat	Wheel painting	Cooking a circular cake	Independence and satisfaction of doing up buttons, wheel painting and making cake Helping to tidy away	Making cake in a very small group

Remember: a plan may well include *where* the activity takes place and which adults and children are involved.

- Ensure some of the pictures are textured. Sam, who is visually impaired, will benefit particularly from these, as will the other children.

- Print simple text under each picture in lower-case lettering.

- Design an attractive cover.

- Have the book ring bound.

- Share the book with the children and make sure it is accessible in the book corner.

Evaluate the processes and the children's reactions to the book, taking into account the original aim and objectives. Discuss the outcome of each objective and any changes that you might have made to the book as a result.

Think about it

The 'circles' topic was very successful with the 1–3-year-olds, and The Ark Day Nursery decided to continue the topic for a further week.

In pairs, brainstorm further activities on the circles topic, or extensions to the activities already done.

A curriculum plan for children aged 3–5 years

Here is an example of a curriculum plan for children aged three to five years at New Road Nursery School. The plan concerned is based on the theme 'Our food'.

Children aged 3–5 years should be offered a curriculum that encourages learning through play in both an indoor and an outdoor environment. For planning purposes the curriculum for this age group is often organised into the six areas of learning. You will remember that they are:

- personal, social and emotional development

- language, communication and literacy

- mathematics

- knowledge and understanding of the world

- physical development

- creative development.

Some children now enter school at the age of four, but it is still expected that they will need the same play provisions as would be found in an early years setting.

Children aged 3–5 years will need:

- a home corner with role-play equipment and dressing-up clothes

- an art area for painting and collage

- a cooking facility with appropriate materials and equipment

- a graphics area

- a construction area (large and small)

- a book corner with listening centre

- a water-play area

- a sand-play area (wet and dry sand)

- a small world play area

- a nature area to grow and observe

- an interest area in order to explore objects

- clay and other manipulative materials

- small and large outdoor apparatus with safety surfaces

- wheeled trucks, tricycles, bicycles, scooters

- a grass area

- a safe surface area.

- computers.

Remember that all key areas must encourage independence so that children can take some responsibility for themselves; that presentation of activities and the way they are set up are essential. Tidying up should also be an important part of each activity, ensuring that children are not rushed and that they know where to place items after use.

Issues regarding gender, culture and disability must always be considered carefully.

The following curriculum plan has been designed for a five-day period at New Road Nursery School.

The long-term plan has been to ensure the six areas of learning are met through the nursery's theme of 'ourselves'. The learning experiences have been discussed in detail to see how the area of learning will be developed. For example, the children's mathematical understanding will be developed through:

- stories
- songs
- rhymes
- board games
- small and large construction
- exploring a range of materials
- outdoor play
- cooking
- shopping
- imaginative play
- 2- and 3-D creative work
- observing number and pattern in the environment

The range of experiences will then be reviewed to ensure the children progress towards their learning goals.

For example, children use mathematical language such as 'bigger than' and 'more than' to describe size and quantity. They compare, sort, match and sequence when using everyday objects, etc.

Resources will be checked – for example, construction equipment, paper of different sizes, sand moulds, cooking equipment, etc.

Medium-term plans have been made to focus on the area of learning – 'people in our nursery'. For example, the mathematical development will focus on 'bigger than', 'smaller than' to describe size, encouraging the children to match and sort heights of people around them.

- The language to be used will be considered.
- The grouping of children appropriately for different activities will be planned.
- The role of the adults will be clarified for each activity.

- Observations will be used to plan and check children's learning.
- Additional learning experiences can be planned.

The **short-term plan** is based on the theme 'our food', relating to the project 'ourselves'. All activities will be well planned and all early years workers will have a clear understanding of the learning potential of each activity.

The curriculum plan opposite covers all the early learning goals including a variety of group size activities to be done indoors or outdoors, including an outing to the local shop.

Think about it

Re-read the weekly curriculum plan based on the theme 'our food'. What factors would the early years workers need to consider to ensure the activities were fully multicultural? Make a note of those factors.

The diagram on page 346 shows a detailed plan of the spaghetti painting to be carried out as a creative activity on Thursday. The aim of the spaghetti painting exercise is to experience a tactile creative activity through spaghetti painting.

The objectives are that children will:

- develop their manipulative skills by squeezing, manipulating, feeling and throwing the spaghetti
- understand the difference between cooked and uncooked spaghetti
- find out about spaghetti's country of origin, and listen to Italian music during the activity
- make letters from spaghetti
- use tactile language, name the pasta and discuss the environmental sign on the label
- learn opposites – wet/dry, fat/thin, short/long, heavy/light and more/less

New Road Nursery School

3–5-year-old group weekly curriculum plan

	Monday	Tuesday	Wednesday	Thursday	Friday
			Weekly curriculum plan based on the theme 'our food'		
Creative	Drawings of vegetables (use crayons)	Make vegetable dyes and dye fabrics Bottle xylophone	Five Currant Buns song	Spaghetti painting	Food pictures collage from magazines
Personal, social and emotional	Bakery in home corner	Bakery Discuss Shrove Tuesday	Bakery Discuss Ramadan	Bakery Share trip to Waitrose	Share food (jam tarts)
Maths	Weigh different foods	Thread pasta	Favourite food graph	Discuss and prepare shopping list	weights and measures in cooking activity
Physical	A treasure hunt for vegetables using pictures	Soapflakes and water Playdough	Bicycles and trucks; shopping trips; large empty food containers	Walk to local shops	Make jam tarts
Knowledge and understanding of the world	Make milkshake IT programme 'Food Mixer'	Cook pancakes It programmes Teddy Bears' Picnic	Observe teabags/ coffee with magnifying glass	Observe change of state of cooked/ uncooked pasta	Cook jam tarts
Language, communication and literacy	The Very Hungry caterpillar Shopsigns	Winnie the Pooh (rabbit hole)	Giant jam sandwich	Sam's shopping list	Food rhymes

- weigh the spaghetti
- make colour choices
- observe patterns made with spaghetti
- listen to sounds made by spaghetti on paper
- take care when throwing spaghetti on paper
- share spaghetti
- take turns
- help to clean up after activity.

Detailed plan of activity

- Discuss plan with supervisor.
- Choose area to carry out activity.

- Prepare table and floor.
- Collect ingredients – cooked and uncooked spaghetti, paint.
- Have bowl of water nearby.
- Prepare protective clothing for children.
- Discuss activity with children.
- Give choice of colours.
- Demonstrate and label activity as it progresses.
- Name each painting.
- Encourage children to clear away.

New Road Nursery School spider plan of spaghetti painting activity

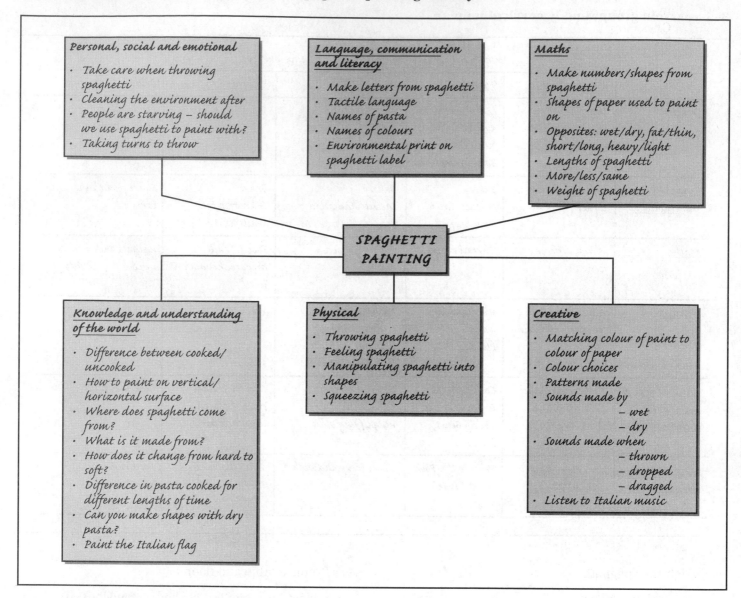

Personal, social and emotional
- Take care when throwing spaghetti
- Cleaning the environment after
- People are starving – should we use spaghetti to paint with?
- Taking turns to throw

Language, communication and literacy
- Make letters from spaghetti
- Tactile language
- Names of pasta
- Names of colours
- Environmental print on spaghetti label

Maths
- Make numbers/shapes from spaghetti
- Shapes of paper used to paint on
- Opposites: wet/dry, fat/thin, short/long, heavy/light
- Lengths of spaghetti
- More/less/same
- Weight of spaghetti

SPAGHETTI PAINTING

Knowledge and understanding of the world
- Difference between cooked/uncooked
- How to paint on vertical/horizontal surface
- Where does spaghetti come from?
- What is it made from?
- How does it change from hard to soft?
- Difference in pasta cooked for different lengths of time
- Can you make shapes with dry pasta?
- Paint the Italian flag

Physical
- Throwing spaghetti
- Feeling spaghetti
- Manipulating spaghetti into shapes
- Squeezing spaghetti

Creative
- Matching colour of paint to colour of paper
- Colour choices
- Patterns made
- Sounds made by
  - wet
  - dry
- Sounds made when
  - thrown
  - dropped
  - dragged
- Listen to Italian music

Knowledge into action

In a group, consider the curriculum plan for thee- to four-year-olds that you have just studied. How could you adapt it to focus on creative development? Carefully read the requirements of the early learning goals with reference to creative development. You may decide to make the plan more detailed with relation to this area of development, the involvement of the children and the involvement of the adults.

A curriculum plan for children aged 5–8 years

The curriculum for children who are just starting school should have an integrated approach, linking subjects together through projects and themes. Children at this stage work towards Key Stage 1 of the National Curriculum. It is often the trained early years workers in a school setting who are able to understand the needs of such young children. As more four-year-olds are being offered places in schools it is the early years workers who are an important link with the early years curriculum and its progression towards the National Curriculum. Although the National Curriculum has legal requirements it is still important for children to be observed and for their individual needs to be met in the planning of any themes or projects. The National Curriculum is known as a *prescriptive* curriculum that must be followed by each child.

Knowledge into action

Evaluate the spaghetti painting activity: take into account the objectives; discuss the outcomes and how a future activity would be planned as a result.

Consider the three plans on pages 348–350 for The Chiltern School, a small primary school. The plans are for a class of five- to six-year-olds.

The 'brainstorm' on page 348 is a result of a group of teachers meeting to discuss 'The Weather', a topic that the school will cover over one term. Plan 2 on page 349 is a plan of the different activities that will meet the key subjects. Plan 3 on page 350 is an example of two weeks' topic planning.

Reading 'Mrs Mopple's Washing Line'

The aim of the activity To read a story relating to the 'weather' to a class of 5–6-year-old children.

The objectives of the story reading activity are that children will:

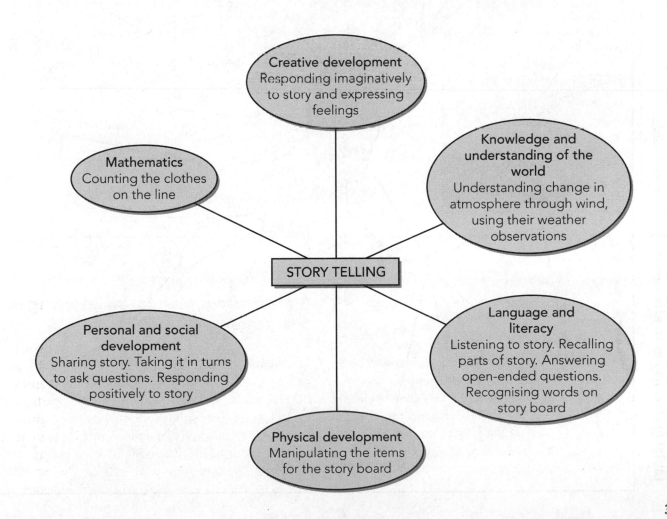

Creative development
Responding imaginatively to story and expressing feelings

Knowledge and understanding of the world
Understanding change in atmosphere through wind, using their weather observations

Mathematics
Counting the clothes on the line

STORY TELLING

Personal and social development
Sharing story. Taking it in turns to ask questions. Responding positively to story

Language and literacy
Listening to story. Recalling parts of story. Answering open-ended questions. Recognising words on story board

Physical development
Manipulating the items for the story board

Stage one
Initial brainstorm of weather project (all ideas listed)

A mind map with **THE WEATHER** at the centre, branching into the following categories and sub-topics:

- **snow** — icicles; winter; blizzards; frozen; warmth; frost; cold — hats, scarves, gloves; clothing; skating; footprints; feelings; sleet; snowflakes; snowmen
- **ice** — freezing melting; ice lollies
- **sun** — holidays; outside; summer; winter; shadows; sundial; warmth
- **rain** — thunder and lightning; rainbows; splashing; other water; noise; hail; water — for life; puddles; reflections; clothing — umbrellas; wellingtons; waterproof; windsocks; streamers; drying; washing (clothes); sky; clouds
- **wind** — stormy; direction; speed; breeze — sailing; kites; parachutes; flying; bubbles — how we blow; seeds in the wind; balloons; windmills; visibility; mist
- **fog** — visibility; mist
- **words** — hot; cold etc.; slippery etc.
- **seasons** — effect of; length of days; changing; plants; flowers; trees; different weather; feel of ground different weather
- **shelter from**
- **feelings**
- **keeping warm**
- **animals** — birds; insects; young; food for; how they keep warm; hot and cold lands; hibernation; poems; stories; dancing
- **work** — measuring weather; weatherman; why do we need weather?; activities; weather games; recording; weather vanes; weather houses; weather in other lands

Plan two

Ideas under curriculum headings

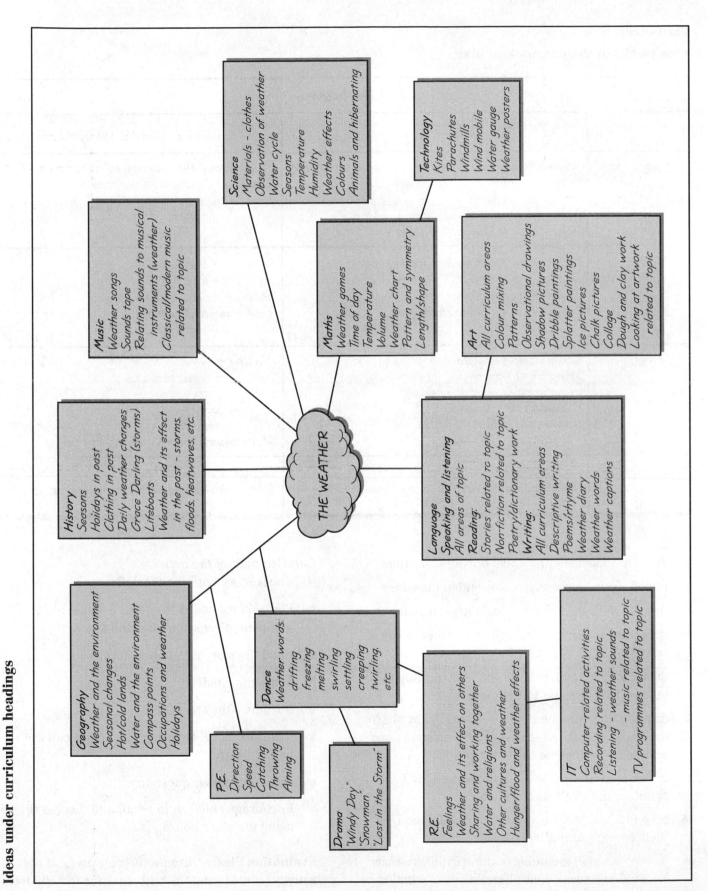

Science
Materials – clothes
Observation of weather
Water cycle
Seasons
Temperature
Humidity
Weather effects
Colours
Animals and hibernating

Technology
Kites
Parachutes
Windmills
Wind mobile
Water gauge
Weather posters

Music
Weather songs
Sounds tape
Relating sounds to musical
instruments (weather)
Classical/modern music
related to topic

Maths
Weather games
Time of day
Temperature
Volume
Weather chart
Pattern and symmetry
Length/shape

Art
All curriculum areas
Colour mixing
Patterns
Observational drawings
Shadow pictures
Dribble paintings
Splatter paintings
Ice pictures
Chalk pictures
Collage
Dough and clay work
Looking at artwork
related to topic

History
Seasons
Holidays in past
Clothing in past
Daily weather changes
Grace Darling (storms)
Lifeboats
Weather and its effect
in the past – storms,
floods, heatwaves, etc.

THE WEATHER

Language
Speaking and listening
All areas of topic
Reading:
Stories related to topic
Non-fiction related to topic
Poetry/dictionary work
Writing:
All curriculum areas
Descriptive writing
Poems/rhyme
Weather diary
Weather words
Weather captions

Geography
Weather and the environment
Seasonal changes
Hot/cold lands
Water and the environment
Compass points
Occupations and weather
Holidays

Dance
Weather words:
drifting
freezing
melting
swirling
settling
creeping
twirling,
etc.

P.E.
Direction
Speed
Catching
Throwing
Aiming

Drama
"Windy Day",
"Snowman
"Lost in the Storm"

R.E.
Feelings
Weather and its effect on others
Sharing and working together
Water and religions
Other cultures and weather
Hunger/flood and weather effects

IT
Computer-related activities
Recording related to topic
Listening – weather sounds
– music related to topic
TV programmes related to topic

Plan three

Two weeks of the curriculum plan

	Week 1 (Wind)	Week 2 (Wind & Windpower)
The Weather		
Language	Writing story about how it feels on a windy day Windy — words Weather — words Poem about the wind 'Mrs Mopple's Washing Line'	Story about the journey of a 'runaway kite' 'Bubbles' descriptive writing
Maths	Number — Washing line items, spots Shapes — for kites Pairs — socks, gloves, etc Days of week & weather	Number — bubbles — kites Shape — sails on boats Time — drying items sailing boats
Science	Observation of weather — Wind direction — using — ribbon on stick & discussion re wind & how we know about it	Making — wind — what moves easier — tissue card foil, etc Discussion about wind power — & uses
Technology	Design & make a fan Make a kite & pattern using shapes	Design & make sail boats Different shapes, sizes, number of sails, etc

- develop their listening skills during story time
- benefit from answering open-ended questions
- develop their memory by recalling parts of the story
- recognise the words from the story on the story board
- develop their manipulative skills by putting the textured pictures on to the story board
- develop their personal and social skills by sharing the story, taking it in turns to ask questions and respond positively to the session
- develop an understanding of numbers by counting the clothes on the line
- respond imaginatively to the story and express their feelings about its content
- develop an understanding of the scientific reasons for wind and recall their observations of windy days.

Detailed plan of the activity

- Check story with the teacher.
- Plan a story board to use as a visual aid to stimulate discussion after the story.
- Read the story carefully beforehand.
- Settle the children.
- Introduce the story.
- Read the story, ensuring each child can see the pages clearly.
- Ask open-ended questions.
- Encourage children to recall and discuss the story using the story board.

Evaluation Clearly discuss the objectives of the activity, considering the outcomes for the children.

Also discuss whether you would alter the activity if it were repeated. Use research in the form of references and bibliography to give depth to the evaluation.

Detailed plan of a resource relating to the storytelling of 'Mrs Mopple's Washing Line'
The aim of the story board is to encourage the children to discuss the story and its contents.

The objectives of the story board are that children will:

- develop an understanding of 'wind'
- recall the story through the activity
- take it in turns to use the board
- recognise the words and pictures used in the story
- listen to each other's comments and ideas
- develop language skills by talking about the objects on the board.

Detailed plan of constructing the story board
- Cut two pieces of MDF approximately 50 cm × 80 cm. Cover with felt or specialist fabric. Hinge the two pieces at the top.
- Make figures relating to the story 'Mrs Mopple's Washing Line'. Add the hooked side of Velcro on the back.
- Clearly print key words on flash cards. Add Velcro.
- Put figures and words in an attractive box.
- Add to box for other stories and projects.

Evaluate the construction of the story board and what the children gained from using it.

Knowledge into action

Re-read the aims, plans and objectives of the storytelling of 'Mrs Mopple's Washing Line'. Using the same approach, construct a plan for a story on the topic of 'ourselves'. You could do this with an age group of your choice.

Routines

Routines are a very important part of a child's day. They give children the security to benefit from the experiences of the day. Routines will vary according to the setting, but will usually revolve around a snack, meal, or sleep.

Changes in routines are a common occurrence and must be dealt with sensitively to enable a child to remain secure. If possible, it is always best to discuss with the children what the change in routine might be, such as a different time for lunch or a different approved person to collect them from nursery. Always encourage children to express their concerns about any impending changes. Unexpected changes in routine, such as an emergency alarm, can be worrying for a child and it is best that children are kept calm and informed about what is happening. If a child has a comforter try to allow him or her to use it at such times. Carefully consider the key principles outlined below.

Some key principles for all routines

Early years workers need a knowledge of:

- ages and stage of development
- social, emotional, physical and cognitive development including language
- safe and hygienic practice
- parental involvement, adhering to parents' wishes within the boundaries of safety and overall well-being of the child
- appropriate play materials including natural materials
- the fundamental experiences a baby and a young child will need – e.g. sound, touch, smell, taste, as well as visual stimulation
- the absolute importance of adult interaction and the need for sensitivity to the child's cues to express his or her needs
- the absolute importance of consistency of adults
- the importance of routine in a child's life
- (and sensitive awareness to) cultural, ethnic and religious needs

- the importance of quiet times for babies and young children

- the value of story telling and reading stories to children

- the child as an individual with mood changes according to temperament and time of day

- the importance of flexibility within a routine.

Routine for a group of children aged 3–5 years in a day care setting

When planning the routine it is important to consider:

- the children's individual needs and care requirements at various times of the day

- provision for the children to have some individual attention throughout the day

- the importance of meeting the children's social and emotional needs

- the importance of parental involvement to respect their wishes.

The children in the setting attend at varying times between 8.00 am and 6.00 pm. Some of the children are preparing for school. Planned activities take place between 9.00 am and 3.00 pm and the rest of the day has a more home-based atmosphere.

The aim of the routine is to provide a stimulating and stable routine for a group of 3–5-year-olds in a day care setting.

The objectives of the routine are that children will:

- feel secure in the routine

- develop through interaction with other children and adults

- enjoy sensory experiences during the routines

- be reassured when changes occur

- feel safe during the routine.

Routine plan	
8.00 am	Welcome to the nursery – free play
8.45 am	Group time – introduction to activities
9.00 am	A variety of planned activities
10.00 am	Group time – story or discussion
10.15 am	Drink and snack in key-worker groups
10.30 am	Outside play
11.30 am	Story or song time
12.00 noon	Lunch
12.30 pm onwards	Children may sleep if parents require, play in garden or with quiet activities
1.30 pm	New arrivals – free play
2.00 pm	Group time – introduction to activities, etc. as in morning session
4.00 pm	After tea, children play in the garden, soft play area or the nursery until collection at 6.00 pm

(Children will go to the lavatory and wash hands according to their needs.)

Evaluating

When evaluating a routine consider the original objectives and discuss the outcomes. Show an understanding of the need to evaluate and update routines and the importance of team work.

Remember that a home setting will also have a pattern or routine. Meal and sleep times are often at similar times, although different activities – such as Tumble Tots and swimming – may occur on different days.

Check your knowledge

- What is baseline assessment?

- What are the main factors that should be considered when planning for babies?

- What factors should be considered when planning a routine for children aged three to five years?

- List the six early learning goals.

- What is the foundation stage?

- Briefly explain why observation is an important part of the planning cycle.

- What is thematic learning?

- Name the national curriculum subjects that children are required to study for Key Stage 1.

- Why is it important to have an aim for any planned activity or experience?

- What is the role of play in children's learning?

- Briefly describe:

  - short-term curriculum planning

  - medium-term curriculum planning

  - long-term curriculum planning.

- Give an example of how a routine activity can play a part in a curriculum plan.

- How would you consider the health and safety of children and adults when planning a water-based activity inside a setting?

- Why are sensory experiences an important part of planning an activity for 0–3-year-olds?

- Briefly describe how the planning for a group of five- to six-year-olds in a school class will vary from the planning for five- to six-year-olds who attend a holiday club.

- What is the rationale of an activity plan?

- What are the main factors that should be considered when planning a curriculum for babies?

- What factors should be considered when planning a routine for children aged three to five years?

- Why should there be an emphasis on the terms *anti-bias* and *world-view* in curriculum planning?

- Why should you consider your own learning when planning a curriculum?

- What is an individual learning programme?

- List six resources that could be used to support a detailed activity plan that is an imaginative play area set up as a hairdressing salon.

Resources

Further reading

Issues series *Education*, Cambridge, Independence Publishers

Nursery World magazine/website

National curriculum publications – QCA/DFEE

QCA/DFEE website

Tassoni, Penny *Planning Play in the Early Years*, Heinemann, 2000

Work with babies 0 to 1 year

CHAPTER 15
Work with babies 0 to 1 year

As an early years worker, you will be caring for babies aged less than a year, and parents will need to feel confident about leaving their baby in your care. This chapter covers the development and care of babies including:

- *normal development from conception to one year*
- *promoting development*
- *care of a baby*
- *requirements of young babies in group care*

Normal development from conception to one year

Conception

A woman's menstrual cycle lasts approximately 28 days, although this can vary considerably. Ovulation (when the egg or *ovum* is released from the ovary) occurs 14 days before the next period is due. Conception occurs when a male sperm fuses with the ovum in the fallopian tube of a woman's body. This is the beginning of the complex and incredible development which will end in the birth of a baby.

Once the egg has been fertilised and has become implanted in the walls of the uterus, the cells begin to divide continually and will form the placenta, membranes, umbilical cord and the embryo.

- The growing baby is called an embryo for the first eight weeks.

- The placenta is attached to the mother's uterus and allows food, oxygen and antibodies (which protect the growing baby from some diseases) to pass from mother to baby through the umbilical cord. It allows waste products to pass from baby to mother. It can also prevent some harmful substances and diseases from passing through.

- There are two membranes that form a sac around the baby and secrete amniotic fluid which protects the growing baby.

- The umbilical cord attaches the growing baby to the placenta.

Development of the embryo

Pregnancy is always measured from the first day of the woman's last period, which is about two weeks before conception. The embryo develops very quickly.

- Week 4 (two weeks after conception): by the time the mother is missing her first period, the embryo has a head and a tail and the beginnings of arms and legs.

- Week 6: at 7 mm long, the embryo's heart starts to beat, the spinal cord, intestines, ears, eyes and nose are forming.

- Week 8: the major organs of the body have formed and facial features are developing. The tail is disappearing, the limbs and hands are developing well, but the feet still look rather like paddles.

Foetal development

After eight weeks the embryo is called a foetus:

- Week 10 (eight weeks after conception): the foetus is about 40 mm long and has definite human

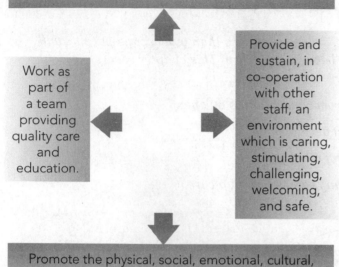

Acknowledge and respect the part played by parents and carers in the child's learning both in the past and as a continuing process by forming a partnership with them, and encourage other active involvement and participation.

Work as part of a team providing quality care and education.

Provide and sustain, in co-operation with other staff, an environment which is caring, stimulating, challenging, welcoming, and safe.

Promote the physical, social, emotional, cultural, spiritual, moral and cognitive development of each individual child and meet his or her needs within the ethos of the establishment.

Growth of the embryo

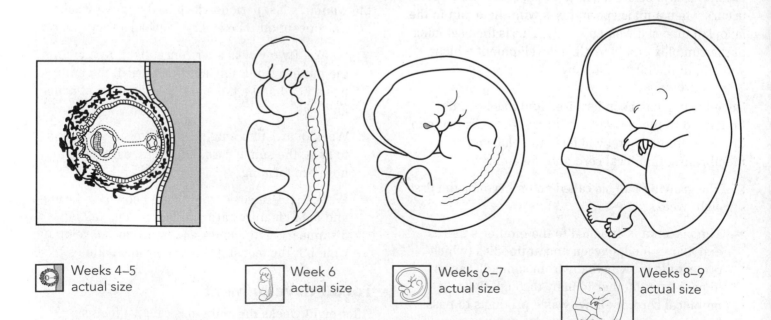

Weeks 4–5 actual size

Week 6 actual size

Weeks 6–7 actual size

Weeks 8–9 actual size

The growing baby

characteristics. The foetal stage is one of growth and perfection of detail. Muscles are beginning to be exercised.

- Week 12: the foetus is now kicking and moving; it frowns, opens its mouth and drinks the amniotic fluid. The milk teeth are forming in the jaw.

- Week 16: arms are now long enough for the hands to grasp each other and vernix is formed. This is a white sticky substance which protects the foetus, and helps maintain an even temperature.

- Week 20: the foetus responds to sound, its mother's voice and light. It has nails and its own fingerprints. The sex of the baby can be seen on an ultrasound scan.

- Week 24: the foetus is now said to be *viable*. This means that the baby could survive if born now, although it would need to spend a long time in hospital. It could breathe but couldn't continue to do this without help.

- Week 28: the lungs have matured. The baby may get hiccups!

- Weeks 28–40: the foetus is now growing, the vernix gradually disappears and fat is laid down under the skin. After week 36, the baby will put on weight by about 28 g a day, and will usually turn upside down, ready to be born.

Factors affecting normal foetal development

There are many things which can affect the normal development of the growing baby during pregnancy and birth. The times in which the baby is most vulnerable are during the first 12 weeks of pregnancy, when all of the organs are being formed, and during labour.

Antenatal care

Before antenatal care first became organised, the death rate among women and their babies was high. Therefore antenatal care aimed to:

- reduce maternal and infant deaths

- increase the health of pregnant women and of their babies

- prepare the mother for having a baby.

Maternal deaths are now very rare in the developed world, thanks to the improved care of pregnant women, and the number of infant deaths has

Screening tests done at every antenatal visit

Test	Reason for test
Blood pressure	To exclude pre-eclampsia, a condition where there is raised blood pressure, protein in the urine and swelling in the ankles in late pregnancy. It can cause poor growth in the baby and can be life threatening to mother and baby if not treated.
Urine test	To detect: ■ protein which could indicate pre-eclampsia (see above) and urine infections which could cause premature labour ■ sugar which could indicate diabetes.
Weight	Too much weight gain could indicate swelling and pre-eclampsia; weight loss may mean the baby is not getting enough nutrients.
Palpation	The midwife or doctor will feel the woman's abdomen to ensure that the baby is growing at the right rate and that the baby is in the right position.
Listen to the foetal heart rate	This can be heard from about 12 weeks using an electronic instrument. A strong regular beat means that the baby is healthy.

dropped too. In order to detect potential problems, the pregnant woman is screened throughout her pregnancy and health education is offered.

As soon as a woman thinks she is pregnant, she goes to see her GP and is 'booked in'. From then on she will be seen regularly by her midwife, with visits also to the GP and/or the obstetrician at the hospital.

Various tests are done regularly, but there are also some which are done only once or twice throughout the pregnancy, for example the ultrasound scan.

Ultrasound scan

Most women have at least one scan in their pregnancy, and it is wonderful for the parents to be able to see their baby on the screen for the first time. This test is done for the following reasons:

- to check that the baby is growing and developing normally
- to detect certain abnormalities

- to show the position of the baby and of the placenta (if this is low, the woman may need a Caesarean section)
- to detect multiple pregnancy e.g. twins, triplets
- to find out when the baby is due (if the woman is unsure of the date of her last period).

Further antenatal tests

A number of other antenatal tests are also carried out during pregnancy (see table below).

Labour and birth

The baby is usually born 38 to 40 weeks after the mother's last period. There are four different ways in which a woman may deliver her baby; the most common, and the safest, is the 'normal delivery' but sometimes a woman will need medical intervention (see page 359).

The mother will know when she is going into labour because one or more of the following will happen:

Antenatal tests

Test	Reason for test
Blood test to detect:	
■ anaemia	■ can cause the mother to feel tired and breathless
■ some sexually transmitted diseases	■ to prevent complications to the baby
■ rubella	■ rubella in the first 12 weeks of pregnancy can cause congenital abnormalities and deafness
■ hepatitis B	■ this may infect the baby
Chorionic villus sampling (CVS) can be done at 11 weeks by passing a tube into the uterus to remove some of the tissue from around the baby. There is a risk of miscarriage.	To detect Down's syndrome and other genetic abnormalities (but not spina bifida).
Amniocentesis (done at 16 weeks), similar to CVS but with less chance of miscarriage, it involves inserting a needle into the mother's abdomen to withdraw some of the amniotic fluid	To detect Down's syndrome and other genetic abnormalities, including spina bifida.
Alpha-foetoprotein, 'double', or 'triple' blood test at 15 to 20 weeks (depending on the hospital).	To detect a risk of spina bifida or Down's syndrome.

ISSUES   Selecting the sex of your child

There have been so many medical advances in recent years, that it is now possible for doctors to help couples have a child of a particular sex. At present this happens only if a serious inherited medical condition might be passed on to a child of one sex.

There is an ongoing debate about whether doctors should be allowed to help all couples have a child of a particular sex. Look at the following views.

■ If couples are able to choose the sex of their child, they will be more likely to love it.

■ In some cultures, boys are more desired than girls and this will mean that more boys will be born.

■ Creating a child of a particular sex is only giving nature a helping hand.

■ Being able to choose the sex of a child is the beginning of a slippery slope – afterwards, parents will want to start choosing the colour of the eyes, etc.

■ If couples already have three boys, for example, it is natural to want to try for a girl.

In pairs, consider what you think about this issue.

■ a 'show', which is a blood-stained vaginal discharge of mucus

■ she will start to have regular contractions. The muscles of the uterus push the baby downwards with each contraction. This opens up (dilates) the cervix

■ rupture of the membranes (often called 'the waters breaking'). The membranes break and the amniotic fluid leaks out.

The stages of labour

There are three stages of labour.

■ **Stage 1**: this starts at the beginning of regular contractions and finishes when the cervix is fully dilated.

■ **Stage 2**: this is the stage when the mother has to push the baby out during her contractions. This can take up to an hour.

■ **Stage 3**: the delivery of the placenta and membranes (sometimes called 'the afterbirth').

Some women are unable to have a normal delivery and need to have help in delivering the baby. There are three ways in which this might happen:

■ *forceps delivery* – large blunt tongs are placed around the baby's head and during contractions the doctor will pull on the forceps while the mother is pushing. This usually involves an episiotomy and later stitches (the vagina is cut to make room for the forceps).

■ *vacuum extraction* – a large cup is placed on the baby's head which is held in place by a vacuum. This is then used in the same way as the forceps. It can cause extensive bruising on the head, but it clears up very quickly.

■ *Caesarean section* – this is an operation which is done either under general anaesthetic or epidural (where the mother is awake but a local anaesthetic in the spine removes the pain). The surgeon removes the baby through a cut made in the mother's abdomen. This is sometimes done as an emergency, if there are problems occurring with the mother or baby. It can, however, be a planned operation and might be done if the baby is in the wrong position, for medical reasons, or if the woman has had a previous Caesarean section.

Apgar score

This is an assessment made by the midwife 1, 5 and 10 minutes after birth. The table below shows what is assessed and the scores given.

The scores are added together and if the total is below 7 at 1 minute; below 8 at 5 minutes or below 9 at 10 minutes, then the baby may need special care.

The scoring system is slightly different for dark-skinned babies as their skin can look grey at birth. Instead of checking the colour of the skin, the midwife checks the mucous membranes: inside the mouth and under the eyes.

This score will be recorded in the baby's Personal Child Health Record (see page 216). The midwife will check over the baby in the first hour after birth and measure the baby's weight, height and head circumference.

Knowledge into action

Ask three mothers about their labours and find out:

How long was the labour?

Did they have anything for pain relief?

Did they have a normal delivery?

How much did the baby weigh?

Low birth weight babies

The main reasons for a baby to be classified as having a low birth weight (below 2.5 kg at birth) are as follows:

- **Prematurity.** When the baby is born between 24 and 37 weeks of the pregnancy. There is obviously a big difference between a pre-term baby of 24 weeks and one of 36 weeks. Babies born very prematurely may not be able to open their eyes, they will be thin and the skin will be smooth, shiny and covered in vernix (a white sticky substance which protects the foetus in the uterus). They may not be able to breathe on their own and will therefore need to be in the Special Care Baby Unit in an incubator (to help them maintain heat) and be on a ventilator (to help them breathe). They may also not be able to suck. These babies may need to be in hospital for some time, but do catch up with their peers during the first year.

- **Small for dates.** The baby is smaller and lighter than would normally be expected at birth. These babies look wrinkled and anxious.

The causes of prematurity and small-for-date babies are often not known but can be due to the mother smoking, taking drugs or drinking in pregnancy; a high blood pressure; a poor diet or maternal illness (such as diabetes) or infection (such as a urinary infection).

Some babies are both premature and small-for-dates. Low birth weight babies are more prone to infections, feeding difficulties and respiratory problems.

Assessed	Score of 0	Score of 1	Score of 2
Heart rate	absent	below 100 beats/minute	above 100 beats/minute
Respiration	absent	irregular, slow, weak	lusty cry
Muscle tone	limp	poor, some movement	strong movement
Reflex irritability (stimulation of the toe)	no response	slight withdrawal	vigorous withdrawal
Colour	blue, pale	pink body, blue hands and feet	completely pink

Apgar scores

Multiple births

Multiple pregnancies are becoming more common due to some fertility treatments but twins are the most common of the multiple births. There are two types of twins:

- **Identical.** This happens when the egg splits completely into two after being fertilised by the sperm to become two separate babies. They will share the same placenta and will be the same sex.

- **Non-identical.** This occurs when the mother produces two eggs and they are fertilised by different sperms. There will be two placentas and the babies may be of different sexes.

Multiple births have a higher risk of being premature; the babies may be delivered by Caesarean section. Some mothers manage to totally breastfeed twins, while others mix breast and bottle feeding, and others chose to bottle feed. Feeding and care routines are obviously much more time consuming and tiring for the parents and there are many national – for example, Twins and Multiple Births Association – and local twins associations that support parents of multiple births.

The developing baby

All babies are unique individuals and will develop at a slightly different rate from each other. During their developmental checks (see page 217), the health visitor will ensure that babies are growing and developing at the right rate.

All newborn babies have some primitive reflexes which should gradually disappear. These are always checked for after birth and during the developmental checks by the paediatrician or GP:

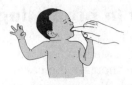

- **sucking**: anything that is put in the mouth is sucked

- **rooting**: the baby turns his head to search for food if the cheek is stroked

- **startle**: throws arms outwards and then back if startled by a sudden noise

- **grasping**: anything placed in the hand will be grasped tightly. This is such a strong reflex that the babies can support their own weight.

- **placing**: when the top of babies' feet touch the underneath of a table, they will lift their feet and place them on top of the table

- **walking**: when held so that their feet touch the ground, babies will make walking movements.

- **Moro**: when babies' heads are dropped very slightly and suddenly (while still being supported), they will fling their arms out with hands open before bringing them back over their body.

The chart on pages 362–365 shows the average age when each baby will reach that stage of development, although this will vary considerably with each child.

Knowledge into action

You're working as a nanny for twins, Duncan and Jessie, and it will soon be their first Christmas. Their mum, Anna, has asked you to make a list of suitable toys that they could be given. Jessie is crawling and Duncan is just walking. She has a total budget of £50.

Look through some catalogues and suggest appropriate toys and state why they are suitable.

The role of the adult in promoting development

Babies are totally dependent on their prime carers to provide all of their needs, including appropriate stimulation. They need plenty of adult attention provided by their prime carers. In order to promote **physical development**, babies need to be given freedom of movement, appropriate support, games and encouragement. Babies will progress at their own pace, so should not be pushed if behind in one area – for example, babies can learn to walk at any time between 8 months and 2 years, and do not need 'baby walkers' to encourage walking.

Language development can be stimulated by talking, having 'conversations', by singing and ensuring eye contact is maintained throughout all communication.

Cognitive development can be encouraged by providing appropriate toys, games and activities for the development stage. In order to promote **emotional and social development**, all babies need plenty of love, cuddles, and to feel secure.

It is important to respect the differing ways in which families choose to care for their children. It may often be very different from your own experiences.

Age	Stage of development	Role of adult	Toys and activities	Equipment needed and safety considerations
Newborn	The primitive reflexes should be present.	■ the newborn is totally dependent on the adult for all needs, which are to be: fed, kept warm and clean ■ the carer needs to talk to the baby while giving eye contact ■ plenty of physical contact to encourage bonding between baby and prime carers.	■ newborn babies will always turn towards the light, so bright and shiny objects hung around the cot will catch their attention. ■ musical mobiles.	Equipment: ■ cradle ■ pram ■ sheets and blankets ■ nappy-changing equipment (see pages 379–380) ■ bathing equipment (see pages 377–379) ■ feeding and sterilising equipment (if not breastfeeding) ■ car seat ■ baby monitor. **Safety:** ■ proper sterilisation of bottles required ■ bottles shouldn't be heated in the microwave ■ general safety measures such as smoke and carbon monoxide detectors ■ always support the baby's head to prevent damage to the neck muscles.

Age	Stage of development	Role of adult	Toys and activities	Equipment needed and safety considerations
6 weeks	■ smiles and coos ■ quietens when picked up ■ recognises the smell of mother's milk ■ follows faces at close range ■ watches mother's face when being fed.	■ to continue to provide milk, warmth and cleanliness ■ continue to talk and sing ■ baby needs plenty of physical contact but also likes to look around ■ massage body and limbs.	■ mobiles with plenty of contrasting colour, such as black and white, or with bright and shiny colours ■ babies of this age love looking at faces and will stare for ages at paper plates with faces drawn on them! ■ music: singing, wind chimes, musical cot toys.	Equipment: ■ pushchair ■ supportive sling could be used instead of a pushchair ■ bouncy chairs – *never* to be left on raised surfaces.
3 months	■ when lying on their front, babies will push up with their arms so that they raise their chest off the surface – head may bob up and down ■ can hold a rattle for a few moments ■ watch and play with their hands and fingers beginning to realise that their hands belong to them, and that they have some control, although hand-eye co-ordination is still lacking) ■ excited by sounds of food preparation (so beginning to recognise routines) ■ vocalises when spoken to – can have a baby 'conversation'.	■ routines provide security, especially at bedtime ■ have conversations with the baby – talk to him, wait while he babbles and when he stops, continue talking ■ experiment with different sounds and music ■ allow the baby to kick with the nappy off and play bicycling games with their legs ■ hold a soft ball so that they can kick it ■ play finger and hand games such as 'round and round the garden' ■ allow babies to lie on their front in order to develop the back and neck muscles needed for crawling	■ different rattles and squeaky toys to hold ■ baby gym and pram toys which will encourage the baby to reach and touch them. This will help the development of hand-eye co-ordination ■ bath toys to kick in the bath to develop leg muscles ■ activity blanket with different textures to feel ■ blowing bubbles for the baby to watch, but not near his face.	**Safety:** ■ ensure that the baby is strapped in the pushchair using a harness ■ bottles should never be left 'propped' up with the baby ■ if playing on their front, babies should be on a blanket or rug because they can hurt their heads if their head bobs or drops down.

Age	Stage of development	Role of adult	Toys and activities	Equipment needed and safety considerations
6 months	■ lift head to look at feet and grasp their feet (now realising that his feet belong to him). ■ may roll from front to back ■ may sit alone for short periods ■ will bounce if held standing ■ grasps objects and passes them from hand to hand ■ will watch a toy fall if dropped (is beginning to learn cause and effect) ■ laughs, chuckles and says a few sounds ■ babies put everything in their mouths (the mouth is very sensitive; so, learning about the world by feeling and tasting).	■ provide safe toys for the baby to put in the mouth ■ tickling and blowing raspberries on the baby's tummy ■ copy the sounds they make and say them back to them ■ point to familiar people or objects and name them ■ nursery rhymes with actions such as 'horsey-horsey' so that they can bounce while you sing ■ place cushions or pillows around them when sitting so that they have a soft landing if they fall ■ when on their front, place toys slightly out of reach to encourage crawling.	■ activity centres ■ suction toys which are attached to a surface and the baby can play with ■ door bouncers.	**Equipment:** ■ high chair ■ bath seats can be used to give the baby more independence. **Safety:** ■ the baby will soon be mobile and therefore safety equipment (see below) is needed before this happens ■ never leave babies on their own in the bath even if they are in a seat – they can still slip ■ always strap the baby into the highchair but never leave them on their own in case they choke ■ wash and sterilise toys which are put into the mouth to prevent germs being spread ■ ensure that all small objects, including older children's toys, are out of reach to avoid choking ■ avoid books with paper. Cardboard books will be chewed ■ never leave babies on a high surface – they can roll off ■ take bib off before sleeping, even if dribbling.

Age	Stage of development	Role of adult	Toys and activities	Equipment needed and safety considerations
9 months	<ul><li>sits well and can reach for toys</li><li>can often get around the floor by rolling, bottom shuffling or crawling</li><li>may pull themselves to standing</li><li>may point at objects</li><li>picks up small objects using finger and thumb</li><li>babbles and understands some words such as 'bye bye' and 'bathtime'</li><li>claps hands</li><li>doesn't like strangers and starts being worried when separated from parents and carers.</li></ul>	<ul><li>routine at bedtime is very important. Because of the baby's anxiety at being left, sleep problems can often develop at this stage</li><li>continue to talk and sing</li><li>peek-a-boo is a favourite game at this age</li><li>clapping games.</li></ul>	<ul><li>bath toys: plastic mugs for pouring</li><li>dial telephone</li><li>toddler trucks and cars</li><li>bricks</li></ul>	**Equipment:** The following equipment needs to be bought before this stage:<ul><li>safety gates</li><li>socket covers</li><li>safety glass in windows and doors</li><li>cooker guard</li><li>fire guard</li><li>fridge, freezer locks</li><li>video guard.</li></ul>**Safety:**<ul><li>ensure that all breakables are out of reach and cleaning products and medicines are locked away</li><li>make sure that the furniture is stable and there are no sharp corners</li><li>be very careful with hot drinks.</li></ul>
12 months	<ul><li>may be cruising around furniture or walking alone</li><li>shows interest and points at pictures</li><li>understands name and can follow simple instructions</li><li>understands the use of some common objects e.g. hairbrush</li><li>may speak 3 or 4 words</li><li>can find a toy which has been hidden</li><li>drinks from cup.</li></ul>	<ul><li>continue pointing to objects and naming them</li><li>repetitive games involving simple instructions</li><li>give opportunities for the baby to feed himself and use a beaker</li><li>outings to a farm or zoo to give new experiences</li><li>read simple books and point to familiar people or object.</li></ul>	<ul><li>toy telephones</li><li>everyday objects which are safe, such as wooden spoons and saucepans</li><li>putting things in and out of containers such as posting boxes and stacking beakers</li><li>trolleys on wheels</li><li>drums, xylophone or anything to bang</li><li>small climbing frame</li><li>sand and water play under strict supervision.</li></ul>	**Safety:**<ul><li>will be able to pull obstacles off tables – remove table cloths and watch saucepans</li><li>supervise carefully, especially when outside.</li></ul>

Observation

At around eight months, babies start to develop object permanence. This means that they will start to look for a hidden object. Ask your supervisor if you can carry out this simple test. If possible try this test on babies of different ages.

Show a baby a new toy, rattle or other safe object.

Carefully record what happens.

Play is always solitary at this age but babies love to watch older children play, and may start to imitate their actions.

Family pressures

Very few new parents realise the impact a baby will have on their lives. Although they love and enjoy their babies, they can feel stressed and under pressure because of:

■ lack of money, especially if the mother has given up work

■ poor housing

■ tiredness

■ lack of support from family

■ the change in lifestyle.

The health visitor will have lists of the many organisations and groups which can provide support to families with young babies, such as parent and toddler and post-natal groups.

Babies need play

In order to develop properly, babies need to be given the time, space and appropriate activities or toys. The toys or activities need to be appropriate for the developmental stage of the child, otherwise the baby may get frustrated.

Babies and children need to repeat activities over and over again in order to 'master' the skill. This is called 'mastery play'. As adults, when we're learning to drive, for example, we need to keep practising gear changes and clutch control again and again so that we become skilled; it wouldn't be safe for us to go out on the road alone after only one lesson! Babies also need to practise new skills over and over before they

go on to the next stage. Learning therefore often appears to be in leaps and starts.

Care of a baby

Babies are very vulnerable and are completely dependent on their carers to provide for every

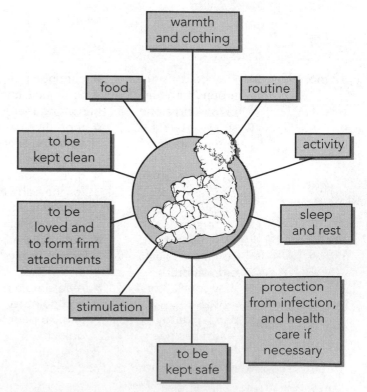

A baby has many needs to be met

need. These needs change as the baby gets older and the carer needs always to be one step ahead and to be able to anticipate needs. This is particularly important in the area of preventing accidents.

ISSUES   Who is the best person to care for a baby?

Twenty years ago, people's answer to this question would have undoubtedly been 'the mother'.

Today, more and more mothers are returning to work and either leaving their partner in charge or organising care for their child. Attitudes towards working parents are divided. Look at the following views.

- People should not bother having babies if they are not ready to stay at home and look after them.

- The idea that the best place for a woman is at home with her children is just a way of keeping women from getting on.

- Babies need the care and attention of just one person – preferably their mother.

- Plenty of babies are cared for by other people and they grow up perfectly fine.

- It is not important whether or not it is the mother who stays with the baby, just that the quality of care is good.

- The idea that parents can leave their babies is just another example of the selfish society where people put themselves first.

- It is better for a baby to have a happy mother rather than one who stays at home just for the sake of it.

In pairs, consider these views and explain what you think.

Observation

Babies learn about their world by using their senses. They are also developing co-ordination. This observation looks at how a baby plays with a new object and also if he has developed the concept of 'object permanence'. (see page 128)

Give a baby a toy or safe object that he has not seen or handled before. Observe carefully using the written record method.

- How does the baby handle the object?

- Is the baby able to pass it from hand to hand?

- How co-ordinated is the baby's movements?

- How does the baby react to the new object – e.g. talking to it, laughing, studying it?

- Does the baby explore the object with its mouth?

- How long does the object hold the baby's interest?

- Take the object and 'hide' it, making sure the baby can see you doing this.

- Observe the baby's reactions to see if he looks in the direction of the object or if he tries to find it.

Interpretation

Read the theories of how children learn before starting this interpretation.

Look also at Freud's stages of development on page 155.

How is the baby learning about the toy?

What physical control has the baby?

Is this similar to other babies of the same age?

Why is it important for babies to be stimulated?

Personal learning and recommendations

What have you learnt about how babies learn?

What have you learnt about this baby?

How can you help this baby's physical skills?

What activities could you provide for the baby?

Why might it be a good idea to observe this baby again?

Importance of routines

Newborn babies very rarely have any sort of routine. In fact, just as one thinks that the baby has finally settled into one routine, it inevitably changes and will end up sleeping and feeding at different times!

Routines are important to both carer and baby because:

■ they provide the baby with a sense of security

■ they allow the baby to begin to make sense of her environment – for example, the baby will understand that being undressed, and hearing the sound of a running tap, is a sign that it is bathtime.

■ they enable the carer to plan the day more efficiently.

By the time babies are about three months old, they are beginning to recognise routines such as

Possible routine for an 8-month baby in a nursery

7.30	Arrive and settle in
8.00	Breakfast
8.30	Nappy change
8.45	Play
10.00	Drink
10.15	Singing time
10.30	Walk in the pushchair
11.00	Nappy change and sleep
12.00	Lunch
13.00	Nappy change and play
14.00	Water play
14.30	Play outside (if fine)
15.30	Drink
16.00	Play clapping games
16.30	Tea
17.00	Home

preparation for bed. This is probably one of the most important routines because tired babies often just don't want to go to sleep! When babies are about seven to nine months old they can become very clingy and, if a routine hasn't been established by this time, a baby can have trouble settling to sleep.

It is always important to follow the baby's routine where possible and to be flexible.

There are, however, a few things that can be done to encourage the baby to settle into a pattern:

■ when the baby sleeps in the day, carry on as normal – don't be too quiet. If babies wake at night, they should be settled quickly, with no games and with the minimum of light: they need to know that they are expected to sleep at night!

■ have a special routine to settle babies to sleep – this is especially important at night time

■ baths and top and tailing (see page 376) could be done at the same time every day.

Knowledge into action

While working with babies, write down the daily routine of one baby for three days. Record the age and then compare the routines with others in the group.

Sleep and rest

All babies are very different in their needs for sleep and rest and in the ways that they can be settled. It is therefore very important to find out from the parents the baby's sleep pattern and methods of getting her off to sleep.

Newborns often sleep for as much as 14–18 hours in the 24-hour period and sleeps during the day will continue into the second and third years.

Parents will vary in where they put their baby to sleep – in a cot, a Moses basket, a cradle, a pram or in the parents' bed at night. Babies vary considerably as to when they start sleeping through the night and the early stages can be very tiring for the parent. It is important to develop a bedtime routine for babies because this helps her to realise that it's time to settle. This routine may include a bath, a drink, a story (for the older baby), and tooth brushing before being put down to sleep. Parents settle their babies in a variety of ways including:

■ cuddling the baby or rocking her to sleep

■ using comfort objects, including soothers, blankets or special toys

■ using noise – some babies will sleep with particular noises especially womb music, the vacuum cleaner, the washing machine or the 'white noise' of an untuned radio!

■ singing

■ walking with the baby.

Feeding

When the baby's umbilical cord is cut, he no longer receives nutrients through the cord and therefore has to become independent from his mother and start to feed. The rooting reflex ensures that the baby will turn to food if the cheek is stroked and the sucking reflex will ensure that he will feed.

Breast or bottle?

During pregnancy, the parents will need to decide how they will be feeding the baby. Their decision will be based on many factors and they will need the

Breast feeding and bottle feeding

Advantages of breast feeding	Advantages of bottle feeding
For the baby: It contains exactly the right nutrients for the baby – these nutrients change as the baby grows older and his needs change. The milk is sterile and at the correct temperature. Because breast milk contains antibodies to protect the baby against infection, there is less gastroenteritis, Sudden Infant Death Syndrome, or respiratory, ear and other infections than in bottle-fed babies. Constipation is very unlikely in breast-fed babies. The sucking required in breast feeding is more vigorous and encourages the healthy development of jaws and gums. A baby's sense of taste is being stimulated more because the breast milk changes very slightly in taste. There is a lower chance of babies suffering from allergies, including asthma and eczema. There is a reduced risk of diabetes.	**For the baby:** The baby is not affected by the mother's health – tiredness and illness can affect the milk production. Alcohol, medication and smoking can affect the breast milk, which doesn't happen in formula milk.
For the mother: The uterus returns to size much more quickly. There is no sterilising and making up feeds – it can therefore be quicker and easier, especially at night or when going out. Breast feeding is cheaper, although the mother has to watch her diet and eat well. Weight loss is usually quicker. Breast feeding reduces the risk of breast and some types of ovarian cancer.	**For the mother:** Anyone can feed the baby. The mother knows how much milk the baby has had. There is no embarrassment when feeding, which some women may feel with breast feeding.

appropriate information so that they can make an informed choice.

Although health professionals would always say that breast feeding is best for the baby, women should never be made to feel guilty about bottle feeding. Some women will be unable to breastfeed because they are taking medication for conditions such as epilepsy. Both methods of feeding have their own advantages.

Breast feeding

The breasts may start to produce a small amount of milk in pregnancy; this is called colostrum and it is the milk which is produced until the baby is three days old. The colostrum is yellow in colour and is rich in protein and antibodies, which help protect the baby from infections. The milk then changes, becoming thinner and paler in colour; this is called mature breast milk.

Breast feeding is not always easy at first, but once established many women really enjoy feeding the baby themselves. In order to produce enough milk, it is important that the mother has a good balanced diet and drinks plenty of fluid.

Expressed milk
In order that the baby may continue to have the benefits of breast milk, some women will express their milk when they return to work. This is usually done by using a breast pump. The milk can be frozen for up to three months and, once defrosted, needs to be used within 24 hours. If breast milk is expressed it can also mean that the father can feed the baby and that the mother is free to go out without the baby.

Bottle feeding

Formula milk is modified cow's milk. Bottle-fed babies should be given formula milk to drink until they are one year old, because ordinary milk doesn't provide the right nutrients, although this milk may be used in cooking at six months. There are a few different brands of formula and the parents' choice should always be respected. See below for more information on bottle feeding.

The most important aspect of bottle feeding is to ensure that all equipment is sterilised, and that good hygiene practices are followed.

Knowledge into action

Ask three mothers how they feed or fed their baby. Find out:

Where did they get their information about feeding from?

How did they feed their baby?

If they breast fed, how long did they do it for and why did they stop?

Did they have any difficulties with feeding?

Good hygiene and sterilising

Babies are particularly vulnerable to infection, and germs can grow quickly in milk and food. It is therefore important to ensure that all feeding equipment is kept as germ-free as possible.

Good practice – bottle feeding

✔ Always wash hands before handling milk or food.

✔ Always wash bottles and feeding equipment in hot soapy water and then rinse carefully.

✔ Use a bottle brush to ensure that bottles and teats are washed properly.

✔ Sterilise all feeding equipment.

✔ Store milk in the fridge for up to 24 hours, but no longer.

✔ Remember that once a baby has started a bottle, anything left after one hour needs discarding.

✔ If going out for the day with a baby, the milk needs to be kept cold and then warmed when necessary.

Equipment

The following feeding and other equipment needs sterilising:

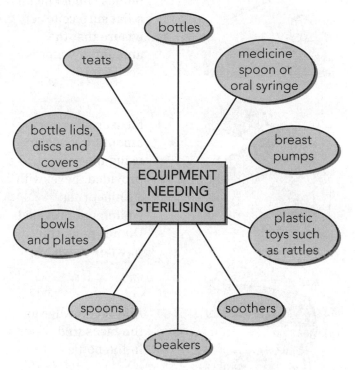

Feeding and other types of equipment must be sterilised

Sterilising equipment

There are three main methods of sterilising: chemical, steam or boiling water. It is also possible to sterilise items in a microwave oven if you have a special unit.

Bottle feeding

Many women choose to bottle feed from birth and others may change from breast feeding after a few months. Some babies may settle into a routine with their feeds but others don't. Babies should be fed 'on demand', which means that they are fed when they are hungry, and should be allowed to have the quantity that they require; they should never be 'encouraged' to finish up the bottle if they have had enough because it will cause the baby to be sick.

Equipment required

The equipment necessary for bottle feeding includes:

- six bottles with lids, discs and covers

- six teats. There are many different types of teat including 'orthodontic teats' which are shaped to be similar to the shape of a nipple.

- bottle brush.

Sterilising methods

Method	Process	Safety points	Advantages
Cold water (or chemical sterilisation)	Sterilising tablets or liquid are dissolved in cold water. Equipment should be fully immersed (leaving no air bubbles) for 30 minutes. Everything will need rinsing with boiled water to remove the bleach solution.	The solution needs changing every 24 hours. Metal will discolour in the solution (take any rings off your fingers).	Cheap and items are always available (though rubber teats perish).
Steam	Place equipment upside down in the unit, ensuring that items are not touching each other and follow the manufacturer's instructions. It will take only a few minutes and will switch off when ready.	Be careful when opening the lid. Only items which are safe to be boiled can be used.	Quick and simple to use.
Boiling water	Equipment is immersed in a saucepan and boiled for 10 minutes.	Ensure that the saucepan doesn't boil dry.	Cheap.
Microwave	Place equipment in the unit upside down and follow the manufacturer's instructions. Leave to cool for a few minutes.	Everything will be very hot. Metal cannot be used.	Quick and easy to use.

Baby milk is also needed. There are many different types on the market, and you should always continue with the one that the baby is used to, unless you are instructed by the parent to change. Soya milk is sometimes used for babies who are allergic to dairy products or who are vegan, but this should be used only if advised by a doctor. After the age of six months, babies may be given a 'follow-on' milk which is for hungrier babies.

Making up bottle feeds

Making up feeds is part of the routine in a home environment, and feeds are usually made up for 24 hours and stored in the fridge. This means that a feed is always available.

Before making up the feed, the bottles need sterilising. It is necessary to find out from the parents how much feed to make up (this depends on the baby's weight rather than its age). Generally, because babies vary in the amount of feed that they take during the day, it is a good idea to make up slightly more feed than is generally needed.

Step-by-step

- Boil the kettle and allow to cool.

- Check the sell-by-date on the tin of milk.

- Read the manufacturer's instructions on the side of the tin.

- Wash hands thoroughly.

- Pour the required amount of water into the bottles (the bottles should be on a flat surface to ensure that the amount of water is accurate).

- Measure the exact amount of powder using the scoop provided. Level with a knife or the equipment provided. **Do not pack the powder down**.

- Add the powder to the measured water in the bottle.

- Screw the top of the bottle on, and shake.

- If not using the bottle immediately, cool quickly and store in the fridge.

Making up a feed

Bottle feeding a baby

In an early years setting, it is always important to record the baby's feeding pattern for the day, in order that the parent knows that the baby is feeding well. If a baby isn't feeding well it can be a sign of illness.

Feeds should be made up before they are needed and stored in the fridge, and marked with the child's name.

Bottle feeding a baby

Follow these guidelines when giving a baby a bottle.

- wash hands
- warm the bottle by standing it in a jug of warm water or by using a bottle warmer. *Do not* warm the bottle in the microwave – it can cause 'hot spots', which might burn the baby's mouth
- change the baby's nappy if necessary
- collect together everything you need to feed the baby, including tissues or bibs
- check the flow and temperature of the milk by testing it on your wrist
- sit comfortably in a chair – you may need to support a small baby on a cushion. (If you find that you are getting backache, change your position, and try to relax your shoulders.)
- gently touch the baby's lips with the bottle, and then place the teat in his open mouth. *Never* force the baby's mouth open
- angle the bottle so that the milk is filling the teat
- allow babies to feed at their own pace
- a young baby will often need frequent breaks for winding, but an older baby will probably break only once. Either hold the baby on your shoulder or support him sitting and gently rub his back. It is always sensible to place a cloth on your shoulder in case the baby is slightly sick!
- throw away unfinished milk
- change the baby's nappy again if necessary.

Feeding a baby should be an enjoyable experience for both the carer and the baby. If possible, choose a quiet place to feed the baby without other distractions and give him all of your attention and eye contact, so that he may feel special and loved.

Feeding difficulties

If there are any concerns about the baby's feeding you should inform the parents in a home setting or the supervisor in a work setting. You should record the difficulty on the feed chart. Difficulties are usually minor and often associated with wind, but can be due to the baby being unwell. Even if a baby has a slight cold, it can cause breathing difficulties when trying to feed.

Colic is one of the most distressing types of feeding problems. It is sometimes called 'three months colic', because it usually lasts for about three months and starts before the baby is three months old. It is characterised by the baby screaming and drawing his legs up and it usually occurs at the same time every day, often in the evening. The parents should see their GP or health visitor for advice and to exclude intolerances, allergies or illnesses. Comfort the baby by cuddling, massaging his stomach and rocking.

Knowledge into action

Design a leaflet explaining the advantages and disadvantages of breast/bottle feeding. The leaflet is to be given to new parents and should be written in a clear, informative way. If possible, use a computer to give the leaflet a professional look.

Weaning

Breast and bottle feeding meets the total nutritional needs of babies until they are six months old. Then they need extra energy, protein, vitamins A and D and particularly iron. Babies therefore need to be introduced to other food in order to meet these needs. This process of gradually introducing the baby to solid food is called 'weaning'.

It is generally recommended that weaning should be started between four and six months because:

- the gut cannot digest food properly before this and there may be a higher risk of allergy if started too early
- the baby needs to be getting extra nutrients by six months or could become anaemic
- the muscles required for speech development need to be developed by chewing
- older babies can find more difficulty accepting solid food.

However, babies do vary in the time they are ready to start weaning and it is important to recognise these signs:

- the baby is hungrier
- the baby is waking at night for feeding

Weaning

Age	Preparation and equipment	Type of food	Drinks	Foods to avoid
4–6 months	Purée or liquidise food using a blender, liquidiser or sieve. Sterilise all feeding equipment: bowl and plastic spoon	Puréed fruit or vegetable; thin porridge made from rice, cornmeal or millet mixed with breast or formula milk. Foods should be warm and introduced one at a time. After about 2 weeks: puréed dahl (lentils) and meat can gradually be added.	Breast or bottle should still be providing the main nutrients initially. Once feeding is established, one milk feed could be dropped, but the baby should be having 500–600 ml of milk daily. Introduce the baby to a beaker with cool boiled water.	Wheat-based foods, cow's milk, eggs, citrus and soft summer fruits, fish and shellfish, nuts and seeds, honey, sugar, salt, spices, beetroot and fatty foods.
6–9 months	Mashed or minced foods	Meat, fish, soft beans, well-cooked eggs, wheat-based foods, and citrus fruits. Cow's milk can be used for cooking. Babies can eat the same food as the family, as long as it is well mashed or minced.	500–600 ml of milk and water from a beaker. Diluted fruit juice can be given, preferably at meal times.	Liver, spices, nuts and seeds, salt, sugar, honey and fatty foods.
9–12 months	Mashed and finger foods	Finger foods such as pitta bread, chapatti, toast, apple, raw carrot can be added.	500–600 ml of breast or formula milk is still needed daily. Cow's milk can be given as a drink when the child is 12 months old.	Nuts, salt, sugar and fatty foods.

- the baby starts to demand feeding more often.

The health visitor will advise the parents when to start the process.

Starting to wean

The first food should be offered during one of the milk feeds in the day at a time when the baby isn't tired; often around lunchtime is the best. Some babies will need some milk first if they're very hungry. Initially it is probably best to put a bib on the baby and sit her on your knee. Place a tiny bit of the

Case study

You're working as a nanny for Isobel whose daughter, Tilly, will soon be one year old. She's having a party and inviting Hamish (10 months), Sophie and Jessica (8 months), William (9 months) who's a vegetarian and Michael (11 months), who is on a dairy-free diet.

What preparation will need to be done beforehand?

Devise a tea which will meet all of the needs of each child and include finger foods.

food on to the tip of a clean sterilised plastic teaspoon and put it gently next to the baby's lips. The baby should suck the food off the spoon. Don't worry if the food gets spat out, try again another time!

4 to 6 months

Once the baby accepts one food, introduce another food a few days later. This allows time to detect whether the baby is intolerant to the food. Over the next few weeks solid food should gradually be introduced so that by the age of six months the baby should usually be having three meals a day.

Some parents may use commercial baby foods for all or part of the baby's diet. It is important to check the ingredients and ensure that the food is suitable for the baby's age. Also check the expiry date, and that seals on the cans and jars are intact.

Example of a weaning plan for a 5-month-old baby	
On waking	Breast or bottle feed
Breakfast	Baby rice mixed with the milk from the breast or bottle feed
Lunch	Puréed chicken or lentils, carrot and potato Cooled boiled water to drink
Tea	Puréed fruit Breast or bottle feed
Evening	Breast or bottle feed

6 to 9 months

From the age of about seven months, babies can start to manage lumps in their food. This next stage should be gradually introduced by mashing foods well and including soft lumps, so the baby can start to chew. Babies will often want to hold their own spoons at this age and should be encouraged to do so, although they will not yet be capable of using spoons properly.

A baby who can sit up can go into the high chair and participate in the family meal. It is very important

that a harness is used every time to prevent the baby from falling out or, later, from climbing out.

Example of a weaning plan for an 8-month-old baby	
On waking	Breast or bottle feed
Breakfast	Cereal mixed with milk from the feed, toast soldiers and milk
Lunch	Mashed fish, green beans and potatoes with peas as a finger food, yoghurt and water to drink
Tea	Sandwiches with savoury spread, stewed apple and a milk drink
Evening	Milk drink if necessary

9 to 12 months

This is the start of the messy stage, where babies want to help feed themselves! In the summer, it can sometimes be best to take all the clothes off while feeding. If not, plenty of bibs, patience and floor coverings are essential!

Example of a weaning plan for an 11-month-old baby	
On waking	Breast feed or milk in a cup
Breakfast	Cereal or a chopped hard-boiled egg, toast and milk
Mid-morning	Piece of apple and water
Lunch	Fish and pasta bake with broccoli, milk pudding, drink of water
Tea	Cauliflower cheese, a mashed banana and milk to drink

Important issues in weaning

There are some important points to remember when helping to wean a baby:

- Avoid sugar and salt in cooking.

- Never give honey to babies under one year because it may contain a type of bacteria which causes problems in babies.

- Never give soft-boiled eggs, unpasteurised cheese, pâtés or liver to babies.

- Always supervise a child whilst eating in case of choking.

- Cover the floor in newspapers at the messy stage.

- Always respect and incorporate any cultural or religious aspects of the diet into the weaning plan. It is possible to meet the nutritional needs of babies on a vegetarian diet if this is carefully planned. Babies on a vegan diet should have a soya-based formula until the age of two years, to supply the necessary nutrients.

- When preparing food always wash your hands first and ensure that equipment is sterilised (at least until 6 months at home or 15 months in a large early years setting)

- Remember that unfinished food needs to be discarded.

- Ensure that food is thoroughly reheated, but do not use a microwave to heat food for babies because 'hot spots' can burn young mouths.

Feeding difficulties and allergies

When the baby is first being weaned, it is important to look for signs of food intolerance. These are easier to notice at this stage than when the baby is taking a wide variety of foods.

If you notice any of these signs, they should be reported. The parents can get advice from their GP or health visitor. Information can also be obtained from the local health promotion unit.

Knowledge into action

In pairs, write down all the advantages and disadvantages you can think of for using home-made and commercial foods.

Ask five parents who have weaned their babies which foods they used and why.

Care of the skin and hair

The purpose of the skin is to protect the body from infections and to help maintain an even temperature. Because babies have little immunity against infection, it is important that the skin is cared for properly. There are two washing routines used for babies: top and tailing (i.e. washing the face and hands, and bottom) and bathing.

It is important to find out about a baby's normal routine from the parent. Some babies, for example, will be top and tailed in the morning and have a bath as part of the bedtime routine. If babies have dry skin they may have baths less frequently. There may also be cultural traditions around bathing, especially in the creams and oils that may be used after bathing.

Top and tailing

This phrase means washing the baby's face and bottom (although the hands are washed too)! This is quite a quick procedure but you still need to be well prepared and have everything ready before you start.

Equipment
The following items will be required:

- changing mat

- nappy-changing equipment

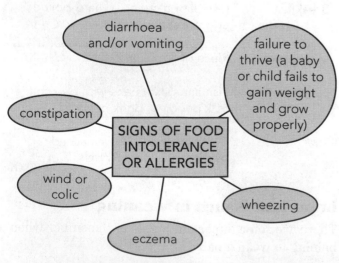

Look out for signs of food intolerance

- clean clothes
- bowl containing warm water and cotton wool (or soft flannel for older baby)
- soft towel.

1 Prepare the equipment needed, wash your hands and remove the baby's outer clothes.
2 Gently clean the baby's face with cotton wool, avoiding the eyes. Use the cotton wool once and then throw away.

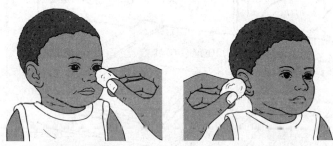

3 Clean around the nose, behind the ears and then the neck, using one piece of cotton wool for each.

4 Dry each area with cotton wool.
5 Wash the hands and pat dry.

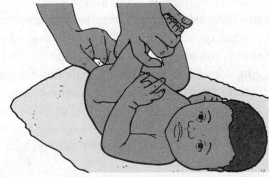

6 Wash the baby's bottom, change the nappy and get the baby dressed.

Top and tailing a baby

Bathing a baby

Bathing a baby is usually one of the most pleasurable of the baby care routines. Some parents bath the baby two or three times a week and top and tail in between. Others will bath daily, often as part of the bedtime routine.

Benefits of bathing

- It cleans the skin.
- Most babies enjoy the experience of bathing.
- It can stimulate all developmental areas:
  - physical: kicking and splashing develops muscles
  - emotional: provides good contact time between carer and baby and can soothe and relax a fretful baby. As part of a routine, it can provide security.
  - cognitive: a baby can explore a new environment and older babies can play with the water, e.g. pouring games.
- Language: bathing is a good time for chatting to the baby; he will soon babble back.

Equipment

It is important to have all the equipment ready for bathing *before* you begin to undress the baby and start the bath.

Procedure

1 Prepare the equipment, wash hands and put on an apron. The room temperature should be about 20°C.
2 Fill the bath with warm water (about 38°C); test this using a thermometer or with your elbow – it should feel lukewarm.

3 Take the clothes off and wrap the baby in a towel leaving the nappy on.
4 Wash face – as in top and tailing. If you are using a baby bath product, which is like bubble bath and doesn't need rinsing off, add this now.

Clean clothes

'Baby bath' product

Baby soap

Bath thermometer

Cotton wool

Baby bath

Towel

Changing mat

Nappy

Barrier cream

Nappy bucket

A number of different things are needed when bathing a baby

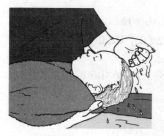

5 Support the baby's head, neck and shoulders with one hand and tuck the body under your arm, so that the baby cannot wriggle.

6 Hold the baby's head over the bath and, using the other hand, wash the hair using shampoo, baby soap or the baby bath product. Dry the hair.

7 Remove the towel and nappy and clean the bottom if necessary. Hold the baby's arm which is furthest from you and support the head with your wrist. Lift the baby into the bath.

8 Use your spare hand to wash the baby. Allow the baby to kick and enjoy the water.

9 Lift the baby back on to the towel and dry thoroughly, especially in the creases. If the baby has dry skin, a moisturising cream may be rubbed into the skin. Afro-Caribbean babies are often massaged with oil. Put a nappy on and dress the baby.

Bathing the older baby
The baby will soon outgrow a baby bath and can be put into a big bath.

There are many products on the market which can be used to help support an older baby in the bath.

- **Always** check that the temperature of the water is about 38°C.
- **Always** prepare the room and equipment carefully.
- **Always** remove jewellery before bathing.
- **Never** leave babies alone near water – even for a second.
- **Never** use cotton buds – they can cause damage.
- **Avoid** using talcum powder – it can be inhaled and cause chest infections.
- **Be careful** of your back when bending and lifting: always bend your knees and keep your back straight.

For older babies:
- **Always** use a non-slip mat in the bath.
- **Make sure** that the taps are tightly turned off and are covered, for example, by a flannel.
- **Always** keep the water shallow.

Knowledge into action

Have a look through catalogues and visit baby care shops.

How many different bath care products can you find?

What equipment and bath toys are available for the older baby?

Hair care

Babies should have their own soft hairbrush and have their hair washed as part of the bath routine. It is important to respect any cultural or religious wishes: some parents will ask for the hair to be oiled, for other children shampoo and soap are never used on the hair.

Nail care

Nails should be cut regularly, using special blunt-ended scissors. It is very easy to damage the skin in young babies, so great care should be taken. In older babies the nails can be cleaned gently using a soft nailbrush.

Care of the teeth

A very few babies are born with a tooth, but most babies cut their first tooth at about six months old. It is important that the habit of caring for the teeth is started early to get the baby used to the brush and to prevent tooth decay. If a baby or young child needs to have a tooth out, the permanent teeth are more likely to be crooked. The following points can help to develop healthy teeth:

- as soon as the teeth appear, use a toothbrush with a small amount of baby toothpaste to clean the teeth and gums

- avoid sugary drinks. Fruit juice should be diluted. Water is the best drink in between meals

- bottles should be used only for milk or water, and the baby should gradually be introduced to a beaker or cup.

Nappy changing

The baby's bottom is the area of skin most likely to become sore and therefore it is important that the nappy is changed regularly and the skin washed and dried thoroughly. Some parents also use a barrier cream to prevent soreness.

There are three main types of nappy:

- disposable nappies, which are the most commonly used, and don't require washing

- terry nappies, which are made of towelling. These nappies need a disposable nappy liner to prevent soreness, and plastic pants over them

- shaped cotton nappies, which don't always require plastic pants and are less bulky than terries.

Most parents choose to use disposable nappies for their baby, although some use a laundry service for terry nappies.

Equipment needed for nappy changing
Whichever type of nappy the parent chooses to use for the baby, it is important to have ready all of the equipment needed and to be well prepared, because the baby should *never* be left alone on a changing mat. Some people prefer to put the changing mat on the floor for safety.

Knowledge into action

Disposable/reusable nappies

1   Ask five parents what type of nappy they use and why.
2   Look in the telephone directory and find out whether there is a nappy service in your area that provides and launders fabric nappies.
3   Work out the cost of providing a newborn baby with nappies for a week based on the cheapest nappies that you can find.
4   Produce a short report of your findings outlining the advantages and disadvantages of disposable nappies.

How to change a nappy

Babies' nappies need changing several times a day, so if you're working with babies it is not something you can avoid!

1   You need to get all of the equipment ready *before* taking off the nappy!

2   Wash your hands and put gloves on.
3   Remove clothes from the lower part of the body and undo the nappy.
4   Using tissues or cotton wool, wipe the faeces off the bottom and place nappy and tissues into a nappy sack.
5   Using wet cotton wool or baby wipes, wash the baby's bottom from front to back and throw each piece away after one wipe. Do not pull a boy's foreskin back during washing.
6   Dry with tissues or cotton wool.
7   Apply barrier cream.
8   Put nappy on and dress the baby.
9   Clean the mat and wash hands.

Don't forget to talk to the baby during nappy changing. Babies also like a chance to kick their legs when their nappy is off !

It is important to note down any changes in the contents of the nappy because it can often be a sign that a baby is becoming unwell. The normal colour of the stools for a breast-fed baby is orange/yellow

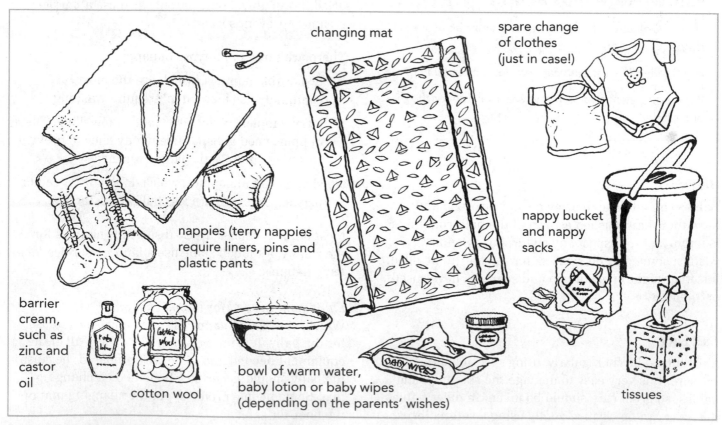

changing mat

spare change of clothes (just in case!)

nappies (terry nappies require liners, pins and plastic pants

nappy bucket and nappy sacks

barrier cream, such as zinc and castor oil

cotton wool

bowl of warm water, baby lotion or baby wipes (depending on the parents' wishes)

tissues

Nappy changing equipment

mustard and watery. Bottle-fed babies produce pale brown, more solid and slightly smelly stools.

The following would need to be reported to the supervisor and the parent:

- any change in colour, frequency or consistency of stools

- green stools (may indicate under- or over-feeding, or infection)

- blood

- watery stools with an unpleasant smell

- passing urine less frequently

- urine which is dark in colour (may be due to dehydration)

- baby has difficulty in opening the bowels or produces stools which are small and hard

- baby cries when opening the bowels

- nappy rash.

Think about it

Make a list of all of the advantages and disadvantages of the different types of nappy. Consider the cost, convenience and the effect on the environment. (One survey stated that it took 200 years for a disposable nappy to disintegrate.)

Nappy rash

Nappy rash

Most babies get a sore bottom from time to time, because the conditions in which bacteria love to grow are all present in a nappy. Nappy rash is much more common in bottle-fed babies, but can be due to a number of reasons (see below).

Health and safety

The Health and Safety Policy in an early years setting will include the following points.

1. Disposable gloves should be worn when in contact with blood, urine, vomit and faeces.
2. Cuts and grazes should be covered by a waterproof plaster.
3. Hands should be washed after contact with spillages (even when gloves are worn).
4. Spillages of blood should be treated as follows:
   - covered by 1% hypochlorite solution
   - wiped over, using disposable cloths
   - these should be placed in the appropriate bag (yellow) for incineration
   - the area should be washed with warm soapy water.

Equipment needed for a baby

The chart beginning on page 362 included the equipment that is needed for a baby at each developmental stage. There is such a variety of different equipment that it is often hard for parents to choose between the different items. When a family or

Reasons why a nappy rash may occur	How to prevent and treat nappy rash
<ul><li>reaction to baby products, such as baby wipes or bath products</li><li>diarrhoea</li><li>nappies left on too long</li><li>poor changing technique e.g. not drying the skin properly</li><li>teething (although some doctors don't agree with this)</li><li>thrush: a raised red rash, which is very sore</li><li>some babies simply seem to be more prone to rashes than others.</li></ul>	<ul><li>change nappy frequently</li><li>ensure skin is washed and dried properly before putting on a new nappy</li><li>use barrier cream</li><li>leave the nappy off for a few minutes as often as possible</li><li>change cleaning products if this is suspected as being a cause of the rash</li><li>fabric nappies need to be rinsed well after being washed in non-biological powder</li><li>thrush needs to be treated with an anti-fungal cream from the GP.</li></ul>

Observation

Ask for permission to observe a baby having its nappy changed. Use the written record method.

- Does the baby make eye contact with the carer?

- Is the baby showing that it has learnt what to do during the process – e.g. lifting legs, lying still?

- Are you able to observe interaction between the carer and the baby – e.g. laughter, speech?

- Does the carer encourage or praise the baby?

- What physical development are you able to observe?

Interpretation

- Consider whether the baby is showing attachment to the carer – e.g. making eye contact.

- Why is this attachment important for young babies (see page 177)?

- Comment on the language and social interaction between carer and baby.

- How has the baby learnt what is expected?

- Why is praise and encouragement important for babies and young children?

- Is the baby's physical development similar to the pattern shown by most babies of its age?

Personal learning and recommendations

What have you learnt by watching this nappy change?

Why is nappy changing so important?

What have you learnt about this baby?

nursery is deciding on the equipment that is needed, it is helpful to make a list of the essential equipment they will require, and then to ask the following questions:

1 How much is to be spent?
2 How much space is available for the equipment and its storage?
3 Is the equipment going to be suitable to meet the needs of the nursery or family?
4 Will the equipment last?
5 How easy will it be to clean and maintain?
6 Is it easy to use and how heavy is it?
7 Is the equipment necessary or a luxury?
8 Is the equipment safe?

Care and maintenance of equipment

This forms part of the setting's health and safety policy and it is often part of the early years

worker's role to clean and check all equipment regularly.

In a work setting, everyone should be taught how to use the equipment safely. If you find any damage to the equipment, you will need to report it to your supervisor and remove the equipment from use and label it.

Clothing and shoes

The layette is the first set of clothing bought for a newborn baby. This usually consists of six stretch suits (or 'Babygros'), four vests, two cardigans, socks or bootees, a hat, gloves and a sun hat. Babies often need a frequent change of clothes in the day and they grow so quickly that new clothes are constantly required.

Maintenance of equipment

Checks on equipment	Cleaning equipment
■ brakes work correctly ■ all moving parts are safe e.g. wheels, hinges ■ stability of equipment, especially if other children could knock it over ■ splits and cracks in equipment e.g. teats ■ all manufacturer's instructions are being followed regarding use, maintenance and cleaning ■ electrical equipment should be checked regularly by an electrician ■ harnesses and reins aren't frayed ■ any signs of wear ■ equipment used is appropriate for the child.	■ manufacturer's instructions are followed for cleaning ■ equipment such as high chairs should be washed after use ■ plastic toys such as rattles and feeding equipment need to be sterilised properly.

It is important to ensure that clothes are:

■ comfortable and have plenty of room for growth (e.g. in the toes of stretch suits)

■ flame retardant and have washing instructions and fabric content attached

■ appropriate for the weather

■ washed in a gentle detergent, such as non-biological washing powder, to avoid skin irritation

■ easy to put on and take off. Babies don't like clothes being put over their heads, therefore cardigans are better than jumpers. Because babies need changing several times a day, clothes which give easy access to the nappy are

necessary. For older babies, dresses are difficult to crawl in – they get tangled around the legs

■ not a danger to the baby – be careful of ribbons, loose buttons which could cause choking, and loose cotton threads inside clothes in which fingers and toes can get caught.

Footwear

At birth, babies have 22 partially developed bones in the feet. This increases to 45 by school age. Babies' feet are very delicate and can easily be deformed by badly fitting clothes and bootees. Stretch suits, socks and bootees should therefore be checked to ensure there is enough room for the growing feet. Remember that socks which are too big can also cause blisters.

Knowledge into action

You've been appointed to work as a nanny in a family who are expecting a baby. They've asked you to research the equipment needed for a baby in the first year of life.

In your group, divide into pairs and choose a different piece of equipment each. Look at the advantages and disadvantages of the different products in the range and at the questions above and decide what equipment you would choose.

Choose from:

■ *cribs/Moses baskets/cots*

■ *car seats*

■ *bedding*

■ *high chairs*

■ *prams/pushchairs*

■ *baby monitors*

■ *bouncy chairs/chairs*

■ *safety equipment.*

Shoes should not be bought for the baby until walking is well established; bare feet or slipper socks are best at first. Shoes need to be properly fitted and should be made of natural materials which allow the feet to 'breathe'.

Health care for babies

It is important that babies are checked regularly to ensure that they are growing and developing normally. This is covered in Chapter 10.

Illness in babies

Babies can very quickly become ill because they are so vulnerable to infection. Babies cannot say when they are unwell, so early years workers need to be alert to signs of illness.

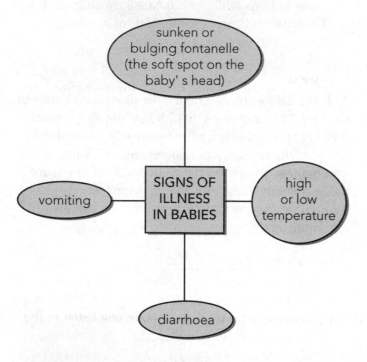

Chapter 10 has details of all of the major and minor common childhood illnesses, who to report to, how to get help and what to do in an emergency.

Sudden Infant Death Syndrome (SIDS)

There has been much research into the causes and prevention of Sudden Infant Death Syndrome, in which babies die unexpectedly in their sleep. The following guidelines are intended to prevent this tragic occurrence.

- Place babies on their backs to sleep.

- Do not allow smoking in the same room as the baby.

- Do not let babies become too hot (room temperature should be 18°C or 68°F):
  - use blankets and not duvets
  - remove outdoor clothes from the baby when indoors, even if it means waking her.

- Place the baby in the 'feet to foot' position in the cot and have the covers no higher than the shoulders. Covers should be tucked in, so that they cannot slip over the baby's head.

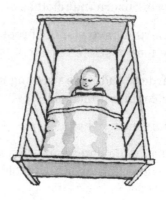

The 'feet to foot' sleeping position is now recommended for babies

- Do not use pillows for babies under one year.

- Seek medical attention if the baby is unwell.

Requirements of babies in group care

In Chapter 8 on emotional development, Bowlby's theory of attachment was discussed, and it has been partly due to his research and because of the Children Act of 1989 that nurseries provide a high ratio of staff to babies (1:2).

Babies develop a strong bond with their primary carer, who is usually the mother, but need also to bond with others in order to develop emotionally and socially. Babies, therefore, can bond with several people, including parents, grandparents and carers, but not easily with more than that.

The **key-worker** system, in which a baby is allocated to one particular member of staff, ensures that the baby can form a strong relationship with one carer, who provides for all the baby's needs. This carer communicates directly with the parent, which ensures that the parent knows whom to see if there are any problems. The carer is therefore able to build up a relationship with the whole family. Most nurseries will also ensure that each baby becomes familiar with at least one other carer, so that when the key worker is on holiday or unwell the baby can feel comfortable with another member of staff.

Because most early years settings have a shift system, babies also need to be able to bond with other staff during the time the key worker is off duty. Some settings, therefore will not only have a primary key worker but also one or more secondary key workers for each baby so that the baby can form attachments to other staff.

Some early years settings also allow their staff to follow the baby into the next section of the setting so that the relationship can be maintained. There are obvious advantages of this for the baby but it can be difficult practically, and does mean that staff need to be willing to work in all areas of the setting.

The needs of babies in group care

A baby's needs in group care must be established when the baby first starts at the setting. The parents will have to complete an extensive questionnaire about all of the baby's routines, including sleeping and eating habits, and any medical history or known allergies in order for the early years workers to help the baby settle quickly into the nursery. The parents may spend one or more sessions with the baby in the setting to help them settle.

Sleep/rest needs

All nurseries will have space for babies and toddlers to rest or sleep and if a baby prefers to sleep in his own pram then this can be brought into the setting. Comfort objects from home will help the baby to settle and the early years workers can settle the baby using the familiar routines from home. The setting will find out from the parent what the baby's bedtime routine is and how to help him to settle.

Feeding needs

If the baby is being breast fed, the mother can express milk which can be stored in the fridge (for up to 24 hours) or frozen (for up to 3 months) for use by the early years workers in the nursery setting. Bottles can also be brought for bottle-fed babies and also food for special diets if necessary, or if the parent prefers. Most settings provide food for the children, but some babies and children prefer food from home.

Nappy changing

The setting will have a special area set aside for nappy changing and it is important that this is always cleaned thoroughly after use to prevent cross-infection. The setting will need to know how the baby's nappy area is cleaned.

Routine

The baby's routine needs to be followed as closely as possible in the setting.

Fresh air

For babies who are in a setting full time it is important, if possible, for them to have some fresh air during the day, in the form of a walk in a pushchair or in the garden.

Adult interaction

In order to develop normally babies need quality time with their early years worker/key worker; this means that the early years worker will talk and listen to the baby, play games, give cuddles, provide stimulating activities, read and sing to the baby as well as perform all of the caring routines.

Stimulation

Some toys and games provide amusement and stimulation time and time again, whereas others should be brought out only occasionally in order to prevent boredom. Many settings use 'heuristic play' daily with their babies. This involves the sensory exploration of natural objects. These objects can include: natural sponges, wooden bricks, a pineapple, large shells, wooden spoons, a pumice stone, and a small tin. It is important to remember that babies will explore with their mouths and therefore checks should be made to ensure that:

- everything is cleaned very thoroughly, according to the setting's policies

- there are no small pieces that could break off and cause the baby to choke

- there is no risk of splinters in the wooden objects

- objects are not too heavy to cause damage if dropped.

These objects are usually kept in a bag or a basket and the adult's role is to allow and encourage the baby to enjoy the experience.

Early years workers should report the following to the parent:

- any changes from the normal routine

- any milestones which the baby has reached – e.g. starting to crawl

- times of feeds and how much milk/food has been taken

- nappy changes and when the baby has opened his bowels

- how much the baby has slept

- activities that the baby has done.

Check your knowledge

- List three tests that are carried out during routine antenatal care.

- Describe three reflexes that newborn babies show.

- What toys and activities can be offered to a three-month-old baby?

- Describe the physical skills of a nine-month-old baby.

- What is colostrum?

- Outline the benefits of breast feeding.

- What types of food could be offered to a seven-month-old?

- What types of food should not be given to babies?

- What should the temperature of bath water be?

- Outline the basic advice given to prevent cot death.

Resources

Further reading

Dare, Angela & O'Donovan, Margaret 1995 *A Practical Guide to Working with Babies,* Cheltenham, Stanley Thornes

Health Education Authority 1988 *A New Pregnancy Book,* London, Health Education Authority

Useful contacts

The Multiple Births Foundation
Queen Charlotte's and Chelsea Hospital
Goldhawk Road
London W6 0XG
020 8383 3519

Twins and Multiple Births Association (TAMBA)
Harnott House
Little Sutton
South Wirral L66 1QQ
0151 348 0020

National Childbirth Trust (NCT)
Alexandra House
Oldham Terrace
London W3 6NH
020 8992 8637

CHAPTER 16

Provision of services in the UK

Families and change

The values and attitudes of societies evolve and change. In Britain we have seen many changes to family life in the last hundred years, some of which would have been hard to imagine just thirty years ago.

The main changes include:

- a decrease in the number of marriages

- more marriages ending in divorce

- an increase in couples living together both before and in place of marriage

- a growth in the number of lone parents (21 per cent of all families)

- a big increase in the number of live births outside marriage

- an increase in the number of one-person households

- a decline in the number of children being born (1.9 children in a family)

- an increase in the number of people aged over 64, as life expectancy has increased.

These changes have dramatically affected the way that we think of the family unit. The number of traditional nuclear families consisting of two married parents and their children has decreased, while the number of step-families has risen. These changes mean that early years workers must not make assumptions about the type of family unit in which children are living. Many children will be living in step-families, with lone parents, and also in extended families.

There are also some cultural differences between the types of family units in which children may be brought up. Statistically, one in ten Bangledeshi, Indian or Pakistani households will be extended. This means that more than one family is living together. Only 25 per cent of households currently fit the traditional nuclear family model. (See pages 426–427 for more information about different types of family structure.)

Women

Social and legal changes in women's roles

It is interesting to see how women's role in society has also changed. More women than ever before work while their children are living at home. In spring 1997, 18 per cent of women with children aged between 0 and 4 were in full-time employment, whereas between 1989 and 1991 this figure was 13 per cent.

The table below clearly shows that more women return to work as their children become older. If this

Type of work	Youngest child aged 0–4	Youngest child aged 5–10
Full-time	18%	23%
Part-time	33%	44%
Total working	51%	67%

Source: *Social Trends 28*, Office for National Statistics, 1998

Economic activity of women: by age of youngest dependent child, spring 1997

trend continues, there will be increased demand for out-of-school care, which may in turn allow some early years worker opportunities in a growing sector. According to this table, 51 per cent of women with children aged 0 to 4 are in some type of employment.

There have been many changes in the role of women in our society. There are often different reasons for these changes but most sociologists include the following:

- an understanding of how to control fertility – leading to lower birth rates

- the development of health and social services

- opportunities during the two world wars for women to do work traditionally carried out by men

- the increase in labour-saving devices in homes, e.g. washing machines, central heating and the decrease in the number of jobs that needed physical labour

- campaigning by women for equal rights and opportunities.

It is worth looking at how women have gradually gained equal status in law and in other areas including employment, over the last few years. Some would argue that there is still not full equality of opportunity, however much has been achieved – as can be seen from the table below.

The change in the role of women in our society has meant that more and more women are working after they have had children. This means that there will be

1928	All women over 21 are able to vote
1945	Family allowances paid directly to mothers
1969	Wives can have legal and financial contracts in their own right e.g. have their own bank account without asking their husband's permission
1970	Equal Pay Act (came into force in 1975). Men and women to get equal pay when doing same or similar jobs
1973	Equal rights of guardianship over children

1975	Sex Discrimination Act – women could not be discriminated against in the fields of training, education, employment and the provision of goods, housing and public services
1983	Equal pay for work of equal value – if the responsibility of the job is similar to another there can be no discrimination on the grounds of gender
1986	Equal retirement ages of men and women
1988	Finance Act (began in 1990) – independent taxation for husband and wife
1993	Trade Union Reform and Employment Rights Act means that women cannot be dismissed on the grounds of pregnancy. Maternity rights extended

an increase in demand for quality child care to support parents who wish or need to work.

Think about it

It is widely accepted that women have more opportunities open to them than in previous years, but have attitudes really changed? Some women feel that equality has backfired because they are working harder than ever before as they are juggling the demands of the home with working outside of it.

In pairs, look at the following statements and consider whether you agree with them.

- Women are generally responsible for organising child care arrangements.

- Women do the cooking and cleaning in households.

- Women are made to feel guilty about working full time and leaving their children.

- Women have to make a choice between career or having a family.

- Most women would prefer to marry a rich man and stay at home.

Social issues affecting families

There are many social issues that affect children's development. In Chapter 2, we looked at the effects of discrimination and prejudice on children's development. In this section, we are looking at the way in which poverty can affect families.

Poverty

What is poverty?
There are different ways of measuring poverty, which means that statistics about how many families are living in poverty will vary.

There are two main ways of measuring poverty:

- Absolute poverty – not enough money to pay for food, water and shelter. This level of poverty is virtually unheard of in the United Kingdom, but exists in some developing countries.

- Relative poverty – this takes into account the standard of living of a country's population;

a person whose income is much lower might be classified as living in poverty.

It is on the principle of *relative poverty* that most of the statistics used by organisations are based.

Causes of poverty
Although there are many reasons why families are living in poverty there seems to be a strong link between employment and poverty. Where families do not have at least one member of the family working full time, they are likely to be living in poverty. The link between employment and poverty is strong, although people can be working but still living in poverty if they are on low wages. Lone parents are often living in poverty as they are unable to afford full-time child care to allow them to work.

Who is most affected by poverty?
There are several groups of people in our society who are more likely to be living in poverty. They are more

---

ISSUES   How the poor actually pay more

If you are living on a low income, you may find that things are more expensive!

In pairs, look at some of the examples below and see if you can think of other ways in which the poor may pay more.

Housing
- Poor-quality housing means that heating is more expensive.

- Poor heating systems mean that more money is spent on fuel.

- House insurance may cost people more if they live in an area with poor housing as these areas are often hit by crime.

Food
- Lack of money means that families are unable to buy food in large quantities or take advantage of offers such as 'buy two, get one free'.

Goods
- Lack of money to pay for goods outright means that poor families borrow money and have to pay interest.

Clothing and footwear
- Lack of money means that cheaper clothing and footwear is bought, which needs replacing more quickly.

likely to be discriminated against in terms of finding employment and also in terms of income.

- **Women** often take part-time work, which tends to be less well paid, in order that they can care for their children.

- **Black and ethnic minority groups** may be discriminated against when looking for work and rates of unemployment are far higher than in the white population.

- **Disabled** people may be discriminated against by employers or may be unable to work due to their disability.

How poverty can affect families

Poverty can affect families in many ways. But, essentially, poverty removes choice from people's lives. They may not be able to choose where to live, where to send their children to school and where to shop. People living in poverty do not have the same choices about lifestyle as others – choice revolves around what they can afford, rather than what they want.

The diagram below shows the practical effects of living in poverty.

Children and poverty

Children are often the real victims of poverty. They are five times more likely to have an accident, their overall life expectancy is likely to be shorter and their achievement in schools is likely to be lower. Poverty is in many ways an equal opportunities issue as children who are living in poverty miss out. Their parents may not be able to afford to pay for them to attend dancing lessons, piano lessons or even the school uniform to make them feel the same as other children.

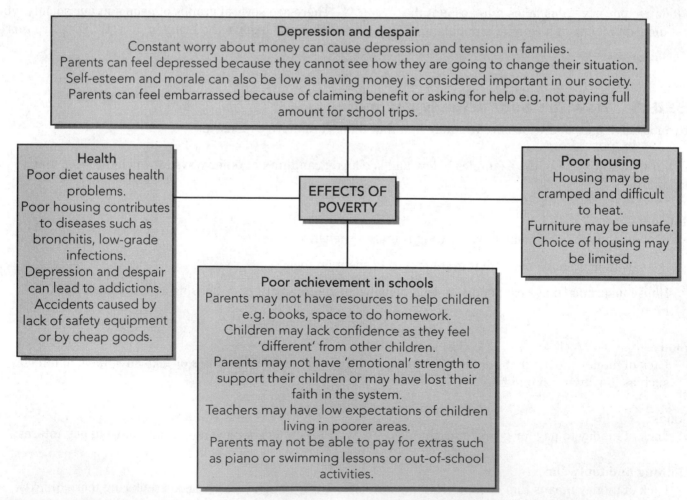

Depression and despair
Constant worry about money can cause depression and tension in families.
Parents can feel depressed because they cannot see how they are going to change their situation.
Self-esteem and morale can also be low as having money is considered important in our society.
Parents can feel embarrassed because of claiming benefit or asking for help e.g. not paying full amount for school trips.

Health
Poor diet causes health problems.
Poor housing contributes to diseases such as bronchitis, low-grade infections.
Depression and despair can lead to addictions.
Accidents caused by lack of safety equipment or by cheap goods.

EFFECTS OF POVERTY

Poor housing
Housing may be cramped and difficult to heat.
Furniture may be unsafe.
Choice of housing may be limited.

Poor achievement in schools
Parents may not have resources to help children e.g. books, space to do homework.
Children may lack confidence as they feel 'different' from other children.
Parents may not have 'emotional' strength to support their children or may have lost their faith in the system.
Teachers may have low expectations of children living in poorer areas.
Parents may not be able to pay for extras such as piano or swimming lessons or out-of-school activities.

Effects of poverty

It is gradually being understood that children living in poverty have lower expectations of what they wish to achieve in their own lives – and this in turn leads to children leaving school early. They may also lack good role models – for example, they may see older children committing petty crimes and come to the conclusion that this is normal behaviour.

Crime, delinquency and socially deviant behaviour

Crime is a social issue that can affect children and their families. It is important to understand the difference between crime, delinquency and socially deviant behaviour as these words are often used incorrectly.

- **Deviance** is any non-conformist behaviour that is disapproved of by society. Deviant behaviour does not necessarily have to be illegal. Spitting is an example of deviant behaviour. It is not illegal to spit, but it is not approved of. Some socially deviant behaviour is illegal, for example, selling drugs.

- **Crime** is behaviour that breaks the law.

- **Delinquency** is crime committed by those between the ages of 10 and 17 years.

Links between crime, delinquency and poverty
There are strong statistical links between criminal acts and poverty. However, this does not mean that all people living on low incomes are likely to be involved in criminal activities! Research into crime shows three main features:

Victims of crime

The Office for National Statistics shows that where you live can make quite a difference when it comes to crime. People living on council estates or in areas of low income are more likely to be victims of crime, especially burglary. Particularly affected are:

- single-parent families
- people living in rented accommodation
- people with no house contents insurance.

1 Most crimes reported are in urban areas (cities, estates).
2 Young working-class males are more likely to commit the crimes.
3 Crimes are often against property, for example, burglaries, vandalism, car theft.

When looking at crime, it is always important to remember that many crimes go either undetected or unreported. This means that we will always have an incomplete picture.

Reasons for the pattern of crimes and socially deviant behaviour
Many reasons are suggested for the link between poverty and criminal activity. These include:

- Poor housing, unemployment and low morale can make young people feel that they want to 'knock' the system.

- Selling drugs or breaking into a house can be a quick way of gaining money and also can give young people a thrill.

- Peer group respect may be gained by committing deviant acts.

- Deviant acts such as taking drugs, smoking and vandalism may become the 'norm' amongst groups of young people. i.e. young people are expected to behave in this way.

How children and families can be affected by crime and deviant behaviour
We have seen that families living on low incomes may find themselves becoming victims of crime. They may also find that their children are exposed to behaviour such as swearing, vandalism and truancy. The danger is that young children often model themselves on older children. If young children see that smoking or drug taking is 'accepted' behaviour, they are more likely to copy it.

Families are also affected in other ways. Children may find that their play area is vandalised. Parents may find that local shops close or raise their prices because of thefts and break-ins. It can be hard for families living in poverty to improve their situation because they may not be able to move.

Think about it

You are passing a play area on the way to work. You see that there are two youths tipping over the litter bin and smashing up the swings.

In pairs, consider the following:

1 Would you tell the youths to stop?
2 Would you report the youths to the police?
3 Would you intervene in any way?

If you do not think that you would intervene – consider the reasons why.

Marital breakdown

Current trends for divorce in the United Kingdom have levelled out at about 40 per cent of all marriages. This means that there are many couples who separate when their children are young. There are also many children whose parents are co-habiting and may separate, also causing family breakdown.

What happens to children when parents separate?
The question of who children will live with after a separation will depend partly on who has parental responsibility. Married couples share parental responsibility, whereas only a mother automatically has parental responsibility when parents are not married. This may mean that if the father does not have parental responsibility, the children will stay with the mother.

The Children Act 1989 is clear that, when parents separate, the needs of the children must be taken into consideration and are 'paramount' when deciding on where children should live. The courts encourage parents to try to agree between themselves on custody arrangements and only step in where parents fail to agree. If parents fail to agree, the court will consider the views of the children, existing arrangements and the needs of the children to see both parents.

Divorce

According to the current system for obtaining a divorce, a court can grant a divorce only where a marriage has irretrievably broken down and this has lasted more than one year. There are five ways of showing this:

■ five years' separation

■ two years' separation if both partners agree

■ two years' desertion

■ unreasonable behaviour of one partner

■ adultery.

ISSUES Separate or stay together?

It was often thought in the past that it was better for disaffected couples to separate, rather than bring up children in an atmosphere of conflict. Research looking at children's performance in schools would suggest that this is not necessarily the case. The Exeter study showed that where children were in families where there was tension and conflict, they generally performed better than children whose parents had separated.

■ What do you think about this?

■ Do you think that divorce is too easy?

■ Do you think that parents should stay together for the sake of the children?

■ If you were able to change the laws about marriage and divorce – what would you do?

You may like to consider these questions in pairs.

How long does it take to get a divorce?
This often depends on whether the divorce is amicable or whether it is contested. The courts will not agree to a divorce until issues regarding children and finances are resolved. This means that some couples divorce quite quickly, within six months of splitting up, if one partner admits to showing unreasonable behaviour.

Attitudes towards divorce and separation
There has been quite a change in society's attitudes

towards divorce. There was a time when being a divorced man or woman was damaging to your reputation. Nowadays, there are so many divorces that there is no such social stigma. However, no one denies that divorce and separation are painful processes and can seriously affect children's well-being.

Social policy and social welfare

It has been said that the mark of any civilised country is the way in which it cares for its poorest members.

In Britain, we have developed a system of health and social services designed to protect the poorest and most vulnerable members of society. This system began following the Beveridge report published in 1942. William Beveridge identified five evils to be eradicated:

- *Ignorance*: lack of education

- *Disease*: lack of health care provision

- *Squalor*: lack of good housing

- *Want*: lack of income

- *Idleness*: lack of employment.

The report went on to look at how these 'evils' could be addressed. Following the report, a social welfare system was developed between 1944 and 1948 when the National Health Service, free education and the social security systems were introduced.

The means of paying for health care and social security followed a simple idea: people who were able to work should contribute into a general pot and when they or their family needed help, either financial or medical, they would be looked after. The money was to be collected through National Insurance and income tax. Health care would therefore be free, people who could not work would be paid and retired people would be given a state pension if they had contributed enough.

Although the original idea was simple and the scheme popular, it has proved to be extremely

difficult to manage and quite expensive for every government.

Economics and social welfare

The difficulty for any government is being able to balance its books and keep its promises! To balance its books every government sets out a budget. In a budget, the government will look to see what money it can raise and also decide where this money needs to be spent.

ISSUES   Political priorities

Every political party has to decide where they would spend money if they were elected. During a general election they write down their ideas in a 'manifesto'. In the 1997 general election, education was mentioned by the three major parties as being extremely important.

Look at some of the spending areas below

1 Health
2 Defence
3 Recreational and cultural affairs
4 General public services
5 Education
6 Social security
7 Housing and community facilities
8 Public order and safety (police and fire)
9 Transport and communication

In pairs, guess the order in which they are usually placed according to how much money is spent. (You can check your answers on page 409.)

If you were in charge of the government in what order would you place them?

Deciding on policies and services

Every government has to decide how best to use the public money it raises. There are some problems that are quite difficult to solve, such as unemployment, and each government will have different approaches to solving the problems. This means that policies which affect families can change – for example, at present the government is prioritising child care and out-of-school care.

Raising income

To pay for services, the government needs to raise money. It does this in several ways including:

- income tax – a tax on a person's income e.g. money they earn or have in savings

- Valued Added Tax (VAT) currently paid on many goods and services at a rate of 17.5 per cent

- National Insurance contributions – this money was originally supposed to be used to pay for benefits, but not enough is raised this way.

The problem for most governments and political parties is that, although voters want services such as the police, health care and free schooling, most voters do not like paying tax! It is not easy for governments to cut spending as many services are *statutory*, which means that by law they must be provided. For example, the law says that state schools should be free.

Statutory services

The role of the government is either directly to provide statutory services or to supervise them through government departments. Each government department is headed by a secretary of state who is responsible to parliament. The Prime Minister chooses the secretaries of state from the members of parliament. They are normally in his political party. Secretaries of state are responsible for making sure that the statutory services are provided. They often do this by supervising the work of local authorities, health authorities and other organisations. Parliament can ask a secretary of state to explain if services are not provided either by asking questions during

parliamentary question time or by asking the secretary of state to appear in front of a select committee.

The role of government departments

The most powerful government department is the Treasury, which controls how much money the other departments are allowed. The amount of money a department is given will affect the services that they can offer.

The main services that families use are health, education and social services. Services and support are provided either directly through central government – for example, social security is directly under government control – or through local authorities.

The role of local authorities in providing services

Many statutory services will be provided by the local authority. The local authority is funded in three main ways from:

- a grant from central government

- householders paying council tax on their properties

- local businesses paying business rates on properties.

There are differences in the ways local authorities work across the country. In some areas, county councils are the main providers of statutory services and other services are provided more locally by district councils. In other areas, there is one unitary authority which provides all the services.

Local authorities provide many services that we take for granted, such as street cleaning, lighting, pest

Government departments relevant to children

Department of Health	Health services
Department for Education and Employment	All aspects of education and employment, including standards in schools
Department of the Environment, Transport and the Regions	Responsible for local government, housing, planning and the countryside

Examples of local government services

DEPARTMENTS OF A BOROUGH COUNCIL

Chief Executive's Department
Personnel Department
Secretary's Department
Economic Development and Estates

Management
Treasurer's Department
Technical Services Department
Housing Department

Rent and Repairs Office
Lifeline
Tourism and Leisure Department
Environmental Services Department

ALPHABETICAL LISTING OF SERVICES IN A BOROUGH COUNCIL

Abandoned Vehicles
Access Officer
Adoption of Roads
Advertisement Control
Allotments
Animal Welfare/Licences
Architectural Grants
Arts Development
Bandstands
Banners and Posters over the
   Highway
Beach Foreshore/Bandstands
Beach Office
Building Conservation
Building Control
Business Rates
Bus Passes and County Cards
Bus Stops and Shelters
Car Parks
Catering (In Style)
Cemetery and Crematorium
Children's Play Areas
Cleansing Services
Coast Protection
Community Charge
Complaints
Conference Promotion
Conservation Areas
Conservation Area Partnership Scheme
Council Tax
Council and Committee Meetings
Country Park
Creditor Enquiries
Dangerous Structure Inspections
Debtor Enquiries
Demolition Notices
Development Control
Divisional Highway Engineer
Dog Control
Drainage – Private Sewers

Ecology Enquiries
Economic Development
Electoral Registration and Elections
Enforcement of Planning Control
Environmental (Green) Information
Estate Management
Fitness Centre
Food Hygiene and Safety
Footpaths
Golf Course
Graffiti
Grants
Grass Mowing
Harassment and Illegal Eviction
Health and Safety
Highway Defects
Highway Drains
Highway Licences
Homelessness
Housing Benefit
Housing Conditions/Grants
Housing – Council
Industrial Estates
Land Charges
Land Drainage
Landslip Inspections
Legal Services
Leisure
Licensing
Lifeline
Listed Buildings
Litter Line
Local Government Review
Marketing (Tourism and Leisure)
Mayoral Services
Museum and Art Gallery
Museum, Old Town
Noise Nuisance
Parking (On Street)
Parks and Recreation

Pest Control
Planning
Pollution Control
Private Tenants Advice
Public Conveniences
Public Entertainment Licences
Recruitment
Recycling Information
Recycling Project
Refuse Collection
Right to buy Council Houses and
   Flats
Roads
Scaffolding on Highways
Seafront
Seafront Concessions
Sheltered Housing – Council
   Properties
Skips on Highways
Sports Centres
Sports Facilities
Street Lighting
Street Naming, Numbering and
   Nameplates
Street Works Supervision
Taxi/Private Hire Licences
Tourism
Tourist Information Centres
Town Centre Development
Trade Waste
Traffic Calming
Traffic Problems
Traffic Signal Faults
Traffic Signs and Road Markings
Trees
Twinning with Other Towns
Vehicular Footway Crossings
Watercourses
Weather (Local Statistics)
Woodland Management

control. They also provide services that are not statutory but are desirable, such as maintaining children's play areas. Just as the government has to decide how to spend their money, the same is true with local government. If local government increases taxes they will be able to provide more services, but if the taxes are too high, local people may decide not to vote for the councillors again.

Services for families

This part of the chapter looks at the services that are most often used by families, such as:

- health services
- education
- social services.

Health services

The aim of the National Health Service is to provide health care for all those who need it, regardless of their ability to pay for it. The difficulty for successive governments is that providing good health care is expensive, particularly new life-saving treatments. The NHS is always under pressure to be as economical as possible. This has meant that new ways of structuring the service are often considered.

Organisation of health services

The Department of Health is the government department responsible for the health service, although it does not directly run the hospitals and other services. To manage the health service, the country has been divided into large areas. Each area has a **Regional Health Authority**, with the exception of Wales where the Welsh Office takes this role. There are currently eight Regional Health Authorities, although this may change.

Every Regional Health Authority is then divided into smaller areas. Each area has a **District Health Authority**. The role of the District Health Authority is to meet the heath care needs of the local population. It uses the funding it receives to buy health care or to run its own services, although most District Health Authorities will buy services from their local Trust.

National Health Service Trusts

In 1990 many health care services, such as hospitals, that had been provided by the District Health

---

ISSUES   Priorities in health care

Providing a health service is expensive – it is the second largest spending area after social security payments.

In order to keep spending within a budget, district authorities sometimes have to make some difficult decisions. In pairs, look at the list below and consider how you would prioritise these areas of spending:

- heart transplants
- research into Aids
- care of premature babies
- breast cancer screening
- infertility treatments
- alcohol and drug rehabilitation.

Do you think that rationing treatment according to age is fair, e.g. a person over 70 may be refused a hip replacement?

Authorities were able to become **National Health Service Trusts**. This means that, in your area, your local hospital may be run by a National Health Service Trust. District Health Authorities now buy the services they want from either their local Trust or from a Trust in another area.

Family Health Services Authorities (FHSAs)
Family Health Services Authorities are responsible for providing health services for families, for example, family doctors, dentists, chemists and opticians. They are responsible to the Regional Health Authority. They work with District Health Authorities to plan the health needs of the local population.

Community Health Councils (CHCs)
Community Health Councils are responsible for representing the views of the local population. They are funded by the Regional Health Authorities, although they are seen as being independent and impartial. They pass on comments about the quality of the services provided and are able to inspect health service premises within their area. Their meetings are open and members of the public are invited to come. Complaints about health services will be dealt with by them.

Costs of services
The National Health Service was designed to give free medical care, but some services, although subsidised, still have to be paid for. These include:

■ dental care

■ prescriptions

■ ophthalmic services, e.g. going to an optician.

To make sure that people on low incomes can still receive these services, the government does not charge everyone. Exemptions from charges include all children under 16 or in full-time education, pregnant women or with a baby under one year, families on income support or family credit.

> Do you know how much one item on a prescription costs?

You'd better go to the doctor before your birthday, otherwise your prescription charge will be my birthday present to you.

Free milk and vitamins for children
A good diet is important for the health of children. This means that the District Health Authorities have to provide free milk and vitamins for children whose parents are on income support or family credit.

Community Health Services
Most families will receive some health care through the community health service. The aim of the service is to provide personal health care for the local community. Teams of professionals work together, although some of them will be funded by the District Health Authority and others by the Family Health Service. The teams are often known as primary health teams (see page 400). Health teams work together to try to prevent illness by giving advice to parents and checking for possible problems. They are often based at the family doctor's surgery or health clinic as it is thought that this may encourage families who are having difficulties to seek help.

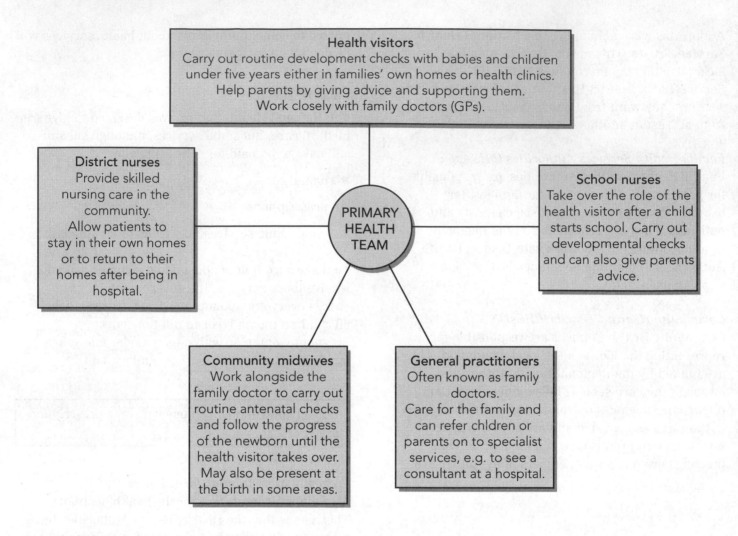

Health visitors
Carry out routine development checks with babies and children under five years either in families' own homes or health clinics. Help parents by giving advice and supporting them. Work closely with family doctors (GPs).

District nurses
Provide skilled nursing care in the community. Allow patients to stay in their own homes or to return to their homes after being in hospital.

PRIMARY HEALTH TEAM

School nurses
Take over the role of the health visitor after a child starts school. Carry out developmental checks and can also give parents advice.

Community midwives
Work alongside the family doctor to carry out routine antenatal checks and follow the progress of the newborn until the health visitor takes over. May also be present at the birth in some areas.

General practitioners
Often known as family doctors. Care for the family and can refer chldren or parents on to specialist services, e.g. to see a consultant at a hospital.

ISSUES   Homework for primary children

The Department for Education and Employment publishes guidelines about the way in which schools are run. For example, they have recently sent out guidelines about homework for primary age children. There are different views about young children being given homework. In pairs, consider the following viewpoints:

▪ Children should be able to play when they have finished a day at school.

▪ Homework will help children get into the habit of studying.

▪ Not all children will do the homework because their parents are not able to support them. This means that they will fall behind the other children.

▪ Homework will encourage children to read more at home.

▪ Homework will give teachers extra pressure.

What do you think about primary children being given homework?

You might like to ask a primary teacher, a parent and a child what they think.

Children and education

The government department responsible for education is the Department for Education and Employment (DFEE). Education is the third largest spending area, following Health and Social Security.

The DFEE oversees the work of several organisations, including:

- **Local Education Authorities** – they are given funds to deliver nursery, primary and secondary education in their areas.

- **OFSTED** – this organisation arranges inspections of schools and nurseries. OFSTED will in future add to its role by taking over the registration inspections that are currently carried out by local authorities.

- **Further Education Funding Council** – the organisation that funds colleges delivering further education and carries out inspections.

School attendance

Children are required to be in full-time education in the school term after their fifth birthday. But in practice many children start school in the year in which they are due to be five (the so-called 'rising fives').

Parents have a duty to make sure that their children are receiving full-time education and local authorities employ Education Welfare Officers to check that children are in school.

Parents can choose to educate their children at home, but they must show that the children are in full-time education.

Types of school

There are many types of schools and the system of education can vary in different parts of the country; for example, in some areas there are middle schools that take children between the ages of 11 and 13, whereas other areas do not have these schools. Parents can choose to have free state education for their children or pay for private education. The Education Act 1980 allowed parents to express a preference for a place at a state school. This means that where a school is oversubscribed, a parent will not automatically be given a place for the child. Occasionally, parents can ask their local authority to pay for a place at a fee-paying school, if they can show that their child has a special need – for example, a child with dyslexia may be able to attend a special fee-paying school.

Children with special needs

The Education Act 1981 introduced the idea of children with 'special educational needs'. This phrase covers all children who need extra support in their education, for example, children with reading difficulties as well as children with disabilities. The Act makes it clear that it is the local education authority's duty to make sure that these needs are assessed and that the children are given the support that they need. The process of assessing children's needs is carried out by a team of professionals and a statement of need is drawn up. This process is often called *statementing*. As well as creating the term 'special educational need', the Act also suggested that children should wherever possible receive their education in an ordinary school, which has meant that there are now fewer 'special schools' although many ordinary schools now have special facilities and units for special needs children (see also page 25).

Nursery education

Every four-year-old is entitled to receive some nursery education. A nursery education grant means that children can have either a part-time place in school or attend some free sessions at a playgroup or nursery. Nurseries and playgroups wanting to receive the nursery education grant have to be inspected by OFSTED and work to the early years curriculum. The government plans to introduce some free nursery sessions for three-year-olds in the near future and from September 2000 will be extending the early years curriculum to this age range.

Education Welfare Benefits

There is some help available that parents on low incomes can ask for while their children are at school. These benefits include:

- free school meals
- help with clothing and uniform

- free school transport
- maintenance and other grants.

Providing the help is the responsibility of the local education authority and the amount of help given will often depend on where a child lives.

Social services

The provision of social services is split between central government and the local authority. Central government is directly responsible for the Benefits Agency and the Child Support Agency, whereas the local authority is responsible for providing a range of personal social services, such as housing, home helps, etc.

Social services – benefits

The Department of Social Security is the department responsible for deciding the rules for claiming benefits; although the actual work of paying out benefits, producing and checking claim forms is carried out by the Benefits Agency. The Department of Social Security also oversees the work of the Child Support Agency. The rules about different benefits are frequently changed and can be quite complex. This means that early years workers should always advise parents wanting information to visit an advice centre or contact the Benefits Agency for further information.

Different types of benefits

There are different types of benefit: contributory and non-contributory.

Contributory benefits

In order to claim contributory benefits, people must have paid sufficient National Insurance contributions. Examples at the time of writing include Jobseeker's Allowance, Statutory Maternity Pay and State Pension.

Non-contributory

These benefits are payable to anyone who meets the criteria. Most of these benefits are '**means tested**'. People have to show how much money they have or are earning before a benefit is paid. Examples of means-tested benefits at the time of writing include Income Support and Family Credit.

A few benefits are **universal** which means that anyone can claim them, providing they meet the criteria. Child benefit is a universal benefit.

Other benefits

Sometimes families who do not claim benefits can lose out in other ways, because claiming one benefit can automatically qualify you for support from other organisations. For example, a family on income support will be able to have free prescriptions, free school meals and even fee remission from college courses.

ISSUES Should child benefit be a universal benefit?

At present, child benefit is paid to the mother, regardless of a family's income. There are advantages and disadvantages to paying universal benefits.

In pairs, consider the comments below:

- Paying everyone is a waste of money, because some families do not need it.
- By paying everyone, it means that there is no shame in getting it.
- Paying everyone child benefit means that there is less money for families who really need it.
- By paying everyone, it means that you can be sure that families who need money actually get it – often benefits go unclaimed.

What do you think about child benefit being available to all families?

Child Support Agency

The 1991 Child Support Act was designed to make sure that absent parents – often fathers – still contributed to the cost of caring for their children. Parents who are claiming benefits are asked for details about the absent parent, so that the Agency can claim some money from them. The Child Support Agency also helps parents who are not on benefits, but whose previous partner is not paying towards the cost of raising the children.

Personal social services

The local authority is responsible for providing many personal social services for families and other vulnerable people in its area.

Housing

Local authorities have a duty to help homeless people in their area. Children and their families are considered to be a priority. Many local authorities do not have enough 'social housing' which means that there are often waiting lists for council homes and other subsidised rented accommodation. Therefore, in some areas, families are put into bed-and-breakfast accommodation.

The local authority is also responsible for paying housing benefit for people entitled to it. Housing benefit can be used to pay for private rented accommodation as well as subsidised housing. Local authorities employ rent officers to check the quality of rented properties and also to help tenants and landlords assess fair rents.

The Children Act 1989 and local authorities

The Children Act 1989 was widely welcomed by most professionals who work with children. It has meant that local authorities now have a responsibility not only for children in their care, but towards all children who live in their area. This means that they are responsible for registering early years settings and childminders.

Social services – social workers

The local authority is responsible for providing social services in its area. This means that the authority employs teams of social workers to work with families who are considered to be in need. Social workers can help families in many ways; for example, giving advice about benefits or arranging child care. They also have a role in preventing child abuse and in protecting children who may be 'at risk.'

Registration of early years settings and people working with children

Local authorities are responsible for annually inspecting people who work with children and in early years settings. This includes childminders, residential homes and any setting that cares for children under eight for more than two hours per day.

Children in need

Under the Children Act, children have a right to basic standards of care, love and upbringing. Where parents are unable for any reason to meet these needs, the local authority has a duty to step in and provide support for these children 'in need'. The Children Act 1989 also defined disabled children as being children 'in need' and local authorities have to keep a register of disabled children in the area.

The Children Act also made it clear that, wherever possible, children should be brought up within their own family.

In order to support children in need and their families, local authorities have to provide three types of service:

- support to help children in need stay with their families, for example counselling, home helps, holidays
- family centres, i.e. places where parents can meet their children, have counselling
- day care, such as nurseries and childminding for children under five and out-of-school care for older children.

'Looked after' children

Some children are not cared for by their families and are 'looked after' by the local authority. There are many reasons why local authorities may be responsible for children – for example, parents may have asked social services to take over their care or the child may be the subject of a care order because the child has suffered harm. (Parents still retain parental responsibility if their children are in care and local authorities should be working in partnership with them. See page 430 on parental responsibility.)

It is interesting to note that since the Children Act 1989 stressed the importance of children remaining with their families wherever possible, the numbers of 'looked after' children has fallen. In 1981 there were 99,000 children in local authority care, while in 1995 the figure was down to 57,000.

Types of care for 'looked after' children

There are several ways in which local authorities care for 'looked after' children. These include:

- local authority homes
- children's homes run by the voluntary sector
- family placements (often known as fostering)
- residential schools
- secure accommodation.

Local authority and voluntary homes

The shortage of placement families has meant that some children are put into children's homes. There are some advantages to this kind of care where there is a lack of placement families, as children will not be split up from their siblings, staff are well trained and there will be some continuity of care for children. There is, however, the danger that children do not get sufficient one-to-one attention and that they may not learn to form deep attachments. (See Chapter 8 on the importance of attachments.)

Family placements

In 1995, 64 per cent of 'looked after' children were placed with families. In theory, this is seen as being the best type of care for children as they can make substitute attachments. In practice, many local authorities have difficulties in finding sufficient families who will take on children. Some children come into placement families with severe emotional and behavioural needs. This can be disruptive to the family's other children and in some cases 'looked after' children are sent to several different families. Another problem for social workers is to find families that are able to take in several children from the same family.

Residential schools

Some local authorities have residential schools for children. Some schools cater for children with severe special needs, whereas others are run for children whose behaviour cannot be coped with in other establishments.

Secure accommodation

There are some centres that provide secure accommodation for children. A court must agree that a child needs to be in secure accommodation and the decision is reviewed every six months. The decision to put children in secure accommodation is not taken lightly. Courts will agree to this step only if:

- a child is likely to harm himself
- a child is likely to harm others through his actions.

Complaints procedures

Local authorities are required to have a complaints procedure for children in their care. This is to protect children from potential physical or other abuse by staff or other children. The complaints procedure has to have an independent element. In addition, children in the care of the local authority can also have their own solicitor as well as a *guardian ad litem* (see page 421).

The role of the private and voluntary sectors in delivering services

Local authorities can pay both the private and voluntary sectors to carry out services for them. This is called *contracting out*. Local authorities are required to make sure that services are good value by seeing who can provide the cheapest and best service. The rules about how they should do this are likely to change in the near future, but at present the organisation that provides the cheapest service is likely to be able to run it. Local authorities still have to make sure that the service meets the required standard. The advantage of contracting out is that the local authority pays only for the services that it needs rather than having to employ people on a permanent basis.

Voluntary organisations

In Britain there is an established network of charities and voluntary organisations. Some charities have been running for long periods of time, when in the past there was no support for vulnerable people. The NSPCC, for example, was founded in 1884 to protect children. When social welfare was introduced in the 1940s, it was thought that there would be no further need for charities. However, charities and voluntary organisations are still needed as in many areas they provide the 'extras' that local authorities are unable to pay for.

Voluntary organisations raise money from the public and their businesses are non-profit-making. They are often run by teams of paid staff and unpaid volunteers. Voluntary organisations can help families and children in many ways :

- providing services, for example, playgroups

- giving advice and support, through freephone advice lines

- campaigning and raising awareness of issues, for example, how to prevent cot death.

Voluntary organisations often support the work of local authorities. Sometimes local authorities will 'buy their services' as they recognise that they have a particular area of expertise – for example, they may ask a playgroup to keep three places for children in need.

How voluntary organisations help children
Many voluntary organisations try to help and support children and their families. There are organisations such as Brownies and Cubs which provide activities for children, as well as organisations that try to help

Name of organisation	Type of work	Contact address
Barnado's	Working for children in the community. Runs residential accommodation for children with severe learning disabilities.	Tanners Lane, Barkingside, Ilford Essex IG6 1QG
Children's Society	Works on many aspects of early years care – including fostering and adoption work and community-based projects.	Edward Rudolf House Margery Street London WC1X OJL
NCH (National Children's Home) Action for Children	Provides residential and community care. Runs family centres and other community child care projects.	85 Highbury Park London N5 1UD
NCT (National Childbirth Trust)	Helps give support and information to parents and parents-to-be. There are 400 branches in the UK.	Alexander House Oldham Terrace Acton London W3 6NH
NSPCC (National Society for the Prevention of Cruelty to Children)	Works to prevent abuse of children. It runs over 100 child protection teams. Offers training to early years professionals.	National Centre 42 Curtain Road London EC2A 3NH
Parentline	Provides support through helplines for parents having any kind of problem with their child. There are also local groups.	Endway House The Endway Hadleigh Essex SS7 2ANN
Save the Children Fund	The aim of this organisation is to work for the rights of children in the UK and overseas.	Mary Datchelor House 17 Grove Lane London SE5 8RD
National Council for One Parent Families	Gives advice on housing, financial and legal issues. The organisation campaigns to improve the social and financial position of lone parents.	255 Kentish Town Road London NW4 2LX

children in distress, such as ChildLine. Playgroups, play schemes and some after-school clubs are often run by voluntary organisations, although they sometimes receive some financial help from local authorities.

ISSUES   Charitable giving

Some people feel that there are too many charities. They believe that the government should pay for the type of work that they do even if this means that taxes should rise.

- Do you give to charities?

- What are your favourite charities?

- Have you ever felt pressured into giving?

- Do you feel the work of charities and voluntary organisations should be taken on by government?

Some voluntary organisations, such as the NSPCC, have a strong role in child protection. Often parents who are finding parenting stressful prefer to get support and advice from them rather than going to social services.

Parents of disabled children often find support groups very helpful and there is a voluntary organisation for most disabilities.

The role of the private sector in providing services

The private sector also has a role in providing some services. Private organisations are profit-making although they may carry out similar work to voluntary organisations. Examples of private sector services include school meals provision, crèches and nurseries. Increasingly, the government is encouraging all sectors to work together and many grants are available only if the private, voluntary and public sectors are working together.

Working in partnership

We have seen that the voluntary, private and statutory sectors all play an important part in delivering services to families. The government is currently working to bring the sectors together to deliver more effective services to families.

National Childcare Strategy

The National Childcare Strategy aims to provide an additional million child care places by the year 2003. The government has asked each local authority to set up an Early Years and Childcare Partnership (EYCDP). The partnerships are made up of a range of people from all sectors of the private, voluntary and statutory services who work with children and their families. Partnerships also include representatives from social services, employment services and training providers. The EYCDPs in each area have to produce a plan each year showing how they will increase the child care places in their area. The government supports the plans with resources towards training and money for developing an infrastructure. As part of the strategy, working parents will also be able to gain some money towards child care costs through the tax system using the Working Families Tax Credit. Information about child care services is also available to parents through the Children's Information Service (see also page 408).

Surestart

This initiative looks at bringing together the health and education sectors in order to provide a better range of services for children under three and their families. It recognises the importance of children's early years in their later education and social development. At the time of writing there are 250 Surestart areas, although this is to be increased in future years. The areas that have been targeted have some level of social deprivation and poverty and the Surestart initiative involves working with the local community. In some areas, Surestart money has been used to provide more parent-and-toddler groups and 'drop-in centres' as well as parenting workshops.

Knowledge into action

Many private organisations provide leisure opportunities for children – for example, swimming lcubs, dance clubs, etc.

- *Look in your local newspaper or telephone directory to find out what leisure opportunities there are for children in your area.*

- *Choose one club or activity and find out the cost per session.*

- *How can children benefit from such activities?*

- *Why might some local authorities decide to supply for children in need?*

Providing information for families

It is unfortunate that many families who need help, advice and support are not aware of some services provided by local agencies and charities. Every year a lot of benefit remains unclaimed. There are many reasons why information does not reach families.

The barriers

The diagram below outlines some of the common barriers to claiming benefits.

Providing information – a new approach

Most charities, local organisations and government departments are now working very hard to provide good information about the services they offer. It is recognised that some of the information and claim forms that were used in the past were not easy to understand. The Benefits Agency, which is responsible for paying most state benefits, is now producing clear information leaflets and claim forms in several languages.

Partnerships

Most organisations which provide advice for families work together in partnerships; this includes government agencies. This has led to many towns and cities developing 'one-stop'

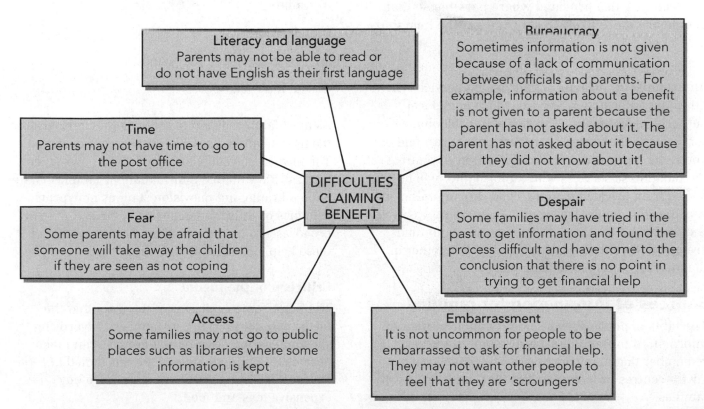

Literacy and language
Parents may not be able to read or do not have English as their first language

Bureaucracy
Sometimes information is not given because of a lack of communication between officials and parents. For example, information about a benefit is not given to a parent because the parent has not asked about it. The parent has not asked about it because they did not know about it!

Time
Parents may not have time to go to the post office

Fear
Some parents may be afraid that someone will take away the children if they are seen as not coping

DIFFICULTIES CLAIMING BENEFIT

Despair
Some families may have tried in the past to get information and found the process difficult and have come to the conclusion that there is no point in trying to get financial help

Access
Some families may not go to public places such as libraries where some information is kept

Embarrassment
It is not uncommon for people to be embarrassed to ask for financial help. They may not want other people to feel that they are 'scroungers'

ISSUES   New Deal for Lone Parents

An example of the way in which advice is provided is the New Deal for Lone Parents. This is an Employment Service initiative which aims to help lone parents get back into employment when they are ready. Research shows that most lone parents want to work and that if they can get back into employment they will be able to escape the poverty trap. The biggest problems for lone parents are often lack of confidence and good child care. The New Deal for Lone Parents means that if a lone parent decides to ask for advice and help, he or she will be assigned a personal adviser. The role of the adviser is to give advice, work out benefits and smooth out the obstacles towards finding a job. This may mean that the Employment Service will pay for some training or child care. The scheme means that every time the lone parent makes an appointment, he or she will always see the same person rather than having to explain the circumstances again each time.

1   Why do you think that the government wants to help lone parents?
2   Why might some lone parents feel that this might be some kind of gimmick?

The Employment Service has arranged special training so that the New Deal Advisers for lone parents are more aware of the some of the problems that lone parents face.

3   Is this type of training a waste of money or can you see why it might be helpful?

advice centres. The aim of these centres is to provide as much help and assistance as possible on one site so that people do not have to travel from office to office. Waiting areas and toys for young children are also provided where possible so that people are more likely to stay and get the help that they need.

An example of this type of information service is the Childcare Information Service, which each local authority is setting up. The aim of this telephone service is to make sure that every parent can find out about the types and cost of child care in their area. To make these services work, information will be pooled from private nurseries, child care organisations, charities and voluntary groups. Partnership working is encouraged by government initiatives and funds are put aside to help local groups work together in the interests of the local community.

Sources of information for families

The table opposite shows some common sources of information for families. It is also important to remember that many towns and cities have local advice centres or local charities that can help families.

The media and information

Families can often find out about services and help from the media. This includes:

- radio
- television
- newspapers and magazines
- the Internet.

As most families listen to radio or watch television, the media can be useful in providing information. The media, especially local radio and newspapers, can provide valuable information for families. Many national radio and television stations now provide helplines or information sheets at the end of their broadcasts to help people find out more. Most of these helplines are freephone numbers.

Criticism of the media

There are some criticisms of the ways that the media can put pressure on families. Advertising showing 'perfect' two-parent families can make parents feel inadequate and adverts aimed at children can put pressure on parents to buy expensive toys and food.

Sources of information for families

Citizen's Advice Bureau	Offers independent advice in legal, social and financial matters.
Public library	Reference sections contain guides to social services and the law that can be helpful. Local voluntary groups often display information in libraries.
Benefit Agency offices	Range of leaflets available and face-to-face advice can be offered.
Law centres	These are found in most cities and are funded by local authorities. They offer free legal advice.
Housing Advice centres	These are funded by local authorities and can help with housing difficulties.
Local councillors	A list of local councillors is available from town halls or county halls. Councillors are often aware of services in the area and can be effective in getting help.
Members of Parliament (MPs)	Writing to Members of Parliament or seeing them at 'surgeries' can be a good way of getting help when bureaucracy seems to be getting in the way. A letter from the local MP often has a curious way of making things happen!
Useful books include	■ *Guide to Social Services* published by the Family Welfare Association. This reference book is published each year and can be found in the reference sections of local libraries. ■ *National Welfare Benefits Handbook* published by the Child Poverty Action group is published each year and explains the benefits that are available.

Some newspapers also give the impression that all lone parents are bad parents and that anyone who is unemployed is scrounging. This type of article is unhelpful and can be one way in which society's prejudices and stereotypes are maintained.

The Internet

The Internet is quickly gaining popularity and most organisations now have a website which provides information. Although the Internet is not widely used by families on poorer incomes at present, it could be a potentially wide source of information. This means that early years workers need to become familiar with how to use the Internet so that they may be able to pass on information.

Criticisms of the Internet
The main problem with the Internet is that anyone can set up a page and paste on information which may not be accurate. It can also take users a long time to reach the information that they want.

Knowledge into action

Choose one of the following charities and, using the Internet, find out if they have a website and find out more about their work.

Kidscape

NSPCC

NCH Action for children

Barnado's

Great Ormond Street Hospital

Answers to question on page 395
6,1,5,2,8,4,7,9,3

Check your knowledge

- Outline three of the main changes to family life in Britain over the last century.

- What is meant by the term 'absolute poverty'?

- How are local authorities funded?

- Give an example of a universal benefit.

- List four different settings in which 'looked after' children may be cared for.

- What are the main reasons why people do not take up the benefits they are entitled to?

- What is 'sure start'?

- At what age must children be in full-time education?

- List four services that local authorities might provide.

- List three effects of poverty on families.

- What is meant by the term 'partnership' in relation to providing services for families?

Resources

Further reading

Donnellan, Craig 1995 *The Poverty Trap*, Cambridge, Independence Educational Publishers

Issues series *Education*, Cambridge, Independence Publishers

Issues series *Homelessness*, Cambridge, Independence Publishers

Office for National Statistics 1998 *Social Trends 1998*, London, HMSO

Useful contacts

Relate
Herbert Grey College
Little Church Street
Rugby CV21 3AP
01788 573241

The Family Law Consortium
2 Henrietta Street
Covent Garden
London WC2E 8PS
020 7420 5000

Child Support Agency
PO Box 55
Brierley Hill
West Midlands DY5 1YL
0845 7133133

Daycare Trust
Wesley House
4 Wild Court
London WC2B 4AU
020 7405 5617

Provision of services and the protection of children in the countries of the UK

CHAPTER 17
The protection of children

This section looks at child protection and child abuse. All carers working with children have to be aware of child abuse and consider their own role in protecting children.

Background to child protection

It seems likely that children have always been abused, although in the past some types of abuse have been accepted and even encouraged – for example, 'spare the rod, spoil the child'. Beating and whipping children was at times considered to be the best way of teaching children right from wrong. Other forms of abuse, such as sexual abuse, were also present in the past, but were hidden away. The position today has changed and society now considers abuse of children to be unacceptable. This change of opinion has been gradual, but children's rights are now well established in law and people working with children are more aware of the importance of making sure that children are safe from abuse.

As an early years worker, you will need to remember that children's needs and welfare must always come first. This means that if you suspect that a child is being abused, you have a duty to act so that he can be protected.

The long-term effects of child abuse

Child abuse has long-term effects on the lives of the victims, which is why children need to be protected. It is generally accepted that repeated abuse is very harmful and causes great psychological damage.

Children's rights

The understanding that children have rights has now been established in law. The Children Act 1989 sets out that children have a right to basic standards of

care, nurture and upbringing. In addition, in 1991 the United Kingdom signed the United Nations Convention on the rights of the child. The convention sets out three main rights that children have when decisions are being made about them:

Non-discrimination All the rights set out in the Convention apply to all children equally whatever their race, religion, language, disability or family background.

Best Interests When adults or organisations make decisions which affect children they must always think first about what would be best for the child.

The Child's Views   Children too have the right to say what they think about anything which affects them.

As well as these three main principles the Convention also sets out the following rights:

- civil and political rights
- name and nationality at birth
- freedom of expression
- freedom of thought, conscience and religion
- meeting other people
- privacy
- access to information
- protection from violence and harmful treatment.

The biggest impact of child abuse is on a child's own self-esteem and self-image. Children may grow up believing that they are worthless and in turn may inflict damage on their own children.

How many children are abused?

There are no firm figures as to how many children are abused. When the NSPCC suggested in 1995 that as many in one in six children may have been abused, there were many protests to say that this was an exaggerated figure covering very minor incidents.

Many people working with abused children have been disappointed by the recent trend to 'put abuse into proportion' – fearing that unless everyone is aware of possible abuse, children may still be in danger.

In 1996–1997, ChildLine, a charity that provides a freephone service for children who are distressed or abused received 103,000 calls from children.

Who abuses children?

It seems that most abuse is carried out by people known to the child, including family members and friends, and in some cases carers.

Abuse can happen in any family and this means that early years workers must not make the assumption

that children in a well-off family will automatically be safe, nor that children will be abused living in a family where money is tight and values are different.

Forms of child abuse

There are considered to be four forms of child abuse:

- physical abuse
- sexual abuse
- emotional abuse
- neglect.

The line between abuse and 'reasonable' discipline

Some countries, such as Sweden, have laws which mean that parents cannot use corporal punishment on children e.g. smacking. The law in this country still allows parents (but not others) to use 'reasonable chastisement' on their children. The test of the term 'reasonable' means what a reasonable parent would impose on a child. A gentle smack may be considered reasonable, but a kick in the stomach is likely to be a criminal offence. Unnatural punishments, such as locking a child in a cupboard, are illegal.

Most child care experts feel that smacking is ineffective and potentially dangerous and organisations such as EPOCH argue that the law should be changed to make smacking illegal.

What do you think about smacking?

Have you ever been smacked?

Physical abuse

Physical abuse takes place when an adult inflicts injuries on a child or does not prevent them – for example, hitting, shaking, or using excessive force when feeding. Giving a child alcohol or drugs would also be physical abuse.

Sexual abuse

The definition of sexual abuse tends to be where an adult has used the child in any way for his or her own sexual gratification. This is quite a wide definition and would cover fondling a child or showing a child a pornographic film, as well as sexual acts.

Most sexual abuse is committed on children by someone they know: only one in six cases is carried out by strangers.

Emotional abuse

This is where adults fail to show children love and affection and where they may continually threaten, shout or verbally abuse a child. This causes the child to lose confidence and become withdrawn and nervous.

The number of children who suffer this type of abuse is hard to measure. It is only recently that it has been recognised as a form of abuse, although its effects are long-lasting as children may find it difficult to form relationships.

Neglect

A child who is neglected is not receiving the basic care needed to thrive. This may mean that children are not given enough food, medical care and warmth. Leaving young children by themselves is also considered as neglect. Sometimes parents neglect children through a lack of knowledge or because they are taking drugs or have a mental illness.

Why do adults abuse children?

It is not completely understood why some parents abuse their children, although research has shown some common themes.

Parent–child attachment

In Chapter 15 we looked at the importance of the parent–baby relationship. There seems to be a link between abuse and the lack of a strong bond between the parent and the child. Even when under stress, most parents are able to protect and care for their children even when their children are also being difficult. This ability to keep caring is thought to be based on the strength of the early attachment that most parents and babies make. Where there are difficulties in this attachment, there is a stronger likelihood of abuse.

There are a number of reasons why the bond formed early in life may not be strong.

Baby and parents have periods of separation
This often happens with premature babies who may need to spend time in special care units or have medical treatment in the months following birth. The increased level of abuse amongst these children has meant that most hospitals try to involve parents in the care of their babies.

Parents are unable to respond to the baby
There are several reasons why parents are unable to make the normal responses to their baby. Sometimes mothers can become depressed after the birth of their child, which is why health professionals always look for signs of post-natal depression.

Some parents are unable to respond to their baby because they have not had the necessary parenting themselves. Statistically, most abusers of children have at some time been abused themselves.

Baby does not respond to the parent
Where a baby is born with a learning difficulty or other disability such as a hearing loss, the child may not respond to the parent's attempts to bond. This can mean that the attachment process is not completed. Many parents of disabled children are still able to love and care for their children, but there are significant numbers of children with special needs who are abused.

Inability to take on the parenting role

Some parents are unable to take on the parenting role. This may happen because the parent's own needs are so great that they cannot cope with the responsibility of caring for their children. There is a higher incidence of neglect and abuse amongst children whose parents are alcoholics, drug addicts or who have depression, or some types of mental illness.

Adults who have been victims of abuse

Not all adults who have been abused become the abusers. Some adults recognise what has happened to them and work hard not to repeat the cycle. For others, the abuse suffered as a child has damaged their self-esteem and understanding of how adults behave. In some situations, abusers may convince themselves that their behaviour is appropriate – believing that they themselves were not harmed by such abuse.

Sometimes parents who have been abused themselves are unable to prevent abuse happening to their children. This may occur because they are attracted to abusive partners and they associate affection and love with being abused.

The realisation that abused children can become abusive parents has led to some organisations trying hard to break the cycle of abuse. Counselling is offered to adults who were abused as children and also telephone helplines are available for parents who feel that they may be close to abusing their children.

Stress

A major factor in some situations where children are abused is stress. Parents who lack some parenting and social skills may abuse their children as a reaction to the stress they are under. Poverty, and a breakdown in family relationships are major causes of stress. Most parents are still able to care for their children in these situations, but where parents have little support and may have received poor parenting themselves, stress may be the trigger for abuse. This is why many organisations working with children, including local authorities, try to help families who they feel may be under stress – for example, by providing playschemes for children in some housing estates.

The role of the early years worker in protecting children from abuse

Everyone working with children has a responsibility to keep children safe from abuse. This section looks at the common ways in which early years workers can protect children by recognising the signs of abuse. Many adults who were abused as children often say that they tried to signal that something was wrong, but they were ignored.

Policies and procedures to protect children

There have been many cases of abuse where children were not identified as having been abused or were not listened to. In some cases, the abuse was 'institutional' which means that it was the staff caring for the children who were actually abusing them. To prevent abuse from happening, it is important for everyone working with children to be able to identify the signs and symptoms of abuse, but also that they should know how to report abuse if they suspect that it is occurring. All early years settings should have a policy in place that should be read and used by all adults in the setting. Ways of reporting abuse may vary from area to area as the Department of Health has set up, using local authorities, Area Child Protection Committees (ACAPs). The aim of the ACAPs is to make sure that everyone in local areas works together and develops a reporting system that will protect children. The policy of an early years setting should therefore reflect what is happening in the local area and cover institutional abuse as well as abuse occurring outside the setting.

Knowledge into action

Find out about your Area Child Protection Committee.

Read your work placement's child protection procedure.

Do you know what you would do if you suspected another adult in the setting of abusing children?

The Department of Health has produced a document entitled 'Working together to safeguard children' which gives guidance to everyone working with children about how to protect them.

This document gives detailed guidance about most aspects of child protection and it is advisable for early years workers to take the time to read it (see end of chapter for details).

A summary of the procedures involved in cases of abuse

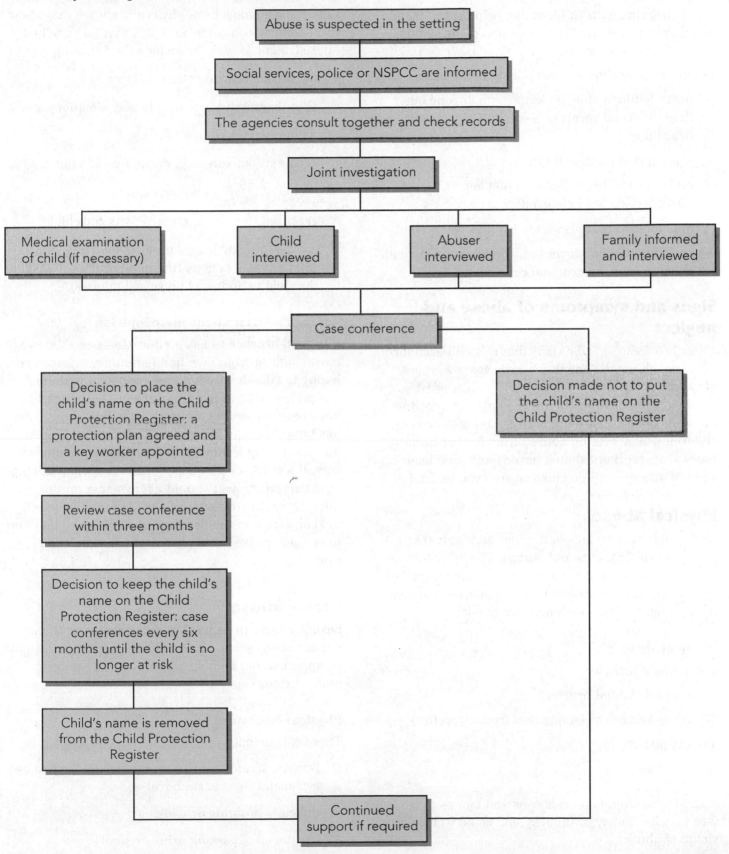

Abuse is suspected in the setting

Social services, police or NSPCC are informed

The agencies consult together and check records

Joint investigation

Medical examination of child (if necessary) — Child interviewed — Abuser interviewed — Family informed and interviewed

Case conference

Decision to place the child's name on the Child Protection Register: a protection plan agreed and a key worker appointed

Decision made not to put the child's name on the Child Protection Register

Review case conference within three months

Decision to keep the child's name on the Child Protection Register: case conferences every six months until the child is no longer at risk

Child's name is removed from the Child Protection Register

Continued support if required

Following procedures

Adults working with children can help protect them by following carefully the procedures of the settings. Common policies include:

- supervising children carefully at home times
- never letting a child go home with anyone other than the usual carer, unless a letter has been brought in
- signing visitors in and out
- making sure that visitors are not left unsupervised with children
- making sure that visitors to settings wear a badge
- checking that employees and people working with children have no criminal convictions.

Signs and symptoms of abuse and neglect

There are some specific signs that relate to each form of abuse, although sometimes early years workers may pick up on signs that the child is distressed through his behaviour. Being vigilant, and knowing the signs of abuse, are important ways of protecting children who are being abused from further harm. Early years workers should never forget that ignoring signs of abuse could, in some cases, even be fatal.

Physical abuse

Most children have falls and minor accidents that result in bruising, cuts and bumps. The difference between genuine accidents and deliberate injuries to the child is often the location of the injuries and also the frequency with which they occur.

Physical signs

These might include:

- unusual-shaped bruises
- scalds and burns (sometimes from cigarettes)
- bite marks
- fractures.

A child who often has black eyes and bumps to the face may be clumsy or unlucky, but could well be a victim of abuse.

Behavioural indicators

Children who have been physically abused may show through their behaviour and play that they are being abused. Signs to look for include the following:

- aggressive towards other children
- show aggressive acts in role-play situations
- withdrawn and quiet
- seems stiff or sore, e.g. doesn't want to sit
- seems reluctant to be with carer
- carer seems to be aggressive with the child
- child frequently brings in notes to excuse him from physical activity (the parent may not wish the child to undress and reveal injuries).

Asking children about their injuries

It is good practice to ask a child about an injury as most children who have had genuine accidents are happy to talk about what has happened to them. Children who have been physically abused might have been told by the abuser not to talk about what has happened and to say that they fell or bumped into something if they are asked about bruising or cuts. If a child seems upset or nervous when talking about an injury, you should always pass on this information to your supervisor. You may be asked to keep a note of the date and type of injury that you have seen, as well as a record of what the child said.

Sexual abuse

Sexual abuse can be hard to detect as the child may not outwardly seem injured. Some physical signs may be apparent, but behavioural indicators can be a more obvious clue.

Physical indicators

These will include:

- bruises, scratches or other injuries unlikely to be accidental (see chart above)
- difficulty in sitting or walking
- frightened of passing urine or stools

- difficulties in passing urine or stools

- frequent urine and genital infections

- frequent toileting accidents.

Behavioural indicators

Children who have been sexually abuse might show the following behaviours:

- babyish behaviour, including comfort habits such as thumb sucking, rocking

- inappropriate behaviour, such as undressing or exposing themselves

- showing sexual behaviour in their play, such as trying to mate two dolls or cuddly animals

- a knowledge of adult sexual behaviour that is unusual for their age

- unwillingness to be with a particular carer

ChildLine reports that sexual abuse often occurs while normal family activities are taking place – e.g. bathing, going to bed, play fights and cuddles. This means that some children may not know that there is anything unusual in the treatment they are receiving from the abuser. Other children may have been told that the activity is a secret and are threatened with the idea that they will be taken away from the family if they tell.

The hidden nature of sexual abuse means that early years workers must listen carefully to children and consider whether the behaviour that they are seeing might be a sign of abuse. If you suspect that abuse is taking place, you should always make sure that you talk to your supervisor about your concerns, or if you are working in a child's home, contact the NSPCC or local authority for advice.

Emotional abuse

There are few physical indicators of emotional abuse, although some older children may show self-destructive behaviour such as trying to cut themselves or drastic dieting. The main indicator of emotional abuse is the child's need for attention and low self-esteem.

Behavioural indicators

Signs of emotional abuse can include the following:

- attention-seeking behaviours, such as being deliberately disruptive

- clinginess and 'hunger' for affection

- telling lies (to gain sympathy or attention)

- babyish behaviour, e.g. sucking thumb, rocking, hair twiddling

- tantrums beyond the age of four

- difficulty in socialising with peers.

Children who are being emotionally abused are very vulnerable because they are happy to receive attention from anyone. This means that some paedophiles can target them as they offer the child love and affection. In the longer term, children with such low self-esteem are likely to underachieve at school and may form intense relationships at an early age. Teenage pregnancies are often a result of children feeling unloved.

Neglect

Parents who neglect their children may have significant personal and other problems of their own. The children might be loved but parents find it hard to provide the basic care that the children need.

Physical signs

These will include:

- frequent accidental injuries (caused by lack of safety devices or supervision)

- children underweight and hungry

- untidy and dirty appearance

- low-grade infections which appear untreated, such as frequent colds, coughing and earaches

- tired (seems to have no particular bedtimes).

Behavioural indicators

These might be signs of neglect:

- children mention being unsupervised

- older children seem to take significant responsibility for younger ones, for example, cooking meals

■ parents rarely appear in settings – for example, for open evenings or to collect children.

Children who are being neglected are at risk of having accidents through being left unsupervised either at home or out playing. They are also vulnerable to attack from strangers. If you suspect that a child is being neglected, you should talk to your supervisor.

Changes in behaviour patterns

Children who are being abused may show behaviour that is not part of their normal pattern or is out of character. This means that a child who has been sunny and outgoing may suddenly be more tearful or aggressive. The change in the pattern of behaviour may be short-lived and a reaction to something specific in their lives, such as the death of a pet, but where behaviour seems to be more long-term and there is no obvious cause, the early years worker should consider the possibility of abuse. This means that the child will be observed more closely for other signs, and early years workers must always pass on their concerns about the child to their supervisor. It is likely that the supervisor will talk to the parents to see if there have been any difficulties at home.

What to do if a child tells you about abuse

There are some simple rules that should be observed if a child tells you she is being abused:

■ Reassure the child that you believe what she is saying.

■ Listen to the child, but do not ask questions.

■ Tell the child that to solve problems, you will need other adults to help you.

■ Reassure the child that she is not in trouble and that she has done the right thing.

Do not:

■ promise the child that you will be able to keep what has been said a secret, otherwise the child will feel that no adult can be trusted

■ question the child or pass any comment other than to reassure the child. If the abuser is taken to court, the prosecution could argue that the child gained ideas from you.

You should immediately find your supervisor and pass on what has been said. You will be asked to keep a record of what the child said as well as the date, time and situation in which the child spoke to you.

If you are working in a home environment, you should seek further guidance from the NSPCC or the local authority.

Confidentiality

At several points during this book, confidentiality is mentioned. In child protection, confidentiality is essential. A careless word might create a situation where a child is put at further risk or may wreck a person's reputation. This means that anything you see, write or read when dealing with child protection issues must be treated as confidential. Information about a child protection issue is generally given on a 'need-to-know' basis. This means that only staff working directly with the child or the parents will be given any information about what is happening. Any records or observations that are made also need to be stored carefully and are extremely confidential.

What happens next

Every early years setting will have a procedure for when children say that they have been abused. The responsibility for contacting the NSPCC or social services is often taken on by the manager or headteacher. If you are working in a home environment, you should make the call if the child tells you that the abuser is the parent.

Once a call has been made, the NSPCC or social services is required to investigate. To do this they will talk to the witness, the child and to the child's family. A case conference will be held to decide what should happen in the child's best interests. Following a case conference, an action plan is agreed and this may mean that a court order is taken out (see page 419).

Contrary to popular belief, many children remain in their own homes, while being monitored by social workers, although the abuser may be asked to leave the family home. Taking a child from home is considered to be a drastic step and perhaps the last resort; the Children Act 1989 maintains that, where possible, local authorities should work alongside parents.

Case conferences

The aim of a case conference is to pool together as much information as possible about the child's situation and well-being. Parents are often invited to case conferences and they are able to bring legal representation if they desire. (The move to involve parents dates from the 1989 Children Act which asks local authorities to work with parents in the interests of the child.)

In addition to social workers and parents, there will also be a range of other professionals present. This may include the child's family doctor, school nurse, teacher or carer and anyone else who may be able to give information about the child. Information is minuted and the meeting has a chairperson. By the end of the case conference, an action plan will be considered and agreed. A date for a further meeting will be set where necessary.

If you are asked to attend a case conference, it is important that any information you give is as accurate as possible. Everything that you learn during the meeting is highly confidential and breaching this would be a disciplinary matter.

Abuse and the Children Act 1989

The Children Act 1989 places a lot of responsibility on local authorities. Under the law all children have a right to basic standards of care, and where parents are unable to meet these the local authority must step in. In child abuse cases, this means that the local authority may at times need either to work with families to prevent further abuse or in extreme cases remove the child from the family.

Taking a child into care

This is considered to be an extreme step as the Children Act makes it clear that, wherever possible, children are best brought up within their own families.

Before a court can make a supervision or care order, it must be satisfied that there are sufficient grounds. This is to prevent local authorities taking children unnecessarily into care.

Courts will decide whether to grant an order based on these grounds: the child has suffered or is likely to suffer

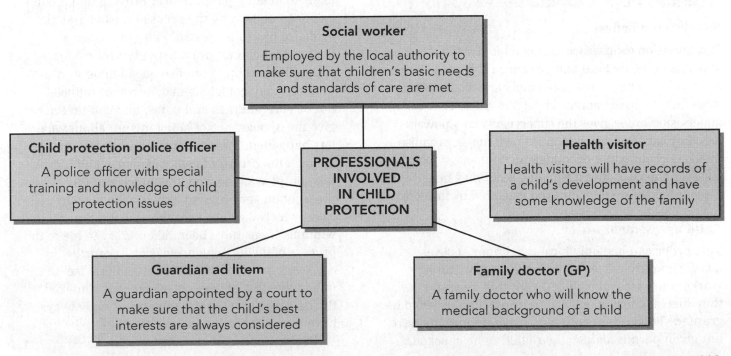

Social worker
Employed by the local authority to make sure that children's basic needs and standards of care are met

Child protection police officer
A police officer with special training and knowledge of child protection issues

PROFESSIONALS INVOLVED IN CHILD PROTECTION

Health visitor
Health visitors will have records of a child's development and have some knowledge of the family

Guardian ad litem
A guardian appointed by a court to make sure that the child's best interests are always considered

Family doctor (GP)
A family doctor who will know the medical background of a child

significant harm because either the harm or likelihood of harm is attributable to the care that the child is receiving; or that the child is beyond parental control.

To show the court that there is enough basis to these grounds, the local authority will have to demonstrate that they carried out some investigations first. This usually means that there has been a case conference which parents were invited to attend.

Child protection orders

There are three types of orders that local authorities and the NSPCC can apply for:

- child assessment order
- emergency protection order
- recovery order.

Care order

A care order places the child in the care of the local authority. The local authority shares parental responsibility with the parents and must try to work with them. A care order lasts until such time as a court discharges it or until the child reaches eighteen. Applications can be made by either the parent or the child to discharge the care order at any time. In addition, the child is appointed a *guardian ad litem* (see opposite).

Supervision order

A supervision order places the child under the supervision of the local authority or probation order, although the child is not taken into care. The supervisor must 'advise, assist and befriend' the child. The supervision order gives the supervisor many powers; e.g. they can visit the child in his own home, organise medical treatment or examination. A supervision order lasts for one year after it is made, but it may be discharged before then, or even extended by the court.

Child assessment order

This order can last only for a maximum of seven days. The purpose of this order is to allow the workers to assess the child. From this assessment, they may ask for an emergency protection order to be granted. This order is often used where parents have not given permission for their child to be checked.

To protect the child's interests a *guardian ad litem* is appointed (see opposite).

Emergency protection order

This order allows the child to be taken immediately into care, although parents can challenge the grounds for the intervention after 72 hours. The order can last for a maximum of eight days and in order to protect the child's interests a *guardian ad litem* is appointed.

Recovery order

This order is used where a child has been abducted or a family is on the run from the local authority. They order the person to produce the child.

ISSUES in child protection – Prosecuting abusers

Although there are laws designed to help children who are being abused, there are relatively few prosecutions each year. It is a difficult process to take to court an adult who is suspected of abuse because our legal system is built on the idea that the prosecution must establish 'beyond reasonable doubt' that a person is guilty. A conviction of child abuse is a serious one and is likely to mean a jail sentence. Proving that a child has been abused by the accused means that all evidence has to be 'tested' and quite often a young child cannot provide the type of evidence that will stand up to intense questioning in court. Children may get frightened, become confused, not be sure of times and dates, and can therefore give the appearance of being unsure about what has happened. To prevent children being put through the ordeal of giving evidence and then the abuser walking free, the police and the prosecution service tend only to take to court cases which they are sure they have a chance of winning. Steps have been taken to try to make the process of giving evidence easier in court, e.g. using a video link; but most experts feel that unless the idea of 'testing' evidence is removed, the defence representing the abuser will always have a strong advantage.

Guardians ad litem

Before the Children Act it was hard for children to have *their* thoughts and feelings listened to. Representatives for children known as *guardians ad litem* are now appointed to represent the child's views in court. Guardians are often family law experts and have access to all the material held on the child. They may talk to the parents as well as to the child. Their role is to make sure that the best interests of the child are being addressed.

Children who have been abused are not meant to receive counselling until after the court process, so that the defence cannot make the case that the child has been influenced by the counsellor. This means that sometimes abusers are not taken to court because it is more in the interests of the child to receive some help straight away.

Preventing abuse

As well as having a role in looking out for signs of abuse, early years workers also need to know how they can protect children from abuse.

This diagram shows the role of early years workers in protecting children from abuse:

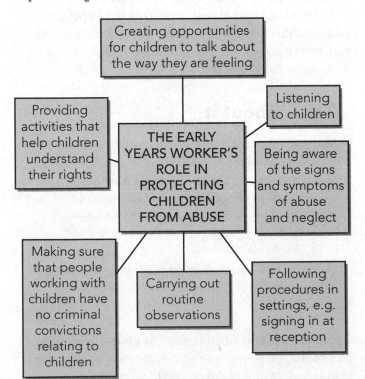

Creating opportunities for children to talk about the way they are feeling

Listening to children

Providing activities that help children understand their rights

THE EARLY YEARS WORKER'S ROLE IN PROTECTING CHILDREN FROM ABUSE

Being aware of the signs and symptoms of abuse and neglect

Making sure that people working with children have no criminal convictions relating to children

Carrying out routine observations

Following procedures in settings, e.g. signing in at reception

Empowering children

There are different types of activities which can be carried out with children of all ages that are designed to help children keep safe from abuse. The charity Kidscape has produced many materials designed to keep children safe. The aim of the activities is to make sure that children feel more confident about themselves and their bodies. Activities should never be carried out in a way that will frighten children, but should provide children with strategies so they know what to do if they have a problem.

Examples of activities include the following.

- Make sure that children know what to do if a stranger approaches them.
- Make sure that children know what to do if they get lost.
- Help children to understand that they have rights over their bodies.
- Help children to realise that they can break 'secrets' if they don't like the secret.
- Encourage children to think about who they can talk to if they have a problem.

Keeping secrets

One way in which some abusers manage to avoid detection is by telling the children that they must keep the abuse a secret. Sometimes children are told that if they break the secret they will be punished. Children need to be told that breaking secrets is not wrong, if the secret is a bad one. To help prevent confusion, it is not a good idea to make children keep secrets – even if they are good ones! It may be better to tell children that you are hoping to give someone a surprise, but if they want to tell someone about the surprise they can.

Giving children confidence

One way in which we can help children protect themselves is by making them confident enough to be able to tell an adult if they are unhappy or being abused. Victims of child abuse often lose their confidence and abusers often tell them that they won't be believed. In some cases, abusers will not choose children who they fear might report them.

There are many ways of giving children confidence, including praise, listening to them and being interested in them. (Confidence and self-esteem are also covered in Chapter 8.)

Encouraging children to think about their own personal safety

Another way in which we can help children is by encouraging them to think about their own personal safety. This is particularly important with older children who may wish to start playing outside or walking home with friends. They need to learn to tell adults where they are going and know that they should not, for example, leave school with anyone other than the person who is due to collect them. It is also suggested that we encourage children to follow their own instincts – so that if they find being with an adult uncomfortable for any reason, they should trust their instinct and tell another adult that they don't feel comfortable.

Child protection organisations

The following organisations have an important role in child protection.

ChildLine

Early years workers may be able to help children by making sure that they know about ChildLine. ChildLine was set up in 1986 and provides a free telephone service which allows children to talk about any problems they are having. They provide 24-hour counselling for children.

NSPCC

The NSPCC was founded in 1884 with the purpose of protection children from cruelty. It plays a strong role in child protection alongside local authorities. It has a child protection helpline which allows people to raise concerns about children or to phone if they feel that they are in danger of harming children.

Kidscape

Kidscape is a charity that was set up in 1984. It produces materials for professionals and parents to use with their children to teach them about bullying, stranger danger and what to do if they have a problem. The aim of Kidscape is to prevent child abuse and bullying by teaching children strategies that will keep them safe. Kidscape also publishes a range of booklets for schools and parents.

(See the end of the chapter for contact information on these organisations.)

Creating opportunities for children to talk

We can help children by encouraging them to talk openly about their feelings. This means that they know that they are allowed to feel angry, sad or afraid. Talking about feelings can open the way for children in future to talk to adults about any problems or difficulties they are facing. It means that a channel of communication has been opened and that they know that, if they are unhappy in some way, they are allowed to share this.

Listening to children

An important way in which we can help children is simply by listening to them. This means that children will learn that you are someone to whom they can turn and will take seriously their news as well as their problems. Early years workers can show children that they care by spending time with them and listening to what they say. This is important, as many children who are abused will often try to say something about what is happening: adults need to be alert to listen to them.

> ## Think about it
>
> You are working in an early years setting and a plumber comes in to mend one of the radiators. You ask him to sign in, but he says there is no point because he is only going to be a few minutes and that with all this fussing he is going to be late for his next job.
>
> Work out how you would convince him that he must sign in and role play this scene with a partner.

Opportunities must be planned to allow children to have some one-to-one attention from workers – for example, hearing children read, carrying out a cooking activity. These types of activity allow children to speak freely to the adults they are with as well as giving children some emotional security.

Carrying out routine observations

Keeping accurate and frequent records of children can protect them. In Chapter 4, we looked at the importance of carrying out routine observations. Routine observations can help us identify changes in children's pattern of behaviour or development. If early years workers are concerned about what they are seeing or the pattern of a child's behaviour, it is important that they dicusss these concerns with their line manager. As mentioned in Chapter 4, it is essential that any records of children are dated, accurate and kept in a safe place. Hearsay observations – for example, recording what someone else has said about the child – are not valid and should not be used.

Helping children who have been abused

It is important that children who have been abused are helped as the effects of abuse can ruin their whole lives. It is recognised that help must be offered to children as soon as possible after the abuse has been detected. There are several specialist professionals who may work with children and often their families as well. These include:

- play therapists (help children by creating play opportunities that encourage children to act out and talk about their feelings)
- psychologists
- child psychiatrists
- family therapists
- counsellors.

Working with children who have been abused

As an early years worker, you may work with a child who has been a victim of child abuse. This could mean that you will have to deal with behaviour which is not 'normal' for the age of the child – for example, a child who has been sexually abused may try to be cuddled in a sexual way. It is important for early years workers to liaise with the professionals working with the children so that appropriate and

agreed strategies are used. In many cases this will mean distracting a child or giving a child attention when he shows appropriate behaviour.

Children who have been abused may show a range of emotions such as anger and fear. Local authorities will often provide extra support for these children such as play therapy or counselling, depending on their age. Through play, children can either learn more appropriate ways of dealing with their feelings or 'play out' their feelings. Children may also benefit from the types of activity outlined in Chapter 8.

Sometimes children who have been abused are very confused about how they should respond to adults – for example, they may alternate between being friendly and co-operative and hostile and resentful. This means that early years workers must be calm and consistently loving in their approach to the children they are working with.

Working with children who have been abused is rewarding but it can also be extremely stressful and, in some cases, distressing. Most settings will therefore provide a 'supervisor' for early years workers so that they can talk about how they are coping.

Knowledge into action

You are working in a nursery attached to a primary school. Tom is four years old and has come into school with a cut above his eye and marks on his face. His older brother who has brought him says that he got the cut by walking into a door. Later on in the day, when you are helping Tom to fasten up his coat, he tells you that his father had got cross with him and had hit him with his belt.

What would you say to Tom?

What would you do next?

Why is it important that Tom's remarks are taken seriously?

Check your knowledge

- List some of the signs that may show that a child has been physically abused.

- What should an early years worker do if he suspects that a child is being abused?

- What is the role of a 'guardian ad litem'?

- Why is it essential that early years workers listen carefully to children?

- What is the aim of a case conference?

- Give examples of the signs that might indicate a child is being physically abused.

- Explain what you should do if a child tells you that he or she is being abused.

- What are area child protection committees?

- Explain two ways in which we can help children to keep themselves safe.

- What is an emergency protection order?

Resources

Further reading

Issues series *Child Abuse*, Cambridge, Independence Publishers

Useful contacts

ChildLine
2nd Floor Royal Mail Building
Strudd Street
London N1 0QW
Freephone for children 0800 1111.

NSPCC
National Centre
42 Curtain Road
London EC2A 3NH
Child protection helpline 0800 800 500.

Kidscape
152 Buckingham Palace Road
London SW1W 9TR
020 7730 3300

Useful websites

BBC Children in Need
www.access.digex.net/~issd/abuse.htm

ChildLine
http://www.childine.org.co/abuse.html

Kidscape
http://www.solnet.co.uk/kidscape/

International Child Abuse Network
http://www.yesican.org/definitions.html

Working with parents

CHAPTER 18
Work with parents

This section looks at the importance of working with children's primary carers, who in many cases will be their parents, although for some children it may be someone else such as a grandparent or foster parent. The ability to relate to and work with parents is an extremely important part of being a professional early years worker.

Why parents and primary carers are important

Parents and primary carers are the most important people in young children's lives. They will have more influence over children's development and identity than anyone else. Children learn about their family history and culture from them as well as the social skills that are needed for their cultural and religious background.

Think about it

Can you do any of the following things?

- play draughts
- wash up
- make a bed
- iron a shirt
- make a phone call
- play cards
- wire a plug
- sew a button a shirt
- use a washing machine.

1 Do you remember where you learnt to do these things?
2 Who taught you?
3 Can you work out five other skills that you have learnt from your family?

Every family has its own rituals, jokes and ways of celebrating. This gives children a strong sense of identity and a feeling of belonging. Parents and primary carers are special for children; they are the people who know them best. This means that parents understand their children well and know what will make them happy as well as what is likely to cause them pain.

Parents are also their children's first teachers. Children often learn many of the life skills that they will need from their parents such as being able to cook, read instructions and use tools. In this way, we can often see that children learn about the interests and hobbies of their primary carers; so children whose parents are interested in pets will know how to feed and care for animals, while children who have a parent who is interested in computers may well be able to mend the classroom computer when it crashes!

Parenting styles

With a few exceptions, most parents love and care for their children. They also want the best for their children, although the way in which parents bring up children can vary tremendously from family to family – for example, some parents may have rigid bedtimes for children, whereas other parents may not feel this is necessary.

Researchers looking at the different ways in which parents discipline and bring up their children have concluded that there are three main styles of parenting.

425

Authoritarian

Authoritarian parents tend to have high expectations of their children and are likely to control and limit their behaviour. They may not spend time explaining the rules and can make statements such as, 'You must do it, because I am telling you to do it.'

Permissive

Parents who are permissive may not take control of their children's behaviour but allow their children a lot of choice and responsibility. Permissive parents may say, 'He will learn from his mistakes.'

Authoritative

Most parents fit somewhere into this band of parenting. They spend some time explaining rules, but will still enforce them. They also spend time listening to their children. It is generally thought that children benefit most from authoritative parenting, because they know the boundaries set for them and so feel secure.

Children are strongly affected by the warmth and quality of communication with parents as well as parental expectations. Parents with high expectations of behaviour and independence are more likely to have children who have a higher self-esteem and are more independent. There are also cultural variations in styles of parenting. Some cultures place an emphasis on authoritarian parenting, but the children do well because of the consistent approach and warmth of communication.

'Goodenough' parenting

Parents tend not to choose their parenting styles. Most parents are influenced by the parenting they received as children and the stresses under which they find themselves.

Most parents are not perfect but are generally 'goodenough'. Increasingly, studies about parenting show that children do not need brilliant parents, but just 'goodenough' parents who are consistent in their care and love.

Different family structures

In today's society, children live in a variety of family structures. The image of a 'normal' family as being children with two parents married to each other is often no longer true. The number of divorces has increased over the past few years and around 40 per cent of marriages now end in divorce, affecting 160,000 children a year.

It is important that early years workers understand that there are many different types of family structures in which children grow up. Most family structures are able to provide the main ingredients for good parenting: love, consistency and physical care.

Nuclear families

This is the family structure that is often portrayed as 'normal' by the media. Parents and their own children live together, with parents having most of the responsibility for caring for their children. Some contact with grandparents and other relatives may take place, although many nuclear families may live in a different town from their relatives.

Extended families

For centuries this was the traditional type of family structure in Britain and in other countries it is still common. Parents, children and other relatives may live together or nearby. Grandparents, aunts or other relatives may help care for the children. Children are seen as the responsibility of the whole family and often children living in extended families feel secure as they have built relationships with several family members.

Reconstituted families

A reconstituted family consists of one natural parent and one step-parent. Where the step-parent has children, the child will have step-brothers or -sisters and if the couple have further children, the child will have half-brothers or -sisters. This is becoming a common type of family structure as many parents divorce or separate and then meet new partners.

Nomadic families

Some families may live by travelling from one place to another. There are two main types of travelling families: gypsies and new age travellers. Gypsies are now recognised by European law as being an ethnic minority and as such are protected from discrimination. They have their own language and cultural identity. They generally travel as extended families. New age travellers are often groups of younger people who wish to find an alternative way of living. Both groups see themselves as separate from society.

Lone-parent families

Lone-parent families consist of one natural parent. There are many different categories of lone parent:

- widowed parents who have lost a partner

- separated or divorced lone parents

- single women who have chosen motherhood

- teenage mothers (statistically, a small percentage of all lone parents).

It is important to understand that not all lone parents have the same needs. The image of all lone parents needing financial support is not always accurate – for example, some women choose to have children without a partner and are financially able to support them.

Adoptive families

Some children live with adoptive families who may or may not also have 'natural' children. Some adoptive children may keep their birth family's surname, whereas others will change their name to their adoptive family's name. As part of the adoption process, most children will spend some time being fostered by their adoptive families before courts grant the adoption order.

Homosexual/lesbian families

Some children live with one natural parent and a same-sex step-parent. Fears amongst the general public that this structure could influence a child's

Think about it

The media often portray parenthood as being a consistently fulfilling and happy experience, although most parents find that there are times when they are exhausted and under pressure. The media also show traditional nuclear families which tends to reinforce people's ideas that this family structure is the most common.

Look at the picture opposite.

What sort of image is it trying to portray?

How might this type of image make children from other family structures feel different?

Why might parents who are lacking in confidence feel threatened by this type of image?

Look through a package holiday brochure and consider the types of images that are being presented.

How many images portray 'happy families'?

Collections/Paul Watts

future sexual identity have not been proven. This being said, adoption of children by homosexuals or lesbians has not been permitted to date.

Communal families

There are a few communes in Britain, where several families who are unrelated live together and act as an extended family for the children. In Israel, there have been many favourable studies which show that children brought up in communes, called kibbutzim, develop well.

Find out more

There is a long-established religious commune in Sussex which produces playthings for children. The Darvell Community welcomes contact from outside bodies and you may like to write for details about their community life.

Darvell Community
Brightling Road,
Robertsbridge
Sussex

Parents as partners in the care and education of their children

There has been a change of attitude about the role of parents in early years settings. Studies show that parents who are involved in the education of their children are more likely to help them to achieve. Parents are now seen as being partners and as having a valuable role to play in the education of their children. This change is reflected in both the law and in the policies of settings – for example, parents are now able to express a preference over which school a child should attend and are also given more information about his or her progress.

As early years workers we should aim to build relationships with parents so that together we can help children to settle in and fulfill their potential. We need to recognise that parents have the long-term responsibility for their children and that they are able

to provide information that will help us care for the child more effectively; for example they will know about any past difficulties that children have had which may affect their behaviour. By trying to work with parents, we will be able to give children more security and stability. (See also ways of relating to parents, page 431)

Parents who do not share the aims of the setting

In an ideal world, parents and carers would enjoy a comfortable relationship. Unfortunately this is not always the case as some parents do not share the aims of the setting where children are receiving care. There can be many reasons for this. For example, a parent may have chosen another school as first preference, or they may be attending a family centre because of a court order. In such situations, parents may feel resentful and might prefer not to communicate with the carers. In such situations, it is important for early years workers to remain calm and friendly. The aim is always to keep the channels of communication open in some way, even if this is simply by greeting and acknowledging parents. In the long term this may help to relax the atmosphere, and will be the best way to help the children to settle.

Think about it

Simon has been told by the court that if he wishes to see his children, he must do so in a supervised setting. He is not very happy about this and hates coming to the setting. He feels watched and suspects that the early years workers are there to report back about him. There is a lot of tension and when Simon arrives he barely nods his head.

1 Why is it important for the staff to try to build a relationship with Simon?
2 How could the tension affect Simon's children?

Early years workers need also to realise that some parents may be afraid of returning to settings, such as schools, where they may have had unpleasant experiences in the past. Most settings try to explain their approaches to parents in a variety of ways, such as at workshops or during open afternoons. This can help to break down potential barriers to communication, although we should always remember that parents are entitled to their own views.

Parents need to be able to voice their views

We also need to understand that even parents who largely support the aims of the setting, may from time to time see things differently. In this situation it is important to listen to parents' concerns and show that we have passed them on. Sometimes the parents can bring about improvements, for example, by showing a setting that they have not provided enough information about their plans.

Think about it

Tinies Nursery has organised an outing to the zoo. One parent comes to you and says that she is unhappy about the amount of money that the trip is going to cost (£8.50).

What should you say to her?

Should her concern be passed on to the supervisor?

Why is it important that parents are listened to?

Parents under stress

The way in which parents cope can depend on their life circumstances. When parents are under stress, they may find it harder to respond to their children's needs or manage their behaviour. Some stresses that families find themselves under are short-term, such as changing accommodation, while others are long-term, for example, long-term illness. These may affect the parents' ability to cope.

Many parents are able to adapt to changes in their lives and will use their friends and families for support. Other parents may not have a strong network; for example, they may have recently moved to a new area. Early years workers need to understand the pressures families can face, as they may need to support such families, either by offering a friendly ear or by being able to give information about services.

Common factors affecting families

These will include:

- **Financial difficulties**
  Some families may live on low incomes. This might mean that they cannot afford to clothe and feed their children as they would wish. Studies that have looked at families on low incomes have found that there is a link between poor health, depression and poverty. Living on a low income will also affect the type of housing that is available. Parents may find themselves living in cramped temporary accommodation which is unsuitable for children and makes it harder for them to cope.

- **Unemployment**
  When parents lose their job, they not only lose the income but can also feel that they have in some way failed. Tensions between parents can be heightened as a result of one or more parents being unemployed.

- **Changing jobs**
  Starting a new job or changing jobs can put extra pressure on families, although these might be short-term ones. Difficulties can occur when the parent who has previously cared for the children starts to work, as child care needs to be arranged. Young children might not feel happy about separating from their parent, while the parent might feel guilty about returning to work. Older children can also resent being asked to do more for themselves, for example, to get themselves ready for school.

- **Divorce and separation**
  Parents who have recently separated from their partners often find it difficult to manage on a lower income as well as hard to cope with their own feelings. The situation is often made worse because children's behaviour changes as they react to the change in circumstances.

- **Caring for a family member**
  Sometimes a parent also has to care for another family member, for example, another child with severe learning difficulties or an elderly grandparent. This puts a strain on the family as the parents can find themselves emotionally and physically drained.

■ **Long-term illness**

The long-term illness of a family member or the child, can put enormous strains on a family. One parent may need to spend time caring for the family member who is ill or, if that person is a breadwinner, it can leave the family in financial difficulties. If a member of the family is in hospital, this makes it harder as hospital visits have to be arranged and time to spend playing and meeting children's needs can be hard to find.

■ **Bereavement**

Parents can be put under great emotional strain if they suffer the bereavement of a friend or close family member, particularly the death of a child or a partner. They may find it harder to focus on the remaining children as they come to terms with their grief.

■ **Social isolation**

Most parents find that talking with other parents can help them to cope. That is why there are many support networks for mothers and fathers, such as Parent Link, National Childbirth Trust and Families need Fathers. But there are many reasons why some parents are not able to do this. They may not be able to communicate with others, perhaps because they do not speak the language or because they are not accepted by other parents – for example, a prostitute may be rejected by other parents.

Other reasons for isolation include lack of transport, extreme shyness or lack of opportunity. When a family moves to a new area it can take time for them all to settle in and make new friends and contacts.

Parents and the Children Act 1989

The Children Act 1989 is an important piece of legislation as, for the first time, it brought together many laws that affected children and revised them. It is important also because, for the first time, children were seen as having rights and the well-known phrase was used 'the needs of the children are paramount.'

Parents were recognised as generally being the best people to bring up their children and the Act made local authorities and other services work with parents to support them, making separation of children from their parents a last resort.

Parental responsibility

The Act sets out clearly the right and responsibilities of people who are legally caring for children. Under the Act people who are legally bringing up children are given 'parental responsibility'.

What does parental responsibility mean?

In essence, having parental responsibility gives people bringing up children the following rights and responsibilities:

■ to choose the name of a child and to register the child at birth

■ to apply for a passport for the child

■ to choose the religion of the child

■ to make sure that the child is in full-time education beween the ages of 5 and 16 years

■ to choose where the child should live

■ to consent to medical treatment on behalf of the child

■ to appoint a legal guardian

■ to maintain and protect the child.

Once a parent or person has parental responsibility, it lasts until the child is eighteen years of age even if the child is no longer living with them.

Who is given parental responsibility?

It is important to understand that parental responsibility is not a right for all fathers and not for step-parents.

■ Parental responsibility is given automatically to married parents and unmarried mothers

■ Unmarried fathers can apply to the courts or be made a legal guardian by the mother

■ Non-parents can be given parental responsibility if it is considered to be in the child's interest. (This means that occasionally grandparents are granted a residence order which gives them parental reponsibility.)

- Local authorities are given parental responsibility when they are given a care order. In such cases they share parental responsibility with the natural parents who are obliged to work with them.

- Step-parents, even if they marry the natural parent, are rarely given parental responsibility in their own right, although the courts can name them on residence orders which means that while the child is with them they can take on this responsibility.

Relating to parents

This section looks at practical ways in which early years workers can work with and relate to parents in settings.

The importance of building relationships with parents

Until quite recently, the attitude towards parents by some people working in early years settings was definitely one of 'we know best'. This was an unhelpful attitude and created a climate where parents did not feel comfortable talking to carers and felt that their views were not important. Parents did not come into early years settings unless they had an appointment or they had been invited in.

This situation has now generally changed and early years workers recognise that working with parents is an essential part of working with children. As children come into settings with different experiences and different needs, the main source of information about children is often their parents.

Ways in which children benefit when parents and carers work together

- Children will feel more settled and secure if they know that their carers and parents 'get on' well.

- Children gain from having a similar routine or approach – for example, parents will be able to tell carers what time a child normally needs a rest.

- Carers and parents can work together to help a child who has a particular developmental need – for example, a child with a language delay might be learning how to use sign language both at home and in the setting.

- Parents may be the first to notice that something is bothering the child and can pass on their concerns.

Children feel more settled if they know their carers and parents get on well

Ways to build a partnership with parents

There are many ways in which staff in settings try to build up a relationship between a child's home and the setting.

The open door policy

In order to work effectively with parents, most settings operate an 'open door policy'. The idea of the 'open door' is to make parents feel that they are able to come and talk to staff whenever they wish. This means that instead of making parents wait until a parents' evening before raising a concern or passing a comment, they are encouraged to talk to a member of staff straight away. The open door policy also makes parents feel that they can trust the setting as they know that they can pop in and have an informal word or look at their children's work whenever they wish. Children benefit from this relaxed approach as they can sense that the important adults in their lives work together. It also means that children can show their parents what they have been doing in their 'other world'.

Getting to know parents

Staff need to be friendly and acknowledge the importance of parents so that channels of communication are established. Once parents and carers have built up a relationship, it is easier for both parties to bring up concerns that they may have – for example, a carer may need to remind a parent about the no smoking rule on the site, or a parent may tell the carer that they have separated from their partner or that the family pet has just died.

Just as we accept that all children are different and have their own needs, the same is true of parents. Parents who are leaving their child for the first time in a setting will have different needs from parents who have used the setting before. Relating well to parents is just as much a skill as working with children. Some parents may feel uncomfortable talking to members of staff while others are friendly and relaxed. As an early years worker, you will need to learn how to talk and listen to parents, although most workers find that their confidence increases as they become more experienced.

Talking and listening to parents

As an early years worker you will need to learn how to talk and listen to parents. Listening is an active skill and is different from merely hearing. *Active listening* is the way in which you encourage someone to talk to you by showing that you are interested and truly understand what they are saying. It can be done by making eye contact and by nodding or smiling when appropriate.

Active listening is important because parents need to feel that they can trust you. Sometimes parents who are shy or unsure will talk to early years workers about something that is less important before plucking up the courage to mention their real concerns.

Other tips for good communication are:

- Reflecting back: this means repeating back what someone has said to you, so that they know that you have been listening. For example:

Parent:	Michael seems to be really unhappy at the moment and I am finding that it is hard to get him here in the mornings.
Early years worker:	That must be hard for you if you he doesn't want to come in the mornings.
Parent:	Yes, he normally can't wait to get here . . .

- Speak clearly, making good eye contact with the listener. This is particularly important if you are talking to someone with a hearing impairment or whose first language is not English.

- Make sure that you are giving parents ample opportunity to explain themselves or to check that they are happy with any solution you are proposing.

Early years worker:	Would it be an idea if I had a chat with Michael this morning and kept an eye on him during the session or would you prefer me to see how it goes tomorrow?
Parent:	I don't really know. I am finding it so hard at the moment. This morning he cried and cried and I ended up crying myself.
Early years worker:	I am sorry to hear that; Michael is normally so happy. I think it might be an idea if I talk to Michael, keep an eye on him and have a quick word with you later on; that way we can decide what to do next.

- Reassure parents, but don't make them feel that you are not taking the problem seriously.

Early years worker: It must be hard for you to see Michael upset in the morning, but with a bit of luck, we will soon work out what it is that is upsetting him. I will keep a close eye on him and let you know how he is. A lot of children do go through a stage of not wanting to leave their parents, especially if they have just had a nice weekend with them.

Good practice – communicating with parents

✔ Always find out how parents would like to be addressed, for example, by their first names or with a title, such as Mr Smith. (Never assume that the children you work with will share their parent's family name.)

✔ Always acknowledge parents, even if it is just a nod and a smile in their direction because they are talking or you are surrounded by children.

✔ Make sure that you do not appear to have 'favourite' parents.

✔ When talking and listening to a parent, make good eye contact and show that you are listening to them by nodding your head or by smiling.

✔ If you cannot give an answer to a question, always refer the parent on to the supervisor or jot it down and say that you will get an answer to them.

✔ Comment positively to parents about their children.

✔ Do not talk to parents about other children or their parents.

Reasons why communication between settings and parents can be difficult

There are many reasons why it can be difficult to establish a relationship between parents and settings. This makes it harder for settings to communicate with parents and most settings have to consider other ways of keeping up some kind of contact.

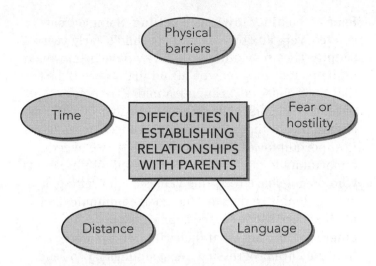

Physical barriers can prevent communication – for example, lack of space where parents can talk to staff privately. Recently, many early years settings have had to introduce security systems which can make it harder for parents to feel that they can just pop in. Most settings try to overcome these difficulties by displaying children's work and by reassuring parents that they are always welcome.

Time is often a real barrier to communication. Parents may be in a hurry to drop off their children at the start of the session, because they need to get to work, or early years workers may be surrounded by children at the end of the session. Where early years workers sense that parents want to discuss an issue, they may need to be prepared to stay on after the session ends. It is important that parents feel that staff will make the time to talk to them.

Distance can be a problem. Some parents are unable to come into the settings themselves for many reasons. They may have other children that need to be dropped off or a child may be brought into some settings by taxi. In these circumstances, the policy might be to try to keep in contact using a *home book* in which staff and parents jot down comments about the children.

Language can also be a barrier to communication. Some parents may not speak the language used in the setting or they may be deaf and sign to communicate. Settings can overcome these difficulties by trying to find an interpreter or by learning some simple signs or words.

Fear or hostility towards a setting Some parents can feel very anxious about their child's early years setting. They may not feel that they have been valued in the past or they may be afraid that they will be told that their child has been in trouble. For some parents, being asked to talk to a member of staff has always meant that something is wrong. This is why it is important for early years workers to use every opportunity to talk positively to parents. With parents who do not share the same values as the setting, it will be doubly important that good communication methods are used – as these parents may not otherwise find out what their children are doing or how they are progressing. Most settings try to send out newsletters or notes to parents they do not see often.

Methods of communication with parents

We have looked at some of the difficulties that can prevent parents and settings from working well together. Most settings have several ways of exchanging information with parents and keeping them in touch with the progress of their children.

Pre-school settings: day care settings, nurseries, crèches and childminders
Pre-school settings often have more contact with parents than settings which work with older children. It is commonplace to see parents talking with staff at the start and end of sessions, although most settings exchange written information and also plan times where parents can talk to staff.

School settings, after-school clubs and play schemes
It can be harder for settings that care for older children to keep in contact with parents. Some parents are in employment work and may not be able to come into settings, while some parents may not feel comfortable in educational settings. Older children are often reluctant to tell parents what they have been doing at school and some children are surprisingly good at losing notes and letters! Some settings send out letters and other notices by post if they are concerned that information is not getting home or add a slip at the bottom of the letter which parents fill in and return to say that they have received the information.

Ways of relating to and exchanging information with parents

Early years settings use different ways of relating to parents and exchanging information with them. These methods might include the following.

■ **Activity slips**
These are used to give parents information about what their child has been doing during the day or session. They are often used in daycare settings. Slips often record how much sleep and food a child has had, as well as activities that the child has enjoyed.

■ **Newsletters**
Some settings send out regular newsletters as a way of keeping in contact with parents they might not see. They can give information about dates of trips, closures, etc.

■ **Letters**
Letters are often sent home with children or by post. They are used to send out a variety of information, for example, about trips or concerts.

■ **Open days**
Open days or afternoons allow parents to come and watch their children during a session. They also allow parents opportunities to meet each other. Parents who work or who are new to an area can find this particularly helpful.

■ **Steering groups**
Some pre-school settings have steering groups which meet regularly with the staff. They represent a parent's perspective on the setting's activities and are useful as a way of allowing parents to give honest feedback in a constructive way.

■ **Fundraising groups**
Some settings will need extra financial support in order to keep fees down or to buy equipment. Fundraising groups form a link between parents and staff. They can also provide a social point of contact for parents.

■ **Parents' evenings or afternoons**
Many settings set aside regular times to meet with parents. It is an opportunity for parents to find

out about their children's progress. It can also be helpful for the setting to find out about how the child is coping from the parent's point of view.

- ### Workshops and information days
  Many settings run workshops or information sessions on particular topics that might interest parents. Popular sessions might include, 'how to help your child learn to read' or 'preparing your child for school'. Workshops can help parents to understand the approach that the setting uses.

- ### Home books
  Some settings send out 'home books' with children, which allow parents and staff to communicate. These are particularly used with children who have learning difficulties and who may not be able to tell adults about what they have been doing. Home books are also used where parents are not able to come into the setting because the children are transported by taxi or by bus – for example, if a child lives in a rural setting.

- ### Concerts, parties and other celebrations
  At different times of the year, parents are invited into settings to look at particular pieces of work or to see their children perform in a play or concert. These occasions are normally very positive and allow parents who otherwise might not feel comfortable to talk with staff in an informal way.

- ### Accident slips
  These are used to let parents know if a child has had a slight injury. They include basic information about the type of injury, how it was dealt with, and at what time it occurred.

- ### Notice-boards
  Many settings use notice-boards as a way of passing on information. These are often put up in areas where parents might be waiting for their children and are a good way of keeping parents informed about future events. For example, a notice might say 'Class 3 is going on their trip on Monday. Please remember that each child will need a packed lunch.'

The advantages and disadvantages of written information

Many of the methods mentioned above use written information as a way of maintaining contact with parents. Although there are many advantages to using writing as a way of communicating with parents, early years workers must understand that not all parents are at ease with the written word.

Advantages

- Parents can read notes and letters when it is convenient for them.

- Newsletters and slips can be kept for reference.

- Some parents use activity slips, reports and home books as a record of their child's progress.

Disadvantages

- Not all parents may be able to read or understand the language – for example, a parent may be visually impaired or may not share the language of the setting.

- Parents may be afraid of communicating in writing as they are not sure of their spelling or grammar.

- If letters and reports are sent out with children, they may get lost.

- Written communications can sometimes sound unfriendly and may not contain all the information a parent needs.

- Some parents prefer face-to-face contact with carers so that they can ask questions or add comments.

Writing letters or messages to parents

Early years workers can often need to write a letter, activity slip or other message to parents as part of their job. It is important that the message is clear, legible and easily understood. A common mistake is to try to use impressive words rather than keeping a message simple. You should remember that the written word can be powerful and might sound unfriendly, so it is a good idea to ask a supervisor to check it through before it is sent home. Some settings have a policy that the manager should see *any* written correspondence before it is sent out.

Good practice – communicating in writing

✔ Clearly address the note or letter.

✔ Make sure that spellings and punctuation are correct.

✔ Keep the language clear and simple.

✔ Make sure that the information is accurate.

✔ Date it and keep a copy of the information sent.

Knowledge into action

Sunil's mother has written in asking for the date of the next parents' evening as she has lost the newsletter.

Write a short letter back to her. You may choose your own times and dates.

Conveying negative information

There may be times when negative information has to be passed on to parents – for example, to inform parents that their child has had a toileting accident or has been aggressive. Sometimes, it is not possible to see parents face to face and so a written communication is needed. It is important to remember that most people will concentrate on negative comments, which means that extra care is needed with the language used – especially if we are writing.

For example: Tom is four years old and has been wetting himself frequently at nursery. His key worker has decided to write a note home to let his parents know that she is concerned, as he is often brought into the setting by an au pair.

Look at the two letters that have been written.

> Dear Mr and Mrs Roberts,
>
> I am writing to tell you that Tom has wet himself every day this week. I am extremely concerned about this and feel that you may wish to consider if this is normal for a boy of his age.
>
> I look forward to hearing from you.
>
> Yours sincerely,

> Dear Mr and Mrs Roberts,
>
> I am writing this note to you because I haven't been able to catch up with you recently.
>
> I feel that you should know that Tom has had quite a few accidents this week, which is unusual for him. It may be that he is not feeling settled or that he is coming down with something. Otherwise he seems quite happy and is really enjoying the new home corner that we have installed!
>
> I look forward to hearing from you and hope to see you soon.
>
> Best wishes

Think about it

Part 1

In pairs, look at the two letters above.

What might be the reactions of the parents to each?

Why is it sometimes easier to convey negative information in a face-to-face situation?

Part 2

Tom still seems unsettled, although he is no longer wetting himself. You have noticed that he has become slightly aggressive with the other children and today he has bitten another child during an argument in the home corner. This is the second time in ten days that he has tried to bite. The au pair is still bringing Tom into nursery and you are concerned that Tom does not always want to go home with her. You have promised Tom's parents that you will write to them, if you are still concerned about his behaviour.

In pairs again, write a note home to Tom's parents.

Exchanging emergency information

There may be times when parents will need to be contacted quickly, for example, if a child is feeling poorly. It is important that early years workers have the correct information to hand: emergency numbers and addresses are usually exchanged as part of the admissions procedure.

Most settings store information in the event of emergencies in a central place. As the information needs to be up to date, most settings regularly send out a form to check for any changes. Where children are being cared for in their own homes, it is a good idea to keep the information by a telephone or in an agreed place.

Settings should also make sure that parents know how to contact them in the event of an emergency, for example, if they cannot collect their children because their car has broken down. This means that telephone and fax numbers should be given to all parents and that the phone should be answered promptly – even if it rings during a lunch break!

Communicating in an emergency

If a parent needs to be contacted urgently, it is important that this is carefully handled so as not to cause unnecessary worry. Remember the following points:

- stay calm

- make sure that you are talking to the correct person

- clearly identify yourself and your role

- explain why you are calling

- give clear and accurate information as to how the situation is being dealt with

- if you have to leave a message, be brief and make sure that you leave a contact number.

Encouraging parental involvement

It is considered to be good practice to involve parents as much as possible in the running of early years settings as, where there is a close partnership, children seem to be happier and are more likely to fulfill their potential.

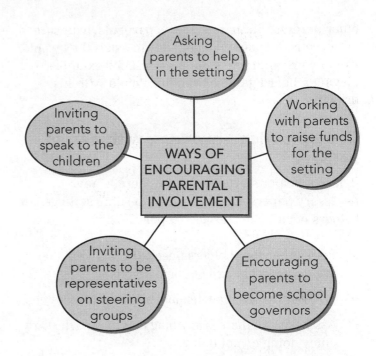

Parents often have a lot to offer settings, in terms of their knowledge, interests and experience. Working together can bring the community closer, particularly in areas where there are several cultural groupings.

Involving parents as helpers

Many settings find that parents who come into settings as helpers are able to bring in many skills and different areas of expertise. Some parents are able to help regularly while other parents prefer to help out occasionally. A good working partnership between parents and settings should mean that parents enjoy coming in while the settings value their time and help and the children are able to benefit from having extra adult attention.

A one-sided relationship, where parents feel used but not valued by the setting will result in them deciding not to offer their services again. Early years workers therefore need to be skilful in directing and supporting helpers effectively. It is important for staff to realise that, for some parents, coming into the setting can be nerve wracking. They may be worried that they will get something wrong or that they will not be good enough. A friendly welcome will be much appreciated. Some parents find that working as helpers can boost their confidence and gives them the chance to meet other parents. If a parent seems particularly unsure or nervous, it is often a good idea to ask if they would like to work with one child at a time, for example, playing a board game or helping a child with his drawing.

Good practice – working with parent helpers

Before a helper starts, find out if there is any necessary paperwork to be done. In some settings, *all* helpers need to be checked by police.

✔ Remember that helpers need to enjoy what they are doing – they are not being paid!

✔ Where possible, give helpers a choice of activities.

✔ Ask helpers if there is anything that they particularly enjoy doing or not doing.

✔ Decide with the helpers if they would like to work with their own children. If it is not appropriate for them to do so, explain why this is not possible.

✔ Allow enough time to explain an activity to the helpers.

✔ Make sure that helpers understand the task that you are directing them to do.

✔ Praise helpers for their efforts.

✔ Always thank helpers for their time at the end of each session.

Many parents enjoy helping in settings

Parents who rarely attend the setting

Early years workers may work with children whose parents rarely come into the setting. This can make it harder to communicate and build a relationship with them, but we should not assume this means that these parents do not care for or love their children.

Some parents may find it hard to take and collect their children because they are working; others might not feel a need to come into the setting, because they know that their children seem happy. It is important that when these parents do come into the setting they are welcomed and not made to feel guilty. Positive remarks about their children generally act as a good starting point – for example, 'I am so pleased that you were able to come, because Junaid has been such a pleasure to work with.'

It is a good idea to remind parents that they can always phone in if they have any concerns or comments and it might be appropriate to suggest a home book system.

Parents who seem negative about their children

Some parents seem to lack interest in their children or are very negative about them. They may make comments such as, 'I suppose he's not done so bad then', or 'I don't expect that he'll be very good at reading.'

Such comments can reflect parents' worries about their children or their own lack of self-esteem. It is important to look at ways of making these parents feel more confident about themselves by trying to develop a relationship with them. This can help parents to become more interested in the setting and feel more relaxed when they come in. So an early years worker could say to a parent, 'Thank you for coming in today, I was looking forward to meeting you as Ravi is such fun to have here', or 'Jade seems to be good at drawing, I was wondering if this is something you are good at.'

Understanding the role of the early years worker when working with parents

To be a professional early years worker, you will need to understand what the boundaries are when working with parents. The relationship with parents needs at all times to be a professional one. Workers must not breach confidentiality and should never be seen to have favourites among parents.

Confidentiality and parents

Confidentiality is mentioned several times in the book, because it is a very important part of being a professional early years worker. In order for parents to trust workers, it is very important to respect their right to privacy and confidentiality. There will be occasions when parents tell you about their personal difficulties – for example, parents may tell you that they have left their partner and you must reassure them that this will be confidential.

Most settings have policies about confidentiality and if you are at all unsure about a situation, you should always check with your supervisor.

- Find out about your setting's policy on confidentiality.

- Anything you learn about parents' or children's backgrounds in the course of your work is likely to be confidential.

- Never listen to or be part of any gossip. Most breaches of confidentiality happen through thoughtlessness.

Maintaining a professional relationship

Early years workers must realise that being friendly with parents is not the same as being friends. Friends share each other's problems, give advice and socialise together. This is not the relationship you should have with parents when you are there to care for their child. Professional boundaries must be maintained. Where this line is crossed, workers can find themselves in difficult positions. Consider this example: a parent brings her unwell child into the setting and begs the early years worker to let the child stay. In this case the worker knows that this is against the setting's procedures and could spread an infection, but she has in the past been to this child's house for tea. She doesn't want to break the rules, nor does she want to upset her friendship with the parent.

Many live-in nannies and their employers find it difficult to maintain a professional relationship as

they may spend some time together socially. This can make it harder for them to talk about issues which are bothering them.

Good practice – confidentiality

✔ Do not tell your personal problems to parents.

✔ Refer parents on to services that might help them with financial, emotional or other problems.

✔ Avoid giving advice about personal issues to parents.

✔ Make sure that you have a contract which covers pay and conditions – especially if you are working as a nanny.

Think about it

Anne Marie is working as a nanny. This is her first live-in job and she has been really happy. Her employers treat her like one of the family and she has been invited out for meals with them and even on holiday. She has not asked for a contract because there did not really seem any need for one. However, in the last few weeks, her employers have been asking her to babysit more and more. At first she said that she didn't really mind because she was in anyway, but now she is finding that she hardly has any evenings free. Her employers have not paid her for the extra babysitting, but have bought her a bunch of flowers. She wants to mention how she is feeling to the parents, but feels embarrassed.

What mistakes has Anne Marie made?

In pairs, role play what Anne Marie should say when her employers next ask her to babysit.

Giving information to parents

We have said that parents and early years workers need to share and exchange information. The way in which this is done is important so that the confidentiality of neither the parents nor the setting is broken. Most settings have a system of line management which means that workers know what their roles and responsibilities are when passing information on to parents. The amount of or level of information you should receive or give out will depend on your position in the workplace. Students, for example, should always refer parents to their supervisors.

Challenging discriminatory or oppressive behaviour

Discriminatory or oppressive behaviour may come from parents in a variety of ways. Often such behaviour is a result of the parent being under stress or feeling insecure and vulnerable. Early years staff may find that they need to challenge this behaviour directly from time to time as there may be occasions when parents come into the setting feeling very angry and aggressive. Handling this type of situation requires sensitivity and skill. It is important to remain calm and not 'fuel' parents' anger. Comments that are discriminatory or offensive should not be tolerated and may require a response such as 'I understand that you are upset and I want to talk this through to find a way forward, but I cannot discuss this further until you are able to talk to me more calmly.'

The other way in which early years staff might have to challenge discriminatory or oppressive behaviour is when children routinely exhibit it and it becomes obvious that they have learnt it from their parents. In these situations, it is important not to alienate parents but to discuss with them the behaviour of their child and the difficulties being caused by the children imitating their behaviour. It might be a good idea to inform parents that swearing or discriminatory remarks might mean that their child will find it harder to make and keep friends. This can be effective as most parents only want the best for their children and may not realise how their child might lose out through showing anti-social behaviour.

Helping parents find out information

Sometimes parents will ask for some general information – for example, about health topics, social benefits, etc. This means that early years workers should know where parents can get information from in their area, although they must be careful that they do not act as agony aunts! (Remember, it is possible to sue someone for giving incorrect advice!)

Job	Role in relation to parents
Student	Students are not members of staff and they must *never* give this impression to parents. They may be asked to wear a badge identifying them as students. If parents ask for information they must refer them to a staff member. Students need to be friendly, yet understand the setting's code of confidentiality. They need to work under the direction of their supervisor.
New member of staff	New members of staff need to make relationships with existing parents. They need to appear confident and friendly and must learn about the general routine of the day quickly so that they can give out accurate information. They should always check with other staff if they are unable to answer a query. They must know when to refer parents to children's key workers or their supervisors, e.g. if a parent wishes to find out more about their child's progress.
Key worker	Key-workers need to form close relationships with the children they are responsible for and the children's parents. They must make sure that they are keeping up-to-date records and can discuss the children, showing good knowledge. The information they keep about the children is confidential and is likely to be discussed only with parents and their manager. They need to work closely with their manager/supervisor.
Supervisor/ manager	The supervisor or manager of the setting needs to know all the children and their parents well. Because they are responsible for all that happens in the setting, they need to be kept up to date with any incidents that happen during the day so that they can discuss them with parents if needed, e.g. if a child is feeling unwell or has fallen over. They will also have access to all information available about the children, including emergency contact numbers.

Some settings that are based in the community, such as a playgroup or playscheme, may have notice boards or areas where written information can be displayed.

The table below shows where parents may be able to get advice or help.

Source	Information
Telephone book	Most telephone books have a section called Useful Numbers in the front. This includes the numbers of the Benefits Agency and employment service, hospitals and advice lines.
Library	Libraries have a range of leaflets from government departments as well as charities. Libraries can also be good sources of information as they contain many books and also CD-ROMs.
Citizen's Advice Bureau	These are centres where people can see someone to get advice about many topics, such as housing, benefits, debt, divorce. The advice is confidential and free. Appointments are not always necessary to get advice. CABs also run debt clinics to help people in financial difficulties.
Health centres, clinics and doctors' surgeries	Most of the leaflets available are about medical conditions or support groups. Appointments to see a doctor or nurse are generally necessary to get advice.
Chemists	Many chemists stock a range of leaflets about health issues, although sometimes they are produced by manufacturers and may not be independent.
Helplines	Helplines are run by many organisations, such as charities and health authorities. They are meant to give immediate advice or information to the caller e.g. Crysis, which is a helpline for parents whose babies keep crying. Sometimes the numbers are free or some are charged at local rate.
Local newspapers	Newspapers often have a local information page. It may include the names of chemists that are open after hours as well as events happening in the local area

Knowledge into action

Kerry's mother has come into the setting this morning looking rather tearful and worried. When a worker asks if everything is all right, she breaks down and says that the building society has written saying that they are going to repossess the house. She doesn't know what she should do next and her partner left her two weeks ago. She realises that he probably left because he knew that the mortgage had not been paid.

Why is it important that this parent is given accurate advice?

Where might the early years staff be able to direct her?

How might Kerry be affected by this crisis?

How can the early years workers support this family?

The importance of admissions procedures

In Chapter 3 we looked at the difficulties that some children and parents have in separating. This section looks at how settings can establish an admissions procedure to help children to leave their parents.

What is an admissions procedure?

An admissions procedure is the process by which:

- parents can find out more about the setting

- settings can learn more about the child

- children are settled in to a new setting.

Although every setting will have slightly different procedures, most settings usually include one or more of the following in their admissions procedure:

- **Prospectus**
  This is often a booklet which gives parents information about the aims of the setting and the number of places available as well as practical details about costs, hours of opening, etc.

- **Initial visits**
  Parents with or without their children can visit the setting. Initial visits allow parents to ask questions, meet the staff and to talk about their child's particular needs.

- **Admissions forms**
  These provide the setting with some basic information about the parents and the children. Emergency numbers are recorded, along with details of any medical conditions or needs that a child may have.

- **Home visits**
  Some workers from pre-school settings will visit children in their own homes as a way of getting to know the children and building a relationship with them and their parents. It allows parents the opportunity to ask questions or to give information in the privacy of their home. It also gives early

---

Farningdon House

Admissions Policy

Applications for places in the nursery should be made to the House Manager.

Places will be allocated on the basis of:

- places available
- position on waiting list
- siblings of those who attend the nursery

Any parents who choose not to take up an offered place will immediately go to the end of the waiting list.

Notice should be given, in writing, to the House Manager one month in advance. Any parents failing to give notice will still have to pay for the time the child does not attend.

Payment is required for any sessions missed – whether due to illness, holidays or any other reason for failure to attend.

Any small changes to sessions will be publicised by the House Manager on the notice board.

Parents will be notified of any major changes, four weeks in advance, in the form of a letter which will be posted rather than handed to children.

Parents requiring extra sessions can book these at short notice subject to availability.

No charges will be made for Bank Holidays as the nursery is not open on these days.

Parents will not be charged for settling sessions.

The nursery will never exceed its registered numbers.

---

years workers more information about the child's home background.

- **Contract**
  Some fee-paying settings send parents a contract which sets out the fees to be paid and the conditions – for example, food may be included in the prices, but nappies may not.

- **Accompanied sessions**
  Many settings ask parents to attend a session with their child before the child actually starts, in order to help him or her settle in. This allows parents and staff a further opportunity to discuss the child's needs. It also helps the child to become familiar with the setting.

A good admissions procedure should help the staff in a setting form a good relationship with parents and allow parents to feel more confident in the setting.

Meeting the needs of parents and children on entry to early years settings

The first few weeks in a new early years setting can prove difficult for some children and their parents. This is why early years workers need to make sure that they work with parents in overcoming any potential difficulties. There are many sources of 'teething' difficulties – for example, it might take children time to settle in or parents might find that the setting works differently from other settings that they have been used to.

It is essential to work closely with parents and to talk to them about how their child is settling in and to encourage them to bring up any concerns that they may have. The chart below shows the types of 'teething' problems and ways in which early years workers might manage them.

Finding a balance between the parent's needs and the child's needs

It can be very hard for parents when their children do not settle in straight away, especially if they are using the setting to provide child care while they are working. In some cases, working parents may be under pressure from their employers and will not have the flexibility to spend long periods of time settling their children in. Taking time off work might mean taking a day's holiday or a reduction in income. However, in situations where children are distressed by the separation process, we must put their needs first and try to negotiate ways of moving forward

How to overcome common settling-in difficulties

Difficulty	Way in which it may be overcome
Child cries on separation and is unsettled	Parents need to be kept informed about how the child is being looked after and the strategies that the setting is using. The child should be allocated a key worker and the key worker should build a relationship with the child and the parent. If the child's distress is acute, the parents should be encouraged to return. The settling-in process may need to be reviewed with the parent with the aim of 'building up' the amount of time the child is separated over a longer period of time.
Child complains of having no one to play with or talk to	Parents will require reassurance that their child is being adequately supervised. Settings might need to make sure that the key worker is keeping an eye on the new child and is working alongside him in order to help him play with other children. The key worker will need to talk to the parent about the activities that the child has taken part in and how the child is beginning to relate to other children.
Parent is concerned about the structure of the day	In some cases, parents might have experienced a different style of provision. It is important to explain the setting's aims and values to the parent and how these will contribute to the child's overall well-being. It is also important for the setting to evaluate its own work, as an issue brought up by a parent might reveal an area of weakness in the setting.
Parents feel that they do not have enough information	In some cases, parents might feel they are not getting enough information about their child's care and education. This is important for parents at all times, but particularly when a child starts at a new setting. It is therefore important that the child's key worker passes on some information at the end of each session and, if he is unavailable to speak personally to the parent, that the supervisor of the setting takes on this role.

with their parents. We may need to explain to parents that in the longer term, their children will settle in more quickly if the process is a gradual one and that, by ignoring a child's distress, the child may react badly to any future separations.

Liaison with other agencies

As part of the process of helping children to settle in, it can be helpful to exchange information with or gain information from other agencies – for example, with a previous setting that the child has attended or with a portage worker. Other professionals might be able to give us advice as to how to meet the child's needs or suggest strategies that they used which were helpful. They might also have some observations or notes about the child that it will be appropriate for us to see. It is usual that parents know, and are happy for information to be passed across from one agency to another and only in exceptional cases – for example, where abuse is suspected – should this be done without parental consent.

Check your knowledge

- Give three examples of family structures.
- What is meant by an authoritative style of parenting?
- Describe three factors that may cause parents to be under stress.
- What is 'parental responsibility'?
- Explain why some parents might find it difficult to come into a setting.
- Describe three ways in which settings might try to build relationships with parents.
- What are the main disadvantages of written communications?
- Describe the common elements of an admissions procedure in a nursery setting.
- Why is it important that early years workers remain professional in their contacts with parents?
- List three sources where parents may be able to gain information about services for families.
- Why might it be useful for early years workers to find out information from other agencies when helping a child to settle in?
- Describe two potential difficulties that might occur when a child first starts in a setting.
- Why is it important to give regular feedback to parents during the settling-in period?
- What are the benefits to children when early years workers and parents work well together?

Resources

Further reading

Issues series *Single and Lone Parents*, Cambridge, Independence Publishers

Useful contacts

EPOCH (End all Physical Punishment of Children)
77 Holloway Road
London N7 8JZ
020 7700 0627

NSPCC (National Society for the Prevention of Cruelty to Children)
National Centre
42 Curtain Road
London EC2A 3NH
020 7825 2500

National Council for One Parent Families
255 Kentish Town Road
London NW5 2LX
020 7267 1361

Parents Anonymous
6–9 Manor Gardens
London N7 6LA
020 7263 8918

Family Welfare Association
501–505 Kingsland Road
London E8 4AU
020 7254 6251

Useful websites

Citizens Advice Scotland
www.cas.org.uk

Family Mediators Association (FMA)
www.familymediators.co.uk

Relate
www.relate.org.uk/bookshop

Preparation for employment

CHAPTER
19
Preparation for employment

The world of employment can often be a confusing one for a newly qualified early years worker. There is a wide variety of career options available in the early years professions which can be entered into immediately after qualifying or after a further qualification has been gained. It can be daunting for newly qualified workers who will quickly be expected to make decisions and take responsibilities in their chosen profession.

This chapter will explore the variety of early years careers in both the private and public sectors and the importance of preparing for all aspects of employment, to include:

- organisations and job roles in the early years profession, including different types of employment available

- preparing for employment and the recruitment process – from first reading the advertisement to accepting a position, including terms of employment

- working as a professional and how it affects the early years worker in the work setting

- working as part of an effective team, including dealing with conflict

- trade unions and professional associations that are available to support early years workers

- the opportunities for professional development for those who wish to develop their qualifications and experience.

Organisations and job roles in the early years profession

Different establishments will provide different job descriptions for early years workers, but the *main role* of the early years worker will *always* be to:

Acknowledge and respect the part played by parents and carers in the child's learning both in the past and as a continuing process by forming a partnership with them, and encourage other active involvement and participation.

Work as part of a team providing quality care and education.

Provide and sustain, in co-operation with other staff, an environment which is caring, stimulating, challenging, welcoming, and safe.

Promote the physical, social, emotional, cultural, spiritual, moral and cognitive development of each individual child and meet his or her needs within the ethos of the establishment.

Employment in the early years profession

There are now many employment opportunities open to early years workers. Some have an increasingly high public profile, such as working as a nanny or as an early years worker in a day nursery, but it is important to understand what each area of employment involves. The differing nature of child care organisation means it is impossible to make a specific list of what each area of employment may require, but instead the possible advantages and disadvantages of each area are discussed. See below for some specific examples of job roles.

ISSUES   Child care qualifications

Many child care qualifications are accepted by inspection units. Requirements can vary from area to area.

Many employers and parents find it difficult to know what type of qualification they should look for.

Below is a list of qualifications.

BTEC Diploma Childhood Studies
CACHE Diploma in Nursery Nursing (NNEB)
CACHE Certificate in Childcare and Education
NVQ Level 2 in Early Years
NVQ Level 3 in Childcare and Education
PPA Advanced Diploma in Playgroup Practice

Find out what these qualifications mean and what period of study is required to gain them.

Private day nursery/day care

There is a wide range of opportunities available in day nurseries that are solely owned by commercial groups or charitable trusts. The standards of these nurseries can vary tremendously, but all of them will be regularly inspected and supported by their local day care advisory team and by OFSTED inspectors if there are three- to five-year-olds on the premises.

Sophie, who worked for a rural day nursery for one year after gaining her CACHE Diploma in Nursery Nursing and NVQ 3 in Child Care and Education, says:

'I felt that working in a day care nursery gave me the opportunity to provide young children with a caring and stimulating environment which will give them a positive start in life. I particularly enjoyed the creative side of my job and was delighted to be given the responsibility for display in my nursery.'

Nursery and primary school

There are many opportunities for early years workers to work alongside teachers in private, voluntary or local authority schools. In nursery schools, early years workers and teachers have traditionally taken joint responsibility for the care and education of three- to five-year-olds in their setting. As more four-year-olds are given places in primary schools, there is an increasing demand for early years workers in these reception classes.

All nursery schools and primary schools will be inspected by OFSTED inspectors and the National Curriculum will be delivered under the guidance of the Quality Curriculum Authority (QCA). Any school, whether state or independently controlled, must meet certain Department for Education and Employment (DfEE) guidelines.

Private day nursery/day care

Opportunities	Concerns
To be promoted to managerial level	Can be long working hours
Variety of professional training funded by nursery or Early Years Development Partnerships (EYDP)	A large administrative workload to meet nursery, social services and OFSTED requirements
To mentor and support trainees or students	Demanding parents or carers
To specialise in the care of one group such as babies or 4- to 5-year-olds.	Limited funding
	Fundraising may be an essential part of providing quality equipment and materials and therefore can be time consuming.

ISSUES   Early years workers in schools

With the introduction of the National Curriculum in the 1988 Education Reform Act, and more recently the literacy and numeracy hour, more early years workers in primary schools increasingly find themselves undertaking what would have formerly been called a teaching role. They are often involved in planning and delivering learning activities and assessing, usually by observation; also keeping records of children's learning. This involves a good understanding of the National Curriculum – both pre-school and at Key Stage 1.

With the launch of the new early years National Training Organisation (NTO) the qualifications of child care workers are being mapped and opportunities identified. It is hoped that eventually those early years workers who may wish to train as teachers will be given some form of Accredited Prior Learning (APL) for their experiences in nursery or primary school.

Melissa is currently working as part of a team in an independent primary school whose classes follow the National Curriculum and whose reception class undergoes a regular OFSTED inspection.

'Young children have one chance in their early years education and I am passionate about giving them a positive experience at school – this is what I try to achieve in my work. I have good GCSE grades, a good NNEB pass and A-levels so I may use my qualifications and experience to train as a teacher later on in my career.'

Nursery and primary school

Early years worker in a nursery

Hospital/community work

While early years workers are not as widely employed on hospital maternity wards as in the past, there are still employment opportunities on children's hospital wards and play schemes. These opportunities are very different from those in settings where the relationship with the children may be more long-term. An exciting development in the employment of early years workers is the chance to work in the community alongside health visitors who are supporting parents/carers and their children under five years old.

Opportunities	Concerns
To work in a multi-disciplinary team	Limited progression (this is currently under review)
A variety of professional development and training	Limited pay scale
May benefit from term-time work pattern	Lack of recognition of professional skills
A chance to mentor student and trainee early years workers	Skills not always fully employed.
A chance to plan and deliver the curriculum as part of a team.	

Hospital/community work

Opportunities	Concerns
May lead to other professional qualifications	Varied hours
Multi-disciplinary team work	Stressful situation of working with sick children
A chance to develop new skills	Limited salary
Possible to work on an individual basis with a child	Career development may be limited.
To meet a variety of people	
Lots of variety in the work.	

Special needs care and education

The early years worker has always had an important role to play in supporting children with a variety of special needs in a school, hospital, nursery, day care or community setting. Some early years workers work in a multi-disciplinary team in a school with children who may have severe learning difficulties, or in a unit attached to a nursery school to support children with hearing or visual impairment. These are just two examples of the employment settings for early years workers who want to work in a special needs environment. It can also be expected that early years workers will come into contact with children over eight years old in a special needs environment.

Special needs care and education

Opportunities	Concerns
Career satisfaction	Can be stressful
To work in a multi-disciplinary team	Pay can be low
	Can be physically exhausting.
To assume an adequate amount of responsibility.	

The home environment

A number of qualified early year workers work as nannies in private homes. Statistics are not conclusive but early research shows that a large number of children are looked after in the home and many of the carers are unqualified.

Knowledge into action

It might be useful to research the different types of employment that are available in your area for early years workers wishing to work with children who have special needs. You could contact:

- *the careers adviser*
- *the community health department*
- *the special needs department of your local education department*
- *special needs schools*
- *local hospitals*
- *day care advisers*
- *specific charitable trusts.*

Experiences of working as a nanny can be varied but many parents and nannies enjoy a positive working relationship in which the needs of the children come first. Sometimes a nanny may work alongside a parent while others are given 'sole charge' – which means that the early years worker is expected to look after the children without either parent present during her hours of work. Nannies may be either residential or attend the home on a daily basis. Many newly qualified nursery nurses take on nannying as a passport to international travel. Such work requires a visa and sometimes a work permit outside the European Union.

ISSUES   Early years regulation

Nannies are the only group of early years workers who are not regulated in any way. There are many pressure groups such as PLAYPEN who are currently calling upon the government to set up a national register for all child carers, to include nannies. This would mean that employers could effectively check the suitability and qualifications of prospective employees.

Case study

This is a daily routine for Jo, a residential nanny who has sole charge of James aged two and Emma aged five. She has the CACHE NNEB Diploma and has been qualified for four years.

7.30 am Brief talk to parents over breakfast about the day ahead. Children and Jo wave goodbye to parents.

8.00 am Dress children, encouraging Emma to dress herself for school.

8.30 am Put both children in car seats in the car and drive for twenty minutes to Emma's school. Settle her into classroom and talk to teacher about the fact that Emma will have to be collected at 3 pm as she has a dental appointment.

9.30 am Arrive at local tumbletots group with James. Take part with him for one-hour session.

11.20 am Arrive home. Take James, who has fallen asleep in the car, and place him in the cot. Tidy children's playroom. Prepare a finger lunch for James and a spaghetti bolognese for the children's tea.

1.00 pm James wakes up and they have lunch together.

2.00 pm After clearing away the lunch, James and Jo read some books and play with a puzzle. Jo takes two telephone messages for her employers and prepares James to go and collect Emma.

2.40 pm Arrive at school. Collect Emma from class and drive to dentist. Jo encourages Emma to talk about the visit.

3.00 pm Jo and James accompany Emma into the dentist. They all receive stickers and James is allowed to sit in the chair!

3.30 pm Arrive home. Jo gives the children a drink and some sliced apple. As it is a sunny day they all play in the garden.

5.00 pm Jo gives the children their tea outside. She fills in the daily diary for the parents while the children play safely in the garden.

6.00 pm Bathtime. Jo prepares the children's bath and afterwards prepares them for bed.

6.30 pm Parents arrive home and they all have a short time together while Jo and the children talk about their day and share the diary.

7.00 pm Jo says goodbye to the family and goes to her flat at the top of the house.

Jane worked as a nanny before travelling to Japan to work in a day nursery for a year.

'Working as a qualified nursery nurse to three children gave me an interesting insight into family life and the varying needs of pre-school and school age children in the home. I found it very tiring but very rewarding.'

Collections/Fiona Pragoff

The home environment

Opportunities	Concerns
To have an individual relationship with children	May lack employment benefits
To use initiative	May have inexperienced employers who make unrealistic demands
To benefit from pleasant surroundings	
To have a chance to travel	May work long hours
To experience different lifestyles	May have lack of contact with fellow professionals
To meet a variety of people	May be isolated from own family
To have rent and food bills paid if residential.	May not be able to entertain friends if residential.

Think about it

Kate works as a nanny for a single mother who has two girls, aged four and two. Recently the mother has begun to ask Kate to do extra jobs, such as collecting her dry cleaning from the laundry and arranging for the car to go into the garage. These jobs are not written into Kate's contract.

Working in pairs, consider:

1   Should Kate agree to do these jobs? If not, why not?
2   How could Kate handle this situation with her employer?

Childminders

Childminders look after children on a daily basis in their own home and are registered by social services under the Children Act 1989. While this is not a highly paid area of child care it is often an attractive option for qualified early years workers who wish to pursue a career and stay at home with their own children. The regulations for an appropriate environment are strict and the day care advisory service will regularly inspect childminders to ensure that they are providing an appropriate environment.

Childminders

Opportunities	Concerns
To have a chance to care for and educate a small group of children	Pay may be low
Access to some quality training	Hours may be long
Work at home	Will have to draw upon individual resources for a greater part of the day
Care for children with specific needs at home	May be lonely
Communicate with other childminding professionals.	May have to deal with demanding parents/carers
	May have to make a substantial initial outlay to set up as a childminder.

Chris Lawrence, Course Manager for The Chiltern College and former Under Eights Adviser says, **'Childminding provides a large proportion of the child care in this country. However childminding can still be an undervalued profession'.**

The National Childminding Association is a respected body in the early years world and has worked hard to raise the profile of childminders. They have also produced some excellent training programmes and collaborated with awarding bodies such as CACHE to provide specific childminding qualifications.

Holiday companies

Working as an early years worker in a holiday company is a popular choice. It can be an exciting opportunity for those with the CACHE Diploma in Child Care and Education (DCE) or the equivalent. Successful applicants will usually care for children in a crèche, either in a sunny climate or at a winter ski resort. Accommodation, travel and food are usually provided and there are managerial opportunities to coordinate and take responsibility for a group of crèches.

Zoe worked for a UK holiday company and describes her job in a winter crèche.

'You need to have a team spirit and stamina. If you are shy, it may be hard, but it is such a lovely atmosphere that you'd overcome it. You also need the initiative to get on with things and to be flexible,

Holiday companies

Opportunities	Concerns
The chance to work abroad	Extremely hard work
To learn to ski and combine love of children	Low pay
To introduce a child to a new environment	Transient relationship with children
To have a good social life	Away from home for long periods.
Enjoy working in a team	
Prospects of promotion.	

because you may need to meet people at the airport or go to another resort to cover for a sick colleague.'

(*Nursery World*, 13 August 1998)

Preparing for employment

How to find the right position

A good starting point for deciding which area of work to apply for can be your work placements. Any prospective child care applicant will have to consider:

■ preferences in early years environment

■ age group of children preferred

■ personal strengths and weaknesses.

After you have thought about the first two areas, it is a good idea to make a checklist of your personal strengths and weaknesses.

Here is a list of questions you could consider when deciding whether to apply for a position:

■ age of children preferred

■ setting preferred

■ areas of children's development I found most interesting

■ do I enjoy working in a team or as an individual?

■ am I ambitious?

■ do I want to progress to managerial roles?

■ how do I rate my skills in the following areas?
    – written skills
    – oral skills
    – am I reliable?
    – do I have a sense of humour?
    – my self-presentation
    – leadership skills
    – response to criticism
    – ability to take initiative
    – flexibility
    – punctuality
    – what strengths did my placement reports note?

Consider the following case study of how Simon chose an area of child care in which to work.

Case study

Simon decided to make a list of his personal strengths and his child care preferences. He knew that he had enjoyed his placement in a state nursery school and particularly enjoyed helping to plan and prepare activities for three- to five-year-olds to meet the learning outcomes of the early years curriculum. He also knew that he wanted to work in an inner city setting.

Simon looked at two reports and noted that they all commented upon his reliability, flexibility and punctuality. He felt that these strengths would make him a suitable team member. His sense of humour and enthusiasm for any task were well known.

Last term he led a project about 'Gardens' and organised the planting of a vegetable garden in his nursery placement; he felt that this was evidence of his ability to take the initiative and lead. However, Simon is aware that his presentation is not always professional and that he needs to develop his written skills in preparation for things such as report writing and record-keeping. If he can address these areas of concern Simon feels he will be able to search for employment in a state nursery school in the city centre.

Knowledge into action

Consider the areas of employment discussed. Choose one in which you are interested and make a list of why you think you would enjoy this area and what you might find difficult. If your negative list is longer than the list of positive aspects, choose another area of employment and carry out the same exercise until you find an area where your positive list outweighs the negative aspects.

Sources of employment

The process of finding the right position to apply for can be confusing and sometimes frustrating. Unfortunately, no job-hunting is completely guaranteed but there are techniques and guidelines that will help to avoid time being wasted and mis-directed applications being sent.

Sources of prospective employment can be found through:

- newspapers, magazines and journals
- agencies
- personal recommendation
- individual advertisements.

Newspapers, magazines and journals

Advertisements for early years workers may be placed in local newspapers or specialist journals such as *Nursery World*. Advertisements should meet the advertising standards requirements but it is important to remember the following points:

- *read between the lines of an advertisement*. For example, 'energetic nanny required for hectic household – sole charge' could indicate a job with long working hours

- *an advertisement should give the name of the organisation* – it is certainly worth researching to find out more about the organisation

- *equal opportunities* – it is preferable to find a statement referring to equal opportunities such as 'an equal opportunities employer'. Why?

- *salary/hours* – if these are stated try to discuss them with other professionals to see if they are fair. As yet there is no recognised pay scale for early years workers.

Look at these examples:

Well-established 25-place family-run day nursery in South East London requires a newly qualified NURSERY NURSE with CACHE Diploma, BTEC or NVQ III to take charge of baby room.

Enthusiasm, energy and ability to work in a team are essential.

£8,500 per annum. 35 hours per week.

For further information please telephone 020 7410 6622

This advertisement is informative and clearly written. An interested applicant may want more details about the age of the children in the baby room, what 'family-run' implies, and what further conditions such as sick pay, holiday pay and entitlement and shift patterns apply.

This private advertisement is not informative. Is the nanny to live in? What are the working hours? What is the salary? More general information about working conditions should be requested.

SURREY Sole charge required for new baby and 2-year-old boy. Flexible working hours. Attractive salary. Non-smoker. Call 0162 40006

Agencies

Agencies are frequently used to find employment in the child care sector. However it is very important to ask some questions of the agency such as:

- do they check child care qualifications?

- do they meet prospective employers and employees?

- are they child care specialists?

- what type of ongoing support will they give both employer and employee?

- do they provide the employer with contract and salary guidelines?

The Federation of Recruitment and Employment Services (FRES) produces a directory of membership. This is not a foolproof form of quality assurance but a well-designed selection service using this may help.

Personal recommendation

This may come in the form of recommendation from a friend or colleague about an early years employment opportunity. It is always advisable to research such opportunities in the same detail as any other form of advertisement. To take a position purely on personal recommendation, without any research, could prove to be embarrassing.

Individual or private advertisements

This type of advertisement, whether found in a newspaper or shop window, has no professional assurance. The applicant will have to work hard to check the credentials of the employer through references, talking to colleagues and recent employees, if at all possible.

Applying for a job

Any application for employment must be:

- legible
- clear
- free of spelling and grammatical errors.

A high standard of verbal or written communication is essential when applying for employment.

Letters

Two different types of letters may be used when applying for jobs: a letter asking for further details, and a full letter of application. All letters should:

- be clearly word-processed or handwritten
- be professionally laid out
- use concise language
- use correct modes of address.

Formal letter checklist

Have you included the name, title and address of the person you are writing to?

Is the purpose of your letter clear?

Have you used new paragraphs to state new points?

Did you proofread for spelling, punctuation and grammar errors?

Is the writing or printing clear?

Did you use the correct ending? (i.e. 'yours sincerely' or 'yours faithfully'.

The letter above is asking for further details or an application form.

If Julia had been asked to send a full letter of application her letter might have read as page 456:

2 Princess Road
Bluetown
B17 6TM

4 March 1999

The Head Teacher
Siren School
Bluetown
B17 6TP

Dear Sir/Madam

I am writing with reference to the post of Nursery Nurse as advertised in The Bluetown Post on 3/3/99. I would be grateful if you would send me further details and an application form.

Yours faithfully

JULIA PIKE (Ms)

Knowledge into action

Practise writing letters in response to an advertisement of your choice or use the advertisements on page 454. Follow the letter styles given above and overleaf. Write a full letter of application for the South East London advertisement, and a letter asking for further details for the nanny advertisement.

Proofread your work carefully, checking for any spelling, grammar and punctuation errors or ask a colleague or tutor to do so.

Telephone

It is sometimes necessary to ring for further details or an application form when applying for a job. It is always a good idea to make notes of what you plan to say before you phone. Remember that your voice should be clear and concise. Take notes to check details. A business-like manner is essential when making such telephone calls.

2 Princess Road
Bluetown
B17 6TM

4 March 1999

Miss Benton
The Head Teacher
Siren School
Bluetown
B17 6TP

Dear Miss Benton

I am writing to apply for the post of Nursery Nurse in your primary school as advertised in The Bluetown Post on 3 March 1999.

I have just completed the CACHE Diploma in Nursery Nursing (NNEB). My extensive training has included a placement in a primary school, working alongside a teacher in a class of five- to six-year-old children.

During this placement I planned a variety of activities to meet the needs of the children in the learning areas of the National Curriculum Key Stage 1. I particularly enjoyed a clock activity based upon the class 'time' project. The children designed and made their own clocks which they were able to use to help them to learn to tell the time.

I have enjoyed the variety of my training and feel that the academic part of the course has prepared me to make effective written records and observations on children. I also hope that I have the flexibility, reliability and initiative to be considered for a position in your school.

I have enclosed my CV which gives extra information. I hope this will be helpful.

Yours sincerely

JULIA PIKE (Ms)

Case study

Anna is telephoning Jollwell Hospital for an application form for the position of nursery nurse on the Crawford children's ward.

Anna: Good morning. My name is Anna White and I would like to be sent an application form for the nursery nurse position on the Crawford children's ward.

Personnel: Certainly, may I take your address?

Anna: 4 White Cottage, Millson, Flondshire, 5TP 1WS. May I ask when the closing date is for applications?

Personnel: 4th June.

Anna: Thank you. I look forward to receiving the form. Good bye.

Note that Anna was very clear, polite and concise and used her time effectively to gain the information she needed.

Curriculum vitae

A *curriculum vitae* (CV) is the Latin for 'a story of your life' and may be requested when you apply for a position. A CV is a brief explanation about your career and education. It should be brief, clearly written and focused upon the position applied for. Make sure that your most recent details are placed at the top of each section.

Listed below are the ten most common CV mistakes as listed in *The Perfect CV* by Tom Jackson.

1 Too long (preferred length is one page).
2 Disorganised – information is scattered around the page and hard to follow.
3 Poorly typed and printed – hard to read – looks unprofessional.
4 Overwritten – long paragraphs and sentences – takes too long to say too little.
5 Too sparse – gives only bare essentials of dates and job titles.
6 Not orientated for results – does not show what the candidate has accomplished for the job – frequent platitudes disconnected from specific results.
7 Too many irrelevances – height, weight, sex, marital status are not needed on today's CVs.
8 Mis-spellings, typographical errors, poor grammar – CVs should be carefully proofread *before* they are printed and posted.
9 Tries too hard – fancy type setting and binders, photographs and exotic paper detract from the clarity of presentation.
10 Misdirected – too many CVs arrive on an employer's desk unrequested and with little or no apparent connection to the organisation – a good covering letter is needed.

Emma Willmington

Education	1997–1999	Newtown College	Newtown

- CACHE Diploma in Nursery Nursing (NNEB)
- NVQ III Early years care and education

	1990–1997	Newtown High School	

• A levels: English; Sociology; French			C; D; D
• GCSEs: English Literature; English Language; French; Geography; Information Technology; Mathematics; Art; History; German			A; A; A B; B; B C; C; C

Experience	Nov 98–	Farningdon House	Newtown

Trainee Nursery Nurse
- Prepared and carried out activities.
- Cared for children aged two to four year.

	Sep 98–Nov 98	Mr & Mrs Sandringham	Newtown

Trainee Nursery Nurse
- Looked after one-month-old twins in home environment.

	July 98–Sep 98	Farningdon House	Newtown

Trainee Nursery Nurse
- As before

	Feb 98–Jul 98	Newtown Primary School	Newtown

Trainee Nursery Nurse
- Worked in classroom alongside teacher.
- Prepared and carried out activities to fit with National Curriculum.

	Sep 97–Feb 98	Purley Nursery	Newtown

Trainee Nursery Nurse
- Looked after three- to five-year-olds following early years curriculum.

Interests	cookery; tennis; painting; Secretary of local French Society

References	Manjit Bhandra, Head of College Newtown College 32 Redbriar Road NEWTOWN NT5 6PB	Callum Prior, Headmaster Newtown Primary School Yew Tree Road NEWTOWN NT3 4RS

Application forms

Application forms will vary according to the position that you are applying for. Some forms are so detailed that you will have no need to send an accompanying CV. It is very important that you take great care when filling in any form and that you consider the following:

- the form is free of spelling and typographical errors

- the language, particularly in a personal statement, is clear and direct

- the information provided is honest and accurate.

It is often worth photocopying an application form first so that you can practise filling it in neatly.

Note You are obliged to disclose *any* medical information that may affect your performance and any criminal convictions you may have. All people working with children – except as a nanny – will be checked by police through their social services department.

References

You may be asked to supply the names of 'referees'. These are people who will write a reference for you.

Make sure you choose referees who are familiar with your recent work and who will be positive about you. An example of a referee might be your college tutor or the supervisor of your work placement. It is always polite to check with the referees before including their name on the application form.

Knowledge into action

Photocopy the application form on pages 459–461 or send off for you own form from an advertisement of your choice. Use the information that you have gathered for your CV to fill in the form. Ask one of your college tutors to discuss the results with you.

Interviews

Preparation

If you are fortunate enough to be called for an interview after submitting a CV and application form, there are ways in which you can ensure that you are fully prepared for the interview. The checklist below would be a useful guide before your first interview for any early years position.

Once you have fulfilled the checklist criteria you will be ready for the interview. If you are very nervous before the interview ensure that you arrive early enough to go to the cloakroom, take a few deep breaths, gather your thoughts and remind yourself that *you* are the best person for the position!

During the interview

It is impossible to predict exactly what will happen during an interview. However, by completing the *Interview checklist* and thinking about the questions you may be asked you should have prepared yourself well enough. Remember that first impressions are crucial at an interview: the way that you dress, the body language you use and the way that you walk into the room will be remembered. So:

■ Walk into the room confidently. Shake hands firmly. Smile and greet the interviewers.

■ Sit upright in your chair with your hands in your lap. Avoid crossing your arms as this can indicate a defensive or hostile attitude.

■ Look directly at the person who is asking you questions.

■ Don't accept a cup of tea or coffee if you are nervous and your hands shake!

Interview checklist

1 Have I found out enough information about the position and the place of interview? ☐

2 Do I know exactly how to get to the place of interview and how long the journey will take, allowing for any delays? ☐

3 Do I know who will be interviewing me? ☐

4 Have I prepared relevant material to take with me such as:

■ National Record of Achievement ☐

■ relevant certificates ☐

■ examples of work I have prepared and successfully implemented with children ☐

■ successful reports? ☐

5 Are my interview clothes smart but comfortable, particularly if I am to spend some time with children? ☐

Check:

■ hair is clean and tidy ☐

■ nails are short and unpolished ☐

■ make-up (if appropriate) is kept to a minimum ☐

6 Have I prepared some questions to ask at the end of the interview? ☐

During the interview, use your *previous experiences* in placements when answering child care questions. By referring to your experiences as much as possible during the interview you will emphasise your knowledge and show that you understand the link between early years care and education

APPLICATION FORM FOR EMPLOYMENT

PLEASE WRITE CLEARLY IN BLOCK CAPITALS   **PRIVATE AND CONFIDENTIAL**

Employment required

Position applied for:	
Where did you hear about this vacancy?	
Other employment interests:	
When could you start?	
Would you work full-time?	☐ YES ☐ NO
If part-time, state days/hours:	
Have you previously worked for us?	☐ YES ☐ NO If yes, when?

Personal details

Full name: Title: Surname:	Forename(s):
Home address:	
	Postcode:
Home telephone:	Work telephone:
Date of Birth:	
Are you legally eligible for employment in the UK?	☐ YES ☐ NO
Do you require a work permit to work in the UK?	☐ YES ☐ NO

Is your ability to perform the particular job for which you are applying limited in any way?
If so, how can we overcome this?

Do you have a relevant current driving licence?	☐ YES ☐ NO
Please give details of any driving offences	

Note: If you are invited for interview, and your driving licence is relevant to your application, it will be necessary to bring it with you.

Provide details here of any unspent criminal convictions (as in accordance with the Rehabilitation of Offenders Act 1974)

Employment

List your present and past employment, beginning with the most recent:

Name and Address of Employer	From: Month Year	To: Month Year	Starting Salary	Leaving Salary	Name of Manager
			£	£	
			per	per	
	Job Title:				
	Describe your work:				
Telephone:					
Type of Business	Why did you leave?				

Name and Address of Employer	From: Month Year	To: Month Year	Starting Salary	Leaving Salary	Name of Manager
			£	£	
			per	per	
	Job Title:				
	Describe your work:				
Telephone:					
Type of Business	Why did you leave?				

Education, Qualifications and Training

Starting with the most recent, give details of your education, qualifications and training to date, including the places you attended.

School/college attended	Dates From/To	Qualifications gained:

Please use this section to outline the skills, abilities and experience which make you suitable for the post for which you are applying. Attach another page to this form if required.

Please give the name and address of two employment referees.

First Referee:	Second Referee:
Name:	Name:
Position Held:	Position Held:
Address:	Address:
Post Code:	Post Code:
Telephone No.	Telephone No.

I declare that to the best of my knowledge and belief the information given in this application is correct:

Signed: .... Date: ....

theory and practice. The interviewers will find out about your relevant experience only if you inform them!

It is also important to avoid closed replies which do not encourage a flow of conversation. A 'yes', 'no' or short answer can be a lost opportunity to promote your suitability for the position you are being interviewed for.

Consider the following as an example.

Maria was applying for a position as an early years care and education worker in a state nursery school. She was interviewed by the head teacher and an experienced level three nursery nurse. This is a short extract from the interview:

Head teacher: Have you had any experience of planning art activities for three- to five-year-olds, Maria?
Maria: Yes I have.
Nursery nurse: Would you like to tell us a little more about one of these activities?
Maria: Yes, I did a bubble painting activity last year.

Maria was not doing herself justice in this part of the interview, despite the fact that the nursery nurse was encouraging her to expand upon her experience. What Maria did not tell the interviewers was that she had planned the activity while on her six-week block nursery school placement. She should have further explained that the paintings were part of a 'rain' display that she was mounting with the children, as part of the nursery curriculum theme of 'weather'.

It is also important to avoid vague or imprecise answers that are not relevant to the question and which may include long-winded anecdotes! You should show that you are enthusiastic about the job throughout the interview – a negative attitude can give the impression that you are not really interested in the position.

Note It is important to know that not all interviewers are trained and sensitive professionals. Some of them can talk too much, are ill-prepared, unsympathetic and fail to provide necessary information. If you are unfortunate enough to experience an interview like

this you will have to take every opportunity to promote your knowledge and experience.

At the end of the interview you will probably be asked if you have any further questions. It is acceptable to plan these and write them on a piece of paper to take to the interview. Some of the questions may have been addressed during the interview. Try not to ask them again!

Listed here are some questions that you could ask at the end of an interview.

- How long was the previous nursery nurse in the position? Why did she leave?

- Would there be a period of induction at the beginning of my employment?

- How soon will you expect the appointed person to take up the position?

- Are there any opportunities for promotion in this establishment?

- How/when will I find out the result of the interview?

- What are the training opportunities in this establishment?

- Could you tell me a little more about the history of this establishment?

After the interview

After the interview you may have to wait to be informed of the outcome.

If you are not successful, it is worth calmly reviewing the interview and considering the way you conducted yourself and responded to the questions you were asked. You may not have even wanted the position very much, but if you did, try not to take the result personally. There is often little to choose between good candidates and the post may have been offered to someone with more experience.

Different types of interview

There are different types of interview that you might attend in the private, voluntary or public sectors.

Public or *voluntary sector* interviews may take place in environments such as schools, hospitals or family centres. Such interviews are likely to provide clear job specifications and descriptions, brochures about the establishment and its policies. Interviews, offers of employment and contracts will probably follow statutory guidelines and procedures.

Private sector interviews may be in a day nursery or school and will probably be as well planned as a public sector interview. However, interviews for a position in a private home may be more informal and less professional, as the prospective employers may never have had experience of leading an interview. In such cases it is helpful to seek guidance from college careers tutors, colleagues who have experienced similar interviews, reputable agencies who will support candidates and prospective employers through the process and professional associations such as PANN (the Professional Association of Nursery Nurses).

The questions that you prepare to ask at the end of an interview in a private home may be different from others you have thought of. Listed below are some questions that you could ask:

- Will you expect me to prepare the children's meals?

- If I have access to a car will it be appropriately insured?

- Am I allowed visitors in the evening (if residential)?

- How often will I be expected to babysit? Will this be part of my weekly duties or will I receive extra pay for this?

- Will I be expected to record a daily diary of the child/children's day to share with you at the end of the day?

- When will I receive a contract of employment?

- Please explain how my salary will be paid, along with income tax and National Insurance deductions.

Employment offers and contracts

When a position is offered verbally it should be confirmed afterwards in writing. A letter to offer a job should state:

- the job title

- the starting date

- salary, and scale if appropriate

- working practices, holiday and sickness leave

- probationary period if applicable.

When an offer is accepted a prospective employee might be asked to sign such a letter as an acceptance of the conditions of employment until a contract is signed. The signing of a full-length contract will often take place at the end of a probationary period.

Employment contracts

Contracts can be permanent or temporary. It may not be appropriate to offer a permanent contract if the employer knows that the job will last for only a certain amount of time. Maternity leave is a good example of this. In a temporary contract the date that the contract will end is often stated on the form.

> 'Trade unions generally have expressed concern about the increased use of casual and fixed term contracts which they regard as offering inferior conditions of employment to their members. They are particularly concerned about renewing fixed term contracts on an annual basis which is common practice in schools. This is often regarded as representing indirect sexual discrimination since most staff employed on fixed term contracts are part-time and female.' (*Croner's Early Years Care and Education Management* February 95.)

ISSUES Short-term contracts

There are some short-term contracts which have a specific purpose:

- special needs support – where a certain child who may be statemented requires specific support

- maternity leave cover – until the teacher on maternity leave returns to her post

- externally funded post – where funding is available for a limited amount of time.

Terms and conditions

On pages 465 to 466 is one type of contract. There are many ways in which contracts are presented but they are all 'an agreement between two or more parties that are enforceable by law'. (*Croner's Early Years Care and Education Management* February 95)

The contract sets out the *terms* and *conditions* of employment and outlines what is expected of both employee and employer. Under the 1978 Employment Protection Act and Employment Acts of 1980 and 1982, employers must draw up a contract with any employee who works more than 16 hours per week.

The terms of contract include:

- *express terms*: these may include nationally agreed pay scales and conditions of service such as School Teachers' Pay and Conditions of Service.

- *implied terms*: these may not be written down, such as covering for absent colleagues. However, it is advisable that *all* terms are written down – in the case of a dispute any court will have to take a view on implied terms.

- *statutory terms*: such terms will *have* to appear in the contract because of government legislation. These include maternity leave, notice period for dismissal on the grounds of redundancy, and so on.

The Trade Union and Reform Act 1993 specifies information that must be included in a written contract:

- names of employers and employees
- the date when employment began
- the date when continuous employment began (including any employment with a previous employer which counts towards that period)
- hours of work
- remuneration and intervals when paid
- holiday entitlement
- sickness entitlement
- pension arrangements (if any)
- the length of notice to be given by the employee and by the employer in order to terminate the contract
- title of the job
- place of work
- collective agreements
- details of disciplinary and grievance procedures.

Knowledge into action

Using the list of terms and conditions check the contract on pages 465 to 466 to see if it meets the requirements of the 1993 Trade Union and Reform Act.

This list will be a useful guide when checking any future contracts.

The contract on pages 465 to 466 is for employment as a nanny in a home. It should ensure that both parties have the same expectations of the position and that it meets the same conditions as any other contract. FRES (The Federation of Recruitment and Employment Services) will be happy to provide its members with sample contracts as will professional associations such as PANN (Professional Association of Nursery Nurses).

'The secret of being a successful nanny is to find out exactly what is expected of you and to make sure that there is a written agreement between you and your employer.' (Penny Tassoni: *Child Care and Education*)

Salaries

When you have been offered a job it is important to find out how your salary will be paid. An employer is required by law to provide an employee with a pay slip, to include notification of earnings and details of deductions that may be made.

CONTRACT OF EMPLOYMENT

DATE OF AGREEMENT ....

BETWEEN:

NAME OF EMPLOYER ....

ADDRESS ....

....

AND

NAME OF EMPLOYEE ....

ADDRESS ....

....

1 WHERE IT IS AGREED AS FOLLOWS:

      POSITION ....

      DATE OF START ....

      DURATION OF CONTRACT ....

REMUNERATION:

The salary will be .... per week

The employer will be responsible for accounting for the employer's and employee's National Insurance contribution and Income Tax.

The salary will be reviewed once/twice per year on ....

2 There will be a .... trial period during which on giving .... days notice, either party may terminate the contract.

3 After the .... trial period ....weeks' notice must be given in writing by the employer or employee in order to terminate this contract. In the event of termination pursuant to this clause, the employer shall pay the return travel expenses. The employer shall be liable to pay the employee's return travel expenses in the event that the employee terminates the contract due to unreasonable conditions or if the terms of contract differ from those laid down in his contract.

4 During any period of absence due to sickness, the employer will continue to pay the employee's salary for a total of .... weeks. Thereafter, the employer will continue to pay half of the salary for a further period of .... weeks. If the employee's absence exceeds .... weeks (i.e. the combined total of the above period) the employer shall be entitled to terminate the appointment and the provision of clause 5 shall apply.

5 The employer shall fully pay the employee's transport to and from the destination save that it is understood that should the employee in any way seriously breach the law of the land in which they work, or commit any act of gross misconduct, the employer would be entitled to send the employee's back to .... at their expense.

6 Employment in a private household is such that it can be difficult to define hours or work and free time. However, the employee will be allowed .... free days per week and .... free weekends per month, commencing Friday at .... pm and returning Monday at .... am. These hours can be changed only by mutual agreement. In addition, the employee will be allowed .... weeks' paid holiday. Paid compensation is not normally given for holidays not actually taken. Holidays may be carried into the next contractual period only with the written permission of the employer.

7 The employee shall be entitled to:–

Bedrooms .... Bathrooms ....

Sitting room .... Kitchen ....

Motor Insurance Contribution

....

Other Insurance

....

8 Duties expected/and or any extra instructions:

....

....

....

....

....

GRIEVANCES

If the employee has any grievances against the employer he/she has the right to go direct to ....

DISCIPLINE

Reasons which may give rise to the need for disciplinary measures include the following:–

(a) Job incompetence

(b) Unsatisfactory standard of dress or appearance

(c) Conduct during or outside working hours prejudicial to the interest or reputation of the employer

(d) Unreliability in time-keeping or attendance

(e) Failure to comply with instructions and procedures or to respect the wishes of the parents in child-rearing

(f) Breach of confidentiality

In the event of the need to take disciplinary action the procedures will be:

Firstly – Oral Warning
Secondly – Written Warning
Thirdly – Dismissal

Employer's signature .... Date ....

Witnessed by .... Date ....

Employee's signature .... Date ....

Witnessed by .... Date ....

A contract for employment as a nanny

The government has now declared a statutory minimum wage for all people of employed status.

On your payslip you will expect to find:

- date of payout – when your salary is paid into your bank account

- pay number – when working for a large organisation this will indicate a payroll number which can be quoted if any queries or arise

- tax code – this is designated by your tax office and is the rate at which you are expected to pay tax on your earnings

- National Insurance – your monthly or weekly contributions towards national insurance. You will have an NI number on a plastic card. These contributions ensure that you are entitled to unemployment benefit, maternity allowance, incapacity benefit and basic retirement pension (currently under review)

- superannuation – this will be your contribution towards a pension scheme if your employer operates one

- further deductions – these will vary according to employment but could include meals, accommodation, etc.

- gross pay – the amount earned before deductions

- net pay – the actual amount of money paid into your account

- special additions – may include overtime payments, travelling expenses or refunds such as tax.

The salaries of nursery nurses vary but those working in the public sector will receive wages that relate to recognised pay scales for educational, health or social services. PANN (Professional Association of Nursery Nurses) has a leaflet about public sector salaries and the average earnings expected for residential nannies and those who are non-residential.

ISSUES   Employment status

There are certain issues to be considered about the employment status of nannies. Stephen Vortron of Nannytax states that, with the exception of maternity nurses and some nannies who do a lot of temporary work in short-term placements, nannies are considered to be employees and do not meet the Inland Revenue criteria for self-employment.

'It is your employer's responsibility to sort out (and pay) your tax and NI and if they fail to do so it is they (and not you) who the Inland Revenue will chase for any outstanding tax and NI liability. This could result in their facing fines and penalties.'

(Stephen Vortron of Nannytax – *Nursery World* 1998)

Working as a professional

When you take up a position as an early years worker you will immediately be expected to behave in a professional way by working as part of a team and:

- respecting principles and codes of confidentiality

- meeting all the needs of the children in your care

- working with parents as partners

- showing commitment to your position as laid out in your job description.

Respecting principles and codes of confidentiality

As a professional early years worker, in whatever setting, you will be expected to arrive on time for work, be flexible, and communicate clearly with all those whom you meet. You will also be expected to present yourself well and adhere to any dress code that your employer may ask you to follow. Many settings may have policies relating to professional behaviour and confidentiality. CACHE (Council for the Awards in Children's Care and Education) issues a 'Statement of Values' to all its students and this is a useful guide when starting in any area of early years employment.

The CACHE candidate will:

Put the child first by:

- ensuring the child's welfare and safety
- showing compassion and sensitivity
- respecting the child as an individual
- upholding the child's rights and dignity
- enabling the child to achieve his or her full learning potential

Never use physical punishment

Respect the parent as the primary carer and educator of the child

Respect the contribution and expertise of staff in the child care and education field and other professionals with whom they may be involved

Respect the customs, values and spiritual beliefs of the child and the family

Uphold the Council's Equality of Opportunity policy

Honour the confidentiality of information relating to the child and the family, unless its disclosure is required by law or is in the best interest of the child.

Meeting all the needs of the children in your care

First and foremost, you have to ensure the health and safety of the children in your care and work closely with their parents or carers. You will also be expected to observe, assess, monitor and maintain records of the progress of the children (as discussed in detail in other chapters of this book). Your setting should have a number of policies and procedures that will help you create the best environment for the children. These should include:

- *Health and Safety Policy*: to ensure that health and safety guidelines are monitored and maintained

- *Equal Opportunities Policy*: to ensure that every child is treated according to its needs
- *Behaviour Management Policy*: to ensure that ways of managing behaviour are sensitive and acceptable
- *Parents as Partners Policy*: to recognise the vital role that parents play in the care and development of their children
- *Admissions Policy*: to ensure fair admissions through waiting lists and availability of places
- *Child Protection Policy*: to ensure a safe environment where children are safe, and in which concerns are dealt with promptly and appropriately
- *Special Needs Policy*: to ensure children with special needs are appropriately supported.

All procedures are ways of approaching issues that arise from the policies. (See also page 470.)

Working with parents as partners

The importance of working with parents is emphasised throughout this book and is an essential part of any early years position. There will be policies and procedures to guide you and confidentiality must always be observed. If, at any time, you feel you have to share a confidence with a colleague you must inform the parents concerned and reassure them that their child will benefit from such action.

An important part of communication with parents is to keep them in touch with their child's activities during the day. In a school or nursery this may take the form of daily records or diaries, while in a home environment a daily diary might be set up and discussed at the end of the day.

Remember that written communication should be:

- clear and legible, in short sentences
- correctly spelt and with correct grammar
- objective
- focused on the issue.

Verbal communication should be:

- clear and articulate
- objective
- precise
- accompanied by appropriate and positive body language.

For more information on communication, see Chapter 17 Work with parents, page 435.

Commitment to employment

The details of exactly what an employer will expect of you should be outlined in a **job description** and clarified through an **induction process**. This is a planned period during which new employees are introduced to the place of work and can find out how the role and responsibilities of the employee should be implemented. An **employer's handbook** may be available for staff to remind themselves of the policies and procedures of their work setting.

A job description can also be used as the basis for an **appraisal**, which is a formal opportunity for an employer and employee to discuss and review the employee's job description, their training needs and chances of promotion.

Teamwork

To carry out the duties any job description effectively, you will be expected to be:

- reliable
- supportive
- an effective time manager, working within a variety of time constraints
- able to follow instructions clearly.

These requirements are an essential element of working as part of an early years team – whatever the setting.

One of the most useful pieces of advice that you can be given about team work is **there is not an 'I' in the word 'team'**.

Wherever you work you will be expected to be aware of the responsibilities of the other people in the team. When you become part of an organisation you will work with other people to ensure that the children in your care are looked after to the highest of standards. In order to work satisfactorily as part of a team you should understand:

- how you fit into the structure
- who you are responsible to
- who, if anyone, is responsible to you.

There is a variety of professional people who will make up a multi-disciplinary early years team or professionals whom the early years worker may come into contact with:

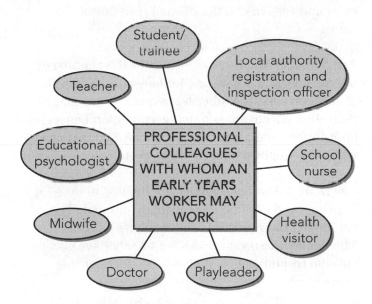

Working as part of an effective team

Management structures

There are many types of management structure, depending on the type of organisation, its function and its size. Within a large team there can often be smaller teams who work together on the daily running of the organisation.

The structure of an organisation should enable each member of staff to focus on specific tasks and to be aware of his or her responsibilities. In an effective team each team member will be aware of who he or she is responsible *for* and who he or she is responsible *to*. Many early years settings have a *hierarchical* structure, which means that the person or people in the top management positions will make the final decisions and take the ultimate responsibility for what happens in the setting. When working in a home environment you will also experience a type of management structure, even if it is a very small and informal one.

Look at the examples of management structures outlined on page 471.

Look carefully at the management structure of the Bluebell Day Nursery and consider carefully the roles and responsibilities of each member of the team.

The Manager will be responsible for the running of the nursery and answering to the owner. She will also ensure that the other team members manage their time effectively and that each person has an appropriate amount of responsibility. The manager will be the highest paid member of staff.

The Deputy Manager will be responsible to the manager and assume responsibility of the daily running of the nursery in the manager's absence. The deputy manager will also probably have some specific responsibility, such as duty rotas or the nursery curriculum.

Experienced nursery nurses are department leaders who are experienced early years workers, responsible to the deputy manager and manager. They will lead their teams in the daily running of their departments, having initial contact with children and parents.

Nursery nurses will usually have less experience and are responsible to their department leaders. They will help to implement the care of the children in the nurseries, liaise with parents and key workers (see next column) and work within the guidelines of the nursery's policies and procedures. They may help to mentor any students or trainees in their care.

Students/trainees will be closely monitored by a staff member who will help them with their professional development.

Administration, catering and domestic staff are responsible to the manager and deputy managers, ensuring that the administration of the nursery is smooth, that it is kept clean and that the food provided meets nutritional requirements.

Children and parents: parents will feel confident that their children will have a safe and stimulating stay in the nursery if the team implements their areas of responsibility efficiently and the team members communicate clearly with each other.

Key workers

The key-worker system is often used in nurseries so that one particular early years worker is responsible for each child. That staff member will greet the child at the start of the day and will communicate with the parents regarding their child's day in the nursery.

The early childhood unit at the National Children's Bureau is currently studying the *key-person* system which is concerned with staff forming close relationships with children to support their care and learning in more depth.

Knowledge into action

Consider an early years organisation where you have spent some time. Draw up a plan of the management structure, showing clearly the lines of responsibility and communication.

Management styles

There are four main styles of management, as shown in the diagram on page 472.

Policies and procedures

Whatever the management style of an organisation it will be effective only if the team has clear policies and procedures and a **mission statement** to guide

Management structures

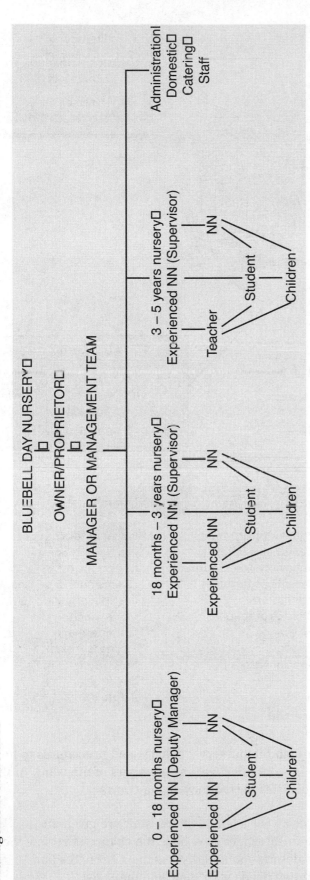

BLUEBELL DAY NURSERY☐

OWNER/PROPRIETOR☐

MANAGER OR MANAGEMENT TEAM

0 – 18 months nursery☐
Experienced NN (Deputy Manager)
            NN
Experienced NN
   Student
   Children

18 months – 3 years nursery☐
Experienced NN (Supervisor)
            NN
Experienced NN
   Student
   Children

3 – 5 years nursery☐
Experienced NN (Supervisor)
            NN
Teacher
   Student
   Children

Administration☐
Domestic☐
Catering☐
Staff

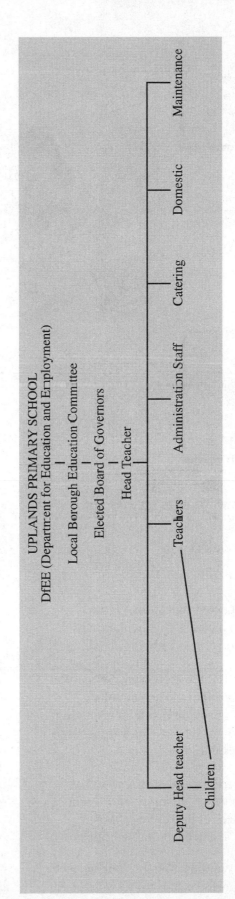

UPLANDS PRIMARY SCHOOL
DfEE (Department for Education and Employment)

Local Borough Education Committee

Elected Board of Governors

Head Teacher

Deputy Head teacher
   Children

Teachers

Administration Staff

Catering

Domestic

Maintenance

THE RAY FAMILY
Parents/carers

Nanny
   Children

Domestic help

Laissez-faire

Team-run setting and no strong leadership.

Messages can be confused. No clear aim.

Democratic

Decisions are made by the team.

No person takes ultimate responsibility.

Consultative

Teams are consulted but manager makes final decision.

Those whose decision is not used can be upset.

Autocratic

Decisions are made by one person, such as the manager.

Can cause resentment amongst staff.

them. There should be two types of policies and procedures:

- those that affect the children
- those that affect the staff.

When nurseries are inspected by Under Eights advisers and OFSTED inspectors they will expect effective policies and procedures to be in place.

Consider the case of the Rainbow Nursery School for children aged three to five years. The school's mission statement is, 'To provide a safe, stimulating and reassuring environment where children are free to learn through structured and unstructured play'.

Visitors to the school, parents and staff know that learning through play is the philosophy of the school. The Rainbow Nursery School has policies and procedures to cover the areas in the table opposite.

All staff in the Rainbow Nursery School undergo a three-month induction period when they are guided

For Children and Parents	For Staff
Equal Opportunities	Equal Opportunities
Health and Safety	Health and Safety
Behaviour Management	Dress Code
Parents as Partners	Claims and Expenses
Admissions	Disciplinary and
Child Protection	Grievance
Grievance	Confidentiality
Emergency	Sickness Absence
Special Needs Policy	Emergency
	Security
	Appraisal

through the nursery's policies and procedures to help them work effectively as members of the team. At the end of this period they sign a contract.

After a year's employment, staff are given an appraisal where they have the chance to review their job description and discuss their strengths and training needs with their line manager.

It is obvious that this is a well-run nursery school where staff have clear guidelines to follow and an opportunity to review their performance.

The role of the team members

A successful team depends on the co-operation and skills of team members.

Being a good team member

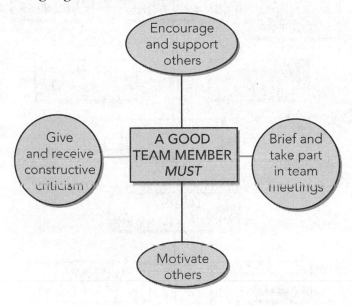

Encourage and support others

This happens through encouraging colleagues to express their own ideas and allowing them to develop. It is important to create an atmosphere where people are happy to be honest and take risks.

Give and receive criticism

Members of a team need to get feedback on their job performance and the chance to improve it. It is important to try to handle criticism yourself before giving it to others. The following may help.

Giving criticism	Receiving criticism
Choose a good moment	Listen carefully and respond only to the facts
Avoid being personal and stick to the facts	Be fair – the criticism may be deserved
Make sure you are honest	

Giving criticism	Receiving criticism
Allow other people to express themselves	Perhaps you have a genuine problem and could discuss it
Discuss how improvements can be made	You may be able to obtain advice which will help you
Do not criticise in public	Be positive
Remain polite and keep calm even if you are nervous.	Remain calm to earn respect
	Ignore rude and abusive criticism.

Motivate others

Everyone responds to praise and most people want to do a job well if they are respected and valued. It is amazing how important a simple 'thank you' can be.

Team meetings

Effective team meetings are an essential element of a successful organisation, along with motivated staff, happy children and satisfied parents.

Meetings may take place for a variety of reasons and can require the presence of every member, not just the team leader. It is important to remember that being a good team member is a collective responsibility.

Keeping meetings to a schedule is very important. Therefore an *agenda* is often created, which states what will happen or be discussed at the meeting. This will be circulated beforehand.

Overleaf is an agenda for a meeting of the Pondlesham Playgroup committee.

A *chairperson* will be in charge of the meeting and will encourage everyone to follow the agenda. A *secretary* will record what is said in the meeting in the form of *minutes*.

Those attending meetings will either be team members (to represent others and to participate in the meeting) or observers (to find out more).

PONDLESHAM PLAYGROUP COMMITTEE
AGM

Agenda

Meeting to be held in playgroup hall on 26th
September at 6.00 pm.

1. Apologies for absence *(explanation in advance
    from absentees)*

2. Minutes of last meeting *(record of last meeting
    to be approved)*

3. Matters arising *(from minutes of last meeting)*

4. Annual Report from Chairperson

5. Playgroup accounts and Treasurer's report

6. Activities for new year

7. Any Other Business *(members given a chance
    to discuss items not on agenda)*

8. Date of next meeting.

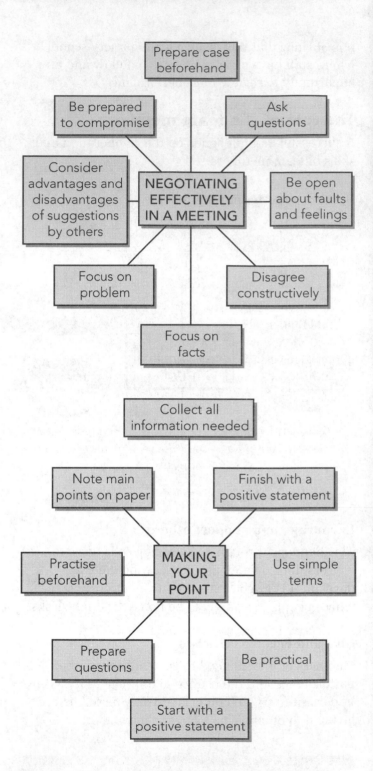

When you are attending a meeting it is important to
use questions appropriately:

■ Check knowledge by asking, 'Do you mean . . . ?'

■ Gain more information by asking, 'How . . . ?'
  'Why . . . ?' 'When . . . ?' 'What . . . ?'

■ Exchange ideas with people, 'What do you think
  about . . . ?'

■ Obtain advice, 'How could I have . . . ?'

■ To see if someone agrees, 'Do you agree . . . ?'

Negotiation skills can be useful in a meeting and
result in people reaching an agreement from two
different starting points. The two diagrams opposite
show ways to negotiate effectively and make your
point.

In order to operate effectively, a good manager will
make sure that his or her team is briefed before a
meeting (or at other times). This is an opportunity to

let people know what is happening and so team
members are more likely to be co-operative (and
gossip is reduced).

Problems

No team can ever operate harmoniously without
some differences of opinion. These can stimulate

positive changes in a team but sometimes *serious conflicts* may arise. These have to be dealt with sensitively and sometimes formally. It is vital to ensure that such conflicts are dealt with swiftly and professionally so that the work of the organisation is not disrupted. Conflicts may arise because of:

- gender differences
- cultural or racial differences
- different working practices
- personality differences.

Disciplinary and grievance procedures

Every organisation should have in place a policy for dealing with disciplinary and grievance procedures so that the aggrieved person can take the appropriate action. Such a procedure should identify lines of management as well as the rights and responsibilities of individuals.

Students and trainees are often the ones who appear vulnerable and need most guidance. A *mentor* could be provided. A mentor is

'To be a fount of knowledge and perfection embodied while always remaining approachable' (Oxford Dictionary).

Think about it

Practise your skills in negotiation and giving/receiving criticism. In pairs, role play these scenarios:

1 Brett has worked as a nanny for a family for three years, during which time he has not had a pay rise. Otherwise he is extremely happy.

Role play Brett and his employer.

2 Hina is the supervisor of the 18 months–3 years nursery team. Natasha is a student in the team. Although enthusiastic and cheerful, she is very untidy and leaves others to tidy up after the activities. The other team members have now complained about this to Hina.

Role play Hina and Natasha.

Stress

Working with colleagues can be very rewarding but is sometimes stressful. It can be difficult to support colleagues under stress in a busy atmosphere where the needs of the children must come first. However, time should be given to a colleague who is suffering from stress and help offered where appropriate. This could include counselling, assertiveness training or medical help.

Stress can be revealed in a variety of ways. A colleague may be tearful, constantly tired, lacking concentration, sleepless, tense, anxious or indecisive. Sometimes such symptoms can lead to serious illness if the person is not supported. Your supervisor or manager will be the first point of contact if you are concerned about a colleague.

Trade unions and professional associations

These are organisations to support people working in child care. They give advice and training. Sometimes workplaces have their own trade union representatives.

Trade unions have been in existence since the nineteenth century when employees were exploited and unprotected, leading to a campaign for better working conditions. Such associations and unions will offer protection to those treated unfairly at work. However, it is not mandatory to join and it is possible to get advice from other organisations. See the end of the chapter for useful contacts.

Professional development

Professional development is important for an early years worker. A Level 3 qualification can lead to a variety of positions in early years after extra training. These include:

- teacher
- nurse
- social worker
- under-eights adviser

■ nursery manager

■ hospital play specialist.

A variety of courses can be taken at post-Level 3 qualification, such as: the Advanced Diploma in Child Care and Education; 60-hour professional courses; Specialist Teacher's Award and the NVQ Level 4 in Child Care and Education from CACHE (Council for Awards and Children's Care and Education, 8 Chequer Street, St Albans, AL1 3XZ). Other organisations, universities and colleges will have early years departments.

ISSUES

The recently formed Early Years National Training Organisation is committed to developing a national training framework to enhance career progression. The new framework is now available.

It is important to keep informed of current issues in child care and education by attending short courses, talking to colleagues and reading journals such as *Nursery World* or *The Times Educational Supplement*.

Check your knowledge

- What are the main advantages of working in a day nursery?

- What are the main disadvantages of working as a nanny?

- What is a CV?

- List three ways in which you can prepare yourself for an interview.

- Why is it important to have a contract of employment?

- What is meant by the expression 'implied terms'?

- What type of information should a payslip contain?

- What are the disadvantages of a consultative style of management?

- Describe some of the factors that should be taken into consideration when giving criticism.

- What is a mentor?

- Why is it important to be reliable as an early years worker in any team?

- How would you, as an early years worker, use a professional organisation or trade union?

- Which Act ensured the registration of child minders?

- What is a short-term contract?

- Why is a child protection policy important in any early years setting?

- Briefly describe the strengths and weaknesses of democratic management.

- What is the role of the Early Years National Training Organisation?

- What is an agenda?

- Briefly describe the role of a chairperson in a meeting.

- Why is it important for a setting to have a grievance and disciplinary procedure?

Resources

Further reading

Johnstone, Judith 1997 *Applying for a Job*, Oxford, How To Books Ltd

Johnstone, Judith 1997 *Passing that Interview*, Oxford, How To Books Ltd

McGee, Paul 1998 *Writing a CV*, Oxford, How To Books Ltd

Useful contacts

The Professional Association of Nursery Nurses
St James' Court
Friar Gate
Derby DE1 1BT
0133 343029

Unison
1 Mabledown Place
London WC1H 9AJ
020 7388 2386

Practice assignment tasks

These practice assignment tasks will give you practice in the new form of assessment in the CACHE Diploma in Child Care and Education.

Chapter 2 – Anti-discriminatory practice

Produce a file about anti-discriminatory and anti-bias practice in early years settings for a new early years worker. The file should contain:

- an introduction explaining the importance of promoting equality of opportunity

- information about the legislation that is in place to promote equality of opportunity

- ideas on how settings can make sure that they are promoting anti-discriminatory and anti-bias practice

- information about the role of the adult in promoting equality of opportunity in early years settings.

Chapter 3 – Foundations to caring

1 Design a guide for a new child care and education student about maintaining hygiene and safety in early years settings. The guide must contain:

- an explanation of why hygiene and safety are important

- practical examples of how to maintain a hygienic and safe environment

- information about regulations relating to health and safety.

2 Produce a file about food and nutrition for child care and education students. The file should contain information about:

- the nutritional requirements for children

- the importance of working closely with parents

- how to plan meals, snacks and drinks

- how to encourage children to enjoy mealtimes.

Chapter 5 – Physical development

1 Design a leaflet that explains how children's growth and physical development are measured. Your leaflet should include information about:

- the importance of measuring children's growth

and development

- the variations between individual children's growth and development

- ways of recording children's growth and development.

2 Produce a guide for child care and education students about their role in promoting children's physical development. The guide should include information about:

- the benefits of physical activity for children

- the role of the adult in promoting physical activity

- practical ideas for activities for children aged three to seven years.

Chapter 6 – Cognitive development

Produce a guide for a parent interested in finding out more about children's cognitive development. The guide should include information about:

- sequences and stages of development

- the role of memory, attention and perception

- different theoretical approaches to how children learn

- examples of activities that might stimulate children's cognitive development.

Chapter 7 – Language development

1 Produce a guide about language development for child care and education students. The guide should include information about:

- how children learn language

- stages and sequences of language development

- the role of the early years worker in promoting children's development

- ideas for activities to stimulate children's language.

2 Produce a letter page about language development for an early years magazine. The letters and the answers must provide information about:

- children who have more than one language

- identifying children who may have a hearing impairment

- working with children who stutter

- the role of the adult in promoting language with children aged 0–7 years.

Chapter 8 – Emotional and social development

1   Produce a file about promoting children's emotional and social development. The file should include information about:

- the expected stages and sequences of children's emotional and social development

- theoretical perspectives on personality development

- the role of the adult in promoting children's emotional and social development

- ideas for activities.

2   Produce a guide to help child care and education students understand attachment and separation. The guide must include information about the:

- theories of attachment

- effects of separation on children

- role of the adult in helping children to separate.

Chapter 9 – Understanding the behaviour of children

1   A nursery has asked you to design a leaflet for new child care and education students about managing children's behaviour. The leaflet should include information about:

- the role of the early years worker in managing behaviour

- reporting and recording children's behaviour

- factors that might affect children's behaviour

- the importance of following policies and procedures.

2   Produce a letter page for an early years magazine about managing children's behaviour. The letters and the answers should cover the following topics:

- attention seeking

- swearing and offensive remarks

- behaviour modification

- strategies for encouraging positive behaviour.

Chapter 10 – Health and community care

Produce a guide to help a child care and education student care about caring for sick children.

Your guide must include the following information:

- signs and symptoms of common childhood illnesses

- how to obtain help

- ways of monitoring children's health

- basic procedures in settings when children are not well

- the importance of good hygiene routines

- ways of helping children who are feeling unwell.

Unit 6 – Play, curriculum and early learning

Produce a guide to help a child care and education student understand the role of play in supporting early years curricula. Your guide should include information about:

- the role of play in promoting children's overall development

- the different types of play

- the role of the adult in supporting different types of play

- five practical ideas for activities that will promote the overall development of children aged three to five years.

Chapter 11 – What is play?

Produce a leaflet to help a child care and education student understand the different types of play. Your leaflet should include information about:

- creative play

- physical play

- manipulative play

- imaginative play

- the role of the adult in promoting these types of play.

Chapter 12 – Learning through play

Produce an information sheet for child care and education students that will help them to understand how to set out play materials for children. The information sheet should deal with:

- the importance of attractively setting out materials

- how to create a stimulating environment

- the difference between structured and spontaneous activities.

Chapter 15 – Work with babies 0–1 year

1   Produce a guide to help a child care and education student who is working with babies aged 0–1 years in a group day care setting. The guide must include information about:

- the development of babies aged 0–1 years

- the role of the adult in promoting and stimulating babies' development

- the importance of working in partnership with parents.

2   Produce a step-by-step file about babies' physical care needs. The file should include information about:

- nappy changing and bathing

- sleep and rest for babies

- meeting babies' nutritional needs

- the role of the adult in ensuring babies' physical comfort

- the importance of working with parents.

Chapter 16 – Provision of services in the UK

Produce a leaflet to help a new child care and education student understand the services that are available for children and their families. The leaflet should include information about:

- the roles of the voluntary, private and statutory sectors

- the types of services that these sectors provide

- where parents and others can get further information.

Chapter 17 – The protection of children

Produce a guide to help a new child care and education student understand the importance of child protection. The guide should include information about:

- the long-term effects of child abuse on children

- the categories of abuse

- the role of the early years worker in identifying that abuse might be occurring

- strategies to help children protect themselves.

Chapter 18 – Work with parents

1   Produce a guide for child care and education students about working with parents. The guide should include information about:

- the role of parents in children' lives

- the benefits of working in partnership with parents

- the role of the child care and education student when working with parents.

2   Produce a letter page for an early years magazine about working with parents. The letters and answers should cover the following aspects of working with parents:

- the importance of involving parents

- the rights and responsibilities of parents under the 1989 Children Act

- working with parents who do not share the setting's aims

- ways of involving and communicating with parents

Chapter 19 – Preparation for employment

Produce a poster for people considering a career working in early years. Your poster should include information about:

- the types of employment opportunities open to them

- the qualities and skills that early years workers need to have

- details of training courses and where to get further information.

Key skills assignment – Child safety

Background to the assignment

Child safety is an important issue for early years workers and parents. The statistics for the Child Accident Prevention Trust (CAPT) for 1998 suggest that over 2.5 million children visit accident and emergency units in hospitals each year. Some more information taken from their April 2000 briefing sheet is given below (reproduced with permission from CAPT).

About this assignment

This assignment can provide you with evidence of key skills in three areas:

- Application of Number – Level 2
- Information Technology – Level 2
- Communication – Level 3

In order to gain these key skills, it will be important to follow advice from your tutor and look at the step-by-step guide on pages 483–484. The step-by-step guide shows how you can build your key skills into this assignment. You must work with your tutor to make sure that you are collecting sufficient evidence to meet the level requirements.

Selected causes* of unintentional injury death, children under 15 years, UK region, 1998

	England and Wales		Scotland		Northern Ireland	
	under 5	5–14	under 5	5–14	under 5	5–14
poisoning	7	5	0	6	0	2
falls	5	13	0	0	0	0
fire and flames	29	10	4	9	1	1
drowning	16	10	2	1	3	1
inhalation, ingestion and suffocation	30	18	6	4	2	1
other	16	18	0	3	1	0
total	103	74	12	23	7	5

*all unintentional injury deaths except transport accidents (ICD codes E800–E848) and E878 and E879. Sources: ONS, GRO Scotland, GRO Northern Ireland

Estimated number of children aged under 15 years requiring treatment at A and E departments, UK, 1998

	Birth–4 years		5–14 years	
	home	leisure*	home	leisure*
falls	229,308	75,490	152,931	459,660
striking a person or object	136,974	44,778	140,421	381,569
cutting, piercing or crushing injuries	54,312	14,715	66,270	70,033
suffocation, choking and asphyxiation	3,388	354	2,206	1,733
suspected poisoning	33,273	1,516	3,565	1,497
thermal injuries	34,829	1,989	13,671	3,920
all other mechanisms	93,437	25,275	70,644	149,385
total	585,523	164,120	449,711	1,067,799

*a 'leisure' accident is classified as not in the home, not at work nor a road accident. Based on the number of accidents recorded in a sample of 18 hospitals throughout the UK.
Source: Department of Trade and Industry, Directorate of Consumer Affairs Home Accident

Trends in death rates by region, children 1–14 years

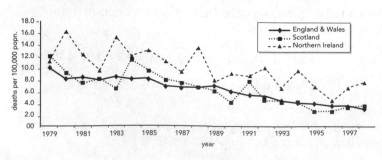

Home and leisure accidents by age, UK 1998

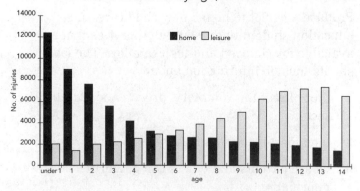

Task

Research the following areas in relation to child safety:

- Accident and mortality rates in childhood

- Safety equipment to prevent accidents.

1 Present your findings in an information session to other students and your tutor. You should produce at least two overhead transparencies to accompany your presentation, one containing a graph or table.

2 Produce an information sheet to accompany your presentation.

3 Produce an evaluation of this assignment

Where to get information

- The Internet should provide you with plenty of information about these topics.

- Books are a good source of reference and many books, such as this one, include contacts for useful organisations.

- Health promotion units in your local area should also provide you with information.

- You should also use and interpret the data provided at the beginning of this assignment.

A step-by-step guide to working through this assignment

No.	Task	What to do	Key skill link
		To gather your key skill evidence, you should always keep any notes, sums and disks that you used in your preparation for this assignment. This means that you should keep your workings of any calculations that you have made.	
1	Gather information using IT	Use the Internet to search for information about your specific topic. Use a variety of websites and methods of searching. Find examples of statistics or graphs that will add depth to your presentation. Highlight sections of information that are useful, download them and save them on a disk.	Information Technology 2.1 Communication C3.2
2	Gather other information	Find out about the types of safety equipment available in your local area. Find out the cost of equipping a family home with safety equipment for children aged 0–3 years using three different suppliers – e.g. two different shops and a catalogue.	Application of Number 2.1, 2.2
3	Handle information	Produce a bar chart showing the costs of buying equipment from three different suppliers. Work out the average or 'mean' cost of buying equipment by adding together the costs from each supplier and then dividing by three. Represent the costs of equipment from the different suppliers. Plot this 'mean' line on to your graph. What saving in percentage terms could a family make by shopping around? Show this by producing a simple diagram. Using the information provided at the beginning of this assignment, produce a pie chart that shows the categories of accidents that children under four years might have at home.	Application of Number 2.2, 2.3

No	Task	What to do	Key skill link
4	Produce information	Using IT, produce your graph and/or pie chart and print it out. Put this on to an overhead transparency so that you can explain your results during your presentation.	Information Technology 2.3
5	Preparing for your presentation	Using the graphs and tables at the beginning of this assignment, analyse the information and draw some conclusions from it for use in your presentation	Application of Number 2.1
6	Preparing for the presentation	Using the computer to help you, produce an overhead transparency that will help you during your presentation – e.g. it might have bullet points on it. Think about an issue that you want your audience to discuss. Here are two examples – should reins on young children be compulsory when they are out near the road? Should the government provide families with safety equipment free of charge? You should also write some notes to help you remember what you want to say and your feelings about this issue. Make sure that you give some reasons for these feelings.	Information Technology 2.3
7	Produce an information sheet	The information sheet should be at least 1000 words in length. It should give information about the importance of child safety – you can use some statistics here – and the types of equipment that can help prevent accidents. You must use the information that you gathered during your Internet search and show how you have used other information. You can do this by keeping notes of where you have found your information. You should write about some of the issues that might affect child safety, such as poverty and gender. You must produce the information sheet on a computer and bring in images or text that you have downloaded from the Internet or from other software packages such as Clipart.	Information Technology 2.2, 2.3 Communication 3.2, 3.3
8	Carrying out your presentation	You need to explain what you have found out during your research and make sure that you explain your graphs and other statistics. You should also invite discussion on an issue that has come out of your research. Make sure that you have practised your presentation skills beforehand.	Communication 3.1a, 3.1b Application of Number 2.1, 2.3
9	Writing your evaluation	Once you have carried out your presentation, write a short evaluation (around 300 words) about what you have learnt from carrying out this assignment and how you would approach similar assignments in the future. Produce this evaluation on a computer and incorporate an image into the text. In the evaluation you should explain the sources of information that you used to produce your information sheet and why you chose them. Write about how you have used the IT equipment and what you have learnt from this.	Information Technology 2.2, 2.3 Communication 3.3

Appendix

Early learning goals for the foundation stage (from Sept 2000)

Foreword

Early childhood is a crucial stage of life in terms of children's physical, intellectual, emotional, and social development and of their well-being. Growth is both rapid and differential. A significantly high proportion of learning takes place from birth to age six. It is a time when children particularly need high-quality care and learning experiences.

The aim of the Government's early years policy is to provide a comprehensive range of services for young children. This includes integrated early years education and childcare provision which will make a positive contribution to children's early development, enabling them to build on this foundation throughout their lives, so providing a sound basis for lifelong learning. High-quality care and education for young children will give parents peace of mind and help them to balance their work and family lives.

Education begins in the home and continues there and in a range of settings. Through initiatives including Sure Start and Early Excellence Centres, the Government is pioneering ways to improve support for families and children before and from birth. The aim is to work with parents and children to promote the development of pre-school children – particularly those who are disadvantaged – to ensure that they are ready to thrive when they get to school.

Since September 1998, a free, part-time early years education place has been made available for all four year old children whose parents want one. The proportion of three-year-olds with a free, part-time early years education place is planned to rise from the present one-third to two-thirds by 2002. These places are in a variety of settings. Most children transfer to the reception year in a primary school during the year in which they reach compulsory school age, the term after their fifth birthday.

The period from three to the end of the reception year is described as the foundation stage. It is a distinct stage and important both in its own right and in preparing children for later schooling. The early learning goals set out what is expected for most children by the end of the foundation stage.

Principles for early years education

Effective education requires both a relevant curriculum and practitioners who understand and are able to implement the curriculum requirements. Children develop rapidly during the early years physically, intellectually, emotionally and socially. They are entitled to provision which supports and extends knowledge, understanding, skills and confidence and helps them to overcome any disadvantage.

Early years experience should build on what children already know and can do. It should also encourage a positive attitude and disposition to learn and aim to give protection from early failure.

No child should be excluded or disadvantaged because of his or her race, culture or religion, home language, family background, special educational needs, disability, gender or ability.

To be effective, an early years curriculum needs to be carefully structured. In that structure there should be three strands: provision for the different starting points from which children develop their learning, building on what they can already do; relevant and appropriate content which matches the different levels of young children's needs; and planned and purposeful activity which provides opportunities for teaching and learning both indoors and outdoors.

A well-planned and well-organised environment gives children rich and stimulating experiences. It provides the structure for teaching within which children explore, experiment, plan and make decisions for themselves, thus enabling them to learn, develop and to make good progress. There should be opportunities for children to engage in activities planned by adults, and those which they plan or initiate. Children learn through play and in other ways. They do not make a distinction between 'play' and 'work', and neither should practitioners. Children need time to become engrossed, work in depth and complete activities.

Practitioners must be able to observe and respond appropriately to children, informed by a knowledge of how children develop and learn.

Well-planned, purposeful activity and appropriate intervention by practitioners will engage children in the learning process, and help them make progress in their learning.

Practitioners need to ensure that all children feel included, secure and valued. They must build positive relationships with parents in order to work effectively with them and their children.

Children, parents and practitioners must work together in an atmosphere of mutual respect.

Above all, **high-quality care and education by practitioners will lead to effective learning and development for young children.**

Early learning goals for personal, social and emotional development

By the end of the foundation stage, most children will:

- continue to be interested, excited and motivated to learn;
- be confident to try new activities, initiate ideas and speak in a familiar group;
- maintain attention, concentrate, and sit quietly when appropriate;
- have a developing awareness of their own needs, views and feelings and be sensitive to the needs, views and feelings of others;
- have a developing respect for their own cultures and beliefs, and those of other people;
- respond to significant experiences, showing a range of feelings when appropriate;
- form good relationships with adults and peers;
- work as part of a group or class, taking turns and sharing fairly, understanding that there need to be agreed values and codes of behaviour for groups of people, including adults an children, to work together harmoniously;
- understand what is right, what is wrong, and why;
- dress and undress independently and manage their own personal hygiene;
- select and use activities and resources independently;
- consider the consequences of their words and actions or themselves and others;
- understand that people have different needs, views, cultures and beliefs, which need to be treated with respect;
- understand that they can expect others to treat their needs, views, cultures and beliefs with respect.

Early learning goals for communication, language and literacy

The objectives set out in the National Literacy Strategy Framework for Teaching for the reception year are in line with these goals. By the end of the foundation stage, most children will be able to:

- enjoy listening to and using spoken and written language, and readily turn to it in their play and learning;
- explore and experiment with sounds, words and texts;

485

- listen with enjoyment and respond to stories, songs and other music, rhymes and poems and make their own stories, songs, rhymes and poems;
- use language to imagine and recreate roles and experiences;
- use talk to organise, sequence and clarify thinking, ideas, feelings and events;
- sustain attentive listening, responding to what they have heard by relevant comments, questions or actions;
- interact with others, negotiating plans and activities and taking turns in conversation;
- extend their vocabulary, exploring the meanings and sounds of new words;
- retell narratives in the correct sequence, drawing on the language patterns of stories;
- speak clearly and audibly with confidence and control and show awareness of the listener, for example by their use of conventions such as greetings, 'please' and 'thank you';
- hear and say initial and final sounds in words, and short vowel sounds within words;
- link sounds to letters, naming and sounding the letters of the alphabet;
- read a range of familiar and common words and simple sentences independently;
- know that print carries meaning and, in English, is read from left to right and top to bottom;
- show understanding of elements of stories, such as main character, sequence of events, and openings, and how information can be found in non-fiction texts to answer questions about where, who, why and how;
- attempt writing for various purposes, using features of different forms such as lists, stories, instructions;
- write their own names and other things such as labels and captions and begin to form simple sentences, sometimes using punctuation;
- use their phonic knowledge to write simple regular words and make phonetically plausible attempts at more complex words;
- use a pencil and hold it effectively to form recognisable letters, most of which are correctly formed.

Early learning goals for mathematical development

The key objectives in the National Numeracy Strategy Framework for Teaching Mathematics for the reception year are in line with these goals. By the end of the foundation stage, most children will be able to:

- say and use number names in order in familiar contexts;
- count reliably up to 10 everyday objects;
- recognise numerals 1 to 9;
- use language such as 'more' or 'less', 'greater' or 'smaller', 'heavier' or lighter', to compare two numbers or quantities;
- in practical activities and discussion, begin to use the vocabulary involved in adding and subtracting;
- find one more or one less than a number from 1 to 10;
- begin to relate addition to combining two groups of objects, and subtraction to 'taking away';
- talk about, recognise and recreate simple patterns;
- use language such as 'circle' or 'bigger' to describe the shape and size of solids and flat shapes;
- use everyday words to describe position;

- use developing mathematical ideas and methods to solve practical problems.

Early learning goals for knowledge and understanding of the world

By the end of the foundation stage, most children will be able to:

- investigate objects and materials by using all of their senses as appropriate;
- find out about, and identify some feature of, living things, objects and events they observe;
- look closely at similarities, differences, patterns and change;
- ask questions about why things happen and how things work;
- build and construct with a wide range of objects, selecting appropriate resources, and adapting their work where necessary;
- select the tools and techniques they need to shape, assemble and join the materials they are using;
- find out about and identify the uses of everyday technology and use ICT and programmable toys to support their learning;
- find out about past and present events in their own lives, and in those of their families and other people they know;
- observe, find out about, and identify features in the place they live and the natural world;
- begin to know about their own cultures and beliefs, and those of other people;
- find out about their environment, and talk about those features they like and dislike.

Early learning goals for physical development

By the end of the foundation stage, most children will be able to:

- move with confidence, imagination and in safety;
- move with control and co-ordination;
- show awareness of space, of themselves and of others;
- recognise the importance of keeping healthy and those things which contribute to this;
- recognise the changes that happen to their bodies when they are active;
- use a range of small and large equipment;
- travel around, under, over and through balancing and climbing equipment;
- handle tools, objects, construction and malleable materials safely and with increasing control.

Early learning goals for creative development

By the end of the foundation stage, most children will be able to:

- explore colour, texture, shape, form and space in two and three dimensions;
- recognise and explore how sounds can be changed, sing simple songs from memory, recognise repeated sounds and sound patterns and match movements to music;
- respond in a variety of ways to what they see, hear, smell, touch and feel;
- use their imagination in art and design, music, dance, imaginative and role play, and stories;
- express and communicate their ideas, thoughts and feelings by using a widening range of materials, suitable tools, imaginative and role play, movement, designing and making, and a variety of songs and musical instruments.

Index